The Future of Domestic Capital Markets in Developing Countries

THE WORLD BANK GROUP

THE INTERNATIONAL MONETARY FUND

THE BROOKINGS INSTITUTION

This book is based on the fifth annual financial markets and development conference bearing the name of this volume and held April 14–16, 2003, in Washington, D.C. The conference was jointly sponsored by the World Bank Group, the International Monetary Fund, and the Brookings Institution.

The previous volumes in this series are available from the Brookings Institution Press:

Financial Markets and Development: The Crisis in Emerging Markets (1999)

Managing Financial and Corporate Distress: Lessons from Asia (2000)

Open Doors: Foreign Participation in Financial Systems in Developing Countries (2001)

Financial Sector Governance: The Roles of the Public and Private Sectors (2002)

ROBERT E. LITAN
MICHAEL POMERLEANO
V. SUNDARARAJAN
Editors

The Future of Domestic Capital Markets in Developing Countries

BROOKINGS INSTITUTION PRESS
Washington, D.C.

ABOUT BROOKINGS

The Brookings Institution is a private nonprofit organization devoted to research, education, and publication on important issues of domestic and foreign policy. Its principal purpose is to bring knowledge to bear on current and emerging policy problems. The Institution maintains a position of neutrality on issues of public policy. Interpretations or conclusions in Brookings publications should be understood to be solely those of the authors.

1775 Massachusetts Avenue, N.W., Washington, D.C. 20036
www.brookings.edu

Library of Congress Cataloging-in-Publication data

The future of domestic capital markets in developing countries /
Robert E. Litan, Michael Pomerleano, V. Sundararajan, editors.
p. cm.
Includes bibliographical references and index.
ISBN 0-8157-5299-7 (pbk. : alk. paper)
1. Capital market—Developing countries. 2. Capital market—Government policy—Developing countries. 3. Capital market—Law and legislation—Developing countries. I. Litan, Robert E., 1950– II. Pomerleano, Michael. III. Sundararajan, Vasudevan. IV. Title.
HG5993.F87 2003
332'.041'091724—dc22 2003015766

9 8 7 6 5 4 3 2 1

The paper used in this publication meets minimum requirements of the American National Standard for Information Sciences—Permanence of Paper for Printed Library Materials: ANSI Z39.48-1992.

Typeset in Adobe Garamond

Composition by Circle Graphics
Columbia, Maryland

Printed by Victor Graphics
Baltimore, Maryland

Contents

PART FIVE
Looking Forward

Foreword

Limited access to capital presents a critical challenge to growth and stability. Well-functioning markets ensure that corporations efficiently mobilize capital for growth and that markets price risk well, so that valuable projects will be financed. Most important, countries that do not have access to equity capital face higher costs of capital, often leading to segmentation of markets. In this context, the World Bank, International Monetary Fund, and Brookings Institution organized a global conference focusing on the future of domestic capital markets in developing countries. Participants addressed the challenges that developing and developed country markets face from globalization, technological changes, and weaknesses of corporate governance.

This conference is the fifth in an annual Financial Markets and Development series, which brings together senior policymakers, financial executives, and researchers each year to address cutting-edge issues facing the financial development community. This annual program aims to foster an ongoing dialogue and exchange of complementary perspectives across regions and between emerging and developed economies.

Many individuals contributed to the success of the conference and to this volume, including the formal discussants and authors of the papers contained here. Special thanks are also owed to Colleen Mascenik at the World Bank, who, along with the editors, helped organize the conference.

In addition, Alicia Jones and Sandip Sukhtankar at Brookings provided valuable assistance throughout the planning and organizing of the conference. Christopher Lyddy provided critical assistance in drafting the summaries of the panel discussions that appear in the volume. We also acknowledge the editorial, proofreading, and indexing assistance of Elizabeth Forsyth, Tanjam Jacobson, Inge Lockwood, and Enid Zafran.

Funds for the conference were generously supplied by the World Bank Group, the International Monetary Fund, and the Brookings Institution.

STROBE TALBOTT
President, Brookings Institution

CESARE CALARI
Vice President, Financial Sector
The World Bank

STEFAN INGVES
Director, Monetary and Exchange Affairs Department
International Monetary Fund

ROBERT E. LITAN
MICHAEL POMERLEANO
V. SUNDARARAJAN

1 *Introduction*

It is now well understood that economic development requires healthy growth of a nation's financial sector. Initially, nations tend to channel their savings and investment primarily, if not almost exclusively, through banks. But over time, savers in search of higher returns and firms seeking capital provide the foundation for the development of capital markets. Here, too, a sequence is evident: first, the issuance and trading of bills and bonds of national governments, followed by the issuance and trading of bonds and equities of publicly held corporations.

Capital markets cannot function effectively, however, unless a number of elements are in place. Exchanges and clearing and settlement systems must exist to enable trading, and money market arrangements are needed to facilitate settlements. A legal system must exist to enforce contracts. Information about the financial soundness and future prospects of companies must be made available on a timely basis to give investors confidence to purchase corporate instruments (both debt and equity). Corporations must be governed in a fashion that also gives investors confidence that their funds will not be wasted or stolen.

Events in recent years in both the developed and less developed world have underscored the importance of these straightforward propositions. In the wake of the Asian financial crisis of 1997–98 and follow-on crises in Russia and Latin America, experts from developed countries lectured those in the affected countries about the importance of ensuring transparency and avoiding "crony capitalism." Yet only a few years later, the United States and, to a lesser extent, some European nations suffered their own embarrassing failures in corporate disclosure. Equity investors in each of these domestic capital markets suffered as a consequence.

It is appropriate, therefore, that the Fifth Annual Financial Markets and Development conference sponsored by the World Bank, the International Monetary Fund (IMF), and the Brookings Institution, held in Washington on April 14–16, 2003, focused on the future of domestic capital markets in developing countries. As in earlier years, this conference was attended by nearly 200 financial experts and policymakers from around the world. Attendees heard presentations of papers and comments from experts in various panels on aspects of the theme chosen for this year's conference. In this introduction, we highlight key features of those papers (and invite readers to review the panel summaries at the end of each section of the volume).

* * *

Gerd Häusler, Donald Mathieson, and Jorge Roldos from the International Monetary Fund open the book with a broad overview of trends in capital markets in developing countries. Several points emerge from this survey.

In the aggregate, national bond markets in developing countries have doubled in size since 1993, from 18 to 36 percent of gross domestic product (GDP). This is still well below the average for developed countries, however, at 120 percent of GDP. As one would expect, most of the growth in domestic bond markets has occurred in government bonds, with corporate bonds lagging. Moreover, despite much of the attention given to sovereign indebtedness in various developing countries, domestic bond issues by governments have outpaced foreign currency issues by a factor of thirteen.

Equity markets in developing countries emerged as a serious alternative to local financing only in the 1990s, doubling from half of domestic credit in 1990 to an amount roughly equal to domestic credit by 1994. As a result of various financial crises throughout the decade, however, equity as a source of finance also was highly volatile.

What policies have been most effective in stimulating domestic capital markets? The authors suggest that there is broad agreement on the importance of sound market infrastructure, transparency, and corporate governance. Although the evidence is less clear-cut on other issues, they offer some conclusions.

One notion is that, while the existence of indexed instruments and derivatives can help to lengthen the maturities and deepen liquidity in the fixed-income market, these financial innovations require careful monitoring to prevent excessively leveraged positions and undesirable mismatches in the maturities of assets and liabilities. A second conclusion is that, although stock market reforms aimed at improving the conditions under which corporations issue and trade shares are desirable, governments should not protect local exchanges or the domestic brokerage industry from local or foreign competition. Third, foreign investors should be welcomed into domestic capital markets since they can deepen liquidity in those markets, even if they may add volatility in the process.

The next two chapters analyze domestic bond markets, in particular, in greater detail. Clemente del Valle, chairman of the Securities and Exchange Commission in Colombia, and Piero Ugolini of the IMF provide an overview of the key policy initiatives and reforms that are necessary for the development of government bond markets. They then survey the status of those efforts in seven regions of the world.

In the authors' view, the foundation of an effective government bond market must rest primarily on macroeconomic stability, a clear definition of the government's debt strategy (including the sale of "benchmark" obligations that are viewed as useful anchors for privately issued debt and the auction of initial government bond issues), a transparent and effective legal framework supporting bond issues and their subsequent trading in secondary markets, the presence of a wide investor base for purchasing the bonds (including an array of institutional investors), and a stable and liquid money market overseen and managed by the nation's central bank. The authors also emphasize the importance of having systems of taxation that do not penalize interest income and an efficient settlement system (ideally one that settles transactions in real time).

Although government bond markets in emerging-market countries still have a long way to go to reach the sophistication of developed-country markets, some country markets are considerably more advanced than others. Two of the most advanced government bond markets (among emerging-market countries) are in Mexico and Singapore. Somewhat less advanced, but still well ahead of many developing countries, are the markets in Brazil, Colombia, Korea, Morocco, and Turkey.

Government bond markets differ not only in their depth, but along other dimensions as well. For example, government securities in East Asia are primarily long term in maturity, with fixed interest rates, while those in

Latin America tend toward shorter- and medium-term maturities, often with variable interest rates.

Despite their differences, emerging-market bond markets face similar challenges: they need to diversify the investor base (beyond banks); tax policies must achieve neutrality between interest and other income, while not disadvantaging foreign purchasers; settlement infrastructure requires further development, especially to facilitate secondary-market trading; and governments need to upgrade their debt and cash management capabilities so that the market has both a credible supply of securities issued and a strategy that supports development of the market.

Philip Turner of the Bank for International Settlements addresses issues relating to emerging-country bond markets more broadly. He begins by documenting the significant growth in these securities in emerging markets, which doubled in volume outstanding to over $2 trillion at year-end 2001 in just seven years (from year-end 1994). Although debt issuance increased throughout the world, it was especially pronounced in East Asia, where governments ran large fiscal deficits following the financial crisis in 1997. Perhaps most significant, the total volume of domestic debt issued by emerging-market borrowers now exceeds that of foreign currency debt.

Turner argues that, although bond markets are central to the development of an economic system, a number of obstacles inhibit such markets in developing countries in particular. These include high and variable inflation (which deters investment in bonds), various forms of interest rate or loan market controls, narrowness of the investor base (attributable in part to investor tastes and in part to limited development of institutional investors), regulatory policies that inhibit secondary-market trading (such as accounting policies that recognize gains and losses only on sale rather than periodically as market values change), and tax policies that reduce liquidity.

Other government policies can hamper the development of domestic bonds, such as the now ill-advised attempts by governments to borrow abroad excessively in foreign currencies and at short maturities. Turner discusses in some detail how government decisions relating to the sterilization of excess reserves over the monetary base—a common situation in East Asia, where reserves exceed domestic currency by almost $400 billion—can influence the development of local bond markets. In particular, governments that issue bonds against these reserves can further the development of their own local bond markets. Of course, if that path is chosen, decisions must then be made about who issues the bonds (governments or central banks) and at what maturities, and these decisions can affect the liquidity and depth of markets.

Turner also comments on the dangers that local debt markets run into when local currency debt is too short term, requiring constant rollover—a problem that exists in countries with a history of high and volatile inflation. The transition to long-term, fixed-rate debt must, however, be gradual. Part of the transition may entail some indexing of the debt to inflation and adoption of variable rates during some interim period.

Governments should also seek to promote liquidity in their debt markets by fostering effective institutional and operational arrangements for secondary-market trading. In particular, tax systems must not inhibit trading. Turner discusses the pros and cons of various other government measures to foster debt markets, including adopting monetary policies aimed at smoothing volatility in interest rates; establishing a primary dealer system; fostering repurchase transactions (in which government securities are used as securities for collateral); adopting more liberal attitudes toward short selling (which facilitates arbitrage and adds to liquidity); and building up benchmark security issues. Encouraging the development of nonbank financial intermediaries, especially insurance companies and pension funds, is also an important way of fostering local demand for domestic debt issues (by both government and private sector borrowers).

How large does a country have to be to maintain a well-functioning bond market? Turner argues that the existence of liquid bond markets in many countries of different sizes suggests that most medium-size emerging-market countries can sustain more liquid bond markets than currently exist.

Turner concludes by advising small developing countries where debt markets are necessarily limited in size to eschew policies requiring local investors to invest in home-country bonds as a way of supporting local bond markets. Such policies deprive domestic investors of opportunities for useful diversification. Instead, small (and other size) emerging-market countries should follow outward-looking policies that welcome foreign banks and securities firms, which can bring investors from abroad as well as valuable expertise, while allowing local investors to diversify by investing abroad. Such capital account opening, however, calls for careful sequencing and coordination of a range of financial policy and macroeconomic measures to help manage the associated risks, a topic discussed in the next section of this volume.

* * *

What policies are most appropriate for enhancing the development of financial systems in developing-country markets, while ensuring financial stability? The chapters in the second part of this volume address this question.

Three experts from the Bank of England—Glenn Hoggarth, Patricia Jackson, and Erlend Nier—examine the extent to which financial markets can contribute to financial stability by fostering market discipline, resulting in sounder banks and thus a safer financial system. The authors begin by laying out the channels through which, at least in principle, the market can exert discipline against excessive risk-taking by banks and other financial institutions: through changes in equity prices (for publicly held financial intermediaries), an intermediary's counterparties, and holders of subordinated debt. Whether and to what extent market discipline is effective depends on the quality and timeliness of information available and whether the parties supposedly supplying the discipline are protected against loss (as is the case with depositors in many countries).

The authors test the hypothesis that banks, in particular, have incentives to hold more capital as market discipline becomes more effective—since, then, the managers and shareholders of the bank want more protection against default. Confirming this hypothesis, one test finds a negative relationship between an index of depositor protection, which should weaken market discipline, and average bank capital-to-asset ratios, by country. Another test finds the expected positive relationship between per country bank capital ratios and the amount of disclosure. The authors find similar relationships for banks within individual countries.

These tests underscore the need for governments to create the right environment for market discipline to be effective. Among the conditions that the authors favor are keeping any depositor protection and financial safety net to a minimum; avoiding state ownership of banks and other financial institutions; keeping the domestic financial market open to foreign entry and competition (which enhances discipline); and maximizing disclosure about the financial condition of banks and other financial intermediaries (as the proposed revisions to the Basel international bank capital standards arguably would do).

Finally, the authors consider whether bank supervisors should be using market prices as guides to risk. Although, in principle, market measures are contaminated by the presence of the safety net, which may limit their usefulness to supervisors, the prevailing studies—for both the U.S. and European markets—provide mixed evidence about the added predictive value of market prices of bank equity and subordinated debt (which, in theory, should not be infected by any safety net since its holders are not protected by deposit insurance). The authors conduct their own empirical tests, finding their market indicators for banks in the United Kingdom to be of only limited predictive value of bank risk and, perhaps most important, to contain large amounts of "noise," with large movements in prices often seemingly not related to a large subsequent event. In other words, the market data generate substantial "false positives," which, in the authors' view, limits their predictive value for supervisors.

The usefulness of disclosure about financial intermediaries is also the subject of the next chapter in this volume. Alan Cameron, deputy chairman of the Sydney Futures Exchange, distinguishes between two models of regulation: "merits" regulation, which in the financial context might take the form of regulators screening which companies can access the capital markets, and "disclosure" regulation, which requires public entities to disclose pertinent financial information about themselves but does not entail prior regulatory approval for capital offerings or other activities by regulators. Developed economies, such as the United States and Australia (the author's home country), have adopted the disclosure model for capital markets, but only a few developing countries have done so.

The line between the merits and disclosure models is not as clear as it may appear, however. Developed-country securities regulators rely primarily on disclosure, but they also engage in some screening of prospectuses (for fullness of the disclosure, but not worthiness of the investment) before companies are permitted to sell their shares to the public.

Cameron considers in some detail the disclosure system relating to "penny stocks" trading on the Hong Kong stock exchange, a subject he studied as part of a larger expert group. The group found that the overall standards for listing in that market were too low, allowing the trading of too many weak companies that later failed. While failure is an inherent part of capitalism, the group concluded that excessive failure of companies listed on stock markets can damage the reputation of all stocks traded on an exchange, not just those that fail. With this in mind, the group urged that the quality of overall listing standards be raised in the future.

Can the kind of disclosure used in developed-country capital markets be applied in the same fashion to emerging markets? Cameron suggests several reasons for being cautious. For one thing, the infrastructure necessary to support disclosure—well-trained legal, accounting, insolvency, and securities analysis personnel—is much weaker in developing economies. Equally important, investors in emerging markets tend not to be as well educated about the methods for assessing the relative merits of different classes of assets. Where governments are owners of listed companies, as they are in many developing countries, this can distort incentives for adequate and timely disclosure. For all these reasons, Cameron counsels emerging-market countries not to rely exclusively on disclosure when constructing and maintaining their capital markets; there is a need, in his view, for some merits-based regulation—prescreening of prospectuses, in particular—as well.

Peter Henry and Peter Lorentzen of Stanford University ask a related, fundamental question in their contribution to the volume: given the turbulence of capital flows to developing countries, is it a good idea for those countries to integrate their capital markets with the rest of the world? The answer to that all-important question is a nuanced one.

Too much of the recent criticism of developing countries for accepting foreign money has focused on debt finance, especially when it is denominated in foreign currency. The Asian financial crisis, and subsequent crises in Russia and Latin America, confirms the riskiness of that strategy. Accordingly, the authors urge emerging-market countries to liberalize their dollar-denominated debt flows slowly and cautiously.

Accepting equity capital, whether through stock market investment or foreign direct investment, has been much more attractive than borrowing from abroad. Nonetheless, less capital has flowed from rich countries to poor-country equity markets than has been implied by economic theory, which suggests that rates of return in developing countries, with less capital intensity, are likely to be higher, even when adjusted for risk, than rates of return in rich countries. As it turns out, however, rich-country suppliers of capital have been unusually hesitant to commit funds in emerging-market equities, where actual returns have proved to be unusually low. The authors suggest that developed-country investors are worried about adverse selection and agency problems, especially where information is less than transparent and protection of minority shareholders is not as well established as in richer countries.

In fact, cross-country econometric research has documented the importance of information problems as a key impediment to foreign investment in emerging-market equity markets. What limited empirical data exist suggest that local equity markets are likely to be larger, more efficient, and more stable as legal protections of investors increase. Perhaps the best approach to securing such protection is to provide strong disclosure laws, backed by penalties in civil court for failure to adhere to them. As countries deepen their equity markets relative to debt, their economies are also likely to be more stable through time and less subject to repeated bouts of financial distress and crisis.

One especially important role for equity markets is to provide a venue for new companies to raise capital through initial public offerings (IPOs). In her chapter, Reena Aggarwal of Georgetown University assesses this function in emerging-market equity markets.

Taken together, equity markets in emerging markets have grown in importance through time. In 1970, stocks listed on U.S. equity markets constituted 78 percent of total world capitalization; by 1999, this share had fallen to just 45 percent. Aggarwal notes that a significant amount of the decline was attributed to the growth in capitalization of companies listed on exchanges in emerging markets or depository receipts traded on U.S. exchanges.

At the same time that equity markets are becoming more global, companies originating from emerging markets—Latin America—are finding it increasingly easy and attractive to abandon their listings on local exchanges in favor of listings in developed-country markets, especially the United States. This affords them access to a global roster of investors rather than the more limited set associated with domestic exchanges. But the adverse consequences for local exchanges are apparent, with declining numbers of listings over time, which in turn spells trouble for the ability of these exchanges to foster IPOs from local companies in the future.

Because listing revenues are likely to continue to decline, emerging-market exchanges must find other ways to generate revenue if they are to survive and, indeed, even prosper. The most likely prospects are trading and other services. In addition, exchanges in emerging markets are likely to seek out alliances with exchanges in neighboring countries as a way of cutting costs, although this avenue for survival is fraught with its own set of difficulties (as past attempts at alliances among European exchanges attest). Aggarwal concludes her analysis by considering a range of options that governments can pursue to encourage new listings and activity on their local exchanges.

In the last chapter in the second section of this volume, Cem Karacadag, V. Sundararajan, and Jennifer Elliott of the IMF discuss what they believe to be the appropriate sequencing of financial sector reforms to develop domestic financial markets while ensuring financial stability. The topic merits attention, in their view, because the financial crises of the 1990s demonstrated that a weak institutional structure—in particular, failure to adequately supervise financial institutions and markets, excessive government involvement in the financial sector, poor central bank policies in an environment of weak money, exchange, and government debt markets, and the absence of reliable and timely information on both the financial and nonfinancial sectors—contributed to and exacerbated financial and economic risks in the course of financial market liberalization. As a corollary, the reforms to develop financial markets and institutions should be coordinated and combined with measures to monitor and mitigate the associated risks in order to realize the full benefits of liberalizing financial markets and capital accounts (to permit mobility of capital into and out of the country). What is the optimal path and sequencing of these reform measures, and how should reforms be coordinated with capital account liberalization?

In order to address these questions, the authors identify a hierarchy of financial markets, reflecting the degree and complexity of the risks created by each market and the technical interdependence among markets. At the base are the money and foreign exchange markets. The money market precedes all others given its central role in price discovery and in the setting and transmission of interest rates. An active money market is a prerequisite for the development of markets in foreign exchange and government securities. A well-developed government debt market, in turn, facilitates the development of markets in corporate debt, equity, and asset-based securities.

This hierarchy is based on two considerations: first, risks evolve into more complex forms and grow in magnitude as new markets develop, especially as new instruments and institutions emerge. Second, depth and liquidity in one market are linked to depth and liquidity in other markets due to shared infrastructure and behavioral linkages. These considerations imply that risks in any one market cannot be effectively managed, and its depth and liquidity adequately built up, in the absence of well-functioning markets at earlier stages in the hierarchy. In addition, a critical mass of reforms encompassing both market development and risk mitigation at every stage in the market hierarchy is necessary to avoid exacerbating financial system fragility and macroeconomic vulnerability.

Against this background and drawing on country experience, the authors review the range of specific operational and structural measures that need to be implemented to build up each market segment, illustrating the hierarchy and interdependence of markets. They stress that such private markets are essential to ensuring financial stability over the long run, because they enable countries to reduce their dependence on bank-intermediated finance, which has its own vulnerabilities to financial crises. The authors also review the additional dimensions of risks introduced by the development of each market in this hierarchy—both financial and macroeconomic risks—and the associated risk mitigation policies that governments can pursue. Given the importance of ensuring financial stability, the authors urge emerging-market countries to sequence the establishment of the various financial markets so that the risks of each market are managed before other markets are developed and maintained. Although countries are likely to be in the midst of various stages of market development and risk mitigation, the proposed approach to sequencing and coordination of reforms can help to prioritize future financial reforms.

The authors conclude by combining the analysis of market development measures and risk mitigation policies into a set of general principles for sequencing financial market development and capital account liberalization. They stress that the liberalization of capital flows by instruments and sectors should be sequenced in a manner that reinforces domestic financial liberalization and allows for institutional capacity-building to manage the additional risks. In rough outline, this means that countries should not liberalize all at once and should seek to implement a critical mass of reforms at each step so that adequate depth and risk management capacity are achieved in each market segment.

* * *

How are equity markets—exchanges in particular—changing in developing countries? What are the challenges facing regulators? And how, if at all, has corporate governance improved? These are among the questions explored in the next section of the volume.

Ruben Lee of the Oxford Finance Group provides an overview of changes in market structure, especially the trends toward "demutualization" of equities exchanges, in emerging markets. He also lends his perspective on the future of the trading of securities in these markets. In brief, he reaches several conclusions.

One is that the volume of trading on exchanges in many developing-country markets is small, in part because of the small number of public companies and also because of concentrated share ownership. Furthermore, as Aggarwal points out in her chapter, some of the more successful local companies increasingly have wanted listings on the larger developed-country markets (especially the United States).

Notwithstanding these real threats to their commercial viability, emerging-market exchanges nonetheless have the advantage of "network externalities"—being the only "game in town," they tend to attract all the local business, making it difficult or impossible for others to enter the exchange market. As for local companies listing off-shore, trading of their shares abroad may actually encourage trading of shares in home-country markets.

Still, the options for local exchanges to earn additional revenues are limited. The trend toward demutualization means that exchanges may not be able to rely on membership fees. If listing is provided by government, then revenues from listing can disappear. Although clearing and settlement revenues are attractive, most exchanges do not provide those services (and where this happens, it may invite antitrust scrutiny). Technology is forcing down the level of transaction fees, one of the primary sources of exchange revenue. Perhaps the most promising source of future revenues is the provision of quote and trade data, but this depends on regulatory approvals.

One possible response to these threats to their viability is for exchanges to achieve greater economies of scale through linkages, alliances, or even mergers with other exchanges. Lee notes, however, that most attempts at linkages have failed so far, for various reasons. He pays special attention to the lessons of the linkage among five Scandinavian exchanges, NOREX, which has had both successes and difficulties. Lee also reviews a number of exchange mergers, which he suggests may hold greater financial promise. He points out that mergers can be constructed so that the national identities of the different exchanges are preserved.

Lee concludes his analysis by surveying the costs and benefits of demutualization. He is skeptical that demutualization will prove to be as attractive or as widespread as many of its advocates claim.

Demutualization of exchanges is often touted for the improvements it may bring in corporate governance. How does corporate governance relate to the performance of public companies that may be listed on exchanges? Amar Gill of Credit Lyonnais Securities Asia addresses this important question in his chapter, concentrating on the evidence for emerging markets in particular.

Using his company's own scoring system for corporate governance, which covered more than fifty issues, Gill and his research team ranked companies in emerging markets and assigned them to quartiles. Gill then compares the corporate governance rankings to the returns on equity for the same companies. The results broadly confirm the view that investors value good corporate governance, at least over a three- to five-year time horizon (but not in the short run). The firms in the top quartile of the corporate governance rankings tend to have superior equity returns than firms ranking lower in corporate governance.

Next, Olivier Frémond and Mierta Capaul of the World Bank examine how capital structures and control rights interact within corporations. The authors outline four basic patterns of ownership and control: dispersed ownership and diffused control, dispersed ownership and concentrated control, concentrated ownership and diffused control, and concentrated ownership and control.

The first two scenarios, where ownership is dispersed, foster portfolio diversification and liquidity. In this circumstance, it is more efficient for shareholders who are disaffected to "vote with their feet," or "exit," than to exercise "voice" by seeking to influence the way the company is managed. In contrast, in the third and fourth scenarios—where ownership is concentrated—liquidity is impaired, making exit comparatively more difficult, while voice, at least in principle, is a more effective mechanism to ensure that management does not expropriate shareholders' investments.

The concentrated ownership scenarios are especially important in the emerging-market context, where many firms are family controlled. Under this circumstance, the best way to ensure that minority shareholders have adequate voice is to provide one vote per share. The authors cite numerous organizations, largely in the developed world, that support "one share, one vote" as a matter of principle. Yet the authors also show that there are substantial deviations from this principle in many emerging markets: among other things, through the use of multiple-voting shares, nonvoting shares, shares with preferential rights, and cross-shareholding arrangements. The result is control by the few, even though there may be ownership by the many.

Surprisingly, the authors conclude from their review of the relevant literature that not all deviations from one share, one vote detract from value. Some studies show that firms that deviate from the principle actually outperform those that do not. Other studies, however, conclude the opposite.

The authors therefore identify a policy trade-off: between promoting capital market development and creating an environment where companies can achieve the highest returns. Can these two objectives be achieved simultaneously, and what do voting and control mechanisms have to do with the effort? The authors wrestle with this trade-off, noting that the protection of minority shareholders remains paramount if countries want to attract both domestic and foreign investors to the capital markets.

What kinds of risks do the financial systems of emerging-market countries pose to the global financial system, and how can regulators and international financial institutions recognize them sufficiently in advance so as to prevent undue damage if they do occur? Patrick Conroy and Arne Petersen of the World Bank address these questions in the final chapter in this section.

The World Bank and the IMF developed the Financial Sector Assessment Program (FSAP) to address issues of country-specific vulnerability and to stimulate constructive dialogue between the officials of relevant countries and the international financial institutions. Since FSAPs were introduced, sixty-five countries have been assessed for their compliance with international financial standards, specifically those developed by the International Organization of Securities Commissions (IOSCO) and by the Basel Committee for International Bank Supervision (bank capital standards). Most countries formally comply, through legislative mandates, with the IOSCO standards in particular, although it can be difficult to assess the degree of compliance in actual practice.

The FSAP process has also revealed a number of generic weaknesses, including nebulous divisions of regulatory responsibilities between agencies, lack of adequate staffing in regulatory agencies, limited options for regulators to impose administrative penalties for noncompliance, inadequate supervision of risk management practices within financial intermediaries, and insufficient mechanisms to detect market manipulation and other unfair practices.

Regulators must also respond to financial crises of various sorts. The authors emphasize the importance of adequate disclosure as a way of warding off crises and refer to the ongoing efforts of IOSCO to improve transparency by private market actors. The authors also note that the faster pace and higher volume of cross-border financial activity underscore the need for regulators in different jurisdictions to cooperate with one another to address, and ideally prevent, cross-border financial contagion.

Over the longer run, both the World Bank and the IMF have stepped up their financial technical assistance to developing countries through the Financial Sector Reform Strengthening Initiative (FIRST). Meanwhile, regulators in developing countries themselves must respond to the need for more consistent and accurate disclosure by publicly traded corporations, as the accounting scandals in even as sophisticated a financial market as the United States have revealed.

* * *

Equities markets exist to provide a means of financing for public corporations. If companies' shares cannot be traded, they are much less likely to be issued and bought.

But to what extent do corporations in emerging markets rely on external financing, and how, if at all, do they differ from firms in more developed economies? Jack Glen of the International Finance Corporation and Ajit Singh of Cambridge University address these questions by reporting the results of their analysis of financial statements of nearly 8,000 companies in forty-four countries during the 1994–2000 period. Their chapter contains numerous empirical findings, only a few of which we summarize here.

As a threshold matter, the authors report that the size of equity markets in the two different parts of the world is very different. In 1994, total world stock market capitalization was approximately $15 trillion, of which about $2 trillion was in emerging markets. By 2000, the disparity between the capitalization of stock markets in developed countries and that of markets in developing countries had grown significantly: whereas total world stock market capitalization had more than doubled, to $32 trillion, emerging-market capitalization had crept up to just $2.7 trillion.

The disparity in market capitalization for exchanges as a whole is mirrored at the company level as well. By and large, companies in emerging markets were smaller in the authors' sample than companies in developed countries, although there is significant variation across countries (the sample companies in Mexico, for example, are larger than those in the United States, while the companies in Peru are much smaller).

The authors investigate differences in capital structure in companies in different countries, since the amount of leverage can have a significant bearing on the exposure of the companies and their local economies generally to external shocks. Here, too, there is great variation across countries, within both the developed- and developing-country samples. Nonetheless, not surprisingly, the authors find a statistically significant greater leverage ratio at the beginning of the period, 1994, for companies in emerging-market countries relative to firms in developed economies. However, in the wake of the financial crises in Asia and other emerging markets in the latter part of the 1990s, firms in emerging markets were forced to deleverage, and this result shows up in the authors' data.

The authors also find a lot of cross-country variation in rates of return. But, again not surprisingly, the data reveal that, on average, returns on assets and equity for developing-country firms were below those for developed-country firms during the sample period.

How did firms in the two parts of the sample finance their growth, at least during the sample period? Consistent with the deleveraging of firms from 1994 to 2000, the authors find that firms in emerging markets, on average, financed much less of their growth with debt than firms in developed countries. Of course, there is significant variation across countries in this respect as well.

The authors conclude with perhaps a paradoxical observation: the differences between firms in emerging markets and developed economies are not as significant as they expected. In this regard, the view held in some quarters that firms in emerging markets are subjected to less competition than firms in other countries may not be valid.

The finding that firms in developing countries have performed poorly in recent years is confirmed in the chapter by Dilip Ratha and Philip Suttle of the World Bank and Sanket Mohapatra of Columbia University. These authors find that the profitability of these firms was declining even before the Asian financial crisis. Since the crisis, despite the efforts of many surviving firms to pay down debt, the corporate sector in the affected countries remains highly leveraged and exposed to sudden withdrawals of capital by foreign suppliers. Indeed, companies in Latin America and Eastern Europe, also highly leveraged, have increased their dependence on foreign finance.

Of course, relying on foreign borrowing entails both benefits and risks. It is beneficial to the extent it is provided at lower cost than domestic funds. But it can be highly risky if short term in nature and denominated in foreign currency, thus exposing the borrowers to the risk of exchange rate depreciation. Problems among Asian companies—before the 1997–98 crisis—dramatically illustrated both risks.

As for the future, the authors stress the need to improve both the quality and timeliness of corporate financial reporting in developing countries, a challenge underscored by similar problems experienced in the United States.

* * *

It is one thing for corporate borrowers to need funds, but capital markets need suppliers of funds as well. One critical challenge for all emerging-market economies is to develop a base of domestic institutional investors who will buy the securities that local public companies issue. The concluding chapter by Alberto Musalem of the World Bank and Thierry Tressel of the IMF examines this important challenge.

The authors begin by surveying the theoretical and empirical literature on the linkages between institutional investors—pension funds in particular—and economic growth. There should be a positive relationship between the two if contractual savings systems increase saving, as they should do if the systems are mandatory. Even if participation in pensions is voluntary, the plans may have a salutory demonstration impact on savings. Surveying the evidence, the authors study Southeast Asian and Latin American plans that are fully funded and report that they appear to enhance national savings. Furthermore, developing countries that shift from a pay-as-you-go pension system to one that is fully funded tend, over time, to experience an increase in saving, although initially such reforms may reduce saving.

Contractual savings institutions deepen the demand for securities and thereby enhance securities markets, a theoretical outcome that has some empirical support. In addition, the presence of institutional investors can indirectly improve domestic financial stability by signaling to foreign investors that a country is a safe place in which to invest. This stabilizing effect can be reinforced to the degree that institutional investors insist on transparency and sound governance by the firms whose equity or debt they purchase.

The authors report previous econometric work they conducted to assess the impact of contractual savings institutions on firms' capital structures. In brief, they find that, after controlling for firm characteristics, macroeconomic factors, and financial system characteristics, the level of development of contractual savings institutions is positively related to leverage and maturity of debt. That is, the deeper a country's institutional investor base, the better able are its firms to borrow, and the more likely are they to do so at longer maturities.

The authors also report on their previous study of the linkages between the development of a country's contractual savings institutions and characteristics of its banks. Among other things, they find that such development tends to reduce net interest margins by banks (due to the competitive pressure applied by the contractual institutions), lengthen loan maturities, and reduce credit risk.

The authors conclude with some thoughts about the policy implications of their work. They suggest that only countries with sustainable macroeconomic outcomes—especially low inflation rates—are likely to enable the growth of institutional savings systems. The authors caution against limiting the asset choices of institutional investors, as these can harm their beneficiaries or clients.

* * *

In sum, emerging markets require healthy capital markets if they are to reap full advantage of finance in promoting real growth in their economies. The chapters in this volume offer a guide for both policymakers and actors in the market about the progress that has been made toward development of capital markets in emerging-market countries and what policies might be employed to further their development in the future.

PART I

Capital Market Development around the World

GERD HÄUSLER
DONALD J. MATHIESON
JORGE ROLDOS

2

Trends in Developing-Country Capital Markets around the World

One of the key structural changes in a growing number of emerging markets has been the rapid development of local securities markets since the mid-1990s. This change has reflected both policy efforts by the authorities in major emerging markets and trends in global financial markets. In this paper, we review some of the trends in the development of local markets as well as some key policy issues, as reported in several of the International Monetary Fund's Global Financial Stability Reports.[1]

The efforts to develop local securities markets have been motivated by a number of considerations, especially the desire to provide an alternative source of funding in order to self-insure against reversals in capital flows. One motivation has been a desire to stimulate domestic saving by offering savers new financial instruments that broaden the set of investment opportunities and allow for better portfolio diversification. In many emerging markets, for example, domestic residents traditionally have had access to only two types of domestic instruments—bank deposits and domestic equities—and have had little access to international markets. Another consideration has been to improve the intermediation of domestic savings and attract foreign investors. This has become particularly important as a

1. International Monetary Fund (2002a, 2002b, 2002c).

greater number of emerging markets have privatized their pension systems. In some countries, such as Chile, the private pension funds and insurance companies have been key sources of demand for high-quality corporate bonds, reflecting a desire to achieve a rate of return higher than can be obtained on bank deposits and also to access longer-duration assets (which better match their long-duration obligations). Moreover, emerging markets have sought to develop alternative sources of funding for both the public and corporate sectors to either domestic bank lending or international capital markets.[2] In addition, local derivatives markets have been seen as providing a vehicle for managing financial risks, especially those related to exchange rates and interest rates.

The measures adopted to further the development of local securities and derivatives markets have typically encompassed efforts to strengthen market infrastructure and create benchmark issues, expand the set of institutional investors, and improve corporate governance and transparency. However, there are several key policy areas where no consensus has emerged regarding either the factors that will influence the likely outcomes or the most appropriate policies. Issues remain regarding the following:

—The use of instruments indexed to changes in such variables as the price level and exchange rates,

—The government's role in promoting the development of local equity markets,

—The role of foreign investors in local securities markets,

—The sequencing of reforms in local securities and derivatives markets.

The paper is organized as follows. The first section reviews recent trends in the development of local capital markets in the major emerging markets and draws some comparisons to the mature markets. This is followed by an analysis of the role that local markets have played as an alternative source of funding in the absence of access to international markets or the banking system. Next, the main policy measures undertaken to promote the development of these markets are reviewed, as well as some areas where there is less than full consensus in the policy community. We conclude with some final thoughts on the future of these markets.

2. Drawing on lessons from recent emerging-market crises, Greenspan (1999) notes that well-developed bond markets can act like a "spare tire" and substitute for bank lending as a source of corporate funding when bank lending dries up.

Recent Trends in Emerging Local Securities Markets

Local bond markets in emerging markets have grown considerably over the last decade, but they are still much smaller than bond markets in the G-7 countries. Although emerging local bond markets have nearly doubled in size since 1993, to roughly 36 percent of gross domestic product (GDP), they are still a long shot from developed-country bond markets (see table 2-1). Mature markets average 122 percent of GDP, although this is influenced by the large 151 percent of the United States, with euroland showing a lower figure of around 88 percent of GDP.

Until the mid-1990s, emerging local bond markets were generally underdeveloped, with restricted demand for fixed-income products, a limited supply of quality bond issues, and inadequate market infrastructure. However, particularly in the period after the Asian crisis, many governments have made determined efforts to overcome these limitations. Nonetheless, there are regional differences in how rapidly the markets have developed. In Asia, the growth of local bond issuance has been driven by the need to recapitalize banking systems and, more recently, to finance expansionary fiscal policies. The lack of bank credit has also contributed to some increase in corporate bond issuance, not just in Asia but also in Latin America. In the latter region, the rapid growth of local institutional investors, together with the large refinancing needs of the corporate sector in a difficult external environment, have driven the growth of local bond markets. Finally, the buildup of institutions, such as debt management agencies, and the harmonization of regulations in the process of accession to the European Union (EU), have contributed to the growth of local bond markets in the Czech Republic, Hungary, and Poland—the so-called CE-3 countries.

A number of countries have made substantial progress in the development of government bond markets, but progress has been somewhat slower in corporate bond markets.[3] Although this has been the sequence of market development observed in many countries, there is nevertheless a risk that improved bond markets and debt management strategies could lead to excessive issuance of government debt and crowding out of the corporate sector. It has been the case, however, that the efforts of authorities to develop

3. As in previous reports, only a select sample of emerging markets is covered in this chapter. These countries are those that have been visited by the staff in the past two years and where information on recent developments is most up-to-date. As a result, some markets, such as South Africa, are not included.

Table 2-1. *Amount Outstanding in the Local Bond Market, by Region and Type of Issuer, 1993–2001*

Percent of GDP

Issuer	*1993*	*1994*	*1995*	*1996*	*1997*	*1998*	*1999*	*2000*	*2001*
All issuers									
All domestic bonds	91.1	95.7	94.6	96.6	96.5	106.4	108.8	106.0	108.9
Public sector	57.8	61.3	60.2	61.2	60.5	65.4	66.8	64.1	65.9
Financial institutions	22.6	23.9	24.2	24.9	25.2	28.4	28.3	27.8	28.2
Corporate sector	10.7	10.5	10.3	10.6	10.8	12.7	13.7	14.1	14.7
Developed countries									
All domestic bonds	100.9	106.0	104.8	108.1	109.0	118.9	120.6	118.4	121.5
Public sector	63.9	68.0	66.7	68.3	67.9	72.8	73.7	71.1	73.0
Financial institutions	25.2	26.4	26.8	28.0	28.8	32.0	31.7	31.5	32.0
Corporate sector	11.8	11.7	11.3	11.8	12.3	14.1	15.1	15.8	16.4
United States									
All domestic bonds	138.9	139.2	142.4	144.7	145.1	149.5	152.3	147.7	150.6
Public sector	90.0	90.1	90.2	90.0	87.5	87.2	87.4	81.7	83.8
Financial institutions	25.3	26.4	29.2	31.8	35.0	38.6	40.9	42.0	42.8
Corporate sector	23.6	22.7	22.9	22.9	22.6	23.6	24.1	23.9	24.0
Euroland									
All domestic bonds	79.9	89.7	88.2	88.8	87.7	94.5	86.1	90.7	87.6
Public sector	46.4	53.7	53.3	54.5	54.1	58.2	52.1	54.5	52.9
Financial institutions	31.1	33.4	32.6	31.8	31.1	33.4	30.4	31.2	28.9
Corporate sector	2.5	2.5	2.3	2.5	2.5	2.9	3.6	5.0	5.9
Emerging markets									
All domestic bonds	20.4	23.9	25.3	26.8	24.2	32.1	33.5	33.2	35.6
Public sector	13.3	14.3	14.7	16.3	15.9	20.0	21.8	22.0	23.7
Financial institutions	4.5	6.8	7.3	7.0	5.8	8.0	7.0	6.5	6.9
Corporate sector	2.6	2.9	3.2	3.5	2.6	4.1	4.7	4.7	5.0
Asia									
All domestic bonds	24.1	26.4	26.8	27.6	21.4	33.2	35.5	35.9	37.8
Public sector	13.3	13.9	13.4	13.9	11.4	17.3	19.7	20.5	21.5
Financial institutions	6.5	7.6	8.1	7.9	6.0	9.0	8.6	8.4	8.9
Corporate sector	4.2	4.9	5.2	5.6	3.8	6.8	7.1	6.9	7.4
Latin America									
All domestic bonds	15.0	20.9	23.4	26.4	28.8	31.8	31.3	29.6	32.3
Public sector	12.0	13.7	15.8	19.3	21.7	23.0	24.6	23.8	26.2
Financial institutions	2.3	6.5	7.1	6.5	6.0	7.7	5.4	4.4	4.5
Corporate sector	0.7	0.6	0.5	0.6	1.0	1.1	1.3	1.4	1.5
Eastern Europe									
All domestic bonds	21.8	21.9	21.8	21.5	21.1	25.5	26.5	27.8	31.9
Public sector	21.6	21.1	20.3	19.8	19.1	23.5	24.4	25.4	29.8
Financial institutions	0.1	0.6	0.8	0.9	0.9	1.0	1.0	1.0	0.9
Corporate sector	0.1	0.2	0.5	0.6	0.9	0.9	1.1	1.3	1.1

Source: Bank for International Settlements and International Monetary Fund staff estimates.

local bond markets, combined with the efforts of corporates to diversify away from refinancing and foreign exchange risks, also have contributed to the expansion of local corporate bond markets in most emerging markets—with the exception, perhaps, of countries in Central Europe. Despite this growth, access to local bond issuance has been restricted to top-tier corporates, and it is unclear whether these markets are resilient and large enough to be considered a meaningful alternative source of funding.

Although the recent development of local bond markets in emerging-market countries has been in large measure a consequence of conscious policy action, the development of the equity market as an alternative source of funding to banks has been influenced by both global and local market trends. The use of equity markets as a serious alternative source of financing for emerging-market corporates began in earnest in the mid-1990s. This period coincides both with significant financial market liberalization in many emerging-market countries and with a marked increase in the interest of international money managers in emerging-market equities. To provide some numbers to capture these developments, stock market capitalization of the main emerging markets was just half of the value of outstanding domestic credit in 1990. By 1994, stock market capitalization was a bit higher than the total value of domestic credit in the main emerging markets, as a combination of increases in equity issuance (associated in part with privatization) and increases in valuations dramatically pushed up the value of total market capitalization. For instance, the average value of market capitalization of the Standard & Poor's/International Finance Corporation Investible (S&P/IFCI) Composite Index more than tripled from about $200 billion between 1990 and 1994 to about $700 billion between 1995 and 2000 and has been broadly at that level recently. While much of the increase in market capitalization in the latter half of the 1990s was in Asia and Latin America (Malaysia and Mexico, for instance, witnessed a tripling of their ratios of stock market capitalization to GDP in this period), the more recent increases in market capitalization have occurred in the transition economies of Central Europe and Russia.

Despite its importance as a source of funding for corporates in emerging markets, the stock market has become more volatile as a result of a string of financial crises, starting with Mexico in 1995, then Asia during 1997–98, Russia in 1998, Brazil in 1999, and, in more recent years, Argentina and Turkey. These crises culminated in severe contractions in economic activity, and the currency depreciations that accompanied them seriously dented the stock markets. The ratio of market capitalization to

GDP in a number of emerging markets, such as Brazil, Malaysia, and Mexico, have reverted to their pre-1995 levels. As the result of negative returns on the S&P/IFCI Composite Index over the past five years, the significant increase in the volatility of returns, and the drying up of initial public offerings (IPOs), emerging stock markets have experienced a significant decline in liquidity. This has made it difficult recently even for well-functioning corporates in emerging markets to tap the equity market as a source of funding.

Local Capital Markets as an Alternative Source of Funding

Given the efforts to develop local securities markets, to what extent have these markets begun to provide an alternative source of funding to either domestic bank lending or international capital flows for both the private sector and the public sector? A number of key conclusions emerge from the data on local and international issuance during the period 1997–2001. First, there has been a surge of local corporate bond issuance, particularly in Asia and Latin America. Indeed, local corporate bond issues grew by a factor of 10 between 1997–99 and 2000–01. Second, local bond markets have been the dominant source of funding for the public sector in all regions. Third, while emerging markets have traditionally been viewed as bank-dominated financial systems, local bond markets have become the largest single source of domestic and international funding. As already noted, this primarily reflects the heavy reliance of the public sector on bond issuance. Nonetheless, domestic corporate bond issuance rose from 5 percent of total corporate domestic and international funding in 1997–99 to 31 percent in 2000–01, whereas domestic bank credit fell from 52 percent of total corporate funding in 1997–99 to 40 percent in 2000–01.

For the private sector, figure 2-1 compares the domestic issuance of corporate bonds, equities, and bank lending with the issuance of international corporate bonds, equities, and syndicated loans for select emerging markets across different regions for the period from 1997 until 2001.[4] During this

4. The economies included in the figures are China, Hong Kong SAR, Malaysia, Singapore, South Korea, and Thailand; Argentina, Brazil, Chile, and Mexico; and the Czech Republic, Hungary, and Poland. The countries were selected on the basis of the availability of data on corporate bond issuance. The data on local bond issuance include various types of instruments, including fixed-interest-rate bonds, floating-interest-rate bonds, and bonds indexed to such items as the price level or the exchange rate. In general, it is not feasible to segment the data by type of instrument.

period, domestic bank lending was the dominant source of corporate funding, accounting for 48 percent of total domestic and international funding. Nonetheless, domestic corporate bond issuance rose from an annual average of $11 billion in 1997–99 to $106 billion in 2000–01, and, for the period as a whole, domestic corporate bond issues represented just under 17 percent of total funding. Domestic equity issues accounted for only about 11 percent of total funding.

International issues of bonds, equities, and syndicated loans by the corporate sector accounted for just over 25 percent of total funding between 1997 and 2001 (see figure 2-1). However, international corporate bond issues amounted to only roughly half of such bonds issued domestically. Indeed, while the annual average value of domestic corporate bond issuance rose between 1997–99 and 2000–01, the annual average value of international corporate bond issuance declined from $28 billion to $26 billion, respectively. Moreover, international equity issuance amounted to about half of domestic equity issuance, while syndicated lending was equivalent to around 20 percent of the extension of domestic credit.

Thus, while domestic bank credit has been the primary source of corporate funding for this group of emerging markets, domestic bond markets have been an increasingly important source of funding. Indeed, domestic corporate bond issues rose from 5 percent of total corporate domestic and international funding in 1997–99 to 31 percent in 2000–01. During the same period, domestic bank credit fell from 52 percent of total corporate funding in 1997–99 to 40 percent in 2000–01.

Between 1997 and 2001, the pattern of corporate funding revealed sharp regional differences. In Asia, domestic bank lending accounted for 65 percent of total domestic and international financing. Moreover, domestic equity issuance was the second largest source of corporate funding ($112 billion) and slightly exceeded corporate bond issuance ($97 billion). Nonetheless, domestic corporate bond issuance rose from an annual average of $276 million in 1997–99 to $48 billion in 2000–01. International issues of equity, bonds, and syndicated loans represented about 17 percent of total corporate domestic and international funding in 1997–2001.

In Central Europe, domestic bank lending was also the largest source of corporate finance during 1997–2001, but privatization helped to make domestic equity issuance ($13 billion) the second largest source of funding. Domestic bond issuance remained limited.

In contrast to other regions, domestic bond issues ($147 billion) became the dominant source of corporate funding in Latin America between 1997

Figure 2-1. *Private Sector Issuance, in Billions of U.S. Dollars, 1997–2001*

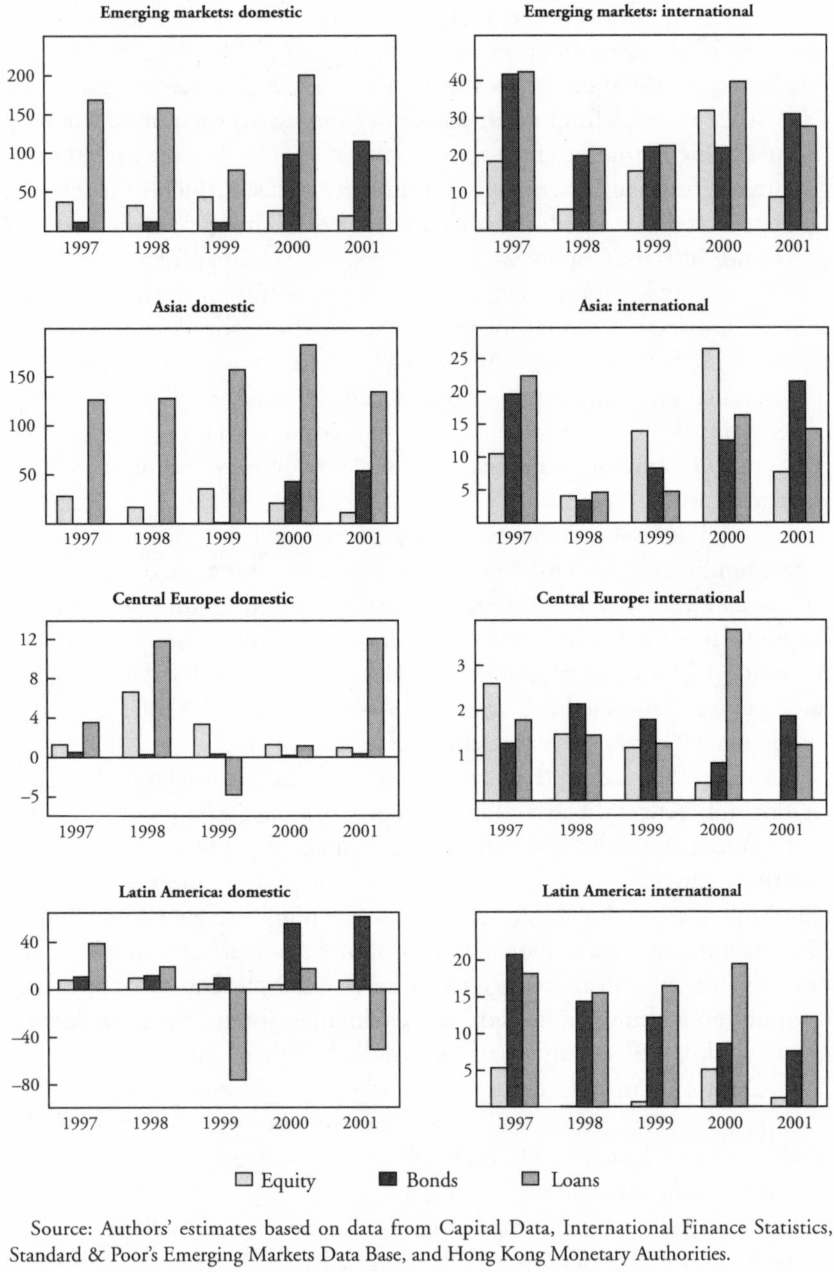

Source: Authors' estimates based on data from Capital Data, International Finance Statistics, Standard & Poor's Emerging Markets Data Base, and Hong Kong Monetary Authorities.

and 2001. Indeed, local bond issues nearly equaled the total of international issues of bonds, equities, and syndicated lending ($157 billion). Moreover, domestic bank lending contracted (by $51 billion).

While local securities markets played an increasingly important role as an alternative source of funding for the domestic corporate sector, they were an even more important source of funding for the public sector (see figure 2-2).[5] Domestic government bond issues clearly were the dominant source of funding for the public sector throughout 1997–2001. Indeed, public sector domestic bond issuance was nearly thirteen times larger than international foreign currency bond issues. This primarily reflects the heavy reliance on domestic bond issuance in Latin America and, to a lesser extent, Central Europe. Nonetheless, even in Asia, domestic bond issuance is the largest single source of public sector funding.

Despite the dominant role of domestic bond markets in all regions, the financing mix for the public sector has differed sharply across the three regions. In Asia, the public sector relied more on credit from the banking system than in other regions. Moreover, the public sector in Asia met a great proportion of its financing from international sources (17 percent) than in other regions. In contrast, the public sectors in Latin America and Central Europe obtained most of their funding through domestic bond issuance (93 and 95 percent, respectively). Indeed, Latin American authorities issued nearly fifteen times as many domestic bonds as international foreign currency bonds.

Despite the rapid expansion of local bond markets (see figure 2-3), it remains unclear whether local securities markets have developed to the point that they will be able to offset either weaknesses in the banking system that curtail bank lending or a loss of access to international markets.[6] Moreover, emerging markets will need ongoing access to global capital markets if they are going to receive the transfers of technology and capital needed for sustained growth and development. Nonetheless, the continued development of local securities and derivatives markets could eventually provide an additional "cushion" by developing a longer-duration domestic

5. The public sector is defined to consist of the central government, government-owned financial institutions, and public sector enterprises.

6. The role of local derivatives markets in supporting both local market activities and capital flows is discussed in IMF (2002c, chap. 4). Indeed, a strong banking system is likely to play a key role in facilitating the development of local securities and derivatives, since banks in emerging markets often are key underwriters of securities, investors in bonds, providers of credit to securities houses, and suppliers of over-the-counter derivatives products.

Figure 2-2. *Public Sector Issuance, in Billions of U.S. Dollars, 1997–2001*

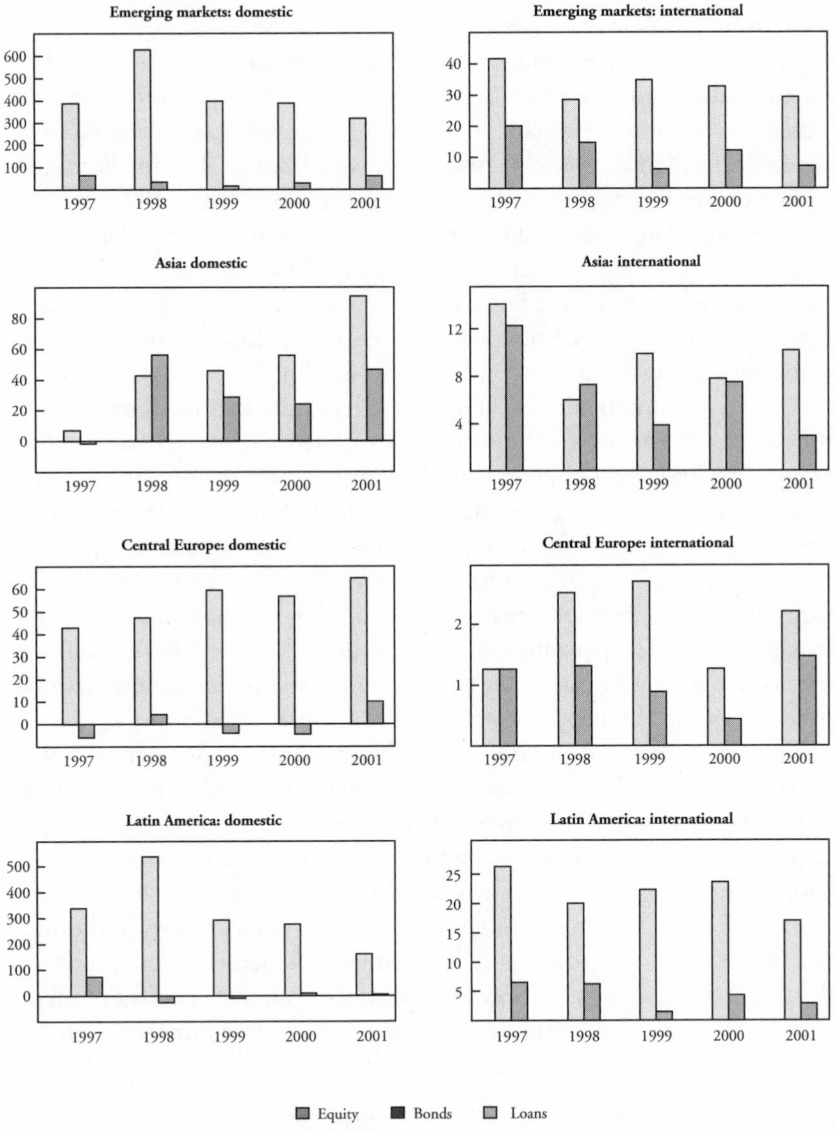

Source: Authors' estimates based on data from Capital Data, International Finance Statistics, Standard & Poor's Emerging Markets Data Base, and Hong Kong Monetary Authorities.

Figure 2-3. *Overall Issuance, in Billions of U.S. Dollars, 1997–2001*

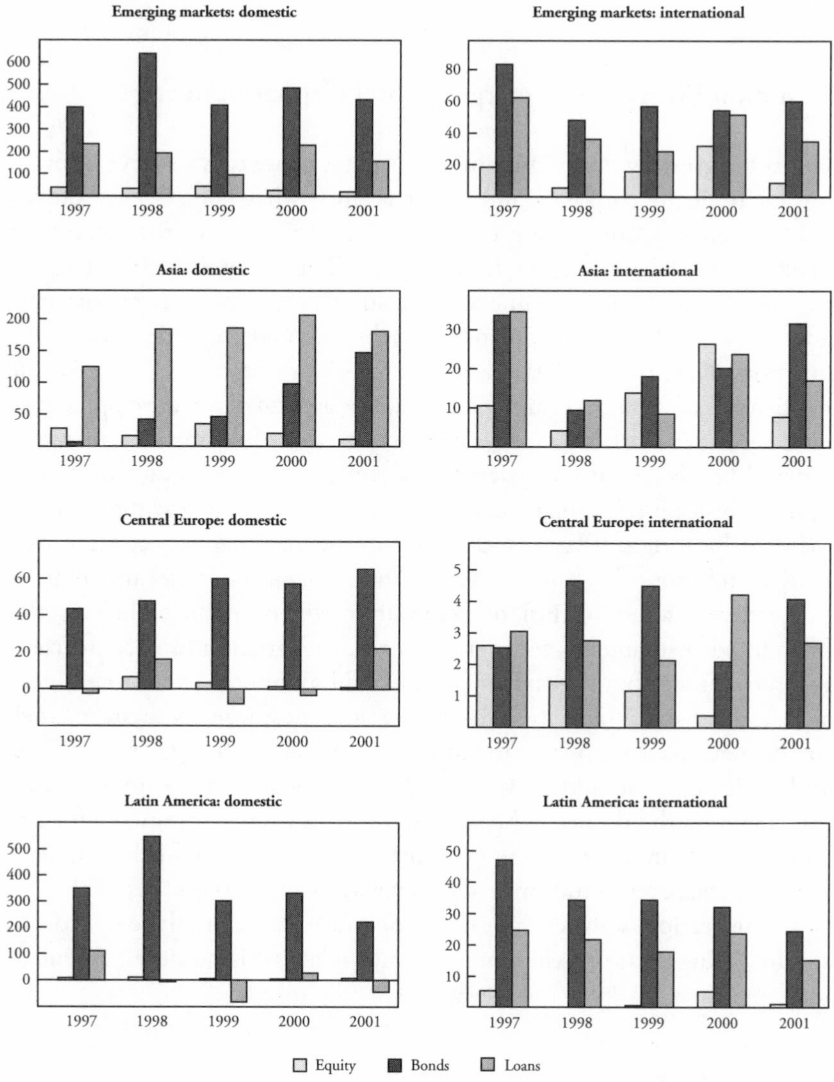

Source: Authors' estimates based on data from Capital Data, International Finance Statistics, Standard & Poor's Emerging Markets Data Base, and Hong Kong Monetary Authorities.

source of funding that may not immediately dry up when a crisis occurs and by providing some vehicles for hedging risks prior to a crisis.

Common Practices in Emerging Local Capital Markets

Given the growing importance of local capital markets as a source of funding for both the corporate and public sectors, what policies have proven most effective in stimulating their development? Some of these common practices are reviewed briefly in this section. There is broad agreement that improvements in market infrastructure and transparency, better corporate governance, and the development of benchmarks and domestic institutional investors all contribute to the development of local securities markets. The net benefits are less clear-cut regarding other aspects of the development of local securities markets (the so-called gray areas). These include the use of indexed bonds, credit risk pricing, government policies toward the development of local stock markets, the role of foreign investors, the development of local derivatives markets, and the sequencing of local securities markets reforms. Nonetheless, despite the ambiguities concerning policies in these areas, some conclusions seem warranted. For instance, the existence of indexed instruments and derivatives can lengthen and deepen fixed-income markets, but they may require careful monitoring to prevent undesirable mismatches and excessively leveraged positions. Moreover, stock market reforms that improve the conditions under which corporations issue and trade shares should be welcomed, but they should not protect local exchanges or the domestic brokerage industry from domestic or foreign competition. Similarly, foreign investors can contribute to the deepening of local markets, even if they may add to volatility during episodes of crisis.

In this section, some of these common practices are briefly reviewed.[7] In the following section, select policy issues related to the development of local securities markets (the gray areas) are discussed.

Market Infrastructure and Benchmarks

A large number of emerging markets have improved the market infrastructure for local securities and have established relevant benchmark yield

7. Surveys on some of these issues, mostly for local bond markets, include World Bank and IMF (2001); Bank for International Settlements (2002); OECD (2001).

curves.[8] Although the provision of a robust financial infrastructure for trading, clearing, and settlement of transactions is generally considered to be a public good, many authorities have felt that the establishment of a liquid government security benchmark yield curve to facilitate the pricing of corporate securities is also a desirable policy objective.[9] In principle, benchmarks could be provided by other instruments issued by quasi-public entities (such as the mortgage agencies in the United States) or even private instruments (including swaps), but it is unlikely that they would reach the level of issuance and liquidity needed to perform benchmark functions.[10]

Institutional Investors

Many emerging markets have realized the importance of developing a local institutional investor base to support local securities markets. The growth of such an investor base has usually been slow, however, and tight regulations on asset allocations have constrained the potentially beneficial role that they could play in local securities markets.

Local pension funds have made a particularly important contribution to the development of local securities markets in Latin America and Central Europe, and their role is beginning to be felt in some local markets in Asia. Following the lead of Chile in the 1980s, most Latin American countries have established private pension funds that have become important sources of demand for local securities as well as for the development of market infrastructure and improved corporate governance and transparency. Similar trends are emerging in Central Europe, where mandatory private pension funds were introduced somewhat later. The provident funds in many Asian countries are largely under public administration and to date have not played a very active role in local market development, but some countries are gradually outsourcing funds to private asset managers.

Corporate Governance and Transparency

A number of countries have adopted measures to improve transparency and corporate governance, which they see as critical for local capital market

8. See IMF (2002b).

9. See, for instance, Yam (2001).

10. Even in the mature markets, the low credit risk and high liquidity of government securities have made them natural providers of benchmark interest rates (see IMF 2001).

development. Studies have shown that countries with less protection for minority shareholders have less developed equity markets, and that firms in these countries use less outside finance and have higher debt-equity ratios, making them more vulnerable to shocks.[11] In response to this evidence, as well as to high-profile shareholder conflicts, some countries have recently changed the laws governing capital markets (including Brazil, Chile, the Czech Republic, and Mexico), while others (including Korea, Malaysia, Hong Kong SAR, Poland, and Singapore) have approved codes of best practice designed to improve disclosure, protect minority shareholders' rights, and maximize shareholder value.

Other Policy Issues

While the development of market infrastructure, institutional investors, and transparency is a necessary step, countries' experiences and the arguments behind some other aspects of the development of local securities markets are less clear-cut. This section considers other policy issues related to the development of local securities markets, in particular those issues that could affect macroeconomic policies or financial stability and capital flows.

Indexed Bonds

The development of indexed bonds, in particular inflation-indexed (or inflation-linked) bonds, has contributed to the development of local bond markets, especially in high-inflation emerging markets. Although there is some discussion about the macroeconomic consequences of indexation, there is almost a consensus that inflation-linked bonds provide risk-sharing opportunities to investors and issuers alike and that they contribute to complete asset markets in an efficient way. Recent experiences in Latin America provide some useful insights on the costs and benefits of inflation-linked bonds as well as on other aspects of indexation. In particular, they show that indexation to inflation could help to deepen and lengthen both

11. See La Porta and others (2000). Corporate governance and the development of local capital markets have been associated with macroeconomic outcomes such as output growth and the severity of exchange rate crises and output volatility (see Johnson and Shleifer forthcoming and references therein).

private and public bond markets, but that indexation to the exchange rate could lead to unstable macroeconomic and financial conditions. In other words, the introduction of indexed instruments needs to be complemented with stable macroeconomic policies and capital market reforms that favor the creation of a large institutional investor base.

The creation of the Unidad de Fomento (UF), a unit of account indexed to the consumer price index, together with the development of a strong institutional investor base, has played a central role in the development of the local bond markets in Chile. In particular, most corporate bonds in Chile are indexed to the UF, and this has contributed to the recent growth and long maturities of the corporate bond market. Analyst argue that, had it not been for the fact that the UF is mandatory for many financial contracts and for the development of a UF-denominated government bond market, the fixed-income market would have developed toward shorter-term, dollar-denominated securities.[12]

This conjecture is confirmed by the experience of Brazil, where efforts to deindex the stock of domestic debt during the successful Real Plan of 1994–98 led to a relatively large share of fixed-rate debt (approximately 60 percent of the total, see figure 2-4) by mid-1997. However, increased instability in the wake of the 1998–99 financial crisis drastically reduced the share of fixed-rate bonds, and the authorities had to increase the supply of bonds indexed to overnight interest rates and the U.S. dollar in order to reduce refinancing risk. While dollar-linked debt provides a foreign currency hedge for investors, it can lead to financial instability if the excessive use of this instrument results in sizable currency mismatches that create solvency concerns about the issuers—like the sovereign or nonexporters, whose tax revenues or receipts are mostly denominated in local currency.[13] The higher volatility of the exchange rate vis-à-vis the price level, especially during capital flow reversals, causes a deterioration in these issuers' balance sheet positions that is likely to magnify the initial problem of lost access to international capital markets and capital outflows.[14]

The issuance of dollar-linked debt in local markets compounds the problem that most emerging markets cannot issue international bonds

12. See Walker (2002).

13. Similar issues arise in economies with dollarized deposits; see IMF (2003) for a discussion of prudential and crisis management aspects of dollarized banking systems.

14. Experience shows that the consumer price index is less volatile than the exchange rate, especially during crises; price indexation is also a superior alternative to indexation through floating interest rates, as the latter are quite volatile in emerging markets.

Figure 2-4. *Composition of the Domestic Federal Debt in Brazil, 1997–2001*

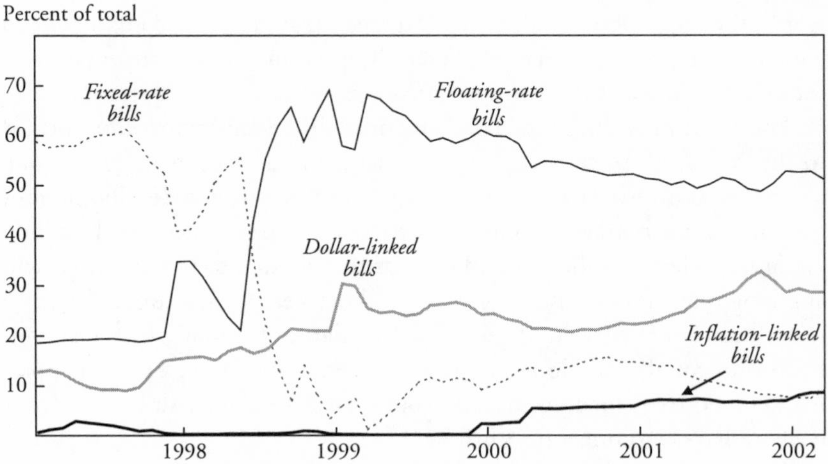

Source: Authors' estimates based on data from Capital Data, International Finance Statistics, Standard & Poor's Emerging Markets Data Base, and Hong Kong Monetary Authorities.

denominated in their own currencies, a fact that Eichengreen, Hausmann, and Panizza refer to as the "original sin."[15] These economists argue that the large share of foreign-currency-denominated emerging-market debt is not just a result of weak macroeconomic policies and underdeveloped local markets but also a consequence of the limited incentives for currency diversification by global investors. As a result, they recently proposed that the World Bank and other regional development banks sponsor a mechanism that would allow emerging markets to issue more debt denominated in their own currencies.[16]

The proposal involves a number of steps. The first step involves the development of a currency basket index including a well-diversified set of emerging-market currencies. The next steps have the World Bank and other international financial institutions (IFIs) issue debt denominated in the index, eventually followed by similar efforts by the G-10 countries.

15. Eichengreen, Hausmann, and Panizza (2002).

16. The proposal is inspired by the fact that international financial institutions issued almost half of all internationally placed bonds in exotic currencies during 1992–98. In most cases, the debt-service obligations were swapped back into U.S. dollars, providing additional support to foreign currency swap markets.

The World Bank could convert the U.S. dollar loans made to the countries in the index into local currency inflation-linked loans and eliminate the currency mismatch generated by the issuance of the proposed bonds, while the G-10 countries could undertake currency swaps with each individual country in the index, allowing the former to eliminate the currency mismatch and providing the latter with a useful hedge against their original sin.

The proposal is innovative, but analysts are skeptical about its implementation and acceptance by investors, as well as its remaining risks for the international financial institutions. In particular, market participants, IFI representatives, and academics are concerned that the proposal may reduce incentives to address the more fundamental issues preventing a number of emerging markets from issuing bonds in their own currencies: namely, weak macroeconomic policies and poorly developed local financial markets. In addition, potential borrowers may prefer to use their access to IFI loans in terms of foreign exchange at favorable interest rates than raise local currency loans. Analysts are further worried about international investors' lack of appetite for emerging-market inflation-linked bonds. They also suggest that, despite the adjustment of the index to each of the countries' consumer price index, emerging markets could have an incentive to depreciate their currencies in the days before the coupons are fixed, in order to lower their debt obligations. Moreover, they are concerned that the index would provide incentives to do this in a concerted fashion, creating another channel for contagion in foreign exchange markets. As a result, the stronger emerging-market players may not find it advantageous to participate in the index.

Credit Risk Pricing

Market participants regard the lack of sophistication in pricing credit risk as a major constraint on the growth of emerging corporate bond markets. But the development of a credit culture takes time, and it is unclear how much the authorities can do to speed up this process. A few aspects of the institutional structure that could be improved include the standardization of securities contracts, the requirement of ratings, and appropriate incentives for independent research on securities.

The standardization of bond contracts could contribute to a more accurate assessment of credit risk, but it could also constrain the issuer's financial flexibility. In several emerging markets, bond contracts have a variety of features—coupons linked to different reference rates, embedded options and other enhancements, and different types of collateral, covenants, and priority rules—that make it difficult to price the credit risk associated with the bond. Some degree of standardization and homogeneity in bond contracts would facilitate the pricing of credit risk, and securities regulators could ensure a minimum set of guidelines for such contracts.

Rating agencies appear to be useful in credit markets, but it is unclear to what extent regulations would have to force market participants to use their services or whether market participants themselves would find their credit assessments useful in their pricing or allocation decisions. The requirement that local pension funds invest only in rated instruments has contributed to the development of a rather sophisticated credit risk culture in Chilean local markets. Several other emerging markets are also requiring that issuers obtain one or two ratings for their corporate bond issues.

Finally, independent research would contribute to better credit risk assessments and pricing, but regulatory authorities can do little in this area.

Local Equity Markets and the Role of Stock Exchanges

The sharp fall in domestic equity issuance in 2000–02, combined with structural developments in global equity markets, has raised doubts about the long-term prospects of initial public offerings in local markets as an alternative source of funding in emerging markets.[17] The bear market in equities has shrunk trading volumes literally everywhere, and the combination of a drop in IPOs associated with the reduction in privatization and a spate of delistings has called into question the viability of many stock exchanges in emerging markets. Moreover, the competitive pressures created by declining costs—associated with automated electronic trading systems and the migration of listings toward exchanges with greater liquidity and a lower cost of funding—have stimulated both changes in the governance of stock exchanges and an increase in the international integration of exchanges. These developments, in turn, have raised the issue of the proper role of the public sector in either facilitating or promoting these structural changes.

17. These concerns are particularly serious in the case of small stock markets. See IMF (2002a) for further details on domestic equity markets as a source of funding and an investment alternative for international investors. Structural issues in global and emerging equity markets are dealt with in IMF (2001).

While a well-functioning stock exchange can yield efficiency gains by providing a key source of funding for the corporate sector and of liquidity for investors, there has been considerable debate about the extent of public sector involvement in helping to develop stock exchanges. There is general agreement that the development of equity markets will be facilitated by a sound macroeconomic environment, open access to foreign investors, political stability, and enforceable property rights. Properly designed and executed privatization programs can also stimulate the development of equity markets, and improvements in corporate governance and the protection of minority shareholders' interests are generally moves in the right direction.[18]

There are, however, several gray areas where there is much less of a consensus about the appropriate degree of official intervention.[19] For example, while everyone agrees that appropriate accounting standards should be put in place, there is considerable debate about whether these should follow generally accepted accounting principles or international accounting standards. In the end, either standard would probably work well as long as it is generally applied and enforced.

Similarly, there is no general agreement about the degree to which consumer protection and more general supervision of the exchanges should be undertaken by self-regulatory organizations or by the authorities. Whatever mix is decided upon, it is generally agreed that regulation and supervision should not be designed to stifle competition.

Perhaps the most contentious issue in many emerging markets is the role of the authorities in promoting changes in the ownership structure of the stock exchanges, particularly from a mutual to a publicly owned corporate structure. A growing number of analysts are recommending that the authorities support the demutualization of their exchanges. In many instances, this intervention is justified on the basis of a collective action problem, namely, that under a mutual ownership structure some vested interests (particularly small brokers) may block the adoption of new computer and telecommunication technologies that allow for more efficient trading platforms, because such platforms would allow for more direct

18. Claessens, Klingebiel, and Schmukler (2002) show that countries following these types of policies tend to have larger and more liquid stock exchanges. However, they also show that as such fundamentals improve, the degree of migration to other exchanges also increases.

19. The focus here is on structural policies. The issue of official intervention in stock and bond markets in the context of speculative attacks is dealt with in IMF (1999, chap. 5).

access to the trading floor, which could reduce brokerage revenues.[20] However, others argue that these decisions should be left up to the exchanges themselves and that competitive pressures (especially from abroad) will bring about the necessary changes.

The Role of Foreign Investors in Local Markets

Foreign investors are an important source of demand for local securities, and several developing countries have opened their local markets to foreign investors in an attempt to widen and diversify the investor base. Foreign participation appears to be larger in local equity markets than in local bond markets, but measurement of the latter is generally problematic and tends to underestimate foreign presence.[21] Although different types of foreign investors may have different investment strategies, market participants perceive foreign investors as playing a supportive role in local markets. For instance, recent inflows to Central European countries, motivated by the prospect of convergence with the European Union, have generally been perceived as driven by "real money" institutional investors that have a positive long-term view on the region and contribute to the depth of local markets. Also, foreign investors usually impose positive pressure for developing robust market infrastructure and transparent market practices.

Some analysts are concerned, however, that foreign investors may be less informed than local ones and may contribute to market volatility and crises. The empirical evidence on this, however, is rather limited and inconclusive. Some argue that foreign investors seeking diversification benefits may not have an incentive to invest in the necessary information required to understand local markets and may be more prone to herding behavior; others state that because foreign investors tend to be quite sensitive to risk and to actively manage their portfolios, they may make local markets more volatile and prone to crises. These hypotheses are difficult to test empirically, and only a couple of experiences may shed light on the issue.

Sequencing

The development of local securities markets raises a number of interesting questions about the optimal sequencing vis-à-vis the development of other

20. See, for instance, Steil (2001).
21. See IMF (2002b).

financial markets and institutions—such as money markets and banks—as well as other macroeconomic and regulatory policies. Broadly speaking, a comparison of different types of financial systems, and their evolution over time, is a complex issue, and there are no simple answers as to what would be an optimal development strategy.[22] Nevertheless, a gradual and complementary approach is beneficial as a general rule, although in some cases a given sequencing may be preferable.

Some analysts suggest that it may be optimal first to develop a deep local debt market, before opening up the capital account. An example of the former strategy is the path followed by Australia, which has developed a deep local bond market and has some 44 percent of its external debt denominated in local currency.[23] This also seems to be the path chosen by two large emerging markets, China and India, that have sizable local debt markets and have not yet fully opened up to foreign investors.[24] The potential benefits of developing local markets in isolation from international markets have to be weighed against traditional arguments against capital controls (such as misallocation of resources, increased costs of funding, and evasion) as well as the fact that market participants argue that controls have in some instances reduced liquidity and hence hindered the development of local securities markets.[25]

The development of well-functioning money markets appears to be a critical first step in developing corporate bond markets as well as derivatives markets.[26] Money markets provide an anchor to the short end of the yield curves and are critical for the pricing of fixed-income securities and derivatives. Korea and Thailand provide examples of the difficulties of developing a secondary bond market and the associated derivatives markets without the support of a money market.[27]

Although local securities markets can provide an alternative source of funding to the banking sector, especially during banking crises (Greenspan's "spare tire"), a sound and well-regulated banking system can be a

22. See Allen and Gale (2000).

23. See Eichengreen and Hausmann (1999), who caution, however, against attempts to follow this path—namely to reverse the opening of the capital account—for countries that have followed alternative sequencing strategies.

24. See IMF (2002b); Bank for International Settlements (2002).

25. See Dooley (1996). Chile is sometimes mentioned as an example; see Cifuentes, Desormeaux, and González (2002).

26. On corporate bond markets, see Schinasi and Smith (1998).

27. See Cha (2002); IMF (2002b).

necessary complement to the development of local securities markets.[28] Banks can play a number of supporting roles for securities markets: they can be large holders of securities, underwriters and market makers, issuers, and guarantors, as well as arrangers of securitizations.[29] The large involvement of banks in the securities business requires appropriate regulations ("firewalls") to prevent the issuance of bonds to repay loans and the subsequent sale of the bonds to an asset manager subsidiary at higher-than-market prices. Banking and bond markets could be developed in tandem, building an appropriate regulatory and institutional framework to encompass both. However, in the absence of a large institutional investor base, domestic debt holdings may become too concentrated in the banking system. This, in turn, could constrain the resolution of debt crises, as haircuts on the debt could compromise the solvency of the banking system.

Finally, local securities markets remain highly segmented in most regions, and a number of measures would have to be undertaken to develop fully integrated regional markets. Despite their recent growth and deepening, Asia's domestic currency bond markets, for instance, are largely insulated from each other. Domestic investors in several countries are not allowed to invest in international markets, and foreign investors are not attracted by the low yield and costly hedges. Analysts note that, besides the removal of controls and harmonization of taxes, several institutional aspects of bond markets—such as contracts, underwriting, and settlement conditions—would have to be standardized to some extent before a pan-Asian market could be created.[30] However, a series of overlapping proposals to develop a regional bond market may focus the authorities' efforts on the removal of some of these barriers and contribute to speeding up the process.[31]

28. Greenspan (1999).

29. See Hawkins (2002).

30. See, for instance, Parsons (2001).

31. These include work aimed at developing local bond markets by the Asia Pacific Economic Cooperation (APEC), the Association of Southeast Asian Nations (ASEAN) + 3 group, and a recent proposal by the Asian Cooperation Dialogue (ACD). The latter would involve a set of Asian governments launching a regional bond fund, financed by Asian central banks, that would "catalyze" larger investments from institutional investors and would invest initially in U.S. dollars, euros, and other nonregional currency bonds, later diversifying into local currency bonds from government and corporate issuers.

Concluding Remarks

Local securities markets have grown substantially over the last five years. Despite the rapid expansion of local markets—in particular, local bond markets—they have not yet developed enough to provide full insurance against the closure of banking or international markets. Nonetheless, continued efforts to develop these markets could eventually provide a significant cushion against future closures. In particular, these efforts should focus on continuing to adopt measures geared toward strengthening market infrastructure, developing benchmarks and local institutional investors, and improving corporate governance and transparency. Moreover, despite the existence of ambiguities concerning some policies related to the development of local securities and derivatives markets, several measures could still be undertaken, while monitoring and controlling their potentially negative side effects. For instance, indexed instruments contribute to increasing the duration in fixed-income markets, but excessive indexation to foreign exchange could lead to balance sheet mismatches and unstable debt dynamics and hence should be discouraged.

References

Allen, Franklin, and Douglas Gale. 2000. *Comparing Financial Systems.* MIT Press.

Bank for International Settlements. 2002. *The Development of Bond Markets in Emerging Economies.* BIS Paper 11. Paris: Monetary and Economic Department, June.

Cha, Hyeon-Jin. 2002. "Analysis of the Sluggish Development of the Secondary Market for Korean Government Bonds, and Some Proposals." Seoul: Bank of Korea, Financial Markets Department, May.

Cifuentes, Rodrigo, Jorge Desormeaux, and Claudio González. 2002. "Capital Markets in Chile: From Financial Repression to Financial Deepening." In Bank for International Settlements, *The Development of Bond Markets in Emerging Economies,* BIS Paper 11.

Claessens, Stijn, Daniela Klingebiel, and Sergio L. Schmukler. 2002. "Explaining the Migration of Stocks from Exchanges in Emerging Economies to International Centers." Washington: World Bank. Available at econ.worldbank.org/files/13265_wps2816.pdf.

Dooley, Michael. 1996. "Capital Controls and Emerging Markets." *International Journal of Finance and Economics* 1 (July): 197–205.

Eichengreen, Barry, and Ricardo Hausmann. 1999. "Exchange Rates and Financial Fragility." Working Paper 7418. Cambridge, Mass.: National Bureau of Economic Research.

Eichengreen, Barry, Ricardo Hausmann, and Ugo Panizza. 2002. "Original Sin: The Pain, the Mystery, and the Road to Redemption." Paper prepared for the Inter-American

Development Bank Conference on Currency and Maturity Matchmaking: Redeeming Debt from Original Sin. Washington, November 21–22. Available at ksghome2. harvard.edu/~.rhausma.cid.ksg/Publication/Original%20Sin/pub8.pdf.

Greenspan, Alan. 1999. "Lessons from the Global Crises." Remarks before the World Bank Group and International Monetary Fund Annual Meetings, Program of Seminars. Washington, September 27. Available at www.federalreserve.gov/Boarddocs/Speeches/1999/199909272.htm.

Hawkins, John. 2002. "Bond Markets and Banks in Emerging Economies." In Bank for International Settlements, *The Development of Bond Markets in Emerging Economies,* BIS Paper 11.

IMF (International Monetary Fund). 1999. *International Capital Markets: Developments, Prospects, and Key Policies.* World Economic and Financial Surveys. Washington.

———. 2001. *International Capital Markets: Developments, Prospects, and Key Policies.* World Economic and Financial Surveys. Washington.

———. 2002a. *Global Financial Stability Report.* World Economic and Financial Surveys. Washington, June.

———. 2002b. *Global Financial Stability Report.* World Economic and Financial Surveys. Washington, September.

———. 2002c. *Global Financial Stability Report.* World Economic and Financial Surveys. Washington, December.

———. 2003. "Financial Stability in Dollarized Economies." Unpublished manuscript. Washington: Monetary and Exchange Affairs Department.

Johnson, Simon, and Andrei Shleifer. Forthcoming. "Privatization and Corporate Governance." In Takatoshi Ito and Anne O. Krueger, eds., *Governance, Regulation, and Privatization, East Asia Seminar on Economics,* vol. 12. Massachusetts Institute of Technology and Harvard University, September.

La Porta, Rafael, Florencio López-de-Silanes, Andrei Shleifer, and Robert Vishny. 2000. "Investor Protection and Corporate Governance." *Journal of Financial Economics* 58 (1, October): 1–25.

OECD. 2001. "Bond Market Development in Asia." Paris.

Parsons, Nick. 2001. "The Bond Markets in Asia." *EuroWeek* (June).

Schinasi, Garry, and R. Todd Smith. 1998. "Fixed-Income Markets in the United States, Europe, and Japan: Some Lessons for Emerging Markets." IMF Working Paper 173/98. Washington: International Monetary Fund.

Steil, Benn. 2001. "Borderless Trading and Developing Securities Markets." In Robert E. Litan, Paul Masson, and Michael Pomerleano, eds., *Open Doors: Foreign Participation in Financial Systems in Developing Countries.* Brookings.

Walker, Eduardo. 2002. "The Chilean Experience with Completing Markets with Financial Indexation." In Fernando Lefort and Klaus Schmidt-Hebbel, eds., *Inflation and Monetary Policy*. Santiago: Central Bank of Chile.

World Bank and IMF (International Monetary Fund). 2001. *Developing Government Bond Markets: A Handbook.* Washington: World Bank.

Yam, Joseph. 2001. "Developing and Positioning Hong Kong's Bond Market." Speech delivered at the Forum on China's Government Securities Market in the New Century, Bank for International Settlements, Hong Kong, November 19. Available at www.bis.org/review/r011123a.pdf.

CLEMENTE DEL VALLE
PIERO UGOLINI

3

The Development of Domestic Markets for Government Bonds

The World Bank and International Monetary Fund (IMF) agree that the development of domestic bond markets deserves high priority on the financial sector development agenda.[1] On the one hand, bond markets are essential for a country to enter a sustained phase of development driven by market-based capital allocation and greater avenues for raising debt capital. On the other hand, the role of domestic bond markets in markedly strengthening the resilience of a country's financial system and insulating it against external shocks, contagion, and reduced access to international capital markets is tantamount. The World Bank and International Monetary Fund have dedicated substantial human and financial resources toward restructuring financial sectors and reducing financial vulnerability. A key component of these efforts has been strengthening capital markets, in particular domestic bond markets.

The importance of government bond markets in catalyzing the growth of overall bond markets is recognized and accepted. Although there is no general development philosophy that can be applied to developing domes-

The authors wish to thank Ashok Bhundia, Mats Filipsson (IMF consultant), Rodolfo Maino (IMF), and Vidhya Rustaman (World Bank consultant) for their contributions to this chapter.

1. As emphasized in the foreword of the International Monetary Fund and World Bank handbook *Developing Government Bond Markets* (IMF and World Bank 2001a).

tic bond markets, the task is too important not to tackle head-on. Many insights, lessons, and strategies can be gleaned from the market development experience of both developed and emerging markets in this area.

As national economies become increasingly open and interlinked with a market-oriented global financial architecture, it is imperative that domestic financial sectors become market based as well. Many economies that suffered during the Asian financial crisis were borrowing from international debt markets while running semi-controlled local financial sectors. This weakness cost them dearly.

In this context, the first section of this chapter provides an overview of the policy framework and building blocs for reform that are necessary to develop a government bond market.[2] The second section provides a snapshot of the development situation in several regions, encompassing the areas of institutional, legal, and regulatory frameworks for debt issuance, size and composition of government debt, primary and secondary markets including market infrastructure, the base of investors, and some relevant macroeconomic linkages.[3]

Prerequisites for Success in Developing a Government Bond Market

Developing domestic bond markets is a complex process involving challenges in several areas, including initial conditions that are essential for success. First, macroeconomic stability and clear debt management objectives are necessary stepping stones toward developing a market for domestic government bonds, as illustrated by various examples in the second section of the paper. However, dealing in government bonds is not a sufficient condition on its own, and complementary policies, which are discussed in the following subsections, are needed to jump-start the process.

Macroeconomic Stability

Macroeconomic and financial stability are essential for developing a well-functioning government bond market and for establishing government's

2. Details are provided in IMF and World Bank (2001a).

3. The information was collected as part of regional workshops held by the World Bank and International Monetary Fund in Brazil, Shanghai, Tunisia, and Turkey. A workshop for the Africa region is being planned.

reputation as an issuer of debt. In particular, developing a track record for macroeconomic stability enhances the reputation and credibility of the government's willingness and ability to repay creditors.

In general, macroeconomic instability deters investment in government bonds. If macroeconomic management is poor, then the risks of currency devaluation, for example, may be perceived as high, effectively shutting the door on the government's ability to sell bonds as a form of budget financing. As an example, vis-à-vis other emerging markets, longer-term maturities are characteristic of East Asian countries, signaling low expectations of inflation, devaluation, or risks of default. Emerging countries that have begun to develop a domestic government bond market have experienced improved macroeconomic stability, notwithstanding short periods of instability in the 1990s.

Macroeconomic instability may also "force" the government to rely on the issuance in the local market of foreign-currency-indexed debt instruments above and beyond what would be desirable for the currency composition of the country's debt portfolio, making the financial system more vulnerable to external shocks or contagion.

The Government's Debt Strategy

A clear understanding and articulation of the government's debt strategy are critical for development of a government securities market. This includes a precise definition of the objectives and scope of public debt management and a shared understanding of the objectives by debt managers, fiscal policy advisers, and the central bank, given the interdependencies among debt management, fiscal policy, and monetary policy.

The IMF and the World Bank define the objective of public debt management as to "ensure that the government's financing needs and payment obligations are met at the lowest possible cost over the medium to long run, with a prudent degree of risk."[4] Minimizing costs in the short run while ignoring risks for the medium to long run should not be an objective

4. IMF and World Bank (2001b). Risks encountered in sovereign debt management include market risk (risk associated with changes in market prices), rollover risk (risk that the debt will have to be rolled over at an unusually high cost or, in extreme cases, cannot be rolled over), liquidity risk (risk faced by the investor in trying to exit a position and risk faced by the borrower when liquid assets diminish quickly in the face of unanticipated cash flow obligations), credit risk (risk of nonperformance by borrowers on loans or by a counterparty on financial contracts), settlement risk, and operational risk.

of debt management. In this context, developed countries, which typically have deep and liquid markets for their government securities, often focus primarily on market risk. In contrast, emerging-market countries, which have only limited (if any) access to foreign capital markets and which also have relatively undeveloped domestic debt markets, should give higher priority to rollover risk.

Where appropriate, debt management policies to promote development of the domestic market should also be a prominent government objective. This is particularly relevant for countries where market constraints are such that short-term debt, floating-rate debt, and foreign currency debt, in the short run at least, are the only viable alternatives to monetary financing.

As a matter of fact, the two objectives are closely linked. Indeed, a most effective way for debt managers to minimize cost and risk over the medium to long run is to ensure that debt policies and operations are consistent with the development of an efficient government securities market. In particular, it is important to discontinue recourse to captive sources of funding and to adopt a firm commitment to market-based funding. Also, it is indispensable to have a wide base of investors and to take their needs into consideration.

Several techniques can be used to boost the liquidity of government bonds, in order ultimately to reduce the government's funding costs. Benchmark bonds can be used to build up large maturities at key points along the yield curve, therefore reducing the number of outstanding securities and concentrating borrowing at these points. One benefit of benchmark bonds is that they tend to be used to price other instruments. A benchmark yield curve can help to develop other segments of the market—corporate bonds and the derivatives markets being examples.

As a selling technique for government bonds, auctions are regarded as a cost-effective and transparent market-based method. Nowadays, auctions are the dominant selling technique in domestic government bond markets. Predictability and transparency in the auction process are crucial to buttress market confidence. This can be reinforced by having a preannounced calendar of auctions (that is, a yearly calendar) and by timely reporting of aggregate information on the results of the auction. Timely and systematic disclosure of information is highly desirable because it enhances transparency of policies, reduces uncertainty, allows investors to make well-informed business decisions, and ultimately lowers borrowing costs.

Although primary dealer arrangements are becoming more widespread, the list of countries allowing noncompetitive bidding is still short. The primary dealer arrangement, a method often used to sell government bonds to final investors, helps the absorption and distribution of bonds. In many countries, primary dealers also act as market makers in the secondary market, thereby contributing to market liquidity. A primary dealer system can also act as a platform on which to develop the market, by concentrating both liquidity and competence on a group of market makers. A potential downside of a primary dealer system is that competition may be limited, which can hinder the development of an efficient market structure, especially if there are few market players.

Legal and Regulatory Framework

Developing a domestic securities market involves addressing, even in the nascent stages, the legal, regulatory, and supervisory framework with a view to ensuring transparency and predictability for investors. An important component of the legal and regulatory framework has to do with the provision of adequate information; therefore, the legal framework should define the requirements for information disclosure.

In this context, an early step in developing securities market regulation to support the issuance and trading of government securities is to establish a legal framework for securities issuance. This framework should clarify the authority to borrow and issue new debt, invest, and undertake transactions on the government's behalf.[5] Counterparties need assurances that the sovereign debt managers have the legal authority to represent the government and that the government stands behind any transactions into which its sovereign debt managers enter. An important feature of the legal framework is the authority to issue new debt, which is normally stipulated in legislation authorizing borrowing with a preset limit or a debt ceiling.

There is also a need to develop a regulatory environment that fosters market development and enables the enforcement of sound supervisory practices. In particular, market regulation should ensure that secondary-market trading is conducted in a transparent and efficient manner. This includes, for example, prohibiting improper trading practices, such as insider trading, fraud, and market manipulation.

5. Ministries of finance and economy generally retain significant leeway concerning debt management decisions, although central banks—with a prominent role as fiscal agents for the issuer—share debt management responsibility for auction administration, record keeping, disbursements, and interest payments. Responsibilities are shared in Brazil, while Hungary places the debt management functions in an independent entity, the Government Debt Management Agency.

Countries usually regulate and supervise the market through a national securities agency, often jointly with other government bodies such as the central bank, acting as fiscal agent for the government, and the ministry of finance. The securities regulatory authority should have the legal authority to write and enforce rules and regulations related to market and business conduct, market intermediaries, and trading systems. According to the principles set by the International Organization of Securities Commissions (IOSCO), the securities regulator should be operationally independent from government, preferably with autonomy over its budget and "accountable for its functions and the exercise of its power."[6] The regulatory authority's powers should be set out clearly in legislation, along with provisions for accountability, transparency of rule-making, transparency of enforcement, and reporting requirements. The securities regulatory authority should have all the necessary authority and resources to carry out its mandate and enforce compliance with its rules.

Finally, there is a need to introduce appropriate accounting, auditing, and disclosure practices for financial sector reporting.

The Investor Base

In the past, some governments used their powers of taxation and coercion to issue nonmarketable bonds to commercial banks and other institutional investors. These policies stifled financial innovation and were not always an efficient mechanism for allocating savings, especially when the government was slow to adjust yields in line with changes in market conditions, risks, or inflation. In this regard, the next section characterizes the challenges confronting many emerging debt markets to diversify their investor base.

The investor base of many emerging debt markets continues to be characterized by captive sources originating in the imposition on banks of minimum reserve and liquid asset requirements as well as the imposition on national provident funds and other social security funds of the indirect requirement to invest in government securities. The move to a market-based system of issuing government debt, which involves a voluntary take-up of government bonds, provides a number of benefits to the economy but also requires a commitment on the part of the government to develop markets for government bonds.

6. International Organization of Securities Commissions (IOSCO), Objectives and Principles of Regulations, 1998.

Having a wide base of investors for government and private securities promotes market stability and the efficient allocation of resources. A wide investor base minimizes the risk of one group of investors being able to manipulate the market and allows an orderly financing of the government's funding requirements. The typical base of domestic investors in mature bond markets comprises financial and nonfinancial entities. Financial entities comprise banks, the contractual savings sector, and collective investment funds, whereas nonfinancial institutions include corporations and individual investors. Collective investment funds include pension and insurance funds that invest their accumulated reserves and mutual funds that invest their pooled funds. These institutions have grown rapidly over the last two decades and typically have had a significant positive impact on capital market development. These include promoting transparency, the flow of information, and market integrity; developing efficient settlement and trading facilities; and promoting innovation in financial productions and trading practices. Institutional investors play a positive role in the development of a government securities market because they tend to prefer low-risk instruments and long-term products.

Foreign participation in the market also helps to widen the investor base and often can bring additional benefits such as advances in financial technology and innovation that boost market efficiency, which encourages active trading in the secondary market. This, in turn, allows for efficient price discovery along the government yield curve, reduces the cost of borrowing, and allows for a more efficient mobilization and allocation of savings. Despite these potential benefits, the participation of foreign investors in government securities markets also brings risks. Their participation can make host economies more susceptible to market volatility because they may withdraw suddenly in response to a deterioration of the macroeconomic framework or contagion. Therefore, the opening of the government securities market to foreign investors needs to be decided in the context of a broader strategy of liberalization of the capital account that takes into account the initial conditions of financial and nonfinancial entities and their capacity to manage the risks associated with international capital flows.

Governments need to understand the preferences of different types of investors and to issue products that encourage wider participation in the bond markets and minimize the cost of funding. Tailoring products to the needs of a wide base of investors also accelerates the pace of financial innovation, providing investors with greater choice of financial instruments.

For example, in some countries, demand from institutional investors stimulated an increase in inflation-linked products.

The Money Market and Monetary Policy

The money market is the cornerstone of a competitive and efficient system of market-based intermediation and should normally be in sound working order before a government bond market is developed. In turn, the central bank's operating procedures greatly influence the stability of the money market as well as banks' incentives to use the money market to manage risks. The management of overall liquidity conditions by the central bank is critical in this regard and should aim to maintain the level of excess reserves very close to that desired by banks and required for the smooth operation of the payment system. Also the structure of the reserve requirements can contribute to money market stability, such as when the reserve requirement can be met on average over the maintenance period.

Effective liquidity management by the central bank requires that the government have an efficient cash management policy and that monetary policy operations are coordinated with the funding of government operations. In particular, it is important for the government to provide cash flow projections to the central bank, so that the central bank can effectively manage overall liquidity conditions in the system. This, in turn, helps to reduce volatility in interest rates and the risk associated with transacting in the money markets, thereby encouraging participation. One way to facilitate coordination between the government and the central bank is to set up coordination committees.

Finally, it is important to note the potential benefits for the central bank and the conduct of monetary policy of a well-functioning government securities market. In particular, government securities are often the most common form of collateral used by the central bank in its discretionary monetary operations—in particular, repurchase operations.[7]

Other Issues: The Tax System and Settlement Infrastructure

The taxation of financial securities can also influence bond market development. The design of the tax system affects investment decisions and the

7. The second section of this paper provides several examples of countries holding portfolios of government securities to conduct outright or repo sales or purchases for monetary policy transactions. This is common in Europe and Central Asia and in the Middle East and North Africa.

allocation of savings. Poor tax policies can be a major impediment to a properly functioning financial market.

In general, it is desirable that transactions taking different forms but having the same economic consequences be treated equally for tax purposes and not be affected by the tax structure. This ensures that the tax regime does not influence the allocation of savings across different financial products. For example, different tax rates on interest income from bonds and bank deposits will affect the competitive relationship between banks and other financial institutions. Capital gains, withholding taxes, and turnover taxes are least common in some countries of the Middle East and North Africa, while turnover taxes, which tend to discourage the development of secondary-market liquidity, are still enforced in several countries. Therefore, to encourage competition, the government should try to equalize effective tax rates across various capital and income structures, between corporate and noncorporate capital, and between debt and equity finance.

Nevertheless, it is not uncommon for interest income from government bonds to be taxed at a lower rate than interest income from private sector debt. Favorable tax treatment, and even tax exemption, is often used to promote government bonds in an effort to widen the base of investors and promote market development. However, in a competitive market, interest rate arbitrage should ensure that after-tax rates of return are equalized, which may diminish the desired effect. The advantages to governments of favorable tax treatment have to be balanced against the disadvantages, which include the risk of crowding out more efficient private sector investment.

To achieve neutrality between capital and other sources of income, many tax systems treat all sources of income—such as wages, dividends, and interest—earned by the same taxpayer as a single income and tax all of them at the same, often progressive, rate. However, withholding taxes is a common practice in many countries because it is relatively easy to administer and makes tax evasion more difficult. On the downside, imposing a withholding tax—such as is the case in some Latin American and East Asian countries—may also discourage foreigners from buying domestic bonds if the tax is applied to nonresidents. Even in some cases, like the Philippines, where the nonresident withholding tax is recoverable by law, in practice the government's collection process discourages foreigners from buying domestic bonds.

The settlement infrastructure is another ingredient of efficient and well-functioning bond markets. Moving to paperless records with a central electronic depository helps to improve the efficiency and speed at which transactions are executed and reduces settlement risk.

Recording transactions in electronic bond accounts helps to minimize operational risks such as theft and the destruction of records associated with paper transactions. This can be done through a central depository where market participants can settle their transactions, take delivery of their bonds, and make payment. Such a depository should be based on the delivery versus payment principle to minimize settlement risk; it can be located and managed by the central bank or administered by an independent entity. The setup should allow for sound oversight of its activities, the membership rules should be transparent, and the law and regulations should allow for proper governance. Moreover, any changes to the settlements infrastructure should be reflected in the legal framework so that, for example, electronic record keeping is recognized in the case of bankruptcy settlement procedures.

In the past, many countries used a multilateral net settlement system for settling bond transactions. In such a system, payment obligations are accumulated over a settlement period. At the end of the period, the net settlement of each participant against the entire system is calculated and executed. This type of system is subject to considerable settlement risk, which could result in a systemic problem if large interconnected participants default on their obligations. To address this problem, the focus has been on adopting a real-time gross settlement system in which transactions are settled bilaterally through depositories or subdepositories of cash and bonds as promptly as is feasible. Settlement arrangements between institutions holding securities accounts in the over-the-counter (OTC) market have achieved real-time gross settlements with delivery versus payment in most regions covered in the following section.[8]

Snapshots of Regional Development

This section provides a snapshot of the government securities markets in emerging regions, encompassing East Asia and the Pacific, Latin America and the Caribbean, Europe and Central Asia, and the Middle East and North Africa. The objective is to illustrate the stage of development of gov-

8. This has been the case in countries such as Czech Republic, Indonesia, Korea, Latvia, Lebanon, Malaysia, Morocco, the Philippines, Singapore, and Thailand.

ernment securities markets in each region using the framework presented in the recent IMF and World Bank publication, *Developing Government Bond Markets: A Handbook.*[9] Our analysis is based on first-hand information and insights from regulators obtained through survey responses and from workshops on developing government bond markets held in each region between mid-2001 and 2002. The study is part of an ongoing process to assess the relative degree of development of the government securities markets. As such, this section does not provide a detailed or conclusive assessment of the stage of market development or a comprehensive review of how the government securities markets have evolved over time.

The survey reflects the state of development of the government bond markets around the world at a given point in time and identifies the main features of markets in each region, specifically covering the institutional, legal, and regulatory framework for debt issuance; size and composition of government debt; primary and secondary markets including market infrastructure; the base of investors; and some relevant macroeconomic linkages. This section compiles the snapshots for each region, drawing mainly on the survey results relevant to the stage of development of the government securities markets. However, due to improvements and progressive revisions in the survey questions, some information may not exist for all regions, and, in other cases, responses may have been incomplete.

Institutional Framework and Infrastructure

The institutional framework for debt management in emerging regions generally places responsibility for debt management in the hands of the ministry of finance and economy, except in Singapore and Yemen, where this responsibility resides with the central bank. In Brazil, the responsibilities are split: the ministry is responsible for domestic operations, while the central bank is responsible (via an agency contract with the ministry) for operations in international markets. In Hungary, the debt management functions reside in an independent entity, the Government Debt Management Agency. The debt management function is sometimes shared by several divisions in the ministry of finance, and the most common case is a split between domestic and external debt management. In general, however, the ministry of finance has significant leeway for making debt management decisions. It is common for the central bank to share some

9. IMF and World Bank (2001a).

responsibility for debt management, as it assumes the role of fiscal agent for the government issuer, encompassing auction administration, record keeping, disbursements, and interest payments.

Countries are moving toward a more consistent and transparent legal and regulatory framework for debt management. The most common objectives of debt management are to minimize cost and minimize risk. However, some developing markets also emphasize developing an active secondary market for government securities (Bulgaria, Estonia, Latvia, Egypt, Morocco, Lebanon, Singapore, Malaysia, the Philippines) and lengthening the debt maturity or establishing a benchmark yield curve (Lebanon, Egypt, Singapore, Malaysia, the Philippines). For markets in the early stages of development or not yet developing, often the focus is primarily on short-term financing and monetary policy (Yemen). The legal framework in most markets also covers other relevant aspects of debt management such as borrowing authority, limits, and supervision.

Limits on net increase are most common. Borrowing limits, which balance accountability with flexibility, are most desirable in a debt management context. Flexibility is supported by regulating the net increase of debt (as opposed to gross debt amount), which is the most common method used in the emerging markets covered in this survey. However, almost as many countries impose limits on gross borrowing, which is more disciplined yet less flexible. In Europe and Central Asia, it is common to link limits on borrowing to the deficit planned in the annual budget, and in some cases limits on both net and gross amount are imposed. In Latin America, limits on gross borrowing are most common, while in East Asia and the Pacific, limits on different categories of borrowing are mainly used. In the Middle East and North Africa, however, many countries do not impose limits on borrowing.

Supervision is generally delegated to mixed systems—that is, systems involving the central bank, securities commission, or both. In some cases, especially in Europe and Central Asia, the ministry of finance is not involved in the supervision of markets. In some cases, the specialized authority is the sole or main supervisor of markets for government securities (Korea, Croatia, Czech Republic, Hungary, Poland, Slovenia, Jordan, Colombia, Mexico, Peru, Costa Rica), or, alternatively, the central bank plays this role (Singapore, Lebanon, Yemen, Malaysia).

Coordination of debt management and management of the central bank is a priority. The central bank participates in and is responsible for certain debt management operations in most countries. There are some exceptions, such as Tunisia, Croatia, Hungary, and Slovenia, where the central bank does not play a significant role in debt management. Nevertheless, coordination with the central bank on matters pertaining to debt management and monetary policy is necessary. Tangible arrangements are evident across most markets, and some countries have formed separate coordination committees to assist in this function (the Philippines, Malaysia, Indonesia, Colombia, Peru).

Government securities play an important role in monetary policy, especially in Europe and Central Asia and in the Middle East and North Africa (see table 3-1). Where a treasury bill market is lacking, central bank securities are useful for bridging the maturity gap or for conducting monetary policy. However, coordination with the government as an issuer is required. Central bank securities are issued in approximately half of the emerging countries covered, with the exception of countries in the Middle East and North Africa, where treasury bills are the dominant type of government security. Where central bank securities are issued, many countries use them as the main instrument of monetary policy (Chile, Costa Rica, Jordan, Indonesia, Malaysia). In others, the central bank also holds a portfolio of government securities to conduct outright or repo sales and purchases for monetary policy transactions. This is most common in Europe and Central Asia and in the Middle East and North Africa. Most countries in the Middle East and North Africa, with the exception of Morocco and Jordan, use transactions in government securities as a main instrument of monetary policy. In East Asia and the Pacific, only Korea and the Philippines use such transactions as their main instrument. In Latin America, Argentina, Brazil, Colombia, and Mexico—in addition to Chile and Costa Rica—also use transactions in government securities as the main instrument.

Primary issues in emerging regions are generally conducted via auctions, although most markets also use another form of issuance for special occasions (for example, introducing new instruments, market disrupters, and so forth; see table 3-2). The exception is Indonesia, which so far has placed government securities directly for recapitalization and is in the process of arranging auctions. In Algeria, about 90 percent of issued government securities are placed directly, but these securities can be traded later through primary dealers in the secondary market. Multiple price auctions are the most common form and are used extensively in the Middle East and North Africa. Tap issues are used in certain circumstances (Lebanon and Morocco use them to place special six-month treasury bills), after considering market conditions (Turkey, the Philippines), or as supply instruments to

Table 3-1. *Transactions in Government Securities Used for Monetary Policy, by Region*

Number of countries in each region

Region	*None*	*Outright sales*	*Outright purchases*	*Repo sales*	*Repo purchases*	*Used as main instrument*
East Asia and Pacific	2	6	6	6	6	2
Europe and Central Asia	6	8	8	10	10	10
Middle East and North Africa	1	2	2	3	4	5
Latin America and the Caribbean	3	6	4	4	5	6
Total	12	22	20	23	25	23

Source: Surveys and workshops on developing government bond markets held in each region between mid-2001 and 2002.

households (Hungary, Thailand). Syndicated placements are rarely used, except in Latin America. However, countries like Colombia have used this mechanism to introduce instruments such as inflation index securities.

Most countries publicly announce an issuing program on a yearly (or other periodic) basis, with the exception of some countries in Latin America (Ecuador, Honduras, Paraguay), Egypt, Estonia, and Turkey (where the treasury announces a monthly borrowing and repayment program). In addition, most securities are issued on a regular schedule. However, in the Middle East and North Africa, schedules tend to be irregular (or only semi-regular), for example, in Jordan, Lebanon, and Tunisia. This is also the case in Thailand and Croatia (where some securities are issued at irregular intervals). The volume of offered securities is also preannounced, except in Costa Rica and Turkey, although tapping the market for an amount different from the preannounced amount is also common. The announcement is generally made up to one week in advance, although up to two weeks is common in Latin America and in Europe and Central Asia.

In East Asia, participation in auctions is mostly restricted to primary dealers, while in other regions, wider participation is common. For example, in Europe and Central Asia and in the Middle East and North Africa, most banks (nonprimary dealers) are also eligible bidders. Most regions generally allow noncompetitive bids, thus encouraging retail participation and potentially deepening the market for primary dealers. However, this is

Table 3-2. *Primary Method of Issuance, by Region*
Number of countries in each region

Region	*Multiple price auctions*	*Uniform price auctions*	*Syndicated placements*	*Tap issues*	*Private placements or other*
East Asia and Pacific	4	3	1	2	4
Europe and Central Asia	14	5	1	3	n.a.
Middle East and North Africa	7	0	0	2	1
Latin America and the Caribbean	8	6	4	2	n.a.
Total countries	33	14	6	8	4

Source: Surveys and workshops on developing government bond markets held in each region between mid-2001 and 2002.
n.a. Not available.

least common in Latin America, where only five countries allow noncompetitive bidding (Costa Rica, Honduras, Jamaica, Mexico, Panama). In most cases, the noncompetitive bids are restricted by number or size.

The use of primary dealers is becoming more common in emerging regions (table 3-3). In East Asia and the Pacific, most countries use a market-making arrangement, with the exception of Indonesia (which is in the process of implementing one) and Cambodia. Similar to other regions, most countries in the Middle East and North Africa use a primary dealer arrangement; the exception is Yemen. In Latin America, Argentina, Colombia, and Mexico initially introduced a system of primary dealers in the mid-1990s, while Brazil, Peru, and Venezuela are exploring their introduction. In Europe and Central Asia, most countries use a primary dealer system. Only Albania and Latvia do not have such an arrangement. The number of primary dealers varies widely, and among the most common obligations are market making (given limitations on basic hedging instruments, audit ability, ability to quote firm prices), active participation in the secondary market, and provision of market feedback to the issuer. Bulgaria and Hungary explicitly include capital adequacy and liquidity requirements as an obligation of primary dealers, and Colombia has recently introduced the same concept. Exclusive right to bid at auctions is the most common entitlement in East Asia, although many countries also allow primary dealers to participate in the central bank's open market operations

Table 3-3. *Number of Countries with Primary Dealer Arrangements, by Region*

Region	*With primary dealers*	*Without primary dealers*	*Notes*
East Asia and Pacific	6	2	Indonesia (in process) and Cambodia do not have primary dealers
Europe and Central Asia	7	5	Albania and Latvia do not have primary dealers; Turkey and Georgia are in process
Middle East and North Africa	3	3	Yemen does not have primary dealers; Jordan and Egypt are in process
Latin America and the Caribbean	5	n.a.	

Source: Surveys and workshops on developing government bond markets held in each region between mid-2001 and 2002.
n.a. Not available.

(sometimes a separate group of primary dealers is appointed) and to take advantage of preferential financing to support their obligations.

Taxation policies that are neutral and simple are most desirable in developing markets for government securities. However, this is a complex issue to analyze given the limited scope of the survey. Capital gains, withholding taxes, and turnover taxes are least common in the Middle East and North Africa. Turnover taxes, which tend to discourage the development of secondary-market liquidity, are still imposed in several countries, such as Brazil, China, Colombia, Jamaica, Serbia (to be abolished this year), and Turkey. Tax policies in some cases discourage foreign investment by imposing an irrecoverable withholding tax—mainly in some countries in Latin America and in East Asia and the Pacific. However, even in some countries where the nonresident withholding tax is recoverable by law, this process has not been successful in practice (the Philippines).

Reopenings and advance redemptions are most common in Europe and Central Asia and least common in the Middle East and North Africa (see table 3-4). There are few restrictions on reopenings in most markets, with the exception of a few countries in the Middle East and North Africa (Algeria and Egypt) and in Latin America and the Caribbean (Paraguay). Legal restrictions on advance redemptions are more common, especially in

Table 3-4. *Use of Reopenings and Advance Redemptions, by Region*
Number of countries in each region

Region	*Reopenings*			*Advance redemptions*		
	Legal obstacle exists	*Technique is used*	*Comments*	*Legal obstacle exists*	*Technique is used*	*Comments*
East Asia and Pacific	0	5	Not used in Indonesia and China	0	5	Not used in Indonesia and China
Europe and Central Asia	0	11		0	11	
Middle East and North Africa	2	2	Used only in Lebanon and Tunisia	2	2	Used only in Lebanon and Tunisia
Latin America and the Caribbean	1	5	Used only in Brazil, Costa Rica, Colombia, Mexico, Peru	1	5	Used only in Brazil, Costa Rica, Colombia, Mexico, Peru

Source: Surveys and workshops on developing government bond markets held in each region between mid-2001 and 2002.

East Asia and the Pacific. However, in many cases, although no legal restrictions exist, these transactions still do not take place.

Breadth and Depth of the Securities Market

Most of the emerging regions still rely on external debt. Although this is also the case in East Asia, domestic debt currently exceeds external debt in six of the seven countries included in our analysis. In the Middle East and North Africa, Europe and Central Asia, and Latin America and the Caribbean, however, less than half of the countries have domestic debt greater than external debt. Figure 3-1 shows the level of indebtedness of emerging countries. Lebanon has the highest ratio of debt to gross domestic product (GDP), at 170 percent, much higher than other countries in the region, where approximately one-third of debt is from external sources. In Europe and Central Asia, the ratio of external debt to GDP is highest in Estonia (93 percent), followed by Bulgaria (92 percent).

Although the issuance of nonmarketable securities, which tend to segment the market, is not common in emerging regions, there are some

Figure 3-1. *Ratio of Debt to GDP, by Country*[a]

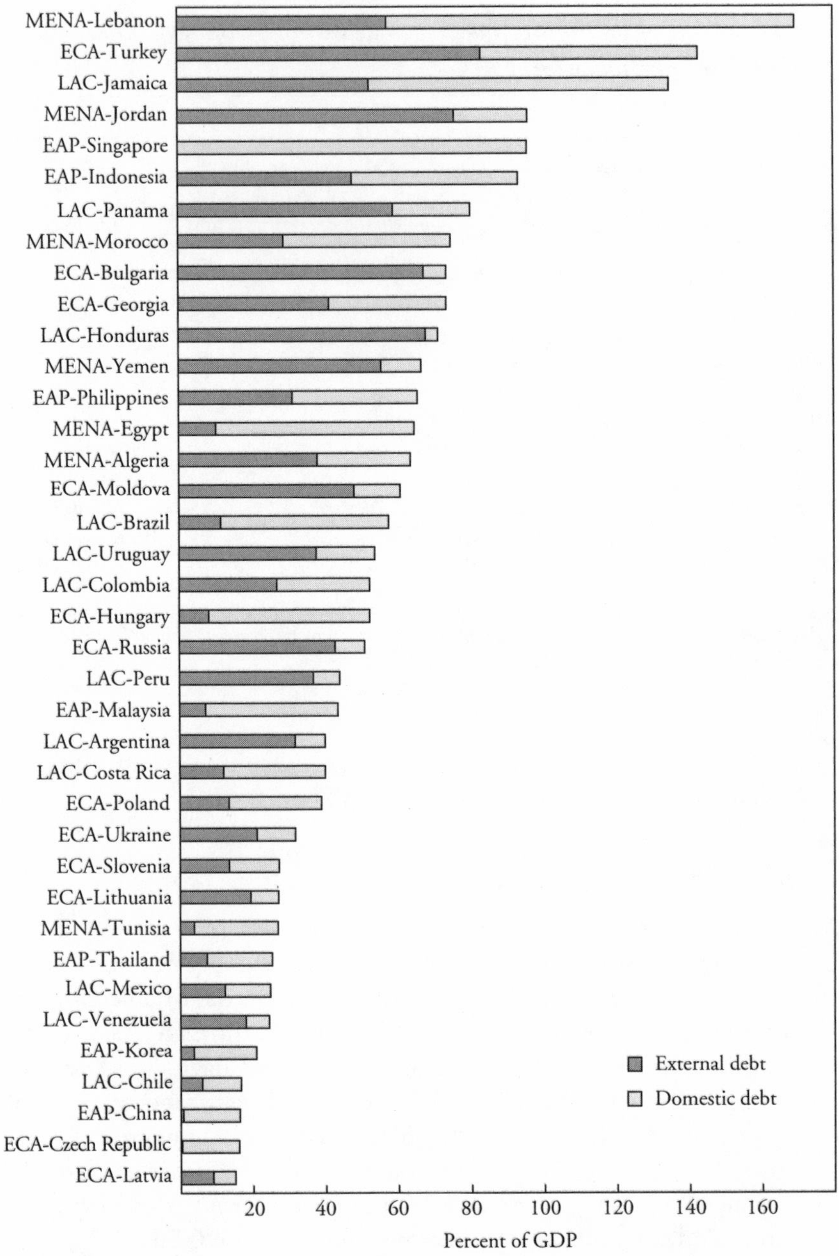

Source: Surveys and workshops on developing government bond markets held in each region between mid-2001 and 2002.

a. Data are as of end-2001; data for Latin America and the Caribbean, Indonesia, and Thailand are for June 2002.

notable exceptions. In East Asia, for example, China and Singapore both issue nonmarketable securities, which currently amount to more than 50 percent of the total public debt securities outstanding. In Europe and Central Asia, nonmarketable securities exist to a lesser extent, although in Estonia 100 percent of domestic debt is in this form (7 percent of total debt), and in Lithuania nonmarketable securities amount to approximately 33 percent of the total (6 percent of total debt).

Although, in general, foreign exchange–denominated securities are not common in the emerging regions included in the survey, there are notable exceptions: Turkey (15 percent of outstanding marketable bonds), Russia and Brazil (20 percent), and Serbia (25 percent).

In Asia and in the Middle East and North Africa, fixed-rate instruments dominate, which is positive for the development of a yield curve (see figure 3-2). While treasury bills dominate in Europe and Central Asia, governments are increasingly issuing medium- and long-term fixed-rate bonds. Turkey and Slovenia issue a large proportion of variable and indexed instruments, but the Czech Republic and Hungary are phasing them out. In Latin America and the Caribbean, floating-rate instruments and inflation-linked instruments have proliferated, as they have been very useful tools for extending the average maturity of the debt despite the long history of high inflation in this part of the world. Brazil and Chile are two good examples of this situation, while countries like Colombia and Mexico have been able to issue ten-year fixed-rate bonds as their macro conditions and debt management system have improved. In Latin America and the Caribbean, the increase in products linked to inflation has been stimulated by demand from institutional investors. In Slovenia, however, variable bonds have been issued as an intermediate step to aid in the transition from inflation-indexed debt to fixed-rate debt.

Longer-term maturities (more than five years) are dominant in East Asia, whereas in other emerging regions, debt securities are mainly short term, and the medium- to long-term markets are still developing (see figure 3-3). Almost an even amount of countries in Latin America have portfolios dominated by medium- or short-term government securities. However, in Europe and Central Asia and in some markets in the Middle East and North Africa, the portfolio is clearly dominated by shorter-term government securities. This is consistent with figure 3-2, which shows that treasury bills are more common in these two regions than in East Asia. In many cases, the dominance of short-term maturities may indicate high expectations of inflation, devaluation, or risks of default and inadequate demand from institutional investors.

Figure 3-2. *Composition of Government Securities, by Type (Coupon) and Country*[a]

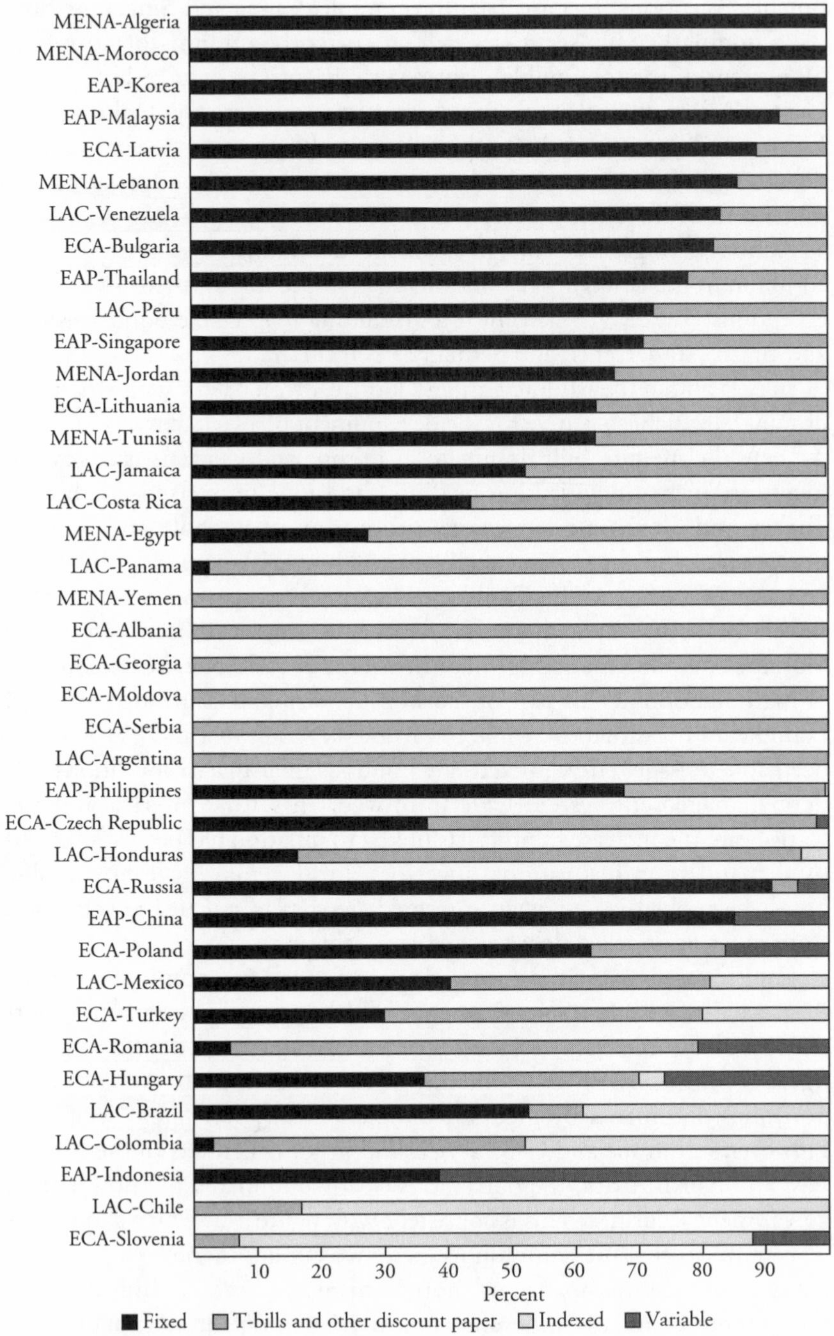

Source: Surveys and workshops on developing government bond markets held in each region between mid-2001 and 2002.

a. Data for Latin America are updated for June 2002.

Figure 3-3. *Composition of Government Securities, by Original Maturity and Country*[a]

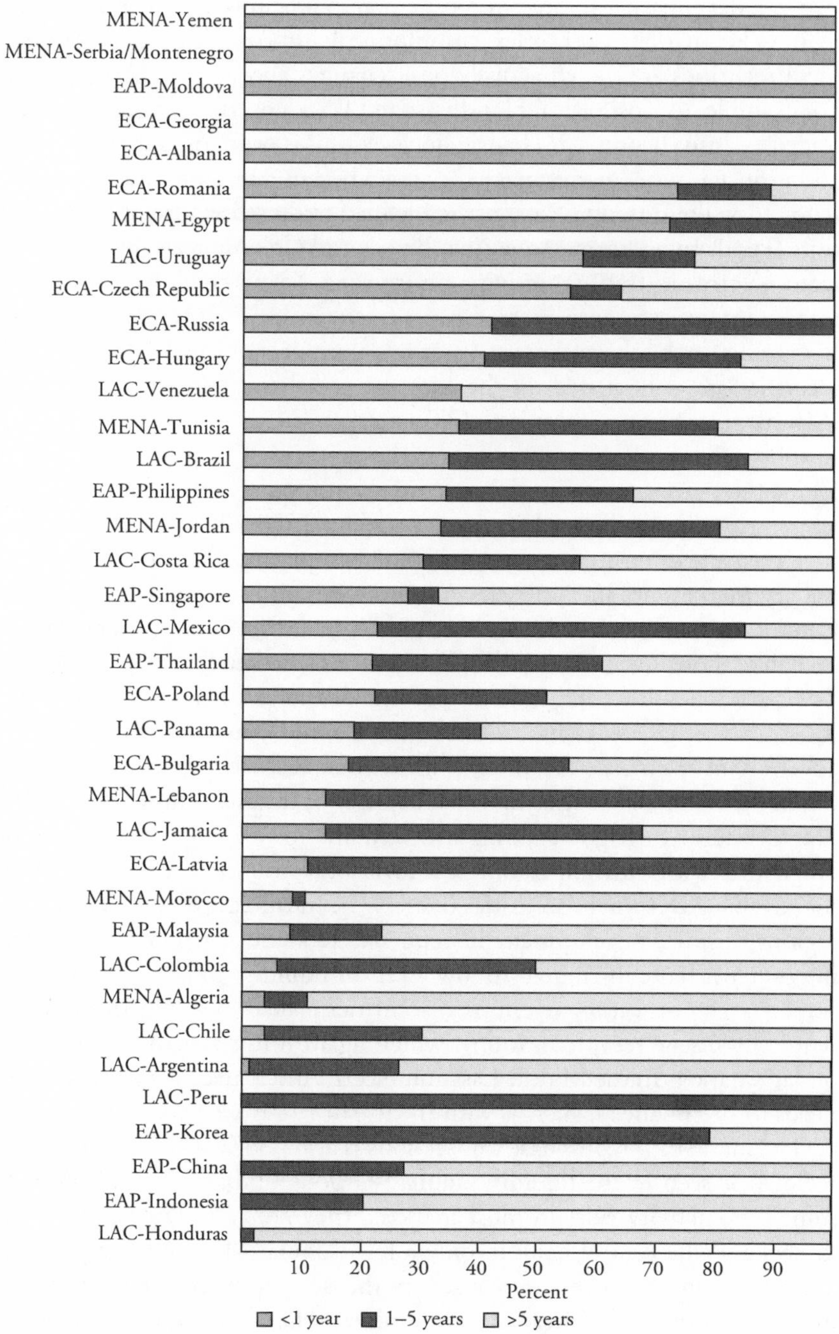

Source: Surveys and workshops on developing government bond markets held in each region between mid-2001 and 2002.

a. For Latin America and the Caribbean, medium-term classification is not inclusive of one and five years. Latin American data are updated for June 2002.

Secondary-market trading in most emerging regions takes place primarily in OTC markets. This is less common in Latin America, where government securities are traded actively on exchanges and electronic platforms. For example, in Costa Rica, Honduras, and Peru, government securities are traded exclusively on the exchange; however, this is primarily a register operation, since intermediaries make the trades because, in some cases, they are required to do so (Costa Rica) or are inclined to do so because of tax incentives (Peru). In addition, Argentina, Brazil, and Colombia also have significant electronic trading activity (more than 15 percent) as a result of important investments in trading infrastructure by the central bank (Colombia) or by the exchanges (Brazil, Colombia). In Russia, government securities are only traded on the Moscow Interbank Currency Exchange (MICEX); in Albania, there is no OTC market. In other regions, a relatively sizable amount of government securities are traded on exchanges, as in China (46 percent), Turkey (30 percent), Korea (4 percent), and Egypt (for all treasury bonds). Secondary-market trading activity is generally shallow, with only a few countries in each region as exceptions. The most active secondary markets are in East Asia and Latin America, while in Europe and Central Asia and in the Middle East and North Africa, trading data, where available, show lower levels of liquidity in most markets.

Figure 3-4 shows that only 20 percent of the countries included have total turnover greater than five times the year-end outstanding marketable government securities. However, a closer look at the composition of trading in these markets reveals that the majority of trading is in repos and the magnitude of outright trading still remains low, except in Korea and Singapore, with outright trading turnover of more than twelve times the marketable government securities (table 3-5). In the case of most emerging regions, limited development in repo markets and other basic hedging instruments has contributed to low levels of liquidity in general. In addition, a large portion of government securities is held by banks (for reserve requirements or recapitalization), which again limits trading in the secondary market. In the Middle East and North Africa, market infrastructure needs to be enhanced, such as with the use of real-time gross settlement.

The market for repurchase transactions is also poorly developed in most regions, as seen in the liquidity figures. Although a basic framework and some repo activity exist in most markets, they are actively used by both dealers and the central bank in only a few (China, Morocco, Singapore). Taxation policy has been an obstacle to the development of repo markets in several countries (Korea, the Philippines, Thailand), but this is being addressed. In the Philippines, for example, taxation policy has hampered

Figure 3-4. *Liquidity of Government Securities Markets (Total Turnover Including Repos and Outright), by Country*[a]

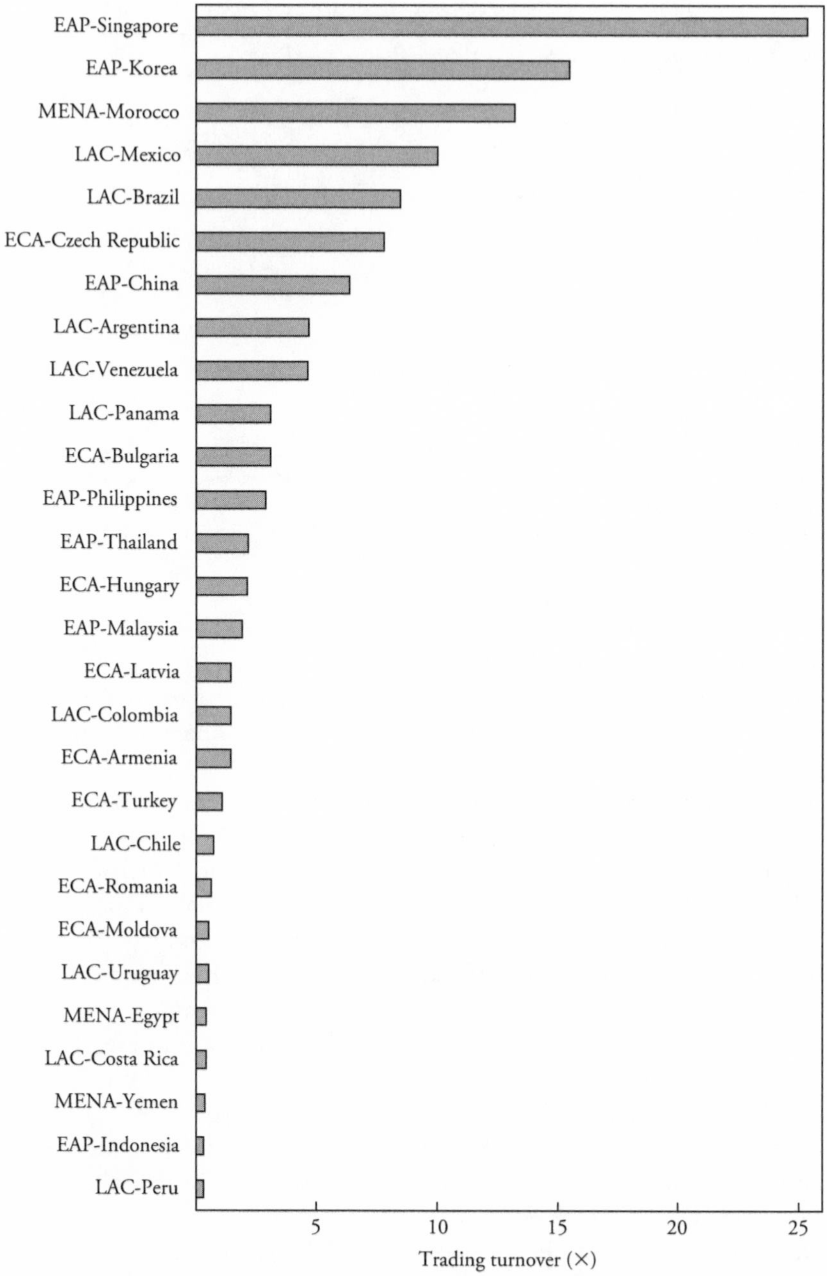

Source: Surveys and workshops on developing government bond markets held in each region between mid-2001 and 2002.

a. Turnover = annual trading volume / year-end outstanding marketable government securities. Excludes Slovenia, the Middle East, and North African countries—Algeria, Jordan, and Lebanon—where turnover is less than 0.1 times (or 10 percent).

Table 3-5. *Liquidity in Select Government Securities Markets, by Region*

Turnover in government securities[a]	*Outright*	*Repos*	*Total*
East Asia and Pacific			
Singapore	12.3	13.1	25.3
Korea	12.0	3.5	15.5
China	0.7	5.6	6.4
Middle East and North Africa			
Morocco	0.7	12.5	13.2
Latin America and the Caribbean			
Mexico	n.a.	n.a.	10.0
Brazil	n.a.	n.a.	8.5
Europe and Central Asia			
Czech Republic	n.a.	n.a.	7.8

Source: Surveys and workshops on developing government bond markets held in each region between mid-2001 and 2002.

a. Turnover = annual trading volume / year-end outstanding marketable government securities.

the development of the private repo market (and, consequently, the ability to sell short and to borrow and lend securities); however, some unofficial repos take place (to avoid taxation). Another common obstacle in most of the regions is the lack of a standardized contract for repo operations, which also explains the lack of liquidity and active trading.

The use of interdealer brokers, who could support and enhance liquidity and price discovery in the secondary market, is also lacking in most emerging countries and is nonexistent in the Middle East and North Africa. Similarly, in Europe and Central Asia, only Hungary and Poland use interdealer brokers. In Asia, however, interdealer brokers are becoming common and are now present in four markets, while two others (Indonesia, Thailand) have plans to implement them. They are common intermediaries in Latin American countries such as Brazil, Colombia, and Mexico.

In most countries, the central bank is the main depository for government securities, which has some advantages (see table 3-6). Although this is clearly the tendency in East Asia, in other regions a large number of countries are using an independent depository institution, such as the central depository or the stock exchange.

Most markets are phasing out paper securities and moving toward full-fledged book-entry securities—in line with the move toward more affordable and efficient settlement procedures. As can be seen in table 3-7, most

Table 3-6. *Institutions Holding Central Depository Functions, by Region*

Region	*Central bank*	*Securities depository*	*Both or other institution*
East Asia and Pacific	Singapore, Thailand, Malaysia, Indonesia	China	Korea, Philippines
Europe and Central Asia	Albania, Armenia, Bulgaria, Georgia, Moldova	Estonia, Hungary, Lithuania, Russia, Serbia, Slovenia	Czech Republic
Middle East and North Africa	Yemen, Lebanon, Algeria	Morocco, Tunisia	Egypt, Jordan
Latin America and the Caribbean	Brazil, Colombia, Honduras, Uruguay	Argentina, Chile, Ecuador, Mexico	Costa Rica, Panama, Peru
Total number of countries	16	14	9

Source: Surveys and workshops on developing government bond markets held in each region between mid-2001 and 2002.

countries have more than 90 percent paperless securities, although in Latin America the average proportion is much lower. In the Middle East and North Africa, Egypt is the only country without book-entry securities; however, once the book-entry system starts operating, all new treasury bills will be issued in this form.

Settlement arrangements between institutions holding securities in the OTC market have achieved real-time gross settlement with delivery versus payment in most regions (see table 3-8). However, real-time gross settlement with delivery versus payment is still rare in the Middle East and North Africa, except in Lebanon and Morocco. In Europe and Central Asia and in East Asia and the Pacific, the majority of countries have achieved real-time gross settlement with delivery versus payment, although several East Asian countries have indicated the need to improve the functioning of existing arrangements. In addition, many countries in these regions still use gross settlement without delivery versus payment. To enhance efficiency, most countries maintain cash accounts with the central bank for settlement, with the exception of China, Hungary, and Russia.

Exacerbating the lack of liquidity in the secondary markets are restrictions on liquidity-enhancing transactions such as forward trading, lending and borrowing securities, and short selling (see table 3-9). In Egypt, all three types of transactions are restricted, while in Tunisia this is the case for all but one of these. However, restrictions on such activities are least com-

Table 3-7. *Paperless Securities as a Percentage of Outstanding Debt, by Region*

Region	*0 percent*	*More than 0 percent, less than 50 percent*	*More than 50 percent, less than 90 percent*	*More than 90 percent*
East Asia and Pacific		China	Korea	Indonesia, Singapore, Malaysia, Philippines
Europe and Central Asia	Turkey		Hungary	Armenia, Poland, Albania, Bulgaria, Georgia, Latvia, Lithuania, Moldova, Slovenia
Middle East and North Africa	Egypt			Jordan, Lebanon, Morocco, Tunisia, Yemen
Latin America and the Caribbean	Costa Rica, Ecuador, Jamaica, Paraguay	Panama, Uruguay		Argentina, Brazil, Chile, Colombia, Honduras, Mexico, Peru

Source: Surveys and workshops on developing government bond markets held in each region between mid-2001 and 2002.

mon in Europe and Central Asia and in Latin America. Although such transactions are not restricted in some countries (such as China, Indonesia, Morocco, the Philippines, Yemen), they do not take place.

The base of investors of many emerging debt markets is characterized by captive sources originating from the imposition of minimum reserve and liquid asset requirements for banks as well as indirect requirements on national provident funds and other social security funds to invest in government securities (Malaysia and Singapore). The large proportion of bank holdings may also indicate weakness in the primary lending function, as is the case in many East Asian countries. In Latin America and the Caribbean, Colombia, Costa Rica, Honduras, Jamaica, and Panama rely heavily on public sector investments that constitute captive sources of funding (through a requirement for state companies to invest surplus finances in government securities).

There are only a few countries where banks or the public sector do not constitute the majority investors in domestic government securities. In Hungary, for example, foreign investors, which can provide an important source of demand for government securities, hold 25 percent, while retail

Table 3-8. *Settlement Arrangements in OTC Market*

Region	*Real-time gross settlement with delivery versus payment*	*Net settlement with delivery versus payment*	*Gross settlement without delivery versus payment*
East Asia and Pacific	Indonesia, Korea, Malaysia, Philippines, Singapore, Thailand		China, Indonesia
Europe and Central Asia	Armenia, Bulgaria, Czech Republic, Hungary, Kazakhstan, Latvia, Poland,	Poland, Romania, Lithuania, Estonia	Serbia, Moldova
Middle East and North Africa	Lebanon, Morocco	Jordan,[a] Tunisia[a]	
Latin America and the Caribbean	n.a.	n.a.	n.a.

Source: Surveys and workshops on developing government bond markets held in each region between mid-2001 and 2002.

a. Sometimes without delivery versus payment or settlement with delivery.

n.a. Not available.

investors hold another 20 percent. However, insurance companies are required to hold at least 40 percent of their insurance reserves in cash and government securities. In Tunisia, the clients of primary dealers, which are mainly retail investors, nonfinancial enterprises, and institutional investors, hold 67 percent of outstanding government securities. In Yemen, there are no restrictions or requirements on investments, although institutional investors hold approximately half of government securities. In Malaysia, however, holdings of the Employees Provident Fund are not broken down separately, but they do constitute a captive source of funding. Such is also the case in Morocco, where pension and insurance companies are obliged to invest in government bonds for prudential reasons. In Latin America, important reforms of the pension system have been implemented to introduce private asset management companies and force the contributions to achieve a fully funded system. As a result, these vehicles have become some of the major holders of government securities in the region. In Mexico, regulations force the pension funds to hold at least half of their portfolio in government bonds, while in Colombia pension funds are required to have no more than half of their portfolio in government bonds.

In the move to diversify the base of investors, most countries have developed, or are in the process of developing, securities specifically targeted to

Table 3-9. *Restrictions on Basic Hedging Instruments*
Number of countries in each region

	Legal restrictions exist?			Trading activity exists?		
Region	*Forward trading*	*Lending or borrowing securities*	*Short selling*	*Forward trading*	*Lending or borrowing securities*	*Short selling*
East Asia and Pacific	1	1	2	5	4	4
Europe and Central Asia	1	2	2	n.a.	n.a.	n.a.
Middle East and North Africa	2	2	3	n.a.	n.a.	n.a.
Latin America and the Caribbean	0	1	0	n.a.	n.a.	n.a.
Total	6	7	8	n.a.	n.a.	n.a.

Source: Surveys and workshops on developing government bond markets held in each region between mid-2001 and 2002.
n.a. Not available.

retail investors. Although retail investors are considered a relatively stable source of funding, distribution is often costly. In Latin America, for example, some countries are exploring the possibility of issuing securities via the Internet, opening auctions up to retail investors (Argentina, Brazil, Uruguay). In East Asia and the Pacific, the Philippines has implemented an electronic small investor program. Although government securities targeted to retail investors are currently less than 10 percent of outstanding government securities in Malaysia, the Philippines, and Thailand, two particular cases are exceptions—Korea, with national housing bonds of 25 percent of total government securities, and China, with national savings certificates (nonmarketable) of 43 percent of total government securities. In Europe and Central Asia, sizable retail securities are also issued in Hungary (also nonmarketable: 12 percent of marketable debt), Romania (20 percent), and Lithuania (9 percent).

Concluding Remarks

Bond markets, as avenues for raising debt capital, are key tools for a country to diversify risks and enter a sustained phase of development. Recently, the development of domestic bond markets has been receiving increasing attention as part of the financial sector development agenda. Domestic bond markets offer resilience and insulate a country's financial system against external shocks, contagion, and diminished access to international capital markets. In addition, by catalyzing market-based capital allocation and other instruments for raising capital, a domestic bond market allows the authorities to diversify their sources of borrowing and reduce any potential recourse to central bank financing and its inflationary consequences. Domestic government bond markets also facilitate the use of indirect monetary instruments and strengthen the transmission mechanism of monetary policy.

Increasing interlinkages of national economies with a market-oriented global financial architecture underscore the importance of strengthening the market-based pillars of domestic financial sectors. In this vein, a market for government bonds is an essential precursor to the development of a market for other fixed-income securities such as corporate bonds, which are normally priced off a government bond yield curve. Countries like Egypt, Lebanon, Malaysia, the Philippines, and Singapore showed the importance of lengthening debt maturity and establishing a benchmark yield curve.

Governments in many emerging countries still rely on external borrowing. By issuing domestic currency–denominated bonds, both the government and the private sector become less reliant on foreign sources of finance and avoid the associated currency risk that has been a dominant feature of some recent financial crises. Moreover, a sound debt management strategy can reduce a government's exposure to interest rates, currency, and other financial risks. In some Latin American countries, like Brazil and Chile, floating-rate instruments have been useful in extending the average maturity of debt. Markets that allow government and corporate bonds to be traded also permit consumption and investment smoothing.

The development of a corporate bond market helps the private sector to diversify its sources of funding and, at the same time, generates competition in financial services. It does this by including lower transaction costs for the domestic banking industry, which results in potential efficiency gains and improvements in the delivery and range of financial services. When commercial banks are faced with increasing competition from the development of a domestic capital market, they may be forced to develop new products that provide greater choice and flexibility in the management and flow of financial resources. The emergence of a benchmark government yield curve can encourage the development of new financial products, including repurchase agreements, money market instruments, and derivatives, and improve risk management and financial stability.

Based on the information collected by the joint World Bank and International Monetary Fund regional workshops, it appears that the development of bond markets has taken very different courses in different regions at varying stages of development. In general, however, most bond markets are in the early stages of development. In this category fall small economies where the size of the financial system does not support the infrastructure required to develop a bond market or countries that have not begun to develop a bond market. Included in this group are Cambodia, Estonia, Georgia, Moldova, Panama, and Peru. Some emerging-market countries have taken significant steps to develop a bond market. Included in this broad grouping are Brazil, Colombia, Korea, Mexico, Morocco, Singapore, and Turkey. However, these countries are still far from reaching the level of sophistication of developed markets.

For those countries with more developed government securities markets, the stage of development also varies, although further groupings are not so clear-cut. For example, some of the more advanced markets in this group are Mexico and Singapore, while at the other end of the spectrum are countries such as Indonesia and Yemen. The structural and economic difference in the countries—most especially in terms of coordination of debt management and management of the central bank—also underlies the uneven development of bond markets in each region as well as the state of the banking systems. For example, there is a higher propensity to save in East Asia than in other emerging regions as well as a larger role for securities issued by entities other than the government, such as corporations. Many of the banking systems in East Asia, however, are still undergoing some restructuring as a result of the financial crisis of 1998 (for example, Indonesia, Korea, and Thailand). In other countries, such as China or some of the economies in transition in Central Asia, the process of financial liberalization still is in an early stage—which represents a major obstacle for the development of secondary markets for securities of any type. In addition, the extent to which each country or region meets basic economic prerequisites will affect the level of development of the government securities market. For instance, these prerequisites might include macroeconomic stability; sound fiscal and monetary policies; an effective tax, legal, and regulatory infrastructure; implementation of smooth and secure settlement arrangements; and attention to further development of the money markets. Developing deep and liquid domestic government bond markets clearly has a number of benefits, which have been discussed in this paper. This paper also has highlighted a number of complementary policies and structural developments that are important for encouraging and enabling the development of government bond markets.

In addition, different countries are at different stages of market development as far as their government bond market is concerned. The development of government securities markets in emerging regions has also taken varying paths. Government securities in East Asia, for example, are primarily fixed term and long term, while in Latin America they are primarily short and medium term, with a greater proportion of indexed and variable securities. Trading is predominately OTC, although Latin America has a significant proportion of exchange-based trading in government securities. Secondary-market liquidity is also more developed in East Asia and Latin America than either in Europe and Central Asia or in the Middle East and North Africa. East Asian governments have sought to develop domestic bond markets and infrastructure in an effort to respond to the Asian financial crisis of 1998; emerging countries in other parts of the world historically have sought to do so in response to growing fiscal deficits.

Despite these differences, emerging regions face many similar challenges. Among them is the need to diversify the base of investors and increase the participation of institutional investors. Apart from lowering the cost of government debt and reducing the volatility in yields, this promises to open up opportunities for financial innovation. Moreover, apart from reducing the reliance on captive markets, taxation policies in most regions must be given attention to achieve neutrality and simplicity (especially with regard to nonresidents). In addition, settlement infrastructure can be enhanced to facilitate more liquid secondary-market activity, initially by achieving smooth operation of real-time gross settlement and delivery versus payment. This will be aided by the development of money market and basic hedging instruments (as well as derivatives and futures markets), which in some markets has been hampered by restrictions (Middle East and North Africa) or by lack of appropriate infrastructure (East Asia). In addition, organization of the trading market, use of interdealer brokers, and stronger market-making ability, among other factors, will assist in this area. Finally, all the countries surveyed need to upgrade the debt management and cash management capabilities of their government institutions. This is a key to providing the markets with a credible supply of securities and to implementing an issuing strategy that will clearly provide the conditions to support development of the market. These factors also will contribute to the development of a yield curve, which is lacking in most emerging countries.

To conclude, there are many common elements in all the countries surveyed, and policies to encourage development of the bond market should include the following elements:

—A stable macroeconomic environment that minimizes the risks of holding government securities,

—Monetary policy operating mechanisms that encourage banks to hold government securities as part of their liquidity management operations. Markets for government bonds tend to operate more efficiently when there are strong linkages with the money market.

—The design of the legal, regulatory, and supervisory framework should ensure transparent and efficient markets, provide protection for investors, and reduce systemic risks.

—The infrastructure for payments and settlements needs to be updated to allow for the electronic transfer of ownership of securities and their safekeeping and to minimize settlement risk.

—Wide participation among banks and nonbanks, including private individuals, should be encouraged. This will improve market depth and liquidity and allow for an improved process of price discovery resulting in a more efficient allocation of resources.

References

IMF (International Monetary Fund) and World Bank. 2001a. *Developing Government Bond Markets: A Handbook.* Washington.

———. 2001b. *Guidelines for Public Debt Management.* Washington.

PHILIP TURNER **4**

Bond Market Development: What Are the Policy Issues?

Why should governments want to issue bonds in their own markets? The simplest reason historically is that bonds have become more attractive or feasible than other methods of finance. Under the highly regulated financial regimes prevalent before the 1980s, governments in many emerging markets could meet much of their borrowing needs by simply forcing local banks to hold government paper, usually to meet demanding reserve requirements. In many countries, inflation "financed" part of the government deficit. Foreign borrowing often seemed an attractive alternative in a world of fixed exchange rates. But such methods of financing were undermined by the progressive liberalization of financial markets and of capital flows, by the adoption of anti-inflationary policies, and by the move to more flexible exchange rates. Governments were increasingly forced to borrow from domestic markets.

This chapter draws heavily on recent discussions among central banks on this issue, which are reported in Bank for International Settlements (2002). Useful suggestions and comments from Pablo Graf, John Hawkins, Robert McCauley (particularly his recent unpublished work on central bank balance sheets and the sterilization of external inflows), Dubravko Mihaljek, M. S. Mohanty, Pascual O'Dogherty, Marcio Silva-de-Araujo, and Peter Stebbing are acknowledged with thanks. I am also grateful for discussion with participants at this conference and at a conference at the Hamburg Institute of International Economics. Thanks are also due to Philippe Hainaut and Michaela Scatigna for work on the tables and graphs and to Lisa Ireland for secretarial assistance.

Yet there is also a much deeper reason. A well-balanced and stable financial system needs debt markets, and a government bond market almost always plays a central role in such markets. Successive crises in the emerging markets have brought home this lesson to governments in countries without adequate debt markets. Major reforms have indeed taken place in many emerging markets, and several have established programs to nurture local bond markets.[1] But in some ways the results have been disappointing: despite a huge increase in issuance, market liquidity has not developed as much as had been hoped.

Why such limited success? The central theme of this chapter is that the development of bond markets raises issues and policy dilemmas across a broad spectrum of policies—fiscal, monetary, and financial. In many cases, these dilemmas are resolved in ways that undermine market development. Quite often bond markets are stifled by the unintended consequences of seemingly unrelated government policies.

The chapter is organized as follows. The first section summarizes the main trends over recent years. The second outlines the strategic value of bond markets and considers some main impediments to their development. The third looks at the role of government borrowing strategies and considers the possible implications of the financing of huge increases in foreign exchange reserves in many countries (especially in Asia). This is followed by consideration of improvements in the structure of domestic debt and by a summary of the steps that can be taken to foster a deep and liquid government bond market. How to widen the base of investors and issuers is examined next, followed by discussion of the development of bond markets, which represents a major challenge for banks. A final section concludes.

Summary of Major Trends

By the end of 2001, outstanding domestic debt securities in the emerging markets amounted to more than $2 trillion, up from $1 trillion at the end of 1994. The country-by-country data are shown in table 4-1. Each major region saw a substantial rise in bonds as a percentage of gross domestic product (GDP), but the most significant rise was in Asia, a direct result of

1. Many of the details in this paper are drawn from the country papers in Bank for International Settlements (2002).

Table 4-1. *Domestic Debt Securities Outstanding, by Region, 1994–2002*[a]
Billions of U.S. dollars

Region	*1994*	*1995*	*1996*	*1997*	*1998*	*1999*	*2000*	*2001*	*2002*
Latin America[b]	274	318	395	468	518	446	483	508	393
Argentina	30	26	29	34	40	43	47	37	26
Brazil	173	231	297	345	391	294	298	312	212
Chile	25	29	32	37	34	33	35	35	34
Colombia	4	5	7	8	10	12	15	18	18
Mexico	37	22	24	38	38	57	74	88	89
Peru	1	1	1	2	2	3	4	4	4
Venezuela	n.a.	n.a.	5	4	4	5	10	14	11
Asia, larger economies									
China	66	93	119	162	228	293	355	403	412
India	64	71	81	75	86	102	114	130	150
Korea, Rep. of	185	227	239	130	240	265	269	293	381
Taiwan, China	68	76	100	101	124	126	123	124	141
Hong Kong	17	24	34	41	40	42	43	44	45
Singapore	20	23	25	24	29	37	43	52	58
Other Asia[b]	94	106	118	85	108	121	127	141	153
Indonesia	0	1	0	0	2	1	n.a.	n.a.	n.a.
Malaysia	54	62	73	57	62	66	75	83	83
Philippines	26	26	28	18	21	22	20	22	22
Thailand	14	16	17	10	24	32	31	36	47
Central Europe[b]	40	49	53	51	67	69	72	89	125
Czech Republic	7	12	12	12	22	25	23	26	43
Hungary	12	12	15	14	16	16	16	19	31
Poland	21	25	26	25	29	27	32	44	51
Other									
Russia	3	17	43	65	8	9	8	5	7
Israel	86	94	103	103	98	101	103	101	106
Turkey	16	21	27	30	38	43	55	85	92
South Africa	97	98	79	80	69	69	58	39	53
Total of all the countries shown	1,029	1,215	1,416	1,415	1,654	1,723	1,851	2,015	2,116
Developed countries									
Australia	181	176	198	170	168	206	172	170	208
Sweden	242	282	285	241	250	238	197	160	208

Source: Central banks; International Monetary Fund; Bank for International Settlements.

n.a. Not available.

a. By country of issuer; outstanding positions at year-end.

b. Sum of the countries shown.

the large fiscal deficits that followed the 1997 crisis (see figure 4-1).[2] As Häusler shows in chapter 2 of this volume, these markets are still much smaller than in the major industrial countries. Nevertheless, recent development has been rapid.

The volume of outstanding domestic debt issued by emerging-market borrowers now exceeds that of international debt. One recent estimate suggests that total international trading in emerging-market domestic debt is now larger than trading in international bonds, even though international bonds are still much more liquid instruments. Figure 4-2 illustrates one assessment of the relative size of international and domestic debt that is tradable.

The Strategic Value of Bond Markets

Bond markets are central to the development of an efficient economic system.[3] The most fundamental reason is that they help to make financial markets more complete by generating market interest rates that reflect the opportunity cost of funds at a wide range of maturities. This is essential for efficient investment and financing decisions. The absence of such markets either constrains investment possibilities or leads to dangerous financing decisions. If firms or households are unable to finance the acquisition of long-term assets with long-term debt, then their decisions may be biased against long-term investment. If borrowers finance long-term investments with short-term debt, they become exposed to significant mismatches between their assets and their liabilities. Alternatively, if firms attempt to compensate for the lack of a domestic bond market by borrowing in international bond markets, they may expose themselves to excessive foreign exchange risk. In addition, as bond markets become more liquid, the hedging of maturity risks becomes cheaper and more reliable.

A second reason is that the development of bond markets can avoid concentrating intermediation on banks. It is better to spread some corporate risk in capital markets than to concentrate *all* corporate risk in the banking system. Such concentration of risk no doubt accentuated the 1997–98 Asian crisis. There is also a governance issue that can be very

2. Including large-scale bond issuance to finance bank reconstruction. In addition, some countries without fiscal deficits set out to develop bond markets.

3. Herring and Chatusripitak (2001) provide a convincing exposition of the importance of bond markets.

Figure 4-1. *Domestic Bonds Outstanding as a Share of GDP, by Region, 1994–2002*

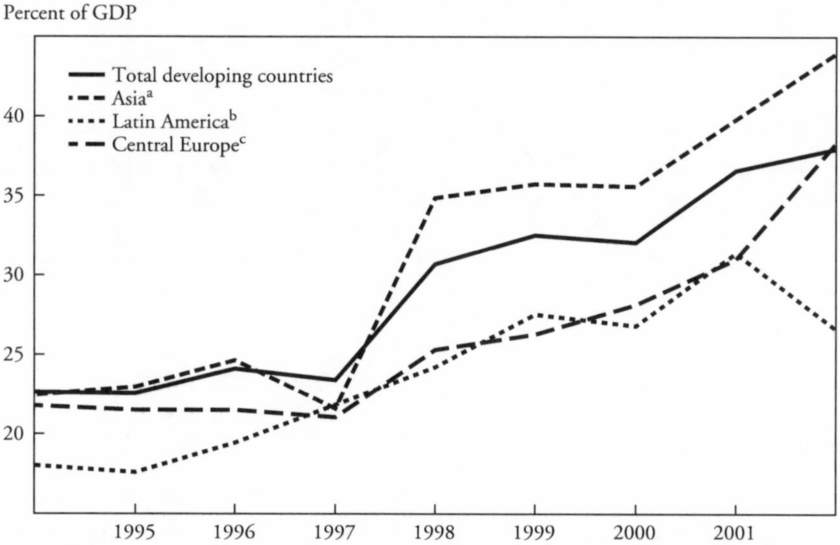

Source: Central banks; International Monetary Fund; national data; Bank for International Settlements.

a. China, Hong Kong, India, Indonesia, Korea, Malaysia, the Philippines, Singapore, Taiwan (China), and Thailand.

b. Argentina, Brazil, Chile, Colombia, Mexico, Peru, and Venezuela.

c. The Czech Republic, Hungary, and Poland.

important in countries where banks are public sector entities or where they are subject to official "guidance" to invest in "socially desirable" projects. Analyzing the performance of India's public sector banks, Patil argues that one way to limit the growth of nonperforming assets is to slow the growth of bank deposits by encouraging households to shift their savings into capital market instruments.[4]

A third reason is that bond markets can provide useful guidance for the setting of macroeconomic policy. Because bond markets react quickly to policy decisions, policies can be adjusted at an early stage. Governments can be sent a clear and immediate message about the sustainability of their fiscal policies. The political impact of higher bond rates can be all the

4. Patil (2001).

Figure 4-2. *Tradable Debt in Emerging Markets, 1996–2001*

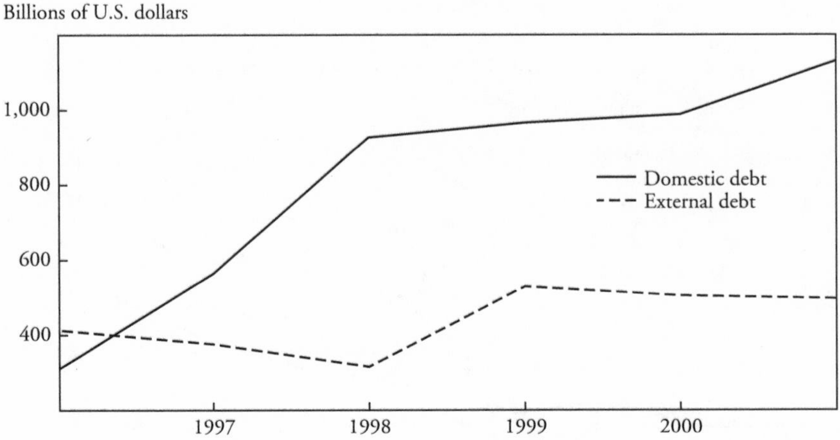

Source: Merrill Lynch (2002).

greater when household mortgages are linked to bond rates: voters usually will not welcome greater government borrowing if it means they have to pay more for their mortgages. A similar discipline is exerted on monetary policy. Excessive monetary expansion can worsen inflation expectations and drive up long-term rates. In markets with inflation-indexed bonds, the difference between the yields on such bonds and classical nominal bonds of the same maturity provides a simple measure of market expectations of inflation, which can change immediately in response to policy decisions. Such "messages" from the market can have a salutary effect on the policy debate.[5]

A final reason is that liquid debt markets facilitate the operation of monetary policy. A well-functioning money market is essential for the smooth transmission of policy moves in a framework that is increasingly reliant on indirect instruments of control.

What are the impediments to bond market development? The factors generally cited as standing in the way of bond market development often suggest some shortcomings in government policies rather than any intrin-

5. Sokoler (2002) cites Israel's experience in 2001, when a substantial rise in the government borrowing requirement led to a substantial rise in the long-term rate, with immediate consequences in the mortgage market, where rates followed the long-term rate. He concludes, "The 'bill' to the government was 'presented' immediately."

sic reason why such markets could not develop. Recent studies have attempted to examine empirically why bond markets develop in some countries but not in others. Although decisive conclusions are not yet possible, several suggest that domestic policies are important.[6]

The first factor is a history of *high and variable inflation*, which undermines the demand for local currency paper. In many cases, this has gone together with very marked volatility of the exchange rate. These factors have often meant that even short-term interest rates have had to be held well above levels prevailing in international markets. This phenomenon has been particularly marked in Latin America: the calculations in table 4-2 for the period 1990–2001 show that rates were high in real terms (particularly in Argentina and Brazil). When the differential between nominal local rates and dollar interest rates is large and when market participants expect that foreseeable movements in the exchange rate will not offset this differential, it is obviously tempting to borrow in dollars.

Even allowing for periodic devaluations, dollar-denominated borrowing would have been significantly cheaper in some countries. This would have been true for most of Latin America, Central Europe, and Indonesia, as shown by the local currency cost of dollar borrowing in table 4-2.[7]

The second impediment is a system of controls that constrains the price mechanism in the allocation of funds. This can involve interest rate controls, the nonmarket pricing of loans, and "captive market" arrangements that force local financial institutions to buy government bonds.[8]

The third major reason for the lack of a bond market is the *narrowness of the local investor base*. Part of this reflects consumer behavior. The nonbank savings of Asian households, for instance, have often gone into property or equity rather than into bonds. This reflects an inadequate realization of the diversification benefits that bonds offer in low-inflation environments—typically rising in value when property and equity values fall.[9]

6. See, for example, Burger and Warnock (2003).

7. This calculation involves comparing interest rates on local currency instruments (which may include some default risk premiums) with virtually risk-free rates in the major currencies. In addition, borrowing choices should take account of the variance as well as the mean of borrowing costs: the variance of dollar borrowing is much higher because of large movements in the exchange rate.

8. Only when the compulsory investment by financial institutions in public sector bonds was eliminated did the primary and the secondary markets in Japan "burst into life." See OECD (1995).

9. Several of the central banks that met at the Bank for International Settlements in December 2001 noted the importance of efforts to educate the public about the value of investments in bonds. They also said that local banks were reluctant to advise their customers to buy bonds, sometimes because banks saw such fixed instruments as direct threats to their own products.

Table 4-2. *Short-Term Interest Rates in Domestic Currency, by Region, 1990–2001*[a]

Region and country	*Nominal*		*Real*[b]		*Local currency cost of dollar borrowing*[c]	
	Mean	*Standard deviation*	*Mean*	*Standard deviation*	*Mean*	*Standard deviation*
Latin America[d]	22.1	7.4	8.4	4.9	20.9	10.5
Argentina[e]	9.7	3.6	9.8	4.2	4.8	0.9
Brazil[e]	25.8	10.1	15.9	8.5	23.4	20.1
Chile	16.0	10.4	5.1	5.8	12.9	7.6
Colombia	24.8	7.6	3.9	5.0	22.3	12.0
Mexico	23.1	11.3	4.3	6.8	19.3	26.5
Venezuela	28.1	13.0	–7.9	14.9	41.0	46.9
Asia, larger economies[d]	8.5	2.8	1.6	4.1	13.0	10.2
China	7.1	3.2	0.4	6.3	12.9	16.0
India	11.0	4.9	2.2	4.4	15.1	11.4
Korea, Rep. of	11.9	3.9	6.3	2.9	12.1	19.8
Taiwan, China	6.8	1.7	4.2	1.7	7.2	7.5
Other Asia[d]	14.5	5.7	5.2	3.6	22.0	48.3
Indonesia	19.9	9.7	6.3	6.5	33.9	85.6
Malaysia	6.2	2.1	2.8	1.3	8.7	15.9
Philippines	13.2	5.0	4.0	2.8	13.6	16.3
Thailand	9.8	5.1	5.1	3.1	11.0	19.3
Central Europe[d,f]	19.4	5.1	2.9	3.9	16.9	9.7
Czech Republic	10.0	3.9	1.3	3.8	8.6	10.7
Hungary	19.6	7.0	2.1	3.5	21.0	8.8
Poland	22.7	6.3	3.6	5.3	18.9	12.5
Other						
Israel	11.8	2.7	2.2	3.8	12.0	5.8
Turkey	70.0	17.6	–1.7	9.7	81.6	41.8
Saudi Arabia	5.7	1.4	4.7	2.6	4.8	1.3
South Africa	14.1	3.1	4.6	3.1	16.1	10.0
Developed countries						
United States	4.8	1.3	1.7	1.1	4.8	1.3
Japan	2.4	2.6	1.5	1.6	4.4	12.7
Germany	4.6	2.0	2.0	1.1	6.7	10.9

Source: National data.

a. The data are based on monthly averages. Rates on short-term government paper or those paid on three- to six-month deposits.

b. The real interest rate is the nominal rate deflated by year-on-year change in the consumer price index.

c. U.S. three-month treasury bill rate corrected for changes in the dollar exchange rate over the past twelve months.

d. Weighted average of countries shown, based on 1995 GDP and purchasing power parity exchange rates.

e. To exclude the periods of hyperinflation, the period of observation for these countries is restricted to mid-1995–2001.

f. To exclude the immediate transition years, the period of observation for these countries is restricted to 1993–2001.

But the narrowness of the local investor base partly also reflects a comparative lack of institutional investors. The assets managed by institutional investors are much smaller as a proportion of GDP in emerging markets than in the major industrial countries (table 4-3). Institutional investors that need to hold long-dated debt can play a major role in the development of debt markets. In addition, a culture of fixed-income investment is often lacking among households, and regulations sometimes hinder the functioning of mutual funds, which are an efficient vehicle for small-scale personal investment. But the situation in emerging markets is changing, a subject I return to later in the paper.

Even when the outstanding stock of bonds grows, official policies may reduce liquidity. Certain *regulatory provisions* often inhibit active trading by institutional investors. Accounting rules can have such an effect. In many countries, institutional investors such as pension funds and insurance companies are allowed to carry bonds on their balance sheet at historic cost irrespective of market price developments. Under this system, valuations change only on sale. On the face of it, such an accounting rule can, of course, be defended: institutional investors should, the argument runs, take the long-term view and avoid much-aligned "short-termism." But there is a major drawback. Because historic cost accounting means that losses or gains are registered only on trading, trading tends to be avoided because it makes the reported income and balance sheet more volatile. The absence of mark-to-market accounting therefore tends to inhibit trading in most markets.[10] This is a major loss. Because long-term investors such as pension funds and insurance companies do not have the same need for liquidity as many other participants in financial markets, they would be particularly well placed to trade by buying illiquid bonds that have become relatively cheap (so earning the liquidity premium) and selling highly liquid issues. Such activity could make bond markets as a whole more liquid. In several countries commercial banks became much more active traders once they were required to mark at least part of their portfolio to market. Institutional investors might respond in much the same way. In many countries, savings institutions designed for small savers—and holding a significant proportion of government bonds—are often exempt from the mark-to-market rules that apply to banks.

Another rule that can inhibit liquidity is the prohibition (or discouragement) of the short selling of government bonds. The ostensible reason for such rules is to limit leverage and so contain systemic risks. In practice, however, they often reflect a wish to insulate the financial system from

10. For a summary of current mark-to-market practices, see Mohanty (2002, table 7).

Table 4-3. *Assets of Institutional Investors as a Share of GDP*
Percent

Market and period covered	*Insurance companies*	*Pension funds*	*Pooled investment schemes*
G-10 countries, 1990–97	62.4	46.0	13.5
Emerging markets, 1990–97	10.8	n.a.	n.a.
Chile			
1981	3.1	1.2	2.6
1990	6.7	24.2	3.2
2000	16.7	53.8	7.7

Source: Cifuentes, Desormeaux, and González (2002); Karacadag and Shrivastava (2000).
n.a. Not available.

shocks and sometimes a wish of the government as borrower to keep long-term interest rates below their market equilibrium.

Taxation arrangements can also make markets less liquid. Taxes on the transfer of financial instruments—even at very small rates—work against frequent trading. Capital gains taxes on instruments that should have a high turnover reduce the incentives for arbitrage and so make markets less liquid. Withholding taxes on nonresidents (and complex procedures for eventual reimbursement) also inhibit liquidity.

Financing Decisions of the Government and Central Bank

Government decisions about their own borrowing strategy have a major impact on the development of local debt markets. Local bond markets are unlikely to develop if governments rely either on short-term debt or, when they borrow long term, on foreign currency–denominated borrowing. The case against a heavy reliance on short-term borrowing is that using short-term finance for long-term investments exposes the borrower to greater interest rate as well as refinancing risks.

What about resort to foreign currency borrowing? Should governments borrow abroad in foreign currency, or should they borrow at home in domestic currency?[11] Although there are no hard-and-fast rules, two

11. There is not, of course, a one-to-one correspondence between locality and currency of denomination—foreign currency debt can be issued at home and conversely—but there is a broad correspondence in most emerging-market countries.

analytic approaches to this question suggest that it is more prudent for governments to issue local currency debt.

The first approach is the balance sheet perspective: the currency denomination of government liabilities should depend on the currency denomination of government assets. Such an approach was explicitly implemented first by New Zealand, where an effort was made to relate government debt management to an overall government balance sheet, encompassing not just financial assets and debts but also physical assets (for example, schools and roads) and future liabilities (for example, pensions).[12] The logic of this approach is that only borrowing aimed at acquiring foreign currency assets (for example, the exploitation of natural resources) should be denominated in foreign currency. Borrowing to finance local currency assets (whose value is insensitive to exchange rate movements) should be in local currency. Since most public sector investments are in the latter category, this argument suggests that most government borrowing should be denominated in local currency. The fact that governments collect taxes in local currency (and often exempt exports from taxation) should further tilt the policy choice toward borrowing in local currency.

The second approach is to compare the macroeconomic consequences of different borrowing strategies. The main macroeconomic difference between domestic and foreign borrowing in the short term is that government borrowing locally pushes up domestic interest rates and so crowds out private sector borrowing (perhaps forcing the private sector to borrow abroad). In the short term, foreign borrowing tends to avoid this crowding-out effect. Over time, however, repayments rise, exerting a deflationary drag on the economy. Such a pattern of short-term benefits and long-term costs has tempted many governments to rely too heavily on foreign borrowing, and this has often made governments and their electorates too complacent about the size of fiscal deficits. Ensuring that the unpleasant consequences of heavy government borrowing are felt immediately (that is, through higher domestic interest rates) may be more conducive to sound policymaking than resorting to devices such as foreign borrowing that can postpone the pain. In addition, countries with fixed exchange rates are less vulnerable to sudden changes in sentiment if foreign borrowing is limited.

These arguments do not imply an *exclusive* reliance on local currency borrowing. Some foreign currency borrowing might be part of a prudent diversification strategy. Or it may be required to ensure a sovereign credit

12. See Anderson (1999).

rating in international markets, which establishes a benchmark for private sector issues.[13] In addition, occasions of marked exchange rate volatility can require increased reliance on foreign currency borrowing, at least for a time. Governments can react to an "undervalued" exchange rate by issuing foreign currency debt. If their judgment is vindicated, they can economize on financing costs. But the inherent risks in such strategies if the government's expectations prove wrong (for example, the exchange rate falls further) argue for only sparing and limited use of foreign currency borrowing.[14]

How the monetary authorities finance foreign exchange reserves has become much more important as the levels of reserves have risen. Before 1990, the value of foreign exchange reserves in the developing world was less than the public's holdings of bank notes, which sometimes was the largest single liability on the central bank's balance sheet. In such circumstances, the management of the central bank's balance sheet had relatively few consequences for financial markets. This position changed radically during the 1990s. Aggregate foreign exchange reserves in emerging Asia (excluding the international financial centers Hong Kong and Singapore) now exceed aggregate domestic currency by more than $400 billion (see figure 4-3). In some countries, reserves exceed domestic currency by several multiples. In many countries, foreign exchange reserves have grown well above aggregate reserve money.

Huge reserves on the asset side of a central bank's balance sheet mean that there is a large stock of liabilities on the other side. The form these liabilities take has a major impact on the development of financial markets. Yet in many cases, central banks simply absorb the excess liquidity arising from foreign exchange inflows by taking (usually fixed-term) deposits from

13. Cifuentes, Desormeaux, and González (2002) cite this as an important reason in Chile.

14. Very large exchange rate depreciation can create difficult dilemmas for policymakers. Brazil's experience during 2001 when financial market conditions were very difficult illustrates some of the issues involved. The Brazilian currency depreciated sharply during much of 2001 (about 40 percent from end-2000 to September 2001), and this had the mechanical effect of increasing the share of outstanding foreign currency debt in total debt. At the same time, the high yields on domestic paper made borrowing in domestic currency very expensive; it seemed all the more expensive to those who believed the exchange rate had fallen too far and was likely to bounce back. A further consideration was that exchange rate volatility—and the prospect of still further weaknesses—increased the private sector demand for exchange rate hedges. The government decided to increase its issuance of dollar-linked notes, in effect allowing local companies to hedge. The Brazilian real did indeed appreciate in the months that followed, appreciating 17 percent against the dollar between October 2001 and March 2002. In retrospect, then, local currency borrowing during mid-2001 proved to be much more expensive than dollar-denominated borrowing.

Figure 4-3. *Net Foreign Assets Less Currency Held Outside Banks, by Region, 1990–2002*

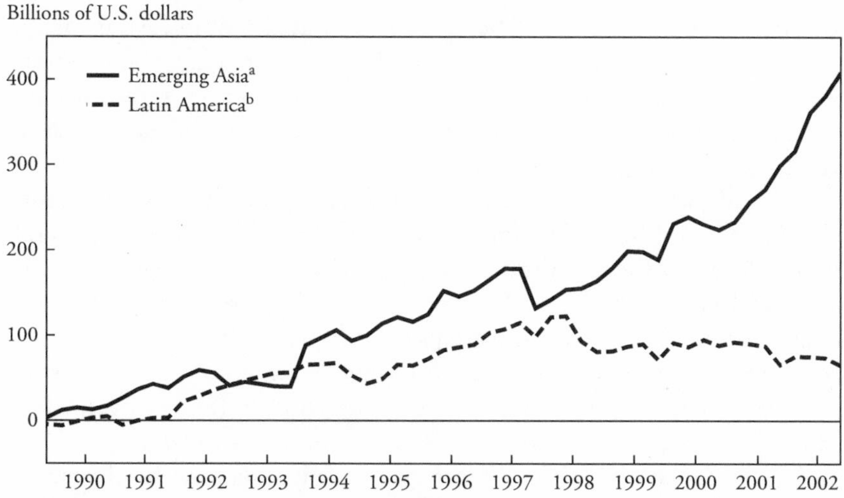

Source: International Monetary Fund; national data.

a. China, India, Indonesia, Korea, Malaysia, the Philippines, Taiwan (China), and Thailand.

b. Argentina, Brazil, Chile, Colombia, Mexico, Peru, and Venezuela.

the commercial banks. In some cases, commercial banks can be forced to make such deposits. Conducting operations through the issuance of marketable debt probably would help to deepen local debt markets. If marketable debt is to be issued, what should be its duration? There is probably a general presumption that the issuance of longer-term paper is more effective. In the early 1990s, for instance, some Latin American central banks found that using the short-term debt instruments at their disposal (bond markets being relatively underdeveloped) was often unsatisfactory. Issuing short-term paper tended to drive up short-term interest rates and encourage further inflows into such paper. This risked biasing the structure of inflows toward the short end. Sterilization through the sale of bonds could reduce such a risk, and this encouraged some countries to seek to develop bond markets.[15]

At the same time, policies need to take careful account of interest rate risks that could arise from maturity mismatches—either at the central bank

15. Frankel (1993) provides a good summary of these issues.

or with commercial banks. Issuing long-term debt to finance short-term reserve holdings (usually short-term treasury papers issued by the reserve currency countries) would expose the central bank to a maturity mismatch. On these grounds, it could be argued that, as the duration of foreign exchange reserves increases (as the level of reserves rises), there may be scope for lengthening the corresponding liabilities. However, issuing long-term paper could expose commercial banks—normally the main buyers—to interest rate risks.

If bonds were to be issued, an important question is whether they should be issued by the government or by the central bank. One possibility would be for the government to issue the bonds and redeposit the proceeds with the central bank. This probably would present few problems in countries with sizable borrowing requirements.[16] Another possibility would be for the central bank to issue its own paper. Economies without a history of fiscal deficits to generate "natural" government debt (for example, Chile, Hong Kong) tend to rely on paper issued by the central bank.

One trap to avoid is that of fragmenting the market for official paper by issuing both government and central bank debt. If the government is issuing debt to finance a fiscal deficit, then the central bank should use government-issued paper. This would require careful coordination between the treasury and the central bank; the failure to resolve differences between these two institutions often induces the central bank to issue its own paper. For instance, a central bank may want to issue bonds at a particular time or with particular characteristics, but the government might balk at this because such issuance competes with its own borrowing plans.[17]

16. If the central bank pays a short-term interest rate on government deposits but earns a long-term rate on the government bonds it holds, the yield curve profit is in essence transferred from the government to the central bank. But arrangements could be made to prevent this (for example, the interest paid by the central bank on government deposits could be aligned with the cost to the government of issuing bonds).

17. An additional consideration not directly relevant to the development of bond markets is whether the government or the central bank should show the financing cost of accumulating reserves (as the interest rate on domestic paper usually exceeds that of international paper in which the reserves are invested). Since it is government that usually decides to build up reserves, accountability would argue for costs being shown in the government accounts. Forcing the central bank to bear the loss can have a severe impact on central bank profitability. Such losses weaken the central bank's balance sheet and can damage its reputation and credibility. Further, actual and prospective losses can eventually lead the central bank to be less resolute in pursuing its monetary policy objectives. If losses persist or are expected to persist, it would be quite natural for profitability considerations to loom larger and larger in *all* decisionmaking processes in the central bank, with potentially damaging consequences for the central bank's policies and the national economy.

How these various dilemmas are resolved in practice differs markedly from country to country. India, for instance, has taken advantage of the strong demand of commercial banks for bonds (reflecting weak demand for loans) to issue long-term debt without causing substantial increases in yields. Mexico, by contrast, has relied on floating-rate debt. Sidaoui notes that the Central Bank of Mexico started to issue its own securities in 2000 to sterilize the continuous increase in foreign exchange reserves—so-called "Brems," one- and three-year floating-rate bonds with coupons linked to the overnight rate.[18] The central bank took the view that continuing to sell long-term government debt would have had a larger impact on the yield curve and did not wish to put further upward pressure on bond yields.

The Structure of Domestic Debt

Poor debt structures exacerbated several recent crises in the emerging markets.[19] Efforts therefore have been made in recent years to improve the structure of domestic debt securities—lengthening maturities and developing local currency debt instruments. Yet many emerging markets are still vulnerable to debt that is too short term, particularly in Latin America and Central Europe. Although the proportion of total domestic debt securities that is short term has fallen in recent years, it is still relatively high. In Latin America, 37 percent of domestic debt securities were short term in 2000, down from 53 percent in 1995, but still higher than in Asia or Central Europe.

Moreover, 28 percent of Latin American debt was indexed to inflation in 2000, and 22 percent was linked to the exchange rate. In Asia, however, debt is more long term, and relatively little is indexed to inflation or the exchange rate. Floating-rate debt remains a high proportion of total debt (figure 4-4). This means that the average duration of debt has increased less than has the average maturity.

Countries with a history of high and volatile inflation cannot move to classical fixed-rate nominal debt in one step. Rather the development of "better" debt structures needs to proceed in stages. Many countries therefore have found that some form of indexation and recourse to floating-rate debt was a desirable transitional phase in moving to longer-term debt. For

18. Sidaoui (2002).

19. See, for example, Financial Stability Forum (2000).

Figure 4-4. *Type of Domestic Debt Securities at Issue as a Percentage of Total, by Region, End-2000*

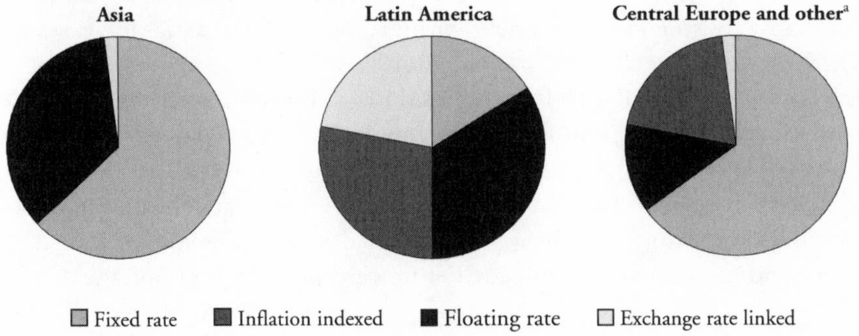

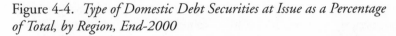

Source: Mihaljek, Scatigna, and Villar (2002).
a. Includes Israel and Saudi Arabia.

instance, Mexico moved away from dollar-linked debt and toward inflation-linked or floating-rate debt after the 1994 crisis. More recently, the government has issued marketable long-term fixed-rate debt.

Brazil also has sought to develop a more sustainable debt structure in stages. At the end of 1999, the treasury and the Central Bank of Brazil set a number of guidelines for domestic debt management, including lengthening the average maturity of debt, increasing the share of fixed-rate securities, and reducing the share of dollar-linked or overnight rate–linked debt. Some progress in achieving these aims was made during 2000 and (for some of the objectives) part of 2001, but the more difficult international and macroeconomic environment thereafter created dilemmas for the authorities, who partially reversed the earlier movement away from dollar-linked debt.

Imagination in the design of debt instruments can be very helpful.[20] Different investors have different tastes, and instruments can be tailored accordingly. The use of inflation index–linked bonds is a case in point. Such bonds not only assure investors in inflation-prone countries but also are useful even in more stable economies. The yield differential compared with nominal bonds provides information about inflation expectations—

20. The use of alternative debt instruments for international issues by emerging markets (for example, with state contingent options or warrants, paper with embedded put options, collateralized paper, and so forth) is analyzed in IMF (2002).

at least in a liquid or nonsegmented market.[21] Several economists have argued that governments should issue bonds with returns that vary directly with economic developments and thus their ability to service debts. One suggestion has been to issue bonds indexed to commodity prices.[22] Such bonds give foreign investors the possibility to "buy" some upside risk in particular commodity prices, and they give commodity-exporting borrowers an offset when commodity prices fall. A more general suggestion has recently come from Borensztein and Mauro, who argue that developing countries can "self-insure against economic growth slowdowns" by issuing bonds indexed to GDP.[23]

These ideas merit serious consideration. New types of instruments make financial markets more complete. Nevertheless, three caveats need to be borne in mind. The first is that the prices of GDP-indexed bonds are likely to be more closely correlated with equity prices and thus offer investors less diversification than classic bonds (which often rise in price when equity prices fall). The second is that market practitioners do not like complex instruments, the pricing of which not only involves computational costs but also depends on the (uncertain) quantification of macroeconomic outcomes. In addition, arbitrage operations across different types of bonds become more complex. This is probably why inflation-indexed bonds took some years to become established. The third is that a greater variety of issuance inevitably reduces the liquidity of each particular type. It is possible that only rather large bond markets can maintain the liquidity of different forms of bonds; if so, governments of smaller countries will have to choose which form suits them best.

Fostering Deep and Liquid Government Bond Markets

Although the aggregate value of bonds issued by governments in emerging markets has grown substantially over the past decade, liquidity in most markets remains rather low.[24] Market participants and issuers frequently

21. When markets are segmented (for example, some classes of investors buy nominal debt, and others buy index-linked debt), then movements in the yield differential can reflect developments specific to particular institutions.

22. Bonds indexed to the price of oil (Mexico) and copper (Chile) have been issued.

23. Borensztein and Mauro (2002).

24. The comprehensive handbook of the World Bank and IMF (2001) and APEC (1999) examine the practical steps involved in fostering government bond markets in useful detail.

complain that liquidity in most markets is still quite limited. Liquidity does vary over time, and its measurement is far from straightforward. Subject to these caveats, table 4-4 provides some common summary measures. Spreads for off-the-run issues tend to be larger in emerging than in industrial countries, the depth of the secondary market (as measured by the ratio of turnover to average outstanding stocks) tends to be low, and liquidity tends to be concentrated in only a few benchmark issues.[25]

Illiquidity in government bond markets is in part a function of the size of the market. McCauley and Remolona, looking at bid-ask spreads and the success of futures markets in G-10 markets, suggest that there may be a size threshold that lies around $100 billion to $200 billion.[26] Government bond markets below this size may tend to be somewhat illiquid.

What can or should the central bank (or government) do to make government bond markets more liquid? There is no easy answer. One view is that the authorities need to concentrate on removing artificial constraints on bond trading. Taxation should not discourage trading. As issuance increases, liquidity will follow naturally. The other view stresses that central banks and treasuries need to take the "necessary first steps" to get the market started—and perhaps be prepared to do so over several years.

Is the more interventionist view justified? It is quite true that the public sector often has taken a leading role in developing an institutional structure for a liquid bond market. And economies of scale may indeed justify an "infant industry" argument for trading structures, which become self-sufficient only once a certain level of trading has been reached. But there are major dilemmas. For example, the direct public control of trading structures creates a conflict between ownership and regulation/supervision. For that reason, it is desirable for government to withdraw gradually from market infrastructure institutions.[27] The following paragraphs consider the pros and cons of specific steps that deserve consideration and underline the dangers of governments becoming too closely involved.

25. In mature bond markets a wide range of benchmark issues (for example, one, two, five, ten, and thirty years) are highly liquid, but in many emerging economies only one or two issues are highly traded.

26. McCauley and Remolona (2000).

27. Reddy (2002) explains that the Reserve Bank of India promoted the Discount and Finance House of India to develop the money and treasury bills markets and the Securities Trading Corporation of India to develop the secondary market for government securities. But the Reserve Bank of India divested most of its holdings in these institutions as markets became more developed.

Table 4-4. *Indicators of Liquidity in Government Bond Markets*

<table>
<tr><th rowspan="2">Country</th><th colspan="2">Typical bid-ask spread[a]</th><th rowspan="2">Turnover as a percentage of average outstanding stock in 2000</th></tr>
<tr><th>On-the-run bonds</th><th>Off-the-run bonds</th></tr>
<tr><td>Emerging markets</td><td></td><td></td><td></td></tr>
<tr><td>India</td><td>1</td><td>n.a.</td><td>3.0</td></tr>
<tr><td>Hong Kong</td><td>5–10</td><td>n.a.</td><td>22.0</td></tr>
<tr><td>Singapore</td><td>5</td><td>10–15</td><td>4.7</td></tr>
<tr><td>Indonesia</td><td colspan="2">n.a.</td><td>0.5</td></tr>
<tr><td>Korea</td><td>1</td><td>1</td><td>9.1</td></tr>
<tr><td>Philippines</td><td colspan="2">25–50</td><td>n.a.</td></tr>
<tr><td>Thailand</td><td colspan="2">2–3</td><td>1.1</td></tr>
<tr><td>Brazil</td><td>2</td><td>50</td><td>n.a.</td></tr>
<tr><td>Chile</td><td colspan="2">n.a.</td><td>3.5</td></tr>
<tr><td>Colombia</td><td>40</td><td>n.a.</td><td>0.2</td></tr>
<tr><td>Mexico</td><td>10–15</td><td>10–25</td><td>2.5</td></tr>
<tr><td>Peru</td><td colspan="2">n.a.</td><td>n.a.</td></tr>
<tr><td>Czech Republic</td><td colspan="2">20</td><td>1.0</td></tr>
<tr><td>Poland</td><td colspan="2">5–25</td><td>31.0</td></tr>
<tr><td>Israel</td><td colspan="2">n.a.</td><td>46.0</td></tr>
<tr><td>Saudi Arabia</td><td colspan="2">20</td><td>0.5</td></tr>
<tr><td>Developed markets</td><td></td><td></td><td></td></tr>
<tr><td>United States</td><td>3</td><td>6</td><td>22.0</td></tr>
<tr><td>Japan</td><td>7</td><td>7</td><td>6.9</td></tr>
<tr><td>Germany</td><td>4</td><td>5</td><td>n.a.</td></tr>
<tr><td>United Kingdom</td><td>4</td><td>4</td><td>7.0</td></tr>
</table>

Source: Mohanty (2002, table 1).
n.a. Not available.
a. In basis points.

Ensure Bond Rates Are Market-Determined

Markets in financial instruments develop best when the prices of such instruments are free. In practice, however, many governments have often sought to hold the interest rate on government bonds below the market-clearing level. Attempting to do this over prolonged periods of time will hinder the development of bond markets, and most emerging markets have moved away from such policies.

A more difficult question is how far the central bank (or the government) should go to smooth short-term volatility in bond rates in order to further develop the bond market. A high degree of volatility in government bond rates can be problematic because such rates tend to become the market benchmarks (for example, affecting mortgages) so that the effects are transmitted throughout the economy.

One view is that "new" bond markets tend to be very unstable because market participants do not have a long history to guide their decisions. In such circumstances, expectations may be destabilizing—a falling price engenders expectations of further falls. Preventing such extreme volatility reduces the risk premiums and increases the underlying demand for bonds. This may be particularly true of banks, which are typically highly exposed to interest rate risk. If they can be assured that official action will, on occasion, moderate extreme volatility of bond prices, the argument runs, then they will be more willing to hold bonds.

The counterview is that official attempts to smooth interest rates simply "featherbed" the banks, giving them less incentive to put in place proper risk management mechanisms. It could also impede the market development of hedging instruments. The balance of arguments depends on circumstances. Thin or nascent markets may require more intervention. Exogenous shocks (for example, reflected in periods of unusual volatility in international capital markets) can justify intervention. But such intervention should be subject to constraints if the market determination of bond prices is to be preserved. Noting that the Reserve Bank of India deliberately moderates sharp movements in yields that could emerge in auctions, Reddy says that such policies are essentially an "intra-year smoothing process" and not an attempt to manipulate prices.[28] The important general point is that intervention to moderate volatility in thin markets should not degenerate into attempts to resist the underlying trend of prices.

Develop Liquid Money Markets

In many countries, the extreme volatility of money market rates adds to the risks of bondholders: the daily carrying cost of long-term paper becomes much more uncertain. The absence of a relatively stable and complete money market yield curve can hamper hedging strategies. Karacadag, Sundararajan, and Elliot in chapter 9 of this volume rightly stress that the money market is the foundation of all financial and capital markets.

The volatility of daily interbank rates in emerging markets (as measured in table 4-5 by the standard deviation of interest rates) is much higher than

28. Reddy (2002).

Table 4-5. *Volatility of Short-Term Interest Rates, by Region, 1996–2002*[a]

Region	*1996*	*1997*	*1998*	*1999*	*2000*	*2001*	*2002*
Asia[b]	1.0	3.6	4.1	2.1	0.5	0.7	0.5
Latin America[c]	2.1	2.1	4.2	3.7	1.0	2.7	5.1
Central Europe[d]	1.2	2.0	2.4	1.4	0.6	1.0	0.9
G-3[e]	0.2	0.2	0.2	0.2	0.4	0.6	0.1

Source: Bloomberg; Datastream.

a. Volatility is measured by the standard deviation of daily interbank or call money rates.

b. Unweighted average of China, Hong Kong, India, Indonesia, Korea, Malaysia, the Philippines, Singapore, and Thailand.

c. Unweighted average of Argentina, Brazil, Chile, Colombia, Mexico, and Peru.

d. Unweighted average of the Czech Republic, Hungary, and Poland.

e. Unweighted average of Germany, Japan, and the United States.

in three major economies. Volatility was particularly high during the various crises of the 1990s; since then, however, volatility has declined in Asia and in Central Europe but remains high in Latin America. One major reason for high volatility even during normal times is the lack of depth in money markets, which in turn reflects high reserve requirements (or a relatively short reserve compliance period).[29]

Establish a Primary Dealer System

Many countries have found that establishing a primary dealer system is essential for creating the necessary liquidity in government bond markets. And primary dealers often help the central bank to understand the market. In addition, the two-way quotes provided by primary dealers play a significant role in developing a transparent secondary market. Bond market turnover increased significantly in several countries after primary dealers were introduced. In most countries, primary dealers were extended some privileges, including the exclusive right to bid at the primary market, access to noncompetitive bids, access to security-lending facilities from the central bank, or certain tax exemptions.[30] Inviting foreign firms to become primary dealers on the same basis as domestic firms can help the transmis-

29. These aspects are discussed further in Mohanty (2002). Uribe and Gutiérrez (2002) explain the measures taken to make the money market in Colombia more stable.

30. For a summary of the obligations and privileges of primary dealers in particular countries, see Mohanty (2002, table A2).

sion of best international practice in the local market. Some developing countries are perhaps not as demanding of primary dealers as are the authorities in industrial countries: obligations could include bidding regularly at auction, offering continuous two-way quotes, and promoting bonds among retail investors.

Foster a Repo Market in Government Bonds

Central banks can enhance liquidity in secondary markets by using government securities as collateral for their lending operations. Moreover, repurchase transactions ("repos") are more market-neutral than outright transactions because they do not affect bond prices (except indirectly) and have only a temporary impact on liquidity.[31] Developing a repo market in government bonds is essential for facilitating arbitrage across the yield curve and thus absorbing excess liquidity in the market. Yet repo markets remain underdeveloped in most emerging economies. The interbank repo market tends to be very short term, rarely going beyond overnight. A lack of good collateral and the inclusion of repo transactions in eligible assets for reserve requirements sometimes limit the development of repo markets.

Adopt a More Liberal Attitude toward Short Selling

The ability to short sell a security makes markets more complete. In particular, the ability to short sell and "borrow" a security promotes market liquidity: the risk of settlement failures is reduced, and arbitrage opportunities are increased. The favorable impact on liquidity was a major reason why many industrial countries relaxed their restrictions on security-lending transactions during the 1990s. Yet most emerging markets continue to restrict short selling. Several reasons are put forward for this. One is that local risk management practices cannot cope with the need to continuously monitor other credit risks (if one counterparty fails to deliver) or market risks (if the value of the collateral changes). Another is that the payment and settlement system is not sufficiently developed to deal with the complex settlement procedures involved. A third is that allowing short selling may entail systemic risks by increasing leverage and creating an addi-

31. See Figuereido, Fachada, and Goldenstein (2002) for a discussion of Brazil's preference for repos over outright transactions.

tional channel through which shocks can be transmitted in the financial system. These reasons, however, do nothing to weaken the general case for allowing short selling. Rather they point to the need for better regulation and supervision of the financial system.

Develop Benchmarks

In many cases, the fragmentation of government debt outstanding into a large number of distinct issues hinders liquidity: one symptom of this is often a very bumpy yield curve. Concentrating issuance on a few benchmark securities typically improves liquidity. When government debt managers are fearful that they will not be able to place all the paper they need to issue, there is a temptation to come to market too frequently with many small issues, often with terms tailored to attract investors at that particular time. The result is often a very heterogeneous outstanding stock of government bonds with many different payment periods.[32]

Increasing the size of issuance and reopening existing issues can make a useful contribution to liquidity.[33] One simple idea is to define issues in terms of a common *maturity date* (for example, June 30, 2008) rather than in terms of a common maturity period (for example, five-year paper with the maturity being defined as five years from the issuance date). This would allow paper with an identical date of maturity to be issued steadily for prolonged periods, simplifying pricing enormously. Equally, a policy of consolidation by the government debt manager or by the central bank (that is, buying back illiquid issues and selling popular issues) can also make the yield curve much smoother and thus provide a better benchmark.[34]

Many countries have adopted such strategies in order to develop benchmarks. Teo explains that Singapore recently switched to buyback operations in order to develop benchmarks. Thailand has introduced legal changes to help the debt manager to buy back securities.[35] Many countries have launched new instruments (zero-coupon bonds and "stripping") to broaden the range of instruments. In addition, many have emphasized the development of a futures market. In Korea, trading in bonds received a

32. For a thoughtful discussion of these issues in the Brazilian bond market, see Gragnani, Amante, and Araujo (2003).

33. For a discussion of recent experience, see Mohanty (2002, pp. 66–67).

34. See Stebbing (1997, fig. 2) for an account of Australia's experiences that draws many useful implications for emerging-market economies.

35. Teo (2002); see Chabchitrchaidol and Permpoon (2002).

boost after the establishment of a bond futures market. A similar trend has also been noted in Singapore.

Widening the Investor Base: Nonresidents, Households, and Institutional Investors

Many countries have found that allowing nonresident investment makes local bond markets more liquid. Choy notes that foreign banks are likely to want to invest their idle cash balances in highly marketable securities such as government bonds in the countries of their operation.[36] Sidaoui notes that foreign banks in Mexico, especially the smaller ones, derive their revenue from actively trading securities rather than holding them.[37]

Much can also be done to foster the local investor base. Because institutional investors such as insurance companies and pension funds need to hold long-dated debt, many see such institutions as key to the development of debt markets. There has been a lively debate about the role of mandatory contributions to pension plans; Musalem and Tressel discuss this issue in chapter 16 of this volume. The development of funded pension schemes is likely to exert a particularly powerful influence; the accumulated funds of pension schemes when fully mature often approach an amount equivalent to the size of annual GDP.[38] Moreover, the net demand for assets in a "young" pension fund is substantial during the process of maturation. If local bond markets are underdeveloped, institutional investors may be induced to hold short-term paper. Pension funds in some countries have an incentive to hold short-term paper either because of an inverted yield curve or because money market instruments can be traded more readily than long-term paper.

The most cited example of pension fund development in emerging markets going hand in hand with bond market development is that of Chile, which launched a funded pension system in 1981. This contributed to a long boom in Chilean asset prices, led to pension funds holding (by 2000) the equivalent of more than 50 percent of GDP, and made the Chilean capital market one of the most developed in Latin America (table 4-3).

36. Choy (2002).

37. Sidaoui (2002).

38. For a good recent discussion of the policy issues raised by institutional investors, see Carmichael and Pomerleano (2002, pp. 108–10). This book reviews recent studies, which show that the growth of pension schemes helps financial markets to develop.

The use of inflation-indexed debt was a central feature of this success. The pension reform also led to the creation of rating agencies.

Cifuentes, Desormeaux, and González note that pension fund investments in local bond markets continued to rise in a period when other investors were pulling out, suggesting that pension funds lend stability to the market.[39] But they also stress the importance of a broadly based investment industry where institutional investors other than pension funds play an important role. This may be difficult to achieve. The pension fund industry in Chile has become a virtual monopsony among institutional investors because of the small size of mutual funds and investment funds.[40] This is a general shortcoming in many emerging markets.

The importance of institutional investors is such that rules governing portfolio decisions can raise wider issues. Rules forcing institutional investors to hold a high proportion of their assets in government bonds can create a "captive" market. This can undermine the creation of a true market in bonds and in effect deter other investors. Rules often restrict mutual funds' investment in short-term instruments, usually to limit how far mutual funds can compete with banks for household deposits by offering funds invested in short-term paper. Such restrictions can stunt the growth of such funds and prevent them from playing a more active role in government bond markets.[41]

A second issue concerns rules governing the credit quality of their investments. In order to protect investors, rules are often imposed to prevent or limit investment in noninvestment-grade paper.[42] Such rules could, however, have several consequences that may inadvertently undermine financial stability: they could magnify the impact of credit downgrading on a company's bonds as institutional investors are forced to sell downgraded bonds, and poorer credits could, in effect, be forced onto the banks, a process of adverse selection.

Another issue concerns investment in foreign securities. This is often prohibited or restricted on the grounds that forcing institutional investors

39. Cifuentes, Desormeaux, and González (2002).

40. Pension funds hold 70 percent of outstanding central bank and government bonds in Chile. See Cifuentes, Desormeaux, and González (2002, fig. 2) for a measure of increased concentration in the pension fund industry.

41. See Sidaoui's (2002) discussion of this issue and reforms in Mexico.

42. An alternative rule might be to allow institutional investors to invest as they please, but to impose higher reserve requirements or provisions against investment in riskier assets. Choy (2002) points out that this approach is applied in Peru. Another approach is to limit what institutional investors buy rather than what they hold.

to buy domestic securities helps to deepen local financial markets. Two reservations can be raised about such reasoning. The first is that small countries typically have a greater need for diversification and hence for investment in foreign securities. A high proportion of institutional investor assets held abroad (denominated in foreign currency) can give a country a buffer against the volatility of exchange rates. In extreme cases, financial institutions that are over-invested in local government bonds may face a "run" when investors lose confidence in local paper. The second reservation has to do with the size of the domestic market. If pension funds are forced to put all their assets in domestic securities, they acquire ever-larger shares of often rather small domestic markets. This could create major distortions in the functioning of local markets.

A much more promising avenue for widening the investor base for small bond markets in Asia and Latin America would be to standardize the institutional aspects of bond markets—taxes, contracts, underwriting, settlement procedures, and so forth. In chapter 2 of this volume, Häusler notes that very different institutional arrangements serve to unnecessarily segment local securities markets. This puts off potential foreign investors and makes it more difficult for them to pool and hedge investment risks. He notes in particular that Asia's domestic currency bond markets are largely insulated from each other.

Widening the Issuer Base: Corporate Bond Markets

With the exception of a few Asian countries, corporate bond markets traditionally have been underdeveloped in most emerging markets. This usually reflects the dominance of bank lending—and the close relationship between corporates and banks. Another reason is that the quality of corporate disclosure is too poor to support the public issue of corporate debt. In some cases, corporations try to evade the strict disclosure requirements for public issuance by relying on private placements. This raises the question of how far such placements should fall under the purview of the supervisory authorities.[43]

A controversial issue is the role that credit-rating agencies should play. One implication often drawn from U.S. experience is that a key prerequisite for the development of a corporate bond market is the existence of

43. Reddy (2002) offers an illuminating discussion of this point.

some form of independent credit risk assessment. For this reason—and because of the greater reliance on external assessment envisaged in the proposed new Basel Accord—most countries have reinforced efforts to develop credit ratings in their country. How successful have these efforts been? In most countries, this is difficult to judge because the practice of the independent credit rating of corporations is still rather new. The historical record of the correspondence between default rates and credit ratings in a number of emerging economies is mixed: for example, in Korea the default rate for borrowers rated BB has been lower than that of borrowers rated A.[44]

The greater prominence of credit ratings (and their wider use for regulatory purposes) has raised the issue of the role of government in fostering the development of private credit-rating agencies. Is it possible to reconcile the overriding need to promote objective ratings with more activist official policies (for example, to promote credit-rating agencies or subject their performance to official audits)? The experience of Chile is that the state gradually came to intervene less in the decisions of private agencies. At first, ratings by private agencies were revised by the Risk Rating Commission; nowadays the commission can order a third rating if original ratings differ considerably. In Peru, any private debt security must be rated by at least two rating agencies; of the three domestic agencies operating in the country, two are associated with international credit-rating agencies.

The Challenge for Banks

The development of debt markets gives corporations an alternative source of finance, and this often places welcome competitive pressure on banks. This not only stimulates greater operational efficiency in the banking industry (so that costs fall) but also forces banks to improve their processes for monitoring risks, which they are forced to price more keenly.[45] In this way, a significant contribution can be made to the soundness of the banking system.

Does this increased competitive pressure go too far? Bond markets, it is often claimed, take away the safest business and leave banks only with the

44. See Kim and Park (2002, pp. 141–42).

45. See Sokoler (2002). Hawkins (2002) surveys the many links between banks and bond markets. See also Hawkins and Mihaljek (2002).

riskier loans. Does the regulatory framework contribute to this outcome? If banks are forced by regulation to hold excessive capital against loans to low-risk borrowers, this can force an unwarranted migration of "good" borrowers from banks to markets. This is a distortion and can be inefficient. Moreover, it could raise systemic dangers in concentrating the poorer risks on the banks. There are reasons to believe that the present rules on capital for banks (which do not differentiate sufficiently across credit risks) can have this effect. Indeed, the Basel Committee's proposed revision to the Capital Accord explicitly sets out to put this right and aims to align capital requirements more closely with actual risks. It should go a considerable way to correcting current distortions.

In practice, the relationship between banks and capital markets is more symbiotic than the old adversarial model would allow. First, banks are major holders of bonds. A recent survey by the Bank for International Settlements finds that banks in the emerging markets hold about one-third of domestic bonds outstanding; in Asia, the proportion is larger than half; see figure 4-5.

Not only do bonds constitute a significant proportion of banks' balance sheets, but business related to the issuance of bonds has become a more important element of the earnings of banks. Many have argued that banks can flourish only if they learn to play a major role in capital markets, a conclusion reached in several international forums in the emerging markets, notably in Asia.[46] According to this view, banks need to be fully involved in bond underwriting and in the sale of capital market products to households.

This presents a major challenge to commercial banks, particularly in those countries with only a limited investment banking culture. The need to educate commercial banks in the skills—and pitfalls—of investment banking is a common theme. Worries about relying exclusively on foreign institutions whose activities are imperfectly understood by local entities (public as much as private) have also surfaced from time to time. Three important issues require attention.

The first relates to the pricing of loans. Traditionally, loans have been nonmarketable and held on the balance sheet at historical value. As corporate customers increasingly issue bonds that trade in secondary markets, however, this basis of valuation will become more questionable: market-

46. See, in particular, Yoshitomi and Shirai (2001). APEC (1999) enunciates thirty-six key elements for developing bond markets.

Figure 4-5. *Holders of Domestic Debt Securities as a Percentage of Total Domestic Debt Issued in a Country, by Country or Region, End–2000*

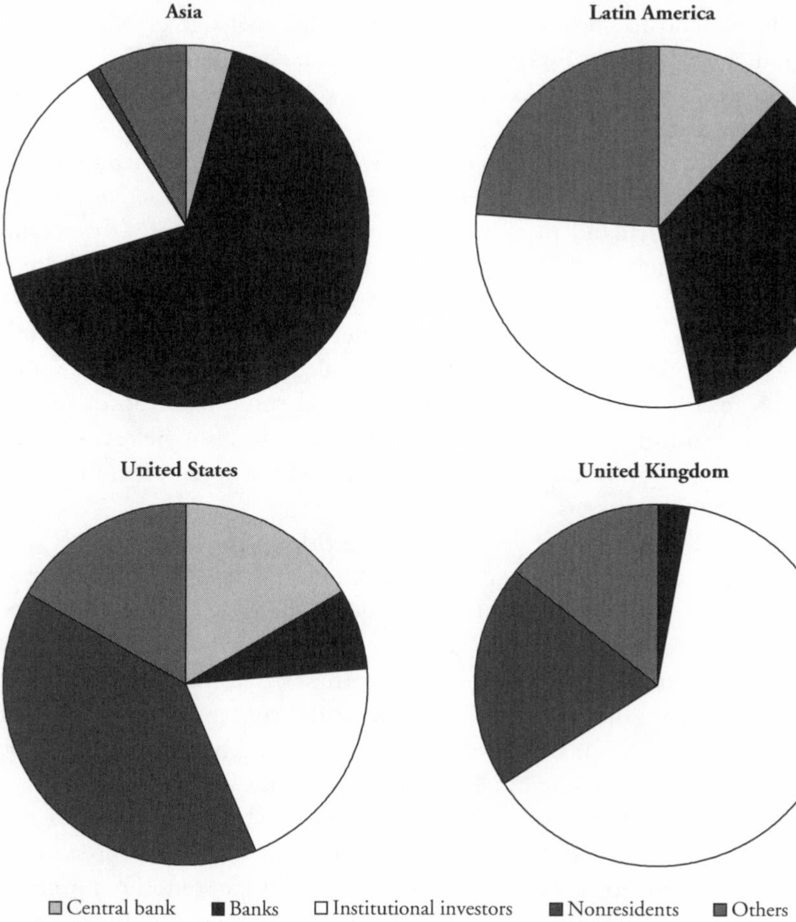

Source: Mihaljek, Scatigna, and Villar (2002); Bank for International Settlements (2001).

based prices of credit risk will become more widely available than at present. This means that banks and their regulators will have to develop mechanisms that incorporate such new information in ways that encourage market discipline but do not unduly destabilize banks' reported earnings.

The second issue is securitization. As in major developed markets, banks in emerging markets will have to become more adept at bundling bank loans into packages to be sold in the market. This can work best for home mortgages and consumer credit, two areas of recent strong growth in several developing Asian economies, because decisions about the pricing of such loans tend to depend not on any special knowledge or relationship but rather on "objective" criteria (such as income, valuation of the collateralized asset, and so on). As this process develops, new debt instruments come onto the market.

At present, the securitization of bank assets is still rather uncommon in emerging economies.[47] This is partly because, in the current environment of weak credit demand in many emerging-market economies, banks are very liquid. In such circumstances, they do not need to get loans off their balance sheet in order to seek new business. But it is also partly because there are significant (and undesirable) barriers to the securitization of bank loans in emerging markets. Reforms are needed to facilitate the development of mortgage-backed securities (collateral rules, bankruptcy procedures, and so forth). The lack of a benchmark long-term yield curve (for example, from government bonds) also restrains the development of markets for securitized assets.

The third issue is unhedged interest rate risk on the balance sheet of a bank. Under earlier highly regulated regimes, interest rates typically did not serve a major allocative function and tended to be rather stable over time. Long-term rates were frequently kept above short-term rates, so that banks could safely finance long-term assets with short-term liabilities. And exchange controls often insulated domestic rates from international capital markets. Under the more liberal regimes prevailing nowadays, however, interest rates have become much more volatile. This means that banks are becoming much more exposed to interest rate risk, which they are not always well equipped to manage. In addition, there is a lack of suitable hedging instruments in many countries, and banks are sometimes prohibited from participating in interest rate derivatives markets.[48] In many cases, banks do not hedge their interest rate exposures that arise from holding government bonds. Al-Jasser and Banafe note that when banks in Saudi Arabia hedge interest rate risk, they tend to use the U.S. dollar futures mar-

47. One exception has been Korea, where the market for asset-backed securities is well developed. See CGFS (2003, app. 4) for further discussion.

48. Cifuentes, Desormeaux, and González (2002) show that the depth of the interest rate derivatives market increased sharply in the two years following the relaxation of rules limiting banks' participation.

ket or fixed versus floating interest rate swaps—an imperfect hedge given the different currencies.[49]

Conclusion

The record of bond market development in emerging markets over the past five or six years has been somewhat mixed. In terms of market size, lengthening of maturities, and number of countries developing their own markets, the record has been one of success. Yet in terms of liquidity, the results have been somewhat disappointing.

Why has the large increase in bond issuance not led to deeper and more liquid markets? It is sometimes argued that some countries are too small to develop their own bond markets. A country with a small investor base and few market traders will find it harder to develop competitive markets for bonds. The dominance of a few large players would inevitably leave the market open to manipulation. And small markets tend to be illiquid.

There is no simple answer to the question of how large a country needs to be in order to develop its own bond market. Nor is there good reason to suppose the threshold is constant over time. Some have argued, for instance, that lower transaction costs that come with developments in information technology can increase the number of active participants in any given market, making it more competitive and liquid.

However, the existence of liquid bond markets in many countries of quite different size suggests that most medium-size emerging-market countries can develop bond markets that are much more liquid than at present. But to realize this potential, countries need to reassess a wide range of policies or practices that hinder the development of bond markets. Three simple guidelines are useful. First, governments should attempt to meet most of their borrowing requirements in local capital markets. Second, issuance policy should avoid fragmenting the local debt market. The fear of government debt managers that the failure of one large issue could damage confidence often leads to the flotation of too many small issues. The nature of bonds issued (for example, taxable versus nontaxable, nominal versus index linked, floating versus fixed rate) is also often diverse. And different public sector bodies often issue different papers. Such procedures inevitably fragment the bond market—and the smaller the market, the

49. Al-Jasser and Banafe (2002).

more concerned the authorities should be about any steps that fragment the market and so compromise liquidity. Third, regulations of financial institutions that deter bond trading need to be carefully reviewed.

A final thought is that a "small" country conscious of the limits of its own size can adopt either an inward-looking strategy or an outward-looking strategy when developing its debt markets. The inward-looking strategy would be to force local investors to invest in local instruments. The error of such a policy is that it deprives local investors of the opportunity to diversify their investments—and the need for diversification is all the greater the smaller the country. Several crises in emerging markets were made much worse when local financial institutions suffered heavy losses on their holdings of (devalued) local paper.

The outward-looking strategy would be to allow foreign banks and securities firms into the local financial sector and to allow local investors to diversify by investing abroad. The smaller or the more local the market, the greater the incentive to standardize the local bond market, aligning it with the procedures in place in the major centers. Such reforms could do much to counter unnecessary market segmentation.

Foreign institutions have much to contribute both to the working of bond markets and to the bringing of investors from the rest of the world. It is true that the recent volatility of international capital markets has given foreign investors a bad name in much of the world. But it is equally true that the search for yield in developed markets, combined with a strategic shift by some major institutional investors from equities to bonds, provides a particularly favorable climate for attracting foreign investors into domestic debt markets in many developing countries. And flat yield curves in many countries offer debt managers a good opportunity to lengthen the maturity of their debt.

References

Al-Jasser, Muhammad S., and Ahmed Banafe. 2002. "The Development of Debt Markets in Emerging Economies: The Saudi Arabian Experience." In Bank for International Settlements, *The Development of Bond Markets in Emerging Economies*, pp. 178–83. BIS Papers 11. Basel, June.

Anderson, P. 1999. "Sovereign Debt Management in an Asset-Liability Management Framework." Paper presented to Second Sovereign Debt Management Forum, World Bank, Washington, November 1–2.

APEC (Asia-Pacific Economic Cooperation). 1999. *Compendium of Sound Practices: Guidelines to Facilitate the Development of Domestic Bond Markets in APEC Member Economies.* September.

Bank for International Settlements. 2001. *The Changing Shape of Fixed-Income Markets: A Collection of Studies by Central Bank Economists.* BIS Papers 8. Basel, July. Available at www.bis.org/publ/bispap8.htm [June 26, 2003].

———. 2002. *The Development of Bond Markets in Emerging Economies.* BIS Papers 11. Basel, June.

Borensztein, Eduardo, and Paolo Mauro. 2002. *Reviving the Case for GDP-Indexed Bonds.* Policy Discussion Paper PDP/02/10. Washington: International Monetary Fund.

Burger, John D., and Francis E. Warnock. 2003. *Diversification, Original Sin, and International Bond Portfolios.* International Finance Discussion Paper 2003-775. Federal Reserve Board, April.

Carmichael, Jeffrey, and Michael Pomerleano. 2002. *Development and Regulation of Non-bank Financial Institutions.* Washington: World Bank.

CGFS (Committee on the Global Financial System). 2003. *Credit Risk Transfer.* Working Group Report 20. Basel: Bank for International Settlements, January.

Chabchitrchaidol, Akkharaphol, and Orawan Permpoon. 2002. "Development of the Thai Bond Market." In Bank for International Settlements, *The Development of Bond Markets in Emerging Economies,* pp. 190–200. BIS Papers 11. Basel, June.

Choy, Marylin. 2002. "The Development of Debt Markets in Peru." In Bank for International Settlements, *The Development of Bond Markets in Emerging Economies,* pp. 165–75. BIS Papers 11. Basel, June.

Cifuentes, Rodrigo, Jorge Desormeaux, and Claudio González. 2002. "Capital Markets in Chile: From Financial Repression to Financial Deepening." In Bank for International Settlements, *The Development of Bond Markets in Emerging Economies,* pp. 86–103. BIS Papers 11. Basel, June.

Figuereido, Luiz Fernando, Pedro Fachada, and Sérgio Goldenstein. 2002. "Public Debt Management and Open Market Operations in Brazil." In Bank for International Settlements, *The Development of Bond Markets in Emerging Economies,* pp. 81–86. BIS Papers 11. Basel, June.

Financial Stability Forum. 2000. *Report of the Working Group on Capital Flows.* Paris: Bank for International Settlements, April. Available at www.fsforum.org/publications/publication_16_5.html [June 26, 2003].

Frankel, Jeffrey. 1993. *Sterilisation of Money Inflows: Difficult (Calvo) or Easy (Reisen)?* Research Paper C93-024. University of California, Berkeley, Center for International and Development Economics, October.

Gragnani, J. A., A. O. Amante, and M. S. Araujo. 2003. "Improving the Brazilian Domestic Security Market." Mimeo. Brasilia: Central Bank of Brazil.

Hawkins, John. 2002. "Bond Markets and Banks in Emerging Economies." In Bank for International Settlements, *The Development of Bond Markets in Emerging Economies,* pp. 42–48. BIS Papers 11. Basel, June.

Hawkins, John, and Dubravko Mihaljek. 2002. "The Banking Industry in the Emerging Market Economies: Competition, Consolidation, and Systemic Stability: An Overview." In Bank for International Settlements, *The Banking Industry in the Emerging Market*

Economies: Competition, Consolidation, and Systemic Stability, pp. 1–44. BIS Papers 4. Basel, August. Available at www.bis.org/publ/bispap04.htm [June 26, 2003].

Herring, Richard, and Nathporn Chatusripitak. 2001. "The Case of the Missing Market: The Bond Market and Why It Matters for Financial Development." Working Paper 1-08. University of Pennsylvania, Wharton Financial Institutions Center.

IMF (International Monetary Fund). 2002. "Alternative Financial Instruments and Access to Capital Markets." Global Financial Stability Report. Washington, March.

Karacadag, Cem, and Animesh Shrivastava. 2000. "The Role of Subordinated Debt in Market Discipline: The Case of Emerging Markets." IMF Working Paper 00/215. Washington: International Monetary Fund, December.

Kim, Sungmin, and Jae Hwan Park. 2002. "Structural Change in the Corporate Bond Market in Korea after the Currency Crisis." In Bank for International Settlements, *The Development of Bond Markets in Emerging Economies,* pp. 130–47. BIS Papers 11. Basel, June.

McCauley, Robert, and Eli Remolona. 2000. "Size and Liquidity of Government Bond Markets." *BIS Quarterly Review* (November): 52–60.

Merrill Lynch. 2002. *World Bond Markets 2002.* April.

Mihaljek, Dubravko, Michaela Scatigna, and Agustín Villar. 2002. "Recent Trends in Bond Markets." In Bank for International Settlements, *The Development of Bond Markets in Emerging Economies,* pp. 13–41. BIS Papers 11. Basel, June.

Mohanty, M. S. 2002. "Improving Liquidity in Government Bond Markets: What Can Be Done?" In Bank for International Settlements, *The Development of Bond Markets in Emerging Economies,* pp. 49–80. BIS Papers 11. Basel, June.

OECD (Organization for Economic Cooperation and Development). 1995. *Securities Markets in OECD Countries: Organisation and Regulations.* Paris.

Patil, R. 2001. "Changing Scenario of Industrial Finances and Capital Markets in the New Millennium." Mumbai: Shroff Memorial Trust.

Reddy, Y. V. 2002. "Issues and Challenges in the Development of the Debt Market in India." In Bank for International Settlements, *The Development of Bond Markets in Emerging Economies,* pp. 117–27. BIS Papers 11. Basel, June.

Sidaoui, José Julian. 2002. "The Role of the Central Bank in the Developing Debt Markets in Mexico." In Bank for International Settlements, *The Development of Bond Markets in Emerging Economies,* pp. 151–65. BIS Papers 11. Basel, June.

Sokoler, Meir. 2002. "The Importance of a Well-Developed Bond Market: An Israeli Perspective." In Bank for International Settlements, *The Development of Bond Markets in Emerging Economies,* pp. 127–30. BIS Papers 11. Basel, June.

Stebbing, Peter. 1997. "Debt Management Practices in Australia: Some Recent History." Paper presented at the International Monetary Fund and Bank of Korea seminar on Fiscal and Monetary Policies and Public Debt Management in Asian Transition Economies, Seoul, November.

Teo, S. L. 2002. "Debt Market Development in Singapore." In Bank for International Settlements, *The Development of Bond Markets in Emerging Economies,* pp. 183–90. BIS Papers 11. Basel, June.

Uribe, José Dario, and Juan Camilo Gutiérrez. 2002. "The Colombian Government Bond Market." In Bank for International Settlements, *The Development of Bond Markets in Emerging Economies,* pp. 200–12. BIS Papers 11. Basel, June.

World Bank and IMF (International Monetary Fund). 2001. *Developing Government Bond Markets: A Handbook.* Washington.

Yoshitomi, Masaru, and Sayuri Shirai. 2001. "Designing a Financial Market Structure in Post-Crisis Asia: How to Develop Corporate Bond Markets." Working Paper 15. Tokyo: Asian Development Bank Institute, March.

PANEL SUMMARY

Country Experiences with Capital Market Development

Clemente Del Valle, chair of the panel and chairman of Colombia's Securities and Exchange Commission, initiated the discussion by commenting that financial systems in most developing countries are fundamentally banking systems and that developing-country governments now recognize the need for capital markets. Yet despite this understanding, developing countries confront many problems as they attempt to cultivate their domestic capital market. The financial culture is so focused on banking that an investor base fails to develop and grow, as would-be investors are not accustomed to evaluating and buying securities. Many countries consequently lack the strong intermediaries and brokers that are keys to fostering growth in capital markets. Moreover, although market infrastructure has improved in the developing world, a clear segment of intermediaries and brokers has not yet emerged, and securities and exchange commissions need to have institutional capacity if they are to supply proper regulation while simultaneously facilitating market growth. In practice, it can be very difficult to strike the proper balance between these two.

Del Valle then prompted the speakers to address the successes their countries have experienced in developing their markets, to explain how they have approached the obstacles to development, and to share their personal experience as regulators.

Khalid Mirza, sector manager of the World Bank's Financial Sector and Private Sector Development, East Asia Region, detailed his three-year tenure as chairman of Pakistan's Securities and Exchange Commission (SEC), during which he revamped and upgraded the commission, the nation's regulatory structure, and the stock exchanges. When he took the reins in March 2000, the commission's regulatory capacity was weak or nonexistent, its reputation was undistinguished, and its capacity to undertake surveillance, monitoring, and enforcement was feeble. During his term in office, Pakistan's SEC underwent a massive reorganization and revamping of staff as well as complete automation; however, much work remains to be done.

The national stock exchanges had laid the groundwork for a strong capital market, including reasonable trading and settlement systems, automation, a smattering of strong brokerage houses with adequate research capabilities, and a cultural willingness of financial players to enact concrete solutions to deal with problems. Yet Pakistan faced a crisis of investor confidence, which impeded the country's ability to attract capital and develop a capital market. Two core issues affected investor confidence. First, there was little public faith in the integrity of the market, particularly with regard to price discovery and settlement. The public believed that the market was run by brokers, for brokers. Second, companies were highly opaque, which led to the perception that they were being managed solely for the benefit of majority owners, not all stakeholders; the average investor and even the creditors enjoyed few of the gains.

Given the imperfect state of the marketplace, Mirza sought to implement a radical reform agenda that addressed governance and risk management at the stock exchanges in order to improve market integrity. Ironically, a crisis caused by over-trading and weak risk management at stock exchanges took place a few months after he took office and gave the commission a mandate to implement these reforms, which were undertaken with the grudging collaboration of the exchanges. Among the highlights of the restructuring were placing independent, professional chief executive officers at the stock markets, greatly strengthening the margin requirements, imposing capital adequacy limits for the exposure of brokers equal to twenty-five times the capital employed in the firm, and redefining net capital and raising it tenfold to bring the definition roughly in line with international standards. Other important reforms included devising proper regulation for short selling, imposing appropriate circuit breakers, implementing a T+3 system to replace the archaic London-type structure, developing and implementing a national clearing and settlement system, requiring brokers to register with the SEC to create a nexus between the two, and requiring brokers to adhere to a code of conduct issued under the broker registration rules.

The commission issued numerous rules and regulations to protect investors, ensure transparency, curb insider trading, prevent money laundering, improve the reputation of the market, and bring the market closer to international respectability. By the end of these reforms, Pakistan complied with almost all thirty regulatory principles of the International Organization of Securities Commissions (IOSCO). Pakistan's markets also comply with thirty-eight of forty-one international accounting standards, including IAS-39, the mandatory publishing of quarterly financial statements. Listed companies must now release audit papers to enhance quality control reviews of auditors. Set in place before the post-Enron reforms in the United States, auditors may no longer engage in other services for corporations and must rotate every five years. Auditors found guilty of professional misconduct are banned from auditing companies for a period of up to three years. Auditors also must verify that companies have complied with regulations regarding pricing methodologies, accounting policies, disclosure requirements, and record maintenance pertaining to transactions with related parties.

Next, Mirza laid out the numerous reforms and developments that he believed should be done expediently. Stock exchanges need to demutualize or at a minimum reorganize so that their business is fully independent of their members' conflicts of interests. He would like to see an electronic communications network (ECN) with self-regulatory status emerge to provide investors with an alternative trading platform, pressuring the traditional exchanges to demutualize. To encourage the existence of mutual funds, the legal and regulatory framework for fund management will have to be overhauled and improved. The Pakistani takeover law needs to be revamped to provide equality for all shareholders and provide a basis for evaluating how portfolio investors should share a takeover premium. Continuing efforts are needed to deepen the market and improve risk management. Auditing practices need to be strengthened, and international accounting standards need to be strictly enforced. Pakistan's corporate governance standards have to be clarified, reinforced, and enhanced. The development of retail demand should be encouraged, where possible. One approach would be to encourage firms to establish branch networks, agents in smaller towns, and telecommunications links.

Mirza also shared his personal experiences with reforming Pakistan's financial environment. He encountered tremendous resistance from many sides, including from within the SEC, the government, and the media, and was barraged with personal attacks. He acknowledged that the regulated tend to have a short-term viewpoint, while the regulator must have a long-term perspective. Developing a common vision for both sides, without seriously compromising the end objective of the regulator, is both essential and very difficult. In the end, the regulated entities in Pakistan publicly recognized the value of the reforms undertaken, and such acceptance, he felt, is the final test of a regulator.

According to Dieter Linneberg of Chile's Superintendency of Securities and Insurance, Chile's strong macroeconomy, including robust growth, low inflation, long-run fiscal discipline, free trade agreements, and no foreign exchange restrictions, has created an environment conducive to vibrant capital markets. As an impressive demonstration of that, institutional funds in Chile hold $80 billion of assets, equal to roughly 80 percent of the nation's gross domestic product (GDP). The corporate bond market issued $5 billion in the first quarter of 2003 alone. Various indexes that measure competitiveness, transparency, financial sector development, and corruption rank Chile quite favorably.

This success is due, in part, to recent reforms of Chilean markets. In 2000 the capital gains tax on stocks was eliminated, while the withholding tax on local bonds held by foreign investors was slashed from 35 to 4 percent. The modifications made the location of personal savings more flexible, and this has benefited the market. A second stage of reform, in its nascent stages, is likely to foster new initial public offerings (IPOs) and provide even greater flexibility in vehicles similar to the 401(k). In light of Chile's very recent market scandals, reforms may also entail an increase in regulations. Despite Chile's regulatory inertia, the country clearly is headed toward liberalization.

Chile is also working to regain market confidence, particularly by improving corporate governance in the areas of ownership, board and disclosure practices, institutional investor practices, relations for intermediaries, and enforcement divisions in the SEC. Finally, Chile needs to supervise conglomerates in a coordinated manner.

Mallam Suleiman Ndanusa, director general of Nigeria's Securities and Exchange Commission, described Nigeria's capital market, touching on the legal and regulatory framework, institutional and market development, and the challenges facing Nigeria. Founded in 1946, the market is small—

at $7 billion equity capitalization—and yet one of the leading markets of sub-Saharan Africa. Market capitalization is equal to approximately 10 percent of GDP, driven by 192 percent growth in local currency terms over the five years ended in 2002. The impressive expansion was due to new listings and enhanced market confidence, made possible, in part, by better market infrastructure. New listings have come from a range of sectors, and the capital raised from listing has been put to a variety of ends.

Raising funds through the capital market has been growing in popularity, largely as a result of several factors: Nigerians have improved their awareness of the market as an alternative fund-raising vehicle, equity has the benefit of no repayment obligation and no fixed, high repayment rates, and trust in the capital market has burgeoned. All this has made the market stronger and more resilient. Privatization has also positively affected the market, as fifty-four formerly state-owned companies have issued shares on the market, and more utilities are preparing to follow suit. Nigeria's low 10 percent withholding tax and lack of capital gains taxation also have contributed to growth.

Nigeria's capital markets are guided by an extensive securities law, enacted in 1999 to correct weaknesses and strengthen the legal and regulatory environment to match principles. Typical of laws of this type, its core objectives include investor protection, market integrity, development of the capital market, and appropriate empowerment of the SEC to regulate markets.

The commission has established an interesting enforcement structure to minimize the settlement of capital market disputes through the regular court system. The Administrative Proceedings Committee, the first tier of the structure, serves as a quasi-judicial body to adjudicate major breaches of the law. Its decisions can be appealed to the Investment and Securities Tribunal, which enjoys the authority of a high court and adjudicates all types of capital market disputes. Its judgments can only be appealed to the federal court of appeals.

In 2002 Nigeria also liberalized restrictions prohibiting universal banking to encourage bank participation in capital market activities, enlarge underwriting capacity, enhance competition, and promote efficiency. However, the major banks are now crowding out smaller nonbank players from other financial services.

The Nigerian stock exchange has automated trading, clearance, and settlement and is preparing for the eventual introduction of remote trading. Most operators are fully automated, and the SEC is partially automated and is still improving its information technology capacity.

To date, the Nigerian market is preponderantly an equities market, with stocks constituting more than 95 percent of both volume and capitalization. Trading in bonds and rights derivatives is also currently available, and a committee is investigating the introduction of new instruments for trading. The use of industry committees to examine and report on specific market aspects is commonplace in Nigeria; current committee topics include bonds, corporate governance, and unclaimed dividends.

Despite these improvements, Ndanusa sees numerous challenges for Nigeria's SEC. As of now, adequate funding for the commission must come from increased government outlays, because the current market-generated fees are sufficient only to fund the commission's regulatory activities and not to accomplish its developmental mission. This may limit the independence of the SEC in the future. On a related front, the SEC is working to create a paradigm shift from banking-centered policy to greater awareness of the importance of capital markets and their role in economic development; this is not an easy task. Ndanusa, as many others in the country, would like to improve investor confidence and increase business participation in capital markets. The local business segment, in particular, could be improved in this regard, because it is culturally habituated to operating without external accountability. In particular, small and medium-size enterprises should be encouraged to open themselves to improved governance, possibly through fiscal incentives.

Jacek Socha, chairman of Poland's Securities and Exchange Commission, discussed the state of Poland's capital market, beginning with a bit of historical context. The Polish market was created in 1991, after the fall of communism, with the modern foundations of full democratization of securities, equal access to information on public companies, and strong supervision over the markets. The Warsaw Stock Exchange handles more than 90 percent of capital market turnover, supports trading in bonds, securities, and derivatives, and operates an over-the-counter market and a national depository for securities. Its market capitalization stands at $29 billion currently, equal to roughly 17 percent of Poland's GDP, with 48 percent of the listed value from the banking sector. Capitalization and GDP were slightly higher in recent years, but Poland's economy has shared in the global economic downturn.

The Warsaw Stock Exchange remains one of the largest exchanges in Eastern Europe, with a size and volume roughly on par with the Vienna Exchange. While its derivatives volume is a fraction of that in major

European markets, the amount dwarfs that found in midsize exchanges in the region courtesy of a rapid deepening of the domestic market for such instruments. In relation to comparable exchanges, the average size of companies listed on the exchange is somewhat small, but mean capitalization is expected to increase as Poland privatizes more large public companies in the near future.

One key to healthy capital market development is firmly in place: a solid base of investment infrastructure and culture. Over the past decade, the number of personal investment accounts and brokerage houses has been fairly stable, and many are linked with listed banks. There has been and continues to be a prominent increase in the number of institutional investors. Currently, 124 mutual funds manage $6 billion in assets, complementing the roughly $9 billion in pension assets invested in the Polish market. By 2009, when distributions from these pensions will first be paid out, the pension system will have $30 billion in assets under management. However, the growing influence of institutional investors will not overtake the role of individual domestic and international investors.

The development of the capital market has slowed relative to the early 1990s, although technological and regulatory catch-up is partially responsible for this. Several international arrangements are expected to integrate Poland's market with the global economy and revitalize its maturation. Poland remains open to cooperation with international organizations such as IOSCO and is negotiating memorandums of understanding with several of them. Poland is also rapidly harmonizing its securities regulations with European Union directives and seeks to achieve full compliance by the beginning of 2004, in advance of Poland's integration with the European Union later that year.

From the start of its capital market in 1991, Poland has modeled its Securities and Exchange Commission on the U.S. SEC, so the great similarities between the two are not surprising. Like its U.S. counterpart, Poland's SEC has recently devoted much effort to developing codes of corporate governance, which are key to a solid market. The Warsaw Stock Exchange accepted these codes in 2002.

The future of Poland's capital market appears quite promising. The market will remain open to all investors, both domestic and international, and there are no restrictions on investment or repatriation of profits. It will continue to be both competitive and cooperative internationally and is well along the path to integration with the European Union, overcoming creative accountancy issues and hosting strong institutional investment. This bodes well for the market. Poland's growth, which measured only 1.2 percent in 2002, is expected to reach 2.5 percent in 2003, and this growth is vital for development of the domestic capital market.

A question-and-answer session followed the presentations. One participant wondered why Poland had experienced such a large increase in net assets invested in mutual funds. Socha replied that, initially, investment sponsors created instruments that provided a tax shield for deposits in the banking sector, but as time went on many investors realized that funds were simply an effective way to invest in Poland, whether they were tax preferred or not. Investments in funds have proven to yield greater returns than investments in individual stocks.

Ravi Narain of the National Stock Exchange of India wondered if the shortening investment horizons around the world would have a long-term structural impact on markets. One panelist replied that the long-time horizons inherent in the pension system could help to stabilize markets, particularly emerging ones.

Robert Sherretta of *Institutional Investor* asked if the panelists won any unexpected allies to their respective reform movements. Mirza replied that he had enjoyed surprisingly few allies, and those he had were allies only of convenience and the moment. He was singularly unsuccessful in building a coalition of support for the SEC in Pakistan. Since the reforms he attempted were aimed over a broad front, that left him with few supporters.

Ndanusa encountered similar problems, but as shareholders recognized the benefits of his efforts, they became surprise allies. He managed to enlist them in challenging other shareholders and institutional investors to support the good-faith reforms of the commission. Additionally, he was able to convince the Nigerian Congress that the SEC reforms were for the public good, and legislators passed the requisite laws to aid the SEC in its efforts. In the end, policymakers in the government are the most important allies to win over, as they are in a position to develop a regulatory framework facilitating the evaluation, mobilization, and allocation of capital.

Another participant asked which structures enabled the SEC to place accountants and auditors under its jurisdiction and, consequently, its control. Mirza replied that, in Pakistan, control of corporate law, insurance, and accounting was outsourced to the SEC by the Ministry of Finance, which provided the necessary legal jurisdiction. However, he believed that financial independence from the central government, and the political strings attached to it, was as essential as legal jurisdiction. Therefore, he fought to keep the miniscule fees that the regulated entities paid to the SEC, which helped the commission to maintain some degree of sovereignty. Once that battle had been won, Pakistan's SEC began applying the law to its maximum extent and stretching its scope, where necessary, to fill the gaps between regulations. The courts did not support the agency's liberal legal interpretations initially, but eventually began acknowledging that the agency was genuinely regulating in the interests of the public and the capital market; the judiciary subsequently reversed itself and began consistently upholding the agency's interpretations. To regulate auditors and accountants, Mirza took full advantage of the law, sought financial independence of his agency, and hired good lawyers to help him.

Del Valle asked the panel if they had employed self-regulation to support their SECs in supervising or performing surveillance on their markets. One panelist replied that his agency had facilitated the creation of new self-regulatory trade groups in the stock market, including the registrar, trustees, accountants, and securities lawyers. This minimized the regulatory burden and hands-on work that the SEC needed to do, allowing it to regulate only a few groups, as opposed to thousands of individuals.

Finally, del Valle asked the panelists whether they had witnessed a conflict between the objectives of monetary policy and financial market development in their countries. Mirza, Linneberg, and Socha answered that they had not. According to Socha, monetary policy actually created stability in Poland's capital and financial markets and therefore supported their development. Mirza added that there was a prevailing, misguided notion in the government that interest rates drive the market, and the securities commissioner must continually correct legislators in this respect. In contrast, Ndanusa said that he faced this conflict in Nigeria because the nation's strictly bank-centered monetary policy neglected to account for other elements of the financial sector. Instead, he felt, the government should look at how such policy affects the entire market system.

PART II

Integrated Supervision

GLENN HOGGARTH
PATRICIA JACKSON
ERLEND NIER

5

Market Discipline and Financial Stability

This paper contributes to understanding the role that capital markets play in fostering financial stability by considering the channels through which the markets, including debt and equity markets, can exert discipline on banks. In particular, it explores whether market discipline is effective in influencing bank behavior.

Effective market discipline depends on a number of important elements. The market must have the information to be able to assess the riskiness of the banks relative to capital. Market participants must be at risk of loss if the banks fail, or they will not act on the information.[1] For the threat of market discipline to affect bank behavior, a third element is necessary as well: the cost to the bank of an adverse market view must be significant. The paper considers whether there is a link between risk-taking by banks and factors that would reduce the effectiveness of market discipline, such as wide deposit protection schemes and limited disclosure. It finds that these factors are related to higher risk-taking. The broad policy implications are drawn out. The paper also looks at whether supervisors can harness the capital markets in their assessment of the riskiness of regulated firms. It considers whether various market indicators, drawn from

1. These two conditions are widely recognized; see Morgan and Stiroh (1999).

the debt, equity, and options markets, reflect the riskiness of individual banks and therefore could provide a cross-check on supervisory judgments.

Channels for Market Discipline

The market can exert discipline on banks or other financial intermediaries through several channels. But public policies can influence their effectiveness, for example, by bailing out banks or protecting some depositors.

The equity price is important to the bank's management because it determines the cost and availability of new capital. Perhaps, in terms of management incentives, the risk of becoming a takeover target if the share price is weak may be of even greater importance. Growing use of share options as part of remuneration also gives senior management a direct interest in the share price, although this does not mean that their incentives and those of shareholders are aligned because the horizon may be different.

One drawback of the share price as a channel for market discipline is that the incentives of shareholders are not aligned with those of the authorities and creditors because of shareholders' limited liability. If the bank fails, the shareholders lose the value of the shares but do not have to meet the debts. When a bank is weak, this could make gambling for resurrection potentially attractive by increasing risks in exchange for the possibility of greater returns. Shareholder assessment of risk also is affected by the perception of the likelihood of a bailout and whether, if some action were taken, shareholder value would be kept intact. Some authorities have made clear that shareholders should expect to be penalized if a bank has to be supported.[2] A number of theoretical contributions have focused on the effect of the safety net on the incentives for banks and their shareholders to take excessive risk. In particular, starting with Merton, a number of authors have analyzed incentives created by flat-rate deposit insurance schemes.[3] Such schemes create a subsidy to banks that is more valuable if a bank engages in riskier activities. Shareholder vigilance in monitoring a bank can also be affected by the regulatory framework if that is perceived as likely to prevent a failure. Shareholders might in effect "subcontract" monitoring of extreme risks to the regulator. There is some anecdotal evidence that this is the case, with shareholders focusing on expected earnings rather than on risks.

2. George (1994).
3. Merton (1977).

A more effective route for market discipline may well be a bank's counterparties. The cost and availability of funding are clearly important because they directly affect a bank's ongoing profitability and its ability to grow. All deposits can potentially run, but the most sensitive are likely to be those from other banks because of access to better information and more regular monitoring. Retail depositors are only likely to react in a nuclear way when concerns have reached the press. In addition, the incentives of retail depositors are affected by the existence of deposit protection schemes. Nozaki and Blum emphasize that deposit insurance per se removes the incentive of depositors to monitor banks and may, in the presence of limited liability, result in excessive risk-taking.[4] Bank counterparties have a much more fine-tuned response to perceived risks.

Access to swap and other derivatives contracts is of almost as much importance as funding. Sophisticated banking operations give rise to myriad exposures that need to be hedged, and access to these contracts is an essential part of risk management. It is possible for a bank to hedge interest rate risk in the banking book by match funding, ensuring that there are no gaps between the refix dates on the funding and each loan, but this is cumbersome. A sophisticated bank that suddenly has no access to the swap market probably will find it almost impossible to continue in business. In the case of swaps, as well as deposits, limits seem, from anecdotal evidence, to be more responsive than price. For community banks, which have access to large quantities of retail deposits and for whom sophisticated hedging might be less assiduously carried out, this route to market discipline is less effective.

A number of developments in recent years have started to limit interbank exposures. The introduction of real-time gross settlement for most major payment systems in the late 1990s has eliminated gross intraday exposures between members. Continuous linked settlement, which started in 2002, enables banks to avoid foreign exchange settlement risk, and increasing use of repo has reduced interbank exposures between banks. Also the development of netting arrangements for swaps, using standard legally tested documentation, has meant that each firm is more protected in the case of the failure of a counterparty. Paradoxically, these measures, which make the system less vulnerable to a shock (which is clearly very important), may also, eventually, make market discipline less effective.

4. Nozaki (2002); Blum (2002).

But even with the current strong incentives banks have to monitor the riskiness of their counterparties, as with any other channel of market discipline, the effectiveness will be contaminated by any expectations of government support. Indeed, the external ratings, which the market uses to assess risk at least in part, explicitly reflect the rating agencies' assessment of the likelihood of support from a parent or, in the case of a large bank, from the government.

Subordinated debt may also provide market discipline. At present, banks can use subordinated debt meeting particular requirements for up to half the minimum capital required under the Basel Capital Accord—the minimum ratio is 8 percent: 4 percent has to be Tier I capital (such as shareholders' funds), and 4 percent can be subordinated debt and general provisions. Discussions with banks indicate that they target the Tier I ratio, which is important for their solvency and their rating, but use subordinated debt as a flexible buffer above this target level. This is borne out by the fact that banks hold proportionately more excess in Tier I capital. For the large U.K. banks, the average Tier I ratio is currently around 8.75 percent (against a minimum of 4 percent), and the other tiers (Tier II and Tier III) account for a much smaller proportion (the ratio of Tier II plus Tier III to risk-weighted assets is less than 4 percent). Given the relatively modest use of subordinated debt (for the U.K. banks it accounts for only around 3 percent of total liabilities), it is a limited channel for market discipline, although it does give the banks added flexibility with regard to their capital requirements.

At present, the channels most likely to exert pressure on banks in a graduated way are the equity market and bank counterparties; of these, the one with interests most closely aligned with the authorities is the interbank market.

The Effectiveness of Market Discipline

It is clearly important for public policy that there be a graduated response from the market to the onset of problems, with management picking up early warning signs in time to influence its behavior rather than participants reacting in a nuclear way to signs of severe difficulty. But this implies considerable transparency about the nature of risks faced by a bank. Large market reactions to relatively small events may reflect substantial asymmetries of information between the shareholders and the banks.[5]

Even with adequate disclosure of information, for market discipline to be effective in enhancing financial stability at least one of two conditions needs to be met. First, bank management must react to the *potential* threat that discipline will be applied if the market realizes that risks are high relative to capital by adjusting their behavior, thereby reducing the likelihood that banking problems will arise. Or, second, management must react to market discipline quickly to reduce the likelihood of banking problems becoming severe.

A small literature examines the extent to which banks respond to changes in the yield of their subordinated debt. Covitz, Hancock, and Kwast provide evidence that banks' decision to issue additional subordinated debt is influenced by yield spreads.[6] Increases in yield are associated with reductions in new issues of debt. However, Bliss and Flannery fail to find any evidence that managers respond to a change in yield spreads by changing their banks' balance sheet allocations.[7] From this evidence, it is not clear that subordinated debt is an effective route for market discipline. Given the modest reliance on this type of debt, such results may not be entirely surprising. In particular, changes in subordinated debt spreads may not be sufficiently costly to the bank and its management to result in effective market discipline. In addition, as pointed out by Evanoff and Wall, these studies are attempting to capture one aspect of discipline imposed by the debt market—ex post discipline.[8] It may well be difficult to identify the exact timing of any management reactions to the application of market discipline, let alone the threat.

However, it is possible to be fairly sure that market discipline will be more effective if banks publish core statistics on their financial condition. The issue that might be tested is therefore whether transparency affects risk-taking. A small theoretical literature looks at this question. Cordella and Yeyati assume that bank deposits are uninsured but that banks enjoy limited liability, which induces them to prefer higher risk for given return.[9]

5. For example, NatWest became a takeover target after making a relatively small loss because of a problem with an option pricing model.

6. Covitz, Hancock, and Kwast (2000).

7. Bliss and Flannery (2002).

8. Evanoff and Wall (2000).

9. Cordella and Yeyati (1998).

They show that if depositors can observe banks' behavior, banks will take on an efficient amount of risk. Bank managers will know that the more risks they take, the greater the compensation required by the depositors. However, if the amount of risk-taking is not observable, then limited liability will induce the bank to choose a higher risk profile at the expense of depositors.

In a similar vein, Boot and Schmeits present a theoretical analysis of the incentives of banks to take risks and relate these to the degree of bank transparency.[10] The degree of transparency determines the sensitivity of the bank's cost of funding to its risk-taking behavior. In their model, bank managers have to exert effort in order to reduce risk. Since effort is costly, in the absence of transparency, the manager will choose lower levels of effort, thus resulting in higher risk. As transparency increases, effort and thus risk become more observable, implying that banks will face a higher short-term funding cost for low levels of effort. Consequently, managers will choose higher levels of effort and thus lower levels of risk when transparency is high than when it is low.

Empirical studies of the effect of transparency on risk-taking have been limited. In this section of the paper, we draw on research carried out by Baumann and Nier in the Bank of England.[11] They construct a large cross-country panel data set consisting of observations on 729 individual listed banks from thirty-two countries. Although this panel data set is unbalanced, it typically comprises observations from 1993 to 2000. We use the same data set to examine cross-country differences in the relation between capital ratios and market discipline variables.

Measures of the Strength of Market Discipline

The data set allows us to consider the impact of a number of market discipline factors on bank behavior. The market discipline variables considered relate both to the strength of the safety net and to the transparency of banks' risks (disclosure). In this section, we examine depositor protection, the safety net, disclosure, and listing.

DEPOSITOR PROTECTION. Depositor protection is likely to weaken market discipline. Demirgüç-Kunt and Sobaci provide a data set on the

10. Boot and Schmeits (2000).
11. Baumann and Nier (2003).

existence and extent of deposit insurance schemes across countries.[12] Using this data set, an index of the extent of depositor protection (*depins*) has been constructed. It takes into account the features that will affect market discipline from depositors: coverage of interbank deposits, coinsurance (that is, less than 100 percent payout on the portion of deposits covered), and unlimited coverage:

depins = sum of *depins2*, *depins3*, *depins4*, *depins5*
depins2 = 1 if there exists an explicit deposit insurance scheme, 0 otherwise
depins3 = 1 if there is no coinsurance, 0 otherwise
depins4 = 1 if interbank deposits are covered, 0 otherwise
depins5 = 1 if coverage is unlimited, 0 otherwise.

The higher the value of the index, the lower the discipline exerted by depositors on banks.

THE SAFETY NET. An important issue is the extent of perceived governmental support for a bank. The Fitch rating agency assigns a support rating that reflects the probability of support from a parent or the government. For most large banks, only the latter is important. The support rating ranges from 1 (near certain bailout) to 5 (bailout very unlikely). Baumann and Nier use the Fitch support rating to create an indicator of expected government support. The value of the indicator is 1 if the public support rating indicates that a bailout is very likely (support rating equal to 1 or 2) and 0 if the public support rating indicates a low probability of a bailout (rating is 3, 4, or 5).[13]

DISCLOSURE. Another important element is likely to be the amount of information disclosed. Baumann and Nier constructed an index of disclosure by measuring the amount of information available from banks' published accounts, as represented in the Fitch BankScope database.

The disclosure index records whether or not the bank provides information on eighteen categories of core disclosure in its published accounts (as represented in the BankScope database). All of the eighteen categories are related to one or more dimensions of the bank's risk profile (interest rate risk, credit risk, liquidity risk, and market risk) or the capital reserves it

12. Demirgüç-Kunt and Sobaci (2001). Using this data set, Demirgüç-Kunt and Detragiache (2003) provide evidence that explicit deposit insurance tends to increase the likelihood of banking crises in a sample of sixty-one countries over the years 1980–97.

13. While the study by Gropp, Vesala, and Vulpes (2002) suggests the use of an indicator variable, an alternative is to use the support rating as assigned on the scale from 1 to 5. The results are not materially affected by whether one uses one or the other.

holds to back the risk. For each category a value of 1 is assigned if the bank provided information and 0 if the bank did not provide information. The disclosure variable (*disc*) is normalized to take values between 0 and 1 and is available for each bank in each year of our sample. A total of eighteen subindexes are created that reflect whether the bank's accounts (as presented in BankScope) provide any detail on each dimension. The subindexes are then aggregated to form a composite disclosure index.

The composite index is defined as $\text{DISC} = \frac{1}{20} = \sum_{i=1}^{18} s_i$, where each subindex, s_i, can be related to one or more sources of risk or the buffers against risk. The definition and ordering of the subindexes follow the presentation in the BankScope database. Table 5-1 lists the subindexes used to construct the composite disclosure score. For all subindexes, 0 is assigned if there is no entry in any of the corresponding categories and 1 otherwise, except for the capital subindex. For this 0 is assigned if there is no entry in any of these categories, 1 if there is one entry only, 2 if there are two entries, and 3 if there are three or four entries. The maximum attainable score on the sum of the subindexes is 20.

LISTING. Market discipline may be affected by whether or not a bank has a U.S. listing. Disclosure requirements of the Securities and Exchange Commission may mean that a U.S. listing improves disclosure when compared to alternative disclosure regimes. The variable *list* takes the value 1 if the bank is listed on the New York Stock Exchange, Nasdaq, or the Amex.[14]

Country-Level Evidence: Stylized Facts

A key variable that determines a bank's risk of default is the amount of capital it holds as a buffer against adverse credit events. Our main hypothesis is that if factors are present that are likely to increase the effectiveness of market discipline, banks will have an incentive to hold more capital, all else equal. In this section we look at the correlation across banking systems of capital ratios and various factors related to the strength of market discipline.

Figure 5-1 illustrates the degree of correlation between the average capital ratios—defined as the inverse of the leverage ratio (equity / [assets – equity])—by country and depositor protection, as measured by

14. We have also assigned the list variable to U.S. banks on the grounds that U.S. banks listed on a primary U.S. exchange are subject to the same disclosure regime as foreign banks listed on a U.S. exchange.

Table 5-1. *Subindexes Used to Construct the Composite Disclosure Index*

	Subindex	Categories
Assets		
Loans	s_1: Loans by maturity	Below three months, three to six months, six months to one year, one to five years, five or more years
	s_2: Loans by type[a]	Loans to municipalities or government, mortgages, home purchases or leases, other loans
	s_3: Loans by counterparty[a]	Loans to group companies, loans to other corporate, loans to banks
	s_4: Problem loans	Total problem loans
	s_5: Problem loans by type	Overdue, restructured, other nonperforming
Other earning assets	s_6: Securities by type (detailed breakdown)	Treasury bills, other bills, bonds, certificates of deposit, equity investments, other investments
	s_7: Securities by type (coarse breakdown)	Government securities, other listed securities, nonlisted securities
	s_8: Securities by holding purpose	Investment securities, trading securities
Liabilities		
Deposits	s_9: Deposits by maturity	Demand, savings, below three months, three to six months, six months to one year, one to five years, five or more years
	s_{10}: Deposit by type of customer	Banks deposits, municipal or government
Other funding	s_{11}: Money market funding	Total money market funding
	s_{12}: Long-term funding	Convertible bonds, mortgage bonds, other bonds, subordinated debt, hybrid capital
Memo lines		
	s_{13}: Reserves	Loan loss reserves (memo)
	s_{14}: Capital	Total capital ratio, Tier I ratio, total capital, Tier I capital
	s_{15}: Contingent liabilities	Total contingent liabilities
	s_{16}: Off-balance-sheet items	Off-balance-sheet items
Income statement		
	s_{17}: Noninterest income	Net commission income, net fee income, net trading income
	s_{18}: Loan loss provisions	Loan loss provisions

a. The categories chosen reflect the presentation in the BankScope database. As a result, the split into the two dimensions "loans by type" and "loans by counterparty" is not exact.

Figure 5-1. *Capital Ratio and Deposit Insurance across Countries*

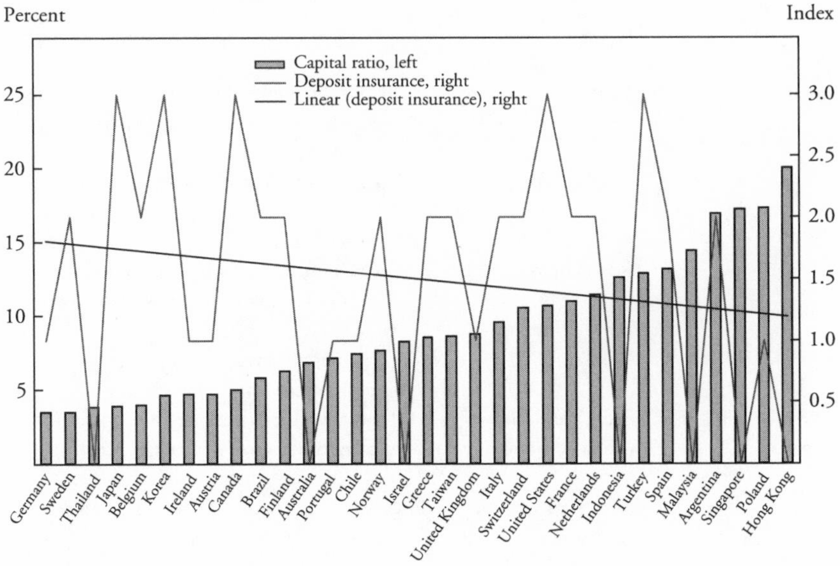

the index. Countries are ordered by the size of their average capital ratios in 1997, from countries with low average capital ratios to countries with high capital ratios in ascending order. The same chart shows the level of the deposit insurance index for each country, where high values correspond to more generous schemes with presumably greater moral hazard incentives. A trend line through the observations for the deposit insurance scheme reveals the degree of correlation between the deposit insurance index and the average capital ratio. Its negative slope implies that there is a negative correlation between depositor protection and average capital ratios. Table 5-2 confirms that the correlation coefficient is negative. However, the *P*-value indicates that the correlation is not quite statistically significant.

Figure 5-2 shows the degree of correlation between average capital ratios and the average public support rating for the sample of banks in the particular banking system. The markedly downward-sloping trend line suggests a strong negative correlation between the average support rating and the average capital ratio. This is confirmed by table 5-2, which shows that the correlation is negative, sizable, and statistically significant at the 1 percent level.

Table 5-2. *Cross-Country Correlations*

Indicator	*Deposit insurance*	*Support rating*	*Disclosure*	*U.S. listing*
Correlation coefficient	–0.26	–0.49***	0.24	0.05
P-value	0.1543	0.0054	0.1945	0.773

*** Statistically significant at 1 percent.

Figure 5-3 illustrates the degree of correlation between the average disclosure index and the capital ratio by country. In line with expectations, the trend line shows a positive slope, indicating a positive correlation between average disclosure levels and average capital ratios. Table 5-2 suggests that this correlation is less strong, with a *P*-value in excess of 10 percent.

Finally, figure 5-4 shows the correlation between the average capital ratio and the fraction of firms in each country that are listed on a primary U.S. stock exchange. The trend line suggests that the correlation is mildly positive, which again is confirmed by table 5-2.

Bank-Level Evidence: Panel Data Analysis

By using aggregate data on the banking system, within-country differences between banks on the factors determining the size of capital buffers averages out. A disadvantage of country-level analysis, however, is that cross-country differences in capital ratios may be due to factors other than market discipline effects. For example, in 1997 a number of countries in the sample faced a banking crisis. This would have resulted in a higher incidence of nonperforming loans, which, in turn, could have affected average capital ratios. Moreover, the average bank size is likely to vary across country. To the extent that a bank's size is a determinant of its desired capital buffer—for example, due to diversification effects—this could also affect the conclusions to be drawn from the evidence on country averages. We therefore augment the findings on country averages by reporting results that Baumann and Nier found from panel regressions at the bank level. These regressions test whether market discipline variables affect the size of individual banks' capital buffers, controlling for bank risk and other factors affecting a bank's capital, such as gross domestic product (GDP) growth and bank size. In using information on the entire time

Figure 5-2. *Capital Ratio and Support Rating across Countries*

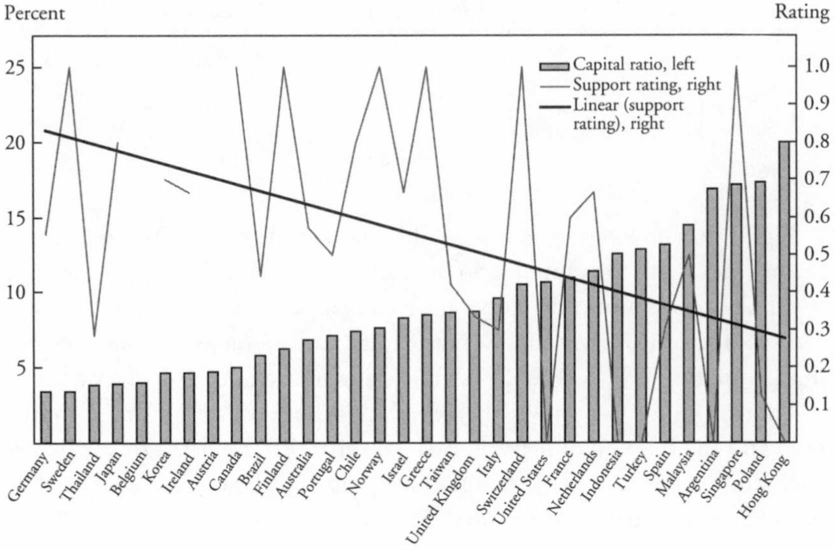

series from 1993 to 2000, these regressions also allow more precise estimates of the effects of market discipline on the capital buffers of banks.

In particular, the basic relationship Baumann and Nier estimated using a two-stage least squares approach is

$$CAP_{it} = f(\underset{(+)}{RISK_{it}}, \underset{(+)}{MKD_{it}}, Z_{it}) + u_{it}, \tag{5-1}$$

where *i* denotes group (bank) and *t* denotes time (year). Baumann and Nier found that both deposit insurance (*depins*) and expected government support (*supp*) have a statistically significant negative effect on bank capital buffers, reflecting the moral hazard incentives arising from explicit or implicit government insurance. They also found that both the U.S. listing variable and the disclosure index had a statistically significant positive coefficient, suggesting that more disclosure leads banks to hold larger capital buffers.

There may also be reason to believe that investors have more information about a bank if the bank is rated by a major rating agency. The argument is that rating agencies act as intermediaries in the disclosure process. They gain access to information that is not publicly available to investors

Figure 5-3. *Capital Ratio and Disclosure across Countries*

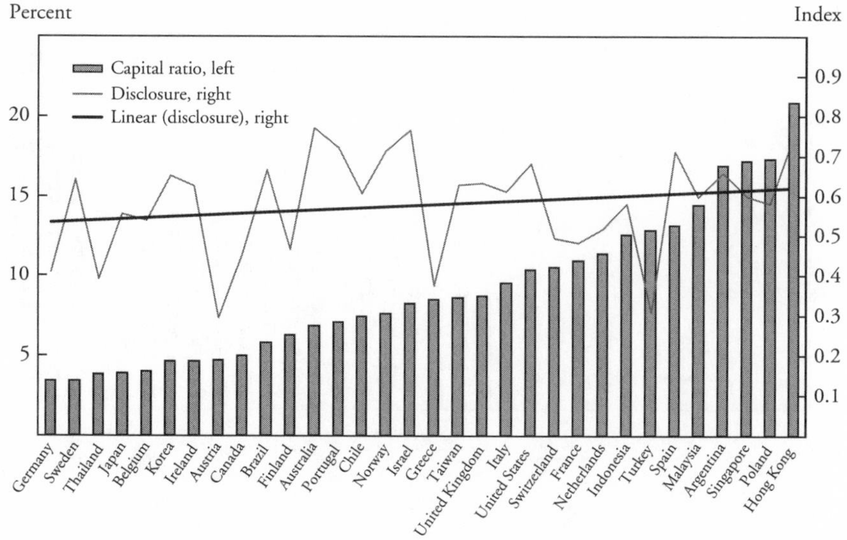

and feed this information into the rating.[15] Baumann and Nier investigated the effect of a variable that captured whether or not the bank was rated by a major credit rating agency and failed to find any strong evidence for a disciplining effect of this variable. This suggests that a rating does not substitute for disclosure to the public at large.

In sum, the results of this study are consistent with the notion that market discipline affects the incentives of banks to limit their risk of insolvency. They show that explicit and implicit government guarantees—measured by a deposit insurance index and the Fitch public support rating, respectively—result in lower capital buffers, everything else equal. There is also evidence that banks that disclose more information—measured by whether a bank has a U.S. listing or by the disclosure index—have higher capital buffers and thus more protection against unexpected losses than banks that disclose less.

Implications for Public Policy

These results underline the importance of governments creating the right environment for market discipline to be effective. Safety nets and

15. See Kliger and Sarig (2000).

Figure 5-4. *Capital Ratio and U.S. Listing across Countries*

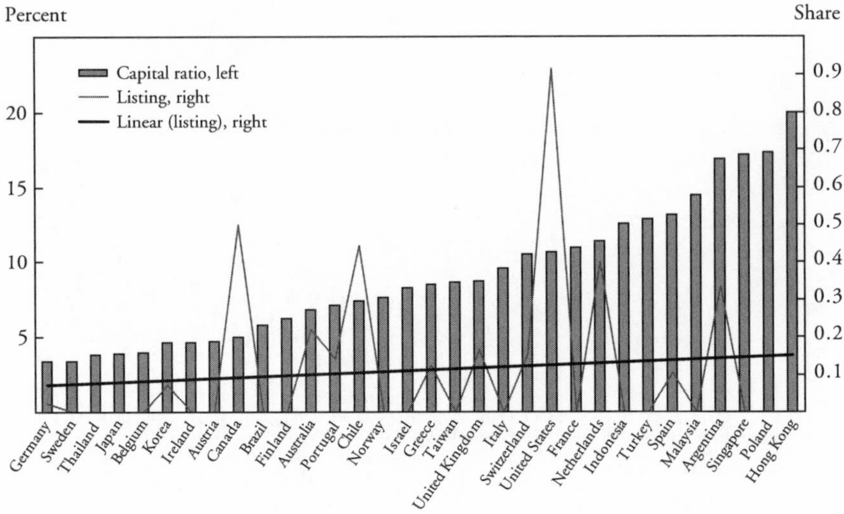

deposit protection schemes need to be kept to the minimum. In addition, state ownership of banks should be avoided. An open market allowing takeover of weak banks by foreign banks will also enhance the threat of market discipline. Where it is difficult politically or for financial stability to move away from wide safety nets, authorities need to realize that the onus of discipline will rest largely with the supervisors. This might well need to influence the way that supervision is carried out.

With wide safety nets, it is even possible that a bank in difficulty, rather than experiencing deposit outflows, might have net inflows because it may be willing to pay more for its funds—a case like this has been seen in the London market, where part of the group benefited from a wide safety net in one overseas country and another part did not. There were net inflows into the one part and substantial net outflows from the other.

The close link between information disclosure and risk also highlights the importance of the authorities encouraging greater disclosure by banks. Research carried out by the Bank of England into the timing of changes in disclosure by a very limited sample of large U.K. banks indicates that the timing was driven by external requirements. U.S. and U.K. accounting standards have developed in a similar way over the past twenty years, with the United States leading the way, making a U.S. listing important. This research indicates that banks react to new requirements promptly (sometimes a year ahead of the required date) but do not provide more capital than is required. This is also supported by evidence from the worldwide sample. There are a number of German banks in the sample, and disclosure of the Tier I ratio (that is, shareholders' funds to risk-weighted assets), which is the key measure of a bank's solvency, is limited largely to banks with a U.S. listing.[16] There could be a coordination issue in which banks only disclose information if other banks have to as well.[17] Mandatory requirements could therefore be important.

Several arguments have been put forward that might discourage the authorities from requiring greater disclosure. One is that if banks are rated, they disclose private information to the rating agencies, making disclosure of public information less important. In fact, the Bank of England research on the effect of disclosure finds that the existence or not of a rating is less important in a bank's risk profile than the amount of disclosure to the market as a whole. This may be because of the effect that implied support has on the ratings, limiting their usefulness as an assessment of intrinsic creditworthiness.

Another argument against mandatory requirements relates to the possibility that more information disclosure might increase the volatility of markets. Morris and Shin, looking at the game theoretic implications, argue that more disclosure might exacerbate sudden market movements but that the general effect is ambiguous.[18] Sometimes greater provision of information is beneficial, but sometimes it is detrimental. It must be the case that disclosure of severe problems might add to volatility, although in bad times banks and investment banks under market pressure or subject to rumor tend to disclose much more information. Generalized concerns about risks in particular areas of activity also have led to increased disclosure. For example, concerns about overheating in the U.K. mortgage market led to material new disclosures by major players.

Information asymmetries in periods when concerns are being raised about particular firms or market segments therefore seem to be adding to market volatility for some firms. Probably here the important issue is to ensure sufficient information at all times for there to be a graduated market response to developing problems.

16. See Jackson, Perraudin, and Saporta (2002).

17. Shaffer (1995).

18. Morris and Shin (1999).

For disclosure to reduce asymmetries, the type of information disclosed is critical. It is not enough for banks to increase the amount of qualitative information about risk and risk management or the production of a range of disparate measures. They need to produce hard disclosure that is directly comparable across banks and encompasses the measures of importance to the market—for example, the Tier I ratio, not Tier I plus Tier II. The Basel Committee on Banking Supervision, as part of the introduction of the market risk amendment to the 1988 Capital Accord, allowed banks to use internal value-at-risk (VaR) models to assess market risk. Banks using this approach were required to estimate losses over a ten-day holding period, with a 99 percent confidence level. As part of the allowance that a bank could use internal models, the committee recommended hard disclosure of the VaR estimates but did not prescribe the actual measure.[19] Banks have chosen to disclose VaRs on many different bases, making any comparison across banks impossible. The following table sets out the basis for the VaRs published by the large U.K. banks and shows a substantial variation in approach; the same is also true of U.S. banks:

Lloyds	*HSBC*	*Abbey*	*Standard Chartered*	*Barclays*
95 percent, 1 day	99 percent, 10 days	95 percent, 1 day	97.5 percent, > 1 day	98 percent, 1 day

Banks might argue that they are showing the VaR that they use for internal purposes, but under the market risk amendment, if they are using VaR to set capital requirements they should also use that model for their own internal purposes.

Hendricks shows that it is not possible to convert a 95 percent VaR accurately to 99 percent using the normal distribution; the errors could be very large.[20] VaRs on different confidence levels therefore cannot be put on a comparable basis. Duffie and Pan do, however, show that scaling up the one-day VaR by $\sqrt{10}$ is a reasonable approximation for moving from a one-day to a ten-day holding period, making the differences in this aspect less important.[21]

The problem regarding the confidence interval underlines the importance of the authorities requiring core disclosures on a comparable basis to enable differences across banks to be assessed.

19. Firms should provide daily information on profits and losses on trading activities, combined with daily value-at-risk numbers. See Basel Committee (1999).

20. Hendricks (1995).

21. Duffie and Pan (1997).

One of the huge benefits of Basel I is that it offers the markets a way of comparing the capital of the banks according to the risk-asset ratio—the ratio of capital to risk-weighted assets. A standard set of weights is applied to the portfolio and the capital that is recognized in the numerator is also laid down. But even with this standard metric, not all banks disclose the Tier I ratio.

Over time, even the Tier I ratio has become less useful as a common metric, as banks, particularly in the United States, have securitized a large proportion of their higher-quality loans. By March 1998, outstanding non-mortgage securitizations by the ten largest bank holding companies amounted to around $200 billion—more than 25 percent on average of these banks' risk-weighted loans.[22] This increased these banks' level of risk relative to a given risk-asset ratio.

With pressure on the Capital Accord, the committee has reacted by developing a revised approach, Basel II, with a much more fine-tuned approach to measuring the risks on the banks' portfolios. Under the more advanced internal ratings approaches, the risk weights for loans will reflect a detailed assessment of risk, which will, in turn, make the Basel ratio for banks on this approach a more comparable risk metric. However, this will depend on the way that standards for internal processes are applied in different countries.

But much further than this, the committee is also requiring banks to disclose much more about their risks and the capital that they have to back them. Banks will have to disclose the composition of capital, including not just the Tier I element but also any innovative instruments included in Tier I. On interest rate risk, banks will have to show the increase or decrease in earnings or economic value that would result from an interest rate shock applied to the banking book. The interest rate shocks will vary across banks, reducing comparability but disclosing the size of the shock. On credit risk, all banks will show provisions and past-due assets by geographic region and type of industry. Banks using internal systems to assess the riskiness of their loans will have to publish information on the breakdown of loans by probability of default band and default out-turns for the main portfolios—corporate, sovereign, or interbank portfolios and the main retail portfolios. For each portfolio, they also will have to disclose a weighted average loss given default per probability of default band. Comparability will be enhanced by the standards that underpin the basis of

22. Jackson and others (1999).

the estimated probability of default and loss given default, because these will be used to set the capital requirements under the more sophisticated approaches. Again the committee has developed a common language for credit risk (probability of default, loss given default), which then can be used as a common metric. Banks also will have to show information on credit risk mitigation—collateral and credit derivatives.

The International Accounting Standards Board is also focusing on the need for enhanced disclosure. In the European Union adherence to international accounting standards will be mandatory for listed companies by 2005. The proposals for added disclosure are in terms of general principles, but the current focus by the market on the Basel ratio for banks indicates that comparability should not be forgotten. This could perhaps be achieved with greater guidance and recommendations.

The industry is resisting requirements for comparable disclosure on the grounds that tailoring the disclosure to a bank's own circumstances and systems is important. But the huge focus given to the Basel ratio, because it is broadly comparable, highlights the importance of publishing other common measures.

The widespread resistance to comparable disclosure is rather hard to understand—banks with low risk profiles might be expected to be in favor of it. However, given the cyclical nature of banking, all banks may believe that they will experience difficult times on occasion. Clearly there are costs regarding disclosure, and the private benefits may not be seen as outweighing them. However, several papers have shown a link between lower disclosure and higher costs on funding, which should influence the banks.[23] The authorities, of course, have to take into account the public benefits as well.

Evidence on Risk Sensitivity of Prices

Another rather different question is the extent to which supervisors can and should be using market prices as an additional guide to the riskiness of the banks they supervise. The market view of the riskiness of a bank may supplement the balance sheet and other information to which the supervisors have access.[24] As with all measures of market discipline, market prices

23. Botosan (1997); Sengupta (1998).

24. Although a study on emerging-market economies finds that in the recent Southeast Asian crisis, information on bank equity prices did not outperform backward-looking information contained in balance sheet data (Bongini, Laeven, and Majnoni 2002).

will be contaminated by expectations of a safety net and by deposit protection arrangements. Prior questions with regard to any market indicator therefore are whether the market believes that particular banks would be allowed to fail and whether equity holders and subordinated bond holders would be bailed out. Most of the detailed evidence we present is for the United Kingdom, where the authorities have gone to some lengths to minimize any expectation of bailout.[25] The results could well be substantially different for markets with different expectations. But papers looking at other markets also indicate that market indicators can play a useful role.

In a comprehensive survey of market indicators of banks in the United States, Flannery concludes that markets have, in general, reflected actual or prospective bank risk.[26] Both equity- and bondholders react promptly to new information about bank risk and make rational inferences about the implications of that information for other banks. Also (equity) market variables provide relatively good information on *future* bank performance. More recently, Evanoff and Wall find that subordinated debt spreads are better than reported capital ratios at predicting banking problems, while Swidler and Wilcox find that implied volatilities from equity prices contain information over and above that from changes in share prices and subordinated debt yields.[27]

There have also been two recent studies on European data. Sironi considers the *information content* of subordinated debt spreads for European banks.[28] He examines new debt issues to assess whether investors were discriminating among banks according to credit quality and uses credit ratings and published accounting data as a measure of bank riskiness. His results support the hypothesis that holders of subordinated debt rationally discriminate between the risk profiles of private sector banks. He also finds evidence that the risk sensitivity of spreads increased during the 1990s, perhaps reflecting a reduction in the perceived public sector safety net. Gropp, Vesala, and Vulpes assess the leading indicator properties of two market indicators—equity-based distance to default and bond spreads—for European banks.[29] They find that distance to default is a good longer indicator (six to twelve months) and bond spreads are a good shorter indicator (six months or less) of bank default, proxied by Fitch financial strength ratings downgrades to C or below. The bond

25. See George (1994).
26. Flannery (1998).
27. Evanoff and Wall (2002); Swidler and Wilcox (2002).
28. Sironi (2003).
29. Gropp, Vesala, and Vulpes (2002).

spread results are strongest for banks that least expected to receive official support (that is, those with the lowest support ratings).[30]

Therefore, although there seem to be different views over which particular market data are most useful in assessing bank risk, the evidence from the United States and Europe suggests that market data of one type or another tend to reflect changes in bank risk or can predict future bank vulnerabilities.

It is difficult to judge whether market prices are an accurate indicator of bank failure in the United Kingdom given the relatively small number of cases. To the extent that failures have occurred—with the exception of Barings—they have generally been smaller banks that do not issue publicly traded bonds or equities.[31] However, a number of listed commercial companies have failed in the United Kingdom, and Tudela and Young find that Merton-based probabilities of default provide a strong signal of their future failure. In particular, they find that over the 1990–2001 period for a large sample (7,500) of companies, the mean value of the one-year probability of default for twelve months before the default date is 32.0 percent for defaulters and 5.2 percent for non-defaulters.[32] Moreover, this market information adds predictive power on future company failure over and above the information from company balance sheet data.

Nonetheless, it is possible to look at the extent to which market prices do reflect the riskiness of a bank. The market prices that we assess are bond spreads and three equity-based indicators (real equity prices, implied volatilities, and implied probabilities of default)—for seven major U.K. banks.[33] We have adopted two separate approaches to assessing the value of the prices as indicators. The first looks at whether there is an econometric relationship over time between each market indicator and banks' accounting ratios that may serve as a proxy for vulnerability. The second looks at

30. Gropp, Vesala, and Vulpes (2002) also find that bond spreads for large U.K. banks are significantly higher—around 100 basis points—than for other European banks. They interpret this as the perception that the support of a safety net is smaller in the United Kingdom than elsewhere in Europe.

31. See Logan (2001).

32. Tudela and Young (2003).

33. Bond spreads are measured as the difference between a five-year bond and a risk-free government bond of similar maturity, implied volatilities are a forward-looking measure of equity volatility derived from the price of an option contract, and implied probabilities of default are calculated over a fixed five-year horizon from a Merton model. The seven banks are Abbey National, Barclays, Standard Chartered, NatWest/Royal Bank of Scotland, HSBC/Midland, Bank of Scotland, and Lloyds TSB.

how the indicators have reacted to discrete known events that would have been expected to increase bank fragility.

The *econometric approach* investigates whether changes in market indicators are statistically significantly associated with current or future changes in certain banks' balance sheet data—proxies for underlying bank fragility. The proxies used for actual bank risk are the ratio of excess capital over the supervisory trigger (a measure of the bank's ability to withstand shocks), provisions as a percentage of total assets (ex post credit risk), and the ratio of risk-weighted to unweighted assets (a broad measure of the riskiness of the bank using the existing Basel risk weights).[34] The panel regressions were carried out for the seven original largest U.K. banking groups on half-yearly data over the period first-half 1995 to second-half 2002.

The method attempts to reveal (a) whether there is a contemporaneous relationship between market indicators and accounting information of bank risk and (b) whether market information provides *leading* information on actual bank risk over and above that obtained from past information on actual risk. Given that banks' accounts are published with a lag of one to two months, evidence of a contemporaneous relationship may suggest that market data are a short leading indicator of the *published* balance sheet data.

The results provide some evidence for contemporaneous relationships between changes in market indicators and proxies for actual risk. Changes in all four market indicators have a statistically significant association in the expected direction with current movements in one or more of the balance sheet risk measures—implied probabilities of default and implied volatilities with excess capital; real equity prices with provisions; and bond spreads, real equity prices, and implied volatilities with risk-weighted to total assets (see table 5-3). That said, only a small part of the variation in the market indicators is due to changes in these balance sheet measures.

The *leading* indicator properties of the market data are tested by seeing whether lagged changes in the market indicators can explain current changes in the actual risk measures over and above what is explained by past changes in actual risk. None of the four market indicators is found to have predictive power (and be correctly signed) up to one year ahead for actual risk, at least looking at the whole sample period (table 5-4). In sum,

34. The (twice yearly) data to construct these accounting ratios are based on confidential returns by the U.K. Financial Services Authority.

Table 5-3. *Contemporaneous Relationships between Balance Sheet Measures and Market Indicators*[a]

	Bond spread		*Real equity price*		*Implied volatility*		*Implied probabilities of default*	
	Mean of period (1)	*End of period (2)*	*Mean of period (3)*	*End of period (4)*	*Mean of period (5)*	*End of period (6)*	*Mean of period (7)*	*End of period (8)*
Excess capital	–0.001 (0.46)	–0.005 (1.61)	0.010 (1.45)	0.003 (0.39)	–0.001* (1.71)	0.000 (0.27)	–0.000* (1.80)	–0.000 (0.62)
Number of observations	53	53	91	91	44	44	82	76
Number of banks	6	6	7	7	6	6	7	7
Provisions to total assets	–2.861 (0.12)	4.741 (0.15)	–105.723** (2.00)	–16.670 (0.26)	8.249 (0.95)	9.075 (1.03)	0.046 (1.47)	0.034 (0.92)
Number of observations	54	54	99	99	51	51	84	77
Number of banks	6	6	7	7	6	6	7	7
Risk-weighted to total assets	2.796* (1.76)	3.352 (1.62)	–8.344** (2.19)	–1.122 (0.24)	0.925** (2.33)	0.716 (1.61)	0.003 (1.47)	0.003 (1.11)
Number of observations	48	48	84	84	47	47	75	68
Number of banks	6	6	7	7	6	6	7	7

* Significant at 10 percent level.

** Significant at 5 percent level.

*** Significant at 1 percent level.

a. Coefficients and their associated standard errors (in parentheses) from a random-effects regression of the change in each market indicator on the change in three proxies for bank risk between first-half 1995 and second-half 2002. The regression being estimated is $\Delta\ Market\ Indicator_{it} = \mu + \alpha_1 \Delta\ Risk\ Indicator_{it} + \upsilon_i + \varepsilon_{it}$. All variables are in first differences.

market information seems to be a reasonably useful reflector of current balance sheet measures of bank risk, but not of future risk.

One problem with the analysis is that the balance sheet measures may not really reflect the risk of the bank—risk-weighted assets under Basel I are a limited assessment of true risk (although actual provisioning is closer to a true risk measure). Another way to assess the extent to which market prices reflect risk is to look at the reaction to news. We adopted an *event approach* to see whether bank market indicators react to significant bank-specific, banking system, or macroeconomic events. There are certain caveats to this analysis. First, these events are qualitative measures; therefore, there is some subjectivity over whether an event should be regarded as significant or not. Second, there may be some ambiguity over the expected impact on market prices. For example, assuming that it is a significant event, is the announcement of the chief executive's resignation bad rather than good news? Third, some events might have been expected and thus factored into the market. Therefore, the occurrence of the event may not have any impact on market prices.

Bearing these caveats in mind, we look at the behavior of the market indicators in a week when twenty known significant adverse events occurred. They include fifteen events affecting specific banks, one shock affecting the banking sector (the release of the Cruickshank review saying that the banks were making "excessive" profits), and four broader macro shocks (the bailout of Long-Term Capital Management, devaluation of the Russian rouble, the events of September 11, 2001, and the announcement of Enron's bankruptcy).

In the face of adverse events, all four market indicators usually move—around 73–85 percent of the time—in the expected direction (that is, they move in the wrong direction 15–27 percent of the time). They are also generally more sensitive to idiosyncratic shocks than broader ones. Among the indicators, on balance, implied probabilities of default and implied volatilities most frequently move in the expected direction. This is especially true in the case of implied volatilities if the release of the Cruickshank report is excluded—an event where the expected directional impact on financial markets is not clear-cut. Another stylized fact is that bond spreads are more sensitive to macroeconomic events than bank-specific news, whereas the opposite is true for equity-based measures.[35]

35. Correlations of movements in market indicators across the seven largest U.K. banks also suggest that debt-based measures have responded more to common shocks than equity-based measures in recent years (since 1997). The average bilateral correlations between banks for bond spreads and credit default swaps are around 0.8–0.9 but only 0.5–0.6 for the three equity-based measures.

Table 5-4. *Leading Indicator Properties of Market Indicators*[a]

Market indicator	*Excess capital*	*Provisions to total assets*	*Risk-weighted to total assets*
Bond spread			
Mean of period	0.1502	0.7386	0.4025
End of period	0.1295	0.6335	0.5773
Real equity price			
Mean of period	0.6584	0.7344	0.6074
End of period	0.2621	0.3380	0.8802
Implied volatilities			
Mean of period	0.007***[b]	0.5124	0.4616
End of period	0.0678*[b]	0.8678	0.6697
Implied probabilities of default			
Mean of period	0.9538	0.2177	0.3428
End of period	0.3363	0.3460	0.2304

* Significant at 10 percent level.

** Significant at 5 percent level.

*** Significant at 1 percent level.

a. Results from a chi-squared test on whether the coefficients on the lags of the market indicator variable are equal to zero in a Granger causality test on the bank risk proxies (figures shown are probabilities). The regression being estimated is $\Delta\ Risk\ Indicator_{it} = \mu + \alpha_1 \Delta\ Risk\ Indicator_{it-1} + \alpha_2 \Delta\ Risk\ Indicator_{it-2} + \beta_1 \Delta\ Market\ Indicator_{it-1} + \beta_2 \Delta\ Market\ Indicator_{it-2} + \upsilon_i + \varepsilon_{it}$, with the null hypothesis of H_0: $\beta_1 = \beta_2 = 0$.

b. Coefficients are counterintuitively signed.

Within the macroeconomic events, all three equity-based measures, unlike bond spreads, moved sharply in reaction to the events of September 11. In contrast, bond spreads rose dramatically in reaction to events at Long-Term Capital Management, but the equity-based measures moved only modestly. This may reflect equity prices reacting more to events that could affect earnings and bond prices reacting to changes in risk.

Another way of assessing the usefulness of market information is the number of false signals (Type II errors), measured here by the number of times (weeks) in the year that the market indicator moved more than during the week of the specified adverse event. On this criterion, the market indicators seem to be quite noisy. The size of moves in the adverse-news weeks was, on average, larger than in 70 percent of the other weeks, but this leaves 30 percent (fifteen) of non-adverse-news weeks with larger movements. Not surprising, September 11 is an exception in that the financial market indicators generally moved by a larger amount than in all the other weeks of 2001. But, even here, bond spreads moved more in eight other weeks of the year than during the week of the attack.

So although market indicators usually move in the expected direction in reaction to specific large events, they often move by a large amount that cannot be related to events. In other words, although Type I errors are quite small, Type II errors seem quite large. In order to investigate the scale of Type II errors in more detail, for each of the four market indicators we look at whether the largest ten market movements for each bank can be related explicitly to news events. Again there is a subjective judgment over what entails an actual event, and we have erred on the side of including some smaller events. Overall, we cannot explain around 20 percent of large market movements, confirming that Type II errors are quite large. Of the market movements that we can explain, macroeconomic events account for some 50 percent across all indicators. But for bond spreads, they account for 90 percent of the movements that we can explain.

In summary, the econometric analysis provides some evidence that movements in all market indicators reflect contemporaneous changes in balance sheet measures of bank risk. But the event studies suggest more strongly that implied volatilities are the best reflectors of risk. The results also suggest that, although market indicators more often than not react in the expected directions to adverse events, the indicators appear to be noisy, with large movements often seemingly not related to a large event—that is, Type I errors are quite small, but Type II ones are quite large. Also, in recent years at least, debt-based market indicators appear to be more sensitive to macroeconomic risks than bank-specific ones, whereas the reverse is the case for equity-based indicators.

Given the usefulness of debt indicators, the introduction of mandatory issuance of subordinated debt has been advocated as a way of giving access to improved information on the views of a class of investor whose interests are aligned with those of the authorities. Calomiris and Powell find that various measures taken in Argentina to increase market discipline, including mandatory subordinated debt requirements, have worked reasonably well.[36] Banks in Argentina were required to issue subordinated debt for 2 percent of their deposits each year. That said, in periods of market stress—the East Asian crisis in 1997 and the Russian crisis in 1998—debt issues were very difficult for banks. Therefore, the central bank put back

36. Calomiris and Powell (2001).

the compliance date for mandatory subordinated debt several times and increased the range of liabilities that banks could issue to satisfy the requirement.

This section has focused on information from widely traded securities. Given the importance of bank counterparties in market discipline, one area that could be pursued is whether a sharp reduction in issuance of certificates of deposit, for example, is a good leading indicator of problems. There is some anecdotal evidence that if the price is likely to rise, banks stop issuing.

Conclusions

Across the globe supervision is used to reduce the likelihood of bank failures and to avoid widespread banking crises. Market discipline has an important role to pay in this by encouraging more prudent behavior and reducing reliance on intervention by the authorities. There is evidence, for example, that those banks that disclose more and therefore are more subject to market discipline tend to hold more capital. The converse is that supervisors need to be particularly vigilant regarding banks for which market discipline will not be effective:

—Where the safety net or deposit protection is wide or banks are state owned,

—Where banks are protected from takeover,

—Where the bank can rely on community deposits to reduce market discipline from bank counterparties.

The authorities need to try to take action in good times to increase market discipline by reducing safety nets and improving disclosure, particularly key elements of comparable disclosure such as those tested in this paper. The authorities have an important role to play in developing common measures of disclosure. Where increased disclosure standards are laid down, emphasis needs to be placed on the use of a common metric for core parts of the disclosure. In terms of coordination, this probably is a role that only the authorities *can* play.

Market prices can also be used to supplement other supervisory information in assessing the riskiness of banks. Equity-based indicators seem to be more sensitive to bank-specific information, with bond indicators picking up macroeconomic information.

But thought perhaps needs to be given to how the authorities can take advantage of information on the views of bank counterparties, probably through indicators of volume.

References

Basel Committee. 1999. "Recommendations for Public Disclosure of Trading and Derivatives Activities of Banks and Securities Firms." Basel: IOSCO, October.

Baumann, Ursel, and Erlend Nier. 2003. "Market Discipline, Disclosure, and Moral Hazard in Banking." Working Paper. Bank of England.

Bliss, Robert, and Mark Flannery. 2002. "Market Discipline in the Governance of U.S. Bank Holding Companies: Monitoring versus Influencing." *European Finance Review* 6 (3): 361–95.

Blum, Jürg. 2002. "Subordinated Debt, Market Discipline, and Banks' Risk-Taking." *Journal of Banking and Finance* 26 (7): 1427–41.

Bongini, Paulo, Luc Laeven, and Giovanni Majnoni. 2002. "How Good Is the Market at Assessing Bank Fragility? A Horse Race between Different Indicators." *Journal of Banking and Finance* 26 (5): 1011–28.

Boot, Arnoud W. A., and Anjolein Schmeits. 2000. "Market Discipline and Incentive Problems in Conglomerate Firms with Applications to Banking." *Journal of Financial Intermediation* 9 (July): 240–73.

Botosan, Christine A. 1997. "Disclosure Level and the Cost of Equity Capital." *Accounting Review* 72 (3): 323–49.

Calomiris, Charles W., and Andrew Powell. 2001. "Can Emerging Market Bank Regulators Establish Credible Discipline? The Case of Argentina, 1992–99." In Frederic S. Miskin, ed., *Prudential Supervision.* Cambridge, Mass.: National Bureau of Economic Research.

Cordella, Tito, and Eduardo Levy Yeyati. 1998. *Public Disclosure and Bank Failures.* CEPR Discussion Paper 1886. London: Centre for Economic Policy Research.

Covitz, Daniel, Diana Hancock, and Myron Kwast. 2000. "Market Discipline, Banking Organizations, and Subordinated Debt." Paper presented to the 2000 Global Finance Association Meetings, Chicago, April 21.

Demirgüç-Kunt, Aslı, and Enrica Detragiache. 2003. "Does Deposit Insurance Increase Banking System Stability? An Empirical Investigation." *Journal of Monetary Economics.* Forthcoming.

Demirgüç-Kunt, Aslı, and Tolga Sobaci. 2001. "Deposit Insurance around the World: A Data Base." *World Bank Economic Review* 15 (3): 481–90.

Duffie, Darrell, and Jun Pan. 1997. "An Overview of Value at Risk." *Journal of Derivatives* 4 (3, Spring): 7–49.

Evanoff, Douglas D., and Larry D. Wall. 2000. "The Role of Subordinated Debt in Bank Safety and Soundness Regulation." In *Proceedings of the Thirty-Sixth Annual Conference on Bank Structure and Competition.* Federal Reserve Bank of Chicago.

———. 2002. "Measures of the Riskiness of Banking Organisations: Subordinated Debt Yields, Risk-Based Capital, and Examination Ratings." *Journal of Banking and Finance* 26 (5, May): 989–1009.

Flannery, Mark J. 1998. "Using Market Information in Prudential Bank Supervision: A Review of the U.S. Empirical Evidence." *Journal of Money, Credit, and Banking* 30 (3): 273–305.

George, E. A. J. 1994. "The Pursuit of Financial Stability." *Bank of England Quarterly Bulletin* (February): 60–66.

Gropp, Reint, Jukka Vesala, and Guiseppe Vulpes. 2002. "Equity and Bond Market Signals as Leading Indicators of Bank Fragility." Working Paper 150. European Central Bank.

Hendricks, Darryl. 1995. "Evaluation of Value-at-Risk Models Using Historical Data." In *Risk Measurement and Systemic Risk, Proceedings of a Joint Central Bank Research Conference.* Board of Governors of the Federal Reserve System, November.

Jackson, Patricia, and others. 1999. "Capital Requirements and Bank Behaviour: The Impact of the Basle Accord." Working Paper 1. Basel: Bank for International Settlements, Basel Committee on Banking Supervision, April.

Jackson, Patricia, William Perraudin, and Victoria Saporta. 2002. "Regulatory and 'Economic' Solvency Standards for Internationally Active Banks." *Journal of Banking and Finance: Special Issue on Banks and Systemic Risk* 26 (5, May): 953–76.

Kliger, Doron, and Oded Sarig. 2000. "The Information Value of Bond Ratings." *Journal of Finance* 55 (6): 2879–902.

Logan, Andrew. 2001. "The United Kingdom's Small Banks' Crisis of the Early 1990s: What Were the Leading Indicators of Failure?" Working Paper 139. Bank of England.

Merton, Robert C. 1977. "An Analytic Derivation of the Cost of Deposit Insurance Loan Guarantees." *Journal of Banking and Finance* 1: 3–11.

Morgan, Donald, and Kevin Stiroh. 1999. *Bond Market Discipline of Banks: Is the Market Tough Enough?* Staff Report 95. Federal Reserve Bank of New York, December.

Morris, Steven, and Hyun S. Shin. 1999. "Risk Management with Interdependent Choice." *Oxford Review of Economic Policy* 15 (3, Autumn): 52–62.

Nozaki, Masahiro. 2002. "Banking with Adverse Selection." Unpublished manuscript. Brown University.

Sengupta, Partha. 1998. "Corporate Disclosure Quality and the Cost of Debt." *Accounting Review* 73 (4, October): 459–74.

Shaffer, Sherrill. 1995. "Rethinking Disclosure Requirements." *Federal Reserve Bank of Philadelphia Business Review* (May–June): 15–29.

Sironi, Andrea. 2003. "Testing for Market Discipline in the European Banking Industry: Evidence from Subordinated Debt Issues." *Journal of Money, Credit, and Banking.* Forthcoming.

Swidler, Steven, and James A. Wilcox. 2002. "Information about Bank Risk from Option Prices." *Journal of Banking and Finance* 26 (5, May): 1033–57.

Tudela, Merxe, and Garry Young. 2003. "A Merton Model Approach to Assessing the Default Risk of U.K. Public Companies." Working Paper. Bank of England. Forthcoming.

ALAN CAMERON

6

Supervision at the Micro Level: Do Disclosure-Based Regimes Work?

My background is as a former practitioner of regulation, now subject to regulation, rather than as an academic, but in recent years, since giving up the active practice of regulation, I have been fortunate to observe very closely capital market regimes in both developed and emerging markets. This experience has convinced me that disclosure-based regulation remains the preferred regulatory approach for developing markets to adopt as quickly as possible, despite the perceptions of its recent failings in developed markets. But developing markets do need to understand its full ramifications—namely, that the credible threat of enforcement is needed to ensure that such a system works—and that is the hard part.

I do not claim that any of this is original thinking on my part. Consider the following quotation:

> Securities markets are the capital-raising vehicle of choice today for companies in both developed and developing countries. New markets are springing up around the globe as countries move towards market economies. Indeed, both as vehicles for government-sponsored privatisation or simply as means for capital raising, the role of bank financing has been vastly overshadowed by the direct use of the securities markets.[1]

1. Mann (1993, p. 178).

That was the then-head of international relations for the U.S. Securities and Exchange Commission (SEC), Michael Mann, speaking in 1993. The same approach was followed in many emerging markets through the rest of the 1990s, actively supported by the aid programs of governments and international financial institutions and by less formal aid from the securities commissions of the major markets, bilaterally or through the International Organization of Securities Commissions (IOSCO). But was bank financing effectively replaced, or did it even experience meaningful competition from the capital markets in that period?

First, I look at some of the theory and recent practice of disclosure versus merits regulation in the fund-raising context in emerging markets and in my own market, Australia. I then note the recent loss of confidence in disclosure as a regulatory tool in other market contexts and its consequences. Finally, I address some of the difficulties that adoption of a pure disclosure model (if that were possible) might have in emerging markets in particular.

Recent Experience with Disclosure Regulation in Fund-Raising and Some Theory

Capital markets are critical to the future of developing countries, and their development, in turn, depends on a system of supervision that involves disclosure. A review of the Asian financial crisis sums up the position in these words:[2]

> The relative immaturity of many East Asian capital markets contributed significantly to the financial crisis. Many enterprises relied on foreign borrowing, volatile foreign portfolio flows, and highly leveraged short-term bank loans. Therefore, strengthening Asia's capital markets is important to prevent further financial crises and mobilise funds to assist sustainable recovery. Deeper capital markets also will improve investment efficiency and expand funds for long-term investment.
>
> Bank loans dominate financing in East Asia. . . . However, healthy capital markets are critical to sustain recovery. They reduce reliance on predominantly short-term local and foreign bank borrowing, as

2. Department of Foreign Affairs and Trade, East Asia Analytical Unit (1999, p. 103).

> primary equities and bonds markets allow issuers to raise long-term funding. . . . Secondary markets in equities and bonds also are important in allowing investors to restructure the maturity and level of their share and bond holdings. . . . Healthy secondary markets also will help keep East Asian capital in the region rather than encouraging its flow to highly liquid markets like the United States. . . . Well-developed capital markets also put competitive pressure on banks to cut their lending margins. . . . Over time, well-supervised capital markets can improve corporate governance and disclosure standards.

This suggests that we need to look beyond the dominance of bank lending to the role played by international lending, but it does not address the question of what style of capital markets might be appropriate. I argue that well-supervised capital markets do not improve corporate governance and disclosure standards so much as *require* such improvement.

Emerging markets might be tempted to abandon or delay their transition to a disclosure philosophy because "disclosure" has had a few troubled years—and certainly not just in the United States. Some of the difficult issues with disclosure were glossed over during the long bull market of the 1990s, as discussion of disclosure tended to focus on establishing common principles to permit cross-border offerings to be made as efficiently as possible.[3]

But the fact is that merits regulation in capital-raising has a perfectly respectable justification in appropriate cases. It was practiced for many years in what are now the major markets. William O. Douglas (later the second chairman of the SEC, but at the time a justice of the Supreme Court) has argued that a disclosure-oriented approach is inadequate. In his view, the legislation should directly involve the federal government in identifying companies that should be permitted to approach investors with public offerings, and the government should be permitted to favor companies that would have an active role in channeling capital into industries that the government wishes to promote.[4]

Such an approach must sound perfectly sensible to politicians in emerging economies today and even to politicians elsewhere, who are frequently unable to resist picking winners, especially when allocating public resources

3. Consider, for example, IOSCO's International Disclosure Standards for Cross-Border Offerings and Initial Listings by Foreign Issuers (IOSCO 1998).

4. Douglas (1934, p. 521).

to support emerging technologies or attract new industries to their political domain. But Douglas's view did not ultimately prevail. As Mann observes,[5]

> By focusing on market integrity and full disclosure, the regulatory system can foster growth and development without running the risk of becoming out-dated and unresponsive. Indeed, for the past sixty years, securities regulation in the United States has embodied clear principles that are recognised as forming the backbone for the evolution of the U.S. securities markets—into the largest and most sought after in the world. . . . From Democrat Franklin Roosevelt, who was President when the SEC was created, to Republican George Bush, the SEC's basic policy tenets have remained constant—market integrity and a dedication to the principles of full disclosure.

Mann refers not simply to full disclosure but also to market integrity, an indicator that disclosure alone is not enough. Nor is merits regulation without its advantages. These include the ability to incubate new businesses that are seen as socially desirable but that are too risky or too long term in their returns to be financed commercially; to ensure that scarce capital is not allocated to second-order priorities; and to avoid unaffordable losses due to pure speculation. But the disadvantages include less-than-ideal capital allocation, the "government picking winners" approach to governance in general, and the legal and moral hazard for the government and the regulator in the process.

We now know that investors even in markets perceived to be sophisticated may display a willingness to suspend their skepticism and to indulge in irrational exuberance in their approach to prices at which they buy shares. Whether the damage done and losses suffered as a result of that naivety or credulity warrant a departure from disclosure as the guiding philosophy for regulation even in those markets is, for now, a rhetorical question. But how realistic are those assumptions about emerging markets?

A few emerging markets have explicitly adopted disclosure, perhaps with foreign prodding. For example, the disclosure principle is now enshrined in law in Indonesia. The definition section in the Capital Markets Law no. 8 of 1995 describes it as the general guideline that requires an issuer (and others) to disclose to the public material informa-

5. Mann (1993, p. 178).

tion with respect to their business or securities, when such information may influence the decisions of investors. Article 75 then requires the regulator, BAPEPAM, to consider the completeness, adequacy, objectivity, comprehensiveness, and clarity of the prospectus *in order to ensure that it fulfills the disclosure principle* and not to evaluate the merits and weakness of the security.

BAPEPAM faces a substantial difficulty in attempting to carry out its role under Article 75. To fulfill its task in considering completeness, it must learn about the relevant industry as well as the issuer—both could be daunting tasks even if the regulator were well resourced. Ideally, the registration process would not take too long, as delay in raising capital is an extra cost. And, finally, the regulator is not to evaluate the merits, but distinguishing that from the positive tasks set out in the article is not always easy.

More merits regulation may be implicit in the regulatory approach even in major markets than is generally recognized, as an examination of what happens in practice may show. For example, the issues that confront the Indonesian regulator arise for all capital market regulators in such situations. How does one articulate the respective roles of issuers, their advisers, and the regulators? I look first at that question and then discuss the recent experience in Hong Kong when its system of market regulation came under scrutiny.

The Australian Regulatory "Hands off "Approach

A recent Australian government policy paper describes the issues concerning the allocation of responsibility around new issues as follows:[6]

> Given the important role of disclosure in the market, prospectus regulation must be efficient. Prospectuses should provide comprehensive, readily understandable information to investors and professional analysts and advisers alike. The cost of undertaking due diligence and preparing a prospectus cannot be justified unless, in practice, it facilitates informed investment decisions. The Law should promote the presentation of reader-friendly information to each of the likely audiences for a prospectus.

6. Commonwealth of Australia, Corporate Law Economic Reform Program (1997, p. 6).

> Retail investors do not generally require the same level of detail as professional analysts and advisers. These investors should not be discouraged from reading prospectuses due to their length and complexity.

The primary obligation regarding prospectus disclosure in many countries, including Australia, is that the prospectus must contain the information that investors and their professional advisers would reasonably require, and reasonably expect to find in the prospectus, for the purpose of making an informed assessment of the assets and liabilities, financial position, profits and losses, and prospects of the corporation and of the rights attaching to the securities. Under this test, the prospectus must include information known to persons involved in its preparation and information that they could reasonably obtain by making inquiries. The regulator relies on the issuer and its advisers and is expected to do so.

Where Australian law and practice part company with those of many other jurisdictions is that prospectuses are no longer required to be registered at all and are not routinely the subject of any examination. They must be lodged with the regulator (for record purposes), they are made available publicly, and applications cannot be accepted until seven days have passed after lodgment.

The theory behind this system (which may strike many readers as high risk!) is that during that exposure period (which can be extended), the contents are public and can be the subject of criticism by analysts, brokers, competitors, anyone—and if a deficiency is discovered, the regulator can intervene with a stop order. This is in some ways a high-water mark of reliance on disclosure as a primary tool of regulation in primary markets and is based on the assumption that the *system*, not just the regulator, will catch up with those who make inadequate disclosure and that the efficiency gains from rapid exposure of the product outweigh any losses brought about by enforcement after the event.[7]

7. The approach also reflects experience in Australia over many years, which showed that the process of checking prospectuses routinely did not reveal sufficient matters of substance to justify the effort, because of the prior work done by investment banks, lawyers, and so on. Further, a significant proportion of fund-raising documents are rollover issues, meaning offers of investment products designed to be continuously available and therefore regularly reissued after annual updating. However, ASIC did review prospectuses for very large floats, as the risks and costs of a dispute over an accounting treatment—for example, in a document going to millions of households—were unacceptable.

First, the Australian Securities and Investments Commission (ASIC) carries out a risk-based review of select fund-raising documents.[8] ASIC identifies areas where the risk of poor information may be greater than usual and reviews documents in those areas to ensure that they comply with the law by including all the information an investor would reasonably require to make an informed decision about whether to invest. ASIC explicitly states that it is not allowed "to judge the merits of a proposal or the value of an investment. We can't 'approve' a prospectus in the sense of giving it a tick or a cross as a 'good' or 'bad' investment offer." How different in practice is its regime from the Indonesian? It provides a fair deal of information about what it does, which enables a judgment to be made.

Since July 1, 2002, following its risk-based methodology, ASIC has issued fifty-one interim stop orders and eight final stop orders on prospectuses. Of these, 26 percent resulted from the failure of the company to disclose its financial position and prospects in the event that the offer was not fully subscribed.

More interesting, 16 percent of the interim stop orders resulted from defective disclosure related to the provision of prospective financial information. Examples of defects identified by ASIC include stand-alone, unsubstantiated statements, such as "the directors expect that the company will become profitable by the end of the 2004 financial year"; insufficient distinction between hypothetical assumptions and assumptions as to future matters that management expects to take place; and lack of reasonable grounds for predictions beyond two years, such as the absence of an independent expert's report or the absence of contracts relating to forward sales or future expenses.

One example is a company involved in a business of marketing a tee-booking management system for the golf industry and sought to raise up to $3 million for the purpose of marketing and developing the booking system. ASIC issued an interim stop order as a result of concerns that the offer document contained several forward-looking statements regarding the company's revenues and cash flows that did not have any reasonable basis.

Another is an aquaculture company based in Port Stephens, New South Wales, involved in farming snapper and mulloway fish. It was seeking to list on the Newcastle Stock Exchange via a $2.5 million share issue. ASIC

8. This description draws largely on a recent press release by ASIC dated March 10, 2003, which discusses both the law and the recent examples of stop orders. See www.asic.gov.au.

formed the view that the prospectus contained inadequate disclosure about prospective financial information relating to the company. The interim stop order was revoked following the lodgment of a replacement prospectus.

A third example is Argus Solutions, a company involved in "iris recognition technology" for the security and information technology industries that was seeking to raise approximately $5.5 million to purchase a technology license and to develop and market new products. ASIC placed an interim stop order on the prospectus as a result of concerns that it contained insufficient disclosure about the assumptions underlying prospective financial information that was included in the prospectus and insufficient disclosure about various agreements to which Argus was party. Argus lodged a replacement prospectus that adequately addressed ASIC's concerns.

A possible interpretation of these outcomes is that ASIC spotted high-risk or speculative investments and imposed a kind of merits test in requiring a high level of disclosure, especially for businesses without a track record—under the rubric, if not the guise, of a judgment about what reasonable investors would expect to find. Any investor should be able to see that a new high-tech company without a track record is a high risk. Too many investors seem incapable (or unwilling?) to observe the distinction between a forecast (a prediction of what might reasonably be expected to happen based on stated assumptions believed to be reasonable), on the one hand, and a mere projection (a mathematical extrapolation from assumptions that are not asserted on any degree of likelihood), on the other. Perhaps that is a typical example of what is a technical difference for lay participants in the markets but is a critical point of distinction for lawyers, regulators, and clever promoters. If the disclosure principle is absolute, then whatever they choose to reveal is enough, and investors can decide for themselves whether that disclosure is enough for them.

It is true that the Australian system looks quite different from the U.S. system, where the SEC continues its close examination of fund-raising documents. A major reason for the Australian approach is to enable a judgment to be made about which fund-raising documents justify the use of scarce regulatory resources. This may now receive the close attention of the new SEC chairman as he seeks to restructure the world's leading securities regulator to meet the challenges of a new era. After all, the risk of aggressive and expensive civil suits is at least as effective a regulatory weapon in inducing attention to detailed and effective disclosure as is pre-vetting by a bureaucratic regulator.

I conclude this section by noting briefly the particular role that regulators play in this context. Regulators have been saying for years that they did not take responsibility for the contents of prospectuses; why, then, did so many spend so much time and so many resources checking them? In the United States, the active role of the SEC in monitoring prospectuses is well known. As can be seen from the foregoing, Australia has the least supervision of prospectuses before offers open, relying on public exposure prior to applications being accepted and on post-vetting and strong enforcement action after the event if prospectuses are false or misleading.

Similarly, with respect to financial reporting generally, judging by some commentary, only after Enron did anyone apparently notice that regulators were not checking the financial statements of issuers on any routine basis. My semi-serious response is, "Well, of course, they weren't. Auditors did that." But there is some truth in that response, notwithstanding what we now know of the notorious deficiencies in the audit practices in some cases. Regulators are not resourced to be, and are not meant to be, super auditors and should resist the pressure from politicians, the media, and investors who have suffered losses to accept such a role. Their role is to monitor the system, including the qualifications and behavior of auditors and perhaps the standards by which they are bound, not to take over their work. When company directors and management—and auditors—let the side down, the regulator should act strongly to enforce the rules and to encourage others to follow the rules next time, but the regulator must make it clear that it is not responsible for those accounts or their audit.

The Penny Stock Incident in Hong Kong and Its Aftermath

The penny stock incident arose from a consultation paper issued by the Hong Kong Exchange raising the possibility of delisting stocks that traded at very low prices over a period of time and were not consolidated into units that traded at higher prices.[9] The release of the paper triggered a run on some small stocks, which led to the appointment of an inquiry; the report of that inquiry recommended a further review of the system, which was undertaken by an Expert Group.[10]

9. A detailed review of this incident is beyond the scope of this paper. For a lengthy, full account, see Kotewall and Kwong (2002).

10. I chaired the Expert Group appointed by the Hong Kong government to review the operation of the system of market regulation, and that report was published on March 21, 2003 (Expert Group 2003). Even when based on that report, the discussion that follows is, of course, my sole responsibility.

In the course of reviewing recent listings on the exchange, the Expert Group commented as follows:

> In a disclosure-based listing regime where caveat emptor (or buyer beware) is the guiding principle, there are obvious risks if the quality and veracity of information disclosed fall short of acceptable standards. In an attempt to build critical mass for competitive purposes, the trade-off between quality and quantity is an important one. If too many poor-quality companies are allowed to list, then a market's reputation can be tarnished, and it can have negative critical mass. Such an approach, where quantity is emphasised and quality addressed by relying on others to police wrongdoing, would be, in our opinion, fundamentally flawed and would operate to the long-term detriment of Hong Kong as an international financial centre.[11]

A sample of other comments in the report that also raise the issue of "quality" is as follows:

> There has been rising concern both in Hong Kong and overseas about the quality of the listings coming to the HKEx [Hong Kong Exchange] in recent years. Indeed, the origins of the Penny Stocks Incident itself reflected an effort by all parties concerned to address this issue. . . .
>
> Our study has revealed that there is a widespread belief that in the effort to achieve critical mass and maximise the quantity of new listings, the quality of the new listings on the HKEx has been seriously compromised. . . .
>
> It is inherent in a capitalist system, and in a stock market, that there will be both "good" and "bad" companies and that some companies will succeed and some will fail. No system can entirely prevent poor-quality companies from listing. . . .
>
> There are already signs that the high standing of the market as a whole is being tainted by the performance of many of the poor-quality stocks. In the long term, this could lead to lower valuations, reduced liquidity, and a higher cost of capital. . . .

The Expert Group was critical of the overall standards of new listings, not the Hong Kong market as a whole. And Hong Kong is not the only

11. Expert Group (2003, executive summary, para. 19), available at www.info.gov.hk/info/expert/summary-e.pdf [May 15, 2003].

market where these issues of "quality" arise and where decisions have to be made about entry criteria and how they will be administered. In the present context, the question is whether "raising" the level of listing criteria in some way to raise the average standard of listed companies amounts to a departure from disclosure regulation and a move to a merits system.

I argue that it does not. The Hong Kong government had set specific objectives for its market, which has a statutory monopoly as a stock exchange in Hong Kong, and the work of the Expert Group was directed toward ensuring that the system was structured to achieve those objectives. The adoption of those objectives required a value judgment on their part as to the kind of market they wanted—namely, a market that would attract high-quality issuers and a high level of participation in the market by international investors, including institutions. The adoption of that objective did not, however, mean that a merits approach was being taken to individual stocks; rather a merits approach was being taken to the *market* overall: What kind of market did Hong Kong want?

Disclosure Regulation More Broadly: Under an Enron Cloud

Disclosure and its twin, transparency, are probably the two most used words in financial markets today. In recent times, they have appeared in connection with diverse issues:

—The transparency of trading conducted on organized markets,

—The timely release of price-sensitive information about listed companies,

—The disclosure of circumstances giving rise to conflicts of interest among investment analysts or advisers,

—The obligation on providers of financial services to notify customers about the terms and conditions attached to those products and of their rights to complain or to have their disputes resolved by an independent complaint-handling agency,

—The ways in which boards of directors are structured and operate,

—Executive remuneration at listed companies, and

—Financial accounting and reporting generally as well as in fund-raising.

In this section, I look at the ways in which disclosure works in some of these areas and show that it is not a straightforward picture of beneficial outcomes in all situations: other values frequently are at work as well.

Executive Remuneration

The common thread is that transparency is assumed to be good—that is, presumably, likely to produce outcomes that "the market" will welcome—but that, in some cases, is not obviously so. The most striking example is executive remuneration. The requirements to disclose more and more, and in greater detail, about executive remuneration, including perks of office, have been growing steadily in all markets, perhaps on the assumption that disclosure will impose some restraint. But the early warnings that it might provoke exactly the opposite—namely, a tendency for executives to ratchet their claims higher and higher—have been realized.

Transparency of Trading

A less dramatic example concerns the call for greater transparency of trading or intended trading on organized markets. IOSCO Principle 27 baldly states, "Regulation should promote transparency of trading."[12] And adds this explanation:

> Transparency may be defined as the degree to which information about trading (both for pre-trade and post-trade information) is made publicly available on a real-time basis. Pre-trade information concerns the posting of firm bids and offers, in both quote- and order-driven markets, as a means to enable investors to know, with some degree of certainty, whether and at what prices they can deal. Post-trade information is related to the prices and the volume of all individual transactions actually concluded.
>
> Ensuring timely access to information is a key to the regulation of secondary trading. Timely access to relevant information about secondary trading allows investors to better look after their own interests and reduces the risk of manipulative or other unfair trading practices.
>
> Where a market permits some derogation from the objective of real-time transparency, the conditions need to be clearly defined. The market authority (being either or both of the exchange operator and the regulator) should, in any such event, have access to the complete information to be able to assess the need for derogation and, if necessary, to prescribe alternatives.

12. IOSCO (2002).

Note the explicit acceptance that there may be some derogation from "the objective of real-time transparency." Greater transparency can be in conflict with increased liquidity, another aspiration for well-regulated and efficient markets. This is expressly acknowledged in the explanatory memorandum to the Australian law that introduced a requirement for market licensees to promote "fair, orderly, and transparent markets":

> 7.37 The word "transparent" is included in the light of the overwhelming support of Australian and overseas commentators for the value of a transparent market. . . .
>
> 7.38 In interpreting the phrase "fairness, orderliness, and transparency," it is desirable that all the words in the phrase be considered together. One word taken out of context may lead to a course of action which conflicts with the other words in the phrase. Thus, transparency may on occasions be in conflict with liquidity, yet liquidity is needed for an orderly market. The tensions between the three words need to be resolved sensibly, so that an appropriate balance is struck between the demands of different market participants. This is specifically acknowledged in the clause to the extent that those objectives are consistent with one another.

Continuous Disclosure

Late disclosure of price-sensitive information has to be a priority for the regulator because it gives rise to the fear that insider trading could have occurred during the period of delay, and this does great damage to the credibility of the market. A regulator with a reputation for dealing with that will be seen to have a good marketplace. It is curious that it is only now, in the aftermath of the recent series of collapses, that IOSCO has published a set of principles relating to continuous disclosure: its Principles for Ongoing Disclosure and Material Development Reporting by Listed Entities.[13]

Corporate Governance

A merits basis has been inherent in some of the recent changes in the secondary-market context, involving new corporate governance requirements on listed companies. Post-Enron, many markets have reconsidered their minimum requirements for listed companies. For example, a pure

13. IOSCO (2002).

disclosure approach would say that a listed company might have to disclose whether it has an audit committee and, if so, how it is constituted. The New York Stock Exchange now requires that every company have such a committee and that it comprise a majority of independent directors defined in a specified way. All of the judgments made in those requirements are merits based. By way of contrast, the Australian and U.K. approach is to require companies to comply or to explain why they do not comply—that is, a disclosure approach. In both places there are concerns that, in practice, the approach is becoming prescriptive, because of the detailed nature of the guidance and the likelihood that institutional investors will become intolerant of departures from the prescribed "best practice," even when an apparently adequate explanation is given.

The disclosure principle in the context of financial reporting assumes that investors can trust that financial statements of companies have been prepared on a fair and transparent basis in accordance with generally accepted accounting principles and have been audited by independent professionals; that there will be and has been prompt disclosure of material events about listed companies; that dispassionate analysts issue reports about these companies to ensure that investors are fully informed and can decide whether to invest or not, with the benefit of such advice; and that there has been prompt disclosure of price-sensitive information about the company on an equal and fair basis to all market participants. All of that information is supposed to be factored into the pricing of the securities. The inability to realize those expectations has caused the dramatic loss of confidence in world equity markets in recent years.

Some Difficulties with the Disclosure Approach in Emerging Markets

The adoption and practice of the disclosure approach in emerging markets remain even more problematic, however. In this section, I look at some of the specific issues in connection with emerging markets, before drawing some conclusions.

Infrastructure

The first problem is that if there is no legal, accounting, insolvency, securities analysis, or media infrastructure that is capable of preparing, issuing, and digesting financial statements in that way, then the system will not work well, if it works at all. I have included an appendix describing the position in East Asia, the major region with which I am most familiar. These descriptions are not my own; rather they are those of Australia's Department of Foreign Affairs, Economic Analytical Unit.[14] The position as described may surprise some readers, positively, by presenting a more favorable view of the content of the *rules* already operating in East Asia concerning disclosure, accounting, and auditing, but the main conclusion tallies with my own: the crux of the issue is the enforcement of those rules.[15]

Education

The second problem is that investors must be capable of understanding all of this disclosure. This may be the greatest difficulty of all in both developed and emerging markets, yet regulators and others have been slow to recognize or address it in any meaningful way. The theory underlying a disclosure system is that investors are capable of using, and do use, the disclosures made by issuers to price securities efficiently, yet few investors even understand that they are expected to read the material. Investor education is an explicit objective, and an important activity, of the U.K. Financial Services Authority, but whether it is a role for a regulator has been a controversial question at least until recently. The annual conference of IOSCO, to be held in October 2003, will include a plenary session on the subject, which is welcome.

In my own country, attention is being paid to whether disclosure is working. A recent report on disclosure of fees with respect to managed investments notes,[16]

> Product Disclosure Statements (PDS) . . . must contain [the information required by law] and that the information must be worded and presented in a clear, concise, and effective manner [emphasis added]. Presentation can be taken to include such matters as layout, format, typeface, graphics, colour, indexation, ordering, and lexicon.

14. The appendix reproduces a section of a report of the Department of Foreign Affairs and Trade, Economic Analytical Unit (2002, pp. 37–44), with liberal edits. Regrettably, only the executive summary and chapter 1 are available online.

15. In developed markets as well, of course; see Benston and others (2003).

16. Ramsay (2002, pp. 53–54), known as the Ramsay Report.

It can also be a reference to the use of appropriate and useful examples, tables and illustrations, or any other thing that aids comprehension. Additionally, it can encompass the consideration of giving appropriate weight and prominence to those matters which require to be elevated in prominence due to their significance or nature. "Effective" also requires a consideration of the type of person who will read the PDS.

Expectation Gaps

Politicians and the media need to understand the disclosure theory so that they do not have unrealistic expectations of any of the players, especially the regulators. Among other things, this requires that it be explicitly legislated, so that politicians have to confront the issue openly and cannot rely on a version of what is sometimes called constructive ambiguity to trap issuers, advisers, or even regulators after the event. Again, my own country provides an example of this in recent laws concerning the sale of financial products, where the law sought, as one of its core objectives, to provide such disclosure to investors across a range of financial products.[17] The explanatory memorandum to the bill in 2001 stated that the broad objective of point-of-sale obligations is to provide consumers with sufficient information to make informed decisions in relation to the acquisition of financial products, including the ability to compare a range of products. The regulator then issued a policy statement outlining six good disclosure principles that it encouraged financial product issuers to consider when preparing a product disclosure statement. The good disclosure principles are:

—Disclosure should be timely,
—Disclosure should be relevant and complete,
—Disclosure should promote product understanding,
—Disclosure should promote comparison,
—Disclosure should highlight important information, and
—Disclosure should have regard to consumers' needs.

Role of Governments

Further, since in many developing markets governments are major owners of listed companies, they have a large role in disclosure but are unlikely to

17. This description is based on Ramsay (2002).

be comfortable with that responsibility. After most major privatizations of government enterprises were complete, the Australian government eventually legislated to remove its own immunity from suit if the disclosures in the listing documents it had issued were false or misleading—better late than never.[18]

To similar effect, in many such markets, businesses are controlled by families, who have a natural reluctance to share information they instinctively see as private. Until that attitude changes, legislative requirements will be seen as technical requirements to be overcome by clever legal maneuvering, if observed at all, not as a threshold for the provision of meaningful information designed to inform a wider pool of investors.

Role of Accountants and Auditors

The expectation of global investors (and, in the United States, post–Sarbanes-Oxley Act of 2002) is that accounts be prepared and audited in accordance with high standards of quality. There are several significant obstacles in the path of what might seem like a modest objective. First, the sheer number of people qualified and available to be accountants and auditors in developing economies makes it difficult, if not impossible. Even in a major developed market like Japan, the number of qualified practicing accountants is too low; this must be an even greater problem in less wealthy countries. I have heard anecdotally that China needs in excess of a quarter of a million additional qualified accountants—in an economy of that size, I doubt that is an over-estimate.

Standards in use in emerging markets need not be identical to international standards, but ideally they will aim to be of similar quality. Eventual harmonization is desirable, as comparability does matter as companies grow and wish to compete in global capital markets. In any event, a transparent approach to setting standards is essential. The World Bank and the International Monetary Fund conduct the Financial Sector Assessment Program and the Report on Observance of Standards and Codes programs, which assess compliance with global standards; in the IOSCO context, this includes whether their accounting standards are of international standing.

Self-regulation of the accountants themselves has proved inadequate or unconvincing in major markets; it is unlikely to be sufficient in emerging

18. The Corporations Act, sec. 5A, chap. 6D, which applies to fund-raising, binds the Crown, meaning the government, but does not render the government liable to prosecution.

markets, where securities regulators frequently will be the obvious and logical candidates to set admission standards and administer registration of auditors. The IOSCO principles include as Principle 6:

> The regulatory regime should make appropriate use of Self-Regulatory Organizations (SROs) that exercise some direct oversight responsibility for their respective areas of competence and to the extent appropriate to the size and complexity of the markets.

This principle does not require self-regulation; rather it permits self-regulation. As the explanation continues,

> The regulator should require an SRO to meet appropriate standards before allowing the organization to exercise its authority. Oversight of the SRO should be ongoing.
>
> Moreover, once the SRO is operating, the regulator should assure itself that the exercise of this power is in the public interest and results in fair and consistent enforcement of applicable securities laws, regulations, and appropriate SRO rules.

In the context, the principle relates primarily to exchanges and associations of securities dealers, who have historically played a major role in the regulation of the traded markets; these words do not in any way *oblige* regulators to defer to accountants' professional bodies in these important matters. It may be sensible, given limited resources, for them to use professional associations as frontline regulators, but they do not thereby escape the responsibility for monitoring their performance of that role.

Role of Regulators

What can one expect of and for regulators in such a system? They need to be credible (well resourced and independent of business interests and of government); they need to be experienced and knowledgeable, so that they can judge the market sensitivity of disclosures substantively, not merely formally; they need to be protected from capricious acts or legal liability for acts carried out in good faith; they need to be accountable according to explicit criteria; they need to have a preference for action over reaction; they need to have a wide range of remedies available to them, including some that many will be reluctant to give them, like the power to impose fines. Many of these attributes can be found in or deduced from the IOSCO Objectives and Principles for Effective Securities Regulation.

In short, what lies at the heart of the disclosure system is the credibility of the threat of consequences for those who break the rules. In a merits-based system, those who are likely to cause losses to investors are supposed to be weeded out early on, if not before they enter. In a disclosure system, problems may take longer to emerge, so the regulator has to be alert and to move quickly and effectively when they do.

IOSCO certainly recognizes that these are critical issues for regulators. As its Technical Committee chairman said to the International Accounting Standards Board World Standard Setters' conference in Hong Kong in November 2002,[19]

> Regulators are at the forefront of investor protection. Detailed approaches to that objective differ between jurisdictions—but there is widespread acceptance that disclosure and transparency are primary regulatory instruments for promoting investor protection. Standards of financial reporting are therefore central to the mandate of securities and corporate regulators. Those wanting evidence to support that supposition need look no further than the October 2002 report from the U.S. General Accounting Office entitled "Financial Statement Restatements." It provides graphic evidence of the correlation between deficient reporting and investor behaviour.

In the same speech, he referred also to the desirability of financial reporting being comprehensible, in these terms:

> I think there is a growing acceptance that the quality of disclosure is at least as important, and probably more important, than the volume of disclosure. This sentiment is influencing regulatory thinking on fund-raising disclosure, financial product disclosure, and consumer protection disclosure. There is, for example, much more emphasis now being placed on consumer comprehension surveys as part of the development of new disclosure requirements.

19. Knott (2002, p. 2).

Conclusions

Disclosure is not as straightforward a concept as might appear at first blush. Its adoption without analysis and consideration of its suitability in particular contexts, and without a careful public explanation of what responsibility the regulator is taking on *and what it does not do*, might produce an appearance of regulatory failure. In emerging markets, as perhaps in others, it is not safe to assume that investors have read the "health warnings" on prospectuses or in annual reports or that the relevant professionals, such as investment analysts, lawyers, or accountants, have the necessary training or experience or are available in sufficient numbers. Too robust an approach to these matters might be a career-limiting move, even in a market that espouses disclosure. Therefore allocating staff to reviewing prospectuses, not simply on a formal basis but to ensure that there is a real commercial basis for the transaction and that the risks are fully described, is likely to be essential. And working out how realistic it is to rely on professionals in the marketplace is an essential preliminary.

Taking as a starting point that they will have limited resources, and adopting and adapting the regulatory approach suggested by Malcolm Sparrow,[20] the best advice for regulators in emerging markets might therefore be as follows:

—Identify the regulatory goals clearly. ASIC never tires of saying, we do not vet prospectuses, because issuers need to be responsible for them. The Hong Kong government set clear objectives for its market, without which judging success would not have been possible.

—Adopt a mixed approach. It is unlikely that a pure disclosure approach will be successful in emerging markets. After all, the growing trend to prescription of company structures and so on may reflect a growing trend toward merits regulation even in major markets. A mixed approach is perfectly respectable, providing it is clearly articulated.

—Explain the goals to relevant stakeholders: investor groups, issuers, the media, intermediaries, and, of course, governments. All these groups have short memories.

—Identify those with whom collaboration is possible, so as to have the benefit of their resources as well, and enter into cooperative arrangements. Professional bodies usually share an interest in good outcomes; where they are prepared to take some of the burden, share it with them *providing* you

20. Sparrow (2000).

can monitor their performance. Fellow regulators in the jurisdiction, as well as foreign counterparts, are all sources of support and good ideas.

—Do not try to do everything. Choose specific areas in which to concentrate and put resources into those. That way you should have some successes; the other way, you will probably just have many failures.

—Publicize the outcomes clearly, to ensure the maximum regulatory effect for each initiative.

What does the most damage to the regulator's credibility, and therefore its effectiveness, is the perception that there are rules, but no enforcement.

Appendix. A Regional Survey

Before the crisis, East Asian corporate transparency and disclosure generally were weak.[21] Complex and opaque links between firms belonging to the same conglomerate demand frequent and comprehensive consolidated reporting of conglomerates' listed and private firm accounts. Most regional economies now require consolidated reporting—the Republic of Korea as of 1998 and Japan as of March 2000.

In all regional economies, listed companies must inform authorities of major transactions, to determine if they are arm's length. Increasingly, commissions such as the Thai Securities Exchange Commission vigorously enforce such regulations. In all major East Asian economies, firms also must inform investors of extraordinary events that may affect the company's value; this is especially important in volatile markets.

Since the currency crisis, several East Asian securities exchange commissions, bank supervisory authorities, and stock exchanges have reviewed disclosure rules, using standards set by leading international financial centers, such as the United Kingdom. Key reforms include requiring disclosure of related-party transactions. Indonesia, Singapore, and Thailand recently have strengthened their disclosure requirements. Hong Kong and Singapore now are market leaders in most areas, using a hybrid system of disclosure- and merits-based systems. Malaysian authorities also are moving toward a disclosure-based system.

Enforcement of disclosure requirements varies widely. Most regulators prefer to threaten to publish details of firms' noncompliance and, in

21. This appendix is taken from Department of Foreign Affairs, Economic Analytical Unit (2002, pp. 37–44), with liberal edits.

extreme cases, fine rather than delist companies. In East Asian economies, where corporate loss of face is a serious issue, public exposure can be very effective.

Hong Kong, Malaysia, and Singapore tightly enforce disclosure requirements, and Japan, Republic of Korea, the Philippines, Taiwan, and Thailand are tightening enforcement. China, Indonesia, and Vietnam have relatively weak corporate disclosure, although the China Securities Regulatory Commission is working hard to improve standards.

Accounting

Before the crisis, accounting practices were problematic in Japan, the Republic of Korea, and many middle-income and all emerging East Asian economies. Since the crisis, most regional professional and quasi-government bodies have reviewed accounting standards, and in China, Japan, the Republic of Korea, Indonesia, and Thailand authorities have upgraded requirements to correspond more closely with international accounting standards. A 1998 survey found Malaysian and Singaporean accounting practices were equal to or above U.K. and U.S. standards, but average East Asian accounting standards were below those levels.[22]

Before the crisis, many East Asian economies' accounting practices were deficient in valuing assets, disclosing off-balance-sheet items, and reporting related-party transactions, including cross-guarantees. Many firms also failed to break down income and expenses in different sectoral activities, potentially concealing from outside investors their exposure to activities concentrated in risky sectors, including real estate. However, since the crisis, most economies have upgraded relevant accounting standards to reduce those practices.

With a few exceptions, East Asian economies' formal accounting requirements now are reasonably sound, but in many, enforcement is problematic. Many firms' financial statements do not comply fully with national or international standards. Very few firms are prosecuted for undertaking fraudulent accounting or for violating disclosure rules, and in the rare cases of convictions, mandated punishments are minimal; this deters authorities from seeking further prosecutions. Very few accountants have lost their licenses to practice, although numbers are up compared with before the crisis.

22. Khan (1999).

However, official and professional bodies are pressing to raise standards. Thailand's peak professional accounting body is encouraging the government to introduce criminal sanctions for fraudulent accounting practices and other failures of fiduciary duty. Professional accounting bodies are also seeking legal authority to enforce ethics and standards; Indonesia's professional body now licenses accountants, and Thailand's professional body is promoting new legislation that would give it this authority.

Auditing

Regional governments also are reviewing auditing regulatory requirements, as these provide an important way of enforcing accounting standards.

In recent years, formal auditing requirements have strengthened markedly, and in most surveyed economies listed companies now must engage independent auditors to undertake external audits of their financial statements. Also, national auditing standards require auditors to detect noncompliance with the country's established accounting standards. Regulators in Australia, Hong Kong, Indonesia, Japan, the Republic of Korea, Malaysia, Singapore, and Thailand also require listed firms to have an audit committee that reports to the board of directors, is responsible for financial reporting, and reviews external and internal audit functions. In some economies, including Japan and Thailand, audit committees must be composed of independent members who are not firm directors. In other economies, audit committee members often hold places on boards of directors.

However, many auditors in East Asia fail to adhere to prescribed reporting standards, due to commercial pressure to return favorable audits, lack of knowledge of standards, ineffective peer review mechanisms, and lack of legal sanctions for noncompliance. Management can exert undue influence on audit committees, or boards can contaminate audits. Many newly formed audit committees have yet to determine their proper role. External auditors lack independence. Some auditors also have close and long-standing ties with the firms they audit. This is of concern to regulators in Indonesia and the Philippines.

The Australian Securities and Investments Commission is inquiring into the independence of auditors of Australia's top 100 companies. Other authorities, including in Hong Kong, also are reviewing similar guidelines.

Since the crisis, regulatory attention has focused on improving auditing standards rather than enforcement. However, enforcement should improve as regional economies' professional accounting and auditing bodies become more active and have more authority. Capital market regulatory authorities also are increasing their surveillance, punishing violations of auditing standards in several economies, including Indonesia and Malaysia.

Although East Asian investors certainly need better access to quality information, this alone will not ensure better investment outcomes. Investors also need safeguards protecting the interests of minority shareholders and creditors.

References

Benston, George, Michael Bromwich, Robert J. Litan, and Alfred Wagenhofer. 2003. *Following the Money: The Enron Failure and the State of Corporate Disclosure.* Washington: American Enterprise Institute and Brookings Joint Center for Regulatory Studies.

Commonwealth of Australia, Corporate Economic Reform Program. 1997. *Fundraising: Capital Raising Initiatives to Build Enterprise and Employment.* Proposals for Reform Paper 2. Canberrapage 11. (Available at http://www.treasury.gov.au/documents/282/PDF/full.pdf

Department of Foreign Affairs and Trade, East Asia Analytical Unit. 1999. *Asia's Financial Markets: Capitalising on Reform.* Canberra, November. Available at www.info.gov.hk/info/expert/expertreport-e.htm [May 16, 2003].

Department of Foreign Affairs and Trade, Economic Analytical Unit. 2002. *Changing Corporate Asia: What Business Needs to Know.* Canberra. Available at www.dfat.gov.au/publications/changing_corp_asia/ [May 16, 2003].

Douglas, William O. 1934. "Protecting the Investor." *Yale Law Journal* 23 (NS): 521.

Expert Group. 2003. *Report of the Expert Group to Review the Operation of the Securities and Futures Market Regulatory Structure.* Hong Kong, March. Available at www.info.gov.hk/info/expert/expertreport-e.htm [May 16, 2003].

IOSCO (International Organization of Securities Commissions). 1998. *International Disclosure Standards for Cross-Border Offerings and Initial Listings by Foreign Issuers.* Paris. Available at www.iosco.org/library/pubdocs/pdf/IOSCOPD81.pdf [May 16, 2002].

———. 2002. *Principles of Auditor Independence and the Role of Corporate Governance in Monitoring an Auditor's Independence.* A Statement of the Technical Committee of the International Organization of Securities Commissions. Paris, October. Available at www.iosco.org/library/pubdocs/pdf/IOSCOPD133.pdf [May 16, 2003].

Khan, Haider A. 1999. "Corporate Governance of Family Businesses in Asia: What's Right and What's Wrong?" ADBI Working Paper 3. Tokyo: Asian Development Bank Institute, August.

Knott, David. 2002. "The Regulatory Perspective." Address to the World Standard Setters' Conference, International Accounting Standards Board, Hong Kong, November 18. Available at www.asic.gov.au/asic/pdflib.nsf/LookupByFileName/HK_speech_181102.pdf/$file/HK_speech_181102.pdf [May 12, 2003].

Kotewall, Robert G., and Gordon C. K. Kwong. 2002. "Report of the Panel of Inquiry on the Penny Stocks Incident." Government of Hong Kong, September 9. Available at www.info.gov.hk/info/pennystock-e.htm [May 12, 2003].

Mann, Michael. 1993. "What Constitutes a Successful Securities Regulatory Regime?" *Australian Journal of Corporate Law* 3 (2): 178–91.

Ramsay, Ian. 2002. *Disclosure of Fees and Charges in Managed Investments.* Report to the Australian Securities and Investments Commission, September. Available at www.asic.gov.au/asic/pdflib.nsf/LookupByFileName/ramsay_report.pdf/$file/ramsay_report.pdf [May 16, 2003].

Sparrow, Malcolm. 2000. *The Regulatory Craft.* Brookings.

PETER BLAIR HENRY
PETER LOMBARD LORENTZEN

7

Domestic Capital Market Reform and Access to Global Finance: Making Markets Work

Over a decade ago, Robert Lucas asked the following question: Why doesn't capital flow from rich to poor countries? His point was simple. Poor countries have lower capital-to-labor ratios than do rich ones. Under standard neoclassical assumptions, the rate of return to capital in poor countries should be higher than in the developed world, attracting capital until risk-adjusted rates of return are equalized. In other words, market pressures should lead to a positive net transfer of resources to less-developed countries, thus boosting their growth rates. Lucas encouraged us to think about the obstacles that prevent this flow from occurring. (Lucas 1990)

At the time Lucas asked his question, the prevailing wisdom was that capital flows to developing countries were a good idea. More than ten years later, intellectual opinion has shifted. A heated debate over capital account liberalization has followed in the wake of financial crises in Asia, Russia, and Latin America. Opponents of the process now argue that capital account liberalization invites speculative hot money flows, increases the likelihood of financial crises, and brings no discernible economic benefits.

Peter Henry gratefully acknowledges the financial support of a National Science Foundation CAREER award and the Stanford Institute of Economic Policy Research (SIEPR), and the Center for Research on Economic Development and Policy Reform (CREDPR). We are grateful to Barry Bosworth and Susan Collins for sharing their growth accounting data.

Some economists have gone so far as to assert that open capital markets may be detrimental to economic development.[1]

With the debate over the wisdom of free capital flows still raging, it is at least a little presumptuous to write a chapter that explains how developing countries can increase their integration with world capital markets without first addressing the underlying assumption that such integration is beneficial.

The chapter is organized as follows. The first section examines capital market liberalization, establishing that there are indeed substantial benefits to increased capital market integration. The increasingly popular, negative view of capital account liberalization comes about partly from a failure to distinguish between equity market liberalization and debt market liberalization. After equity market liberalization, capital becomes cheaper, investment booms, and economic growth increases. In contrast, liberalization of debt markets has often led to great difficulty, as banks, companies, and governments often become vulnerable to changes in financial market perceptions of their ability to pay back loans.

The evidence outlined here can be distilled into two key lessons. First, the liberalization of dollar-denominated debt flows should proceed slowly and cautiously: Countries should refrain from premature liberalization of dollar-denominated foreign borrowing. The second lesson is that countries have thus far derived substantial economic benefits from opening their stock markets to foreign investors; there is no reason to think that future liberalizers will be any different in this respect.

The second section turns to liberalization of the stock market. Although the effects of equity market liberalization are positive and substantial, they fall far short of the torrent of capital flow to the developing world implied by the theory of perfect markets. New theories in economics and finance developed over the past three decades have highlighted the inefficiencies that can result when not all parties to a transaction are equally well informed. Such asymmetric information problems can make investors reluctant to put their money in companies for two reasons. First, they may worry about the adverse selection or "lemons" problem, wherein only the worst companies offer their shares. Second, moral hazard or agency problems raise the concern that even money invested in a good company may be misspent on managerial perks or even stolen outright through accounting tricks.

Over the past few years, cross-country econometric research on corporate governance, law, and finance has provided empirical support for the

1. Bhagwati (1998); Rodrik (1998); Stiglitz (2002).

importance of such information problems. In addition, some of this research hints at the relative effectiveness of different reform strategies for increasing foreign participation in developing-country equity markets. However, given the relatively small number of countries with stock markets and the large number of plausible alternative explanations for large, prosperous equity markets, the statistical robustness of these conclusions cannot be taken for granted. Thus the findings of this research should be treated as tentative. Nevertheless, stronger laws and regulatory institutions that protect investors (whether domestic or foreign) from colluding insiders are strongly correlated with deeper and more robust equity markets. The third section discusses this literature and its policy implications in detail. A fourth section concludes.

Capital Account Liberalizations and Access to Global Finance

Capital account liberalization was once seen as an inevitable step along the path to economic development for poor countries. Liberalizing the capital account, it was said, would permit financial resources to flow from capital-abundant countries, where expected returns were low, to capital-scarce countries, where expected returns were high. The flow of resources into the liberalizing countries would reduce their cost of capital, increase investment, and raise output.[2] The principal policy question was not whether to liberalize the capital account, but when—before or after undertaking macroeconomic reforms such as stabilization of inflation and liberalization of trade.[3] Or so the story went.

In recent years intellectual opinion has moved against capital account liberalization. Financial crises in Asia, Russia, and Latin America have shifted the focus of the conversation from when countries should liberalize to whether they should do so at all. Opponents of the process argue that capital account liberalization invites speculative hot money flows, increases the likelihood of financial crises, and brings no discernible economic benefits. Some economists have gone so far as to suggest that open capital markets may even be detrimental to economic development.[4] Must developing countries maintain financial self-sufficiency even as they reap the benefits of openness to trade? In reality, the choice is not so stark.

2. See Fischer (1998); Summers (2000).
3. See McKinnon (1991).
4. See Bhagwati (1998); Rodrik (1998); Stiglitz (2002).

Recent research demonstrates that the answer to the question "Is capital account liberalization helpful or harmful?" depends critically on the type of liberalization undertaken. While liberalization of debt flows has gotten many countries in trouble, liberalization of portfolio equity flows has been associated with booming stock markets, greater capital investment, and faster economic growth.

In its broadest form, capital account liberalization can be any decision by a country's government that allows capital to flow more freely in or out of that country. Allowing domestic businesses to obtain loans from foreign commercial banks, allowing foreigners to purchase domestic debt instruments (both corporate and sovereign), and allowing foreigners to invest in the domestic stock market are three examples. At a minimum, we need to distinguish between two categories of liberalization: those that involve debt and those that involve equity. Although this is an oversimplification, it is useful for driving home the following point. Debt financing and equity financing are different. This point may seem obvious, but it has gotten lost in the heated debate over whether developing countries should have open capital markets.

A debt contract has very different characteristics from an equity contract. A debt contract requires regular payments regardless of the borrower's economic circumstances, while an equity contract involves risk-sharing—large payouts for shareholders when times are good and little to nothing when times are bad. In other words, unlike debt servicing obligations, which are constant, variations in profits and dividends are procyclical and tend to stabilize the balance of payments.

Liberalization of foreign borrowing restrictions typically leads to an over-reliance on debt financing for the liberalizing countries. In the 1970s countries became over-leveraged as governments obtained large quantities of floating-rate commercial bank loans. The 1980s debt crisis then demonstrated that the fixed-payment schedules of debt contracts can induce large inefficiencies when economic conditions turn out to be worse than anticipated at the time the debt contract was signed.[5]

Nor, as emphasized by John Williamson, "is it just the flow of payments to service the debt that theory suggests is more likely to vary in a stabilizing way for equity than for debt. The debt crisis was caused not just by high and variable interest rates magnifying the service payments due, and by the reduction in export earnings with which to service the debt, but

5. See Fischer (1987).

most immediately and powerfully by the cutoff in new lending without any similar curb on the requirement to pay amortization."[6]

At first glance, it may seem that foreign purchase of equities on the domestic stock market could also be reversed if and when foreign investors become concerned about a country's prospects. But foreigners cannot simply demand their money back. They have to sell their shares. Prices will drop as soon as other market participants (domestic or foreign) anticipate the sudden increase in supply. Furthermore, as prices fall, expected returns rise so that the incentive to sell equity is no longer as strong. Loans, in contrast, have to be serviced even after adverse information becomes known, so that creditors rush to get their money while they can. In other words, the risk-sharing characteristics of an equity contract provide a kind of built-in stabilization mechanism, which suggests that foreign sales of portfolio equity are not likely to pose a particular threat to the domestic economy.[7]

In the 1990s countries turned to bonds instead of bank loans as their principal source of finance, but the outcome was largely the same. A number of economists have documented that excessive short-term borrowing in dollars by banks, companies, and governments played a central role in the Asian financial crisis.[8] In essence, the mismatch between the term structure of borrowers' assets, which were typically long term and denominated in local currency, and their liabilities, which were short term and denominated in dollars, placed these countries in an extremely vulnerable position. Any bad news that made their lenders reluctant to extend new loans created an immediate liquidity problem. A bunching of long-term debt maturity profiles creates a similar vulnerability. Beyond the Asian crisis, it appears that excessive short-term borrowing in dollars played a central role in precipitating almost every emerging-market financial crisis during the 1990s.[9]

Thus a key lesson is that once external debt flows have been liberalized, it is of utmost importance that the magnitude and maturity profile of the country's external debt liabilities be compatible with the magnitude and maturity profile of its assets. That the liberalization of external debt financing can quickly generate liquidity problems for a country is a well-known phenomenon that dates back at least as far as Chile in the late 1970s.[10]

6. Williamson (1997, p. 288).

7. Choe, Kho, and Stulz (1999).

8. See Furman and Stiglitz (1998); Radelet and Sachs (1998).

9. See Dornbusch (2000); Feldstein (2002).

10. See Akerlof and Romer (1993, pp. 18–23); Díaz Alejandro (1985).

The empirical distinction between debt and equity flows is as important as the theoretical distinctions, because the composition of capital flows to developing countries has shifted drastically over the past twenty-five years. Table 7-1 breaks the composition of capital flows to developing countries into five major categories: public and publicly guaranteed debt flows, private nonguaranteed debt flows, foreign direct investment (FDI), portfolio equity, and grants. The sum of the first two categories reflects all debt flows to less-developed countries. There are three salient points to be made about table 7-1.

First, the lion's share of capital flows to developing countries from 1970 to 1984 took the form of debt. The five-year averages from 1970 to 1984 show that debt typically accounted for about 80 percent of all capital flows. Second, there were no portfolio equity flows to these countries from 1970 to 1984. The fact that portfolio equity flows were nonexistent is a direct consequence of the fact that these countries did not allow foreigners to own shares in their domestic stock markets (a point we revisit shortly). Third, a dramatic shift in the composition of these flows took place starting in the five-year period from 1985 to 1989. Portfolio equity flows as a fraction of total capital flows rose from less than 0.1 percent in 1980–84 to 18.7 percent in 1990–95, an almost two-hundred-fold increase. Debt flows as a fraction of total capital flows fell from 82 percent in 1980–84 to 50 percent in 1990–95. FDI flows as a fraction of total capital flows increased from 13 percent in 1980–84 to 28 percent in 1990–95.

One of the principal reasons why countries became so reliant on debt during the 1970s was rather straightforward—foreign shareholding was banned. Countries could not rely on portfolio equity to finance development because their governments did not allow foreign investors to purchase shares in the domestic capital market. The import-substitution development strategy in vogue at the time discouraged integration with the global economy in general, and the writings of academic dependency theorists reinforced concerns about the negative political and economic consequences of widespread foreign ownership in particular.[11]

In the late 1980s and early 1990s, perhaps in part as a response to the debt crisis, countries all over the developing world decided to open their stock markets to foreign investment. Liberalizing the stock market—opening it to foreign investors—is one of the most important domestic

11. See Cardoso and Faletto (1979); Evans (1979).

Table 7-1. *Composition of Capital Inflows to Developing Countries, 1970–95*

	Average 1970–74		*Average 1975–79*		*Average 1980–84*		*Average 1985–89*		*Average 1990–95*	
Category of capital inflow	*Millions of dollars*	*Percentage of total*	*Millions of dollars*	*Percentage of total*	*Millions of dollars*	*Percentage of total*	*Millions of dollars*	*Percentage of total*	*Millions of dollars*	*Percentage of total*
Net resource flows	12,529.1	100.0	32,836.8	100.0	51,604.7	100.0	32,726.2	100.0	90,184.1	100.0
Net debt flows[a]	10,121.3	80.8	27,151.3	82.7	42,374.6	82.1	20,563.4	62.8	45,316.2	50.2
Public and publicly guaranteed debt	5,628.0	44.9	18,014.0	54.9	28,383.4	55.0	14,844.5	45.4	12,820.5	14.2
Private nonguaranteed debt	4,493.4	35.9	9,137.3	27.8	13,991.2	27.1	5,718.9	17.5	32,495.8	36.0
Foreign direct investment	1,798.6	14.4	4,247.2	12.9	6,871.7	13.3	9,006.5	27.5	24,993.8	27.7
Portfolio equity	0.0	0.0	0.0	0.0	27.0	0.1	762.2	2.3	16,855.0	18.7
Grants	609.2	4.9	1,438.3	4.4	2,331.3	4.5	2,394.2	7.3	3,019.0	3.3

Source: Global Development Finance, 1997.

a. Public and publicly guaranteed debt plus private nonguaranteed debt.

capital reforms that developing countries can undertake and a necessary (but not sufficient) condition for increasing their access to global finance.

Stock Market Liberalization

Although numerous studies have shown that premature liberalization of dollar-denominated debt flows in the capital account has deleterious effects, there has been a relative dearth of evidence on the effects of equity market liberalizations. Recent work has begun to address this deficiency, and a consensus is forming that equity market liberalization reduces developing countries' cost of capital.[12]

Identifying the date of stock market liberalization is the first step in determining whether stock market liberalization has any discernible economic effect. Since markets are forward-looking, the most important question is, when does the market first learn of a credible, impending liberalization? In principle, identifying a liberalization date involves simply finding the date on which the government declares that foreigners may purchase domestic shares. In practice, the liberalization process is not so transparent. In many cases, there is no obvious government declaration or policy decree.

When there is no salient liberalization decree, liberalization is taken here to be the date on which a closed-end country fund was established. Closed-end funds are often the impetus for a spate of subsequent market openings, which further increase integration.[13] Table 7-2 presents a list of the eighteen countries in the sample, the date of their first stock market liberalization, and the means by which they liberalized. For example, the table shows that the modal means of liberalization occurred through the establishment of a closed-end country fund.[14]

The establishment of a country fund in particular—and stock market liberalizations in general—may seem like a narrow way to define capital account liberalization, but it is precisely the narrowness of stock market liberalizations that makes them more useful for two specific reasons. First,

12. See Bekaert and Harvey (2000); Henry (2000a, 2000b, 2003); Martell and Stulz (2003); Stulz (1999); Tesar and Werner (1998).

13. Bekaert and Harvey (2000); Henry (2000a).

14. While there is broad agreement that liberalization reduces the cost of capital, there is some disagreement about the exact timing of liberalizations. This matters, in principle, because the estimated size of the reduction in the cost of capital depends on the liberalization date one chooses. However, changing liberalization dates has virtually no effect on the basic conclusion. All of the evidence we have indicates that liberalization reduces the cost of capital and suggests that the effects are economically significant, even if we cannot precisely pin down the magnitudes.

Table 7-2. *Dates of Stock Market Liberalization, by Country*

Country	*Year of liberalization*	*Means of liberalization*
Argentina	1989	Policy decree
Brazil	1988	Country fund
Chile	1987	Country fund
Colombia	1991	Policy decree
India	1986	Country fund
Indonesia	1989	Policy decree
Jordan	1995	Policy decree
Korea, Rep. of	1987	Country fund
Malaysia	1987	Country fund
Mexico	1989	Policy decree
Nigeria	1995	Policy decree
Pakistan	1991	Policy decree
Philippines	1986	Country fund
Taiwan	1986	Country fund
Thailand	1987	Country fund
Turkey	1989	Policy decree
Venezuela	1990	Policy decree
Zimbabwe	1993	Policy decree

Source: Bekaert, Harvey, and Lundblad (2001); Henry (2003).

focusing on stock markets alone helps us to distinguish the consequences of equity market liberalization from those of debt market liberalization. Second, studies that use broad indicators of liberalization focus on cross-sectional data, examining the long-run correlation between average openness and average investment.[15] Examining the correlation between average openness and investment tells us whether investment rates are permanently higher in countries with capital accounts that are more open. The problem with this approach is that economic theory makes no such prediction.

What the theory does predict is that capital-poor countries will experience a temporary increase in investment when they liberalize. Hence the relevant issue is not whether countries with open capital accounts have higher investment rates, but whether investment rates increase in the immediate aftermath of liberalization. The most transparent way of testing this prediction is to compare investment rates during episodes of liberalization with investment rates during periods of no liberalization. Because

15. See for example, Rodrik (1998).

they constitute a radical shift in the degree of capital account openness, stock market liberalizations provide ideal natural experiments for confronting the theory with data.

Stock Market Liberalizations: The Cost of Capital, Investment, and Growth

The data indicate that, on average, opening up to foreign shareholders leads to a 38 percent increase in the real dollar value of the stock markets in liberalizing countries.[16] Stock market liberalization does not alter the functioning of these companies in any way; liberalization only changes the ownership of the shares of the companies listed on a country's stock exchange. Then, is the increase in share prices evidence that liberalization drives domestic stock prices away from the fundamentals and leads to stock market bubbles? Not necessarily.

The price of a stock depends on the expected future dividends to be paid by that stock and the discount rate shareholders apply to those expected future dividends. The discount rate has two components: the interest rate and the equity premium. Liberalization reduces interest rates through the inflow of foreign funds from countries with more plentiful capital. Stock market liberalization also reduces the equity premium, because emerging-market stocks provide diversification benefits for investors in countries like the United States.[17] In other words, stock market liberalization leads to a lower cost of equity capital. Thus there are sound fundamental reasons for share prices to rise when the stock market is liberalized, and we seem to observe this in reality.

Exactly who benefits from the increase in share prices and the decline in the cost of capital? Clearly, domestic shareholders benefit: Those who sell their shares realize capital gains, and those who continue to hold their shares see the value of their portfolios increase. Some foreign shareholders may reap immediate capital gains if they get in early on the country's "initial public offering," but the more important benefit is the long-term reduction in risk they get from diversifying their portfolios.

Domestic residents who do not own shares also benefit from liberalization, although for less obvious reasons. When a stock market increases in value, this is equivalent to a fall in the cost of capital through that market. For a given capital-raising requirement, a higher stock price means that

16. Henry (2000a). This number varies according to the liberalization date. Martell and Stulz (2003) report even larger effects.

17. Chari and Henry (2002).

fewer shares need to be issued. Figure 7-1 illustrates the fall in the cost of capital that occurs when developing countries liberalize the stock market. The figure plots the average aggregate dividend yield across the liberalizing countries in event time (year 0 is the year of liberalization). The average dividend yield falls roughly 240 basis points—from an average level of 5.0 percent in the five years prior to liberalization to an average of 2.6 percent in the five years following liberalization.[18]

Although the immediate effect of liberalization is to raise share prices and lower the cost of capital, this is not the end of the story. The lower cost of capital encourages firms to build new factories and install new machines because some investment projects that were not profitable before the stock market liberalization are profitable after liberalization.

The increased investment that should result from stock market liberalization is particularly important for emerging economies, because more investment should lead to faster economic growth and higher wages for workers.[19] Thus stock market liberalization should generate substantial economic benefits, even for those individuals who did not own shares before the liberalization and therefore do not reap the capital gains associated with the increase in share prices.

It sounds plausible that a lower cost of capital should lead to increased investment, but what is the reality? Figure 7-2 demonstrates that, on average, countries experience an increase in investment when they liberalize the stock market. The growth rate of the capital stock rises 1.1 percentage points in the aftermath of liberalization—from an average of 5.4 percent a year in the period before to an average of 6.5 percent in the period after liberalization.

While liberalization leads to a sharp increase in investment on average, it is also important to know whether this is a uniform effect: Do all countries experience higher investment, or do just a select few drive the results? In order to address this question, recent research looks at the results on a

18. Recall that the dividend yield, D / P, is given by the following formula: $D / P = r - g$, where D is the dividend, P is the price, and g is the expected growth rate of D. It is legitimate to interpret a fall in the dividend yield as a decline in the cost of capital, if there is no change in the expected future growth rate of dividends at the time of liberalization. But, as we discuss shortly, stock market liberalizations usually are accompanied by other economic reforms that may increase the expected future growth rate of output and dividends. Economic reforms do have significant effects on the stock market, but the financial effects of liberalization remain statistically and economically significant, after controlling for contemporaneous reforms (Henry 2000a, 2002).

19. The increase in the growth rate of output will only be temporary. Because of diminishing returns to capital, it is impossible for a country to achieve permanently higher growth rates by simply increasing the capital stock. The gains in the level of GDP per capita, however, will be permanent.

Figure 7-1. *Relation between the Cost of Capital and Liberalization of the Capital Account*

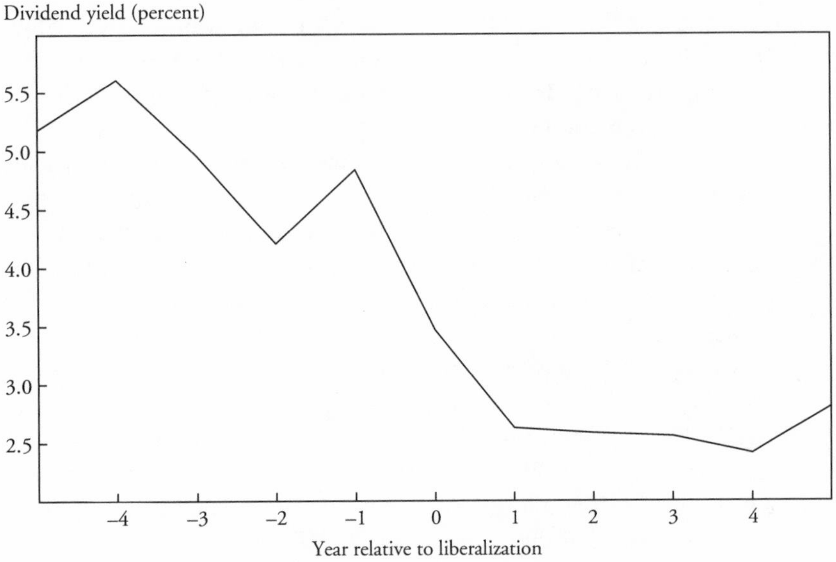

Source: Authors' calculations and Emerging Markets Database, 1998.

country-by-country basis. In one study, only two of the countries in the sample did not experience abnormally high rates of investment in the first year after liberalization. In the second year after liberalization, only one of the countries did not experience abnormally high rates of investment.[20]

Theory also tells us that increased investment should raise productivity and economic growth. Figure 7-3 shows that, as predicted, the growth rate of output per worker rises in the aftermath of liberalization—from an average of 1.4 percent a year in the period before to an average of 3.7 percent a year in the period after liberalization.

Stock Market Liberalization and Other Economic Reforms

Stock market liberalizations are usually accompanied by other economic reforms. Therefore, it is important to ask whether these economic reforms would have caused large increases in stock prices, investment, and growth,

20. Henry (2000b).

Figure 7-2. *Relation between the Growth Rate of Capital and Liberalization of the Capital Account*

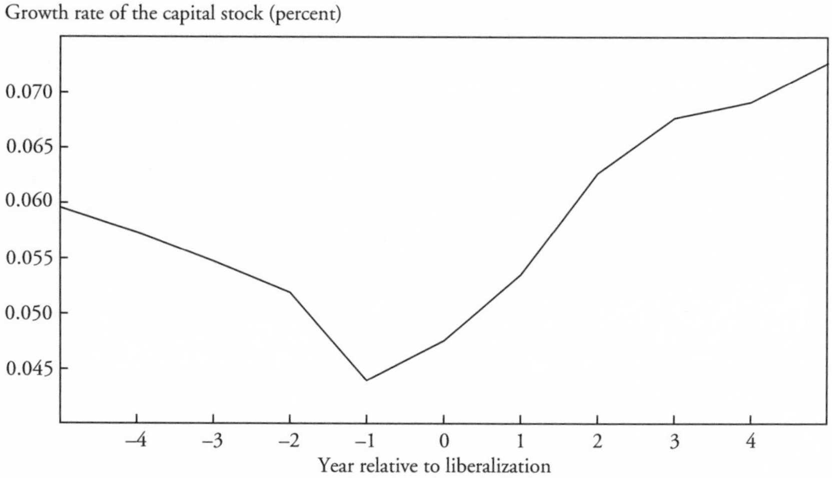

Source: Authors' calculations and Bosworth and Collins (2003).

even if there had not been any stock market liberalization. While the financial and economic effects of stock market liberalization remain statistically and economically significant after controlling for contemporaneous reforms, the other economic reforms are also important sources of growth.

To see the point, consider in greater detail the result illustrated by figure 7-3: per capita gross domestic product (GDP) growth increases following liberalization. On the one hand, there is nothing surprising about figure 7-3. Whereas figures 7-1 and 7-2 document behavioral responses of prices and quantities of capital to liberalization, figure 7-3 simply provides a mechanical check of the standard growth-accounting equation:

$$\hat{Y} = \hat{A} + \alpha\hat{K} + (1-\alpha)\hat{L}, \quad (7\text{-}1)$$

where a circumflex over a variable denotes the change in the natural log of that variable.[21]

21. In words, this equation says that the growth rate of output equals the growth rate of total factor productivity plus capital's share in output (α) times the growth rate of the capital stock plus labor's share in output ($1 - \alpha$) times the growth rate of the labor force. Starting with the standard production function, $Y = AK^{\alpha} L^{1-\alpha}$, taking natural logs on both sides and differentiating with respect to time, yields this equation.

Figure 7-3. *Relation between the Growth Rate of Output per worker and Liberalization of the Capital Account*

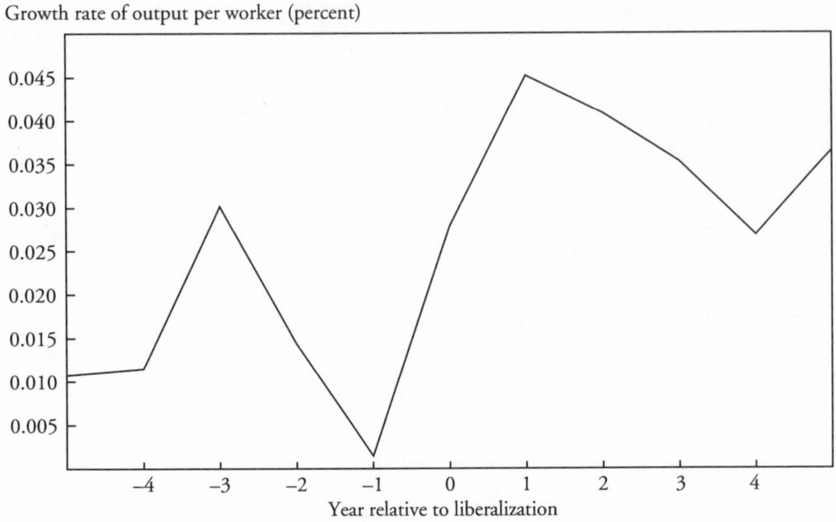

Source: See figure 7-2.

The interesting point about figure 7-3 is that the increase in the growth rate of output per worker is too large to be explained by the increase in investment. A few simple calculations illustrate the point. The elasticity of output with respect to capital, α, is typically around 0.33. So, based on figure 7-2, we would expect the growth rate of output per worker after liberalization to be about 0.363 (0.33 times 1.1) percentage point higher. But figure 7-3 displays a 2.3 percentage point increase in the growth rate of output per worker. All else equal, a 1.1 percentage point increase in the growth rate of the capital stock can produce a 2.3 percentage point increase in the growth rate of output per worker only if the elasticity of output with respect to capital is on the order of 2!

The increase in growth due to liberalization is slightly larger than 1 percentage point after controlling for a number of variables.[22] Nevertheless, this finding still requires an elasticity of output with respect to capital that is greater than 1. What explains the inconsistency of this finding with standard production theory? The answer, of course, is total factor productivity (TFP) growth. Equation 7-1 shows that any increase in the rate of growth

22. Bekaert, Harvey, and Lundblad (2001).

of output that is not accounted for by an increase in the growth rate of capital and labor must be the result of an increase in $\hat{A}$, the growth rate of TFP. While we typically interpret $\hat{A}$ as the growth rate of the stock of productive ideas or technology, any economic reform that raises the efficiency of a given stock of capital and labor also increases $\hat{A}$, even in the absence of technological change.

Economic institutions and social infrastructure can also be crucial in determining the level of human capital accumulation and in turn setting the marginal product of capital.[23] In other words, the rate of return to capital may be low because emerging economies fail to create an environment where (1) entrepreneurs are free to pursue new productive opportunities and (2) lenders have an incentive to extend capital to the private sector.

Consider the gap between G-7 countries and emerging economies using some common measures of institutional development. According to one measure of social infrastructure,[24] the median G-7 country ranks fourteenth of 130 countries, while the median emerging economy ranks sixty-fourth.[25] A look at the Heritage House 2003 Index of Economic Freedom yields similar results. Out of 161 countries, the median G-7 country ranks nineteenth, and the median emerging economy ranks seventy-second.[26]

Stock market liberalization commonly takes place concurrently with a number of other institutional and macroeconomic reforms. Because of this, it is important to think carefully about how to interpret the data. Consider a few simple pictures. Standard trade theory predicts that trade liberalization will increase TFP. As countries tilt production toward their comparative advantage, they experience an increase in output for a given stock of capital and labor. Figure 7-4 plots the average growth rate of output per worker across all of the countries in the sample following trade liberalization.[27] The figure shows that the average growth rate of output per worker rises 1.5 percentage points following trade liberalization—from an average of 0.6 percent a year in the five years preceding trade liberalization to an average of 2.1 percent a year in the five years after.

Stabilizing inflation may also increase TFP, because high inflation generates incentives for workers and producers to divert resources away from

23. Kremer (1993).

24. Hall and Jones (1999).

25. We use the emerging economies listed in table 7-3. These countries, all of which have stock markets, are among the more successful of the less-developed countries. A more complete list of less-developed countries would only make the distinction sharper.

26. These data are available online at www.heritage.org/research/features/index/ [June 6, 2003].

27. The trade liberalization dates are taken from Sachs and Warner (1995).

Figure 7-4. *Relation between the Growth Rate of Output per Worker and Liberalization of Trade*

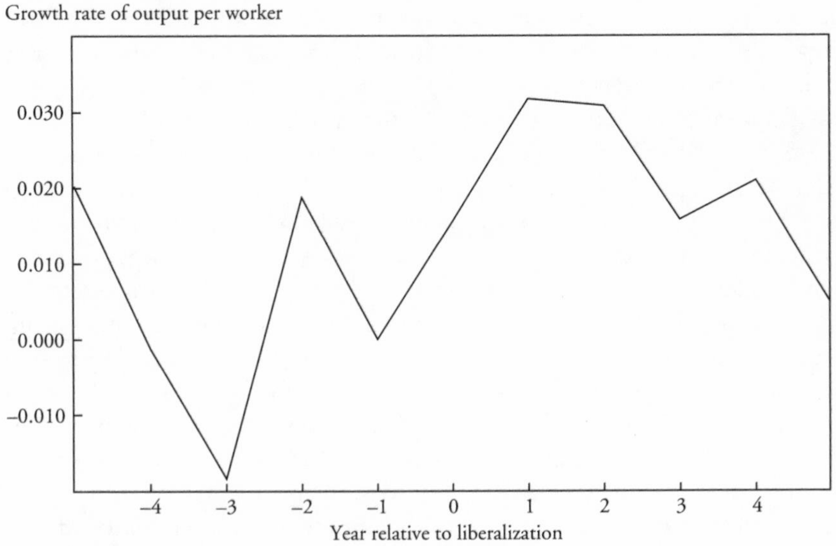

Source: See figure 7-2.

productive activities and toward activities that help them to avoid the costs of high inflation. Economic research has found that stabilizing high inflation is good for asset prices, investment, and output.[28] Figure 7-5 plots the average growth rate of output per worker across all of the countries in the sample following inflation stabilization programs.[29] Figure 7-5 shows that the growth rate of output per worker rises 0.8 percentage point following stabilization programs—from an average of 0.8 percent a year in the five years preceding stabilization to an average of 1.6 percent a year in the five years following stabilization.

Pictures are not conclusive, of course. To reach more reliable conclusions, one must work carefully to disentangle the effects of these and other reforms on growth. Our only point is that there are strong a priori theoretical reasons to expect reforms other than equity market liberalization to have a significant effect on economic growth. The raw data do no

28. Calvo and Végh (1998); Easterly (1996); Fischer, Sahay, and Végh (2002); Henry (2000b, 2002).

29. The inflation stabilization dates are taken from Henry (2002). In countries with multiple stabilization dates, the last date was chosen.

Figure 7-5. *Relation between the Growth Rate of Output per Worker and Inflation Stabilization*

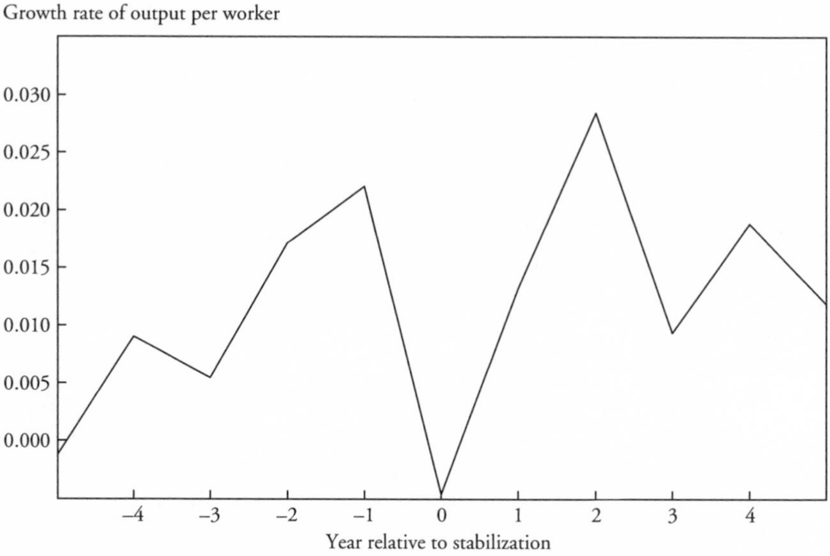

Source: See figure 7-2.

harm to this view and provide strong prima facie evidence that factors not related to capital markets play a significant role in explaining the increase in growth during the period after liberalization.

Hence, although this chapter focuses primarily on the ways in which domestic capital market reforms can improve developing countries' access to capital, we would be remiss not to underscore the following point. Domestic reforms that improve the efficiency with which capital is utilized are at least as important as reforms increasing the quantity of capital that domestic markets are able to attract. In addition to macroeconomic reforms such as inflation stabilization and trade liberalization, reforms that improve the efficiency with which capital gets allocated can also raise TFP growth.

Investor Protection and Access to Global Finance

We have shown that whether liberalization succeeds or fails depends crucially on whether it is equity market liberalization or debt market liberalization. In general, liberalizing debt flows leads to crises, while liberalizing portfolio equity flows is associated with higher asset valuations, greater capital investment, and faster economic growth. The contrasting evidence on the effects of debt versus equity flows suggests that there may be a need for developing countries to shift their financing toward equity and away from debt.

But it is important to remember that international finance is a two-way street—borrowing requires lending. Therefore, policymakers must ask the following: Given the preferences of developed-country suppliers of capital, what steps can be taken to shift the equilibrium financial mix toward equity and away from debt? Permitting foreign investors to hold stocks is a necessary step but is not sufficient by itself. We now explore the potential causes of an over-reliance on debt and suggest some steps that countries can undertake to remedy the situation.

Equity flows to developing countries have fallen far short of what one would expect given the scarcity of capital in these countries. Capital flows may be heavily tilted toward debt over equity because of institutions that intentionally or unintentionally skew the equilibrium mix. Even the initial boom in emerging stock markets led to much smaller increases in valuations (declines in the cost of capital) than one would expect to occur with the entry of foreign investors.[30] Since the initial boom of the early 1990s, the flow of portfolio equity to emerging markets has slowed.[31] While a recent study by the World Bank shows that developing countries' ratios of external debt to equity fell between 1997 and 2001, it is still not clear that they have fallen to prudent levels.[32]

Before one can prescribe a solution to the problem of weak equity flows, however, one must first identify the cause of the problem. At first glance, one is tempted to resort to home bias as an explanation.[33] Does the fact that foreign investors hold far too few foreign securities account for developing countries' high ratios of debt to equity? No. Home bias can help to explain why overall levels of capital flows to developing countries are not what we would expect them to be. But home bias alone cannot explain why the composition of capital flows to developing countries is skewed toward debt over equity.

Put another way, taking the overall inflow of capital to developing countries as given, why do we see so little in the way of portfolio equity inflows

30. Martell and Stulz (2003); Stulz (1999).

31. Akyut, Kalsi, and Ratha (2003).

32. Suttle (2003, p. 9).

33. See Lewis (1999) for a survey of the home-bias literature.

relative to debt inflows? Two linked explanations suggest themselves. First, lack of transparency in equity markets makes investors reluctant to invest in emerging-market stocks; second, weak protection of the rights of equity investors reinforces the tendency of capital suppliers to purchase debt rather than equity. We now discuss the economic theory behind these explanations before moving on to the accumulating empirical evidence supporting them.

Asymmetric Information and Access to Global Finance

New theories in economics and finance developed over the past three decades have highlighted the inefficiencies that can result when not all parties to a transaction are equally well informed. Such asymmetric information problems can make investors reluctant to put their money in companies due to the problems of adverse selection, moral hazard, or both. If good companies are indistinguishable from bad companies, investors can only safely assume that all companies are bad. In that case, good companies will not receive a high enough price for their shares and will not list shares on the market, thus confirming investors' negative beliefs. Second, investors may be concerned about moral hazard or agency problems. Money invested in a good company may be misspent on unnecessary managerial perks or even stolen outright where accounting standards and enforcement bodies do not exist to restrain insiders.[34] These insiders may be controlling shareholders, such as a founding family, a firm's top managers, or both.

A new literature on law and finance has found strong support for the importance of these legal and institutional factors in explaining why the magnitude of capital flows from rich to poor countries is smaller than we would otherwise expect. The degree to which a country's law protects the legal rights of minority shareholders exerts a significant influence on the size and robustness of capital markets.[35] If investors get poor protection from a country, they will stay away. Table 7-3 shows that developing countries rank lower than developed countries on every major measure of investor protection: shareholder rights, creditor rights, efficiency of judicial system, rule of law, and rating of the accounting system. This underscores our point that allowing foreign investors into the country is a necessary but not sufficient condition for increased capital market integration.

34. Jensen (1986); Shleifer and Vishny (1997).
35. La Porta and others (1997, 1998, 2002).

Table 7-3. *Investor Protection, by Country*

Country	*Rule of law*	*Judicial efficiency*	*Contract repudiation*	*Expropriation risk*	*Accounting standards*
Argentina	5.4	6.0	4.9	5.9	4.5
Brazil	6.3	5.8	6.3	7.6	5.4
Chile	7.0	7.3	6.8	7.5	5.2
Colombia	2.1	7.3	7.0	7.0	5.0
Ecuador	6.7	6.3	5.2	6.6	n.a.
Egypt	4.2	6.5	6.1	6.3	2.4
Greece	6.2	7.0	6.6	7.1	5.5
India	4.2	8.0	6.1	7.8	5.7
Indonesia	4.0	2.5	6.1	7.2	n.a.
Jordan	4.4	8.7	4.9	6.1	n.a.
Kenya	5.4	5.8	5.7	6.0	n.a.
Korea, Rep. of	5.4	6.0	8.6	8.3	6.2
Malaysia	6.8	9.0	7.4	8.0	7.6
Mexico	5.4	6.0	6.6	7.3	6.0
Nigeria	2.7	7.3	4.4	5.3	5.9
Pakistan	3.0	5.0	4.9	5.6	n.a.
Peru	2.5	6.8	4.7	5.5	3.8
Philippines	2.7	4.8	4.8	5.2	6.5
South Africa	4.4	6.0	7.3	6.9	7.0
Sri Lanka	1.9	7.0	5.3	6.1	n.a.
Thailand	6.3	3.3	7.6	7.4	6.4
Turkey	5.2	4.0	6.0	7.0	5.1
Uruguay	5.0	6.5	7.3	6.6	3.1
Venezuela	6.4	6.5	6.3	6.9	4.0
Zimbabwe	3.7	7.5	5.0	5.6	n.a.
Mean					
Less-developed countries	4.7	6.3	6.1	6.7	3.8
Developed countries	9.1	9.1	9.2	9.5	6.4

Source: López-de-Silanes (2002).
n.a. Not available.

For example, Shleifer and Wolfenzon show that weaker investor protection may reduce the marginal product of capital and can eliminate the incentive for capital to flow from rich to poor countries. According to their argument, the amount of capital that does flow to emerging economies is only a fraction of what we would see in a world where minority shareholders in these countries enjoyed the same legal protection as their U.S.

counterparts.[36] In other words, stock market liberalization is a necessary but not sufficient condition for increased access to global equity capital.

The drastically lower capital-to-labor ratios in emerging economies may not translate into higher rates of return if there are significant cross-country differences in investor protection. We can think about such a claim in terms of the standard production theory discussed earlier. While economists have traditionally interpreted the parameter A in the production function as the stock of ideas, A is really an index of the efficiency with which a given stock of K and L can be transformed into Y.[37] Therefore, any economic reform that raises the efficiency of a given stock of capital and labor will also increase A, even in the absence of technological change. Holding the stock of ideas constant, government distortions may reduce A and lead to lower rates of return to capital than we would otherwise expect.

Ineffective investor protection is an important example of such a distortion. Since outside investors (whether foreign or domestic) know less about the firm's prospects and the behavior of the managers running it than do insiders, they will demand higher returns or stay out entirely. By mitigating the effects of asymmetric information, strong investor protection may help countries to attract more international capital. More protection should keep mobile domestic capital from leaving or being kept out of the financial markets and saved as cash or in nonfinancial assets (such as land or jewelry). Finally, better disclosure will improve efficiency regardless of whether protections increase the total stock of capital, thus helping countries to make better use of the capital they already have.

Institutions to mitigate moral hazard improve the ability of investors to monitor how their money is being used and make it easier for investors to step in when insiders start to misuse their power. In contrast, if some shareholders have disproportionate influence over the firm's policies, or if minority shareholders face roadblocks to active participation in decision-making, outside investors will hesitate to risk their money at such a firm, thus raising its cost of capital.

Institutions to mitigate adverse selection require firms listing new securities to provide more information and make them legally liable for the quality of this information. Because minority shareholders are unlikely to take an interest in the governance of a single firm when it is easier simply

36. Shleifer and Wolfenzon (2002).

37. Solow (2001).

to sell the shares, it has also been suggested that it would be beneficial to have a strong public regulator with the incentives and capabilities to act on their behalf.

An important point of contention has been over who needs this protection. American research on corporate governance initially concerned itself with the problem of managers of a widely held firm with few concentrated shareholders. Because no individual shareholder owned enough shares of one firm to make it worth the effort to monitor, the concern was that managers would not be accountable. Outside the United States, however, the widely held firm is a rarity. Instead, most firms have a single dominant shareholder or group of shareholders (often the founding family or a government shareholder) that keeps close track of the business and may include the chief executive officer and other top managers.[38] For this reason, we refer to "insiders" in general, leaving open the possibility that they may be managers, large shareholders, or both in any given company.

Firm-level Corporate Governance

One growing body of research has explored the relationship of firm-level corporate governance practices to valuations or performance. While this research points to the value of good governance for firms, it fails to rule out crucial alternative theories and does not indicate whether there is a useful role for governments to play.

In general, firms with better corporate governance practices have better performance and higher valuations, especially in countries where the overall legal system is weak.[39] A study of almost 3,000 Asian corporations found that a mismatch of cash flow rights to voting rights, such as through violations of "one-share, one-vote," through cross-shareholdings, or through pyramid ownership structures, is associated with significantly lower firm valuation.[40] When surveyed, international investors have reported that they would avoid companies and countries with poor corporate governance.[41]

However, the policy implications of this are not entirely straightforward. The most obvious interpretation of the research is that if firms would only

38. La Porta, López-de-Silanes, and Shleifer (1999).
39. Klapper and Love (2002); Newell and Wilson (2002).
40. Claessens and others (1999).
41. McKinsey and Company (2002).

improve their corporate governance, they would have cheaper access to capital. This fails to address the question of why these companies have not done so already. Were they simply unaware that minority shareholders would require a higher return in order to invest in companies with opaque or exclusionary corporate governance practices? Alternatively, we must consider the possibility that these policies were consciously chosen. In that case, we need to understand why firm insiders decided that allowing more outside observation of and influence on corporate decisions was not worth the cost.

One possible cost is that shareholder involvement keeps the firm from making the best strategic decisions. It has been argued that the extra bureaucracy involved with fulfilling corporate governance requirements slows down firm decisionmaking. In a similar vein, the pressure to make quarterly results and to justify corporate decisions to the public could keep executives from taking a longer-term strategy. Another cost is that of disclosure. More public disclosure makes it harder to keep profitable lines of business out of the view of competitors. These costs reduce the value of the firm to all shareholders and hence could be good reasons for the failure to adopt corporate governance "best practices."

A more cynical view is that firms would benefit from the cheaper capital they could receive if they improved their governance but that insiders benefit more from continuing to extract rents from the current "captive" shareholders than they would from taking their honest share of a well-governed firm. Alternatively, there might be some sort of coordination problem. If all firms in a country have significant internal governance problems, the first firm to reform might risk looking worse than other firms. For instance, if most firms in a country are reporting profits, but only because they violate international accounting standards in some respect, the first firm to switch over and admit that it is running a loss may not benefit. If all firms are compelled to switch together, the better firms will stand out.

Thus this firm-level research has ambiguous policy implications. Legally requiring stronger corporate governance measures from every firm in an economy when these firms have already demonstrated through their own choices that they do not want better corporate governance only makes sense under some circumstances. Otherwise it might harm the firms more than help them. The results of firm-level research do not help to answer this question because they are consistent with either hypothesis.

Measuring Investor Protection

In recent years a growing body of econometric research has demonstrated that economies with fewer protections for minority shareholders, with weaker legal systems, or with reputations for corruption have smaller and weaker financial systems and grow more slowly. Such institutional problems not only make it harder for firms to access international capital but also make it harder for firms to convince domestic investors to entrust the firms with their money, reducing growth even in a closed economy.

Both the desired outcome (capital market development) and the proposed influences on it (effective legal systems, transparency, and so forth) can be measured in a variety of ways. The influences are particularly difficult to assess rigorously. Following the example of earlier cross-country research on the correlates of overall economic growth, initial work primarily used general indexes of "law and order," "rule of law," or "corruption" created by private business risk advisory services, by think tanks, or by investment banks.[42]

Such indexes have three main problems. The first is that these measures are somewhat subjective, giving substantial weight to the personal assessments of analysts or surveyed businesspeople. This affects their comparability and obscures what they are actually measuring. The second is that they are not focused on financial markets in particular, which may be more or less law-abiding than other parts of the economy. Finally, and perhaps most important for the present discussion, results based on such studies provide only very general policy implications. A reputation for corruption and an ineffective legal system are bad for the entire economy, not just for the financial sector, and there is no universally accepted "cure" for these ills.

A new wave of economic research has attempted to remedy this deficiency by systematically measuring specific financial regulations and institutions and statistically testing their effects. In the first major effort in this direction, La Porta, López-de-Silanes, Shleifer, and Vishny examine the financial laws and regulations of forty-nine countries to determine what level of protection they afford to creditors and shareholders.[43] This work focuses on aspects of company law that might (in theory) act to mitigate the moral hazard problem.

Shareholder rights are measured by seven indicators, each taking a value of 1 if a particular law works in favor of minority shareholders and a value

42. See, for example, Demirgüç-Kunt and Maksimovic (1998).
43. La Porta and others (1998).

of 0 otherwise. Six of these are summed into an "antidirector rights" score that ranges from 0 to 6. The first antidirector right is proxy by mail. If small shareholders must personally attend annual meetings in order for their voices to be heard, they are unlikely to do so and thus are effectively disenfranchised. The second, "shares not blocked," refers to a requirement in some countries that shareholders temporarily deposit their shares with the company or an intermediary in order to participate in general shareholders' meetings. Such provisions make it more difficult for shareholders to participate in corporate governance and restrict their ability to react to the meeting's events by trading immediately. The third right indicates whether voting rules give small shareholders a good opportunity to get a board representative through proportional voting or other means. Countries earn the fourth point of the antidirector score if minority shareholders have means to challenge the company's or the board's decisions in court. The fifth point comes from requiring a relatively low percentage of shares in order to call an extraordinary shareholders' meeting, and the sixth comes from granting preemptive rights to existing shareholders to buy new issues.

Another crucial shareholder right, "one-share, one-vote," is kept separate from the basic index of antidirector rights because it has a somewhat different nature. This right indicates whether cash flow rights match voting rights. Where these rights do not match, some shareholders have disproportionate control over the firm. If these shareholders act to ensure the firm's long-term profitability and dividend distributions, then any additional voting rights are without value. In practice, a premium usually is associated with multiple voting shares, which suggests that the extra control over the firm pays off through something other than share appreciation or dividends.[44]

Creditor rights are measured with a four-point scale. The first point is earned if restrictions are placed on firms going into reorganization, since reorganization shelters debtors from their obligations to creditors. The second is earned if no automatic stay is placed on secured assets in reorganization, meaning that creditors can reclaim their collateral even in reorganization. The third point comes if secured creditors receive priority over other creditors such as the government or employees. The fourth point is earned if in reorganization management is automatically fired or

44. Dyck and Zingales (2002).

the firm is placed under the supervision of a court or creditor-appointed agent.

There are a number of trade-offs to be made in the choice of data. First, financial laws and regulations in any country are far more complicated than can be represented in a simple index of rights. It might well be that some unique characteristic of the laws of one country gives shareholders much stronger or weaker rights than this index indicates. Alternatively, actual practice may be quite different from the laws on the books, with much stricter or weaker enforcement because of cultural or political factors. However, sensitivity to these nuances has only been achieved by using subjective ratings from country experts, which has a high cost in terms of consistency and comparability across countries.

The other trade-off is that these two measures focus only on the protection of the rights of shareholders and creditors after they have purchased the shares or bonds or made the loans. Although these are crucial in mitigating the moral hazard problem, they do not address the adverse selection problem. Recently, La Porta, López-de-Silanes, and Shleifer have collected a new set of data on laws dealing with the issuing of new securities, one that addresses the means by which securities purchasers can have confidence in the quality of the financial assets they are purchasing.[45] We discuss this at more length, after first examining what researchers have uncovered over the past six years using the initial data set described above.

The central finding of this research is that, as suspected, countries that have put in place fewer of these protections have smaller and weaker capital markets. To evaluate the strength of stock markets, La Porta, López-de-Silanes, Shleifer, and Vishny use three outcome measures.[46] First, they estimate the value of listed shares held by minority shareholders and compare that to GDP. They also look at the total number of listed firms and at the annual number of initial public offerings relative to population—seeing more firms on the market suggests that equity markets have been an attractive and feasible source of capital and seeing more initial public offerings confirms that they remain so. Controlling for rule of law (using a rating from the International Country Risk Guide), GDP growth, and gross national product (GNP), they find that antidirector rights have a statistically significant effect on all three outcome measures but that one-share, one-vote does not.[47]

45. La Porta, López-de-Silanes, and Shleifer (2002).

46. La Porta and others (1997).

47. La Porta and others (1997).

These effects are sharply attenuated or disappear when another factor is taken into account: the origin of the country's company law. Countries that have a company law based on the English common-law model, whether because of colonial legacy or some other connection, have larger capital markets. Countries that follow continental European models based on a civil law tradition, such as the German or French, have significantly smaller equity markets. Although this reinforces the view that law matters for security markets, these measures of investor rights do not capture the most crucial ways in which it does so. As expected, overall rule of law also has a significant effect on the number of listed firms and the number of initial public offerings and, to a lesser extent, on the ratio of market capitalization to GDP.

For credit markets, which are less public and thus harder to measure, La Porta, López-de-Silanes, Shleifer, and Vishny use the sum of all private sector bank debt and all outstanding corporate bonds, divided by GNP.[48] Stronger creditor rights have the expected effect of increasing total debt, but this effect is not statistically significant and is swamped once legal origin is taken into account.

The overall statistical weakness of these results might lead one to discount the importance of the specific shareholder and creditor rights measured, but this would not be the correct conclusion. First, the sample includes only a cross section of forty-nine countries, meaning only the most dramatic effects could be expected to show up as statistically significant. Second, these indexes measure only a few aspects of a variety of complex legal codes and practices. Countries with weaker investor rights by the main measures used may have compensating measures such as mandatory dividends for listed firms or legal reserve requirements for borrower firms.[49] Third, regardless of the control variables used or the outcome variable chosen, strengthening the rights of shareholders and creditors has a positive effect on the size of capital markets. The lesson for policymakers is not that the law and finance research lays out the best recipe for bigger capital markets but rather that protection of minority rights, in one form or another, must be among the ingredients.

Examination of other characteristics of financial systems with different rules reinforces the importance of shareholder rights. Ownership of large public companies is significantly more concentrated in countries with weaker

48. La Porta and others (1997).

49. La Porta and others (1998).

investor protections.[50] This suggests that these firms missed opportunities to bring in more capital for investment through broad issuance of equity shares and that the investors in these firms are less diversified than they could be.

In addition, firms in countries with stronger shareholder rights pay out more dividends than do firms in the same industries in countries with weaker shareholder rights.[51] Perhaps more important, rapidly growing firms in a country with strong shareholder protections pay less in dividends than do slowly growing firms in the same country, but this is not true in countries without such protections. This implies that less-protected investors feel compelled to extract dividends from their investments in high-growth firms every year because they are not certain that these cash flows will be used wisely or distributed to shareholders later. This apparent need to maintain credibility by paying dividends may restrict the ability of firms to raise capital for longer-term investments or to pursue the best opportunities available. Firms located in countries with weaker investor protections have lower market valuations relative to their book assets, again supporting the hypothesis that investors in these countries do not trust firms to use their assets effectively or to pay out profits in dividends.[52]

Other researchers have used this data set to test further implications of the theory. Countries with stronger minority shareholder rights have more efficient capital allocation overall. In particular, these countries see less over-investment in declining industries.[53] In countries with weaker investor protections, insiders are compelled to hold a larger share of their firms (and thus not diversify) as an extra assurance to outside investors that they will run the firm to maximize profits.[54]

Dyck and Zingales analyze transactions in which a controlling stake is sold as a block. They infer that the premium paid in such transactions above the market price reflects the extra value of control rights, as opposed to the cash flow rights of shares sold one-by-one. Where those premiums are high, capital markets are less developed and ownership is more concentrated, suggesting that these premiums are a good measure of market inefficiency. They find that more shareholder rights and more effective law enforcement are associated with lower control premiums. This again supports the idea

50. La Porta and others (1998).
51. La Porta and others (2000).
52. La Porta and others (2002).
53. Wurgler (2000).
54. Himmelberg, Hubbard, and Love (2002).

that controlling shareholders are less able to extract "private benefits" from a company when shareholder rights are in place, which should make investors more confident in investing in such economies. They also find that low private benefits are associated with wide circulation of daily newspapers, high rates of tax compliance, and competitive product markets.[55]

Investor rights not only affect how well markets function in normal times but also play a role in crises. Countries with weak corporate governance were particularly hard hit in the Asian financial crisis of 1997–98. In fact, it has been argued that weak corporate governance played a greater role than did conventional macroeconomic variables such as government budget balance, current account deficits, or foreign debt. This may occur because insiders are more likely to start or increase the pace of expropriation of the assets of a company during a downturn, if investors are unprotected. Knowing this, investors will pull out rapidly when conditions become unfavorable, contributing to a downward spiral such as that observed in Asia.[56]

Mitigating Adverse Selection through Public and Private Enforcement

In their most recent paper, La Porta, López-de-Silanes, and Shleifer turn to securities law relating to initial public offerings.[57] As mentioned, these laws can be viewed as attempts to deal with the adverse selection or "lemons" problem, making investors more confident that a firm issuing new equity has told the truth about its financial situation. In collecting these new data, the researchers address this question at three levels. First, they assess the theoretical arguments that securities laws are potentially harmful because they keep firms and investors from independently making whatever arrangements are best for them. Second, even if law is helpful, it might work through effective public enforcement or it might work through "private enforcement" that makes it easier for private parties to make informed decisions and to take action when deceived. Finally, the researchers go further into the details of specific laws to see which appear to be most effective and whether that varies with context.

This new study analyzes data on twenty-two aspects of securities law, across the same forty-nine countries with large stock markets that were in

55. Dyck and Zingales (2002).

56. Johnson and others (2000).

57. La Porta, López-de-Silanes, and Shleifer (2002).

the earlier database. As in the 1998 study, La Porta, López-de-Silanes, and Shleifer consider the three outcome variables of market capitalization as a fraction of GDP, number of listed firms per capita, and number of initial public offerings per capita.[58] On their first question, whether law matters at all, they answer "a definite yes," echoing their earlier results.

Having dealt with the not-entirely-straw man of the efficiently lawless equity market, they go on to examine what does work in more detail. The obvious theoretical alternative to relying solely on the market is to rely solely on public enforcement, a strong independent government regulator that they call the supervisor. However, they find somewhat mixed evidence for the value of this. Contrary to expectations, it does not seem to matter whether the supervisor is insulated from political influence, nor does it matter if the supervisor's resources are thinly spread across multiple areas of responsibility (for example, both banking and market supervision). Furthermore, the ability of the supervisor to issue criminal sanctions against issuers, distributors, or accountants is not associated with larger financial markets. However, giving the supervisor power to make regulations, to command documents from firms, and to order market participants to take or refrain from taking specific actions (such as disclosing certain information to the public or paying compensation to investors) is associated with larger securities markets relative to GDP.

La Porta, López-de-Silanes, and Shleifer find stronger evidence for the efficacy of a third way, what they call "private enforcement." Laws can facilitate private enforcement first by ensuring that investors have the information they need and second by making it easier for them to take legal action when they believe they have been deceived. This first aspect is measured by tallying up disclosure requirements in the law. Legal systems are ranked higher on this scale for requiring that firms deliver a prospectus to investors before listing, for requiring more detail on directors' compensation, for requiring more detail on the issuer's ownership structure (especially insider ownership), and for requiring disclosure of irregular contracts and related-party transactions. Stricter disclosure requirements are highly correlated with securities market development.

The second aspect of private enforcement is quantified by examining where the burden of proof is placed in civil suits, should the investors believe that material information was left out of the prospectus. In the least investor-friendly regimes, investors must prove that defendants were

58. La Porta, López-de-Silanes, and Shleifer (2002).

grossly negligent or deliberately fraudulent, while at the opposite extreme defendants may be required to prove that they conducted due diligence or may even have no defense if they excluded important information for any reason. These standards are rated separately for distributors, issuers, and accountants. An additional criterion, whether distributors are expected to conduct due diligence on the prospectus, is added together with these to construct a burden of proof index. This index is also highly correlated with strong equity markets.

In addition to measuring the direct effects of these different laws, La Porta, López-de-Silanes, and Shleifer find support for an important interaction effect. Public enforcement works well in countries with an efficient judicial system, but not in countries with a weak judicial system. In contrast, private enforcement works well in either environment. This suggests that developing countries with an imperfect judicial system might find more immediate success facilitating private enforcement, since this could succeed in bringing in more investment even without the broader systemic reforms that might be necessary to fix a dysfunctional judiciary.

Furthermore, unlike the antidirector rights index, these effects do not become insignificant when controlling for legal origin. In fact, the strong negative effect of French legal origin itself disappears in most of the measures. When these securities laws are included in a regression together with antidirector rights, antidirector rights become insignificant. This suggests that all of the earlier results that relied on the shareholder rights indexes may have been proxying for these securities laws. That is, "French legal origin" describes a package of laws and regulations that tend to go together, including weak shareholder rights. Saying a country has "weak shareholder rights" (by the measures of La Porta, López-de-Silanes, Shleifer, and Vishny) is thus nearly indistinguishable from saying a country has a continental European legal origin, especially given the inherently small samples of cross-country regressions. But these newer results suggest that legal origin itself is just a proxy for other aspects of the system, such as these securities laws.

Conclusions

What can developing countries take away from this research? First, they need not forgo the benefits of foreign investment in order to avoid being buffeted randomly by the winds of global investor sentiment. Equity market liberalization appears to be a safe and healthy alternative to debt dependency. Second, developing countries must recognize that opening up to foreign equity investment is necessary but not sufficient to ensure these inward flows. The lists of laws that La Porta, López-de-Silanes, and Shleifer amalgamate into their various indexes might have the appearance of a recipe for strong markets: Put in place these rules, and international capital will flow in. Such a conclusion would be hasty, for a number of reasons. What we can say, however, is that laws, regulations, and government institutions can play an important role in mitigating problems of moral hazard and asymmetric information for investors and that this will help capital markets to grow.

The main problem with drawing direct prescriptions from this research is that it is unclear what the crucial elements are from the whole package of institutional features. With only a cross section of forty-nine countries to compare, we cannot draw a clear statistical distinction between the effects of any of these institutional features. It appears that the positive effect of antidirector rights found with the earlier data might just be a proxy for other aspects of securities law.[59] Thus putting the set of antidirector rights into law without making other changes might have no effect or could even have unexpected negative effects. We might be more confident if we had systematic before-and-after data on put-in-place new laws, but such data have not yet been collected.

Nevertheless, both theory and empirics point in the same general direction. More protection for shareholders is strongly associated with the size, efficiency, and stability of equity markets. The most recent findings of La Porta, López-de-Silanes, and Shleifer also suggest that cheaper reforms might actually be more effective. Rather than setting up a powerful independent supervisor responsible for criminal prosecution of market actors, governments might do just as well by simply requiring more disclosure of firms and making them responsible in civil court for these disclosures. This does not require the creation of a new bureaucracy or the funding of its investigations.

Some scholars instead argue that improving creditor rights and regulation of the banking system should take priority. In this view, equity markets in developing countries are just a sideshow because most financing occurs through banks.[60] While it is true that equity markets as yet play a small role in most developing countries and that an efficient commercial

59. La Porta and others (2002).

60. Berglof and von Thadden (1999); Mishkin (2000).

banking system is very desirable, this does not diminish the value of effective equity market reforms.

Developing-country equity markets are small and often insignificant precisely because they are poorly regulated. If small savers cannot trust that they will get a fair return from equity investments, they will instead deposit their money with a bank or other financial intermediary. Both the theoretical and empirical literature suggest that different types of business will be better served with different kinds of financing.[61] If only bank loans are available, some kinds of businesses may have difficulty getting started or growing. Furthermore, if well-run banks have access to cheaper equity financing, they should be able to expand their size and scope to serve more domestic clients.

As countries continue to open their equity markets to foreign investors and improve the protection of minority shareholders, there is good reason to believe that equity markets will continue to grow in importance relative to debt. In addition to providing additional capital to fund growth opportunities, less reliance on debt financing in the future might also lessen the frequency and severity of emerging-market financial crises.

References

Akerlof, George, and Paul M. Romer. 1993. "Looting: The Economic Underworld of Bankruptcy for Profit." *Brookings Papers on Economic Activity 2,* 1–74.

Akyut, Dilek, Himmat Kalsi, and Dilip Ratha. 2003. "Sustaining and Promoting Equity-Related Finance for Developing Countries." *Global Development Finance: Striving for Stability in Development Finance.* Washington: World Bank.

Bekaert, Geert, and Campbell Harvey. 2000. "Foreign Speculators and Emerging Equity Markets." *Journal of Finance* 55 (2): 565–613.

Bekaert, Geert, Campbell Harvey, and Christian Lundblad. 2001. "Does Financial Liberalization Spur Growth?" NBER Working Paper 8245. Cambridge, Mass.: National Bureau of Economic Research.

Berglof, Eric, and Ludwig von Thadden. 1999. "The Changing Corporate Governance Paradigm: Implications for Transition and Developing Countries." Paper presented at the Annual World Bank Conference on Development Economics, World Bank, Washington.

Bosworth, Barry, and Susan M. Collins. 2003. "Updated Growth Accounts, 1960–1999." www.brookings.edu/es/research/projects/develop/growthaccounts.xls.

Bhagwati, Jagdish. 1998. "The Capital Myth." *Foreign Affairs* 77 (3, May-June): 7–12.

61. Carlin and Mayer (2003).

Calvo, Guillermo, and Carlos Végh. 1998. "Inflation Stabilization and Balance of Payments Crises in Developing Countries." In John Taylor and Michael Woodford, eds., *Handbook of Macroeconomics*. Amsterdam: North-Holland.

Carlin, Wendy, and Colin Mayer. 2003. "Finance, Investment, and Growth." *Journal of Financial Economics* 69 (1): 191–226.

Cardoso, Fernando E., and Enzo Faletto. 1979. *Dependency and Development in Latin America*. Berkeley: University of California Press.

Chari, Anusha, and Peter Blair Henry. 2002. "Capital Account Liberalization: Allocative Efficiency or Animal Spirits." NBER Working Paper 8908. Cambridge, Mass.: National Bureau of Economic Research.

Choe, Hyuk, Bong-Chan Kho, and René M. Stulz. 1999. "Do Foreign Investors Destabilize Stock Markets? The Korean Experience in 1997." *Journal of Financial Economics* 54 (2, October): 227–64.

Claessens, Stijn, Simeon Djankov, Joseph P. H. Fan, and Larry H. P. Lang. 1999. "Expropriation of Minority Shareholders: Evidence from East Asia." Washington: World Bank, Financial Operations Vice Presidency, Financial Economics Unit, March.

Demirgüç-Kunt, Aslı, and Vojislav Maksimovic. 1998. "Law, Finance, and Firm Growth." *Journal of Finance* 53 (6, December): 2107–36.

Díaz Alejandro, Carlos. 1985. "Goodbye Financial Repression, Hello Financial Crash." *Journal of Development Economics* 19 (September-October): 1–24.

Dornbusch, Rudiger. 2000. *Keys to Prosperity: Free Markets, Sound Policy, and a Bit of Luck.* MIT Press.

Dyck, Alexander, and Luigi Zingales. 2002. "Private Benefits of Control: An International Comparison." NBER Working Paper 8711. Cambridge, Mass.: National Bureau of Economic Research.

Easterly, William. 1996. "When Is Stabilization Expansionary?" *Economic Policy* 22 (April): 67–107.

Evans, Peter. 1979. *Dependent Development: The Alliance of Multinational, State, and Local Capital in Brazil.* Princeton University Press.

Feldstein, Martin. 2002. "Economic and Financial Crises in Emerging Market Economies: Overview of Prevention and Management." NBER Working Paper 8837. Cambridge, Mass.: National Bureau of Economic Research.

Fischer, Stanley. 1987. "Sharing the Burden of the Debt Crisis." *American Economic Review, Papers and Proceedings* 77 (2, May): 165–70.

———. 1998. "Capital Account Liberalization and the Role of the IMF." *Princeton Essays in International Finance* 20: 1–10.

Fischer, Stanley, Ratna Sahay, and Carlos Végh. 2002. "Modern Hyper and High Inflations." *Journal of Economic Literature* 40 (3, September): 937–80.

Furman, Jason, and Joseph Stiglitz. 1998. "Economic Crises: Evidence and Insights from East Asia." *Brookings Papers on Economic Activity 2,* 1–114.

Hall, Robert E., and Charles I. Jones. 1999. "Why Do Some Countries Produce So Much More Output per Worker Than Others?" *Quarterly Journal of Economics* 114 (1): 83-116.

Henry, Peter Blair. 2000a. "Do Stock Market Liberalizations Cause Investment Booms?" *Journal of Financial Economics* 58 (1-2): 301–34.

———. 2000b. "Stock Market Liberalization, Economic Reform, and Emerging Market Equity Prices." *Journal of Finance* 55 (2): 529–64.

———. 2002. "Is Disinflation Good for the Stock Market?" *Journal of Finance* 57 (4): 1617–48.

———. 2003. "Capital Account Liberalization: The Cost of Capital and Economic Growth." *American Economic Review* 93 (2, May): 91-96.

Himmelberg, Charles P., R. Glenn Hubbard, and Inessa Love. 2002. *Investor Protection, Ownership, and the Cost of Capital.* Policy Research Working Paper 2834. Washington: World Bank.

Jensen, Michael C. 1986. "The Agency Costs of Free Cash Flow: Corporate Finance and Takeovers." *American Economic Review* 76 (2, May): 323–29.

Johnson, Simon, Peter Boone, Alasdair Breach, and Eric Friedman. 2000. "Corporate Governance in the Asian Financial Crisis." *Journal of Financial Economics* 58 (1-2): 141–86.

Klapper, Leora, and Inessa Love. 2002. *Corporate Governance, Investor Protection, and Performance in Emerging Markets.* Policy Research Working Paper 2818. Washington: World Bank.

Kremer, Michael. 1993. "The O-Ring Theory of Economic Development." *Quarterly Journal of Economics* 108 (3): 551–75.

La Porta, Rafael, Florencio López-de-Silanes, and Andrei Shleifer. 1999. "Corporate Ownership around the World." *Journal of Finance* 54 (2, April): 471–517.

———. 2002. "What Works in Securities Laws." Unpublished manuscript. Stanford Law School.

La Porta, Rafael, Florencio López-de-Silanes, Andrei Shleifer, and Robert W. Vishny. 1997. "Legal Determinants of External Finance." *Journal of Finance* 52 (3): 1131–50.

———. 1998. "Law and Finance." *Journal of Political Economy* 106 (6): 1113–55.

———. 2000. "Investor Protection and Corporate Governance." *Journal of Financial Economics* 57 (1, October): 3–26.

———. 2002. "Investor Protection and Corporate Valuation." *Journal of Finance* 57 (3, June): 1147–70.

Lewis, Karen K. 1999. "Trying to Explain Home Bias in Equities and Consumption." *Journal of Economic Literature* 37 (2, June): 571–608.

López-de-Silanes, Florencio. 2002. "The Politics of Legal Reform." *Economia* 2 (2, Spring): 91–152.

Lucas, Robert E., Jr. 1990. "Why Doesn't Capital Flow from Rich to Poor Countries?" *American Economic Review* 80 (2): 92–96.

Martell, Rodolfo, and René M. Stulz. 2003. "Equity Market Liberalizations as Country IPOs." *American Economic Review* 93 (2, May): 97–101.

McKinnon, Ronald I. 1991. *The Order of Economic Liberalization.* Johns Hopkins University Press.

McKinsey and Company. 2002. "Global Investor Opinion Survey: Key Findings." Available at www.mckinsey.com/practices/CorporateGovernance/Research/ [July 2, 2003].

Mishkin, Frederic S. 2000. "Financial Market Reform." In Anne O. Krueger, ed., *Economic Policy Reform: The Second Stage.* University of Chicago Press.

Newell, Roberto, and Gregory Wilson. 2002. "A Premium for Good Governance." *McKinsey Quarterly* 3.

Radelet, Steven, and Jeffrey Sachs. 1998. "The East Asian Financial Crisis: Diagnosis, Remedies, Prospects." *Brookings Papers on Economic Activity 1,* 1–91.

Rodrik, Dani. 1998. "Who Needs Capital Account Convertibility?" *Princeton Essays in International Finance* 207: 55–65.

Sachs, Jeffrey, and Andrew Warner. 1995. "Economic Reform and the Process of Global Integration." *Brookings Papers on Economic Activity 1,* 1–95.

Shleifer, Andrei, and Robert W. Vishny. 1997. "A Survey of Corporate Governance." *Journal of Finance* 52 (2, June): 737–83.

Shleifer, Andrei, and Daniel Wolfenzon. 2002. "Investor Protection and Equity Markets." *Journal of Financial Economics* 66 (1, October): 3–27.

Solow, Robert M. 2001. "Applying Growth Theory across Countries." *World Bank Economic Review* 15 (2): 283–88.

Stiglitz, Joseph. 2002. *Globalization and Its Discontents.* W.W. Norton.

Stulz, René M. 1999. "Globalization of Equity Markets and the Cost of Capital." NYSE Working Paper 99-02. New York Stock Exchange.

Summers, Lawrence H. 2000. "International Financial Crises: Causes, Prevention, and Cures." *American Economic Review* 90 (2): 1–16.

Suttle, Philip. 2003. "Financial Flows to Developing Countries: Recent Trends and Near-Term Prospects." *Global Development Finance: Striving for Stability in Development Finance.* Washington: World Bank.

Tesar, Linda L., and Ingrid M. Werner. 1998. "The Internationalization of Securities Markets since the 1987 Crash." In Robert E. Litan and Anthony M. Santomero, eds., *Brookings Wharton Papers on Financial Services 1998.* Brookings.

Williamson, John. 1997. "Prospects for Avoiding Crises with Liberalized Capital Flows." *Estudios de Economía* 24 (2): 287–95.

Wurgler, Jeffrey. 2000. "Financial Markets and the Allocation of Capital." *Journal of Financial Economics* 58 (1, October): 187–214.

REENA AGGARWAL

8

Capital Market Development and Nurturing the IPO Market

Strong securities markets are necessary for the economic growth and development of any country. Efficient raising of capital and allocation of financial resources is an integral part of economic development. Recent literature documents the direct link between capital market development and economic growth. It also documents the essential role played by capital markets in improving corporate governance, disclosure standards, transparency in the marketplace, and accounting standards.[1] The optimal amount of transparency and regulation leads to market credibility and results in market growth. A sound regulatory framework is the cornerstone of vibrant financial markets. However, global competition is the force that is driving innovation in the markets.

The purpose of this paper is threefold. First, I analyze the impact of globalization and technological innovation on the development of securities markets, examining both the opportunities and the challenges facing emerging markets.[2] The evidence regarding challenges suggests that not all emerging markets should be lumped together. For example, the paper

1. For details, see Aggarwal (2001); Demirgüç-Kunt and Maksimovic (1998); Henry (2000a, 2000b); Levine (1997); Levine and Zervos (1998); Megginson and Boutchkova (2000).

2. Part of this paper draws on work done for the securities commissions of Ecuador, Mexico, and Peru on market microstructure, regulation, and registration process.

focuses specifically on policies for nurturing the market for initial public offerings (IPOs). However, the number of total listings has continued to grow in Asia but has consistently dropped in the emerging markets of Latin America, and the reasons need to be identified. Second, I briefly examine the changing sources of revenue for stock exchanges. Stock exchanges can no longer rely on their traditional sources of revenue. Listing fees have been a major source of revenue, and if the number of companies that list on the exchange decreases, then this source of revenue is further threatened. Therefore, exchanges must find ways to provide value added services efficiently. Finally, based on future trends in the markets, I offer thoughts on developing a strategy to nurture the market for initial public offerings in emerging markets.

Development of the IPO market is important for three primary reasons. The IPO process allows companies to raise much-needed capital. Small and medium-size companies play a major role in the economic growth of any country, and they need access to capital. Both firms and countries are interested in attracting investment to fuel growth. The additional demand for shares also helps to create liquidity for individual stocks and for the equity market within a country. This additional demand lowers firms' cost of capital and allows them to compete more effectively in the global marketplace, hence benefiting the economy of the country. Successful IPOs also add to the liquidity of the local exchange; hence new offerings generate more revenue from trading activities and contribute to listing fees earned by the exchanges. A vibrant stock market provides investment opportunities to domestic investors so that they can earn reasonable returns and hold diversified portfolios without incurring large transaction costs.

Securities markets are undergoing rapid transformation, brought about by globalization of the marketplace and by technological innovation. Globalization is both good news and bad news for emerging markets, posing both opportunities and challenges. Emerging markets have made significant progress in market infrastructure, institutions, and regulation. Computerized trading systems have been set up with expanded capacity and transparency. Market capitalization and trading volume increased significantly during the last ten years. World market capitalization increased from $9 trillion to $35 trillion between 1990 and 1999, before dropping off to $31 trillion in 2000, as shown in table 8-1. Similar growth is seen in the number of companies listed on stock exchanges. In 1990 a

Table 8-1. *Market Capitalization and Company Listings, 1990–2000*

Year	*Market capitalization (billions of U.S. dollars)*	*Number of companies listed*
1990	9,399	25,153
1991	11,178	24,980
1992	10,671	24,919
1993	13,677	26,453
1994	14,520	27,635
1995	17,124	28,345
1996	19,529	29,544
1997	21,722	30,289
1998	25,425	31,175
1999	34,988	34,548
2000	31,024	35,304

Source: World Federation of Exchanges' website: www.world-exchanges.org.

total of 25,153 companies were listed on exchanges, as reported by the World Federation of Exchanges. The number of companies listed grew to 35,304 by 2000. The depth and liquidity in the markets increased as well. Emerging markets also saw dramatic increases in market capitalization and listings during the early and mid-1990s. This growth in emerging markets was due to several factors, including privatizations, participation of foreign institutional investors, and growth in the base of domestic investors and in the number of issuers going to the market. Clearance and settlement systems became more efficient, and the regulatory framework experienced major changes, with countries adopting new securities laws and setting up independent regulatory agencies.

However, the outlook for emerging markets is not completely bright. The business of stock exchanges and the business of trading are global in nature. There are no "domestic" markets anymore, with the industry becoming truly global. Issuers raise capital wherever it is cheapest, and investors invest their money wherever it is most profitable. Globalization is at the root of some of the change, but technology is at the heart of many of the changes and is clearly the major force in today's marketplace. These developments are posing interesting challenges for emerging markets. Emerging markets have found that the large blue-chip companies have global access to capital and can list on the largest and most prestigious stock exchanges in the world. Even when they continue to be cross-listed on the domestic exchange, little trading takes place there. The stock is trading in the global marketplace, and meaningful price discovery occurs on the foreign exchange. This has dried up liquidity and decreased the number of listings on the local exchange, posing a challenge for domestic emerging-market exchanges. These developments also pose a challenge for small and medium-size firms that are trying to raise capital in the market. These firms do not have access to global capital markets, and a functioning local exchange is critical for their ability to raise capital.

Globalization

Physical trading floors have been replaced by electronic trading systems, and the Internet is playing a crucial role in the globalization of markets. Information is available quickly and cheaply, foreign markets are one mouse click away, and individual investors have as much access to the market as institutional investors. Issuers know of no national boundaries and want to raise capital wherever it is cheapest. Investors also want to invest globally to earn higher returns and diversify their portfolios. The rapid pace of global mergers in the financial services industry underlines the importance of global competition among financial intermediaries.

The U.S. equity markets made up 78 percent of world capitalization in 1970; by 1999, however, this market share had dropped to 45 percent. The share lost by the United States was partly due to the rise of trading in emerging markets. During this period, several new stock exchanges opened, particularly in the transition economies, and the stock markets of Asia and Latin America expanded and liberalized. The globalization of markets is also evident in the growth of depository programs, which have been increasing in both the number of issues and the size of the market (figure 8-1). Large depository programs from several emerging markets exist, and more are added every year.[3] Brazil, Mexico, and Taiwan have some of the most actively traded American Depository Receipts (ADRs). Emerging-market companies that trade in the United States frequently have been some of the most actively traded stocks.

Globalization is changing the nature of capital raising and securities trading. It is creating opportunities but also posing challenges. There is no doubt that emerging markets are integrating into the global financial sys-

3. Bank of New York's website: www.bony.com.

Figure 8-1. *Depository Receipt Programs, 1998–2002*

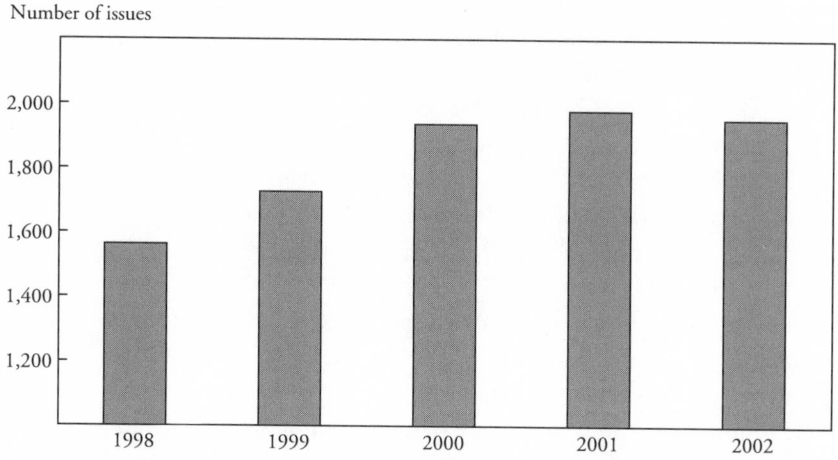

tem, but the real questions are whether they are ready and how they will be affected by globalization. I use Latin America as an example of the impact of globalization. Latin American countries and firms operating in the region have experienced the benefits of globalization, and they have had to deal with the associated challenges. Twenty-four Mexican companies are listed on the New York Stock Exchange, thirty-three trade in the over-the-counter market, eight trade in London, one trades on Nasdaq, and two trade on Amex.[4] The trading activity of foreigners has grown significantly on the Mexican Bolsa. Foreign investors owned 27 percent of Mexican capitalization in 1995, 43 percent in 1999, and 44 percent in the first seven months of 2000 alone. Nine foreign brokers were operating in Mexico: ABN Amro Securities, Bankers Trust, BBV-Probursa, Chase, Deutsche Bank, Goldman Sachs, ING Barings, Merrill Lynch, and Santander Mexicano. Prudential also operates in Mexico as an independent fund manager. The significant participation of foreign investors and financial intermediaries in the Mexican market and the issuance of Mexican ADRs and Global Depository Receipts in foreign markets are evidence of integration.

Latin America also illustrates the challenges of globalization because the region has been hurt by its own success. The loss of trading activity in

4. Presentation by Jorge Familiar Calderón, Comisión Nacional Bancaria y de Valores, Mexico, at Georgetown University's Alternative Structures for Securities Markets International Conference, September 2000.

blue-chip stocks, low liquidity, and decline in the number of primary offerings are raising questions about the future of Latin bourses.

Table 8-2 shows the number of companies listed in emerging stock markets of Latin America and Asia from 1990 to 2000. The number of companies listed declined for almost all markets in Latin America during this period. In Mexico 390 companies were listed in 1990 and only 177 in 2000; in Argentina 179 companies were listed in 1990 and only 125 in 2000; in Brazil 579 companies were listed in 1990 and only 467 in 2000. Listings in Peru peaked at 249 in 1998, dropping to 227 in 2000. Chile reached a high of 294 in 1997, falling to 261 in 2000.

The stock exchanges of Asia have not suffered as dramatically in terms of listings as those of Latin America. Listings in some Asian countries are off their peaks, but not as dramatically as in Argentina, Brazil, and Mexico. The number of listings in Malaysia, the Philippines, and Taiwan peaked in 2000. Korea saw a drop from its peak of 776 in 1997 to 702 in 2000, and listings dropped in Thailand from a high of 454 in 1996 to 381 in 2000. The Asian exchanges were hurt by the Asian financial crisis and the resulting loss of confidence, but the stock exchanges have recovered from those problems. Overall, the scenario does not look too bleak for Asian exchanges with respect to total listings. In particular, the trend is different in Asia than in Latin America, where the number of listings fell consistently. Total listings can decline for two main reasons: (1) new firms are not listing because IPOs are not taking place or (2) existing firms are delisting for various reasons. Some of these delistings are due to mergers and acquisitions. I later examine new listings on each exchange.

Table 8-3 presents the market capitalization of firms listed on the emerging-market exchanges from 1990 to 2000. The market capitalization is presented in U.S. dollars, so the value reflects the performance of the bolsas as well as fluctuations in the local currency relative to the U.S. dollar. Due to the stock market slump and currency movements, market capitalization was lower in 2000 than in 1996 for most Asian countries. The drop in stock prices was of concern to both developing and developed markets during this period. Despite large fluctuations over the years, market capitalization was less problematic than the number of listings. Market capitalization did not follow a consistently downward trend, and many of the large blue-chip companies from emerging markets continued to trade successfully in foreign markets.

Table 8-2. *Total Number of Listings, Excluding Investment Funds, on Asian and Latin American Exchanges, 1990–2000*

Exchange	*1990*	*1991*	*1992*	*1993*	*1994*	*1995*	*1996*	*1997*	*1998*	*1999*	*2000*
Mexico	390	207	199	190	206	185	193	198	195	190	177
Buenos Aires	179	170	170	165	156	149	147	136	131	125	125
Lima	n.a.	n.a.	n.a.	235	220	243	238	248	249	239	227
Santiago	216	223	244	263	277	282	290	294	287	282	261
São Paulo	579	570	565	551	549	544	551	545	535	487	467
Jakarta	123	139	153	172	217	237	252	281	287	276	286
Korea	677	686	688	693	699	721	760	776	748	712	702
Kuala Lumpur	271	321	366	410	475	526	618	703	731	752	790
Philippines	153	161	169	178	189	205	216	221	222	226	230
Taiwan	205	221	256	285	313	347	382	404	437	462	531
Thailand	159	270	305	347	389	416	454	431	418	392	381

Source: World Federation of Exchanges.
n.a. Not available.

Sources of Revenue for Stock Exchanges

Exchanges in emerging markets must find a way to survive in the global architecture. They must respond to change and innovate in order to survive. Traditional methods of trading securities will soon be outdated. The typical sources of revenue (listing, transactions, and information) are likely to decline in importance. For example, there is no reason to believe that listing will continue to be a major source of revenue. Similarly, technology has already made information inexpensive, and exchanges do not have the luxury of relying on the provision of data as a major source of revenue. Systems that can attract trading volume by their design, costs, and ability to provide liquidity will be the winners. These do not have to be exchanges.

Several exchanges around the world have demutualized in recent years. Listing fees are a smaller proportion of revenue for demutualized exchanges relative to other types of exchange structures.[5] In the future, all exchanges

5. World Federation of Exchanges (2001).

Table 8-3. *Market Capitalization on Asian and Latin American Exchanges, 1990–2000*

Millions of U.S. dollars

Exchange	*1990*	*1991*	*1992*	*1993*	*1994*	*1995*	*1996*	*1997*	*1998*	*1999*	*2000*
Mexico	41,054	102,764	138,745	200,865	130,246	90,694	106,770	156,595	91,746	154,044	125,204
Buenos Aires	3,615	18,640	18,623	44,055	36,867	37,784	44,692	59,252	45,333	55,848	45,839
Brazil	11,201	32,152	45,416	96,779	189,303	147,636	216,906	255,478	160,886	227,962	226,152
Lima	812	1,118	2,630	5,113	8,178	10,907	12,583	15,485	9,869	12,092	9,750
Santiago	13,636	27,990	29,595	44,887	68,195	72,928	65,971	72,046	51,866	68,228	60,401
Jakarta	8,081	6,823	12,038	32,824	47,241	66,454	90,857	29,050	22,078	64,045	26,813
Korea	110,301	96,466	107,661	139,584	191,778	181,955	139,122	41,881	114,593	306,128	148,361
Kuala Lumpur	47,869	56,722	91,471	219,759	190,163	213,757	306,165	93,174	95,561	139,908	113,155
Philippines	6,632	10,835	15,335	40,148	56,648	58,780	80,464	31,211	34,911	41,536	25,261
Taiwan	98,927	123,460	100,166	193,252	247,325	187,206	273,776	287,813	260,498	376,508	247,597
Thailand	20,777	37,526	57,278	127,474	125,599	135,774	95,901	22,792	34,118	57,177	29,217

Source: World Federation of Exchanges.

will need to be concerned about the drop in revenue from listing fees because, as exchanges compete for listings, the fee from listing is likely to drop.

The trend in revenue sources is toward a larger proportion being derived from trading and services and a smaller proportion being derived from listing fees. As exchanges are challenged to meet the demands of multinational issuers and international investors, they have converged to form regional and global alliances. These alliances and partnerships become particularly important for emerging markets to reduce costs and offer more services to their clients. So far, there has been a lot of talk about alliances and partnerships and even mergers. In reality, due to political, social, and economic differences, it is hard to make these structures functional. Major regulatory differences between countries complicate the task of harmonization. Even in Europe, integration has been difficult to achieve and has evolved over decades.

The IPO Market

This paper focuses specifically on the new listings market. The primary market is extremely important for raising capital, particularly for small and medium-size firms. When there is no inflow of new companies and large companies are leaving the domestic market and obtaining foreign listings, this creates a real financial problem for the domestic exchanges. Table 8-4 lists the number of new listings in 1995, 1996, 2000, and 2001 to show the trend in new listings during the last six years. In every Latin American country—Argentina, Brazil, Chile, Mexico, and Peru—the number of new listings was lower in 2000–01 than in 1995–96. IPO listings also slowed in many developed markets during 2000–01. However, in the case of the developed markets, large companies are not moving away from the domestic exchange. Also, in the developed markets, the trend is a short-term response to the global economic slowdown. For most countries in Asia, a drop in new listings is observed mainly for 2001. The recent turmoil in the global markets subsequent to the U.S. war on terrorism and the bursting of the Internet bubble has affected both developed and emerging markets adversely.

Primary-market activity requires appropriate policies both at the country level and at the firm level. Exchanges and firms can take several steps to increase primary-market activity. However, these actions cannot be taken

Table 8-4. *Number of New Listings on Asian and Latin American Exchanges, Select Years, 1995–2001*

Exchange	*1995*	*1996*	*2000*	*2001*
Mexico	1	14	2	4
Buenos Aires	7	7	10	3
Lima	31	33	18	12
Santiago	12	14	5	3
São Paulo	24	26	24	10
Jakarta	21	16	21	31
Korea	28	51	5	16
Kuala Lumpur	51	92	38	20
Philippines	16	13	7	3
Taiwan	41	36	80	70
Thailand	28	40	2	10

Source: World Federation of Exchanges.

in isolation. Ultimately, the country's broad macroeconomic policies, legal systems, and equity culture will determine whether primary markets, and therefore the secondary markets, will succeed. Aggarwal, Klapper, and Wysocki examine the attributes of countries and firms to which foreign investors allocate a relatively large proportion of their assets.[6] They find that foreign investors invest more in emerging-market countries that have better corporate governance than in those with a poor record of corporate governance. They also find more investment in firms that have higher transparency and disclosure after controlling for other factors. The authors conclude that steps can be taken at both the country and the firm levels to attract foreign investors. Some of the important factors necessary for primary-market development are discussed below.

Country-Level Factors

Growth in gross domestic product (GDP) and investment are closely related for countries. As growth occurs in any industry segment, demand increases, and this leads to investment by companies. Companies need to finance this investment through either debt or equity. Levine and Zervos find economic growth and stock market development to be significantly related.[7]

6. Aggarwal, Klapper, and Wysocki (2002).

7. Levine and Zervos (1998).

Strong shareholder protection laws that protect the interest of minority shareholders and strong enforcement of these laws are important to gain the confidence of both domestic and foreign shareholders. Research by La Porta, López-de-Silanes, Shleifer, and Vishny concludes that strong investor protection laws and enforcement policies lead to greater capital market development, as measured by the ratio of market capitalization to GDP.[8]

Market- and Firm-Level Factors

Transparency and disclosure are key determinants of asset prices and should play an important role in primary-market development. Investors are more willing to invest if firms are more transparent and disclose more information.

Better information should lead to more primary-market activity if its impact on investors more than offsets the costs that are implied for issuers. Aggarwal, Klapper, and Wysocki find the quality of accounting of companies, as measured by the quality of auditor and accounting standards, to be significant in explaining foreign investment.[9] Firms can adopt strong accounting practices even if they are not legally obligated to comply with international standards.

The cost of equity capital also plays an important role in primary-market activity, as discussed by Aylward and Glen.[10] As the cost of capital increases (decreases), issuers should be willing to issue less (more) capital. If stocks perform well and prices move higher, companies will issue more equity. However, the performance of stock prices is also tied to macroeconomic factors.

Many countries still do not have an equity culture. Companies therefore borrow money rather than raise capital when financing is required.

Capital markets may be over-regulated so as to keep issuers and investors away. Market entry may be restricted in various ways: by type of investor (for example, individuals, corporations, or funds), by the investor's country of origin, or by the class of shares available to foreigners. There may be outright prohibitions on investment in equity, or foreign invest-

8. La Porta and others (1998).
9. Aggarwal, Klapper, and Wysocki (2002).
10. Aylward and Glen (1999).

ment may be subject to discriminatory regulations concerning minimum holding periods or repatriation rights over capital and income.[11]

Policies for Nurturing the IPO Market

This section discusses specific steps that can be taken to strengthen the development of the IPO market. The recommendations are divided into two groups: policies that can be adopted at the country level and steps that can be taken by firms attempting to go public.

Country-Level Issues

Regulators must give careful thought to the information to be reported in the prospectus. There should be sufficient information so that investors can make an educated decision about investing in the stock. This becomes particularly important for IPO companies that are new and about which there is little information.

Underwriters, lawyers, and corporate officers should be held legally responsible for providing accurate information to investors. If investors perceive that the parties involved have not provided all material information or have manipulated the market, they will be less likely to participate.

Liquidity is also important; therefore, it is important for firms to sell a sufficient number of shares in an IPO. The float in emerging markets is on average 40–50 percent, and this itself poses a problem. At the time of the IPO, the float will be even lower, and this may reduce the interest of both institutional and retail investors who need liquidity. If the stock does not have sufficient liquidity, then the stock price may not be a perfect measure of its valuation. Regulators may want to examine the issue of minimum float at the time of the IPO.

The costs of going public are high in most emerging markets, and economies of scale are important. Therefore, it is difficult and costly for very small companies to go public. Regulators should help to reduce these costs. For example, electronic filings and prospectuses should be encouraged in order to save on the costs of printing. Aggarwal and Dahiya discuss the role of the Internet in the capital-raising process.[12]

11. For example, see Aylward and Glen (1999).

12. Aggarwal and Dahiya (2000).

There is considerable discussion and controversy about the method that should be used to go public. The discussion has focused on the benefits of the auction method versus book building. In the auction method, the price is determined using an auction process, and there is little flexibility in allocating shares. In book building, issuers and underwriters have a great deal of flexibility in pricing and allocations. However, the large underpricing of IPOs during the Internet bubble has opened the debate regarding both methods. The two countries that use auctions as the primary IPO method are Israel and Taiwan, both of which ban book building. Most countries, including Argentina, China, Hong Kong, Hungary, Korea, and Peru, use book building as the primary method.[13] Regulators should examine the methods used in their own country and develop an approach that is best suited to the country.

Underwriters should consider a lock-up period during which insiders of the firm are not allowed to sell shares. The fact that insiders are not selling out increases the confidence of investors. However, the lock-up period cannot be too long. In the United States, the lock-up period is typically 180 days. This is not a regulatory requirement, but an agreement between management and underwriters. In India, a three-year lock-up period is required by regulation. This seems excessive and might create incentives for insiders to bypass the requirement in some other way.

Firms should consider granting an over-allotment option to the underwriters. The over-allotment option allows underwriters to buy from the firm additional shares at the offer price. Normally, the over-allotment option has a maximum value of 15 percent. It allows the underwriter to stabilize the IPO indirectly, if needed. However, underwriters should not be permitted to hold these shares for their own account. Regulators should consider the possibility of allowing this option in their countries.

Steps should be taken to develop the investment banking and underwriting industry. Underwriters play an important role in helping companies to go public. Underwriters should be required to perform due diligence, they should be required to be market makers in the stock, and they should be required to provide research coverage for the firm. This would improve the after-market liquidity of the stock and ensure that sufficient information about the firm is available.

Banks frequently have an extensive network in emerging markets. Therefore, the role banks can play in helping to nurture the new issues

13. See Sherman (2002) for details.

market should be explored. Banks might have a lending relationship with the firm going public and therefore be able to monitor the firm better. However, if banks act as lenders and investment banks, conflicts of interest may arise.

Finally, steps need to be taken to develop the venture capital industry further. Venture capitalists eventually need an exit mechanism, and an IPO is a method for them to exit.

Firm-Level Issues

Firms must "prepare" to go public. This might involve changing the corporate structure of the firm; adopting appropriate accounting practices; bringing in venture capitalists; bringing in strategic partners, such as the International Finance Corporation or other large, well-known companies; selecting a reputable investment banking firm; and bringing visibility to the firm and its business.

The IPO needs to be structured properly. The IPO should not be thought of as a one-step process. It is the start of a process and continues after the company has become public. Underwriters can help the firm with the registration process, due diligence, valuation, "selling" of the IPO, market making, and issuance of research reports.[14] The role of the underwriter in market making and research reports after the IPO will be important for after-market liquidity of the stock. It is important to consider the number of shares that will be sold in the IPO, as selling too few shares can create liquidity problems in after-market trading.

With the help of the underwriter, firms must choose the method with which to go public. Auction and book-building methods each have pros and cons that need to be considered. Firms should leave some "money on the table," but excessive underpricing is not in the best interest of shareholders.

The participation of both retail and institutional investors is needed for the IPO market to succeed. Therefore, steps should be taken to encourage participation by both retail and institutional customers. In several emerging markets, IPO activity has been fueled by retail customers rather than by institutional customers.

Firms can take steps to protect the rights of minority shareholders that invest in an IPO. This can be done in several ways. For example, firms

14. The IPO process and the role of the underwriter are discussed in Aggarwal (2000, 2003); Aggarwal and Conroy (2002); and Aggarwal, Prabhala, and Puri (2003).

should be cautious in issuing several classes of stock with different voting rights. The board of the firm can be structured appropriately to address corporate governance issues. It is up to the firm to choose the degree of transparency and disclosure that it wants to provide. The firm does not need to be restricted by the requirements of the country. For example, the firm can use international accounting standards even if this is not a requirement.

Several factors can boost investor interest and result in a successful IPO market in emerging markets. Some factors, such as the level of economic development, the development of the domestic market, the number of restrictions on investors, and the adequacy of investor protection laws for participants in both primary and secondary markets, need to be addressed at the country level. However, firms themselves can take steps to improve the probability that their IPO will succeed.

Market participants have cited a number of reasons for the recent lack of equity issues in emerging markets:

—The window of opportunity for issuing emerging-market equities is typically linked to developments in mature markets. Weak performance and high volatility in mature markets (such as Nasdaq) have a negative impact on emerging-market issuers.

—There is some degree of disillusionment with emerging-market equities because, as an asset class, they have yielded negative returns since 1996 (with the exception of 1999), as measured by the Morgan Stanley Capital International Emerging Markets Free Index.

—The small size of some emerging equity markets (where a few companies represent a large share of market capitalization) and their lack of liquidity are also discouraging foreign investors.

—There is disappointment with the lack of progress in the treatment of minority shareholders, and other concerns regarding corporate governance.

Conclusions

Competition among exchanges is heating up on a global scale. I use the term "exchange" in a broad sense. Securities markets are undergoing tremendous changes. It is not clear who the winners will be five years from now. Will the traditional exchange even survive? How will the role of exchanges be modified? What additional value added services will they provide? Will every country have a stock exchange, and does every country need a stock exchange? How will exchanges in emerging markets compete with the big players? Will there be regional markets? It will be interesting to see what kinds of alliances and partnerships become fruitful and how consolidation in the industry shapes up.

Emerging markets need to have a strategy to compete in this global marketplace. Integration in the global system is a fact; the challenge is how best to prepare for it. The new issues market is important not only for the survival of exchanges but also for their functioning. Exchanges ultimately enable firms to raise capital. In a global marketplace, if large companies move to large foreign exchanges, we must concern ourselves with how small and medium-size firms will be able to raise capital.

The purpose of this paper has been to discuss strategies to foster the primary market. Developing a vibrant IPO market will not be easy: it will require coordinated policies at the country level and steps at the firm level. The local or regional markets are important for the capital needs of small and medium-size firms that do not have access to global capital. These firms are major drivers of economic growth in a country. In addition to development of the IPO market, countries also need to take steps to develop the venture capital industry and the private equity markets.

References

Aggarwal, Reena. 2000. "Stabilization Activities by Underwriters after New Offerings." *Journal of Finance* 55 (3, June): 1075–104.

———. 2001. "Capital Market Development: Strategies for Latin America and Caribbean." Paper prepared for the conference on A New Focus for Capital Market Development in Latin America and the Caribbean, Inter-American Development Bank, Washington, February 5–6.

———. 2003. "Allocation of Initial Public Offering and Flipping Activity." *Journal of Financial Economics* 68 (1): 111–35.

Aggarwal, Reena, and Patrick Conroy. 2000. "Price Discovery in Initial Public Offerings and the Role of the Lead Underwriter." *Journal of Finance* 55 (6, December): 2903–22.

Aggarwal, Reena, and Sandeep Dahiya. 2000. "Capital Formation and the Internet." *Journal of Applied Corporate Finance* 13 (1, Spring): 108–13.

Aggarwal, Reena, Leora Klapper, and Peter D. Wysocki. 2002. "Portfolio Preferences of Foreign Institutional Investors and Corporate Governance." Working Paper. Georgetown University.

Aggarwal, Reena, Nagpurnanand Prabhala, and Manju Puri. 2002. "Allocation and Price Support in IPOs: Who Benefits?" *Journal of Finance* 57 (3, June): 1421–42.

Aylward, Anthony, and Jack Glen. 1999. *Primary Securities Markets: Cross-Country Findings.* IFC Discussion Paper 39. Washington: International Finance Corporation, June.

Demirgüç-Kunt, Aslı, and Vojislav Maksimovic. 1998. "Law, Finance, and Firm Growth." *Journal of Finance* 53 (6, December): 2107–39.

Henry, Peter Blair. 2000a. "Do Stock Market Liberalizations Cause Investment Booms?" *Journal of Financial Economics* 58 (1, October): 301–34.

———. 2000b. "Stock Market Liberalization, Economic Reform, and Emerging Market Equity Prices." *Journal of Finance* 55 (2, April): 529–64.

La Porta, Rafael, Florencio López-de-Silanes, Andrei Shleifer, and Robert Vishny. 1998. "Law and Finance." *Journal of Political Economy* 106 (6): 1115–55.

Levine, Ross. 1997. "Financial Development and Economic Growth: Views and Agenda." *Journal of Economic Literature* 35 (2): 688–726.

Levine, Ross, and Sara Zervos. 1998. "Stock Markets, Banks, and Economic Growth." *American Economic Review* 88 (3): 537–58.

Megginson, William L., and Maria K. Boutchkova. 2000. "Privatization and the Rise of Global Capital Markets." *Financial Management* 29 (Winter): 31–76.

Sherman, Ann E. 2002. "Global Trends in IPO Methods: Book Building versus Auctions." Working Paper. University of Notre Dame, Department of Finance and Business Economics.

World Federation of Exchanges. 2001. *Cost and Revenue Survey.* December. Available at www.world-exchanges.org/WFE/home.asp?menu=11&document=1638 [June 12, 2003].

CEM KARACADAG
V. SUNDARARAJAN
JENNIFER ELLIOTT

9

Managing Risks in Financial Market Development: The Role of Sequencing

Domestic financial markets are a critical pillar of a market-based economy. They can mobilize and intermediate savings, allocate risk, absorb external financial shocks, and foster good governance through market-based incentives. As such, they contribute to more stable investment financing, higher economic growth, lower macroeconomic volatility, and greater financial stability. The development of local financial markets also reduces the risks associated with excessive reliance on foreign capital, including currency and maturity mismatches.[1] Key, but heretofore largely unanswered, questions concern the optimal path and sequencing of reforms to develop domestic financial markets and how these reforms should be coordinated with capital account liberalization. Despite a rich literature on capital account issues, no attempt has been made to provide an overarching framework for financial liberalization, with domestic financial market development at its epicenter.

Strategies to develop local financial markets must revolve around mitigating risks injected into the financial system as markets develop and

1. Prasad and others (2003) note that developing economies have taken measures to "self-insure" against volatile capital flows and asset prices by improving the sovereign management of external asset liability, modifying exchange rate regimes, strengthening banking soundness and the prudential framework, and developing local financial markets.

become more sophisticated. The liberalization of financial transactions and capital flows, aimed at deepening capital markets, invariably increases risks that often result in financial distress and crisis. Domestic and external financial reforms thus need to be sequenced so that the central bank and financial institutions (as well as the infrastructure that supports them) develop the capacity to manage the risks associated with a wider range of permissible financial transactions, investible instruments, and loanable funds. The goal of orderly sequencing is to safeguard monetary and financial stability during financial liberalization and market development.

Against this background, this chapter presents five theses.

First, capital market development–cum–financial stability hinges on establishing the institutional infrastructure for controlling both macroeconomic and financial risks. Macroeconomic risk management requires effective instruments and institutions for the implementation of monetary and exchange policy, including well-functioning money, foreign exchange, and government debt markets.[2] Financial risk management depends on high standards of corporate governance, accounting, and disclosure and high standards of prudential regulation and supervision. These institutional reforms are critical to fostering an environment in which capital markets can grow, without undermining financial stability.

Second, financial liberalization and market development should revolve around the hierarchy and complementarity of markets and related institutional structures. Markets are hierarchically ordered, starting with money markets, followed by foreign exchange, treasury bill and bond markets, and, ultimately, markets for corporate bonds and equity and for asset-backed securities and derivatives. The hierarchy reflects the degree and complexity of risks created by each market. The hierarchy also incorporates the interaction among markets that links the depth of one market to the depth of other markets.

Third, capital market development requires a careful sequencing of measures to mitigate risks, in parallel with reforms to develop markets. Risks evolve into more complex forms and grow in magnitude as markets develop, especially as new instruments and institutions emerge. These risks cannot be managed effectively in the absence of well-functioning markets at earlier stages in the hierarchy. Thus a critical mass of reforms encom-

2. Ishii and Habermeier (2002); Ingves (2002).

passing both market development and risk mitigation at every stage of the market hierarchy is necessary to avoid increases in financial system fragility and macroeconomic vulnerability.

Fourth, institutional development is a critical component of building capital markets and financial risk management capacity. Financial institutions—both bank and nonbank—are the key counterparties in financial markets. They often create and transmit risks. As such, establishing good governance structures, including effective internal controls and risk management systems in financial institutions, is among the most critical of market reforms.

Fifth, capital account liberalization can play an important role in deepening domestic financial markets. However, foreign capital may complement, but cannot substitute for, a domestic investor base. Before capital from abroad can play a constructive role, critical mass must be reached in terms of the depth of domestic markets, the diversity of local investors, the effective oversight and governance of market institutions, and the length and distribution of instrument maturities.

Admittedly, there are trade-offs between having good domestic institutions in place before undertaking capital market liberalization, on the one hand, and opening the capital account to import best practices to strengthen domestic institutions, on the other hand.[3] Thus ultimately, there is no single optimal speed and order of measures to promote local financial markets and their integration with global markets. The pace and sequencing need to be decided in the context of country-specific circumstances and institutional characteristics. This chapter highlights some of the best practices and considerations on sequencing of institutional and operational reforms based on cross-country experience.

The remainder of the chapter is organized as follows. The next section identifies the key institutional reforms needed to develop financial markets. The third section outlines the specific structural and operational steps to build different segments of financial markets, guided by the hierarchy and interdependence of markets. The fourth section focuses on specific additional risks that need to be monitored and controlled when individual markets develop. The final section combines the analysis of market development and risk mitigation into a set of general principles for sequencing financial market development and capital account liberalization.

3. Prasad and others (2003).

Institutional Reforms for Capital Market Development

The financial crises of the 1990s underscored the critical importance of institutional factors in determining countries' vulnerability to economic distress and crisis. Structural weaknesses—including those in prudential supervision, banking soundness, judicial enforcement, and accounting and disclosure—and market failures are among the key sources of financial instability (box 9-1).[4] Structural weaknesses also relate to deficiencies both in the institutional infrastructure for macroeconomic management and control and in the functioning and integrity of financial markets.

A separate strand of literature on capital account liberalization also finds that its intended benefits—financial market development and economic growth—are realized in proportion to a country's level of institutional development.[5] The rule of law, shareholder protection, adequate prudential regulation and supervision, and financial transparency are significant determinants of whether capital account openness benefits or harms financial market development and economic growth. The development and liberalization of financial institutions themselves can lead to the loss of macroeconomic control due to excessive credit expansion and large fiscal deficits (for example, through the realization of contingent liabilities), underscoring the importance of those aspects of institutional reforms that reinforce fiscal and monetary control.

The Hierarchy of Markets and Financial Market Development

Financial markets are hierarchically ordered (figure 9-1). The money market precedes all others, given its central role in price discovery and in the setting and transmission of interest rates. The foreign exchange market's early place in the hierarchy stems from its unique role as the "entry" or "intermediate" market through which nonresidents must pass to enter all other local financial markets.[6] The money market is also critical to devel-

4. See Ishii and Habermeier (2002).

5. See Arteta, Eichengreen, and Wyplosz (2001); Chin and Ito (2002); Edwards (2001). Also see papers cited in Prasad and others (2003) that provide evidence for the view that "countries need to build a certain amount of absorptive capacity in order to effectively take advantage of financial globalization" (Prasad and others 2003, p. 51).

6. Foreign exchange market activity, more than that of other financial markets, is also a function of current and capital account regulations, which determine the permissible transactions and uses of foreign exchange.

Box 9-1. *Lessons from Recent Financial Crises*

Some of the lessons learned from recent financial crises underscore the importance of the following:

—*Instruments and markets for monetary control and sound public finances.* Shortcomings in monetary policy instruments and financial markets—including money, foreign exchange, and government securities markets—can impede monetary control by the central bank as well as price discovery and risk management by financial and nonfinancial firms. They also can lead to excessive government borrowing from the central bank.

—*Effective prudential regulation, supervision, and enforcement.* In particular, prudential regulation and supervision need to be strengthened in line with the growing complexity of financial markets and risks and the diversity of financial institutions and products. Moreover, the supervisory framework and enforcement mechanisms are a critical source of external discipline on banks and essential to developing a credit and risk culture in the financial system.

—*Financial market infrastructure.* Adequate and well-enforced contracts, insolvency procedures, governance structures, and accounting and disclosure standards are necessary to the functioning of financial markets and to the building of confidence in their integrity.

—*Monetary and financial policy transparency, clearly defined institutional responsibilities, and central bank autonomy.* Both the supervisory agency and central bank need the strength and independence to pursue their objectives of financial sector soundness and price stability rigorously and consistently. In this context, the specific rules and lines of accountability for central bank lending need to be established to avoid the loss of monetary control that occurred in some countries during the Asian crisis.

—*Robust payment settlement arrangements.* The absence of reliable and safe payment settlement arrangements can weaken monetary control and exacerbate systemic risks. Such arrangements are critical for ensuring liquidity and the smooth functioning of markets.

—*Reliable and timely information on the financial and nonfinancial sectors.* Central banks, supervisory agencies, and finance ministries rely on financial information to evaluate and monitor financial sector soundness. Similarly, banks and investors rely on financial information to assess and monitor the creditworthiness of counterparties, borrowers, and issuers of shares. Absent high accounting standards and good financial information, neither macroeconomic control nor financial market development can be achieved or sustained.

Figure 9-1. *Hierarchical Order of Domestic Financial Markets*

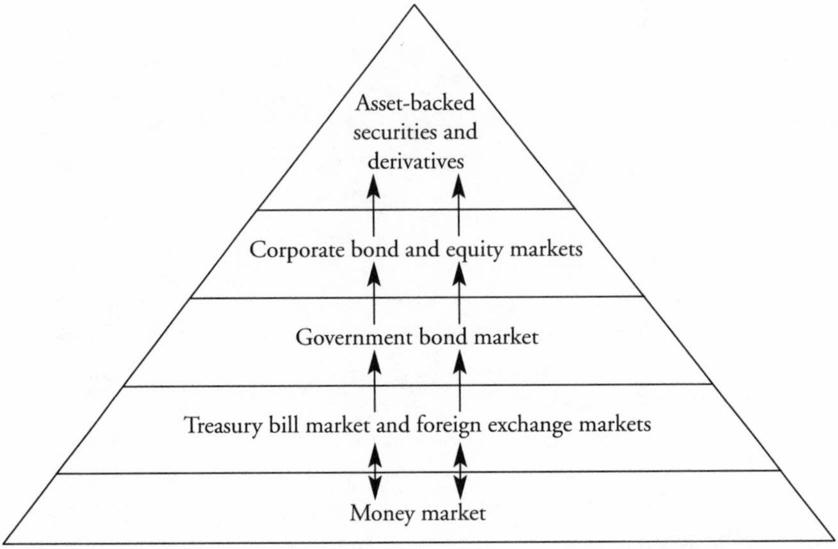

oping the market for government debt securities, first at the short end and then at the long end, given that the market for longer-term securities carries more complex risks than short-term paper and depends on money markets to support the liquidity needs of market makers. A well-developed government bond market, in turn, is a necessary condition for developing markets in corporate debt and asset-backed securities. Finally, the derivatives market requires liquid and efficient markets in underlying fixed-income or equity markets.

Financial markets, particularly money and government bond markets, are also highly interdependent. A liquid money market, for example, helps the operation of the foreign exchange market and the effective implementation of monetary policy, both of which have a strong bearing on the efficiency and depth of the money market itself. At the same time, a liquid money market depends on adequate depth in the government securities market and vice versa. Depth in one market cannot be achieved without depth in the other.

Policies to develop financial markets thus should be sequenced in a manner that observes these hierarchies and interdependencies and takes into account three additional key factors. First, measures that have long gestation periods, such as developing a domestic investor base, restructuring weak financial institutions, and building a robust financial infrastructure (including a legal, accounting, and insolvency framework), need to be initiated early on. Bond and equity market development, in particular, depends on the presence of a domestic investor base. Second, the framework for prudential supervision and market conduct needs to evolve in line with the pace and pattern of market development. Third, the overall strategy for capital market development must take into account the size and wealth constraints of a country.

Money Market Development

The money market is the foundation of all financial and capital markets. It is the medium through which the central bank injects and withdraws liquidity and steers short-term interest rates. It is also the medium through which financial institutions manage their liquidity by lending to and borrowing from one another. As such, it is critical to price discovery in a free interest rate environment and to the transmission of monetary policies through the credit channel. Countries that embark on interest rate liberalization often start with freeing money market rates, followed by lending and deposit rates.

The central bank plays a key role in money market development.[7] Early in the process, the central bank should begin developing new monetary instruments (such as treasury bills, central bank bills, and central bank auctions), reforming the system of reserve requirements, and designing the terms and conditions of access to standing facilities.[8] Central bank policies and standing facilities should be designed and conducted in a manner that creates incentives for market participants to trade money among themselves before trading with the central bank. The central bank must also ensure that there is a two-way market in bank reserves and short-term funds by avoiding protracted periods of excess reserves and by alleviating systemic liquidity shortages. Similarly, it should avoid simply reacting to the initiative of financial institutions, but instead anticipate surpluses and deficits in the market and provide liquidity at its own initiative, leaving market participants to trade among themselves during normal times. To manage systemic liquidity effectively, the central bank must have the technical capacity to forecast liquidity and possess the instruments to inject and withdraw funds from the market.

7. Mehran and Laurens (1997).
8. Bisat, Johnston, and Sundararajan (1999).

Money market development depends on the soundness of financial institutions. In the absence of creditworthy counterparties, market participants would be reluctant to deal in the interbank market, but instead would transact solely with the central bank. Market participants, therefore, should be able to assess one another's creditworthiness on the basis of timely disclosure of reliable financial information, underpinned by high-quality accounting standards and widespread use of external audits. In order to enhance liquidity, participation in the market can be broadened to include sound nonbank financial institutions.

Repurchase agreements (repos) are an essential instrument for money market development.[9] For central banks, repos are a key tool for indirect monetary control and daily liquidity management, especially before an active secondary market for government securities develops.[10] Whereas "outright" purchases and sales of securities by the central bank require a secondary market in (government) securities, repos allow the central bank to adjust its balance sheet and systemic liquidity without a secondary market. Repos also offer flexibility in the duration and timing of the central bank's liquidity management operations, because they can be effected with little notice, for very short periods of time, and without the need to create treasury bills in shorter maturities than those already issued. Reducing the issuance of new treasury bills in different maturities can help to deepen secondary markets in existing securities.

Repos are particularly important in money market development, where counterparty credit risks are high. As collateralized instruments, repos facilitate interbank lending by minimizing the credit risk exposure of each counterparty, which reduces the dispersion of interbank lending rates and the segmentation of the interbank market.[11] If the cash borrower fails to repay its loan, the lending institution is already in possession of the collateral underlying the repo operation. Without secured lending, the interbank market would be adversely affected by bank-by-bank exposure limits. Repos also have the important advantage of facilitating the acquisition of

9. A repo is a collateralized loan that is effected through the sale and subsequent repurchase of a security at a specified date and price. It is a combination of an immediate sale of a security for cash with an agreement to reverse the transaction at a specified future date, typically from overnight to two weeks.

10. Green (1997).

11. Repos may be based on any security, although in practice most repos involve government securities. The absence of a secondary market in government securities is not an impediment to using repos, but it may impair the liquidation value of the underlying collateral, which may result in the application of a larger discount to the collateral by the lender.

credit and interest risk management skills by banks without exposing them to large (principal) losses. From the central bank's perspective, repos have the advantage of enabling liquidity management operations without triggering the unwanted volatility in bond prices and yield curve that outright operations are likely to cause.[12]

Prudential supervision and payment settlement system regulations play important roles in developing the money market by guarding against risky market practices and fraud. For example, participants in the repo market should meet predetermined criteria, such as minimum capital requirements and the capacity to observe market practices and manage market risks. Moreover, regulations, particularly related to the book-entry system for repurchased securities, should ensure that repo transactions are recorded and conducted in a supervised and transparent manner and that the ownership of the related securities is effectively transferred. The design and oversight of the payment system, particularly for settling money market and other large-value transactions, can help to contain systemic risks and foster market liquidity.[13]

An active money market is a prerequisite for the development of markets in foreign exchange and in government securities.[14] The money market not only supports the bond market by increasing the liquidity of securities but also makes it cheaper and less risky for financial institutions to warehouse government securities for sale to investors and to fund trading portfolios of government securities. When the money market is illiquid and interest rates are volatile, investors in bonds face greater market risks, which limit their ability to invest in long-term assets.[15] At the same time, however, money markets are interdependent with securities markets. Deeper money markets can be facilitated by the availability of a wide range of high-grade securities, which can serve as collateral in interbank lending and are easy to liquidate in the event of counterparty defaults.

Foreign Exchange Market Development

The foreign exchange market is similar to the money market but differs in that each transaction involves the simultaneous exchange of local and

12. Mohanty (2002).

13. The Committee on Payment Settlement Systems has developed international standards for the functioning and risk management of systemically important payment systems (Bank for International Settlements, Committee on Payment Settlement Systems 2001).

14. IMF and World Bank (2001a).

15. Mohanty (2002).

foreign currency.[16] The market consists of a wholesale interbank market, where authorized dealers (usually banks and other financial institutions) trade among themselves, and a retail market, where authorized dealers transact with final customers (usually households and firms). The interbank market, in particular, is where price discovery occurs through a decentralized allocation of foreign exchange by market participants on their own behalf as well as on behalf of their customers.

The efficiency and depth of the foreign exchange market hinge on several factors, including the degree of competition, the removal of impediments to price discovery, and the dissemination of information in the market. The introduction and development of a foreign exchange market require that foreign exchange be freely available for various external transactions and, as such, have often moved in tandem with progress toward currency convertibility. At a minimum, exchange controls and regulations affecting foreign exchange dealings should be modified to ensure market-based allocation and pricing of foreign exchange. Structural features of foreign exchange markets, including market microstructure and prudential supervision, also affect the depth and volatility of these markets.[17]

As with money markets, the central bank plays an important role in the development of the foreign exchange market. This includes implementing transparent criteria for licensing dealers, delegating exchange control authority to authorized dealers, improving information technology to facilitate interbank dealings, abolishing taxes and surcharges on transactions, and strengthening payment and clearing systems. In the early stages of development, the central bank could encourage banks to become market makers by limiting its trades to banks that provide firm two-way quotations for a set minimum amount. The requirement to provide two-way quotations may be imposed as part of the licensing process. Moreover, the central bank should not undercut the market-making function of authorized dealers by actively quoting buying and selling exchange rates when it enters the market.[18] Instead, the central bank should be a price taker. It also should buy and sell foreign exchange directly from the market rather than acquire it through surrender requirements or sell it directly to nonbank retail customers. More generally, the central bank should shift its focus

16. This section draws from Kovanen (1996).

17. Ishii and others (2003).

18. The central bank may enter the market for a variety of reasons, which include buying and selling foreign exchange on behalf of the government, reducing exchange rate volatility, correcting exchange rate misalignments, and accumulating reserves.

from directly controlling foreign exchange flows toward general oversight and supervision of the market.

Like all other financial markets, the soundness of market participants and the integrity of the payment and settlement systems are key to development of the foreign exchange market. In many emerging markets, however, significant obstacles remain, including instability in foreign exchange flows, lack of confidence, inefficiencies in the payment systems, and lack of adequate communication technology and computer systems. These obstacles can prevent the emergence of continuous two-way quotations in the market. Market participants thus should be able to evaluate their counterparties' creditworthiness on the basis of reliable and timely information. Similarly, settlement risks should be minimized by improving domestic payments and clearing systems, where local currency—and sometimes foreign currency—transactions are settled.[19]

The dissemination of information is essential for the efficient pricing of foreign exchange. Information systems and trading platforms should enable the provision of real-time bid-and-offer quotations in the interbank market. The retail market should also be well organized to ensure that buying and selling rates are set freely. Building the confidence of retail market customers is particularly important because the retail market is the medium through which foreign currency inflows and outflows are channeled to the interbank market.

Government Bond Market Development

The government bond market is the central pillar of domestic capital markets. It provides a market-determined term structure of interest rates that reflects the opportunity cost of money at each maturity.[20] The term structure of interest rates, in turn, is an essential prerequisite for the development of derivatives markets that enable market participants to manage financial risks. Markets in financial forwards, futures, swaps, and options all depend on the bond market for pricing and for hedging positions.

19. Normally, only the local currency leg of foreign exchange transactions is settled in the domestic payment and settlement system, while the foreign currency leg is settled in the home country of the foreign currency, through correspondent accounts. However, a growing number of central banks in developing countries serve as the settlement agents for foreign exchange, without taking on the risk of either counterparty.

20. Herring and Chatusripitak (2000).

Interest rates along the yield curve also serve as the key link between spot and futures prices in futures and forwards markets.

Fostering government debt markets also enhances the conduct of monetary policy operations by the central bank and liquidity management by financial institutions. Central banks increasingly manage liquidity through open market operations, which involve the outright sale and purchase of securities or the use of repos, where high-grade debt securities serve as collateral. Trends in long-term bond yields, moreover, provide valuable information to the authorities on market expectations and on confidence in macroeconomic policies.[21] Deep debt markets also facilitate liquidity management by financial institutions, which can more easily convert their liquid assets into cash, when needed. Without liquid debt markets, banks may not be able to cash their liquid assets, especially in times of systemic distress.

More generally, the government bond market creates a wide array of positive externalities. An active market in government securities and a benchmark yield curve enable the introduction and development of new financial products, including repos, money market instruments, asset-backed securities, and derivatives, which can improve risk management and financial stability. Government bond yields and yield differentials also provide critical pricing information to the economy at large.[22] Although equity market development is not strictly dependent on the bond market, in the absence of the latter, market participants will lack a benchmark discount rate, which is needed to discount projected earnings to value listed company stocks. Moreover, the differential between risky and "risk-free" bonds reflects the market's view of the risk premium, which can be used to price comparable bank loans.

Establishing a liquid government bond market hinges on several factors.[23] The government must be committed to financing its borrowing requirements at market-based prices, permanently moving away from the use of funding at below-market rates from captive investors. Without credibility in the government's financial policies, investors will be reluctant to invest and trade in government securities. Moreover, the government's ability to borrow from the domestic bond market should be legally well defined and sufficiently broad to achieve a range of objectives. In the same vein, the contractual relationships between the government and under-

21. Turner (2002).

22. Herring and Chatusripitak (2000).

23. APEC (1999); IMF and World Bank (2001a).

writers or winning bidders and between primary- and secondary-market participants should also be well defined. The essential elements of market infrastructure, including the settlement and registration of securities, the use of market intermediaries, and the organization of trading in the secondary market must be put in place.[24]

Bond design features and regulatory incentives also matter. The design of government securities should be standardized and their issuance concentrated in a limited number of popular, benchmark maturities.[25] Issuance on a regular basis at benchmark maturities can help to create a benchmark yield curve, spur greater investor demand, enhance market liquidity, and lower issuance costs. Design should also take into account investor preferences in maturity, coupon, and tax status.[26] Governments can enhance market activity by removing legal and regulatory impediments to competition, rationalizing tax distortions on bond investments and trading, and encouraging transparency and disclosure to protect investors' interests. Given the sensitivity of debt markets to disincentives, capital income taxation should treat incomes of all types of investments and savings, including bank deposits, equity, bonds, and other debt instruments, equitably. To the extent that bonds are disadvantaged in terms of tax treatment, they are less likely to become attractive investment and trading instruments.

Measures to develop the government bond market should place first priority on developing an effective primary market in short-term maturities.[27] Initiatives to deepen the money market, particularly through repos, can reinforce demand for and liquidity in the short end of the market. At the early stage of market development, the infrastructure for trading and settlement should be simple, secure, and capable of handling a sufficient volume of daily transactions. Priority should be accorded to building a safe spot-trading system, leaving the infrastructure for more advanced transactions (for example, swaps, futures, and options) for later. This can be achieved through a simple book-entry system for wholesale market participants.

Consideration should also be given to the use of primary dealers, which can help to build a stable, dependable source of demand for securities. As a small group of committed players responsible for buying and distributing

24. Ladekarl (2002).

25. Typical benchmark maturities are two to three years, five, ten, and, in some countries, thirty years.

26. Schinasi and Smith (1998).

27. IMF and World Bank (2001a).

government securities, primary dealers can greatly facilitate trading, especially in countries where the technological infrastructure is weak and where investors are only accessible through intermediaries. In most of the countries in which they are used, primary dealers are required to participate actively in the primary market by fulfilling a minimum bidding commitment, by underwriting issues, and, in the secondary market, by providing two-way quotes.[28] Primary dealers also build distribution channels, acting as intermediaries, and provide market information, including prices, volumes, and spreads.[29] In return, they are granted certain privileges for their market-making role, including exclusive or restricted access to auctions, access to noncompetitive bidding, and liquidity support from the central bank. The use of primary dealers, however, may reduce market competition and pose the risk of collusion, particularly in countries with small markets, which can be squeezed and cornered. Nevertheless, bond market turnover increased significantly in several countries after the introduction of primary dealers, suggesting that their benefits may outweigh their costs, at least until critical mass is reached in the number of financial institutions with market-making capabilities.[30]

Policymakers should carefully consider other aspects of market structure and their impact on development, including the choice of trading system. For example, in more nascent markets limited participation can be effectively aggregated in a periodic market, whereas in deeper markets and markets with widespread use of hedging strategies, a continuous market will be required. In countries where dealers are few in number and thinly capitalized, an auction market may be more successful. In countries where the market is dominated by large institutional investors, however, a dealer market (which provides immediacy and low-cost transactions) will be more appropriate.[31]

Once the market for short-term securities takes hold, efforts should focus on developing the market for long-term government securities. Making the transition from short-term to long-term instruments may not be easy, particularly for countries with a history of lax fiscal policies and high inflation. This may require intermediate steps, such as issuing floating-rate debt or issuing debt indexed to inflation, the dollar, or short-term

28. Mohanty (2002).

29. Arnone and Iden (2002).

30. Turner (2002). See Arnone and Iden (2002) for a more detailed discussion of the rationale, objectives, and operational issues related to the establishment of a primary dealer system.

31. Dattels (1997).

interest rates, a practice widely adopted by Latin American countries, including Brazil, Chile, and Mexico. A key goal at this stage is to achieve sufficient depth in benchmark maturities across the yield curve in order to create a term structure for "risk-free" interest rates as a basis for developing auxiliary markets in derivatives for hedging purposes.

Developing a liquid market in long-term government bonds, however, requires active participation by intermediaries and an efficient market infrastructure, including well-designed securities settlement arrangements. Market intermediaries, including securities houses, investment banks, brokers, and commercial banks, should operate on a competitive and efficient basis, with adequate capital and risk management practices.[32] As the principal underwriters and investors in bonds and suppliers of credit to securities houses, banks are a particularly important market intermediary. Thus a strong banking system can play a key role in deepening the government securities market.[33] Common problems encountered with intermediaries, including lack of competition, conflicts of interest, insufficient capital, and scarcity of human capital, can be addressed by enforcing strict entry policies (that is, fit-and-proper tests) and by permitting foreign entities to offer brokerage services.

Corporate Bond and Equity Market Development

Corporate bond and equity markets provide additional channels for the intermediation of savings and the transfer and diversification of risk. Diversifying the sources of investment financing and spreading risks more evenly, in turn, reduce the exposure of firms to financial system stress, thus bolstering an economy's ability to withstand shocks.[34] As Greenspan notes, in contrast to East Asia, which "had no spare tires," nonbank financing cushioned the impact of the slowdown in bank lending precipitated by the collapse of collateral values in Sweden and the United States in the late 1980s and early 1990s.[35] Greenspan also acknowledges that building a financial infrastructure is a "laborious process," involving accounting standards that accurately portray firms' finances, legal systems that protect property rights and enforce contracts, and effective insolvency regimes.

32. Ladekarl (2002).
33. IMF (2003).
34. Stone (2000).
35. Greenspan (1999).

Developing bond and equity markets also avoids concentrating financial intermediation in banks.[36] Banks typically lend for periods much shorter than the maturity of long-term bonds, which may bias firms' investments toward short-term assets. As a result, firms may not adequately invest in long-term projects in infrastructure, utilities, and other capital-intensive industries. An over-reliance on banks to provide investment financing also leaves the economy vulnerable to the credit crunches that typically follow financial sector distress and crisis. The absence of bond markets in Asia, for example, deepened the recessions in crisis countries.[37]

To maximize their contribution to intermediation and risk-sharing, it is critical that corporate bond and equity markets develop in a balanced manner. Strong growth in corporate debt securities without matching equity market financing can otherwise lead to excessive leverage in non-financial firms and increase firms' vulnerability to shocks. Equity markets facilitate the financing of high-risk and high-return projects and help to contain overall financial system risks.

The development of a corporate bond market builds on the presence of a strong government bond market and on the infrastructure created to support government securities. However, the involvement of private corporate issuers in the market introduces a wide array of new challenges. Market efficiency and integrity hinge critically on the transparency of financial information and of market prices. Authorities responsible for regulating the market should ensure accurate and timely disclosure of financial information for investors to properly assess issuer creditworthiness, value debt securities, and make informed investment decisions. Similarly, pricing information should be widely available. A transparent market in which pre-trade and post-trade information is disseminated to traders and investors lowers spreads, improves efficiency, and attracts more participants by increasing their confidence in the pricing process.[38] Moreover, market rules should deter, and provide investors effective recourse against, misrepresentation and fraud.

Establishing a corporate equity market, particularly in emerging economies, is equally challenging. In many markets, it is difficult to find a

36. Turner (2002).

37. A survey of Asian countries revealed that the main impediments to the development of domestic markets included the lack of reliable benchmark yield curves, a weak local institutional investor base, insufficient market liquidity, a lack of credible risk assessment, and underdeveloped securities trading, clearing, and settlement systems (APEC 1999).

38. Mohanty (2002).

sufficient number of companies that are large enough to warrant public status. As a result, only a few large stocks are traded on stock exchanges. The evolution of equity markets generally has followed the pattern of slow graduation from privately held status—that is, companies owned by small, often family, groups—to more widely held private corporations (with a few shareholders) and then to widely held public companies with a broad base of shareholders.

The lack of "free-float" capacity—that companies are unwilling to offer a significant portion of ownership to the public—impedes the development of quality public issuers. Until existing owners are willing to cede a meaningful level of corporate control, investors will be reluctant. While public companies have access to a greater pool of capital because ownership shares are available to the public, they are faced with the risks and costs of public ownership, including greater accounting, legal, and reporting costs and less flexibility in decisionmaking. In many transition economies, authorities have attempted to develop equity markets by privatizing state assets, with mixed success. In Hungary, for example, privatization of assets contributed to a relatively robust equity market. In Romania, privatization initially resulted in a very large number of companies being traded on a stock exchange, but without an adequate regulatory system, many of these companies became insolvent, and without a delisting process, the exchange suffered from a serious lack of credibility. (For a discussion of privatization as a development tool, see Berglof and Bolton 2000.)

Equity markets require strong regulatory frameworks and legal infrastructure—equity instruments are private property instruments, which require mechanisms to enforce legal ownership rights and facilitate ownership transfer. If shares are not fully transferable and questions of ownership arise, there will be a negative impact on liquidity and companies' ability to raise financing. Further, if a court system is not sufficiently sophisticated in dealing with complex commercial claims or imposes delays in resolving disputes, property rights can be impeded, and this will deter investment.

The regulatory structure must adequately address corporate governance and disclosure, especially financial disclosure. The attractiveness of a market to investors is dependent on the quality of price discovery in the market—price discovery, in turn, depends on adequate information. As in bond markets, the accounting standards that underpin financial disclosure are crucial to building this credibility. The impact of improved corporate governance and disclosure standards can be illustrated by those large companies in emerging-market countries that have achieved listings on the

New York or London exchanges, where these standards are very high. Companies such as Infosys in India or Gazprom in Russia then have access to liquid markets and cheaper financing.

The imposition of improved corporate governance, disclosure, and accounting standards can be costly to corporations. A balance must be struck between the benefits of standards that establish credibility in the market and the cost of compliance with standards that may cause corporations to avoid the markets. In many countries, this challenge is addressed with lesser standards for small and medium companies than for large public issuers: an over-the-counter market often has fewer requirements than a listed market.

The protection of minority shareholders is a major issue in market development. Many of the minority shareholders' concerns relate to the quality of financial disclosure and corporate governance. The protection of minority shareholders also requires addressing the regulation of takeover bids and related-party transactions, level of free float of ownership in the market, distribution of voting rights, and access to judicial arbitration of shareholder disputes. Because the introduction of minority shareholder protection challenges the rights of existing shareholders, such rules can be difficult to introduce, as was the case in Chile and Brazil, for example, where the attempt to reform minority shareholder rights became a protracted battle (Aninat 2000).

The design of market infrastructure is a key consideration in developing markets. The design of trading systems must be carefully considered in the local context—appropriate designs can vary between continuous and periodic markets, auction and dealer markets, electronic and physical trading. In Poland, for example, where there was limited liquidity, the small stock market chose a periodic auction market rather than a continuous auction market as a means of bringing together all trades at one time—deepening the market for a short period rather than stretching liquidity through a day. This proved an effective way to enhance liquidity. The use of market makers in the trading system also can improve liquidity because these traders take on obligations to meet orders up to certain prices and volumes. Because a market maker takes on risk in doing so, a number of well-capitalized market intermediaries must be available in order to foster the development of market makers. Fragmentation of trading of the same security across more than one market can also affect liquidity—the market may be too small to support trading in more than one venue. A country can address this by supporting centralized trading or centralized information systems.

Equity markets have traditionally developed through stock exchange mechanisms; stock markets bring together investors temporally and therefore aggregate liquidity. The traditional stock exchange provided an auction market for market intermediaries, who were usually also owners of the system. The globalization of investment has challenged the traditional model, and many exchanges are faced with falling liquidity and revenues, because trade volumes are mobile and consequently may conglomerate in major exchanges with deeper liquidity. Many exchanges cannot compete with international listings or alternative sources of liquidity. Policymakers today have some nontraditional options to consider in developing trading systems for publicly traded securities. Many emerging-market countries have been reluctant to allow alternative trading systems because of concerns over further fragmenting liquidity and regulatory burdens. It is important, however, that market design be addressed in a way that does not protect trading systems from competition at the expense of the market as a whole. Shielding local exchanges from both internal and external competition may stifle growth and innovation in the markets. The recent trend toward demutualization of exchanges may foster more competition in trading and listing services, but it also introduces its own governance challenges.

The design of clearing and settlement systems for securities is a crucial factor in market development: the system must be both safe and efficient. Inefficient clearing and settlement will impede development by driving up the cost of investment and tying up capital in the settlement process. Unsafe systems will expose participants to settlement risk, one of the most important risks in the equity markets because the risk of loss can be enormous, especially in the case of derivatives, where losses can be exponential. The design and risk management of clearing and settlement systems recently have been the focus of standard setters. In 2001 the Basel Committee on Payment and Settlement Systems and the International Organization of Securities Commissions published recommendations setting the international standard for clearing and settlement systems.[39] These standards will enhance understanding of the role of regulators and markets in managing the risks of securities settlement.

39. Bank for International Settlements, Committee on Payment Settlement Systems (2001).

Derivatives Market Development

The development of derivatives markets is more difficult to discuss in broad terms and does not fit precisely into a hierarchy of market development. Derivatives markets range from interbank financial derivatives traded over the counter to commodity and financial derivatives traded on exchanges. Derivatives and their underlying markets are interdependent—derivatives require the existence of a liquid market in underlying products, but they also enhance the liquidity and price discovery in those underlying markets.[40] Certain derivatives markets, including interest rate swaps, foreign exchange swaps, and forward contracts, are critical to facilitate risk management for financial institutions and hence foster liquidity and price discovery in markets for the underlying securities. At the same time, derivatives themselves raise other forms of risk. Managing the risks associated with derivatives requires additional infrastructure (for example, in the case of clearing systems for exchange-traded derivatives) and additional ability to understand more complex risks (for example, in the case of accounting for derivatives on bank balance sheets). We do not address these issues in detail, but we raise derivatives as a dimension of market development that must be considered in conjunction with the development of fixed-income and equity markets.

Institutional Investors and Development

Perhaps the most important dimension of domestic capital market development is the need to develop a diversified institutional investor base in the economy. Institutional investors—mutual and investment funds and other contractual savings institutions, such as pension funds and insurance companies—play a critical role in financial market development in a variety of ways.[41] First, they provide an institutional framework for long-term capital accumulation and act as a stable source of demand for long-term debt securities and equity investments. In an empirical analysis of the impact of contractual savings institutions on securities markets, Impávido and others find that an increase in the assets of contractual savings institutions relative to domestic financial assets has a positive effect on the depth of stock and bond markets.[42]

40. Schinasi and Smith (1998).

41. Impávido, Musalem, and Tressel (2003).

42. Impávido, Musalem, and Tressel (2003). For example, in Chile, private pension funds and insurance companies have been a crucial source of demand for corporate debt and stocks (Cifuentes,

Second, institutional investors and contractual savings institutions compete with investment banks, make primary markets more efficient, and enhance financial innovation and modernization of trading systems. For example, in highly developed capital markets such as in the United States, they supported the development of asset-backed securities, structured finance, and derivatives products; the launching of index-tracking funds; and the proliferation of synthetic products designed to protect investors against market volatility.[43] Similarly, institutional investors exert pressure for efficient trading, clearing, and settlement facilities. In several countries, they have promoted the use of block trading, the abolition of minimum commissions, and the automation of trading facilities.

Third, institutional investors enhance market discipline and corporate governance by promoting transparency and shareholder rights. As institutional investors become dominant shareholders of nonfinancial corporations, they collectively have the power to strengthen governance structures and increase the accountability of top managers. In India, for example, which has a number of large institutional investors, the equity market is relatively active. By contrast, Russia, which does not have the same strength and variety of institutional investors, has a small capital market and is often criticized for its poor standards of corporate governance.

Fourth, the development of institutional investors and contractual savings institutions creates the need and strong incentives for the establishment of a robust regulatory and supervisory framework to minimize systemic risks.

Notwithstanding the positive externalities associated with the development of a domestic institutional investor base, several obstacles stand in their way. Pension funds still face competition from pay-as-you-go systems, while both pension funds and insurance companies are subject to strict licensing requirements or, in some cases, excessive portfolio investment restrictions.[44] To the detriment of the growth and diversification of institutional investors, regulators in several countries have followed a rules-based approach to regulating investors, placing quantitative limits on their investments and thus limiting their investment options and creating a bias

Desormeaux, and González 2002). Following Chile's lead, many Latin American and more recently Central European countries have established private pension funds, which are contributing to local capital market development (IMF 2003).

43. Vittas (1999).

44. Mihaljek, Scatigna, and Villar (2002).

toward investing in domestic or government debt. In particular, requiring institutional investors to hold a large share of their assets in government bonds undermines the integrity of the price-discovery mechanism in the market and the credibility of the government's financial soundness and issuance strategy.[45] Public pension funds, moreover, often come under political pressure to invest in certain types of assets, which compromises the rate of return earned for the pension holders.

For institutional investors to enhance market discipline and corporate governance in the economy, however, they themselves must be well run. This, in turn, rests on the degree of reputational risk faced by institutional investors themselves rather than any particular type of governance structure. Buxton and Giles argue that the key sources of discipline for institutional investors include competition, disclosure, and the ability of investors to exit funds.[46] So long as these elements are in place, institutional investors will face real reputational risks and be held accountable for their investment decisions and risk management practices.

Promoting Sound Financial Institutions

The development of active money and debt markets requires sound banking institutions, which can compete effectively in deposit and loan markets through adjustments in interest rates and efficient pricing of risk. In addition to their role in money markets, banks are key players in other financial markets, and their ability to cope with market volatility can be crucial for both market development and sound banking.

The development of a sound banking system and robust supervisory framework thus should be phased in to support financial liberalization.[47] Where systemic weaknesses exist, the authorities must cleanse banks of significant stocks of nonperforming loans; close, restructure, or recapitalize them; and enhance the governance of financial and nonfinancial firms in order to develop financial markets. Sound financial institutions contribute to financial market development through their roles as market intermediaries, providers of back-up lines of credit, and holders and managers of a portfolio of traded securities. Inefficiencies in banking, reflected in part in the high cost of bank loans, for example, have spurred the development of

45. Turner (2002).
46. Buxton and St. Giles (2002).
47. Sundararajan (1999).

debt and equity markets in some countries, but the market depth achieved under such circumstances is neither healthy nor sustainable.

Risks in Financial Market Development and Risk Mitigation Policies

To reap the benefits of financial market development and maintain financial sector stability, the risks introduced by each market need to be managed effectively before other markets are developed and more risks are injected into the financial system (figure 9-2). Market development strategy thus must accord high priority to mitigating the risks introduced by increasingly more sophisticated financial markets and the risks to macroeconomic control from institutional reforms. For example, central banking and money market reforms, including interest rate liberalization, can lead to the release of excess reserves and strong capital inflows, which can stimulate credit expansion, undermine monetary control, and lower the asset quality of banks. Similarly, increased price volatility in equity and real estate markets, particularly in the context of capital account opening, can complicate monetary policymaking as well as the soundness of institutions. Thus in the absence of regulatory and institutional capacities to measure, monitor, and contain financial risks, they can accumulate over time and undermine the policy consensus and commitment to liberalize further.

Financial market development and capital account opening also create common exposures to macroeconomic risk factors such as increased volatility of asset prices, capital flows, and macroeconomic conditions, both locally and in global markets. The impact on financial system soundness could itself feed back into macroeconomic outcomes. Macroprudential surveillance monitors these linkages through an analysis of aggregate information on financial soundness of banks and nonbanks and through stress testing of individual institutions' resilience to certain plausible, but exceptional, common shocks. Such top-down and bottom-up surveillance of vulnerabilities to macroeconomic risk factors is increasingly being recognized as a critical complement to prudential supervision of individual institutions, particularly in a globalized environment.[48]

48. Borio (2003).

Figure 9-2. *Financial Markets and Risks*

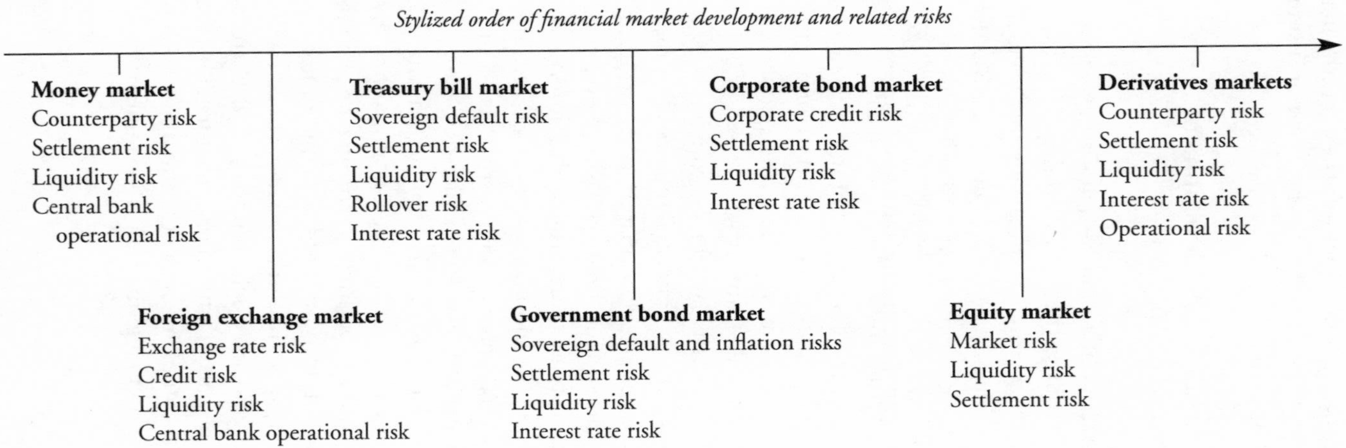

Money Market Risks

Money markets most prominently introduce additional dimensions of credit and liquidity risks into the financial system (table 9-1). Lenders are exposed to the risk of nonrepayment by borrowers in the interbank market. Where interbank loans are securitized, the lender may realize losses from failing to seize posted collateral quickly and at low cost in weak institutional and legal environments. Moreover, even when collateral is seized, the lender may still suffer a loss from potential illiquidity in the market in which collateral is sold. By contrast, borrowers become susceptible to liquidity risks, where short-dated interbank loans may not be rolled over. Thus the use of interbank loans to fund long-term assets leads to maturity mismatches, repricing gaps, and exposure to withdrawals of credit lines, which, in turn, can precipitate failure or large losses on creditor and borrowing banks.

Payment settlement arrangements and the central bank's liquidity management procedures also affect the depth and functioning of money markets. As the monetary authority and lender of last resort, the central bank manages systemic liquidity through the money market and itself faces credit risks through its regular and emergency lending facilities. The central bank's capacity to anticipate and offset shifts in interbank market liquidity is a crucial determinant of money market depth and banks' ability to manage their own liquidity. The parameters of risk control in the payment system (for example, loss-sharing arrangements, size of collateral pool, bilateral exposure limits, and terms of access to central bank credit to facilitate settlements) also affect market liquidity. The design of the payment system thus can amplify risks to financial stability and contagion in times of distress, if interbank exposures are not adequately controlled. This could lead to a loss of monetary control, depending on the extent of access to central bank credit.

Risks in the money market and payment systems ultimately emanate from the soundness of market participants and their ability to monitor and evaluate their counterparties. Accurate and timely information disclosure by banks on their financial condition is thus essential. Equally important is the capacity of market participants to assess credit risks, avoid interbank loan concentration, and minimize maturity mismatches. Ensuring high standards in information disclosure and credit risk analysis, in turn, rests on a strong regulatory and supervisory framework and on enforcement mechanisms for sound banking and payment systems.

Table 9-1. *Money Market Risks and Countermeasures*

Source and type of risk	*Measures and instruments*
Credit risk	Provide detailed financial information disclosure on asset quality, capital adequacy, and liquidity position
	Enhance credit risk analysis and lend against high-quality, liquid collateral
	Strengthen framework for repurchase agreements and collateral seizure
Liquidity risk	Contain maturity mismatches and maintain a minimum level of liquid assets
	Negotiate backup credit lines in the event of market distress
	Strengthen liquidity management skills and techniques
Central bank operating risk	Strengthen central bank operating procedures to manage market liquidity
	Reinforce risk controls and loss-sharing arrangements in the payment settlement system

Foreign Exchange Market Risks

The development of the foreign exchange market introduces further risks in the financial system, mostly revolving around exchange rate risk and, to a lesser extent, credit and liquidity risks (table 9-2). In particular, exchange rate risks can be enormous. As market makers, borrowers, and lenders in foreign exchange, financial institutions create net open positions in foreign exchange, both on and off balance sheet, which give rise to the risk of loss from adverse movements of the exchange rate. Exchange rate risk also heightens banks' credit risk exposure to foreign currency loans extended to unhedged borrowers. The foreign exchange market per se mainly involves settlement risks, which are increasingly being contained by the move toward real-time settlement in many countries.

The potential magnitude of foreign exchange market risks is closely related to the openness of the capital account. An open capital account allows for the flow of capital through which foreign currency exposures are built. Thus the benefits from the free flow of capital from abroad must be weighed against the capacity of the financial system to manage foreign exchange risks and withstand volatility in foreign currency flows.

Table 9-2. *Foreign Exchange Market Risks and Countermeasures*

Source and type of risk	*Measures and instruments*
Exchange rate risk	Establish internal limits and monitoring mechanisms for foreign exchange exposure, including off-balance-sheet items
	Establish net open position limits[a]
	Set capital requirements against exchange rate risk
	Develop instruments for hedging exchange rate risk
Credit risk	Conduct detailed credit analysis of borrowers, with a special focus on their capacities in foreign currency earning and exchange rate risk hedging
	Apply high underwriting standards to foreign currency borrowers
Liquidity risk	Promote liquid market for foreign exchange transactions by fostering efficient and transparent trading and market conduct arrangements
	Establish limits against foreign currency maturity mismatches
Central bank operational risk	Establish transparent objectives for central bank intervention and specific criteria for its timing, amount, and operational modalities
	Avoid providing exchange rate guarantees
	Ensure that monetary and foreign exchange intervention policies and exchange system arrangements adequately support the exchange rate regime

a. See Abrams and Beato (1998) for various approaches to measuring net open positions and the types of internal and prudential limits that may be placed on them.

Foreign exchange markets also involve operational risks for the central bank, particularly when capital market transactions are being liberalized. Central bank interventions, particularly in the forward market, can result in large reserve losses if the intended reversal in market expectations does not materialize and local currency selling pressure continues through the maturity of forward contracts. More generally, like any financial institution, the central bank faces operational risks stemming from potential misconduct or excessive risk-taking by traders and the potential for misjudging the nature of financial shocks, the sources of exchange rate volatility, and prospects for correcting exchange rate misalignments and reducing volatility. These, in turn, can result in the loss of foreign exchange reserves, impairing market confidence.

Debt Market Risks

Debt securities markets introduce a broad array of risks into the system, most prominently involving credit and market risks. While government debt securities pose minimal credit risk in normal times, investors in long-term government bonds are exposed to the risk of high inflation and macroeconomic instability during times of economic crisis and distress, which can erode the value of the bonds, even if they are repaid in full and on time. In addition, sovereign credit risk could arise when debt is denominated in foreign currency and the macroeconomic policy mix leads to unsustainable debt dynamics. Corporate debt securities involve credit risks similar to those related to bank loans, with one important caveat: whereas bank loans tend to be concentrated in a small number of lending institutions, investors in corporate debt securities may be diverse, creating collective action problems during times of distress.

The single most important market risk involving debt securities is interest rate risk. Banks, in particular, are exposed to repricing risk, arising from timing differences in the maturity and repricing of banks' assets and liabilities, and yield curve risk, arising from changes in the slope and shape of the yield curve.[49] This highlights the need for supervisory authorities to enhance monitoring and reporting requirements on the maturity structure of interest-sensitive assets and liabilities by asset class and currency, and for financial institutions to actively manage maturity mismatches and to analyze the sensitivity of balance sheets to changes in interest rates. In times of systemic distress or crisis, interest rate risks can quickly escalate, transform into substantial credit risks, and trigger large-scale defaults.

Governments are the largest issuers in the debt market in most countries and face a number of risks, including market, rollover, and liquidity risks (table 9-3).[50] As the most important and most creditworthy issuer in the market, a government must manage its debt prudently to minimize its exposure to market volatility and potential shocks and to build investor confidence in the market. Market risks stem from potential changes in interest rates, which affect the cost of debt servicing and new issuance. Short-term, floating-rate debt is riskier than long-term, fixed-rate debt. Debt denominated in or indexed to foreign currencies adds risks and volatility to debt-servicing costs related to exchange rate movements. Rollover risk is the risk that debt will have to be rolled over at an unusually

49. Sundararajan, Ariyoshi, and Otker-Robe (2002).
50. IMF and World Bank (2001b).

Table 9-3. *Debt Securities Market Risks to Issuers and Investors and Countermeasures*

Source and type of risk	*Measures and instruments*
Risks to investors	
Settlement risk	Dematerialize securities
	Centralize depository
	Automate settlement on a real-time basis
	Monitor members on the basis of prudential requirements
Liquidity risk	Reduce fragmentation, develop benchmark securities, and use primary dealers
	Make available a collateralized line of credit to support primary dealers
Interest rate risk and rollover risk	Comply with prudential requirements for risk management of portfolios
Market and credit risk	Improve credit-pricing ability by standardizing bond contracts, requiring the use of rating agencies
	Achieve an adequate degree of transparency of large-positions trading data
Risks to issuers	
Rollover risk	Use longer-term instruments as part of a balanced issuer portfolio
	Establish liquid reserves to meet short-term foreign borrowing requirements
Exchange rate risk	Avoid concentration of debt in foreign currency
	Limit foreign currency debt to minimum maturities of three or more years
Interest rate risk	Develop risk management systems, including asset-liability management, stress testing, and value-at-risk measurement of exposures
	Develop hedging strategies

high interest rate or cannot be rolled over at all and is particularly important for emerging-market economies.

Governments can take a number of measures to minimize these risks.[51] First, issuance of short-term debt, which is usually intended to lower the cost of funds, should be balanced against rollover risks. Over-reliance on

51. IMF and World Bank (2001b).

short-term debt can raise the government's exposure to shifts in investor confidence. Second, government liabilities should not be concentrated in foreign currencies, and foreign currency debt issued should have an average maturity of a minimum of three or so years. Governments should also hold liquid reserves sufficient to cope comfortably with new foreign borrowing requirements over a short horizon (one year or so). Third, over time, governments should develop more sophisticated methods of risk management, including asset-liability management, stress testing, and value-at-risk techniques to measure their exposure to market, rollover, liquidity, interest rate, exchange rate, and operational risks. They should also make use of hedging instruments where necessary.

Investors in fixed-income instruments also face a variety of risks (table 9-3). These include (a) credit risks (counterparty risk, borrower risk, sovereign risk), (b) market risks (interest rate risk, price risk, currency risk), and (c) legal, operational, and fiduciary risks. To minimize the risk of financial market disturbances and instability, a core set of risk management practices ought to be implemented at the institutional level by the major private and public investors in bonds to measure, monitor, and control risks effectively. These practices should include the following:[52]

—Senior management should keep the board fully informed, and both the board and senior management should provide effective oversight of the institution's fixed-income investment portfolio.

—The institution should have a sound mechanism for assigning responsibility to different units in charge of implementing investment and risk management policies to ensure adequate checks and balances. The board should be responsible for approving all investment and risk management policies, which should assign clear responsibilities to the front office (dealing functions), back office (settlement and accounting functions), and middle office (independent oversight and audit of risk and measurement and analysis of performance). Risk management policies should also outline the stress-testing framework and frequency as well as accounting guidelines.

—Institutions should develop robust systems of risk measurement, identification, and reporting.

—Institutions should periodically conduct stress tests on their portfolio, identifying its sensitivity to various risks, including those related to inter-

52. APEC (1999).

est rates, prepayment, changes in risk premiums, and shifts in yield curves, and adjust their asset composition.

—Institutions should establish strong internal control and audit systems, which maintain an appropriate segregation of duties, conduct independent reviews of the fixed-income management function, and enforce lines of authority. In particular, personnel responsible for measuring, monitoring, and controlling risks should be independent of the business units that take risks.

Equity Market Risks

Equity markets introduce additional dimensions of market risk and liquidity risk to investors that are strongly responsive to perceived macroeconomic and sectoral prospects (table 9-4). Market risk is the risk that the book value of the instrument suddenly will be unattainable in the market, causing loss to the holder. A sudden drop in asset value can be destabilizing to both financial institutions and nonfinancial corporations. Market risk is exacerbated where there is concentrated exposure to the particular market (as is the case where there are restrictions on investment outside the country or where risk management practices of inside investors are not adequate). Derivatives markets can mitigate some of these risks, but they combine a variety of risks already present in the financial system, and their inherent complexity heightens operational risks in institutions, as the widely known cases of Barings and Allied Irish Bank illustrate.

Market risk is ameliorated through transparency in markets that improves price discovery, through active prevention of market abuse, including reporting of insider trades, related-party transaction rules, and market manipulation rules, and through adequate disclosure requirements and enforcement. In some markets, regulators impose price bands on daily or weekly trading that prohibit large price movements. Although this may prevent a sudden drop in price, it interferes with price discovery. At the institutional level, it is important to address market risk with accounting and valuation requirements and with concentration and exposure restrictions such as those listed above for corporate bond holders. In addition, a strong information infrastructure—notably listing, rating, and public disclosure requirements—backed by high-quality accounting standards is needed to promote sound equity markets.

Equity holdings can also present a liquidity risk: institutions must be able to liquidate equities in order to meet liabilities. This will raise concerns

Table 9-4. *Equity Market Risks and Countermeasures and Instruments*

Source and type of risk	*Measures and instruments*
Counterparty and settlement risk	Regulatory capital requirements, supervision of financial condition, early warning systems
	Membership restrictions in trading and settlement systems
	Central counterparty
	Supervision of clearing and settlement systems; detailed operational requirements
Market and liquidity risk	Accounting and auditing standards ensuring quality of financial disclosure
	Market transparency (pricing, insider trading activity, market abuse)
	Valuation requirements for institutions
	Restrictions on exposure and concentration

during times of distress and downward price pressure in the markets, when institutions are forced to liquidate at low prices. Liquidity risks are managed through appropriate valuation standards (for example, requiring mutual funds to mark-to-market their assets daily) and greater transparency in the market. In many emerging markets, equity markets are relatively illiquid, and consequently financial institutions are prohibited from investing in them or have their investments restricted. This can present difficulties when such institutions are also restricted to domestic investment for capital account and other reasons. A pension fund, for example, that is restricted to the domestic market may have difficulty finding suitable investments and may hold much of its assets in cash, deposits, and government securities.

Equity markets also introduce more complex counterparty and settlement risks: there is wider participation in the market, and participation may be financed by third parties. Counterparty risks are present in the clearing and settlement system, and these become settlement risks. Settlement risks are dealt with in a number of ways. The clearing and settlement system is normally restricted to members that have met financial tests and whose financial condition is constantly monitored (by the system or another regulator). Ideally, clearing and settlement systems are directly connected to payment systems and large value-transfer systems, enabling a quick transfer of funds for the cash leg of transactions. Similarly, for the securities leg, the system must be connected to a depository of securities.

Ideally, this depository would be centralized and connected directly to the clearing and settlement system.

In some systems, a central counterparty is used so that a central system absorbs the risk of failure. Central counterparties are widely used in derivatives clearing and settlement. Settlement risk is further mitigated with the appropriate capital standards for intermediaries. In most systems, access to clearing and settlement systems is limited to intermediaries that meet capital requirements. The strength of the enforcement of compliance with capital standards will have a direct impact on settlement risk.

In systems where capital requirements are not adequately enforced, the system may require up-front payment for trades, which is more expensive and less efficient and which reduces liquidity, since it ties up the intermediaries' capital. In India, for example, the National Stock Exchange introduced an effective clearing and settlement system that relies on up-front payment for trades (payment is made from cash in the intermediaries' account). Although this system is costly, it avoids reliance on capital standards for intermediaries. In contrast, the Bombay Stock Exchange once employed a settlement system known as *badla*, under which settlement was rolling and no up-front payment was required. A crisis in investor confidence in March 2001 caused prices to drop, and undercapitalized firms were unable to meet settlement obligations. The failures to settle drove market prices down much further; caused a number of failures of market intermediaries, spread to small banks that had financed these intermediaries, triggering losses and one bank failure; and ultimately resulted in client losses. The Bombay Stock Exchange is still recovering from this event. The National Stock Exchange, on which many Bombay Stock Exchange stocks are cross-listed, experienced price drops, but no settlement failures.[53]

Counterparty risks also exist between market intermediaries and their clients. These are normally reflected in capital requirements and in margin requirements that restrict the amount of financing an intermediary can extend to a client. This counterparty risk can also be addressed through restrictions on activities between market intermediaries and related entities and through conflict-of-interest rules governing relationships between the intermediary and customers (for example, mutual funds or banks).

Operational risks are also present in equity markets. These pervade all levels of the system, including market intermediaries, trading systems, and

53. Joint Committee on the Stock Market Scam (2002).

clearing and settlement systems. Operational risks are met by entry or licensing requirements governing management and technological capacity, ongoing internal control requirements, inspections, and other means of ongoing supervision of institutions.

Finally, equity markets introduce market risks for the equity issuer. The issuer faces the risk that market prices will negatively affect access to financing. Quality of disclosure and transparency to the market will help to ensure that the issue is accurately priced, but a single equity can still feel the effects of a general shock to the equity market.

Capital Account Liberalization and Sequencing of Financial Market Development

Capital account liberalization and domestic financial reforms need to be approached in an integrated manner.[54] Risks in developing specific types of markets, and the hierarchy of markets in terms of the demands they place on risk management and information requirements, provide certain benchmarks and principles for the sequencing and coordination of financial sector reforms (box 9-2). These principles also apply to the strategy to liberalize capital account transactions, where the key challenge is to identify precisely how foreign capital can enhance market development, and when. Policies to develop markets and manage risks provide a critical mass of reforms in each stage of market development. The matrix of reforms in figure 9-3 illustrates several of the key principles of sequencing:

—Reforms in financial system infrastructure, including the insolvency regime, creditor rights, and accounting and disclosure, should start early in the process of market development, given the time needed to implement these reforms and their importance to financial institution restructuring and good corporate governance.

—A comprehensive approach to risk mitigation requires not only effective prudential supervision and oversight of the payment system but also adequate macroprudential surveillance and the implementation of needed adjustments in macroeconomic policies.

—Capital account liberalization should closely complement the domestic market development strategy. This implies that allowing short-term

54. Johnston, Darbar, and Echeverría (1999).

Box 9-2. *Select Principles of Sequencing*

Sequencing domestic financial liberalization:

—Liberalization is best undertaken in the context of sound and sustainable macroeconomic policies.

—Capital market development–cum–financial stability hinges on establishing the institutional infrastructure for controlling both macroeconomic and financial risks. Financial sector reforms that support and reinforce macroeconomic stabilization and effective conduct of monetary and exchange rate policies should be accorded priority. This entails giving priority to developing monetary policy instruments and money and foreign exchange markets.

—Financial liberalization and market development policies should be sequenced to reflect the hierarchy and complementarity of markets and related institutional structures.

—Market development policies should be comprehensive. Technically and operationally linked measures should be implemented together, and linkages among markets should be taken into account.

—Capital market development requires a careful sequencing of measures to mitigate risks in parallel with reforms to develop markets. Policies to develop markets should be accompanied by prudential and supervisory measures as well as macroprudential surveillance in order to contain risks introduced by new markets and instruments.

—The pace of reforms should take into account the initial financial condition and soundness of financial and nonfinancial firms and the time needed to restructure them.

—Institutional development is a critical component of building capital markets and the capacity to manage financial risk. Establishing good governance structures in financial institutions, including internal controls and risk management systems, is among the most critical of market reforms.

—Operational and institutional arrangements for policy transparency and data disclosure need to be adopted to complement the evolving financial markets.

—The pace, timing, and sequencing also need to take account of political and regional considerations that could strengthen ownership of reforms.

—Reforms that require substantial lead time for technical preparations and capacity building should be started early.

Additional principles for external financial liberalization:

—The liberalization of capital flows by instruments and sectors should be sequenced in a manner that reinforces domestic financial liberalization and allows for institutional capacity building to manage the additional risks.

—Reforms need to take into account the effectiveness of existing controls on capital flows or the implicit restrictions on capital flows due to the ineffectiveness or absence of markets.

—Transparency and data disclosure practices should be adopted to support capital account opening.

Source: These principles are drawn in part from Ishii and Habermeier (2002); Sundararajan, Ariyoshi, and Otker-Robe (2002).

Figure 9-3. *Financial Market Development: Stylized Sequencing of Reforms*

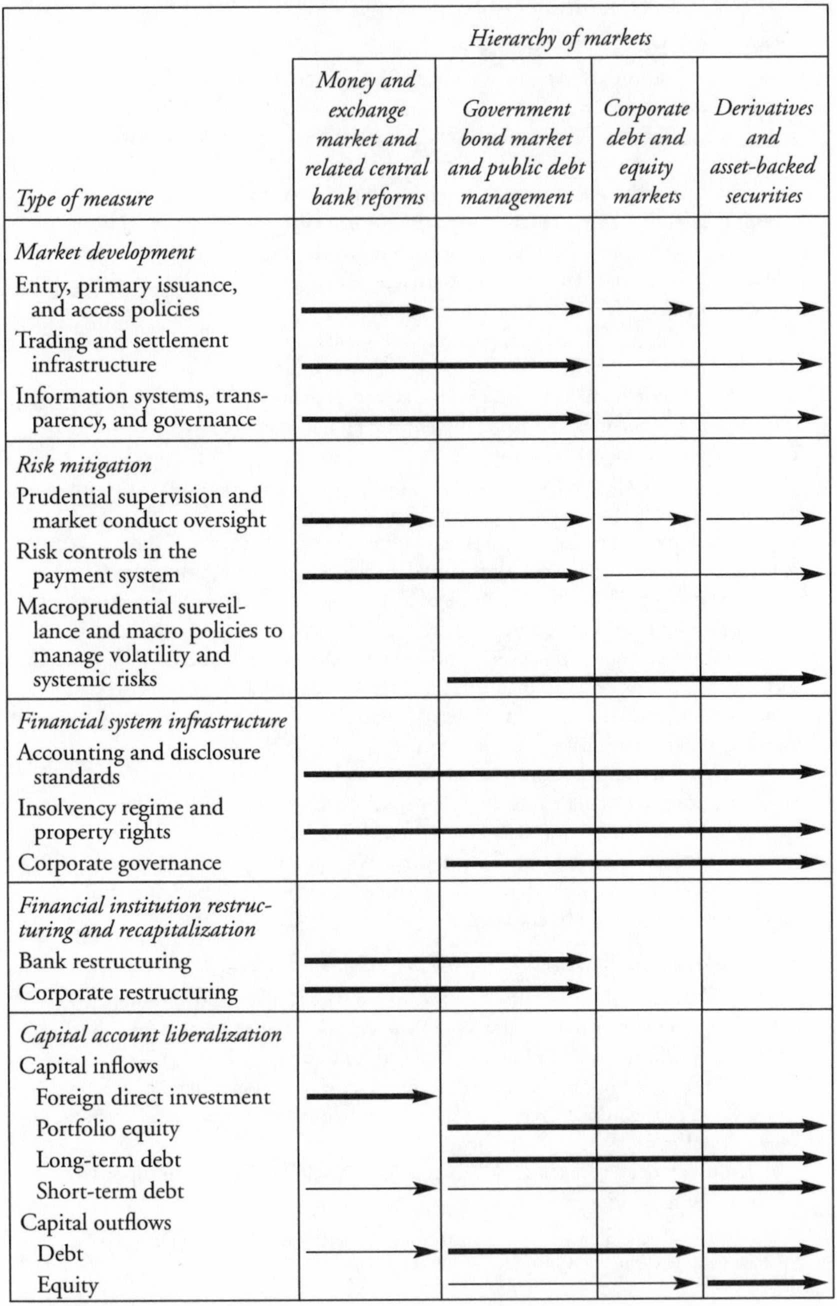
Hierarchy of markets
Type of measure
Money and exchange market and related central bank reforms
Government bond market and public debt management
Corporate debt and equity markets
Derivatives and asset-backed securities
Market development
Entry, primary issuance, and access policies
Trading and settlement infrastructure
Information systems, transparency, and governance
Risk mitigation
Prudential supervision and market conduct oversight
Risk controls in the payment system
Macroprudential surveillance and macro policies to manage volatility and systemic risks
Financial system infrastructure
Accounting and disclosure standards
Insolvency regime and property rights
Corporate governance
Financial institution restructuring and recapitalization
Bank restructuring
Corporate restructuring
Capital account liberalization
Capital inflows
Foreign direct investment
Portfolio equity
Long-term debt
Short-term debt
Capital outflows
Debt
Equity

capital flows for certain instruments and sectors is needed early on in order to support money and exchange market development.

In practice, countries are likely to be in the midst of various stages of market development and risk mitigation, which are out of sync with the hierarchy of markets and sequencing of reforms outlined here. Nevertheless, the proposed approach and principles of market development, risk mitigation, and sequencing can help countries to prioritize future financial reforms, regardless of the pattern of market development in the past.

Foreign capital can play an important role in developing local financial markets. The timing and use of foreign capital, however, should be selected in a manner that maximizes their contribution to domestic market development at the least cost in terms of additional risk. Accordingly, foreign capital first should be used to facilitate real sector and institutional reforms, including banking and corporate sector restructuring through privatization.[55] Capital account liberalization should start with the liberalization of foreign direct investment, which can help to import the superior technology and management expertise needed to implement operational reforms in financial institutions and corporations. Foreign technology and ownership also promote competition and export growth.

Foreign investors can serve also as an important source of demand for local securities.[56] Liberalizing portfolio investment in debt and equity securities widens and diversifies the investor base for local markets and enhances market discipline on issuers and on macroeconomic management more generally.[57] Opening up to portfolio inflows, however, may increase volatility in market prices, at least for emerging-market economies in the short run.[58]

Well-developed risk management capacities of local investors and financial institutions can help domestic financial markets to benefit from foreign capital without subjecting markets to excessive volatility. Cross-border capital flows, in essence, amplify the wide array of risks already prevailing in liberalized domestic financial markets, including credit, liquidity, market, interest rate, exchange rate, and operational risks. For example, access to short-term borrowing by domestic banks within appropriate prudential

55. Johnston, Darbar, and Echeverría (1999).

56. IMF (2003).

57. Sundararajan, Ariyoshi, and Otker-Robe (2002).

58. However, Kaminsky and Schmukler (2003) also find that financial cycles become less pronounced as institutions improve.

limits can facilitate the development of foreign exchange markets and strengthen the links between interbank money and foreign exchange markets. The risk management capacities of financial institutions and domestic investors, however, have to be strong and sophisticated enough to assess and manage higher degrees of risk in all areas. For example, in hindsight, financial institutions and corporations in Korea and Thailand did not adequately assess and manage the risks associated with foreign currency borrowing and lending, which were financed principally by capital flows intermediated through the banking system.

Similarly, it is desirable to achieve some level of depth in domestic financial markets before exposing markets to potentially volatile capital flows.[59] In the presence of domestic institutional investors, local money, equity, and bond markets are likely to be more resilient in the event of economic and financial shocks that may trigger capital outflows. Potential market volatility and high interest rates resulting from a withdrawal of foreign capital are more manageable and short-lived when domestic institutional investors act as counterparties to foreign investors. Thus an adequate base of domestic investors can cushion the impact of external shocks, particularly when the nature of the shock is contagion from abroad rather than domestic in origin, thereby fostering greater financial stability. This, once again, highlights the importance of developing institutional investors as a critical component in the sequencing of financial market reforms and development.

References

Abrams, Richard K., and Paulina Beato. 1998. "The Prudential Regulation and Management of Foreign Exchange Risk." IMF Working Paper 98/37. Washington: International Monetary Fund, March.

Aninat, Edouard. 2001. "Developing Capital Markets in Latin America." Speech to the Inter-American Development Bank. Washington, February 5.

APEC (Asia Pacific Economic Cooperation). 1999. *Compendium of Sound Practices: Guidelines to Facilitate the Development of Domestic Bond Markets in APEC Member Countries.* Manila: Asian Development Bank, September.

Arnone, Marco, and George Iden. 2002. *Establishing a System of Primary Dealers in Government Securities.* Operational Paper 02/02. Washington: International Monetary Fund, Monetary and Exchange Affairs Department.

Arteta, Carlos, Barry Eichengreen, and Charles Wyplosz. 2001. "When Does Capital Account Liberalization Help More Than It Hurts?" NBER Working Paper 8414. Cambridge, Mass.: National Bureau of Economic Research, August.

59. Ishii and Habermeier (2002).

Bank for International Settlements, Committee on Payment Settlement Systems. 2001. *Core Principles of Systemically Important Payment Systems.* Paris, January.

Berglof, Erik, and Patrick Bolton. 2002. "The Great Divide and Beyond: Financial Architecture in Transition." *Journal of Economic Perspectives* 16 (1).

Bisat, Amer, R. Barry Johnston, and V. Sundararajan. 1999. "Sequencing Financial Reform and Liberalization in Five Developing Countries." In R. Barry Johnston and V. Sundararajan, eds., *Sequencing Financial Sector Reforms: Country Cases and Issues.* Washington: International Monetary Fund.

Borio, Claudio. 2003. "Towards a Macroprudential Framework for Financial Supervision and Regulation." BIS Working Paper 128. Paris: Bank for International Settlements.

Buxton, Sally, and Mark St. Giles. 2002. "Governance and Investment Funds." In Robert E. Litan, Michael Pomerleano, and V. Sundararajan, eds., *Financial Sector Governance: The Roles of the Public and Private Sectors.* Brookings.

Chin, Menzie, and Hiro Ito. 2002. "Capital Account Liberalization, Institutions, and Financial Development." NBER Working Paper 8967. Cambridge, Mass.: National Bureau of Economic Research, June.

Cifuentes, Rodrigo, Jorge Desormeaux, and Claudio González. 2002. "Capital Markets in Chile: From Financial Repression to Financial Deepening." In Bank for International Settlements, *The Development of Bond Markets in Emerging Economies.* BIS Papers 11. Paris, June.

Dattels, Peter. 1997. "Microstructure of Government Securities Markets." In V. Sundararajan, Peter Dattels, and Hans J. Blommestein, eds., *Coordinating Public Debt and Monetary Management.* Washington: International Monetary Fund.

Edwards, Sebastian. 2001. "Capital Flows and Economic Performance." NBER Working Paper 8076. Cambridge, Mass.: National Bureau of Economic Research, January.

Green, John H. 1997. "Repurchase Agreements: Advantages and Implementation Issues." Operational Paper 97/03. Washington: International Monetary Fund, Monetary and Exchange Affairs Department.

Greenspan, Alan. 1999. "Lessons from the Global Crises." Remarks before the World Bank Group and International Monetary Fund Annual Meetings, Program of Seminars. Washington, September 27.

Herring, Richard J., and Nathporn Chatusripitak. 2000. "The Case of the Missing Market: The Bond Market and Why It Matters for Financial Development." University of Pennsylvania, Wharton Financial Institutions Center.

Impávido, Gregorio, Alberto R. Musalem, and Thierry Tressel. 2003. "The Impact of Contractual Savings on Securities Markets." Policy Research Working Paper 2948. Washington: World Bank, January.

IMF (International Monetary Fund). 2003. *Global Financial Stability Report.* Washington.

IMF and World Bank. 2001a. *Developing Government Bond Markets.* Washington.

———. 2001b. *Guidelines for Public Debt Management.* Washington.

Ingves, Stefan. 2002. "Meeting the Challenges for the Chinese Financial Sector: What Have We Learned from Other Countries?" Speech delivered to the Second China Financial Forum, South China University, May 16–17.

Ishii, Shogo, and Karl Habermeier. 2002. *Capital Account Liberalization and Financial Sector Stability.* IMF Occasional Paper 211. Washington: International Monetary Fund.

Ishii, Shogo, Karl Habermeier, John Leimone, Inci Otker-Robe, Jorge Ivan Canales-Kriljenko, and Rupa Duttagupta. 2003. *Exchange Arrangements and Foreign Exchange Markets: Developments and Issues.* Washington: International Monetary Fund.

Johnston, R. Barry, Salim M. Darbar, and Claudia Echeverría. 1999. "Sequencing Capital Account Liberalization: Lessons from Chile, Indonesia, Korea, and Thailand." In R. Barry Johnston and V. Sundararajan, eds., *Sequencing Financial Sector Reforms: Country Experiences and Issues.* Washington: International Monetary Fund.

Joint Committee on the Stock Market Scam and Matters Relating Thereto. 2002. "Lok Sabha Report." New Delhi: Lok Sabha Secretariat, December.

Kaminsky, Graciela Laura, and Sergio L. Schmukler. 2003. "Short-Run Pain, Long-Run Gain: The Effects of Financial Liberalization." IMF Working Paper 03/34. Washington: International Monetary Fund, February.

Kovanen, Arto. 1996. "Establishing an Interbank Foreign Exchange Market: Institutional and Operational Modalities." Operational Paper 96/02. Washington: International Monetary Fund, Monetary and Exchange Affairs Department.

Ladekarl, Jeppe. 2002. "Developing Efficient Market Infrastructures." Slide presentation. Washington: World Bank, Financial Sector Department.

Mehran, Hassanali, and Bernard Laurens. 1997. "Interest Rates: An Approach to Liberalization." *Finance and Development* 34 (2, June): 33–35.

Mihaljek, Dubravko, Michela Scatigna, and Agustin Villar. 2002. "Recent Trends in Bond Markets." In Bank for International Settlements, *The Development of Bond Markets in Emerging Economies.* BIS Papers 11. Paris, June.

Mohanty, M. S. 2002. "Improving Liquidity in Government Bond Markets: What Can Be Done?" In Bank for International Settlements, *The Development of Bond Markets in Emerging Economies.* BIS Papers 11. Paris, June.

Prasad, Eswar, Kenneth Rogoff, Shang-Jin Wei, and M. Ayhan Kose. 2003. "Effects of Financial Globalization on Developing Countries: Some Empirical Evidence." Washington: International Monetary Fund, March.

Schinasi, Garry J., and Todd R. Smith. 1998. "Fixed-Income Markets in the United States, Europe, and Japan—Some Lessons for Emerging Markets." IMF Working Paper 98/173. Washington: International Monetary Fund, June.

Stone, Mark. 2000. "The Corporate Sector Dynamics of Systemic Financial Crises." IMF Working Paper 00/14. Washington: International Monetary Fund, June.

Sundararajan, V. 1999. "Prudential Supervision, Bank Restructuring, and Financial Sector Reform." In R. Barry Johnston and V. Sundararajan, eds., *Sequencing Financial Sector Reforms: Country Cases and Issues.* Washington: International Monetary Fund.

Sundararajan, V., Akira Ariyoshi, and Inci Otker-Robe. 2002. "International Capital Mobility and Domestic Financial System Stability: A Survey of the Issues." In Omotunde E. G. Johnson, ed., *Financial Risks, Stability, and Globalization.* Washington: International Monetary Fund.

Turner, Philip. 2002. "Bond Markets in Emerging Market Economies: An Overview of Policy Issues." In Bank for International Settlements, *The Development of Bond Markets in Emerging Economies.* BIS Papers 11. Paris, June.

Vittas, Dimitri. 1999. "Pension Reform and Capital Market Development: 'Feasibility' and 'Impact' Preconditions." Policy Research Working Paper 2414. Washington: World Bank, Development Research Group.

PANEL SUMMARY

Does Integrated Supervision Work in Emerging Markets?

Alan Cameron, chair of the panel, deputy chairman of the Sydney Futures Exchange, and a consultant with Dawson Waldron, asked the panel to discuss the use of integrated supervision in developing countries as a response to the growing complexity of the financial industry from conglomeration, globalization, and the blurring of distinct financial industries. The United Kingdom is the most prominent country to use integrated supervision, but such regulation has long been the model in Scandinavia and Singapore as well.

Daochi Tong, deputy director general of the Department of Listed Companies Supervision in China's Securities Regulatory Commission, observed that China's financial holding-company model may serve as a good model for financial conglomerates in developing markets. This hybrid has the advantages of both integrated and separate financial services: it erects firewalls between subsidiaries to prevent the spread of risks between them yet enables firms to be globally competitive by capitalizing on efficiencies in sharing the client base, information network, and so forth. While this could be an efficient model for firms, it may work especially well for countries that want to adopt integrated supervision but have been unable to do so. While the regulatory structure would permit conglomeration to take advantage of efficiencies of scale and scope, sectoral regulators could effectively regulate each subsidiary component.

He urged regulators in developing markets to prevent the integration of financial services if they lack the appropriate supervisory capabilities for the individual industries. If a nation lacks such capabilities, it might be better served by maintaining a separate regulatory structure and developing its regulatory capacity before seeking to integrate its regulatory agencies and allowing conglomeration in the industry.

Pablo Gottret Valdes, former chair of the Superintendencia de Pensiones, Valores y Seguros in Bolivia and a senior economist in the World Bank's Human Development Network, elaborated on the rationale behind the decision to integrate a financial regulatory system or leave it separate. Among the many motives for integration, a central one is to avoid regulatory arbitrage, such as the circumvention of capital adequacy requirements. For example, integration can produce consistency in agency-specific technical regulations—conflicts of interest, ratings, and portfolio valuation systems—that under separate agencies can be easily manipulated by regulated entities. Integration makes it easier both to share information and thus prevent conflicts of interest and to coordinate policy and regulation.

In Bolivia, similarities between the pension and insurance sectors made integrating their regulatory agencies into a single authority a logical move; creating a single agency ensured adequate regulation and supervision between the two. Integrated supervision also helped Bolivia to handle market crises. Due to political insecurity, the market became extremely volatile, securities values became strongly related to liquidity on a particular day instead of to the underlying quality of the asset, and the market started to collapse. The size of the combined supervisory agency provided the weight necessary to pressure financial industry players to steady the market and secured its managers a place at the table with top politicians and policymakers during the crisis. Supervision of conglomerates also improved because the integrated agency was able to improve its monitoring and to ensure that conglomerates were operating in a transparent and impartial manner.

When Bolivia undertook to integrate the individual ministries of insurance, pensions, and securities into one agency, all the superintendents agreed on a common goal for the new body. The aim was to promote and control the prudent growth of each sector, which Gottret felt is not necessarily a conflict of interest because promoting a transparent and prudent market does not inhibit growth.

The agency adopted the specific goal of convincing insurance and pension companies to channel their long-term internal savings through the capital markets. These funds would flow to the real sector on the basis of risk-rated instruments in a market portfolio and generate a market return for the savings. Although this seems an obvious goal, insurance companies were not investing through the capital markets when Gottret assumed his chairmanship. Even the pension funds were only investing in relatively safe instruments such as demand deposits. There existed no risk-rating agencies or coordinated mark-to-market.

How did the Bolivian government manage to convince firms to invest in the market? The authorities employed the usual assortment of regulations affecting capital markets, pensions, and insurance and set in place a supervisory system intended to minimize disruption to the regulated companies. The government took the essential step of making transparent information available to all market participants. In addition, the government educated insurers and pension fund directors about the benefits of investing in Bolivia's capital markets. The encouragement paid off eventually, as institutional investors began purchasing long-term corporate debt, even in the face of readily available high-interest government debt, the result of deficit spending by the Bolivian government. As a measure of the success of these initiatives, risk-rating agencies have developed, and since 2000 the best Bolivian firms have indeed begun to draw long-term funds from the market, particularly pension and insurance companies, to finance their investments.

Narciso Muñoz, president of the Comisión Nacional de Valores in Argentina, began by observing that the decision to integrate supervision hinges on the nature of financial conglomerates, regulatory arbitrage, and systemic risk in a nation. His presentation covered what financial conglomerates look like in Argentina, the structure of regulators there, and some preconditions for the success of integrated supervision.

Two types of financial conglomerates can be found in Argentina. The first type is centered around a bank and offers at least one other type of financial service; the second is an investment company serving as a holding company for two or more financial services subsidiaries. In Argentina, 42 percent of conglomerates are of the former type; 58 percent are of the latter.

During the 1990s the financial services sector experienced three transformational processes—concentration, an increase in foreign ownership, and conglomeration—that dramatically altered the financial landscape and, in hindsight, may have contributed to the subsequent economic meltdown. Muñoz cited statistics attesting to the intensity of these trends. The number of banks in Argentina dropped from 182 to 109 between 1995 and 2001, while the top-ten banks' share of total deposits climbed from 59 to 74 percent. The top-five pension funds' share of total pension assets jumped from 61 to 80 percent. Foreign-owned banks dramatically increased their share of ownership of total deposits from 31 to 78 percent, and foreign investors owned 81 percent of the conglomerates in Argentina in 2001. Conglomerates clearly had become dominant players by that time, moving 83 percent of total financial resources in Argentina.

Unfortunately, these conglomerates also dramatically increased systemic risk, as all business lines, particularly mutual funds, invested heavily in bank deposits relative to conglomerates in the United States, Chile, Japan, and the Organization for Economic Cooperation and Development. Between the end of 2000 and November 2001, pension funds expanded their investment in bank deposits by almost 20 percent, even as total deposits crashed from $71 billion to $56 billion. Moreover, conglomerates heavily weighted their business toward related subsidiaries. State-owned, domestic private, and foreign private financial conglomerates each invested 76 percent or more of their funds in-house.

Muñoz then turned to Argentina's regulatory structure, which he considered quite unwieldy, with the Parliament and executive branch supervising different areas of financial services. The legislative branch supervises the central bank, which encompasses the Superintendency of Financial and Exchange Institutions. The executive branch appoints the minister of the economy, who appoints the management of the National Securities Commission and names the superintendent of insurance as well as the minister of labor, who appoints the superintendent of pension funds. Each of these groups, in turn, regulates a different sector.

However, there has been initial movement within the government to integrate, consolidate, and harmonize this regulatory structure. In 2001 and 2002, a working group headed by the secretary of finance was established to study and propose reforms of the financial sector. One proposal advocated a thoroughly detailed plan for an integrated regulatory agency responsible for supervising securities, insurance, and pensions. Another working group has been studying the behavior of financial conglomerates and regulatory arbitrage. However, the government has since collapsed and been unable to act on the recommendations.

Muñoz felt that integrated supervision definitely would work in Argentina's market, given the spectacular failure of decentralized supervision. Moreover, integration would work because the entire government is aware of the need for reform. A foundation for such change has been laid, as the regulatory agencies have been collecting information to build a map of the myriad rules and regulations enforced in the different agencies. The eventual goal for such an initiative is to enable the authorities to set proper parameters to prevent regulatory arbitrage and imbalanced enforcement.

Yet although Muñoz felt that integrated supervision remains a necessary correction in Argentina's current system, he contended that some preconditions exist for successful adoption in that market or other emerging markets. Both executive and legislative branches of government must agree that the financial system will operate more soundly under integrated supervision. Users of the system—meaning the consumers, regulated institutions, pensioners, and so forth—must accept that they will benefit more from the reduced systemic risk possible with integrated supervision than from the tighter control possible with sectoral superintendents. Finally, a reform law must be passed without eviscerating other achievements in the nation's legal and economic framework, such as the pension funds and central bank acts.

In the likely event that these desirable conditions are not present, regulators may temporarily coordinate by decrees and resolutions. A less ambitious but more practical approach may be called for, such as modifying large portions of rules with minor changes and immediately responding to problems when detected instead of waiting for crises to instigate change.

Clemente del Valle, chair of Colombia's Securities and Exchange Commission, stated that a big component of the rationale for evaluating the move to integrated supervision in Colombia came from the new government's drive to develop a more efficient government structure across-the-board. Each ministry was given the latitude to evaluate its supervisory and regulatory bodies and to submit a proposal for approval to the president. Del Valle discussed many of the considerations involved in that process.

To understand the decisionmaking process regarding regulatory integration, one must understand the initial regulatory structure that potentially will be modified. Colombia has only two financial sector supervisors. The banking supervisor covers pensions and insurance from a prudential standpoint, and the securities supervisor focuses on market integrity, investor protection, and market development. This structure dates back more than fifty years, so each position has strong historical roots and traditions. According to del Valle, this format creates a great deal of overlap and regulatory arbitrage, because each supervisor regulates by entity, not by activity, and this is a problem the authorities wanted to correct.

What features of the regulatory structure did reformers consider in assessing the present situation in Colombia? They recognized that the framework had numerous problems. It was inducing, or at least conducive to, regulatory arbitrage, particularly with collective investments. Some of these investments were owned by banks, others by securities firms, and these were subjected to two different regulatory regimes and agencies, clearly an undesirable situation. Which supervisor should be regulating a given entity was also ambiguous. For example, which supervisor should regulate a bank engaging in investment banking and trading activity? Such a bank would fall under the jurisdiction of the banking supervisor if regulated by entity, but under the securities supervisor if regulated by activity. Naturally this resulted in inefficiencies and limited the effectiveness of supervision and regulation. The last item of consideration was cost. Consolidating agencies would be an easy way to reduce costs and minimize the size of government, if regulation would be at least as effective after integration as it was before.

These problems clearly demonstrated that the system was unsuitable. Logically, the reviewers first examined the existing literature on the subject. Del Valle lamented that most of the literature discussed why integrated supervision makes sense, and little was available on other schemes for dealing with conglomerates or for blurring activities. The reviewers also assessed in detail their current environment, such as the future agendas of financial institutions and the capacity and strength of the regulatory bodies, taking stock of ongoing and future reforms. One piece of reform was already well under way by this time. The central bank recently had received additional powers to strengthen its supervision of conglomerates, while the securities agency was performing a major overhaul of its regulatory framework, so both agencies were rapidly transforming for the better.

This process of evaluation eventually boiled down to two options. The first proposal was to merge the two institutions into a superintendency like the United Kingdom's Financial Services Agency. The second was to improve both standing agencies and create a dual regulatory structure in which both supervisors would specialize and regulate different activities within an institution simultaneously. This entailed formal coordination between the two supervisors.

Both options had pros and cons. The main benefits of integration, and they were significant, included better supervision of conglomerates, better management of systemic risk, and greater ability to cope with blurred activities. However, despite these important advantages, the downside was also significant. The specialization of each supervisor and agency, an important asset, would be lost in a merger. From a pragmatic perspective, integration would kill the important reform agendas being undertaken in both institutions. Concentrating excessive power in the hands of one institution and supervisor also increased the possibility of industry capture, and the current system produced socially beneficial competition between the two supervisors.

Politically, the securities agency personnel viewed such a move as a takeover that would reduce their standing relative to their banking counterparts, and del Valle shared this view. Precedent existed that such a reorganization would indeed accomplish this, as evidenced by the addition of pensions and insurance to the banking superintendency. Both activities were clearly secondary to banking supervision after the merger, due to the initial failure to complete a functional reorganization of the agencies. According to del Valle, the arrangement has not worked well.

Given these trade-offs, the ministry decided not to integrate and instead reorganized functions between the two supervisors. A senior policy committee was created to help both supervisors to coordinate with the central bank and the minister of finance, effectively granting the Ministry of Finance additional powers for coordinating prudential regulation. Additionally, operational supervision was bolstered through formal memoranda of understanding and cooperation between supervisors. This decision was certainly simpler for Colombia, with only two supervisors, than it would be for nations with more complex supervisory structures.

PART III

Securities Trading

RUBEN LEE

10

Changing Market Structures, Demutualization, and the Future of Securities Trading

It is widely recognized that the pressures of competition, globalization, and technological change are threatening the development, and in some instances the very survival, of many developing capital markets. This chapter examines some options for responding to these pressures that are open to policymakers with regard to their trading infrastructure and exchanges, and also provides some practical comments on how to decide which of these policies to follow.

The chapter is divided into six sections. The first section briefly identifies the key factors threatening the development and survival of securities exchanges in developing markets. The next four sections analyze different policy options that stock exchanges can follow in order to respond to these factors.[1] The second section discusses whether policymakers should continue to support the development of their domestic stock exchanges in isolation, in the belief that they can be self-sufficient. The third examines whether regional linkages or alliances between exchanges should be encouraged, in order to try to build larger virtual markets. The fourth discusses

This paper draws on and extends Claessens, Lee, and Zechner (2003) and Lee (2002b), and the author would accordingly like to thank Stijn Claessens and Josef Zechner.

1. These options have been discussed before. See, for example, Rozłucki (2001) and Szeles and Marosi (2001).

the costs and benefits of mergers between, or takeovers of, stock exchanges in developing markets. The fifth offers some comments on the advantages and disadvantages of demutualizing stock exchanges. The suggestions made throughout the chapter are summarized in the conclusions in the form of six broad recommendations.

Three general comments on the discussion presented here are important. First, given the intense difficulties facing stock exchanges in many developing capital markets, it is not surprising that no easy options are available. Second, the analysis provided in the chapter is not intended to be either definitive or exhaustive. Indeed, the strategy that any particular stock exchange should follow is crucially dependent on its particular circumstances, and thus no single strategy will fit all exchanges. Third, enhancing the domestic provision of trading infrastructure is not sufficient by itself to ensure that a stock exchange in a developing market will thrive. The success of a stock exchange depends on many factors beyond the control of the exchange itself. Relevant issues include the creation and enhancement of domestic institutional investors, which are likely to have natural domestic liabilities, the growth of domestic retail trading, the protection of shareholder rights, the establishment of robust legal systems that allow firms to issue and trade shares, the implementation of high-quality corporate governance, accounting, listing, and transparency standards, and the effective enforcement of securities market legislation and regulation.

Factors Threatening Developing-Market Exchanges

This section briefly identifies a range of factors threatening the development and survival of securities exchanges in developing markets. One central problem is that the number of liquid shares on many such markets is small. There are various reasons for this. In many countries, few companies are large enough and profitable enough to warrant the trading of their shares on a stock market—disregarding the possibility of trading start-up companies on a special board or with reduced listing requirements. A range of potentially attractive companies have not been privatized in many developing markets. The shareholdings of many companies are progressively being concentrated in fewer hands, as the people and institutions seeking control of these companies are gradually buying up their shares. The free float of shares in many companies is therefore declining. Some of the most attractive companies on local domestic markets are also being bought up by bigger foreign firms and are then being delisted.

The prosperity of stock exchanges in developing markets has, in some contexts, also been adversely affected by the trend for domestic stocks to be traded or listed on larger international markets. Such trading or listing can take several forms: it may include dual listing, the use of depository receipt programs, or listing only on a foreign exchange. For all developing markets combined, the ratio of market capitalization listed abroad to total market capitalization jumped from only a few percent in 1989 to about 50 percent currently, with a peak of over 62 percent in 1999.[2] The amount of capital raised abroad, especially for middle-income countries, rivals the amount raised domestically, as large firms, and particularly those firms being privatized, generally include large tranches geared to international markets. The degree of listing of firms on international stock exchanges varies considerably among individual countries. In some cases, more than two-thirds of stock market capitalization is listed abroad as well as domestically.

Firms that seek a listing abroad are typically larger, grow faster, and carry on more international business than their domestic-only counterparts. Such firms are also generally from the better-performing segment of their local market. This reflects both demand and supply factors: better-performing firms are likely to have greater opportunities for growth, which makes seeking foreign financing more attractive. International investors may view these types of firms more favorably. This process of selection means that the firms listed only on the local markets tend to be smaller and perform less well than the firms that can be listed and traded internationally.

Even when the liquidity and price-setting process of a single firm obtaining a foreign listing is not affected, the international listing or trading of specific firms can affect their whole domestic market. More particularly, it may reduce the liquidity of the remaining firms that are only listed domestically in two ways. First, a reduction in the domestic liquidity of the "international" firms may have negative spillover effects on the liquidity of the remaining domestic firms. Second, trading within the domestic market may move away from the purely domestic firms and into those firms that have sought an international presence.[3] Foreign listing of a few large companies can have a large impact, especially on smaller exchanges, given that most trading on such exchanges takes place in precisely these larger shares. The

2. See Claessens, Lee, and Zechner (2003, fig. 4).

3. See Karolyi (2002); Moel (2001).

market capitalization of most companies listed on developing exchanges is small to begin with compared to the size of most companies in which global portfolio investors invest. With further declines in liquidity, the remaining companies may become even more unsuitable for such investment.

Other factors are also threatening the prospects for developing stock exchanges. Regulators in the larger jurisdictions, with the most capital available, rarely allow such exchanges to access their markets directly. Competition with developing-market stock exchanges could, in principle, come from alternative trading systems (ATSs). To date, however, such competition has rarely occurred in developing markets, both because some regulatory authorities ban ATSs and because most developing markets are too small to be profitable for the major international ATSs. If it is allowed, internalization by major financial intermediaries can also pose a threat to developing-market stock exchanges. Developing-market stock exchanges can also be adversely affected by regulatory liberalization. Domestic portfolio restrictions requiring investors to place a specified minimum of their funds in local securities may be abolished. Such deregulation will inevitably increase domestic interest in foreign securities, thereby reducing their interest in the local market.

Self-Sufficiency

The first policy that a threatened stock exchange in a developing market can follow is to maintain the status quo: namely, to seek to prosper by itself in isolation, without any form of linkage with other exchanges. This section briefly surveys some key factors that support the continued existence of domestic stock exchanges in developing markets and then discusses some issues concerning the future sources of revenue for exchanges.

Factors Supporting Developing-Market Exchanges

Several factors support the continued survival of domestic stock exchanges in developing markets, notwithstanding the trends that are threatening the trading infrastructure in such markets. An important one arises from the now widely recognized positive "network externality" associated with order execution.[4] Order flow attracts order flow, and liquidity attracts liquidity. A

4. See Coffee (2001, p. 5).

trading system that already attracts a large amount of orders thus has an advantage over new competing systems. If an exchange in a developing market has most, or even a large part, of the trading in its shares, it is difficult, though not impossible, for other trading systems to capture this liquidity.

Even if competition between a developing-market stock exchange and an international exchange does occur, it is not self-evident that such competition will either undermine the domestic exchange or lead to its demise. The experience of competition between the more developed European exchanges provides an interesting illustration of this. In 1986 the London Stock Exchange (LSE) changed the structure of its market in the so-called Big Bang. Market participants who previously had only been allowed to act in a single capacity, either as a market maker (jobber) or as a broker, were now allowed to act in a joint capacity, namely, to provide integrated market-making and sales teams. In addition, a screen-based system was established for disseminating the LSE's quotes around the market. As a result of these reforms, a significant amount of trading in continental European stocks was attracted to the London market for several years. In response to this competition, all the major continental European stock exchanges automated and liberalized their markets, both by establishing electronic auction mechanisms and by allowing much easier access to their exchanges. The result was that most of the trading that had gravitated to the London market then reverted to the continental European domestic markets.

Although foreign listing may divert trade away from a local exchange, trading in a domestic share on a foreign exchange is not simply a substitute for trading on the local market—it can lead to greater domestic trading if the stock attracts more attention or acquires a better reputation. Trading abroad may also lead to greater trading locally if foreign trading is unwound on the local market.

For many companies—except the truly global ones—the domestic market is the "natural" place to be traded. Domestic traders may be better informed about local companies than foreign investors, and foreign investors know this, thus keeping the trading of companies on the local market. Having no "home listing" may also be a significant problem, especially for small and intermediate-size firms, which tend not to be able to go abroad. These firms, of which there are typically a relatively large number compared to the number of big firms in many developing markets, will often support the operation of some form of domestic stock exchange.

A local stock exchange can adopt a market microstructure by defining market segments or designing listing requirements and fees that best conform to the characteristics of potential listing candidates and investors. Local exchanges can also be more flexible in accommodating channels through which small and medium-size local firms can tap into public securities markets, through securitization, the listing of holding companies, and the listing of private equity funds.

Another factor supporting the continued existence of developing stock exchanges is that the technology of providing trading services continues to advance and relatively low-cost trading systems are now available off-the-shelf. This is making it easier to maintain small stock exchanges in developing markets.

Future Revenues

A key question for many stock exchanges, in both developing and developed markets, is how to remain financially sustainable. In order to prosper by itself in the current climate, a stock exchange needs both to reduce costs and to increase revenues. Options for stock exchanges to enhance their revenues are, however, limited. Historically, exchanges have had seven main types of revenue: membership subscriptions; fees for listing, trading, clearing, and settlement; and charges for the provision of company news and for quote and trade data. A few exchanges have also sought to obtain revenues by selling their technology. For many exchanges, however, many, if not all, of these sources are now under threat.

Membership fees will continue to be paid as long as an exchange has members, but demutualization is bringing this to an end. Exchanges now have customers, not members. In many contexts, listing is subject to intense competition between exchanges, and thus the ability to extract high revenues from the provision of this service is limited. Furthermore, there is debate about whether exchanges should still undertake this function—for example, when they can use it as a competitive advantage against trading systems that do not provide it.[5] There is also growing controversy about whether the listing function is best provided by an independent regulator in order that it not be compromised by the commercial interests of the exchange.[6] One possible source of maintaining a sustainable competitive advantage and a stable source of revenues for an exchange is to provide

5. See Lee (2002a).

6. See Expert Group to Review the Operation of the Securities and Futures Market Regulatory Structure (2003).

clearing and settlement services.[7] However, most securities exchanges do not provide such services, and even for those that do, there is pressure to reduce their costs and charges. The provision of clearing and settlement services is also subject to growing antitrust scrutiny. Only a few exchanges provide company information, and in most environments this is subject to intense competition from the data vendors.

Transaction fees are the largest source of revenues for most exchanges today. However, this may not continue. As the cost of processing an extra marginal trade on most automated trading systems has now become essentially zero, competition between trading systems is pushing transaction fees to this level. Exchanges may be able to attract more trading by allowing remote access to their trading systems. Remote access may allow foreign financial intermediaries easier access to a domestic market. One example where this may happen is in the European Union (EU). If a revised version of the Investment Services Directive (a law affecting the determination of market structure in the EU) is agreed and if it becomes applicable to countries seeking accession to the EU, then all jurisdictions in the EU should be required to allow exchanges from the accession countries to provide remote access to their exchanges. Remote access, however, will not necessarily bring an increase in trading since foreign traders can obtain similar access via local brokers, which establish internal systems for routing orders on a cross-border basis. To date, remote access does not appear to have had a significant impact on exchanges in many developing markets.

One area that may be a viable source of extra revenues for exchanges is the sale of their quote and trade data.[8] Even when a dominant exchange has faced competition from new trading systems, and even if such trading systems have succeeded in capturing some order flow, very rarely has a dominant exchange lost its position as the main source of price discovery for the securities it trades.[9] Revenues from the sale of quote and trade data will therefore be more resilient in the face of competition than those from transaction fees. However, the extent to which revenues from the sale of quote and trade data can be increased will again be critically dependent on regulatory approval, or rather a lack of regulatory price capping, which is most likely to arise as a result of antitrust regulatory scrutiny. Other poten-

7. See Financial Services Authority (1999).

8. There is a fine legal distinction between the terms "data" and "information." See Lee (1998, p. 141).

9. See Shah and Thomas (2000) for an exception.

tial sources of revenues include introducing trading in new instruments such as derivatives or mutual funds.

Although this paper does not discuss in detail the ways of reducing costs for stock exchanges, one is mentioned, as it relates to the other strategies examined. An exchange may be able to reduce the costs it incurs by outsourcing major expenditures. This is often attempted by negotiating with a foreign exchange to use its information technology software and hardware at a lower cost than would be possible if the domestic exchange had to build and operate its own structure. As discussed below, the outsourcing of the supply of key technology may be a precursor to, or associated with, a closer linkage between the participating exchanges or indeed a merger.

Linkages

There is a widely held belief among policymakers interested in promoting capital market development that the survival of many smaller developing markets is in question precisely because they are too small to survive. One obvious response is therefore to consider whether linkages between several such markets could create a larger virtual exchange, which by construction would be more able to survive than the individual and smaller exchanges of which it was composed. This section examines some issues related to the establishment of cross-border associations or linkages between exchanges, in which the various exchanges essentially retain their identities but cooperate in some manner.[10] In order to illustrate the benefits that may be obtained via a linkage between exchanges and some of the strategic problems associated with establishing such a linkage, one example—NOREX—is also discussed.

Linkages between exchanges may work in many ways. Any subset of the various functions undertaken by exchanges can be shared, including marketing, listing, order routing, information dissemination, order execution, matching, clearing, settlement, and administrative services. There are also many different contractual procedures by which shared delivery of these services can be implemented. For example, an exchange may purchase services from another exchange, both exchanges may agree to subcontract delivery to a third party, or a joint venture may be established.

10. See Lee (2001).

The prime aims of a linkage between stock exchanges are to reduce costs and to increase liquidity. Cost savings can arise from many different sources. An exchange may establish an order-routing mechanism or joint clearing arrangement with another exchange in order to offer some of its products to members of the other exchange, without requiring them either to buy a seat on its market or to deal through a local intermediary. This may give traders who are not members of the first exchange cheaper access to its products than would otherwise be available. Economies of scale may be available to cooperating exchanges, if the shared costs in any joint facilities are less than the sum of their separate costs. If the linked exchanges are able to combine the order flows they receive for similar products, they may be able to achieve a more liquid market together than either would be able to realize separately. Sharing standards (for example, on communications, messaging, and technology) can also reduce costs. Achieving these potential gains is not easy, however, and typically requires major managerial and sometimes financial investments.

Of the many attempts at cooperation between exchanges that have been proposed, few have been implemented; of those that have been realized, most have failed.[11] There are many reasons why. Even if several small exchanges operating in the same region were to link up with each other to create a bigger virtual exchange (or indeed were merged to create a larger combined exchange, as discussed below), the new exchange would still be relatively small by the standards of more developed markets. It is therefore questionable whether such a merged exchange would be sufficiently large to interest international investors.

Another factor leading to difficulties in exchange linkages has been associated with the implementation of new technology. Despite continuing advances in information technology, it frequently takes longer and is more expensive to build appropriate technology for market infrastructure projects than is initially anticipated. It is also often cheaper and more efficient to buy a technology package off-the-shelf rather than attempt to develop a new one for a single project. A good time to consider embarking on a cooperative project is when the useful life of a particularly important technological aspect of market infrastructure is coming to an end.

Another critically important factor affecting the development and success of cooperative exchange ventures is the influence of exchange

11. See Lee (1998, ch. 4–5).

governance structures. Linkages are never neutral in terms of their effects on the various constituencies of the participating markets. The governance structures of the collaborating exchanges determine how any benefits obtained by the scheme will be distributed and whether those constituencies that believe their interests might be harmed have the power to change or obstruct its implementation. Joint ventures may give rise to conflict both within a particular institution participating in such a scheme and between the institutions supposedly working together on the project. The resolution of these conflicts may depend not only on the contractual agreements signed between the relevant parties but also on their relative commercial power.

Another problem is the difficulty of creating credible contractual commitments between cooperating exchanges. To achieve this, not only do such agreements have to be initially beneficial for the participants, they have to continue to be so even in a changing environment. If material circumstances vary, as often occurs, one or more of the participating exchanges may decide that the original contractual agreement is no longer appropriate. It is normally hard for the other participating organizations to insist that the dissenting institution honor its original agreement. The costs of enforcing any such contract are typically too high to warrant a legal attempt to do so, particularly in an international environment. More important, however, even if a participating exchange could be forced into an action it perceived as unfavorable, the market participants who trade on the exchange could not be compelled to use the linkage. There is thus little point in forcing an unwilling exchange to continue honoring an initial linkage agreement without the active support of its customers or members.

Other barriers to the successful implementation of linkages between exchanges include legal issues, especially concerning clearing and settlement, and how such linkages should be financed.

Some lessons about the benefits of a linkage between exchanges, and also some of the difficulties in establishing one, can be seen by considering the NOREX project. NOREX is a strategic alliance between four out of the five Scandinavian stock exchanges, namely, those in Denmark, Iceland, Norway, and Sweden.[12] The alliance seeks to maintain the identity of all participating exchanges and is based on the following principles: (a) cross-membership, which means that member firms are encouraged to join all the NOREX exchanges; (b) a single point of liquidity, which means that

12. This is drawn from www.norex.com.

issuing companies are encouraged to list their securities on only one NOREX exchange; (c) a common trading system, which means that trading on the NOREX partner exchanges is executed on a single electronic trading system, allowing the exchanges to take advantage of economies of scale in the development of key technology; and (d) a common regulatory framework, which means that the member countries of the NOREX alliance have harmonized their trading rules and membership requirements as well as the authorization obligations of brokers.

NOREX has had some significant successes. It was founded on January 21, 1998, when the Stockholm Stock Exchange and Copenhagen Stock Exchange signed a formal cooperation agreement. By August 1, 2001, a common set of rules for trading and membership on NOREX had been agreed and implemented, and over this period the SAXESS trading system had also become operational on all four partner exchanges.[13] However, not all its initiatives have been successful. NOREX hoped to attract the three Baltic exchanges to join the partnership, and indeed both a letter of intent and a design study agreement to do so were signed in 2000. After many negotiations, however, the potential cooperation between NOREX and the Baltic exchanges was put on hold a year later and finally was suspended. Among the reasons indicated were that some of the NOREX partners thought the size of the combined Baltic markets was too small to be commercially interesting and that the Baltic exchanges thought the cost of joining NOREX was too high. Subsequently, the only Scandinavian stock exchange that was not a party to NOREX—the Helsinki Stock Exchange operated by the HEX Group—bought up two of the three Baltic exchanges.[14]

Three important and simple lessons may be drawn from the NOREX experience. First, it is possible for different exchanges to agree on a linkage structure that is mutually beneficial. One factor that has led to the success of NOREX has been the long history of cooperation between the Nordic countries in a range of endeavors, which meant that national political concerns about cooperation in the field of stock exchange activity were minimized. Second, at all stages in an alliance between different exchanges, the individual exchanges will consider their commercial incentives and will continue participating only if, on balance, the partnership is believed to

13. On Oslo Börs on May 27, 2002, on ICEX on October 30, 2000, on the Copenhagen Stock Exchange on June 21, 1999, and on the Swedish market on March 12, 1999.

14. After this chapter was written, the OM, the Swedish Stock Exchange, merged with HEX, the Finnish exchange.

further these commercial incentives. Third, balancing the interests of different-size exchanges—in this instance, the larger developed Nordic exchanges and the smaller developing Baltic ones—proved difficult.

Mergers and Takeovers

A third strategy that a stock exchange in a developing market may consider in the face of threats to its prosperity and survival is a merger with, or takeover by, another exchange so as to form a larger, typically regional, exchange. Some brief general issues concerning exchange mergers and takeovers are now raised, and then two examples of such transactions are described—the creation of Euronext and the purchase by HEX of two of the Baltic stock exchanges—in order to illustrate some relevant issues.

There have been only a few mergers and acquisitions between exchanges, and many of the problems associated with linkages between exchanges are also present in such transactions. The difficulties both of agreeing to a merger and of successfully implementing it once agreed are also high. In addition, many other factors can and do obstruct the success of mergers in general and of mergers between securities exchanges in particular, including legal, regulatory, cultural, and political issues.

Politics will indeed be a key factor in determining whether, and how, securities exchanges can agree to merge. In a merger, the identity of the participating exchanges may disappear, and this can cause significant political problems. It is hard to conceive of many jurisdictions, including in developing markets, where the takeover of the national stock exchange would not be considered worrying by its national government, whatever the economic reasons proposed for doing so. This may be particularly true for countries that have been established relatively recently and that see the creation of a local stock exchange as a central plank in their political path to national financial independence. The possibility that their national exchange may be subsumed into a larger market, most likely controlled by one of their neighboring states, is often unappealing.

A merger between exchanges does, however, have three important economic advantages over most types of linkages. First, the distribution of any gains between merged exchanges becomes irrelevant, as they all share in any such gains via their equity in the merged vehicle. In contrast, there is often friction between cooperating exchanges about how to divide up any gains obtained from linkages. The second beneficial attribute of a merger over a linkage is that the credibility of agreements between the elements of a single merged exchange is typically much higher than could obtain in contractual agreements between different exchanges. This is because, while still possible, it is difficult to unwind such mergers. Third, unlike in linkages, contracts between merged exchanges do not have to be fully specified in advance. Internal incentives are normally sufficient for the different components of a merged entity to work together even in changing circumstances.

Two examples of exchange mergers and takeovers are now briefly described in order to illustrate some key aspects of such transactions. Euronext is the result of a merger carried out on September 22, 2000, between the French (SBF), Belgian (BXS), and Dutch (AEX) stock exchanges.[15] The three stock exchanges became wholly owned subsidiaries of a newly created Dutch holding company, Euronext NV, and changed their names to Euronext Paris, Euronext Amsterdam, and Euronext Brussels. Following the merger, Euronext NV became 60 percent owned by former SBF shareholders, 32 percent owned by former AEX shareholders and former holders of participating certificates issued by AEX, and 8 percent owned by former BXS shareholders. Although companies remained listed in their original market, the intention was for all financial instruments to be traded on a single integrated trading platform and for the listing and trading rules of the merged exchanges eventually to be harmonized, resulting in a single market rulebook. Issuers are subject to the supervision and monitoring rules, information obligations, and public offer obligations set by the regulators in the country in which they are listed. Following the merger, the three exchanges retained their separate legal status from a regulatory point of view.

A developing-market example of a merger between exchanges is that of HEX, which has taken over the exchanges in two out of its three neighboring Baltic countries. In April 2001 HEX acquired 62 percent of the Tallinn Stock Exchange in Estonia, and in August 2002 it bought 93 percent of the Riga Stock Exchange in Latvia.[16] The key goal of HEX in doing this was to achieve growth and profitability through internationalization by being the best place to trade Baltic securities. The reasons for the Baltic exchanges to join HEX are illustrated by the Riga Stock Exchange's main

15. Euronext subsequently also bought the London International Financial Futures Exchange and the Lisbon Stock Exchange.

16. HEX has also been in negotiations with the National Stock Exchange of Lithuania.

objectives: to attract a strategic partner or join an alliance in order to obtain a solid investor base and to transfer the know-how of an experienced partner to the Latvian market. When the Riga Stock Exchange saw that NOREX was not going to deliver these objectives at what it believed to be a reasonable price, it decided to join HEX. The Tallinn Stock Exchange and the Riga Stock Exchange still operate independently, but under the brand of HEX. The intention is to provide trading and settlement facilities on a single electronic platform. On February 25, 2002, the Tallinn Stock Exchange and its member firms started using the trading system of HEX, thus creating a common trading environment for securities listed on the Tallinn and Helsinki exchanges.

Several lessons may be drawn from the Euronext and HEX experiences. First, both transactions show that a merger between exchanges can be structured so that the national identities of the constituent exchanges can be retained, or at least continue to be marketed, while creating a new transnational institution. Second, the anticipated technological efficiencies obtainable from a merger, such as the delivery of a single trading platform across several exchanges, can take several years to be realized. Third, the technological aspects of a merger are easier to implement than any regulatory convergence or harmonization that might be needed to exploit efficiencies in having a single regulatory structure govern trading on the merged institution. Indeed, notwithstanding developments in the EU, there is no example of a merger between exchanges in different countries where some form of regulatory framework has been established so that a single national or international set of rules or laws is applicable to all users of the merged institution.

Demutualization

There is now a widespread belief that the demutualization of stock exchanges is both desirable and inevitable, as the following two quotes illustrate. According to Cha,[17]

> Surely it would now be impossible to deny that the securities community has reached an implicit consensus that demutualisation

17. Cha (1999, n.p.).

> maximises efficiency incentives and is critical to the survival of international exchanges.

And according to Cameron,[18]

> Mutuals as a way of operating financial markets were never going to survive corporate membership of exchanges, far less computerisation in the financial sector, the information age, the Internet revolution, or globalisation. They reflected the coffee shop origins of the markets, the shouted order across the crowded, noisy, and frequently smoke-filled room, where every trader knew every other trader and what they were good for. The wonder is not that they are coming to an end, but that they lasted so long.

Notwithstanding this almost universal agreement that the merits of demutualizing securities exchanges are self-evident, there may also be significant costs in such a process. Furthermore, although some of the larger benefits, and specifically those obtained by members of an exchange who choose to sell their shares, are available immediately after the event, the costs that arise from demutualizing a stock exchange will take some time to become apparent. The choice of whether to demutualize a stock exchange is therefore more finely balanced than generally accepted, and indeed there may well be contexts in which it is inadvisable.

Demutualization has a wide range of potential benefits for exchanges.[19] It may allow an exchange:

1. To modernize its technology,
2. To create a valuable currency to develop international strategic alliances and acquisitions by offering equity to relevant parties,
3. To obtain a governance and management structure that is more agile, flexible, and swift in its ability to respond to industry and market conditions,
4. To obtain a governance and management structure that is less susceptible to members' vested interests and conflict between classes of members and, more bluntly, that is not subject to "cumbersome decision-making and strategic gridlock,"[20]

18. Cameron (2002a, para. 1).

19. See BTA Consulting (2001); Cameron (2002b); Karmel (2002a, 2002b); Lee (1998, ch. 2–3); Sydney Futures Exchange (2000).

20. See Grasso (1999).

5. To unlock members' equity and buy out the vested interests of traders,

6. To ensure that those market participants that provide the most business to an exchange have a proportionate say in its control,[21]

7. To avoid concentration of ownership power in a particular group of exchange participants,

8. To spread ownership risk,

9. To reward key market participants in equity, thus giving them a financial incentive to bring business to the exchange,

10. To provide appropriate incentives for, and impose market discipline on, management,

11. To create a catalyst for pursuing new business strategies,

12. To provide both a valuation benchmark and liquidity for investors,

13. To obtain an initial infusion of capital and to gain easier ongoing access to capital,

14. To be more willing to open up access to its markets, and

15. To improve financial decisionmaking by ensuring that resources are allocated to business initiatives and ventures that enhance shareholder value.

A full analysis of all the potential benefits associated with demutualization is beyond the scope of this paper. Nevertheless, four obvious but important and general points are worth noting, and then some more detailed comments on five of the potential benefits listed are also made, given their importance. The four general points are, first, the anticipated benefits may not materialize; second, they may be obtainable with a mutual governance structure; third, there may indeed be costs associated with demutualization; and fourth, some of the anticipated benefits may in fact conflict with each other. More detailed comments on five of the potential benefits—namely, the items numbered 2, 5, 9, 14, and 15—now follow.

The value of benefit number 2—that demutualization may give an exchange a valuable currency to develop international strategic alliances and acquisitions by offering equity to relevant parties—is self-evidently dependent on a prior assumption that an exchange wishes to enter into such an alliance or make such an acquisition. Given the failure of almost all such linkages, exchanges in developing markets may choose not to implement one, which may reduce the anticipated value of demutualization. Furthermore, there are many different contractual procedures by which to effect a linkage between exchanges. A transaction in the shares of the

21. Cameron (2002a, para. 16).

participating exchanges is not a precondition for the success of a linkage between exchanges.

Benefit number 5—that demutualization may allow an exchange to unlock members' equity and buy out the vested interests of traders—normally has different implications for the different types of members of an exchange. Such members may typically be divided into a small group of relatively large firms that provide most of the business on the exchange and a large group of relatively small firms that each provides only a tiny proportion of the business of the exchange. It is this second group of members whose votes normally determine whether an exchange chooses to demutualize or not. Their prime reason for voting for such an outcome is to receive the shares in the demutualized exchange, the value of which is normally relatively large compared to the size of their firms. This is, in fact, a key factor explaining why many exchanges have chosen to demutualize—so that the majority of their members can realize at short notice a large capital gain on the shares of the exchange that they own.

Benefit number 9—that demutualization may let an exchange reward key market participants in equity, thus giving them a financial incentive to bring business to the exchange—is likely to have an unanticipated and paradoxical effect. Many privately owned ATSs and indeed demutualized exchanges have sought precisely to attract trading by giving equity ownership to the largest users of their trading platforms—namely, to the biggest traders in the market. By doing so, however, these providers of trading infrastructure are in effect re-mutualizing their ownership structure, but with a different group of owners than before.

Benefit number 14—that demutualization may make an exchange more willing to open up access to its markets—could be very beneficial both for the exchange itself and for the market in which it operates. In particular, a demutualized exchange may be more responsive than a mutual exchange to the needs of its users and customers, including investors and issuers, and may reduce the need for the exchange to satisfy the interests of the financial intermediaries that were previously its members and owners. This may encourage the exchange to grant direct access to its trading system to market participants other than financial intermediaries.[22] The cost savings to investors, and indirectly to issuers, of having such direct access without any intermediation can be considerable.[23] A nonprofit or coopera-

22. Steil (2001).

23. See Domowitz and Steil (1999, 2001).

tive exchange whose members are financial intermediaries will be loath to grant access to its trading system directly to investors. To do so would disintermediate, and thereby imperil the livelihood of, the members whose very welfare the exchange exists to serve. A for-profit non-member-owned system, in contrast, would have no such qualms, as it would not have to satisfy the preferences of the financial intermediaries trading on its system.

Although this argument is valid, it is not believed determinative, especially in a developing context. The creation of any financial institutions in a developing market is extremely hard, and the development of the institutional investors that would benefit the most from direct access to a stock exchange is frequently much harder than the creation of brokers. Any cost savings that a demutualized stock exchange with direct investor access might bring therefore need to be balanced against the benefits that the presence of brokers, with ownership interests in an exchange, may yield in helping to bring the market into existence.

The last benefit, number 15—that demutualization may allow an exchange to improve financial decisionmaking by ensuring that resources are allocated to business initiatives and ventures that enhance shareholder value—is the most problematic for policymakers precisely because it will come true. A central problem with an exchange demutualizing is if the exchange operates a monopoly. Notwithstanding the current environment in which trading infrastructures are believed to be competing with each other to some extent, there are strong reasons why trading in a particular asset tends to gravitate to a single monopolistic exchange. Order flow tends to attract order flow, making competition with a dominant exchange difficult. A monopolistic for-profit exchange will tend to do what all monopolists do: maximize profits by raising prices, reducing output, and reducing unnecessary expenditures. This will not be desirable either for the users of the exchange or indeed more generally from a public policy viewpoint.

Standard corporate governance procedures operated by a for-profit demutualized stock exchange are unlikely to stop this from happening. A key goal of demutualization is precisely to disperse ownership to a wider group of market participants than just financial intermediaries. However good the corporate governance structure of a demutualized securities exchange, it will therefore be difficult for a wide group of shareholders to exert any influence to stop such anti-competitive activity. Indeed, to the extent that the owners of securities exchanges are not users of the exchanges, they will have no incentive to do so. On the contrary, as shareholders, the owners will benefit from any monopolistic profits that these exchanges are able to obtain.

It is here that the main advantage of the mutual governance structure is evident from a public policy viewpoint. The central attribute of a mutual or cooperative securities exchange is that the users of its services are also its owners. The customers of a cooperative exchange can therefore control the prices the exchange sets and ensure that, even if it operates effectively as a monopoly, by dint of being the dominant provider of execution facilities, the exchange does not charge anti-competitive prices.

This brief summary of some the costs and benefits of demutualizing a stock exchange in a developing market is not meant to be exhaustive. It does, however, highlight one central conclusion: namely, it is not clear that such a policy is unambiguously beneficial, and the benefits of demutualization need to be set off against the costs.

Conclusions

This chapter examines the responses that policymakers in developing markets who are concerned with the future of their domestic securities exchanges can follow in the face of the pressures of competition, globalization, and technological change. Four major policy options are discussed: self-sufficiency of a domestic stock exchange, regional linkages or alliances between exchanges, mergers and takeovers of stock exchanges, and demutualization. The advice presented in the paper may be summarized in the following six broad recommendations:

1. Identify the policy options open to a domestic stock exchange.
2. When assessing any particular option, undertake a realistic cost-benefit analysis of its likely effects.
3. When considering the financial sustainability of a stock exchange, ensure that due account is taken of the likely effects of both competition and regulatory intervention.
4. When evaluating a linkage between exchanges, identify both the initial and the ongoing incentives facing the cooperating institutions, so as to assess whether they are likely to maintain their support for the linkage, and bear in mind that most exchange linkages have failed.
5. When examining the merits of a merger between exchanges, do not underestimate the difficulties either of agreeing to the merger or, once it is agreed, of implementing it effectively.

6. Do not accept unconditionally the belief that demutualizing a stock exchange is clearly beneficial: there are costs as well as benefits associated with such institutional transformations.

Three aspects of these recommendations are noteworthy. First, many people may consider them to be obvious, but that is not sufficient reason to ignore them. On the contrary, the obvious advice is often the most important, is often overlooked, and frequently is not implemented, even if identified. Second, given the intense difficulties facing stock exchanges in many developing capital markets, it is not surprising that no easy options are available. Finally, these recommendations are not intended to satisfy someone seeking specific suggestions that can be implemented in a particular context. This is both because the analysis provided here is neither definitive nor exhaustive, and also—more important—because the strategy that any particular stock exchange should follow is crucially dependent on its particular circumstances. A full examination of the relevant context is therefore required before any specific recommendations can be made.

References

BTA Consulting. 2001. "To Be or Not to Be: Demutualization Survey." London, February.

Cameron, Alan. 2002a. "Demystifying Demutualisation." Available at www.sec.or.th/nbfi_2002/papers/513session5_future_cameron.doc [June 30, 2003].

———. 2002b. "The Future of Stock Exchanges." Presentation at the Regional Seminar on Non-Bank Financial Institutions in East Asia Region, World Bank, Bangkok, Thailand, September 4–6.

Cha, Laura. 1999. "Regulatory Framework after the Merger of the Exchanges." Speech given at the Hong Kong Securities Institute seminar, Hong Kong, October 21.

Claessens, Stijn, Ruben Lee, and Josef Zechner. 2003. "The Future of Stock Exchanges in European Union Accession Countries." CEPR Paper. London: Centre for Economic Policy Research for the Corporation of London, March.

Coffee, John C. Jr. 2001. "The Coming Competition among Securities Markets: What Strategies Will Dominate?" Working Paper 192. New York: Columbia University School of Law, September 24.

Domowitz, Ian, and Benn Steil. 1999. "Automation, Trading Costs, and the Structure of the Trading Services Industry." In Robert Litan and Anthony M. Santomero, eds., *Brookings-Wharton Papers on Financial Services 1999*, pp. 33–92. Brookings.

———. 2001. "Innovation in Equity Trading Systems: The Impact on Transaction Costs and the Cost of Capital." In Richard Nelson, David Victor, and Benn Steil, eds., *Technological Innovation and Economic Performance*. Princeton University Press.

Expert Group to Review the Operation of the Securities and Futures Market Regulatory Structure. "Report to the Financial Secretary of the HKSAR Government." Available at www.info.gov.hk/info/expert/expertreport-e.htm [June 30, 2003].

Financial Services Authority. 1999. *The Transfer of the UK Listing Authority to the FSA.* Consultation Paper 37. London, December.

Grasso, Richard A. 1999. "Public Ownership of the U.S. Stock Markets." Testimony before the Committee on Banking, Housing, and Urban Affairs, U.S. Senate, September 28.

Karmel, Roberta. 2002a. *Demutualization of Exchanges as a Strategy for Capital Market Regulatory Reform.* Washington: Inter-American Development Bank.

———. 2002b. "Turning Seats into Shares: Causes and Implications of Demutualization of Stock and Futures Exchanges." *Hastings Law Journal* 53 (2, January): 367–430.

Karolyi, G. Andrew. 2002. "The Role of ADRs in the Development and Integration of Emerging Equity Markets." Working Paper. Ohio State University, Fisher College of Business.

Lee, Ruben. 1998. *What Is an Exchange? The Automation, Management, and Regulation of Financial Markets.* Oxford University Press.

———. 2001. "Promoting Regional Capital Market Integration." Paper prepared for the Inter-American Development Bank, Washington, January.

———. 2002a. *Central Counter-Parties and the Stock Exchange Industry.* Oxford Finance Group, prepared for the World Federation of Exchanges.

———. 2002b. "The Future of Securities Exchanges." In Robert Litan and Richard Herring, eds., *Brookings-Wharton Papers on Financial Services 2002.* Brookings.

Moel, Alberto. 2001. "The Role of American Depositary Receipts in the Development of Emerging Markets." *Economia* 2 (1, Fall): 209–73.

Rozłucki, Wiesław. 2001. "Developing Stock Markets in Central Europe: Where Do We Stand?" In Lajos Bokros, Alexander Fleming, and Cari Votava, eds., *Financial Transition in Europe and Central Asia: Challenges of the New Decade,* pp. 139–44. Washington: World Bank.

Shah, Ajay, and Susan Thomas. 2000. *Displacing the Liquidity of an Entrenched Market: One Case Study.* Bombay: Indira Gandhi Institute of Development Research.

Steil, Benn. 2001. "Borderless Trading and Developing Securities Markets." Paper presented at the Third Annual Financial Markets and Development Conference, World Bank, International Monetary Fund, and Brookings, Washington, April 19–21.

Sydney Futures Exchange. 2000. "Information Memorandum." Sydney.

Szeles, Nóra, and Gábor Marosi. 2001. "Isolation or Association: A Difficult Choice for a Regional Exchange—The Example of the Budapest Stock Exchange." Josseph de la Vega Prize. Federation of European Stock Exchanges and European Capital Markets Institute, March.

AMAR GILL

11

Corporate Governance Issues and Returns in Emerging Markets

This paper shares my views on corporate governance in emerging markets, focusing on Asia, the region covered by my company. CLSA, a subsidiary of the French banking group Credit Lyonnais, has produced its fourth report on corporate governance. We issued our first report in 2000, just after the financial crisis hit Asia, in response to the belief of our clients—international fund mangers—that this was a key area of concern for emerging markets in Asia. We have since issued a report each year, scoring the companies we cover, as well as markets, for macro determinants on corporate governance.[1]

In this paper, I share some of our findings on the correlation between good corporate governance and share price outperformance. I then provide some views on why this correlation should hold. Then, I discuss the main issues regarding corporate governance in Asia and how they differ from those in developed markets. Finally, I offer some personal observations on why real progress on corporate governance in Asia and most other emerging markets has been slow and what needs to be done for there to be more significant advance in this area.

1. Gill (2000, 2001, 2002, 2003).

Correlation between Corporate Governance and Stock Returns

In our latest report, we find, once again, prima facie evidence that the stocks of companies with good corporate governance tend to outperform the market, particularly over the medium term, that is, three to five years. This is especially true in markets where corporate governance is a concern.

The positive effect of good corporate governance is seen more clearly over three to five years than in the short term. Every year, we rank the companies we cover in each of the markets we cover according to a system for scoring corporate governance. This system scores companies on fifty-seven issues, covering seven key areas of corporate governance: discipline, responsibility, transparency, fairness, independence, accountability, and social responsibility. The analyst for each company scores it based on the best information available to him and on his interpretation of the company's track record. After scoring and ranking the companies, we divide them into corporate governance quartiles.

Returns in global equity markets have been dismal in recent years. Most of our markets in Asia have fallen, whether we look at performance in 2002 alone or in the five years leading up to end-2002. Nevertheless, in 2002, the companies in the top quartile of corporate governance in six of the ten Asian countries under CLSA coverage had stocks that outperformed within their market—most notably in China and the Philippines (see figure 11-1). And over three and five years, the top-quartile corporate governance stocks outperformed in six and seven of the ten markets surveyed, respectively (see figures 11-2 and 11-3). Over the three years to end-2002, on average the top-quartile corporate governance stocks outperformed the average of companies covered by CLSA in each market by 5 percentage points, while over the last five years these stocks outperformed by 35 percentage points.

The bottom-quartile corporate governance stocks underperformed in only five of the ten markets under coverage for 2002—Singapore, Hong Kong, Malaysia, Thailand, and China—but the underperformance was large enough such that, on average, the bottom quartile underperformed the average of all the quartiles of the respective market by almost 4 percentage points on average. Over the previous three years, the bottom quartile underperformed in seven of the markets by almost 8 percentage points on average (the exceptions were Hong Kong, Korea, and Taiwan). And over the last five years, the bottom quartile underperformed the average

Figure 11-1. *One-Year Performance of Companies in the Top and Bottom Quartiles of Corporate Governance in Relation to Country Average, 2002*

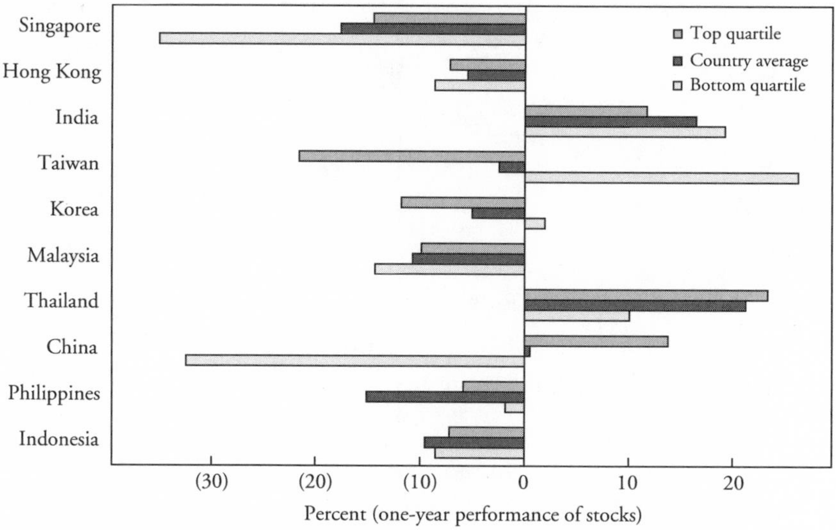

Source: CLSA Emerging Markets calculations using data from Bloomberg.

performance in the market by 25 percentage points (although not in Hong Kong, Korea, Singapore, and Taiwan).

The calculation is based on the simple average performance of the stocks in the top quartile versus the average performance of all the quartiles. A simple average is used within each quartile rather than a market cap–weighted average, so that the performance of the quartile is not skewed by that of any large-cap company: the aim is to examine whether, on average, companies with better corporate governance have stocks that perform well irrespective of size. The comparison is made against the average of the four quartiles rather than against the main country index because the performance of the index is skewed toward the performance of the large-cap firms. Using a simple average calculation for each quartile might show all quartiles outperforming the index if the big-cap index stocks had seen a large fall or, conversely, if the big-cap index stocks had seen a large rise. Hence consistency requires that the simple average performance of stocks in each quartile be compared with the simple average performance of all the quartiles.

For the three years to end-2002, the only markets where the top quartile did not outperform were Singapore (marginally), Taiwan, and Hong

Figure 11-2. *Three-Year Performance of Companies in the Top and Bottom Quartiles of Corporate Governance in Relation to Country Average, End-2002*

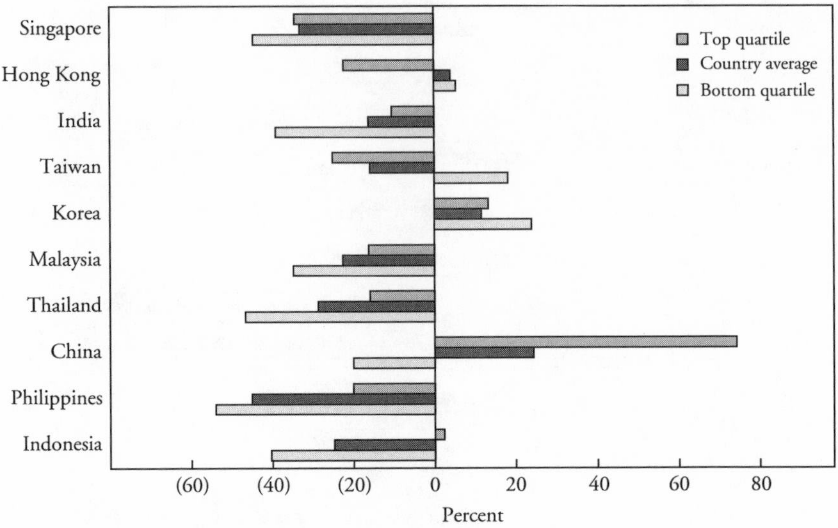

Source: See figure 11-1.

Kong. For the five years to end-2002, the three markets where the top-quartile corporate governance companies did not outperform were Singapore (again very marginally), Hong Kong, and Korea.

For seven of the ten markets, the top two quartiles of corporate governance stocks outperformed the bottom two quartiles in the respective market in 2002; the exceptions were India, Korea, and Taiwan (figure 11-4). The average outperformance of the top-half corporate governance stocks against the bottom was, however, very slight (0.1 percentage point) for the year, because the bottom-half corporate governance stocks—generally companies in sectors other than technology—outperformed quite significantly in Taiwan and Korea. Over the last three years in eight of the ten markets, the top half of the corporate governance stocks outperformed the bottom half—exceptions were Taiwan and Korea—by an average of almost 10 percentage points. In all the markets under coverage except Korea, the top half of the corporate governance stocks outperformed the bottom half over the last five years; on average the top half of corporate governance companies provided 45 percentage points higher returns than the bottom half.

In the countries where the top-quartile companies did not noticeably outperform the bottom-quartile companies, sectoral factors were the key to

Figure 11-3. *Five-Year Performance of Companies in the Top and Bottom Quartiles of Corporate Governance in Relation to Country Average, End-2002*

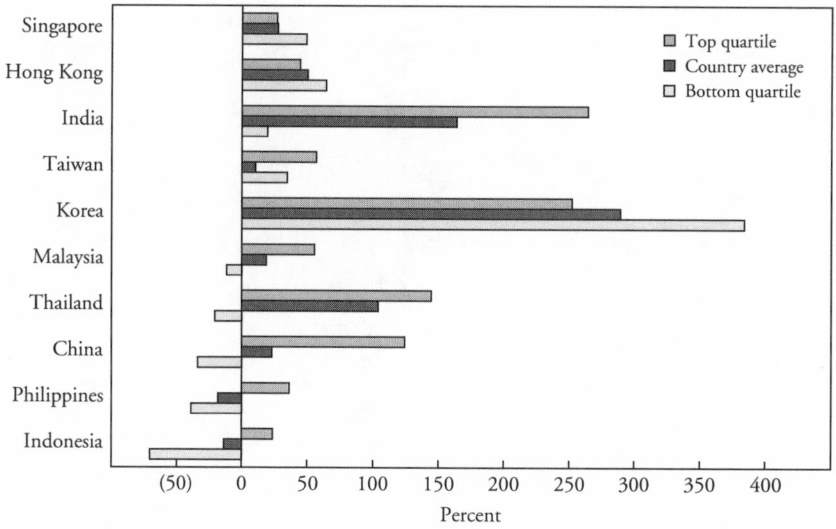

Source: See figure 11-1.

performance—for example, the performance of the technology sector in India, Korea, and Taiwan surpassed the performance of quality companies as represented by good corporate governance.

In addition corporate governance is sometimes not a key factor in the performance of stocks when overall standards of corporate governance in that market are within the expectations of fund managers and there are no major shocks in the companies covered by most investors. Thus in Singapore and Hong Kong, the two markets that rate the highest for macro determinants of corporate governance, the top quartile of corporate governance companies did not generally outperform over the periods examined. Nevertheless, even in Hong Kong, when the performance of stocks is adjusted for beta, the companies with better corporate governance produced better returns.

For the five markets ranked in the lower half of our country rankings for macro determinants of corporate governance—Indonesia, Philippines, China, Thailand, and Malaysia—the top-quartile corporate governance stocks outperformed over one, three, and five years against the country average. For 2002, the top-quartile corporate governance companies outperformed the average of the quartiles in these five markets by almost 6 percentage points, by a much wider 24 percentage points over three

Figure 11-4. *Performance of Companies in the Top Half in Relation to Companies in the Bottom Half of Corporate Governance, by Country, One, Three, and Five Years*

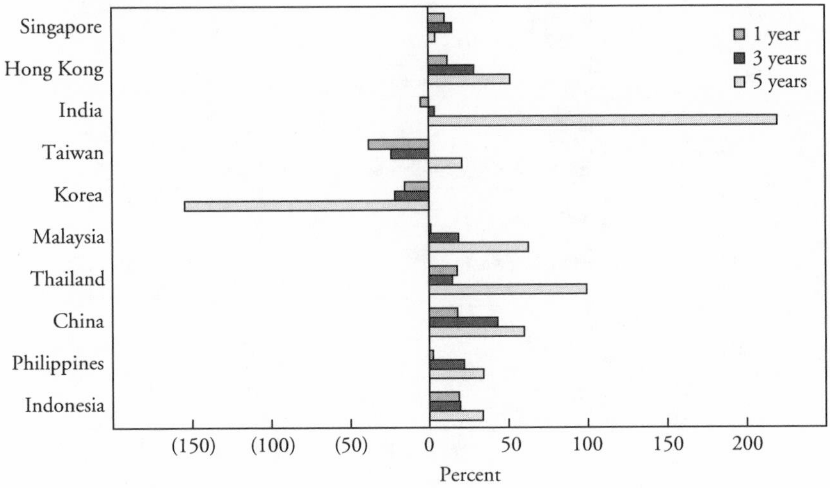

Source: See figure 11-1.

years, and by an impressive 54 percentage points over five years. The top half of the corporate governance stocks in these markets outperformed the bottom half by 11 percentage points in 2002 and by 23 and 58 percentage points, respectively, over three and five years. And the bottom-quartile corporate governance stocks underperformed the respective country average for these five markets by more than double the underperformance of bottom-quartile corporate governance stocks in the overall sample of ten markets, whether for one, three, or five years. Over the last five years, for instance, the underperformance was minus 58 percentage points for the five markets with relatively poor corporate governance versus minus 25 percentage points for the whole basket of markets covered.

Particularly where corporate governance is a big concern, the evidence suggests much greater outperformance of the top corporate governance stocks and underperformance of poor corporate governance stocks over shorter periods of a year and quite certainly over the medium term.

Why Good Corporate Governance Is Correlated with Higher Stock Returns

The reason why corporate governance is correlated with stock performance is, I believe, quite simple. Corporate governance is one of the ways of picking out quality management. Well-run companies give their shareholders what they want, and good corporate governance is one of the key things shareholders want. Well-run companies also churn out better financial ratios. In our 2001 corporate governance report, *Saints and Sinners,* we establish that there is a strong correlation between companies with good corporate governance and high return on equity as well as economic value added and that the converse is true for companies with poor corporate governance.[2]

Because well-run companies have both good corporate governance and higher financial returns, they provide investors with higher medium-term returns and, theoretically, less risk because the companies with good corporate governance should be the companies that are less likely to implode the way Enron did. I say "theoretically" because, in practice, it is very difficult to tell how much of the good corporate governance we detect is simply a front. Hence our latest report is titled *Fakin' It.*[3]

There are also other caveats on whether companies with better corporate governance have stocks that are lower risk in the sense of having a lower beta—that is, a lower correlation with the market overall. The reason why they may not have a low beta is that large-cap index stocks generally have the resources to have more independent directors on the board, getting results out to investors faster, and so forth. But whether beta is a good indicator of investment risk is debatable. No less an authority in the area than Warren Buffet, for instance, believes that market correlations deserve to be chucked into the bin when determining the real risk in investments.

Theoretically, stocks of companies with better corporate governance have lower risk, and in practice they have higher returns over the medium term. That seems inconsistent with the maxim in finance theory that higher returns can only come with higher risk. One might say that the higher corporate governance stocks outperform only in periods when market returns are poor—that is, when safer stocks do better. Although we do

2. Gill (2001).
3. Gill (2003).

not have evidence going back to the bull market in Asian equities, my view is still that as long as the correlation between good corporate governance and high return on equity plus positive economic value added holds—which it should, because the explanatory factor is quality management—then companies that have consistently high returns on equity, the highest economic value added, and the best corporate governance will, in practice, outperform their market.

A company that is able to generate a higher financial return on its equity base, especially when that return is above its overall cost of capital, is continuously generating added value for shareholders. Whatever finance theory says, it is difficult to discount adequately all the future added value that such management can deliver into the share price at any given time. Companies with top-quality management, over time, will surprise investors on the upside rather than the downside. And hence the stock returns of these companies, which also exemplify high corporate governance, outperform.

A second reason for the correlation is that investors are not constrained to particular markets and can avoid stocks and markets where corporate governance is poor. In the early 1990s, dedicated-country and regional funds were popular products. However, such emerging-market investment vehicles were disasters. Had the investors kept their money in their home market, many would have seen much better returns.

While spreading out one's investment geographically and diversifying into emerging markets are conceptually appealing, because doing so promises to provide better performance and spread the risk, the end investor now has much less confidence in being able to pick the right country or region. Hence this responsibility is being moved to the institutional fund manager.

The end investor places funds in international or global accounts rather than in specific country or regional funds. It is then up to the fund manager of these accounts to determine which countries and companies to invest in. The institutional fund manager is not constrained in the way the fund manager of a country fund would be in choosing among what might be the best of a poor lot of companies for corporate governance in a given market. The investor can get the same exposure to a particular industry from companies in other countries where the standards of corporate governance are seen to be higher.

The huge menu of possible stock investments open to the global fund manager means the investor will be much more careful about investing in companies with poor standards of corporate governance, especially if he cannot monitor the developments at each of the companies as closely as a country-dedicated fund manager can. Particularly given the poor record of corporate governance during the Asian crisis, when corporate governance fiascos led to huge deratings of some stocks—and sometimes of the market—investors are generally more alert to the need to invest in companies with a minimum acceptable level of governance standards. Corporate governance has become an investment criterion that determines how much investors are willing to pay up for a stock.

Main Corporate Governance Issues for Developing Markets

The corporate governance issues that arise in emerging markets are different from those that arise in the developed world. Particularly in the United States, but also in most of the developed world, corporate governance issues arise when ownership is separated from control. The managers are in control and hard to check, especially when ownership is diffuse, without any big controlling shareholder. Managers then are able to steer the companies to favor management rather than shareholders generally, through, for instance, expansion and acquisitions for no purpose other than to make the managers even more powerful and compensation schemes that essentially rob the shareholders.

In emerging markets, this is not an important issue because major shareholders exert tight control on companies. The representatives of controlling shareholders generally run the company; they make sure that managers are not stealing from shareholders through outrageous option schemes, off-balance-sheet transactions where the risk remains with the listed company, and so forth. Major shareholders are, generally, in control in emerging markets.

But dominant-shareholder control raises a different set of corporate governance issues, pitting minority interests against majority interests. Controlling shareholders may have other interests that conflict with the interests of the listed company. When it comes to the crunch, the private or other interests of the controlling shareholder usually triumph over the fate of the listed company, as repeatedly occurred during the Asian crisis.

The problem of dominant-shareholder control in emerging markets is not just family, or single individual, control. Quite often, the largest companies in the emerging markets are privatized entities in which the controlling shareholder invariably is still the government, and the government, like other controlling shareholders, often has interests other than maximizing value for the company.

We have seen government-controlled companies not getting the tariffs they were due by tariff formulas that initial public offering prospectuses said would hold or going into massive share purchase schemes of other stocks on behalf of individuals related to the government, or making international investments because the government felt that was the way to go, but at prices that dismayed investors and sent stock prices shuddering down; or being directed by government to buy parts from local vendors even if they were more expensive or to increase capital expenditure to support certain other sectors; and so on. Such actions on the part of government-controlled large companies give the markets an image of poor corporate governance that is often of greater significance than the mismanagement of small, family-controlled firms.

Slow Progress on Corporate Governance in Emerging Markets

In our corporate governance reports, for 2002 and the recent one for 2003, we highlight improving regulations in the markets that we cover. In a number of the markets, there is also greater enforcement of the rules. However, in practically all these markets, investors remain wary about the level of corporate governance. The reason, to paraphrase an old adage, is that you can put garb on a leopard, but the spots are still there. Changing rules may present, superficially, the form of good corporate governance, but the commitment might well be absent. Commitment comes with values—that is, the business culture. And culture usually changes very gradually.

The culture in emerging markets is that the companies are run the way the controlling shareholders want them to be run. If investors do not like that, they can take their money elsewhere. The controlling shareholders see markets going up and down, and they believe that in the end investors will return to their markets and lift all values. So, robbing minority shareholders today may not necessarily affect the market value of the company tomorrow or next year. And if the controlling shareholder does not care to raise more equity capital or to place out existing shares, then he (or the finance minister) may not really care about the market value of the stock.

The image of a market for corporate governance is invariably determined by the worst transgressors. Hence, a few egregious transgressions will give a market a bad name. It is especially disappointing when these transgressions come from the government on the big listed utilities, usually the key index stocks in those markets.

There is another reason why such deals happen. In all the markets we cover, there are no class action suits, which makes it not worthwhile for an aggrieved investor to seek legal redress. He will only get a small portion of the damages, his equity stake in the company, if he can show that the company and its directors did not pursue the best interests of the company, but he has to reckon on paying full damages to the company and its directors if he loses his case. He thus will decide that it is not worth pursuing legal action. From the opposing point of view, the controlling shareholder can almost certainly get away with putting forward deals that are patently negative for the listed company but that benefit him personally; often enough the odds on personal gains versus potential legal damages mean that it is worth shafting minority shareholders.

Finally, if the government is misdirecting a company, and minority investors have to seek redress for grievances in that government's legal system, they will feel mistreated by the authorities. This gives certain markets a very bad reputation that will take years to live down.

What Needs to Be Done?

International investors tend to have relatively small exposure to emerging markets compared to the size of their positions in their domestic market. When the investor's position is relatively small and a corporation transgresses, it is often best to cut the losses and move on. While the controlling shareholder might have gotten the better of the minority shareholders, the portfolio manager and his chief investment officer will place a black mark on those companies and that market. Hence some emerging markets are at valuation discounts and see much lower trading volumes even years after the worst cases of corporate governance were exposed.

But if investors silently bear the brunt of poor corporate governance and do not challenge controlling shareholders, then there is little pressure for the companies to improve their corporate governance. And if there is no such pressure, these companies will make only cosmetic changes, and the overall culture will remain the same.

The key, then, is to create an environment in each of the markets where controlling shareholders have to be concerned about legal redress by minority shareholders. This requires (1) proper rules in place, (2) activist groups on the ground that can pursue the interest of investors, (3) class action suits so that the odds and size of gain versus potential losses do not invariably deter legal action by investors, and (4) a competent and independent judiciary.

Most emerging markets have gone a long way in the last five years to address item 1— having the right rules in place. In some countries, notably Korea, we see item 2—activist groups. Malaysia has formed a watchdog group for minority shareholders, but it needs to have bark as well as bite. There is even progress on item 3 in some markets: Korea and Thailand might soon introduce class action suits. Item 4—the integrity and independence of the judiciary—is often a problem but should improve over time as a country becomes more wealthy, its judges are paid sufficiently, and justice no longer goes to the party who can pay the most.

In summary, there is progress, but much remains to be done to convince international investors that corporate governance is satisfactory and that their rights are protected in emerging markets. The markets making the most progress will be rewarded. Korea has seen the biggest improvement in country scores in our universe and has been the best-performing market in Asia since we started this survey. But if the authorities only make changes to regulations, without addressing the other three key legs of the platform for good governance, then investors will continue to see these markets as having poor corporate governance and high risks. And funds flowing into them will be largely speculative, looking for short-term gains rather than the longer-term returns that come from companies and markets with better corporate governance.

References

Gill, Amar, comp. 2000. *The Tide Is Out: Who's Swimming Naked?* CG Watch: Corporate Governance in Emerging Markets. CLSA Emerging Markets.

———. 2001. *Saints and Sinners: Who's Got Religion?* CG Watch: Corporate Governance in Emerging Markets. CLSA Emerging Markets, April. Available at www.webb-site.com/articles/Saints&Sinners.pdf [May 16, 2001].

———. 2002. *Make Me Holy, but Not Yet.* CG Watch: Corporate Governance in Emerging Markets. CLSA Emerging Markets.

———. 2003. *Fakin' It: Board Games in Asia.* CG Watch: Corporate Governance in Emerging Markets. CLSA Emerging Markets.

OLIVIER FRÉMOND
MIERTA CAPAUL

12

Capital Structures and Control Rights: Patterns, Trade-offs, and Policy Implications

Capital structures and voting arrangements define how control is distributed among shareholders in the corporation. Capital structures may consist of a single class of shares where every share has one vote or several classes of shares with different voting rights. This chapter contributes to the one share, one vote debate by showing that "one size does not fit all" and that effective reform of corporate governance must take into account a country's ownership structure, enforcement capacity, specific policy objectives, and idiosyncratic constraints of the political economy.

The chapter is organized as follows. From a corporate governance perspective, countries can be mapped in a two-dimensional space, with ownership in one dimension and control rights in the other. Four main frontiers arise: (1) dispersed ownership rights and diffused control rights, (2) dispersed ownership and concentrated control rights, (3) concentrated ownership and diffused control rights, and (4) concentrated ownership and concentrated control rights. The topology of ownership and control rights around the world is discussed in detail in the first section.

The authors would like to thank Michael Klein, Neil Roger, Alexander Berg, Harry Broadman, Simeon Djankov, Claire Grose, Cally Jordan, Sue Rutledge, and Richard Symonds for their insightful comments during the preparation of this chapter. Special thanks are also due to Victoria Korogodon and Huiwen Leo for their assiduous work in conducting research.

The simplest way to ensure that shareholders can exercise their voice is to give each share one vote (see table 12-1 for a comparison of how some international and institutional guidelines address the issue of one share, one vote). In this chapter we define the principle of one share, one vote as pure symmetry or equality between cash flow rights and voting rights.[1] Although a country might follow one share, one vote in the sense that each share normally carries one vote, its legal framework or ownership structure may include a mixture of provisions that concentrate and diffuse control rights, such as voting on a show of hands, pyramid structures, or special rights for minority shareholders.

In many countries, cash flow rights often deviate from control rights. This occurs largely because the legal and regulatory framework separates cash flow rights from voting rights. Asymmetries between voting rights and cash flow rights lead to the concentration or diffusion of control, and these asymmetries are discussed in the second section. Capital structures or arrangements leading to *concentration of control rights* include multiple-voting shares, nonvoting shares, shares with preferential rights like golden shares, pyramid structures and cross-shareholdings, shareholder agreements, and other arrangements, such as voting by partly paid shares. The result is control by few and ownership by many. Capital structures or arrangements that lead to *diffusion of control rights* include voting on a show of hands, minimum capital requirements to initiate corporate actions, minority veto rights and supermajority requirements, cumulative or proportional voting, and voting caps.

The Organization for Economic Cooperation and Development (OECD), in its Principles of Corporate Governance, does not advocate one share, one vote. Rather, it recommends that deviations from the benchmark be disclosed to investors. The question arises whether such deviations are fundamentally wrong and should be abolished through strengthening of the OECD principles or whether the OECD principles should remain unchanged. This prompts a thorough analysis of one share, one vote. To put it differently, the question is whether deviations from one share, one vote dilute welfare production, because such deviations do not maximize value. The answer to this question is more complex than anticipated.

Under some circumstances, deviations can enhance value, while in others, they can reduce value. For example, Rose investigates the performance of Danish firms with dual-class structures between 1995 and

1. La Porta and others (1998, table 1).

Table 12-1. *Overview of Select International and Institutional Guidelines on One Share, One Vote*

Guidelines	*Stand on one share, one vote*
Organization for Economic Cooperation and Development (OECD), Principles of Corporate Governance, 1999	Principle IIA sets forth that "all shareholders of the same class should be treated equally." The annotation to the principle notes that participation certificates and preference shares with no voting rights may efficiently distribute risk and reward and affirms that the principle is not intended to take a position on the concept of one share, one vote. Investors should be able to obtain information about the voting rights of all share classes before they purchase.
International Corporate Governance Network (ICGN), Global Share Voting Principles, 1998, and Statement on Global Corporate Governance Principles, 1999	The principles articulate ICGN's adoption of OECD Principle IIA. However, they also go beyond OECD in cautioning capital markets that, if they maintain unequal voting rights, they may not be able to effectively compete for capital. Deviations from one share, one vote should be disclosed and justified.
European Association of Securities Dealers (EASD), Corporate Governance Principles and Recommendations, 2000	The principles disapprove of deviations from one share, one vote but concur with OECD Principle IIA that if deviations are unavoidable, they should at least not apply to the same share class.
Danish Shareholders Association, Guidelines, 2000	Shares with disproportionate voting rights should be abandoned altogether.
Hermes, Statement on U.K. Corporate Governance and Voting Policy, 2001	Article 4.1 disapproves of the issuance of shares with reduced or no voting rights.
Pension Investments Research Consultants (PIRC), Shareholder Voting Guidelines, 1999	Part V states, "Dual share structures with different voting rights are disadvantageous to many shareholders and should be reformed."
Peters Commission, Recommendations on Corporate Governance in the Netherlands, 1997	The commission advocates one share, one vote, except under certain circumstances. Priority shares and preference shares could be used if the annual general meeting agrees.
Hellebuyck Commission, Recommendations on Corporate Governance, France, 1998	Under I.C.3. the commission recognizes double-voting rights as a "way to reward the loyalty of certain shareholders." Nonetheless, it favors one share, one vote, conceding that double-voting rights can be abused and allow firms to be controlled by a few shareholders, "contrary to the spirit of . . . corporate governance."

(*continued*)

Table 12-1. *(continued)*

Guidelines	*Stand on one share, one vote*
Euroshareholders, Corporate Governance Guidelines, European Union, 2000	Guideline II states, "The principle of one share, one vote is the basis of the right to vote. Shareholders should have the right to vote at . . . meetings in proportion to . . . shareholder capital. . . . Certification [the Netherlands] should be terminated, [as] it deprives the investor of this voting right and transfers influence to a trust office which lies within the [firm's] own sphere of influence." Firms also should not issue shares with disproportional voting rights to influence the balance of power with the annual general meeting.
California Public Employees' Retirement System (CalPERS), Global Corporate Governance Principles, United States, 1997	CalPERS has adopted the ICGN statement, adapting it under its own Global Corporate Governance Principles. The major difference is a preferred distinction favoring the term "shareowner" over "shareholder."
International Institute of Finance, Policies for Corporate Governance and Transparency in Emerging Markets, International, 2002	The International Institute of Finance maintains one share, one vote as a top priority and advocates one share, one vote for new issues. One share, one vote capital structures are considered to be the simplest, guaranteeing maximum accountability, as influence is proportional to ownership. Best practice for existing issues is to gradually eliminate nonvoting shares and shares with super voting rights; multiple-voting rights are seen as facilitating abuse and as being generally inconsistent with good governance.

1999 and concludes that firms with one share, one vote do not outperform firms with dual-class shares.[2] Rose argues that other corporate governance mechanisms, including block holding and monitoring, provide sufficient incentives to persuade managers to limit the private benefits of control and invest in value-maximizing projects. Ehrhardt and Nowak come to the opposite conclusion with regard to Germany.[3] They argue that dual-class

2. Rose (2002). We use the term "dual-class structure," regardless of whether the precise mechanism involves nonvoting or multiple-voting shares, because both of these instruments have the effect of concentrating control rights.

3. Ehrhardt and Nowak (2003).

companies underperform both in terms of operating performance and stock returns. This is explained by the fact that minority shareholders do not anticipate correctly the extent to which they will be expropriated.

Policymakers are trying to achieve two fundamental policy objectives through the concentration or diffusion of control rights: portfolio diversification and liquidity through the "democratization" of capital and the highest possible economic returns. In some cases, it may be more sensible to favor one objective over the other because of specific circumstances. For example, in countries where there is a lack of managerial expertise or where the legal and regulatory framework is inefficient, it may be preferable to focus on the second objective. However, in such circumstances, policymakers are confronted with a series of trade-offs. Understanding the trade-offs between concentration versus diffusion of control rights gives policymakers a tool to further their reform agenda and build on the existing regulatory framework. These trade-offs are the subject of the third section.

Topology of Ownership and Control Rights

Countries can be fit into a two-dimensional space, with ownership in one dimension and control rights in the other. Four main frontiers arise: (1) dispersed ownership and diffused control rights, (2) dispersed ownership and concentrated control rights, (3) concentrated ownership and diffused control rights, and (4) concentrated ownership and concentrated control rights. Diffusion and concentration of control rights are a departure from the one share, one vote benchmark. Some countries may straddle two frontiers. For example, corporations with dispersed ownership and diffused control rights are found in countries where ownership is generally concentrated, such as in France. The United Kingdom and United States are examples where both ownership and control rights are dispersed. Shareholders rarely own more than a few percent of the equity of a company, and nonvoting shares, multiple-voting shares, and pyramid structures are rare. The combination of dispersed ownership and concentrated control rights occurs in countries where cross-shareholdings are prevalent (such as Korea), where multiple-voting rights are common (such as Sweden), where proxy collection is widespread (such as Germany and Switzerland), and where shareholder agreements are prevalent (such as privatized companies in Brazil). Concentrated ownership structures and diffused control rights occur in countries with voting caps, such as France, Italy, Spain, the Netherlands, Norway, Poland, Portugal, Spain, Sweden, and Switzerland. The most common situation in industrial and developing countries alike is the concentration of both ownership structures and control rights. This often occurs following a takeover. In each configuration, policymakers are faced with trade-offs in the form of costs and benefits and specific agency costs.

Dispersed Ownership and Diffused Control Rights

This configuration fosters portfolio diversification and liquidity. "Exit" is an efficient alternative to "voice" for outside shareholders because investors can vote with their feet, that is, sell their shares. When dispersed ownership is combined with diffused control rights, the market for corporate control thrives and the threat of hostile takeovers disciplines management.

This configuration leads to lax monitoring of management by shareholders, because of a free-riding difficulty (see box 12-1). The free-riding problem arises because the monitoring shareholder bears the full cost of corporate monitoring, while only enjoying the increase in corporate value in proportion to his own stake. Also, when many are entitled to vote, no one expects a single vote to decide the contest. Consequently shareholders do not have the incentive to study the firm's affairs in order to vote intelligently. The agency problem of this scenario is between management and shareholders.

Dispersed Ownership and Concentrated Control Rights

The benefit of a combination of dispersed ownership and concentrated control rights is that it encourages the monitoring of management, while preserving portfolio diversification and liquidity. Concentration of control rights is achieved most commonly through pyramid structures, which enable certain shareholders to maintain control through multiple layers of ownership, while at the same time sharing the investment and the risk with other shareholders at each intermediate tier of ownership. Other mechanisms to concentrate control with limits of ownership are multiple-voting rights, proxy voting, or shareholder agreements. If the enforcement environment is weak and disclosure and transparency are poor, the most efficient way to monitor the corporation may be to concentrate control in the hands of responsible owners.

Box 12-1. *Free Riding and Collective Action*

Consider a hypothetical motion to vote, which could result in each of the 1,000 voters gaining or losing $1,000. The total corporate gain would be $1 million. If each voter is certain that the results of the election will be the same, whether or not he participates, then the voter's optimal investment in information is zero. Still, if a voter thinks that his vote could make a difference, he may be willing to invest up to $1,000 to make certain that he makes the right choice. However, an investment of $1,000 may not be sufficient to decide whether or not a $1 million investment is warranted. Thus there is a danger that the voter who invests $1,000 dollars will be acting on inadequate information, even though a single investment of $10,000 in information might be adequate. Those who have more shares, such as institutional investors, do not face the collective action problem to the same extent. Nonetheless, no shareholder, no matter how large his stake, has the right incentives unless that stake is 100 percent.

The downside is that the potential for controlling shareholders to expropriate minority shareholders is high, especially through "tunneling." In addition, such structures prevent the development of an active market for corporate control. In this situation, exit is the preferred solution for dissatisfied minority shareholders. The agency problem is between controlling shareholders and minority shareholders.

Concentrated Ownership and Diffused Control Rights

The combination of concentrated ownership and diffused control rights occurs when a company has voting restrictions that limit the number of votes per shareholder in its capital structure, such as voting caps or voting on a show of hands. The benefit is that minority shareholders are protected from abuse by block shareholders.

The downside is that monitoring incentives are low, and management can become entrenched. Portfolio diversification is impaired, and liquidity is low. In addition, the cost of capital for issuers is likely to be high, and the market for corporate control is impeded. In this situation, voice might be preferable over exit for dissatisfied minority shareholders. The agency problem is between management and shareholders.

Concentrated Ownership and Concentrated Control Rights

The benefits of concentrated ownership and concentrated control rights are that the monitoring incentives for controlling shareholders are high. Concentrating control rights in the hands of a controller may be optimal for noncontrolling shareholders, if the agency costs that result from the deviation are perceived to be lower than the transaction costs that would be incurred if power were exercised directly. Ultimately, the decision rests on trust—those who delegate power trust those who assume power to generate returns for all shareholders. Given that the economic stake of the controllers is high, the economic interests of minority and majority shareholders are better aligned than where control is concentrated, but ownership is dispersed.

The downside is that portfolio diversification and liquidity are low, and hostile takeovers do not play a disciplinary role. In this situation, voice becomes critical for dissatisfied minority shareholders. The agency problem is between controlling shareholders and minority shareholders.

Asymmetries between Voting and Cash Flow Rights

This section reviews the occurrence of asymmetries between cash flow rights and voting rights in countries around the world, including high-income, middle-income, and low-income countries. An asymmetry between voting rights and cash flow rights is a deviation from the one share, one vote principle. Another way of looking at asymmetry is as a separation of voting rights and the cash flow rights of risk-bearing capital.

The most commonly used deviations are discussed next. Some of these concentrate control, while others diffuse control.

Concentration of Control Rights

This section focuses on concentration of control rights, discussing nonvoting shares, multiple-voting shares, shares with preferential rights or golden shares, pyramid structures, cross-shareholdings, shareholder agreements, and proxy voting.

NONVOTING SHARES. Nonvoting shares may be ordinary or preference shares. Nonvoting ordinary shares retain their economic right to receive dividends but are stripped of their political or voting rights. In some countries, such as Egypt, bearer shares do not convey a right to vote.

Nonvoting preference shares constitute risk-bearing capital. However, they are quasi-debt instruments, since the absence of voting rights is accompanied by a compensating preferential right to the distribution of dividends or by seniority in the winding up of the company. The dividend for preferred shares can, for example, have seniority over the dividends for ordinary shares or can be fixed as a percentage of the nominal value of shares or as an increment over the dividend payout for ordinary shares. The preferred dividend can be cumulative; if it is not paid one year, during the following year, the unpaid dividend must be distributed in addition to the current year's dividend.

Holders of preference shares also often acquire the right to vote if the preferred dividend is not paid for a number years. For example, in Latvia, if preferred dividends are not paid for three years, the owners of nonvoting preference shares acquire the right to vote at the annual general meeting until a decision is taken at the meeting to resume payment of the preferred dividend.

Usually countries grant limited voting powers to owners of nonvoting preference shares in matters concerning the special rights of their class. In some countries, owners of preference shares have a limited say in the general corporate governance of companies, for example the power to elect *fiscal boards* in Brazil or Mexico.[4] Companies listed on Level 2 of the São Paulo Novo Mercado must even grant nonvoting shareholders a say in fundamental corporate decisions, such as mergers and acquisitions.[5]

Nonvoting shares are an option in most countries surveyed. However, there are exceptions. They do not exist in Denmark, Poland, and Sweden. In Hong Kong, holders of preference shares have the same voting rights as holders of ordinary shares unless the memorandum or articles of association provide otherwise. This option is also available in the United States.

Brazil is perhaps the best-known case for the widespread use of nonvoting shares, representing the majority of traded shares and 46 percent of

4. The fiscal board is not a subcommittee of the board, and its members are not directors of the board. Under civil law in some countries, the fiscal board is elected by shareholders and has potentially wide powers to supervise management, oversee financial reports, consult with external auditors, issue opinions on the annual report and major corporate transactions, report criminal acts, and call the annual general meeting.

5. Companies listed on the São Paulo stock exchange special listing segments must grant voting rights to preferred shareholders in certain circumstances, such as transformations, spin-offs, and mergers, approval of contracts between the company and other companies of the same group, and other matters that may involve conflicts of interest between the controlling shareholders and the company.

the total equity of listed companies.[6] Until 2001, it was possible to structure the capital of a corporation with two-thirds of nonvoting shares, the rest being in the form of ordinary voting shares. Thus a corporation could be controlled by shareholders owning only 16.7 percent of its total share capital. Criticism of this practice by domestic and institutional investors prompted the introduction of an amendment to corporation law limiting the authorized percentage of nonvoting shares to 50 percent for new companies or initial public offerings.[7] In the Slovak Republic and the Czech Republic, the percentage of nonvoting preference shares can represent up to 50 percent of capital. In Morocco, the percentage is capped at 25 percent. In many countries, there is no limit.

MULTIPLE-VOTING SHARES. Multiple-voting shares give their owners the right to cast more than one vote per share. They are powerful instruments that concentrate control in the hands of a few shareholders. Sweden is the most famous case for its use of multiple-voting rights; Swedish companies can issue shares with up to 1,000 times the voting power of ordinary shares.[8]

Multiple-voting shares can protect the corporation from unfriendly takeovers. In France, for example, corporate bylaws may grant double-voting rights to share owners who hold their shares for at least two years. This makes it virtually impossible for a hostile predator to control the nomination of the members of the board of directors and the decisions of the annual general meeting. The corporation is thus bid proof. In Morocco, double-voting rights can be granted to certain registered shareholders in the corporation's bylaws or by decision of an extraordinary general meeting, provided the shares are fully paid up and have been registered in the shareholder's name for at least two years. The double-voting right disappears if the shares are sold or converted to bearer shares.[9]

Countries such as Austria, Belgium, Chile, Colombia, Czech Republic, Georgia, Germany, Greece, India, Ireland, Italy, Luxembourg, Malaysia, Norway, Spain, Ukraine, and the United Kingdom have banned multiple-

6. In Brazil, issuers may offer one of three privileges when issuing nonvoting shares: (a) priority in the distribution of dividends corresponding to at least 3 percent of the net equity value per preference share, (2) "tag-along" rights at 80 percent of the price paid to the controlling shareholder in a change of control, or (c) dividends at least 10 percent higher than those paid to ordinary shares. Most companies opt for the spread of 10 percent.

7. Article 15 of Corporation Law (10,303).

8. For example, Investor, Sweden's biggest industrial-holding group, can have a 22 percent "say" at Ericsson, a mobile-phone company, with only 2.7 percent of its capital.

9. Article 257 of the Commercial Code.

voting shares. In some countries, the law limits the number of votes per share that can be attributed to any class of shares. This is the case in Latvia and Poland, where multiple-voting rights are capped at five and three votes per share, respectively.

In Lithuania, the voting rights attached to each class of shares are determined by their nominal value. The class with the lowest nominal value grants its owners one vote per share. The number of votes attached to the other classes of shares is determined by the ratio of their nominal value to the nominal value of the class of shares having one vote per share.

In Egypt, the legal framework allows for preference shares with multiple-voting rights. Owners of preference shares receive a fixed dividend to be paid before other dividends (which may be cumulative) and have priority in liquidation and capital increases in addition to having multiple-voting rights.

In the U.S. state of Delaware, firms can issue shares with as many voting rights as they want, and bondholders can be given voting rights in addition to shareholders.[10] German firms have altered their share structures in response to pressures emanating from the stock exchange, which changed the rules for calculating its DAX and M-DAX indexes in 2002. By permitting only the free float of one class of shares per company to be included in the index, firms with multiple-class structures saw their weight decrease in the index and, therefore, had an incentive to simplify their share classes.

Recent anecdotal evidence suggests that capital cost plays an increasingly important role in the structure of share classes. For example, in response to a recent decline in its share performance, telecommunications company Ericsson is considering eliminating its B class shares in order to lower its cost of raising new capital.

SHARES WITH PREFERENTIAL RIGHTS OR GOLDEN SHARES. Shares with preferential rights carry more rights per share for certain matters. Typically, the class of shares with preferential rights grants the controlling shareholder the right to elect more board members than is permitted with ordinary shares. Controlling shareholders in Chile and Mexico use preferential shares to secure the control of the board of directors, while letting outside investors enter the corporation's share capital. The risk-bearing capital of the Chilean chemical company SQM, for example, is structured with two classes of shares, A and B shares. Both classes have the same economic rights and the same voting rights at shareholder meetings, except that hold-

10. Del. Code §§ 151(a), 221.

ers of A shares can elect seven out of eight board members, while those holding B shares can elect only one board member.[11]

Golden shares are special shares created by law or by the company's articles of association for the specific purpose of according their holders special rights that go beyond those attached to ordinary shares. Governments typically use golden shares to maintain a degree of control over privatized corporations after their transfer to the private sector. Golden shares are most commonly used for companies in strategic industries, for example in the airline industry, the oil and gas sector, and infrastructure. The United Kingdom was the first country to introduce golden shares, but many countries have followed suit, including Belgium, Brazil, France, Malaysia, New Zealand, Spain, and Turkey. The objective of governments is generally to prevent privatized corporations from coming under foreign control. However, the rights conferred to golden shares can extend to other decisions of the company.

In some countries, such as the United Kingdom, golden shares have a limited life span. They expire after a certain number of years. Since management is, to a large degree, immune from takeovers as long as golden shares are active, their presence diminishes the performance incentives for management and adversely affects the profits of privatized corporations. In addition, as companies are bid proof, their share price is often negatively affected.

Special shares have features similar to those of golden shares; however, their beneficiaries can be the state, a regional government, or even a municipality. Germany, Hungary, Lithuania, and Malaysia have used them. In Lithuania, special shares grant greater rights to the state or municipal holders. The German state of Lower Saxony, for example, may veto certain key decisions of Volkswagen AG, such as a merger or acquisitions.[12]

Some countries, like Egypt, Morocco, and the United Kingdom, allow shareholders to pay for shares in installments. A first installment (usually the nominal value of the share) is paid at the time of issuance, and a second installment is paid some time later. Since the shares are traded at the time of their issuance, this creates an arbitrage situation for investors between the fully paid shares and the partly paid shares until the second payment is due. For example, in 1987 the U.K. government used partly

11. In addition, no one may own more than 37.5 percent of A shares. This means that no one can elect more than three board members, and no one can control the board.

12. Under the 1969 VW Law, Lower Saxony has privileges that function as a special share.

paid shares in the privatization of British Petroleum as a means of attracting small investors.

Partly paid shares may carry the same voting rights as fully paid shares. In Egypt, for example, shareholders who have paid up 50 percent or less of the share issue price have full voting rights, but they receive dividends in proportion to the amount paid up. This creates a distortion between their cash flow rights and their voting rights until the shares are fully paid. Ultimately, the scheme can then be used to control the company.

In Croatia, the company law indicates that voting rights may be acquired only on full payment for shares; however, company statutes may allow voting rights for lower levels of payment proportional to the amount of paid up shares. Singapore also allows for voting rights attached to partly paid shares.

In Morocco, issuers can buy back the economic rights of a share while the voting right attached to the share remains in the hands of the shareholder. This allows certain registered shareholders to recover the nominal value of their shares from the company. Such shares (*actions de jouissance*) then no longer receive dividends but continue to have voting rights.[13]

PYRAMIDS, CROSS-SHAREHOLDINGS, AND SHAREHOLDER AGREEMENTS. Pyramid structures and cross-shareholdings are used around the world to extend a controller's reach, while limiting his or her monetary investment. Pyramid structures are structures of holdings and subholdings by which ownership and control are built up in layers. For example, holding Company A owns 51 percent of Company B, which in turn owns 51 percent of Company C. Therefore, Company A controls 51 percent of the voting rights of Company C, but its cash flow rights in Company C are only 25 percent. Cross-shareholdings are reciprocal shareholdings between two companies. For example, Company A owns 25 percent of Company B, which in turn owns 25 percent of Company A.

When combined with a pyramid structure, cross-shareholdings can be used to create a maze, where beneficial ownership and control are difficult to determine. Cross-shareholdings are particularly common throughout continental Europe and Asia; such practices are widespread in Belgium, Hong Kong, and Korea. While pyramid structures are prevalent in Chile, cross-shareholdings are prohibited. Pyramid structures and cross-shareholdings diminish the capability of noncontrolling shareholders to influence corporate policy. They entrench management and make takeovers potentially costly to those who attempt them.

13. Article 202 ff of SA Law 17/95.

Claessens, Djankov, and Lang explain how typical pyramid and cross-holding structures in East Asia work.[14] Suppose that a family owns 10 percent of the stock of public Company A, which owns 20 percent of Company B. The family also owns 30 percent of Company C, which owns 15 percent of Company B. Summing the ownership stakes of the "weakest" links in the ownership chains—10 and 15 percent—puts the family's *control* of Company B at 25 percent. However, summing the product of the ownership stakes along the two ownership chains puts the family's *ownership* at only 6.5 percent of the cash flow rights of Company B.[15] The pyramid and cross-shareholding structures have allowed the family to gain a degree of control far greater than its equity stake in Company B.[16] Hong Kong's Li Ka-Shing Family Conglomerate is an example of a pyramid and cross-shareholdings' ownership structure (see figure 12-1).

Shareholder agreements bind a group of shareholders, who individually may hold a relatively small percentage of shares in a firm, and enable them to act in concert so as to constitute an effective majority or at least the largest single block of shareholders. This gives shareholders who are parties to a shareholder agreement a degree of power disproportionate to their equity ownership. The parties to the agreement usually agree to vote as a block, in line with the instructions of a lead shareholder.

Shareholder agreements often give the signatories to the agreement the right of first refusal to purchase the shares of a signatory wishing to sell. They may also contain provisions that require the parties not to sell their shares for a fixed period of time (lock-in).

The government of France has used shareholder agreements to put in place so-called groups of stable shareholders in the privatization of corporations through mixed sales.[17] Morocco has used them for the same purpose.

In Brazil, shareholder agreements not only give signatories the right to elect directors to the board but also are binding on board decisions. Board members representing shareholders bound by a shareholder agreement must vote in accordance with the stipulations of the agreement or their vote will not be counted. In the case of abstention, another director representing the shareholder agreement may cast a vote for the silent director in

14. Claessens, Djankov, and Lang (1999, 2000).

15. Ownership relates to cash flow rights, while control denotes voting rights.

16. Claessens, Djankov, and Lang (1999, 2000). The countries surveyed are Hong Kong, Indonesia, Japan, Korea, Malaysia, the Philippines, Singapore, Taiwan, and Thailand.

17. A mixed sale is a privatization where the majority stake is sold to a strategic investor and the rest is sold through an initial public offering.

Figure 12-1. *Li Ka-Shing Family Conglomerate Pyramid and Cross-Shareholding Ownership Structures in Hong Kong*[a]

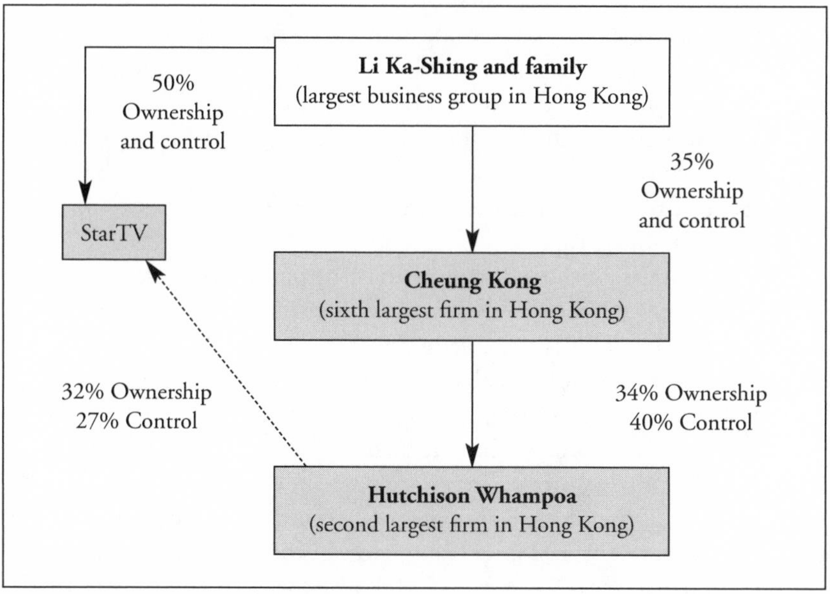

Source: Claessens, Djankov, and Lang (2000).

a. This depicts a partial diagram of the Li Family Conglomerate. Ownership relates to cash flow rights, while control denotes voting rights. The principal shareholders—the Li family—are shown in the white box. Continuous lines denote pyramidal holdings, and the dotted line indicates cross-shareholding. Percentages refer to ownership and control by one level of the next; for example, Cheung Kong owns 34 percent and controls 40 percent of Hutchison Whampoa.

accordance with the agreement's terms. If the shareholder agreement is worded in generic terms, the chairman of the board, who is appointed by the controller, has the power to decide what matters fall under the agreement. This seriously undermines the independence of judgment and fiduciary duties of the board members.

PROXY VOTING. Proxy voting allows shareholders to vote in absentia by delegating their voting rights to a third party, who will attend and vote at the shareholders meeting on their behalf. In some countries, the proxies must be notarized (for example, Bulgaria, Croatia, and Turkey), or there are restrictions as to who may be appointed as a proxy, such as in Egypt.

Proxies can be used as an instrument to concentrate control rights in diffused ownership situations. This is the case in Germany, where banks may vote on behalf of shareholders whose shares they hold in custody. This is conditional on the bank's announcing how it will vote on specific propositions and on a written confirmation by the depositing shareholders permitting proxy voting. Proxy voting also exists in the United States and Switzerland, where management makes propositions for the annual general meeting and solicits proxy votes from the shareholders.

In Egypt, there is a limit on how many votes a proxy may represent; no natural person may represent more than 10 percent of total shares and 20 percent of represented shares at the meeting. This provision, in effect, functions as a voting cap.

In some countries, the shareholder must be physically present to participate in the vote on a show of hands; proxy votes are not taken into account in this procedure. This is the case in South Africa, for example, where the Companies Act provides that shareholders may appoint a proxy to attend and speak at company meetings. However, unless the articles of association provide otherwise, a proxy is not entitled to vote on a show of hands.

In other countries, proxies may vote on a show of hands; however, like all shareholders, they have only one vote, regardless of how many shareholders they represent. In Hong Kong, most of the traded shares are immobilized, and the clearinghouse of the stock exchange appears in the company's register as a member. On a show of hands, the clearinghouse has only one vote, which is cast according to the balance of voting instructions received. Consequently, the votes cast may not reflect the instructions of the beneficial shareholder, unless a poll is demanded.

Diffusion of Control Rights

Provisions that diffuse control rights include voting on a show of hands, minimum capital requirements to initiate corporate actions, minority veto rights or supermajority requirements, cumulative and proportional voting, and voting caps.

VOTING ON A SHOW OF HANDS. Voting on a show of hands means that each shareholder has only one vote, irrespective of the number of shares owned. The practice of voting on a show of hands is a remnant of nineteenth-century corporate governance practices, where investors in a corporation were "members" rather than shareholders. Each member had one vote. Proxy voting did not exist, and votes at shareholders meetings were cast on a show of hands "among gentlemen." The practice has remained in most common-law countries.

Usually, the prevailing company law or commercial code makes provisions for changing the voting procedure from a show of hands to a poll, which grants shareholders a number of votes in proportion to the shares held. For example, in Hong Kong, the Companies Ordinance stipulates that a poll may be demanded by three to five registered shareholders, shareholders owning at least 10 percent of the company's voting capital, or the chairman of the meeting.

In the United Kingdom, under the system of nominee accounts, the nominee votes the shares as she sees fit, unless the beneficial owner gives specific instructions to ensure that the holder votes in line with his wishes. A problem arises when the nominee account is used by more than one shareholder and there is disagreement among them on how to vote. On a show of hands, the nominee or custodian will vote according to the party in the majority. In Hong Kong, this problem is compounded by the fact that the central depository is the member on record for most outside shareholders.

In terms of transaction costs, voting on a show of hands is an efficient means of obtaining shareholder approval of resolutions that have the broad support of shareholders and is less expensive than a poll. In the first instance, a resolution is passed as soon as it is put to the meeting, and shareholders move on to the next agenda item. If a poll is demanded, voting is by secret ballot. The votes must be counted meticulously, and the result can take hours or even days to be announced.

MINIMUM THRESHOLDS TO INITIATE CORPORATE ACTIONS. All corporate governance frameworks give minority shareholders some special powers. Such powers include provisions that allow minority shareholders to call a shareholders meeting, add items on the agenda of the meeting, nominate board members, or seek remedies. To the extent that a minority can impose its will on the majority, this represents a deviation from the one share, one vote principle.

In most countries, the percentage of capital or voting rights needed to call a shareholders meeting is set at 5 or 10 percent. However, there are exceptions. For example, the minimum capital requirement is 20 percent in Belgium, Colombia,[18] Italy, and Luxemburg and 15 percent in Jordan. In the United States, the percentage is usually 10 percent, but it can be as low as 1 percent in some states. Generally, the higher the threshold, the more difficult it is for minority shareholders to initiate a corporate action.

18. Unless stipulated otherwise by company bylaws.

However, depending on the ownership structure of the company and its free float, a 5 percent threshold might be low or high.

Some countries, like Morocco, require that shareholders own a minimum number of shares to attend the annual general meeting. Moroccan law allows companies to request that a shareholder own a minimum of ten shares in order to attend.[19] In this case, minority shareholders can form a pool to gather the required number of shares.

Many countries have provisions that permit shareholders to require the board to add items to the agenda prior to the annual general meeting. Unless the resolution is included in the agenda, it cannot be voted on in most countries.[20] This right may have deadlines or other restrictions attached. In Hong Kong, for example, shareholders representing 5 percent of capital or 100 shareholders owning an average of HK$2,000 of par value may add items, but they must pay the costs of circulating the new agenda as determined by management. Within ten days after publishing the proposed agenda in the official gazette, shareholders in Croatian companies may request amendments or present counterproposals to issues requiring a vote; however, these are not circulated to the other shareholders.[21]

In Brazil, shareholders representing 10 percent of capital may request cumulative voting. In addition, shareholders representing 15 percent of voting capital or 10 percent of nonvoting capital may elect a director to the board.

Traditionally, in civil law countries, only the annual general meeting could initiate legal actions against directors or management. However, to better protect minority shareholders and diffuse control rights, many countries have introduced minority redress mechanisms that allow a certain percentage of shareholders to sue directors on behalf of the company (derivative action). In Chile, for example, shareholders representing 5 percent of capital may sue a party for compensation on behalf of the company.

There are no threshold requirements for shareholders to file suit in the Czech Republic. In Poland, shareholders must hold more than 1 percent of share capital in order to file suit. In Hungary, if a board decision violates the law or minority rights, shareholders with 10 percent (in some cases, 5) may petition the Court of Registration. If a company fails to sue a manager, board member, or auditor, shareholders with at least 10 percent of

19. There is no share minimum for extraordinary meetings per Article 127 of SA Law 17/95.

20. In some countries, 100 percent of shareholders present and voting may lift this prohibition.

21. Current proposals would change this to fifty shareholders.

votes may, within thirty days of the annual general meeting, bring suit in the company's name. In Colombia, the threshold is 20 percent. In Latvia, shareholders representing 5 percent of the company's capital may bring action against the supervisory board on the company's behalf.

Shareholders have other redress mechanisms such as the ability to require an investigation of the company's affairs. In Croatia, a 10 percent threshold is required for appointing a third party to review the financial accounts of the company. In Romania, if complaints are submitted to censors[22] by shareholders holding at least 25 percent of share capital, the censors must present the conclusions of their investigation to the annual general meeting. Shareholders holding at least 10 percent of shares may also request the court to appoint an expert to examine certain operations. The resulting report must be submitted to the censors who review it and propose appropriate actions. Shareholders with 10 percent of shares have the right to ask the court to appoint experts for investigating certain operations of the company.

However, in many countries, the costs and complexities of litigation may be overly burdensome and protracted to make this an effective venue for redress. In India, for example, court proceedings initiated by shareholders can take between six and twenty years to resolve.

The right of minority shareholders to request a vote on related-party transactions represents a diffusion of control rights. This is the case in Chile, where shareholders representing 5 percent of capital may request that a related-party transaction be approved at an extraordinary general meeting with two-thirds majority.

As with all attempts to diffuse control rights, setting low threshold requirements for corporate actions can have unintended consequences. Giving minority shareholders special powers can lead to charges that small numbers of shareholders "greenmail" the company. In Slovakia, for example, a 5 percent threshold for calling an annual general meeting and initiating other shareholder redress was recently introduced. As a result, well-connected small shareholders have attempted to acquire small stakes in order to hold the company "for ransom," and several large companies appear to be delisting rather than face this risk.

VETO RIGHTS AND SUPERMAJORITY REQUIREMENTS. Veto rights and supermajority requirements ensure that certain corporate decisions are taken with the express consent of minority shareholders. Such provisions

22. Censors are the equivalent of examiners or fiscal boards.

include, for example, blocking minority or supermajority requirements for fundamental decisions and opt-out or withdrawal rights.

Supermajority requirements and blocking minority (veto) rights are two sides of the same coin. For example, if the supermajority requirement is 75 percent, then the blocking minority is 25 percent plus one vote. Depending on the voting procedure, however (that is, quorums or procedures for calling a second meeting), there may be subtle differences.

The efficiency of redress mechanisms also seems to influence policymakers in the allocation of minority shareholders rights. For example, in some Latin American countries, like Chile, a supermajority of two-thirds of the shareholders is required to declare a dividend of less than 30 percent of earnings for the year. In Colombia, the minimum mandatory dividend is 50 percent of net profits.[23] A majority requirement to change the minimum dividend is 78 percent of capital.

Certain provisions may allow minority shareholders to block certain fundamental decisions. In most countries, decisions about amendments to company bylaws, winding up of the company, or capital increases allow for a blocking minority veto of 25 percent plus one vote. In the Czech Republic, Egypt, France, and Slovak Republic, this minimum level is 33 percent plus one vote.[24]

The Czech Republic is an interesting case. Czech law recognizes the concept of "legal" minority shareholders (those with 10–33 percent of share capital) in addition to "blocking" minority shareholders (those with 33–50 percent of share capital). "Blocking" minority ownership gives shareholders the right to block some decisions, such as those related to increasing or reducing assets and implementing major changes in business activities that the majority shareholder may strive to implement at the general shareholders meeting. "Legal" minorities may call shareholders meetings and obstruct corporate decisions with protracted litigation.[25]

23. If the sum of all reserves is over 100 percent of subscribed capital, however, the minimum dividend is 70 percent.

24. Germany's 1960 VW Law, in addition to imposing a 20 percent voting cap, also stipulates a supermajority requirement of 80 percent for certain fundamental corporate decisions. The government of Lower Saxony holds nearly 20 percent of capital (and votes) and is entitled to two out of twenty seats on the supervisory board. However, its stake also gives it an effective 20 percent blocking minority and the ability to veto strategic company decisions.

25. Kocenda and Svejnar (2002) report that Czech portfolio companies interested largely in capital gains may buy 10 percent stakes in companies where they can sell their holdings at a premium to the dominant shareholder(s), who may not wish to be subjected to scrutiny by strong minority shareholders.

Another implicit veto right is the right of redemption. In Colombia, Korea, Germany, Mexico, and the United States, corporate law gives dissenting shareholders the right to have the company redeem all of their shares if they did not vote in favor of a merger, a sale or exchange of substantially all the assets of the company, or material and adverse charter amendments. Dissenters' rights are, in effect, one way of ensuring equitable treatment for all shareholders in major corporate decisions. While dissenters' rights may be particularly attractive in developing countries and transition economies, the problem is determining the valuation at which shareholders may exit.

CUMULATIVE VOTING AND PROPORTIONAL REPRESENTATION. Cumulative voting (in conjunction with other factors) helps minority shareholders to elect at least one director to the board, even if one shareholder or a group of shareholders controls an absolute majority of the voting rights. With cumulative voting, there is no deviation from one share, one vote in the sense that some shareholders carry voting rights greater than their cash flow rights. Rather, the deviation occurs as a result of the voting procedure, which allows shareholders to concentrate their voting rights on one preferred candidate. Box 12-2 describes how cumulative voting works.

Cumulative voting may be optional—that is, stipulated in a company's articles of association—or it may be mandatory, as set forth by a special provision in the companies or securities legislation. The procedure is optional in Bulgaria, Canada, Chile, Croatia, Finland, Italy, Latvia, Slovakia, the United Kingdom, and the United States. Sometimes, shareholders representing a minimum percentage of the voting rights may demand cumulative voting. This is the case, for example, in Korea, where shareholders representing 1 percent of voting rights can insist on cumulative voting. However, in Korea, the company can opt out of this option by amending the articles of association; more than 80 percent of listed companies have done so.

In Russia, cumulative voting is mandatory. Under Article 66 of the Joint Stock Company Law, open joint stock companies with more than 1,000 shareholders must have at least seven board members and use cumulative voting in the election of the directors. Companies with more than 10,000 shareholders must have at least nine board members and must also use cumulative voting. Other companies may have fewer board members and may use either proportional or cumulative voting. Cumulative voting has been important in fostering equitable treatment in Russia, particularly

Box 12-2. *Cumulative Voting Procedures*

Imagine a hypothetical board with five seats. All seats are up for reelection at the annual general meeting. For each seat, a resolution proposing the election or reelection of a candidate is put to a shareholders vote. Ultimately, to elect or reelect all five directors, shareholders will vote a total of five times. The procedure for cumulative voting consists of allowing minority shareholders to cast all five of their votes for a single candidate.

Consider what happens if the corporation has two shareholders—one with eighty voting rights and another with twenty voting rights. Without cumulative voting, the majority shareholder will outvote the minority shareholder each time by eighty to twenty, winning all five seats. With cumulative voting, the minority shareholder can cast 100 votes (twenty times five) in favor of a preferred candidate, while the controlling shareholder will cast eighty votes. Thus the candidate of the minority shareholder will win that seat.

since the procedure was combined with a requirement for unanimous board approval for some key decisions.

There are other methods to ensure that minority shareholders are represented on the board. The most common is a system of proportional voting, which gives shareholders representing a fixed percentage of the voting rights—say 10 percent—the right to appoint one board member. This is the case in Mexico and Brazil. Sometimes the law allows shareholders to appoint an additional director for each additional 10 percent holding.

Another method consists of calculating, at the request of a shareholder or group acting in concert, the number of board seats proportional to their shareholding (usually rounding down) and then allowing the shareholder or group to appoint the calculated number of directors.

In Colombia, board members are elected through the "electoral quotient" system. The system was devised to provide a degree of proportional representation on Colombian boards and protect minority shareholders. However, in practice, minority shareholders seldom succeed in electing a board member because the ownership structure of most companies is so concentrated that the electoral quotient system does not work (see box 12-3).

VOTING CAPS. Like the practice of voting on a show of hands, voting caps are remnants of nineteenth-century corporate governance practices. Voting caps are special provisions in the articles of association that limit the

Box 12-3. *Electoral Quotient in Colombia*

In Colombia, shareholders elect board members at the annual general meeting through a system called electoral quotient. In this system, holders of voting shares are requested to cast their votes for competing lists of board members, each list making up the entire board, rather than for individual candidates.

The selection of individual board members takes place as follows. First, the total number of votes present at the annual general meeting is computed and the quotient Q is calculated by dividing this computed number by the total number of seats on the board up for election or reelection and rounding down Q to the lowest integer number. Second, holders of voting shares then cast their votes for the competing lists of board members, and a tally is prepared. Each list, Ln, receives a number of votes, Vn. Third, the number of votes cast on each list is then divided by the quotient Q. The result for a given list is a number consisting of an integer, In, and a fraction, Fn. Fourth, seats are allocated as follows. Each list of board members is first allocated as many seats on the board as its integer number. If the sum of the integer numbers is less than the total number of seats up for election or reelection, the remaining seat(s) are allocated on the basis of the highest fractions, in decreasing order.

Although the system was devised to introduce proportional representation, in practice, board candidates of minority shareholders are seldom elected because of the concentrated ownership structure of companies. Consider the following example. A company is owned 90 percent by a controlling shareholder and 10 percent by minority shareholders. The board of five directors is up for reelection. The total number of votes present at the annual general meeting is 240. There are two competing lists: L1 put forth by the controlling shareholder and L2 put forth by minority shareholders. The following votes are cast: 216 votes for L1; 19 votes for L2; and 5 blank votes. Therefore,

$$Q = 240 / 5 = 48$$

$$L1/Q = 4.50 \rightarrow I1 = 4; F1 = 0.50$$

$$L2/Q = 0.40 \rightarrow I2 = 0; F2 = 0.40.$$

In the first round of allocation, the list put forth by the controlling shareholder (L1) is allocated four seats since I1 equals 4; the list put forth by minority shareholders (L2) is not allocated any seat since I2 equals 0. In the second round of allocation, the extra seat is allocated to L1 since F1 (0.50) is greater than F2 (0.40). Thus in spite of the electoral quotient system, the minority shareholder list of board members is not allocated any seats.

voting rights of shareholders. The limit can take the form of a sliding scale, a maximum number of votes per shareholder, or both.

Voting caps are an option in many countries, including Austria, Belgium, the Czech Republic, Finland (particularly in the insurance sector), France, Germany, Hungary, Ireland, Italy, Korea, Mexico, the Netherlands, Norway, Poland, Portugal, Slovakia, Spain, Sweden, Switzerland, and Turkey. In some countries, like Mexico, Norway, Sweden, and until recently Korea, provisions in the law limit the percentage of shares that can be owned by foreign investors. Such limitations are a form of voting cap.

In France, the articles of association may limit the number of votes that each shareholder has at the annual general meeting, on the condition that the limitation be imposed on all shareholders, with no distinction by classes of shares.[26] The limitation can be expressed as a specific number of votes or a percentage of the total voting rights represented at the meeting. Voting entitlement may also decrease with a sliding scale over the total number of shares held. For example, 100 votes for the first tranche of 100 shares, fifty votes for the second tranche of 100 shares, and ten votes per 100 shares thereafter. In Denmark and Luxemburg, the application of voting caps may be limited to certain major corporate decisions, such as a modification of the articles of association. Voting caps can be used as poison pills to prevent a change of control of the corporation. For this reason, the commercial codes of France and Hungary stipulate that provisions in corporate bylaws that restrict voting rights become null and void if a controlling interest is acquired through a public bid. The controlling interest is defined as 50 percent of the total capital in Hungary and 66 percent in France. Germany's law on control and transparency of companies stipulates the abolition of multiple-voting rights and voting caps by June 2003, with the Volkswagen voting cap regulated by its statute remaining an exception, at least for now.[27] The proposed Directive on Takeover of the European Commission includes provisions to eliminate voting caps in the breakthrough rule (see box 12-4).[28]

Korea has used voting caps in the specific case where companies ask their shareholders to opt out of cumulative voting. In this case, each shareholder's voting rights are capped at 3 percent, irrespective of economic rights in the company.

26. Article L.225-125 of the Commercial Code.

27. KonTraG Article 10, enacted in 1998.

28. McCahery and others (2003).

Box 12-4. *Breakthrough Rule in the Proposed European Directive on Takeover Bids, October 2002*

The directive sought to harmonize takeover regulation across the European Union and to promote an active market for corporate control within the European Union, that is, where hostile takeovers are possible. The proposed directive is based on two principles: (1) shareholder decisionmaking and (2) proportionality between risk-bearing capital and control. Under the proposed rule, there would be no distinction between defensive measures held by public companies (for example, golden shares) and private companies. Additionally, the breakthrough rule applies to defensive measures generally, irrespective of whether they are developed as pre-bid or post-bid devices. The key point is that a level playing field is achieved by introducing a rule that is applied after 75 percent of the risk-bearing capital is acquired. Specifically, under the proposed breakthrough rule, if the acquirer acquires 75 percent of the company's risk-bearing capital, then he or she should be able to exercise a corresponding share of total votes and take control of the company. The bidder will then convene a general meeting of shareholders and impose one share, one vote.

Another type of voting cap is targeted shares, which give the holders financial returns based on the performance of a particular business unit of the listed company. When targeted shareholders vote as a class, they generally have one vote for each share. When they vote in a general meeting, however, their voting rights may be calculated by a fixed ratio to other classes of shareholders or by reference to the relative market capitalization of each class of share. Either method has the potential to disadvantage the holders of targeted shares and cuts across the notion of equality between voting rights and cash flow rights.

All countries combine legal provisions and corporate structures that concentrate corporate control with provisions that diffuse control. The protection of minority shareholders can be strengthened by introducing or modifying provisions to diffuse control in the corporate governance framework. A wide range of instruments are available. These include a decrease in the capital requirements to initiate corporate actions, a prohibition of cross-shareholding, a requirement to disclose shareholder agreements, the introduction of supermajority requirements for certain corporate decisions, and cumulative voting. Some asymmetries can work in both directions. For example, the practice of voting on a show of hands normally diffuses control rights. However, when the registry is the nominee for all registered shares, the result is an increase in the concentration of control rights.

Trade-Offs for Policymakers

Policymakers can build on the existing legal and regulatory framework when pursuing the two fundamental objectives of corporate governance policy: promoting capital market development and creating an environment where companies can achieve the highest possible economic returns for society as a whole. The question is whether policymakers can achieve both objectives simultaneously or whether, in some circumstances, this optimal solution is not possible because of the costs of each objective. In light of their country's specific circumstances, policymakers may choose to maximize efficiency by giving priority to one objective over the other. In all circumstances, policymakers are confronted with trade-offs.

Enhancing liquidity fosters the growth of large institutional investors in charge of welfare provision, in particular pension funds and insurance companies. These institutions need liquid capital markets; they cannot invest in equities unless these can be sold. They also need to be able to diversify their portfolio. Liquidity can be enhanced through legislative reforms that diffuse control rights, such as a simplification of share classes and strong minority protections, including high veto rights and supermajority requirements or cumulative voting. Demand for equities, in turn, allows companies to raise capital at a reasonable cost. However, dispersed ownership may lead to insufficient monitoring of management as a consequence of free riding on control. In countries where the enforcement capacity of the state is low, this may lead to expropriation of minority shareholders and ultimately to suboptimal welfare production at the level of society as a whole.

The case of Eastern Europe offers a lesson for policymakers. In the immediate aftermath of the transformation to a market economy, policymakers decided to foster liquidity by mass privatization and anticipated high returns to society as a whole from the privatization process. Somewhat unexpectedly, this led to extensive expropriation of minority shareholders through theft, "tunneling," and other techniques and to low welfare production for the entire economy. After only a few years, the market started concentrating naturally, and corporations started generating profits, which increased welfare for society as a whole.

The case of Eastern Europe shows that policymakers may be facing trade-offs. Although promoting the democratization of capital is an important objective for capital market development, at certain stages of development policymakers might decide that it is more important to find the right managers to run a company. In such a case, they may favor measures that strengthen the incentives of shareholders to monitor management through the concentration of control rights. This can be achieved by introducing measures in the legislative framework that foster the concentration of control rights, such as a high percentage of nonvoting shares, multiple-voting rights, and shares with preferential rights.

However, swinging the legislative framework toward more concentrated control does not always lead to greater economic efficiency, as the privatization of Teléfonos de Mexico (Telmex) shows. In 1990, control of Telmex was bought up by Carlos Slim, one of Mexico's wealthiest men, after the government deregulated telephone service charges, allowing them to rise substantially. Local calls, for example, increased from 16 pesos per minute to 115 pesos. The price of Telmex's stock increased considerable after the sale, and in 2000, Carlos Slim's personal fortune exceeded the annual income of the poorest 17 million Mexicans combined. The biggest losers from the privatization were consumers, who were worse off by 92 trillion pesos (U.S. $33 billion).[29]

The shareholders who engage in monitoring are compensated by means of the private benefits of control. These benefits are extracted at the expense of firm value accruing to noncontrolling shareholders. In other words, the welfare produced by the firm is skewed in favor of the monitoring shareholder. Examples of such benefits include the ability to influence who is elected to the board of directors or as the chief executive officer, the power to build business empires, the diversion of corporate assets to other corporate entities controlled exclusively by the controlling shareholders, other beneficial related-party transactions, or simply the satisfaction or prestige derived from control.

Various recent studies have attempted to measure the magnitude of the private benefits of control in different countries. One study, by Tatiana Nenova, compares the share price of voting and nonvoting shares for the same company and derives the value of corporate votes and control benefits.[30] Another study, by Alexander Dyck and Luigi Zingales, compares the price of block trades that result in a change of control with the market

29. Tandon (1992).
30. Nenova (2000).

Table 12-2. *Private Benefits of Control as a Share of Total Market Value, by Country*

Country	*Block premium (percentage of market value)*	*Vote value (percentage of market capitalization)*
Argentina	27	—
Australia	2	17
Austria	38	—
Brazil	65	18
Canada	1	2
Chile	15	12
Colombia	27	—
Czech Republic	58	—
Denmark	8	1
Egypt	4	—
Finland	2	5
France	2	27
Germany	10	9
Hong Kong	1	-3
Indonesia	7	—
Italy	37	29
Japan	-4	—
Korea, Rep. of	2	34
Malaysia	7	—
Mexico	34	46
Netherlands	2	—
New Zealand	3	—
Norway	1	6
Peru	14	—
Philippines	13	—
Poland	11	—
Portugal	20	—
Singapore	3	—
South Africa	2	6
Spain	4	—
Sweden	6	1
Switzerland	6	5
Turkey	30	—
United Kingdom	2	9
United States	2	1
Average	14	12.5

Source: Adapted from Dyck and Zingales (2002, table 2); Nenova (2000, table 6). This table presents descriptive statistics by country on select block premiums in a sample of 412 control block transactions. The block premiums are computed taking the difference between the price per share paid for the control block and the exchange price two days after the announcement of the control.

— Not analyzed by Nenova (2000).

value of shares the day after the transaction's announcement, deriving control premiums.[31] Both studies have strikingly similar results, which are summarized in table 12-2.[32] In both studies, the countries with the highest private benefits of control are Brazil, Italy, and Mexico, all countries with concentrated ownership structures and several corporate governance arrangements that render hostile takeover more difficult. The Czech Republic and Turkey also have high private benefits of control, according to Dyck and Zingales (these countries were not studied by Nenova).

According to Dyck and Zingales, the levels of private benefits of control are related to the degree of statutory protection of minority shareholders, but also to law enforcement, the level of diffusion of the press, the rate of tax compliance, and the degree of market competition. Reputational or moral standards and labor also play a role in limiting the consumption of private benefits. Media circulation and tax compliance seem to be dominating factors.

These findings suggest that legal provisions that concentrate control rights do not necessarily lead to high private benefits of control if other mitigating factors are in place, such as high ethical standards, a high level of diffusion of the press, a high rate of tax compliance, and a high degree of market competition. The case of Sweden, a country well known for large deviations from one share, one vote, but also for a high level of enforcement, a powerful press, high tax compliance, and high ethical norms in general, corroborates this inference.[33]

In the late 1980s and early 1990s, a number of countries, such as Korea and Mexico, introduced additional deviations from the one share, one vote principle in their corporate governance framework that led to the concentration of control rights. Such provisions were intended to (a) encourage domestic firms to attract foreign investors without allowing them to gain control or to (b) attract strategic foreign investors. In order to maximize government revenues from privatization, Brazil abolished tag-along rights for minority owners of ordinary shares. More recently, these countries have been trying to attract long-term portfolio capital by introducing policy reforms to enhance the protection of minority shareholders.

31. Dyck and Zingales (2002).

32. In a few cases, the results of Dyck and Zingales differ from those of Nenova. The differences can be explained by differences in the samples used.

33. In Sweden, the control block premium is 6 percent.

In conclusion, the OECD principles are well balanced when advocating the disclosure of deviations from one share, one vote rather than their outright elimination. Fostering both market liquidity–portfolio diversification and management monitoring may not always be possible. In some instances, one objective may be more important than the other. Understanding the trade-offs between concentration and diffusion measures gives policymakers a tool to further their reform agenda. Often, they find that a mixture of concentration and diffusion mechanisms can provide the greatest value and avoid resistance from vested interests.

References

Claessens, Stijn, Simeon Djankov, and Harry H. P. Lang. 1999. *Who Controls Asian Corporations?* Policy Research Working Paper 2054. Washington: World Bank.

———. 2000. "The Separation of Ownership and Control in East Asian Corporations." *Journal of Financial Economics* 58 (1-2): 81–112.

Dyck, Alexander, and Luigi Zingales. 2002. "Private Benefits of Control: An International Comparison." Working Paper 535. University of Chicago Business School, Center for Research in Security Prices.

Ehrhardt, Olaf, and Eric Nowak. 2003. "The Effect of IPOs on German Family-Owned Firms: Governance Changes, Ownership Structure, and Performance." *Journal of Small Business Management* 41 (2): 222–32.

Kocenda, Evzen, and Jan Svejnar. 2002. "The Effects of Ownership Forms and Concentration on Firm Performance after Large-Scale Privatization." Working Paper 471. William Davidson, May.

La Porta, Rafael, Florencio López-de-Silanes, Andrei Shleifer, and Robert W. Vishny. 1998. "Law and Finance." *Journal of Political Economy* 106 (6): 1113–55.

McCahery, Joseph A., Luc Renneboog, Peer Ritter, and Sascha Haller. 2003. "The Economics of the Proposed European Takeover Directive." Centre for European Policy Studies Research Report in Finance and Banking. European Roundtable of Industrialists (ERT) and Standard and Poor's, May.

Nenova, Tatiana. 2000. "The Value of Corporate Votes and Control Benefits: A Cross-Country Analysis." Harvard University and World Bank.

Rose, Casper. 2002. "Corporate Financial Performance and the Use of Takeover Defenses." *European Journal of Law and Economics* 13 (2): 91–12.

Tandon, Pankaj. 1992. *World Bank Conference on the Welfare Consequences of Selling Public Enterprises: Case Studies from Chile, Malaysia, Mexico, and the U.K.*, vol. 1, *Mexico, Background, TELMEX.* Washington: World Bank, Country Economics Department (June 7).

PATRICK K. CONROY
ARNE B. PETERSEN

13

Identifying Vulnerabilities, Promoting Financial Stability, and Other Challenges

The international community has attached increasing importance to identifying vulnerabilities in the financial architecture, finding solutions to address these potential risks, and focusing on other developmental needs. In particular, the Asian financial crisis of 1997 and subsequent, well-publicized market events have highlighted the need to strengthen the functioning of markets and promote financial stability. More subtle actions, primarily concerning efficiency of markets, have also been at work to shore up financial supervisory regimes and promote cross-border financial activity.

Continued turmoil in a number of emerging-market economies is a poignant reminder of the overall economic and societal vulnerabilities posed by financial sectors that lack depth and stabilizing forces. Although many of these crises are likely to be contained relative to historical events, the risk of contagion is ever present. Indeed, it is worth remembering that many industrial countries have also experienced a financial sector crisis in the recent past—the large number of crises, the possibility of far-reaching systemic consequences, and the crisis in confidence resulting from the more prominent financial collapses have provided further motivation to address weaknesses and encourage more sustained market stability.

The invaluable assistance and input provided by Peter Clark of the International Monetary Fund and Melinda Roth of the World Bank are gratefully acknowledged.

Of course, there is no quick fix; nor would it be desirable to eliminate risks from financial markets. The various risks present in a well-functioning securities market are integral to ensuring that the market—and the economy as a whole—remains dynamic and viable. However, systems are needed to mitigate the adverse consequences associated with such risks and achieve stability in the overall financial architecture. Various international initiatives under way are meant to inform authorities and markets of the vulnerabilities and risks present and to reduce the incidence of crises through appropriate policy responses.

Assessment of Risks and Vulnerabilities

The various initiatives to identify vulnerabilities, promote financial stability, encourage greater efficiency in global markets, and foster financial infrastructure development have also brought into sharp relief the need for more focused collaboration among the international financial institutions, national authorities, and standard setters. The International Monetary Fund (IMF) and the World Bank developed the Financial Sector Assessment Program (FSAP) with these goals in mind. Indeed, the FSAP has, in the context of individual country assessments, encouraged dialogue with national authorities on a range of issues beyond the scope of existing surveillance initiatives.

Efforts to strengthen financial systems necessarily require a framework that allows for consistency of assessments and that can be used to determine whether certain policy and operational characteristics are present and effectively implemented in a given jurisdiction. In the case of securities markets, such a framework is provided by the standards promulgated by the International Organization of Securities Commissions (IOSCO)—the Objectives and Principles of Securities Regulation (see box 13-1). The IOSCO principles establish the outline of an effective system of securities regulation and, while not intended to be prescriptive, permit the measurement of market supervisory arrangements against generally accepted international benchmarks.

As the FSAP process evolves with experience and heightened understanding of the diagnosis, mitigation, and management of vulnerabilities, so too will the standards that form an essential component of the program be further fashioned. Ideally, there should be a process of continuous review of all elements of the FSAP to ensure the ongoing relevance and

Box 13-1. *IOSCO Objectives and Principles of Securities Regulation*

The three core objectives of securities regulation are to protect investors, to ensure that markets are fair, efficient, and transparent, and to reduce systemic risk.

Principles relating to the regulator

1. The responsibilities of the regulator should be clear and objectively stated.
2. The regulator should be operationally independent and accountable in the exercise of its functions and powers.
3. The regulator should have adequate powers, proper resources, and the capacity to perform its functions and exercise its powers.
4. The regulator should adopt clear and consistent regulatory processes.
5. The staff of the regulator should observe the highest professional standards, including appropriate standards of confidentiality.

Principles for self-regulation

6. The regulatory regime should make appropriate use of self-regulatory organizations (SROs) that exercise some direct oversight responsibility for their respective areas of competence, to the extent appropriate to the size and complexity of the markets.
7. SROs should be subject to the oversight of the regulator and should observe standards of fairness and confidentiality when exercising powers and delegated responsibilities.

Principles for the enforcement of securities regulation

8. The regulator should have comprehensive inspection, investigation, and surveillance powers.
9. The regulator should have comprehensive enforcement powers.
10. The regulatory system should ensure an effective and credible use of inspection, investigation, surveillance, and enforcement powers and implementation of an effective compliance program.

Principles for cooperation in regulation

11. The regulator should have authority to share both public and non-public information with domestic and foreign counterparts.
12. Regulators should institute information-sharing mechanisms that establish when and how they will share both public and private information with their domestic and foreign counterparts.
13. The regulatory system should allow for assistance to be provided to foreign regulators who need to make inquiries in the discharge of their functions and exercise of their powers.

(continued)

Box 13-1. *IOSCO Objectives and Principles of Securities Regulation* (*Continued*)

Principles for issuers

14. There should be full, timely, and accurate disclosure of financial results and other information that is material to investors' decisions.

15. Holders of securities in a company should be treated in a fair and equitable manner.

16. Accounting and auditing standards should be of a high and internationally acceptable quality.

Principles for collective investment schemes

17. The regulatory system should set standards for the licensing and regulation of those who wish to market or operate a collective investment scheme.

18. The regulatory system should provide for rules governing the legal form and structure of collective investment schemes and the segregation and protection of client assets.

19. Regulation should require disclosure, as set forth under the principles for issuers, that is necessary to evaluate the suitability of a collective investment scheme for a particular investor and the value of the investor's interest in the scheme.

20. Regulation should ensure that there is a proper and disclosed basis for asset valuation and pricing and the redemption of units in a collective investment scheme.

Principles for market intermediaries

21. Regulation should provide for minimum entry standards for market intermediaries.

efficacy of the program to both the jurisdictions being reviewed and the IMF and World Bank, which also have broader macroeconomic and prudential goals. The experience emanating from the FSAP also will complement—and inform—any initiatives among the standard setters to review, update, and, if necessary, sharpen their standards.

Conduct of the Assessments

Identification of vulnerabilities and management of risks in domestic financial systems are, in systemically important countries, also essential to the stability of the financial system as a whole, providing urgency to the task. Since the introduction of the FSAP in 1999, some sixty-five jurisdic-

22. There should be initial and ongoing capital and other prudential requirements for market intermediaries.

23. Market intermediaries should be required to comply with standards for internal organization and operational conduct that aim to protect the interests of clients, ensure proper management of risk, and under which management of the intermediary accepts primary responsibility for these matters.

24. There should be procedures for dealing with the failure of a market intermediary in order to minimize damage and loss to investors and to contain systemic risk.

Principles for the secondary market

25. The establishment of trading systems, including securities exchanges, should be subject to regulatory authorization and oversight.

26. There should be ongoing regulatory supervision of exchanges and trading systems that should aim to ensure that the integrity of trading is maintained through fair and equitable rules that strike an appropriate balance between the demands of different market participants.

27. Regulation should promote transparency of trading.

28. Regulation should be designed to detect and deter manipulation and other unfair trading practices.

29. Regulation should aim to ensure the proper management of large exposures, default risk, and market disruption.

30. The system for clearing and settlement of securities transactions should be subject to regulatory oversight and designed to ensure that it is fair, effective, and efficient and that it reduces systemic risk.

tions have been, or are continuing to be, assessed for a range of standards and codes.[1] Of the sixty-five, around forty-eight have been assessed on the basis of the IOSCO principles.

Although it may not be appropriate to perform IOSCO assessments in all FSAP missions, less than half of the members of the international financial institutions have been assessed for implementation of the IOSCO

1. The standards and codes currently assessed are the Basel Core Principles for Effective Banking Supervision; the Core Principles for Systemically Important Payment Systems; the International Association of Insurance Supervisors Insurance Core Principles; the IOSCO Objectives and Principles of Securities Regulation; and the International Monetary Fund Code of Good Practices on Transparency in Monetary and Financial Policies. Assessments of the Financial Action Task Force Recommendations on Anti–Money Laundering/Combating the Financing of Terrorism are also undertaken in relevant jurisdictions.

principles at this point (see table 13-1). As our experience grows, and as the relevance of the FSAP process and findings to securities regulators, national authorities, and the standard setters becomes more cogent, it is expected that significantly more countries will routinely volunteer for an assessment. We also anticipate that some countries will ask to be reassessed in order to ensure that reforms implemented as a consequence of the initial FSAP findings are appropriately recognized or to provide a fresh review of the jurisdiction in light of its domestic policy prerogatives or international undertakings.

Outcomes of the Assessment Process

Many of the jurisdictions assessed have made significant progress in providing the necessary structures to facilitate regulation of their securities markets. In particular, most countries have in place the general legislative framework necessary for an effective securities regulatory regime—there are adequate laws relating to the establishment and conduct of markets and their principals. Legislation is also largely in evidence to effect, often in the broadest sense, surveillance of the markets in order that breaches of the securities laws might be appropriately sanctioned.

Although the legislative and policy framework is often in place, the merits of such arrangements relative to the particular characteristics of a jurisdiction (for example, size of the market, systemic importance, sophistication of participants, range and quality of financial products) are sometimes more difficult to determine. Given the various levels of economic development evident in the jurisdictions assessed, and the copious nature of the principles themselves, a ready calibration of assessment results is not possible.

It is expected that more formal guidance currently being developed by IOSCO in collaboration with the IMF and the World Bank will provide for greater consistency in the FSAP assessments. Although the IMF and World Bank have sought to equip assessors with as many assessment tools as possible, many of the earlier IOSCO assessments were conducted without the benefit of such a comprehensive assessment methodology. The formulation of appropriate guidance will greatly enhance the quality and consistency of the IOSCO assessments.

It is nevertheless possible to discern a number of common themes from the FSAP assessments that are relevant to strengthening the regulation of securities markets and, as a consequence, improving overall financial

Table 13-1. *Completed or Ongoing IOSCO Principles Assessments through March 2003*

FSAP missions	*Date of first mission*	*World Bank and IMF staff*	*External expert*
Argentina	February 2001	x	. . .
Albania	October 1999	x	. . .
Bangladesh	April 2002	x	. . .
Barbados	March 2002	. . .	x
Brazil	March 2002	. . .	x
Bulgaria	October 2001	. . .	x
Canada	October 1999	. . .	x
Croatia	April 2001	x	. . .
Czech Republic	November 2000	x	. . .
Egypt	April 2002	. . .	x
Estonia	March 2000	x	. . .
Finland	February 2001	. . .	x
Georgia	May 2001	x	. . .
Ghana	June 2000	x	. . .
Guatemala	June 2000	. . .	x
Hong Kong	December 2002	. . .	x
Hungary	February 2000	x	. . .
Iceland	February 2000	. . .	x
India	March 2000	x	. . .
Ireland	September 2000	. . .	x
Israel	September 2000	x	. . .
Kazakhstan	February 2000	x	. . .
Korea, Republic of	October 2001	x	. . .
Latvia	February 2001	x	. . .
Lithuania	September 2001	. . .	x
Luxembourg	October 2001	x	. . .
Malta	October 2002	x	. . .
Mexico	March 2001	. . .	x
Morocco	February 2002	x	. . .
Nigeria	February 2002	x	. . .
Philippines	October 2001	x	. . .
Poland	June 2000	x	. . .
Russia	April 2002	. . .	x
Senegal	November 2000	x	. . .
Slovak Republic	November 2000	x	. . .
Slovenia	April 2001	x	. . .
Sri Lanka	October 2001	x	. . .
Sweden	October 2001	x	. . .
Switzerland	June 2001	. . .	x
Tunisia	February 2001	. . .	x
Ukraine	April 2002	. . .	x
United Kingdom	February 2002	. . .	x
Total	42	25	17

stability. In emerging-market countries, various weaknesses in the regulation of securities markets have been identified (see box 13-2). For example, national authorities often did not respond effectively to the development and proliferation of financial services in their particular jurisdiction. In developed economies, the ability of regulators to appropriately monitor a wide variety of risks, across both sectors and borders, particularly associated with large and complex financial institutions, was often tested.

Assessors have expressed several key concerns that may have implications for overall financial stability. These may be summarized as follows:

—Many jurisdictions, especially emerging markets, are seen as having a nebulous division of responsibilities among the regulatory authorities responsible for financial regulation. Often this is due to the relatively recent establishment of regulators of the securities markets in some countries, although some established regulatory systems also exhibit similar characteristics.

—Skilled staff often are lacking in many agencies: the ability of regulatory agencies to recruit appropriate staff is sometimes hampered by funding difficulties or the availability of only a small pool of skilled job seekers. Weaknesses in the physical infrastructure of various regulatory arrangements thus have the potential to create fissures in the overall regulatory scheme.

—Regulators often have at their disposal limited administrative penalties, such as the imposition of fines or revocation of licenses, leading to ineffective enforcement of securities laws. The range of sanctions available to the regulator is also considered to have a bearing on the deterrence of unfair or illegal market conduct in the jurisdictions concerned—compliance with the securities laws is thus seen as being facilitated by the presence of wide-ranging and sizable civil and criminal penalties. Even where meaningful sanctions and penalties are available, many jurisdictions are simply unable to enforce them.

—Processes for managing risk within market intermediaries, and other prudential controls, are inadequately supervised in many jurisdictions. In particular, capital adequacy requirements, along with other prudential mechanisms, need strengthening in many countries to ensure that failure of an intermediary can be appropriately managed and contained.

—Mechanisms to detect unfair and manipulative market behavior are poorly developed in many countries. This is often due to poor management of information or to a lack of the necessary technology to supervise effectively large volumes of transactions and other types of activity. Moreover, arrangements for information exchange and cooperation

Box 13-2. *Some Challenges for Regulators Identified in the FSAP*

—Institutional support (for example, legal, accounting, bankruptcy professions) was often lacking, in nascent form, or ineffective.

—The role of the securities regulator vis-à-vis other supervisors was sometimes not clearly defined or legislated.

—Regulators often did not have the capacity to adequately enforce laws and administer penalties.

—There were concerns as to the ability of regulators to share information, either domestically or with foreign counterparts. This is of particular concern when one considers the effectiveness of regulatory enforcement.

—The content and timeliness of continuous reporting obligations on firms were inconsistently enforced, or the requirements were unclear.

—The interests of minority shareholders were sometimes given scant regard in the relevant legislation.

—Disclosure and financial reporting obligations were sometimes not subject to sufficient oversight.

—The regulator's ability to effectively supervise risk management procedures and internal organization of firms, along with capital adequacy and other prudential requirements, was sometimes weak.

—The monitoring of market activity, including the ability of the regulator to detect manipulative practices, was often underdeveloped.

—Many jurisdictions did not provide for the adequate oversight of their clearing and settlement functions.

between regulators and self-regulatory organizations are also inefficiently organized in many jurisdictions.

Although the form of the IOSCO principles does not readily provide for such an analysis in the FSAP, there may nevertheless be some utility in pursuing strategies in the conduct of assessments relevant to the specific nature of particular markets and to the generic characteristics of a range of similar jurisdictions. Shaping aspects of the program with developmental and other needs in mind would assist in further calibration of assessment findings across the range of jurisdictions surveyed by the IMF and the World Bank and, as a consequence, might also assist in more readily identifying the vulnerabilities in regulatory systems. Such measures would also help in crafting more relevant technical assistance programs and other capacity-building initiatives.

It is often thought that securities markets, in comparison with the banking sector, are a less accommodative vehicle for the transmission of systemic shocks in the event of a major institutional collapse. Although historical examples may support this proposition, the unprecedented level of participation in the securities markets, coupled with the increasingly cross-sectoral nature of investment products and services, raises the specter of newfound risks to financial stability and significant systemic consequences of shocks in certain markets. The spectacular nature of recent corporate collapses, and the crisis in confidence resulting from such events, is an added imperative.

Staff at the IMF and World Bank are therefore giving priority to the development of methods to link the IOSCO assessments to an overall identification of vulnerabilities in the financial sector. Part of this work will involve a more concentrated effort to articulate the goals of the FSAP as they relate to securities markets. Another aspect of this project will be to identify more clearly the relationship of the FSAP findings to the broader surveillance and technical assistance activities of the IMF and the World Bank.

Other Regulatory Challenges

Regulators not only are confronted with vulnerabilities in their supervisory systems that potentially affect financial stability but also must deal with sporadic institutional and market crises and the consequences of other domestic and global events that affect confidence, stifle innovation, and potentially limit market development. Indeed, many investors are already bruised by the fallout from recent corporate scandals—widespread market malaise may overshadow the significant efforts of securities regulators in many jurisdictions to address the issues raised by these corporate events.

The sheer size and extravagance of recent corporate collapses should, however, ensure that market events—and the actions of regulators—remain topical and well publicized. Regulators, in conjunction with governments, have responded to corporate scandals by reviewing their regulatory frameworks to identify gaps and, where appropriate, elaborate on their own mandates to shore up regulatory defenses. For example, many regulators are now much more engaged in corporate governance issues than previously was the case.

The recent enactment of legislation in various countries to, among other things, promote greater integrity in financial disclosure, as well as more obvious independence in auditing practices, is primarily a response to specific corporate scandals. Although it will likely have significant consequences for the conduct of business in the jurisdictions concerned, its impact on the scope and philosophy of the regulatory function will possibly be just as great. The challenges of implementing the requirements of the legislation and promoting compliance with the law necessarily rest with the regulator—ensuring that these new tasks complement the respective regulatory model will require careful craftwork.

High-profile business failures have also prompted IOSCO and other international bodies to articulate new standards and recommendations. In October 2002, IOSCO released a series of recommendations—in the form of statements of principle—relating to transparency and disclosure by listed entities, independence of external auditors, and the need for independent oversight of the audit function. While broad in scope, the new principles nevertheless complement the range of existing standards adopted by IOSCO.

Given the significance of this new body of work, the three sets of principles should ideally be fully incorporated in the process for implementing the IOSCO principles and, ultimately, within the framework of the FSAP. The dynamic nature of securities markets requires that the assessment process be responsive to regulatory developments. Thus, as markets become increasingly sophisticated, and as the boundaries differentiating aspects of market conduct and participation become increasingly blurred, so too will regulatory mandates be tested and, perhaps, redefined. The challenge for regulators—and for assessors—is to develop linkages between the various responses to major market events and an optimal regulatory model to ensure consistency in approach and continuity in regulatory design.

Regulatory models must also adjust to technological innovation. Rapid advances in trading technology have greatly improved market access as well as access to financial and other information of relevance to investors. The Internet offers greater access to investment portals, yet it also provides fraudsters with a powerful tool to use for personal gain. The proliferation of Internet teams within regulatory agencies—to scan the Internet for fraudulent activity in particular—shows how regulators try to stay abreast and ahead, if possible, of constantly improving technology and its use by market stakeholders.

Securities regulators are thus presented with significant challenges consistent with the growth and complexity of financial market activity. Under the banner of globalization, regulators have been required to cooperate more fully in order to address the myriad issues raised by financial consolidation and innovation. In the context of global financial stability, such collaboration has necessarily extended to other multilateral institutions engaged in efforts to promote soundness of the financial system. Opportunities for regulators and the international financial institutions to engage more actively in stability issues will increase as the role of securities markets becomes more clearly identified with the overall systemic health of an economy.

Addressing Needs: The Role of the International Financial Institutions in Technical Assistance and Other Capacity-Building Initiatives

It is envisaged that the FSAP process will lead to more focused technical assistance initiatives, again in cooperation with the standard setters, with other multilateral agencies, and, which is important, with regional groupings of regulators and authorities. Although requests for assistance in this area have, to date, been limited, it is likely that authorities will increasingly identify technical assistance requirements as a component of the necessary follow-up to the FSAP findings. The IMF and the World Bank, in conjunction with IOSCO, are exploring the various means by which effective technical support might be provided to countries after assessment—it is contemplated that this will occur primarily through other multilateral programs.

One such undertaking is the Financial Sector Reform Strengthening Initiative (FIRST), operated jointly by a number of national government development agencies and by the IMF and the World Bank. FIRST aims to provide funding for technical assistance to address financial sector weaknesses and promote financial system developments in low- and middle-income countries. FIRST is also intended to be a mechanism for exchanging information among beneficiaries and interested participants.

The absence of depth and diversity in financial sector activity among many emerging-market countries limits the ability of firms and individuals in those countries to spread risk and prevents the ready formation of capital for the development of a robust financial sector and economy as a whole. A range of financial instruments, institutions, and mechanisms for intermediation are clearly significant elements in the developmental needs of many jurisdictions—the outcome of an FSAP will, in appropriate circumstances, provide an opportunity for ongoing technical assistance to address these structural shortcomings, either through the FIRST initiative or in some other form.

Other challenges are present in emerging economies: institutional support for market activities, in the form of an adequate legal system, comprehensive accounting, auditing, and bankruptcy practices, and responsive technology systems, is often in a poor state. Although these aspects form the preconditions necessary for an effective regulatory regime, their assessment in the FSAP has, for various reasons, often been rudimentary. An enhanced understanding of their place in the regulatory structure of a jurisdiction not only would benefit the overall appraisal of the jurisdiction's supervisory system but also would lead to more effective technical assistance in the form of institutional capacity building.

Unique Challenges Facing Regulators

The current global economic slowdown has combined with recent corporate scandals to depress the appetite for investment in equities in both developed and developing capital markets. It is unclear when this lull will end given the current state of global economic integration, as well as constantly improving technology, easy access to markets, and the proliferation of new investment opportunities; there do, however, appear to be some positive trends.

These same events, however, have raised important policy considerations for government officials, including regulators and supervisors. Securities regulators, perhaps more than other supervisory bodies, now are called on to address many of the perceived deficiencies giving rise to these events. Areas covered can range from corporate governance and the regulation of accounting and auditing standards to oversight of credit rating agencies and corporate insolvencies.

Although this renewed focus may be somewhat overdue and, to an extent, precipitated by corporate scandals such as those of Enron and WorldCom, it has certainly placed securities markets and their regulation at the forefront of efforts to improve the image and soundness of the global investment environment. For example, the sheer amounts involved in the collapse of Enron force us to focus on the factors giving rise to such a devastating corporate failure. That Enron resulted in some $32 billion in lost market capitalization and the loss of more than $1 billion from employee retirement accounts (most of these accounts clearly were not diversified from the risks of their own company) requires new and innovative approaches on the part of securities regulators.

There has been a tendency to generalize beyond Enron to determine what, if any, lessons can be learned as a result of such corporate scandals. In particular, securities regulators are being asked what might be done in the future to prevent, or at a minimum mitigate, the catastrophic consequences of such failures. The nature of financial markets requires supervisors and regulators to adapt and adjust their regulations and enforcement policies in response to scandals and other significant financial events. This is particularly true on securities markets where market developments more often than not outpace attendant regulatory controls. As such, securities regulators have to keep pace not only with increasing numbers of investors, issuers, and products but also with rapidly advancing technology and clever individuals determined to break the rules for personal gain.

The insider trading scandals that arose in the 1980s and the subsequent enforcement action on the part of regulators, particularly in the United States, are evidence of this responsive trend. In the United States, for example, the Securities and Exchange Commission's Enforcement Division cracked down on insider trading in a number of high-profile cases. Although this pursuit of insiders became something of a global trend, it also revealed that securities regulation in many jurisdictions did not prohibit insider trading. As a result of regulatory action, most jurisdictions now have legislation and other policy mechanisms designed to prohibit insider trading and other forms of market manipulation. We have seen from the IOSCO assessments in the FSAP that changing the regulatory framework is the first step in dealing with the problems of the day. The next, and necessary, step to achieve full implementation is, of course, to implement effectively such regulations.

Regulators are faced with a delicate task: the protection of investors must be achieved in the context of ensuring that markets are fair, efficient, transparent, and, which is most important, viable. The structure of regulation in many markets also presents enormous challenges, given the often complex division of responsibilities between the regulator and self-regulatory organizations, the role of other sectoral supervisors, and the diversity of the stakeholder base. For example, the stock exchange, as a self-regulatory organization, may have oversight over its member firms, but at the same time these members are responsible for the very life of the exchange. It is not uncommon for the self-regulatory organizations to predate the establishment of the regulator and, as such, to retain certain regulatory functions that oftentimes can be inconsistent or in conflict with the regulator's function or at times can serve to diminish the regulator's authority. The demutualization of self-regulatory organizations has further complicated this issue.

Another example of the dilemmas present in the current agenda of securities regulators is related to research analysts. It would appear from recent events that some companies routinely overstate earnings, and, in certain cases, analysts have been unable to perform properly their independent function of following companies and providing accurate and timely information to potential investors. Given that credit-rating agencies have been an integral component of many securities markets (with the number growing all the time) for many years, there is greater pressure than ever on government authorities to ensure that these entities contribute to and do not detract from market integrity. In many cases, securities regulators are being asked to consider how regulatory oversight might be best exercised.

In a speech last year, Federal Reserve Chairman Alan Greenspan provided telling statistics to back up this point. He stated that earnings forecasts over the past three to five years for each of the Standard and Poor's 500 corporations averaged about 12 percent a year between 1985 and 2001. Yet, over that same period, actual earnings growth averaged only 7 percent. Was the 5 percent difference the result of excessive optimism? Or was it merely bias, since the difference between forecasted growth and actual growth was greater when the analyst issuing the report was from the same firm that served as the company's underwriter?

Pressure rapidly mounts for securities market regulators as the overseers of the market to address such concerns. As we have seen not only from the FSAP findings but also from recent events, the challenges are daunting. The wide array of issues now confronting market regulators—governance, accounting and auditing, insolvency, credit rating agencies, as well as traditional securities regulatory issues such as minority shareholder protection, self-regulation, demutualization, derivatives trading, over-the-counter markets, transparency, disclosure of interests, independence of the regulator (both financial and political), consolidated supervision of financial conglomerates, use of the Internet, and integrated supervision—will test the current structure of market regulation and the resources of the regulators themselves.

Our findings from the FSAP show that securities market regulators do need to be distinguished from other financial sector regulators given the dynamic nature of capital markets. The securities markets have been a fertile environment in which to explore new regulatory models such as self-regulation or demutualization. As discussed, in some cases, policymakers and governments have not known exactly where to deal best with a certain issue or scandal, and this has typically meant a greater mandate for securities market regulators. This greater mandate, in turn, puts pressure on how markets are regulated, since the regulators have to adopt constantly to new products and new challenges.

We are clearly at a critical juncture in relation to the manner in which securities markets are regulated, both with respect to domestic concerns but also with respect to the manner in which a particular market is integrated into the global marketplace. The capital-raising needs of both developed and developing countries continue to be substantial, and it is therefore incumbent on those who promote sound and efficient market development to ensure that markets are reasonably well regulated and to offer appropriate protections to investors and other market stakeholders. As we have learned from recent events, it is important to remain vigilant when it comes to effective regulation. History is replete with examples of catastrophic economic failures that could have been mitigated and perhaps prevented if controls already in place had been diligently enforced.

Conclusions

In seeking to promote financial stability in the context of securities markets, the IMF and the World Bank have several aims. Most obviously, a well-functioning securities market is essential for the success of broader public policy goals in relation to sustainable economic development. Just as important, securities markets provide a balance in financial systems, reducing the likelihood that financial distress in the wholesale (banking) sector will cause economic collapse. A third aim is to encourage competition in financial services so as to afford maximum opportunities for participation in the financial system and thus reduce costs and increase efficiencies in the provision of financial products and services.

The increasing complexity and connectivity of securities markets require a more sustained effort on the part of regulators and the international financial institutions to ensure that relevant standards are in place. The international financial institutions also will continue to develop methods to rapidly identify vulnerabilities in regulatory systems and provide timely feedback in order to encourage appropriate policy responses by national authorities. While the FSAP will remain the principal platform for identifying regulatory gaps and, it is hoped, for promoting financial stability in the context of securities markets, other innovative mechanisms to address weaknesses and facilitate development of securities markets will need to be pursued. The international financial institutions look forward to continuing close collaboration with IOSCO and national authorities with regard to this ambitious agenda.

The FSAP and IOSCO assessment exercises have provided a better sense of what implementation of the IOSCO principles really means. In this regard, it is clear that the standard-setting bodies, in addition to national authorities, will need to maintain their dynamism in responding to market events and ensuring continuing relevance of the work on core standards.

Whereas a decade ago it might have been reasonable to assume that the regulatory problems confronting developing markets were considerably different from those facing developed markets, increasing integration of markets has reduced the areas of divergence. Through the FSAP and other financial sector activities conducted by the World Bank and the IMF, we have a unique insight into the common issues that many regulators face. Not only have the markets become incredibly complex and interlinked (such complexity and linkage will only continue to expand), but risks, including inadequate regulation and the speed with which crises can develop, have created an environment where greater vigilance is required.

Although the challenges facing regulators are immense, one should not despair. In many respects, we are better equipped than ever to make meaningful strides in addressing the issues. Through instruments such as the FSAP and the assessments as well the work of national authorities and standard setters, the future should see continued development of sound and efficient securities markets.

PANEL SUMMARY

Approaches to Securities Trading

Ruben Lee, chair of the panel and managing director of Oxford Financial Group, opened the discussion by asking Emmanuel Zamble of the Bourse Regionale des Valeurs Mobiliers in West Africa why West Africa sought to create a regional exchange serving eight countries, one of the few places in the world where such a structure has been attempted. Zamble replied that the countries chose to create an exchange because the nations of the West African Monetary Union wanted to provide their citizens an opportunity to invest in their economies. They considered having eight national exchanges with linkages between them, but since only one of the eight members had an exchange, they decided to pool their resources into constructing a single exchange.

Lee then asked Sergio Luiz de Cerqueira Silva of the São Paulo Stock Exchange in Brazil what he considered to be the greatest threat to his exchange. Silva replied the New York Stock Exchange (NYSE) is São Paulo's toughest competitor, because 35 percent of trades in Brazilian stocks are conducted there.

Does the Brazilian exchange have the capacity to process the 35 percent of trades currently handled on NYSE? If it does not, then Lee suggested that the NYSE in fact adds to trading in Brazilian stocks rather than detracting from it. Silva responded that such trading initially added to Brazilian stock liquidity, but that Brazil's frequent economic crises frightened investors, who subsequently chose to avoid the volatility of the market there. As a result, the São Paulo exchange is unable to maintain adequate liquidity, and thus he believes the NYSE clearly is taking business away from Brazil.

What does the NYSE offer that the São Paulo exchange does not? Silva replied that companies listed on the NYSE prepare financial statements according to generally accepted accounting principles (GAAP). Lee then asked whether requiring Brazilian companies to report in U.S. GAAP would minimize the competitive gap between the two exchanges or whether the U.S. stamp of quality is truly the difference, so the Brazilian exchange would be unable to counter that difference no matter what steps it takes. Silva agreed that the implicit SEC stamp of approval of GAAP is vital, citing German firms that have to redo their statements to satisfy the SEC. He felt that, like Germany, Brazil is incapable of enforcing U.S. GAAP, although the quality of statements prepared under Brazilian GAAP is quite good. Unfortunately, foreign investors do not recognize that quality—or, presumably, the standards and concepts resulting in those statements—and this prevents them from effectively analyzing Brazilian companies.

Lee directed his next question to Ravi Narain, chief executive officer of the National Stock Exchange of India. He asked why the National Stock Exchange, the second major exchange in India, was needed, and whether it is possible to continue having two major players in the country. Narain replied that the country's twenty-two exchanges had been making no effort to upgrade their technology, improve trading practices, or integrate global benchmarks. Such stagnation led to a highly inefficient trading system and left a large gap for the National Stock Exchange to enter. There was a need, as is evident in the exchange's ability to gain significant market share in a short period of time. When asked why the other exchanges failed to respond quickly to this competition, Narain replied that they had indeed improved themselves quickly at the start, but that their management lacked the ongoing drive for self-improvement. The other exchanges adopted best practices, but the National Stock Exchange went beyond this: it had a vision for itself in the future and moved quickly from integrating best practices to expanding into new products and segments and meeting more international benchmarks. It rapidly added new instruments and incorporated equity, then fixed income, then equity derivatives; it now is investigating interest rate and commodity derivatives. In effect, the

National Stock Exchange is attempting to remain three steps ahead of the competition.

Lee asked Alfred Berkeley, vice chairman of Nasdaq, what he considered to be the greatest threats to the Nasdaq today. Berkeley replied that the greatest threat is regulatory arbitrage by brokerage firms licensed to perform market functions. These firms are not required to pay for regulatory inspections, and they are leveraging these savings to underprice the Nasdaq. The electronic communications network (ECN) Instinet is a prime example. This presents a significant competitive disadvantage to the Nasdaq, as roughly 10 percent of its annual revenue goes to pay for regulatory costs. However, to what extent does the technology of these competitors, not their regulatory status, play a role in this competitive gap? The cost of executing trades has declined from $5 in 1995 to only $0.20 today, far exceeding the 10 percent cost spread resulting from regulatory structures. Secondary regulatory arbitrage also has sprung up, as the regional exchanges, such as Boston and Cincinnati, have begun purchasing order flow.

When asked about the exchange's current goals, Berkeley replied that the goal is to trade many companies globally and to push through regulatory walls to offer such a trading arena. He felt that firms in certain nations, such as Japan, are averse to the transparency and competition brought through Nasdaq and therefore seek to block the launch of Nasdaq in their markets.

Lee asked the panel to describe the top three sources of revenue for their exchanges and to address whether they are sustainable or not. At the West African exchange, listing fees account for 60 percent of revenue and trading commissions account for 25 percent. At the São Paulo exchange, trading, vendor, and listing fees account for 60, 20, and 15 percent of revenue, respectively. According to Silva, these revenues are not sustainable unless the exchange can attract more investors. Nasdaq receives 20 percent from listing, 20 percent from data, and 60 percent from trading fees. Given that the NYSE, the regional exchanges, and ECNs compete for those revenue sources, Berkeley was somewhat pessimistic about their sustainability.

What costs do exchanges face? At the West African exchange, because of its newness and the cultural norms of the region, the ratio of fixed to variable costs is relatively high because the number of people trading stocks is so low. At the São Paulo exchange, supervision of trading accounts for much of the costs. At the National Stock Exchange, the costs of technology, upgrading of systems, and product innovation are high, while the costs of regulatory compliance remain low. At the Nasdaq, personnel expenses are low, and the largest cost is $100 million devoted to marketing expenditures. Aimed at building a brand of investors, this marketing seeks to create a group of investors willing to do a lot of investment research, something that will appeal to new, up-and-coming growth companies that the Nasdaq seeks out.

Lee asked about the prospects of survival in the absence of linkages with other exchanges. The São Paulo exchange is trying to attract local and regional investors and their liquidity, but regulation is posing a barrier. For example, Silva felt that Argentine investors should be able to purchase stocks in Brazilian markets, but the present regulatory structure prevents this.

Narain suggested that there are two types of markets: (a) small markets in small economies that may need regionalization to compete and operate effectively and (b) big markets in big economies that have a large pool of domestic liquidity and can compete and survive even without international liquidity. However, even the big markets must eventually compete in the international arena. For example, in India, as the rupee becomes convertible, Indian citizens may want to buy foreign companies, companies may try to buy American Depository Receipts, and the market should provide a structure for meeting these demands. Narain also noted that time zones make a difference in international competition. The National Stock Exchange trades at very different hours than the NYSE, so there is limited competition between the two; the São Paulo exchange has a lot of overlap with the NYSE and therefore goes head-to-head with the largest exchange in the world. Such factors play a role in international markets. Whatever their size or format, exchanges should not be isolated from one another, because isolation tends to block and segment liquidity pools.

How can a stock exchange contribute to growth? Berkeley replied that the introduction of the Nasdaq in the 1970s doubled the return to venture capital by enabling money to be invested earlier. In addition, Nasdaq's fee structure is arranged so that larger companies effectively subsidize the listings of smaller companies, helping them to develop. Narain noted that raising listing standards boosts growth by ensuring a minimal level of quality on the exchange, which improves the returns to capital. The National Stock Exchange also has taken a role in helping companies to publicize themselves to private investors, which assists their development.

How do their organizations view demutualization? Zamble replied that the primary goal of his stock exchange is to reinforce economic integration within the eight member countries and thus aid development. Demutualization would require each country to operate its own exchange, which would run counter to the goal of integration and incur greater costs. The West Africa exchange has no plans for demutualization. Silva replied that the costs of demutualization, which in Brazil stem largely from taxes, clearly exceed the benefits and that his exchange will not be demutualizing anytime soon. Berkeley said that whether an exchange is nonprofit or for-profit has much less of an impact than whether it has the correct regulatory structure. Under prior management, the Nasdaq demutualized and paid a heavy price: the reorganization caused a great deal of regulatory confusion about what the Nasdaq is and the direction in which it should be headed, and it absorbed a large amount of management's time and attention.

In the question-and-answer period, Alvaro Goncalves of Stratus Investments of Brazil predicted that, in the future, the major international markets in New York, London, and elsewhere would draw all the blue-chip firms from around the globe, while local stock exchanges would serve mainly small and medium enterprises. Narain was doubtful about this scenario, responding that the National Stock Exchange has roughly fifteen to twenty companies with American Depository Receipts or Global Depository Receipts, yet the exchange still maintains 80–85 percent of the liquidity in nearly all of them. This is the case despite a lack of direct effort to build liquidity in these stocks, which the exchange is starting to do. Given the competition his exchange faces from the NYSE, Silva agreed that the international trend is indeed in that direction but that making the transition to a small-company market would be challenging, because blue-chip companies are still paying the exchange's bills.

Lee asked Berkeley why the Nasdaq is still trying to open international markets despite continued failures in the United Kingdom and Japan, for example, and whether the exchange could eventually succeed in opening markets? Berkeley responded that Nasdaq is committed to achieving that goal because operating in other markets would create a deeper pool of liquidity and lower the cost of capital for companies that list on the Nasdaq.

Finally, a participant asked about relations between the National Stock Exchange and the many small exchanges in India. Narain replied that the

National Stock Exchange explicitly sought to drive them out of existence and that they responded to this pressure by becoming subsidiaries of the National Stock Exchange. Instead of subsuming each exchange directly, the National Stock Exchange consolidated the order books of each exchange into a single order book. He believed that such a consolidation would have failed if it had been mandated and that only market pressure was capable of achieving an effective consolidation. Narain concluded that the arrangements are working quite well, although the National Stock Exchange profits more from them than do the other exchanges.

PART IV

Private Equity

JACK GLEN
AJIT SINGH

14

Capital Structure, Rates of Return, and Financing Corporate Growth: Comparing Developed and Emerging Markets, 1994–2000

This chapter seeks to establish stylized facts and, where possible, to explain differences between emerging-market corporations and developed-market corporations with respect to accounting ratios derived from balance sheets and income statements. In addition to examining relationships among accounting variables, such as capital structure, asset structure, and return on assets, we also analyze the size distribution of corporations and the manner in which they finance corporate growth. A study of these variables for developing countries is interesting in its own right, but in order to put this into perspective, a comparison with advanced countries is particularly valuable.

The current public interest in corporate finance and corporate behavior in emerging markets is a recent phenomenon that arose out of the East Asian crisis and the view that the "deeper causes" of the crisis lay in the Asian way of doing business.[1] That analysis suggests that poor corporate governance, inadequate competition, high leverage, and "crony capitalism" led to disregard for profits, over-investment, and exploitation of minority shareholders. Hence, in order to forestall future crises, G-7 countries under the New International Financial Architecture have proposed reform of the

1. See, for example, Greenspan (1998); Pomerleano and Zhang (1999); Summers (1998). For critical views of this hypothesis, see Singh (1999); Stiglitz (1999).

corporate system in emerging markets.[2] Whether or not this thesis is correct, corporate reform in emerging markets is now on the national and international agenda. Implementing appropriate reforms, however, requires a body of empirical knowledge that is only now beginning to emerge.

This chapter attempts to further that knowledge by reporting the results of analysis of the corporate financial statements of nearly 8,000 companies in forty-four countries over the period 1994–2000. Although the body of data is large, the sample is not a random selection from each of the countries involved, and, therefore, interpretation of any results must incorporate the nature of the sample and any influence that its selection might have on the results. For that reason, we also draw on what is known about the countries and the sectoral composition of the sample when describing our findings.

At one level, the questions addressed in this paper are simple. For example, does a typical company in an emerging market finance growth from internal or external sources? Are firms in emerging markets larger or smaller than their developed-market counterparts? Are asset and capital structures in emerging markets fundamentally different from those observed in developed markets? Are accounting returns higher and more volatile in the emerging-market countries? However, interpretation of the empirical answers to these questions is far from straightforward, owing, in part, to the issues raised with respect to the sample as well as the ambiguities that exist in the relevant theoretical models.

The findings are both expected and unexpected. We find that emerging-market firms are generally smaller than their developed-market counterparts. We also find that emerging-market firms use lower levels of debt, but the debt level has declined in recent years from much higher levels previously. We also find that emerging-market firms hold higher levels of fixed assets (relative to total assets) than do developed-market firms. The evidence also shows that returns on assets and equity have been more volatile for emerging-market than for developed-market firms and returns have been generally lower. Finally, the analysis shows that emerging-market firms have used much higher levels of external equity to finance growth than developed-market firms.

The remainder of the chapter is organized as follows: the next section outlines a series of analytical issues that one needs to consider when comparing corporate financial choices and outcomes in an international context.

2. For fuller discussion of these issues, see Singh, Singh, and Weisse (2002).

That is followed by a description of the data and the empirical results. A summary, conclusions, and policy implications make up the final section.

Conceptual Issues

Should statistics generated from financial statements about, for example, capital structure and profitability systematically differ across countries? What does economic theory predict? At one level, theory suggests that differences should be immaterial if all countries are subject to the full rigors of competition and market forces. Theory, however, recognizes that, despite vigorous market forces, specific factors may result in differences. For example, the sectoral composition of firms might differ across countries, and owing to risks inherent in a sector, this might result in different corporate choices and outcomes. Other factors that influence corporate outcomes are the macroeconomic environment, the regulatory system, the tax system, institutions (for example, the legal system and system of corporate governance), and the preferences of and options available to investors. For these reasons, one should not be surprised to find differences among countries in corporate finance and corporate behavior. In line with this, interpretation of observed behavior therefore requires careful attention to these factors.

In the particular case of comparing emerging and developed markets—important environmental differences are pertinent to the analysis. First, compared with developed-market countries, most emerging-market countries have markets that are more imperfect and incomplete, including the product market, the labor market, and the capital market. Second, emerging-market corporations tend to be family owned, and there is less separation of ownership and control of the kind found in Anglo-Saxon corporations. Third, domestically owned business groups and conglomerates dominate corporate structures in some emerging-market countries. These conglomerates are quite different in their origin and character than those found in advanced countries, and therefore their behavior might be different. Fourth, there are differences between emerging-market countries and developed-market countries in regulation, in the enforcement of corporate law, in corporate governance, and in governance generally.[3]

3. Laffont (1999) suggests that product market competition in emerging markets is highly imperfect. For a different perspective, see Glen, Lee, and Singh (2001, 2002). For a review of these issues, see

In view of these particular features of emerging-market countries, it would be difficult to maintain a priori the hypothesis that there is no difference between the characteristics of the corporations in the two groups of countries. Differences with respect to any particular aspect, such as profitability or the size distribution of firms, would depend on the relative significance of these factors. We illustrate this by considering the financing of corporate growth.

Myers and Majluf demonstrate that even if managers, acting as agents for owners, are rational maximizers of shareholder wealth, because of asymmetric information between them and the investing public, a pecking order of finance, in which internal equity is first choice, followed by debt and then, as a last resort, external equity, would be optimal.[4] This theoretical analysis should be equally applicable in both groups of countries. However, because emerging-market corporations, even large listed ones, are often family controlled and these families are averse to losing control, companies may have an additional reason to avoid external equity finance. One would therefore expect to find even more emphasis on internal equity finance in emerging-market corporations. In addition, subsidized debt from government-controlled lenders might lead to greater use of debt than equity, relegating external equity to a distant third place.

Another conceptual issue regarding differences between the two groups of countries is that of accounting standards and reporting requirements. In light of recent scandals in the United States and other developed markets, the superiority of developed-market accounting is now much less obvious. Moreover, our data for emerging-market countries pertain to listed companies where, increasingly, international standards are being applied. Despite that, to the extent that emerging-market countries are more inflationary, their accounting data, unless adjusted, could be distorted. For most countries in our sample, however, inflation is not an issue, and, where inflation is a problem, adjustments are the norm.[5] Finally, although many of the questions we address are economic in nature and accounting data are

Tybout (2000). On capital market imperfections in general in emerging markets, see Singh (1997). On groups and conglomerates, see Khanna (2000); Leff (1978); Singh (1995). On implications of regulatory and legal inadequacies in emerging markets, see Shleifer and Wolfenzon (2002). On ownership patterns, see Claessens, Djankov, and Lang (2000).

4. Myers and Majluf (1984).

5. Inflation accounting in some emerging-market countries is well developed. For example, Whittington, Saporta, and Singh (1997) show that the Brazilian method of inflation adjustment deals effectively with the problem.

not designed to deal directly with those economic issues, we must accept that accounting data are the only data available and adjust our interpretation of the results accordingly. Dealing specifically with issues associated with accounting differences between countries is beyond the scope of this paper.

Data Description

The data consist of various accounts taken from the financial statements of listed companies, as reported by Osiris/BVD in their May 2002 CD-ROM. Osiris attempts to provide data on as many companies as possible for each country. Over time, their sample has grown, and this growth has influenced the data used in this study. The sample period used in much of the work that follows is 1994–2000. Data for earlier years are available for some companies, but the number of companies with data prior to 1994 declines, especially for some of the emerging markets. With that decline, one is usually left with results only for the larger companies in each market, which could bias the results. Data also are available for 2001 for some companies, but owing to a lag in reporting, the number of companies drops nearly 40 percent from the number for 2000. For that reason, the sample period ends at 2000.

Table 14-1 presents the number of companies for each year for each country, with the table divided between the two country groups.[6] In total, forty-four countries are represented in the sample: twenty-two developed markets and twenty-two emerging markets. For 2000, 7,968 companies are in the sample, which is down 8 percent from the number in 1999, most likely reflecting lags in reporting, as the number of companies increased each year except 2000. Over 1994–2000 the number of reported companies increased 82 percent; the rate of increase in both groups of countries was large, but the increase in the developed-market group (84 percent) exceeded that of the emerging-market group (75 percent).

The number of companies reported in table 14-1 is well below the total number of listed companies in these markets.[7] Standard and Poor's reports

6. The division into developed and emerging markets is based on the system employed by Standard and Poor's (2001), which follows the system originally developed by the International Finance Corporation in its Emerging Markets Database.

7. As reported in Standard and Poor's (2001).

Table 14-1. *Number of Companies in Developed and Emerging Markets, by Country, 1994–2000*

Market and country	*1994*	*1995*	*1996*	*1997*	*1998*	*1999*	*2000*
Developed markets							
Australia	72	78	81	80	94	92	84
Austria	33	36	41	47	52	49	45
Belgium	38	39	43	55	65	72	68
Bermuda	23	24	28	31	32	42	38
Canada	118	151	176	182	274	286	242
Cayman Islands	6	6	6	7	10	8	10
Denmark	61	63	68	73	77	78	70
Finland	26	26	32	40	58	67	66
France	177	196	224	253	308	359	335
Germany	212	218	242	270	348	382	345
Greece	26	37	51	51	55	53	43
Ireland	17	16	20	22	23	24	22
Italy	30	47	60	62	65	81	79
Japan	344	413	1,177	1,323	1,536	1,540	1,163
Netherlands	57	66	78	87	95	95	86
Norway	24	27	32	40	46	44	35
Singapore	62	60	91	124	153	149	121
Spain	18	20	30	30	46	48	47
Sweden	60	76	95	106	127	119	105
Switzerland	70	88	102	109	124	125	119
United Kingdom	425	476	494	545	557	490	460
United States	1,443	1,604	1,783	1,902	2,108	2,510	2,572
Group total	3,342	3,767	4,954	5,439	6,253	6,713	6,155
Emerging markets							
Argentina	9	10	11	7	9	20	21
Brazil	n.a.	31	39	57	89	97	117
Chile	53	56	64	70	69	68	40
Colombia	8	9	11	41	19	10	50
Czech Republic	14	24	39	68	86	63	73
Hong Kong	102	125	153	164	172	157	132
Hungary	2	3	5	5	10	17	13
India	48	48	71	158	176	114	75
Indonesia	24	26	25	25	27	15	6
Israel	9	11	13	25	39	56	57
Korea, Rep. of	533	619	650	705	735	751	779
Malaysia	136	189	205	184	204	207	142
Mexico	31	38	28	31	42	45	40
Pakistan	2	4	5	7	12	11	8
Peru	1	2	3	62	65	68	64
Philippines	5	5	6	4	7	5	8

Table 14-1. *(continued)*

Market and country	*1994*	*1995*	*1996*	*1997*	*1998*	*1999*	*2000*
Poland	1	1	5	10	26	29	20
South Africa	13	17	39	60	73	69	36
Taiwan	16	20	30	65	92	95	112
Thailand	21	24	28	27	29	19	9
Turkey	5	7	7	6	6	2	2
Venezuela	3	4	3	3	17	8	9
Group total	1,036	1,273	1,440	1,784	2,004	1,926	1,813
Grand total	4,378	5,040	6,394	7,223	8,257	8,639	7,968

Source: Authors' calculations based on Osiris/BVD data.
n.a. Not available.

a total of 25,253 listed companies in all emerging markets in 2000 compared to a total of only 23,996 for developed markets. Both of these numbers increased between 1994 and 2000: the emerging-markets universe increased 76 percent, and the developed-market total increased 39 percent. Clearly, the Osiris database has far to go before it provides complete coverage of these markets.

About 77 percent of the sample companies in 2000 were in developed markets, with the United States alone representing 32 percent of the total. Other significant developed countries in the sample include Japan and the United Kingdom; Germany, France, and Canada have relatively fewer companies. These six countries together represent 61 percent of the total sample for 2000. Among the emerging markets, Korea has by far the largest number of companies in the sample: 779. No other emerging market comes close to this number, with Malaysia and its 142 companies a distant second place.

The disparity in the number of companies in developed and emerging markets in this sample is also matched by differences in their market capitalization. In 1994 total world stock market capitalization was $15.1 trillion, of which emerging-market countries represented just $1.9 trillion, or 13 percent.[8] By 2000 the disparity between the two groups of countries had grown even wider, with total market capitalization growing to $32.3 trillion, of which emerging markets represented just $2.7 trillion, or 8 percent. Taking market capitalization as a reference, emerging markets are more than adequately represented in this sample.

8. Standard and Poor's (2001).

Companies are sorted into eight industrial sectors using NAICS (North American Industry Classification System) codes as reported by Osiris. Those sectors are chemicals, food and beverages, industrial and consumer products, nonmetallic minerals, plastics and rubber, primary metals, pulp and paper, and textiles, apparel, and leather. Companies in the financial sector as well as in services and utilities are excluded from the sample in order to avoid issues related to peculiarities in their reporting and operations relative to manufacturing companies. A summary of the number of companies in each sector in 2000 is presented in table 14-2. Globally, 55 percent of the sample companies are classified in industrial and consumer products, a sector classification that includes a range of products, such as machinery, electronics goods, automobiles, and general consumer goods. A distant second in number of companies is chemicals, which accounts for 13 percent of the total. The pulp and paper sector has the smallest number of companies, 223, representing 3 percent of the global total. The distribution of companies across sectors is roughly comparable in both the developed and emerging markets, although there are fewer industrial and consumer products companies in emerging markets (43 percent) than in developed markets (58 percent), with the difference spread across a number of sectors.

Empirical Analysis

This section reports the results of the empirical analysis. It is separated into subsections that report the size distribution of the companies in the sample, regressions of size on country and sector factors, and regressions that measure the evolution of company size over time. Separate subsections also report and discuss summary statistics on capital structure, asset structure, and returns on assets and equity. The section ends with an analysis of the manner in which the companies in the sample financed growth in their balance sheets.

Size Distribution of Firms

The size of a company, as measured by the total assets on the balance sheet, has potentially important implications. For example, in some sectors size is a determinant of cost structure, as certain technologies require that output be above a minimum threshold in order to be competitive. Even without

Table 14-2. *Sector Composition in Developed and Emerging Markets, 2000*

	Number of companies			*Percent of total number*			*Mean total assets (millions of U.S. dollars)*			*Median total assets (millions of U.S. dollars)*		
Sector	*Developed*	*Emerging*	*Global*	*Developed*	*Emerging*	*Global*	*Developed*	*Emerging*	*Global*	*Developed*	*Emerging*	*Global*
Chemicals	740	289	1,029	12	16	13	2,743	1,020	2,259	187	120	163[a]
Food and beverages	533	194	727	9	11	9	1,892	572	1,539	214	187	209
Industrial products	3,568	776	4344	58	43	55	1,541	436	1,344	102	63	107[a]
Nonmetallic minerals	210	110	320	3	6	4	1,423	636	1,153	119	173	172
Plastics and rubber	207	56	263	3	3	3	764	510	710	172	87	117
Primary metals	271	127	398	4	7	5	1,870	966	1,581	315	154	252[a]
Pulp and paper	160	63	223	3	3	3	2,092	505	1,644	414	133	277[a]
Textiles	466	198	664	8	11	8	395	220	343	92	70	88
Total	6,155	1,813	7,968	100	100	100	1,628	574	1,388	139	93	126

Source: Authors' calculations based on Osiris/BVD data.

a. Indicates rejection of the hypothesis of equal medians at the 5 percent level.

technological constraints, larger firms may have lower net costs as administrative costs are amortized over larger amounts of output. In either case, one might expect emerging-market companies to be at a disadvantage, especially with respect to the larger developed markets, where overall demand for products may be higher. Consequently, one might expect to see smaller companies in emerging markets, and this might have an impact on their competitiveness.

An alternative view is that size, especially as measured by total assets, is not important. The argument here is that firms exploit two sets of assets in their operations: those that are purchased and reside on their balance sheet and those that are represented by the human capital they employ. If human capital is more important in developed than developing countries, this might be reflected in the size of companies as measured by total assets.

There is an additional complicating factor: the extent to which the firms in any given country are subject to competition. In a large market, such as the United States, domestic competition alone might force companies to adopt optimal technologies, and that might determine size. But in smaller and less open markets, where competition is limited, size could reflect factors other than competition. In small, but open, economies, firms would adjust to the comparative advantages of the local resources, and those factors, together with technological considerations, would determine size.

The empirical evidence on the size of emerging-market companies is limited in the academic literature. Roberts and Tybout examine a sample of Chilean and Colombian companies and the impact of trade liberalization on their size, as measured by number of employees at the plant level.[9] Their review of the theory suggests that the impact of trade openness should be to rationalize production, which suggests larger size. In fact, they find that plant size decreases when import competition increases and that the impact increases over time. This effect is measured at the plant and not the company level.

Table 14-2 provides a first glimpse at the size of the companies in the sample. Globally, the average company had total assets of $1.4 billion in 2000, but average size in the sample varies greatly across sectors, with chemicals having by far the largest average total assets and textiles the smallest. As measured by average total assets, the emerging-market companies are only about 35 percent the size of their developed-market counterparts. In this sample, however, mean size is not a good indicator of the

9. Roberts and Tybout (1991).

overall sample, owing to an asymmetric distribution of size across companies. Under these circumstances, the median paints a slightly different picture, as shown in the last three columns of the table. Under that measure, the emerging-market companies are much closer in size to their developed-market counterparts, with equality of medians not being rejected in four sectors. Owing to the differences between mean and median values in this sample, much of what follows concentrates on median values.

Table 14-3 presents the median value of total assets for each country by year. The global median company in 2000 had assets of $126 million, down from $132 million in 1994. This decline likely reflects the expansion in the number of companies in the sample over time. Initially, the largest and most liquid companies were included in the database. Over time, smaller companies were added, pulling down the median value. One can see a similar pattern for the developed-market sample. For the emerging markets, the pattern over time is more complicated; median company size rose through 1996 and then fell in 1997. A large part of the drop in value in 1997 must reflect the Asian crisis and coincident depreciation of the Asian currencies; note in particular the drop in Korea. As these values are reported in U.S. dollars and given the large contingent of Asian companies in the sample, one should expect to see a currency impact at that time. Not all of the impact is from Asia, however; note the decline in the median value for Venezuela in 1998, which has a significant impact on the cross-country mean.

Ignoring the time-series dimension, there are distinct differences between the two groups of countries. In fact, the developed-market median exceeds the emerging-market median in all years, and that difference is statistically significant in all years. Looking deeper at individual countries, however, one can see that the median size in several emerging-market countries is well in excess of that of the larger developed-market countries. For example, Mexico, which had forty companies in the sample in 2000, had a median size of $840 million, nearly four times the U.S. median value and well above that of any developed-market country. In contrast, Peru, which had a sample of sixty-four companies in 2000, had a median value of only $26 million, far below that of any developed-market country. Perhaps sector composition accounts for these country differences.

While the median values are useful for summarizing the sample, they also hide much of the variation that occurs across the sample. Some of that variation is revealed in figure 14-1, which presents a histogram of total assets for the year 2000 for both the emerging-market and developed-

Table 14-3. *Median Assets in Developed and Emerging Markets, by Country, 1994–2000*
Millions of U.S. dollars

Market and country	*1994*	*1995*	*1996*	*1997*	*1998*	*1999*	*2000*
Developed markets							
Australia	223	190	205	216	133	158	194
Austria	207	221	188	155	169	181	191
Belgium	244	279	236	183	157	139	143
Bermuda	133	135	129	114	109	108	115
Canada	136	117	101	119	102	92	83
Cayman Islands	102	103	175	160	252	363	361
Denmark	127	151	135	134	157	166	179
Finland	1,389	1,526	1,091	706	307	138	147
France	244	241	198	142	120	88	102
Germany	333	422	304	225	184	137	148
Greece	63	47	51	54	56	99	106
Ireland	378	398	436	356	365	386	417
Italy	1,265	491	375	360	391	344	340
Japan	1,569	1,215	237	198	265	316	185
Netherlands	243	292	236	200	227	173	236
Norway	117	96	87	106	140	103	122
Singapore	81	107	87	77	72	80	89
Spain	303	339	387	375	317	294	318
Sweden	316	240	177	149	118	105	100
Switzerland	412	339	326	288	297	251	312
United Kingdom	83	77	84	79	84	83	83
United States	70	75	80	89	94	90	116
Group median	159	165	147	139	148	145	139
Emerging markets							
Argentina	984	968	754	904	1,237	516	267
Brazil	n.a.	1,177	895	979	549	387	303
Chile	85	102	112	125	125	129	190
Colombia	249	337	361	169	157	202	113
Czech Republic	31	47	43	40	43	28	26
Hong Kong	120	110	119	119	111	116	128
Hungary	56	60	88	138	104	88	117
India	285	193	183	119	115	141	168
Indonesia	224	295	281	231	212	261	322
Israel	431	302	217	218	201	86	109
Korea, Rep. of	46	59	61	42	45	51	57
Malaysia	89	67	72	57	50	55	74
Mexico	743	659	1,250	1,157	702	650	840
Pakistan	124	114	59	56	60	27	30

Table 14-3. *(continued)*
Millions of U.S. dollars

Market and country	*1994*	*1995*	*1996*	*1997*	*1998*	*1999*	*2000*
Peru	148	84	30	30	24	22	26
Philippines	43	70	65	1,497	239	83	116
Poland	55	75	189	51	51	52	69
South Africa	1,557	957	180	104	65	58	113
Taiwan	368	569	965	443	422	502	446
Thailand	126	162	183	93	95	172	299
Turkey	134	54	61	67	82	38	156
Venezuela	511	990	923	1,054	102	326	277
Group median	81	92	99	77	80	83	93
P value[a]	0.00	0.00	0.00	0.00	0.00	0.00	0.00
Global median	132	139	134	121	128	127	126

Source: Authors' calculations based on Osiris/BVD data.
n.a. Not available.
a. P value presents the results of a test for equality of medians across the two country groups. P values less than 0.05 reject equality at the 5 percent level.

market pooled samples. The figure confirms that the emerging-market sample is much like the developed-market sample, but it does contain more small companies and fewer large companies. More than 35 percent of the emerging-market companies had total assets of $50 million or less in 2000, compared to a bit more than 25 percent for the developed-market sample. At the other extreme, only slightly more than 10 percent of the emerging-market companies had total assets over $1 billion, compared to about 18 percent for the developed-market sample. Except for these extremes, the two distributions look remarkably similar.

Size Regressions

Table 14-3 provides a simple measure of size—median total assets—but that measure suffers from trying to explain the total distribution of firms in a single statistic. It also combines firms across industries within a single country. Given the potential importance for technology-related industry effects, accounting for industry composition within a country is important.

This section reports results from a regression of total assets (expressed in natural log form for 2000) on a set of industry and country dummies. The

Figure 14-1. *Total Assets in Emerging and Developed Markets, 2000*

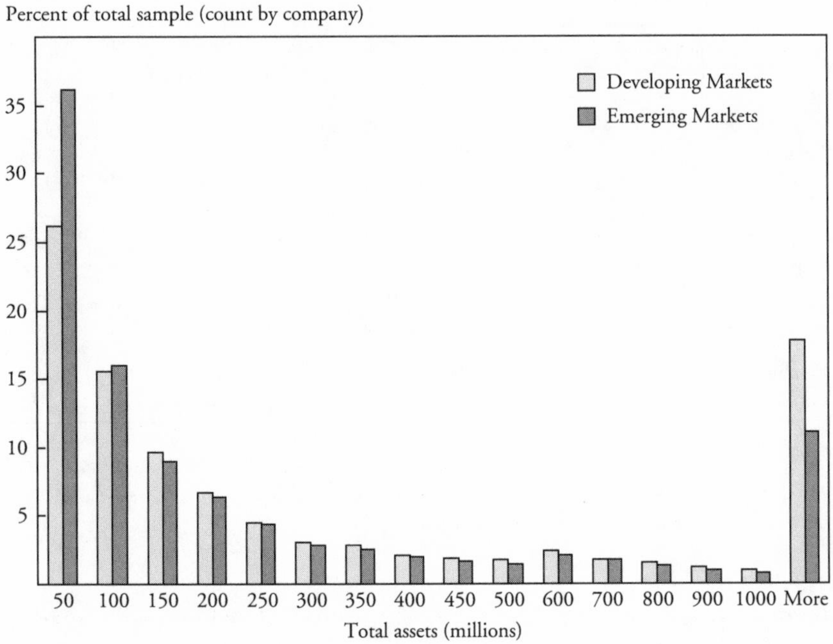

results provide industry and country mean values (adjusted for industry effects) as well as a statistical test of differences across industries and countries. Those results are presented in table 14-4. In the table, the United States and the industrial and consumer products industries are taken as the base levels against which all other industries and countries are measured. Note that the regression employs a total of 3,360 companies and has an overall R^2 of 21.6 percent.[10]

Starting with the industry coefficients, five of the seven industries have coefficients that are significantly higher than the base industry; only one industry—textiles—has a lower value. To give an order of magnitude to

10. The sample used in this and the following regressions differs slightly from the sample used in the other tables. There are two dimensions to this difference. First, the main objective is to produce data for the financing regressions reported later, which require data for both 1995 and 2000; this eliminates 3,863 companies that do not have data for both years. Second, to avoid the impact of a few outliers on the results, the sample excludes 749 companies (18 percent of the sample) where the ratio of financing from any source to total assets exceeds 200 percent.

Table 14-4. *Regression: Ln(Total Assets 2000) on Sector and Country Dummies*[a]

Dummy	β	*t statistic*
Sector		
Chemicals	0.707	6.93
Food and beverages	0.592	5.38
Nonmetallic minerals	0.860	5.26
Plastics and rubber	0.279	1.52
Primary metals	0.686	5.51
Pulp and paper	0.667	3.83
Textiles	−0.358	−3.53
Developed markets		
Australia	−0.365	−1.56
Austria	0.162	0.66
Belgium	0.120	0.45
Bermuda	−0.737	−2.13
Canada	−0.057	−0.29
Cayman Islands	0.044	0.07
Denmark	−0.204	−0.87
Finland	1.436	3.46
France	0.319	1.85
Germany	0.535	3.29
Greece	−0.405	−1.37
Ireland	0.863	3.25
Italy	1.335	3.76
Japan	2.697	19.42
Netherlands	0.830	2.74
Norway	0.393	0.89
Singapore	−0.231	−0.90
Spain	0.595	1.64
Sweden	0.446	1.75
Switzerland	0.673	3.54
United Kingdom	−0.550	−4.56
Emerging markets		
Argentina	0.766	2.73
Brazil	1.076	4.01
Chile	−0.632	−1.74
Colombia	−0.807	−2.08
Czech Republic	−1.473	−2.74
Hong Kong	−0.415	−2.51
Hungary	−1.436	−3.73
India	0.207	0.56

(*continued*)

Table 14-4. *(continued)*

Dummy	β	*t statistic*
Indonesia	0.387	0.82
Israel	0.676	1.46
Korea, Rep. of	–1.255	–14.13
Malaysia	–0.975	–5.90
Mexico	1.036	4.27
Philippines	–0.691	–0.75
South Africa	0.779	2.20
Taiwan	1.432	4.45
Thailand	–0.139	–0.35
Turkey	–2.413	–1.22
Venezuela	1.621	1.14
Constant	12.273	199.39
Number of observations	3,360	
R^2	0.216	

Source: Authors' calculations based on Osiris/BVD data.

a. The United States and industrial and consumer products industries are taken as the base levels against which all other industries are measured.

these coefficients, the mean value of total assets in the base industry-country is $214 million. In the textiles industry, that value is reduced to $149 million, about one-third less. The largest industry is nonmetallic minerals, with mean value of $505 million.

Within the developed markets, nine of the twenty-two countries have mean values (after adjusting for industry effects) that differ statistically from the base case. Only two of those, the United Kingdom and Bermuda, have a value below the base case, with values of $102 million for Bermuda and $123 million for the United Kingdom. The other seven countries have mean values above the base case. Japan has the largest companies, with mean value of $3.2 billion after adjusting for industry effects. However, country size does not correlate well with firm size. Switzerland, which has a small gross domestic product (GDP), has significantly larger companies, on average, than the U.S. base case; the same is true in Ireland. Perhaps this difference reflects the much larger sample from the United States, which allows many smaller companies to be included in the sample.

The emerging markets present a somewhat different picture, with eleven of nineteen emerging markets having coefficients that are statistically different from the base case. Five of those countries have mean values that are above the base case. Taiwan has the largest companies (ignoring Venezuela, which has a small sample and a single large chemical company), with an average value of $895 million, followed by Brazil, Mexico, Argentina, and Israel. In addition, six countries have smaller companies on average, with the Czech Republic having the smallest, with a mean value of $49 million.

Unfortunately, interpreting the regression results in table 14-4 in terms of any of the logical arguments on size determination is difficult, as there are many dimensions to be taken into consideration. In Korea, for example, where firms are subjected to fierce domestic competition and export success is important, firms are generally smaller than average. In contrast, in Taiwan, under similarly competitive circumstances, firms are larger than average. In addition to possible competition effects, sample characteristics also need to be taken into consideration. The larger size of Taiwanese firms may reflect the fact that there are far fewer of them in the sample, whereas the large number of Korean companies may reduce their average size. Clearly, interpretation of the results is difficult.[11]

This regression framework also provides evidence of the relative importance of country and sector effects on company size. To assess these effects, the regression was estimated again with only country and with only industry variables. The results (not reported) show that, of the total explained variation in the regression reported in table 14-4, nearly 85 percent of that amount is accounted for by country effects alone. The framework also permits one to examine the extent to which the industry effects are peculiar to either the developed- or emerging-market companies. Those results (also not reported) show that the industry effects reported in table 14-4 do not change when emerging-market industry dummy variables are introduced into the regression, nor do the additional variables have significant coefficients, suggesting that industry effects are equal in both size and significance in both sets of countries.

Finally, specific firm effects could be an important component of size determination. In fact, the unexplained variation in the regression, which represents 88 percent of total variation, is due to factors other than country and sector. For example, superior management would result in business success and larger size. Firm-specific effects, however, are absent from our specification owing to the decision to examine the size distribution at a single point in time.

11. Aw, Chung, and Roberts (2002) argue that competition is different in Taiwan and Korea: Taiwan is more competitive.

Evolution of Firm Size over Time

An important issue for economic analysis and public policy is the evolution of the size distribution of firms over time and its implications for competition and economic growth. The question of growth becomes relevant as the study of firm size distribution over time essentially involves an analysis of the relationship between size and growth of firms. Is this relationship the same for the two groups of countries?

Economic theory suggests that the simplest hypothesis to start from is the one that regards growth to be a random phenomenon across firms. The specific form of this hypothesis—the so-called law of proportionate effects—asserts that all firms have the same chance of growing by a given percentage during any period of time. If this law holds, it has powerful economic implications, including that there will be a relentless increase in industrial concentration over time.[12]

An economic rationale for this law based on an entirely stochastic model of firm growth can be presented in the following terms. It may be argued that firm growth depends on a multitude of factors—some of which make for positive growth, others for negative growth—and they may be thought of as being individually small and independently randomly distributed. It is difficult to estimate their individual effect, but the combined effect is to generate the stochastic relationship between size and growth of firms as manifest in the law of proportionate effects.

From the perspective of economic analysis, a better theory would postulate that firm growth is subject to both systematic and stochastic forces. The former might be managerial quality or macroeconomic conditions. In empirical terms, the law in this formulation can be tested by a regression of firm closing size on opening size. A regression coefficient of 1 indicates equal growth rates across firms; a coefficient below 1 suggests convergence in size.

The results of these regressions are presented in table 14-5. The main point that emerges relates to the slope coefficient. The law in this strong form fails to be rejected in a large majority of countries in both groups. The hypothesis that the slope is not significantly different from 1 is not rejected in fourteen out of twenty-two developed-market countries and in twelve out of eighteen emerging-market countries in the sample. However, in eight developed-market countries and five emerging-market countries, the

12. See Caves (1998) for a recent review article on the law of proportionate effects and modern theory about size distribution.

Table 14-5. *Size and Growth: Regressions of Firm-Level Total Assets (2000, ln) on Total Assets (1995, ln), by Country*

Market	*A*	β	R^2	*Number of observations*
Developed markets				
Australia	1.96	0.85*	0.77	57
Austria	0.31	0.97	0.85	25
Belgium	1.48	0.89	0.87	31
Bermuda	–2.85	1.24	0.50	14
Canada	3.45	0.76*	0.60	105
Cayman Islands	–2.91	1.24	0.63	3
Denmark	0.43	0.98	0.92	44
Finland	–0.68	1.06	0.95	17
France	–0.19	1.02	0.92	148
Germany	–0.54	1.04	0.80	164
Greece	1.19	0.97	0.62	21
Ireland	4.64	0.70*	0.76	13
Italy	–0.63	1.07	0.89	32
Japan	1.39	0.91*	0.94	128
Netherlands	0.87	0.95	0.87	43
Norway	0.67	0.97	0.89	17
Singapore	0.69	0.95	0.83	38
Spain	–1.15	1.11	0.87	18
Sweden	3.04	0.79*	0.86	57
Switzerland	2.31	0.84*	0.84	74
United Kingdom	2.32	0.84*	0.73	299
United States	2.16	0.88*	0.80	1,150
Emerging markets				
Argentina	3.20	0.76	0.66	8
Brazil	–1.78	1.11	0.90	23
Chile	3.26	0.73*	0.71	26
Colombia	–1.22	1.07	0.98	6
Czech Republic	7.58	0.31*	–0.01	11
Hong Kong	2.69	0.78	0.40	68
Hungary	–3.78	1.37	0.58	3
India	–3.87	1.28*	0.92	14
Indonesia	–0.53	1.01	0.90	6
Israel	–3.14	1.27	0.91	5
Korea	3.39	0.72*	0.74	517
Malaysia	1.87	0.84*	0.65	103
Mexico	1.86	0.91*	0.97	31
Philippines	0.95	0.94	0.84	4
South Africa	–0.93	1.04	0.76	9
Taiwan	–0.50	1.08	0.88	19
Thailand	–5.12	1.41	0.79	4
Venezuela	–1.42	1.11	0.98	3

Source: Authors' calculations based on Osiris/BVD data.

* Significantly different from 1 at the 5 percent level.

slope coefficient is below 1, which suggests convergence in firm sizes in these countries. The slope coefficient of unity or above indicates that, other things being equal, in these economies large firms are growing faster than small firms and concentration is occurring.[13]

Capital Structure

Capital structure has important implications for the vulnerability of firms to exogenous shocks. As noted, high leverage is thought to have contributed to the East Asian crisis. Despite this importance, there is neither theoretical nor empirical consensus on the factors that drive corporate decisions on this matter.[14] In this section, we examine the capital structure of our sample of firms and investigate similarities and differences between the two groups of countries.

LEVERAGE: TOTAL LIABILITIES TO TOTAL ASSETS. Globally, the average company in the sample financed just over half of its balance sheet with liabilities, with a slight decline in the level of liabilities over time for the global average (table 14-6). That global average, however, masks large variations across individual countries and, within those countries, across time. Across the two major groupings of countries, debt levels are much higher in emerging-market countries, which had a median ratio of total liabilities to total assets ranging from 49 percent (in 2000) to 62 percent (in 1994), with a steady decline following the 1997 Asian crisis. In contrast, the ratio of the developed-market group fluctuates between 52 and 53 percent from year to year, with no obvious trend across time. Those differences between countries are statistically significant at the 5 percent level in all years.

Even within these two major groupings, one observes considerable variation. Some of the lowest levels of debt in the developed markets are observed in the United States, where the median company had ratio values of 41 percent in 1996–97. Those ratios grew over the next few years, however, ending the sample period at 45 percent, still well below the level of nearly all other developed markets. For some countries, debt levels dropped over the sample period. For example, in Japan the ratio declined from 62 percent in 1994 to 55 percent in 2000, placing it below the developed-country median. The ratio for German companies also declined but ended the period with a median value of 64 percent, well above the group

13. The other things equal clause is important here since entry and exit patterns, in principle, could reverse the growth of industrial concentration. These phenomena are not examined here.

14. Myers (2001) reviews the literature on capital structure.

median. In other cases, leverage increased, with the median Irish company increasing its leverage ratio from 60 percent in 1994 to 68 percent in 2000, earning it the distinction of having the highest median leverage ratio in the entire developed-market sample for that terminal year.

There is also great variation across countries and over time in emerging markets. Indonesia ended the sample period with by far the highest leverage ratio (89 percent), up sharply from its levels in the first three years of the sample. Following the 1997 crisis, leverage ratios soared in Indonesia as profits turned to losses, thereby eating up equity, with this effect compounded by foreign currency–denominated debt being inflated by an especially weak currency and, possibly, by the large decline in the number of Indonesian companies in the sample. Clearly, however, the impact of the crisis was much different in Korea, which also experienced severe currency weakening, but where the leverage ratio was trimmed from a relatively high value of 72 percent in 1994 to a much more conservative 52 percent in 2000. Thailand represents a third way, with lower levels of debt in the early years of the sample, but higher leverage ratios after the crisis, but not nearly to the extent of Indonesia. Finally, leverage ratios declined in Hong Kong following the crisis, but they increased marginally in Taiwan, one of the few emerging markets in the region that did not experience extreme disruption to its economy at that time.

Some other emerging-market countries also produce interesting results. For example, in Venezuela, which had a weak financial sector throughout this sample period, leverage ratios were consistently low, although there was a sharp drop in 1995, likely reflecting the currency devaluation at that time. Also notable is the trend in Brazil, which adopted its Real Program in 1994 and stabilized inflation: the level of debt held by the median company climbed steadily from a below-average value of 42 percent in 1995 (the first year for which data are available) to an above-average value of 62 percent in 2000. Also note the increase in leverage in Pakistan following its 1998 economic hardships (and currency devaluation) as well as the increase in Poland and the Czech Republic over time as the financial systems in those countries developed and came closer to developed-country standards. Turkey had relatively high levels of debt despite high inflation and correspondingly high levels of real interest rates. These ratios for Turkey do raise the issue of inflation accounting and the impact that restatement of balance sheets has on ratios such as this.

The use of median values in table 14-6 paints a very different picture from what is obtained using mean values, which suffer from the influence

Table 14-6. *Median Total Liabilities to Total Assets, by Country and Year, 1994–2000*
Percent

Market	*1994*	*1995*	*1996*	*1997*	*1998*	*1999*	*2000*
Developed markets							
Australia	51	51	51	51	52	53	55
Austria	66	69	71	66	63	64	63
Belgium	58	56	59	62	60	56	57
Bermuda	54	57	51	49	47	52	43
Canada	52	50	47	48	49	48	48
Cayman Islands	47	51	37	47	48	48	43
Denmark	54	53	51	52	52	54	59
Finland	67	63	61	60	58	59	58
France	62	62	61	62	61	62	62
Germany	71	70	71	70	68	65	64
Greece	56	55	56	58	57	55	57
Ireland	60	62	64	60	65	65	68
Italy	66	65	62	64	62	64	64
Japan	62	62	58	56	57	55	55
Netherlands	58	62	59	59	60	64	61
Norway	59	56	56	55	56	54	58
Singapore	45	44	49	49	52	47	46
Spain	60	58	47	50	52	56	56
Sweden	60	55	53	55	54	54	53
Switzerland	60	60	58	56	57	54	54
United Kingdom	52	54	53	52	53	51	49
United States	44	43	41	41	43	47	45
Group median	53	53	52	52	53	53	52
Emerging markets							
Argentina	46	44	47	46	53	44	41
Brazil	n.a.	42	50	52	51	57	62
Chile	39	40	41	41	42	40	43
Colombia	33	37	38	30	43	34	34
Czech Republic	35	41	40	45	47	49	45
Hong Kong	52	52	51	46	44	42	40
Hungary	42	29	23	23	30	37	35
India	60	57	57	56	55	50	47
Indonesia	54	51	57	71	76	70	89
Israel	54	54	48	56	47	47	40
Korea, Rep. of	72	72	71	72	66	56	52
Malaysia	47	51	48	49	50	48	48
Mexico	51	52	50	52	46	49	56

Table 14-6. *(continued)*
Percent

Market	*1994*	*1995*	*1996*	*1997*	*1998*	*1999*	*2000*
Pakistan	61	68	56	56	59	72	63
Peru	19	28	34	47	48	48	49
Philippines	22	19	17	39	26	22	41
Poland	14	15	16	26	43	48	44
South Africa	57	53	47	46	45	47	51
Taiwan	36	34	41	44	43	44	47
Thailand	52	56	62	72	54	61	62
Turkey	48	61	63	54	59	68	62
Venezuela	53	31	30	27	33	38	34
Group median	62	61	60	58	55	50	49
P value[a]	0.00	0.00	0.00	0.00	0.01	0.00	0.00
Global median	55	55	54	54	54	53	51

Source: Authors' calculations based on Osiris/BVD data.
n.a. Not available.
a. P value reports results for a test of median equality between the two country groups. P values less than 0.05 reject equality at the 5 percent level.

of large outliers. Although mean values of the ratio of total liabilities to total assets are not presented, a few comments highlight their difference with the medians reported in the table. Globally, mean values of the ratio do not differ significantly, with a global mean of 56 percent (in 2000) compared to the 51 percent average median value reported in the table. For some countries, however, there are large differences. In Malaysia, for example, the mean value of the ratio for 2000 is 86 percent, compared to a median value of 48 percent. In many other countries, the mean and median do not differ substantially, but in eight countries the differences are large and always in the direction of lower median ratios than mean ratios.

Differences in medians across the different countries could, in part, represent different industry compositions. To address this issue, table 14-7 reports a regression of the year 2000 ratio of total liabilities to total assets on a size factor[15] and a set of sector and country dummy variables, where the base case is taken to be the U.S. industrial and consumer products sector. The size factor is significant, with larger firms having higher levels of debt. The table provides limited evidence in favor of sector effects on the

15. The size factor is ln(company total assets/global mean total assets).

Table 14-7. *Regression: Ratio of Total Liabilities to Total Assets on Relative Size, Sector, and Country Dummies, 2000*[a]

Variable	β	*t statistic*
Sector		
Chemicals	–9.22	–2.71
Food and beverages	–2.85	–0.65
Nonmetallic minerals	–4.34	–0.68
Plastics and rubber	3.21	0.68
Primary metals	–1.52	–0.32
Pulp and paper	–0.54	–0.14
Textiles	–4.32	–1.27
Developed markets		
Australia	8.27	2.73
Austria	19.76	5.03
Belgium	12.40	2.67
Bermuda	0.14	0.02
Canada	13.71	1.7
Cayman Islands	–10.26	–1.13
Denmark	10.53	4.28
Finland	11.09	3.14
France	15.23	8.7
Germany	18.64	10.93
Greece	8.00	1.99
Ireland	25.04	6.26
Italy	18.24	6.76
Japan	11.05	5.74
Netherlands	14.93	4.46
Norway	11.66	2.08
Singapore	2.78	0.93
Spain	16.18	3.14
Sweden	6.19	2.39
Switzerland	5.89	2.85
United Kingdom	6.17	3.54
Emerging markets		
Argentina	12.07	2.12
Brazil	13.98	2.8
Chile	–5.86	–1.42
Colombia	0.33	0.04
Czech Republic	1.51	0.38
Hong Kong	13.28	1
Hungary	–13.68	–2.12
India	11.53	1.36
Indonesia	38.41	3.32

Table 14-7. *(continued)*

Variable	β	*t statistic*
Israel	12.14	1.55
Korea, Rep. of	13.17	2.34
Malaysia	41.67	1.17
Mexico	9.80	2.53
Philippines	−13.63	−1.21
South Africa	11.43	1.97
Taiwan	3.29	0.85
Thailand	20.32	1.73
Turkey	17.44	9.25
Venezuela	−19.58	−3.82
Constant	49.29	36.39
Size	2.55	5.59
Number of observations	3,360	
R^2	0.014	

Source: Authors' calculations based on Osiris/BVD data.

a. The base case is the U.S. industrial consumer and products sector.

ratio; the chemicals sector has a ratio that is significantly below the level of the other sectors, but no other sector is statistically different from the base sector. Country differences, however, are both large and significant. Among the developed-market countries, sixteen countries have mean ratios that exceed the level of the U.S. base case. For some of those—for example, Ireland, Austria, and Spain—the differences are economically very large. No developed market (except the Cayman Islands) has a ratio that is statistically below the level of the United States. Among the emerging markets, six countries have ratios significantly above the level of the United States; Indonesia has the largest difference, but the sample is small. Only Hungary and Venezuela have a ratio that is significantly below the level of the United States.

The regression was also estimated for 1995 (not reported). The estimated coefficients for that year do not differ notably from those reported in the table. One important difference, however, is in the amount of explained variation (R^2). For 2000, reported in table 14-7, the regression explains less than 2 percent of the total variation in the data. In contrast, for 1995 a similar regression explains 15 percent of the variation. This enormous difference in the two samples is also reflected in the sample statistics for the two periods. The standard deviation of the ratio for 2000 is four times the level for 1995 globally. Nearly all of the higher level of volatility is in emerging markets; the standard deviation in emerging markets increases by a factor of eight, compared to an increase of 55 percent in the developed markets.

Closer scrutiny explains much of the difference between the 1995 and 2000 samples. Regressions of the two groups of countries reveal that the developed-market results did not change much between the two years, whereas the emerging-market results differed notably. Breaking the emerging-market sample down further, one learns that most of the difference in the two years can be accounted for by a large shift in the distribution of the Korean population over this time period. That shift is documented in figure 14-2. Apparently, Korean companies entered the mid-1990s with high levels of liabilities; for nearly 30 percent of the sample, liabilities financed 71–80 percent of total assets. Following the 1998 crisis, however, Korean companies deleveraged their balance sheets, with that shift occurring across nearly the entire distribution of Korean companies. That deleveraging, however, was accompanied by a high level of dispersion in the distribution of leverage ratios, accounting for much of the lower level of explanatory power in the year 2000 regression.

CURRENT AND NONCURRENT LIABILITIES. Globally, current liabilities represent about 30 percent of total assets, well above the 15 percent of total assets (in 2000) represented by noncurrent (or long-term) liabilities. Current liabilities represent a combination of both trade and other nonmarket sources of credit, as well as the current portion of bank lending and bonds. Noncurrent liabilities represent long-term credit from either banks or markets. Together, these two ratios constitute the ratio of total liabilities to total assets reported in table 14-6.

The level of current liabilities does not differ greatly between the two major subgroups of countries, with emerging-market countries, on average, financing about 30 percent of total assets with current liabilities, as compared to 28 percent in developed-market countries (in 2000). There is no apparent trend in the time-series behavior of this ratio in the developed-market countries; however, there appears to be a tendency toward lower levels of current liabilities in the emerging-market countries over the sample period: current levels fell steadily from 39 percent in 1994 to the current level.

The ratio of noncurrent liabilities to total assets, reported in table 14-8, reveals a similar time pattern. The ratio remained steady in the developed-market countries: in the range of 15–18 percent, with no obvious time

Figure 14-2. *Ratio of Total Liabilities to Total Assets for 516 Companies in Eight Manufacturing Sectors, Korea, 1995 and 2000*

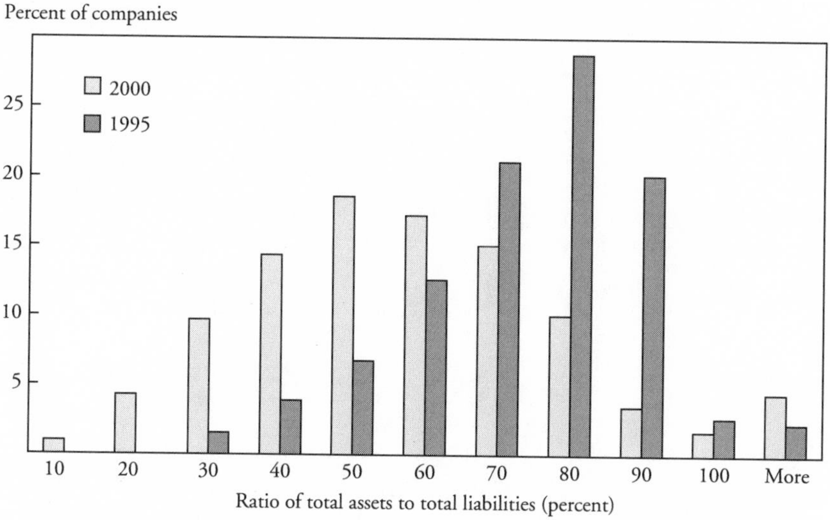

pattern. In the emerging-market countries, however, the ratio started out at a high of 19 percent and then declined following the 1997 crisis to 13 percent. With the exception of 1994 and 1998, the ratios in the two groups are statistically different at the 5 percent level. In a regression framework with size, sector, and country factors (not reported), however, the emerging-market group average is not statistically different from the developed-market group average.

Within the two country groups, one observes considerable cross-sectional variation, with several countries in both groups producing single-digit levels of noncurrent liabilities, including the most recent year for the United Kingdom, a country with a relatively well-developed domestic bond market and with a large number of reporting companies. Even the United States, which has perhaps the most developed corporate bond market in the world in addition to a well-capitalized and competitive banking sector, had noncurrent liabilities of only 13 percent in 2000, well below, for example, Brazil.

In several other countries in the developed-market sample, one sees much higher levels of noncurrent liabilities, particularly in Germany (31 percent), with its bank-based financial system, in the Nordic countries, and in Austria and Ireland. In the emerging-market group, one finds

Table 14-8. *Ratio of Median Noncurrent Liabilities to Total Assets, by Country and Year, 1994–2000*

Percent

Market	*1994*	*1995*	*1996*	*1997*	*1998*	*1999*	*2000*
Developed markets							
Australia	20	18	20	22	22	23	21
Austria	45	40	39	38	33	29	25
Belgium	22	22	20	20	18	16	16
Bermuda	8	7	5	5	6	3	3
Canada	22	21	19	18	17	17	19
Cayman Islands	9	9	13	12	13	17	16
Denmark	19	19	20	18	17	20	18
Finland	32	28	23	26	26	24	23
France	23	21	21	20	19	19	20
Germany	39	38	38	37	33	32	31
Greece	9	8	6	7	9	10	10
Ireland	26	26	22	19	31	27	28
Italy	22	19	18	19	18	18	18
Japan	20	18	14	13	15	15	14
Netherlands	24	21	23	21	19	18	17
Norway	28	26	24	25	25	26	25
Singapore	9	11	9	10	9	9	9
Spain	18	18	15	20	16	18	19
Sweden	22	20	21	22	27	27	26
Switzerland	30	28	28	27	25	23	21
United Kingdom	10	10	10	10	11	10	9
United States	15	14	12	12	14	16	13
Group median	18	17	15	15	17	17	16
Emerging markets							
Argentina	15	11	16	21	9	9	10
Brazil	n.a.	17	22	24	23	24	25
Chile	9	13	15	15	15	15	19
Colombia	18	15	18	10	12	9	15
Czech Republic	1	3	3	7	6	5	2
Hong Kong	9	10	8	7	6	6	6
Hungary	16	8	5	3	5	6	4
India	35	31	28	19	22	16	11
Indonesia	15	16	14	19	11	11	46
Israel	17	13	21	18	14	13	12
Korea, Rep. of	23	22	23	24	20	17	14
Malaysia	8	8	7	7	8	7	9
Mexico	31	27	28	29	26	27	32
Pakistan	10	16	12	15	17	13	16

Table 14-8. *(continued)*
Percent

Market	*1994*	*1995*	*1996*	*1997*	*1998*	*1999*	*2000*
Peru	2	6	17	12	10	9	9
Philippines	0	0	0	18	2	1	12
Poland	0	0	3	4	5	7	13
South Africa	18	17	12	10	11	8	10
Taiwan	8	15	19	14	15	16	17
Thailand	8	17	16	16	10	17	20
Turkey	8	11	13	17	13	10	10
Venezuela	29	18	15	14	11	14	18
Group median	19	18	19	17	16	14	13
P value[a]	0.23	0.04	0.00	0.00	0.23	0.00	0.00
Group median	19	18	19	17	16	14	13
Global median	18	17	16	16	16	16	15

Source: Authors' calculations based on Osiris/BVD data.

n.a. Not available.

a. P value reports the results of test for equality of medians for the two country groups. P values less than 0.05 reject equality at the 5 percent level.

relatively high levels of noncurrent liabilities in Mexico, where the ratio remained stable across the sample period, and in Brazil, where the ratio increased rapidly following the currency stabilization program introduced in 1994. In Korea, noncurrent liabilities actually declined in importance following the 1997 crisis, as companies deleveraged themselves; a somewhat similar pattern emerges in Indonesia, albeit with a twist in 2000, as the number of reporting companies dropped sharply.

Asset Structure

Asset structure—the relative amount of fixed and current assets—can provide information on operational efficiency and the choice of technology. However, disentangling these two dimensions is difficult. For example, high levels of current assets may suggest over-investment in inventory. Alternatively, the combination of lower levels of fixed assets combined with high levels of human capital, which do not appear on the balance sheet, can produce the same result. In this section, we document the relative amounts of current and fixed assets used in our sample of countries.

CURRENT AND FIXED ASSETS TO TOTAL ASSETS. Current assets, which consist primarily of cash, liquid securities, inventory, and trade receivables, constitute roughly half of all assets on a global basis, and this level of current assets has been maintained consistently across the sample period. There is, however, considerable variation across the countries, with the developed-market countries holding, on average, about 57 percent of their assets in this form, as opposed to a much lower level of 45 percent (in 2000) for the emerging-market countries.

As the complement to current assets, fixed assets also represent about half of the total (table 14-9). Here one sees a marked difference in the level of the ratio in the two groups of countries, with emerging-market countries holding much higher levels of fixed assets than their developed-market counterparts, and these differences are statistically significant. This difference is highlighted by the remarkably low levels of fixed assets in two leading developed-market countries—the United States and Germany—both of which have ratios below both the global and developed-market average. The difference extends much deeper, however, as only four of the developed-market countries have fixed asset ratios in excess of 50 percent (Australia, Canada, Cayman Islands, and Ireland), while only four of the emerging-market countries have ratios below 50 percent (Hong Kong, Israel, South Africa, and Turkey).

Differences between the countries might reflect sector or size effects, but regressions (not reported) that control for these effects do not support that view. For 2000 a regression of the ratio of fixed assets to total assets on country and industry variables and a size factor shows that, although both size and sector effects are statistically significant, country effects are also significant. Specifically, among the emerging-market countries, eleven countries have ratios that are statistically larger than that of the United States, and only a single emerging-market country—Turkey—has a ratio below that of the United States. Among the developed-market sample, two countries have ratios above that of the United States, and five have ratios below that of the United States. Apparently, even controlling for sector and size effects, the emerging-market group holds higher levels of fixed assets than the developed-market group, and that difference is statistically significant.

This result is at odds with one view of the world that posits higher levels of current assets in emerging-market countries as a result of poorer inventory management skills, combined with a need for precautionary balances of both cash and inventory. The result could be consistent with a view that the reporting companies in the developed-market group are more mature and that, therefore, their fixed assets are more fully depreciated,

Table 14-9. *Ratio of Median Fixed Assets to Total Assets, by Country and Year, 1994–2000*

Percent

Market	*1994*	*1995*	*1996*	*1997*	*1998*	*1999*	*2000*
Developed markets							
Australia	51	54	52	52	52	58	54
Austria	48	48	47	48	47	45	47
Belgium	45	42	41	39	40	43	44
Bermuda	41	47	40	42	45	34	33
Canada	50	49	50	49	52	54	53
Cayman Islands	59	60	45	42	59	61	67
Denmark	40	40	36	40	42	42	43
Finland	51	53	50	46	48	44	43
France	34	34	34	32	32	31	32
Germany	40	39	39	37	37	39	40
Greece	31	33	33	34	38	42	39
Ireland	46	45	44	41	45	53	55
Italy	36	32	33	37	37	37	35
Japan	42	43	42	42	44	44	46
Netherlands	44	43	44	42	42	40	41
Norway	45	44	43	43	42	41	44
Singapore	47	49	48	50	50	49	49
Spain	54	55	53	52	52	54	48
Sweden	38	41	42	41	46	43	41
Switzerland	45	44	45	46	46	46	44
United Kingdom	37	35	35	35	38	43	42
United States	38	37	36	37	39	40	40
Group median	40	40	40	40	42	43	43
Emerging markets							
Argentina	60	59	60	58	65	64	63
Brazil	n.a.	74	71	65	65	61	61
Chile	57	58	57	57	57	62	63
Colombia	78	82	84	78	75	80	74
Czech Republic	58	54	58	54	54	55	55
Hong Kong	43	45	45	45	45	45	46
Hungary	47	46	46	40	53	54	52
India	48	48	50	57	57	63	67
Indonesia	53	57	57	62	57	64	67
Israel	49	48	45	40	38	34	28
Korea, Rep. of	48	47	49	48	52	51	50
Malaysia	50	49	48	50	53	54	52
Mexico	73	71	73	72	72	69	69

(*continued*)

Table 14-9. *(continued)*

Market	*1994*	*1995*	*1996*	*1997*	*1998*	*1999*	*2000*
Pakistan	47	49	36	68	54	53	58
Peru	58	51	56	52	56	56	60
Philippines	57	61	64	68	48	54	62
Poland	40	44	47	49	53	51	52
South Africa	40	44	44	42	39	41	42
Taiwan	65	60	64	61	61	62	63
Thailand	56	59	58	58	57	67	58
Turkey	28	29	29	37	40	39	29
Venezuela	65	73	79	82	68	76	76
Group median	49	50	50	51	54	54	55
P value[a]	0.00	0.00	0.00	0.00	0.00	0.00	0.00
Global median	42	42	42	43	45	45	45

Source: Authors' calculations based on Osiris/BVD data.

n.a. Not available.

a. P value reports the results of test for equality of medians between the two country groups. P values less than 0.05 reject equality at the 5 percent level.

leaving them primarily with current assets on the balance sheet. But that view fails to account for the fact that most companies are constantly investing and that depreciation actually does represent the consumption of capital over time, thereby requiring the acquisition of new and undepreciated equipment. What may be observed instead is a world in which highly skilled and highly paid labor in developed-market countries acts as an additional form of capital, but one not counted on the balance sheet. In contrast, the low-wage unskilled worker in the emerging-market countries must be combined with higher levels of fixed assets.

Return on Assets and Equity

Returns on assets are of central importance in a market economy. Allocation of capital on the basis of risk and return is the foundation for financial economics and has obvious policy implications. In this section, we examine the differences among the accounting returns of the various countries and sectors in our sample.

Ignoring potential impacts from various accounting standards on the calculation of income, a major difference across countries in calculating returns is the impact of local inflation. For that reason, the statistics on returns reported in table 14-10 have been adjusted for the difference between the local rate of inflation and the U.S. rate of inflation for the corresponding year, so that all returns are reported in U.S. nominal terms. This adjustment does not account for currency movements, which also could be significant, because the reported returns are accounting returns, not market returns. Adjusting for the impact of currency movements on accounting returns is delicate, and no obvious methodology is available. For that reason, we rely on a simple inflation differential adjustment.

The global median return on assets (inflation adjusted) ranges from 1.8 percent to 4.2 percent over the sample period, with the high in 1996 and the low in 1998. The difference between the developed-market and emerging-market median values is significantly different in all years except 1999, when they are equal. In all years except 1999 the emerging-market returns are below the developed-market returns. Notably, returns in emerging-market countries are near zero over 1994–97, with a sharp drop in 1998 as the Asian crisis both reduced nominal returns and increased inflation in several emerging-market countries. Both the inflation and nominal return effects were transitory, however, and emerging-market returns increased in 1999–2000.

The variation across individual countries is substantial. Note, in particular, the higher incidence of negative values in the emerging-market sample, but also bear in mind that many of these countries have relatively small numbers of companies, which should result in higher volatility in the median over time. In a few countries, volatility is relatively low—Australia, Denmark, France, Japan, and Taiwan are examples—whereas in other countries higher volatility prevails—Italy and Mexico are examples. Cyclical patterns are discernible; a slowdown in the returns provided by U.S. companies is evident in 1998–2000 after four years of higher returns. In Malaysia, returns were high through 1997 and lower in subsequent years, but a similar pattern is not obvious in either Thailand or Korea, both countries that fell prey to the Asian crisis of 1997.

Differences at the country-group level also are evident at the sector level, as reported in figure 14-3, which shows the (inflation-adjusted) returns on assets for 2000 for each of the eight sectors for the two country groups. Returns in the developed-market sectors are consistently in the 4–5 percent range, with the notable exception of textiles, which returned just over 1 percent. There is considerably more variation in emerging-market returns, although within the same range as the developed-market group. In part

Table 14-10. *Median Return on Assets and Equity by Country and Year (Inflation Adjusted), 1994–2000*

Percent

	Assets							*Equity*						
Market	*1994*	*1995*	*1996*	*1997*	*1998*	*1999*	*2000*	*1994*	*1995*	*1996*	*1997*	*1998*	*1999*	*2000*
Developed markets														
Australia	5.4	3.3	4.9	6.5	4.4	4.5	2.8	10.5	7.8	8.8	11.8	8.5	9.7	7.3
Austria	1.3	3.5	3.6	4.5	4.3	4.6	5.1	5.0	11.4	8.0	12.4	12.8	10.0	9.6
Belgium	3.4	5.9	4.7	5.7	4.6	4.3	4.6	8.7	11.4	12.7	13.8	10.5	10.2	11.3
Bermuda	4.0	1.6	3.9	5.1	1.4	4.9	4.8	6.8	3.7	8.8	8.6	2.3	9.7	7.7
Canada	7.4	6.1	5.7	4.0	2.7	2.4	3.1	13.4	11.9	11.0	9.4	7.6	5.5	6.6
Cayman Islands	10.9	3.4	7.3	2.2	2.5	0.1	2.4	20.6	5.4	15.0	3.7	3.4	2.7	7.2
Denmark	6.0	6.9	5.8	5.2	5.1	4.8	3.8	12.2	12.5	12.5	11.3	12.2	11.7	8.9
Finland	4.9	5.9	6.6	7.3	5.2	6.1	5.7	9.8	12.1	14.3	16.6	12.1	13.4	13.9
France	3.6	4.2	4.2	4.6	4.4	5.0	4.9	8.9	9.6	10.2	11.9	11.0	11.4	10.7
Germany	2.0	4.1	4.0	3.5	4.0	4.3	4.3	6.6	10.3	10.1	10.5	11.5	10.0	10.2
Greece	–2.2	1.4	1.0	3.5	3.1	6.5	6.6	9.6	13.2	13.2	15.7	13.4	15.5	14.4
Ireland	7.0	7.4	9.1	8.5	5.7	7.5	2.9	16.9	19.6	19.1	19.5	17.1	20.6	14.0
Italy	–0.3	–0.1	1.9	3.6	2.3	4.0	3.7	3.6	5.4	7.7	9.5	8.5	10.2	9.4
Japan	2.8	4.3	4.5	2.0	1.7	3.7	5.5	4.6	6.6	7.1	4.1	2.9	5.4	7.4
Netherlands	5.0	6.9	6.8	6.7	5.8	5.0	6.0	14.1	16.8	15.0	16.2	15.6	14.2	15.8
Norway	7.2	6.4	6.9	3.8	3.2	1.9	0.9	17.1	16.2	13.2	11.3	9.6	5.6	1.9
Singapore	5.1	5.2	5.6	3.9	5.1	6.8	5.8	8.7	9.0	9.3	7.9	8.4	10.7	9.3
Spain	2.4	3.2	4.6	5.2	5.3	5.0	4.6	7.2	10.8	9.5	11.6	11.7	11.8	11.6
Sweden	7.4	9.2	8.3	6.4	5.8	5.5	7.1	18.4	19.6	15.3	13.1	13.3	11.4	13.6
Switzerland	5.5	5.2	6.4	7.1	6.5	6.6	7.4	11.2	10.8	12.6	14.7	13.4	13.6	14.1
United Kingdom	5.6	5.1	6.5	5.3	2.8	4.6	3.8	11.9	11.9	13.5	11.5	8.2	9.4	7.4
United States	4.9	5.4	4.9	4.7	3.0	1.8	1.1	10.6	10.6	9.8	9.8	6.8	5.0	3.3
Group median	4.3	4.8	4.9	3.7	2.7	3.7	4.2	9.4	10.1	9.0	8.0	5.9	6.8	7.4

Emerging markets														
Argentina	3.9	3.6	9.5	5.2	5.0	4.1	7.4	9.0	6.3	15.6	9.9	8.7	4.7	9.0
Brazil	n.a.	–60.9	–10.9	–2.4	0.0	–0.1	–1.5	n.a.	–58.7	–9.0	0.5	2.5	3.5	4.5
Chile	–1.3	1.5	0.3	1.3	1.3	3.2	2.4	3.1	5.9	4.7	5.1	4.5	6.1	4.9
Colombia	–16.1	–16.2	–15.3	–14.7	–16.3	–7.9	–3.4	–13.8	–15.3	–14.8	–14.2	–15.2	–6.8	–1.4
Czech Republic	–6.6	–6.1	–5.5	–5.1	–8.5	0.2	0.5	–6.2	–6.0	–4.6	–3.7	–8.1	0.7	2.1
Hong Kong	0.3	–1.5	2.1	0.4	0.6	9.5	10.0	7.9	3.2	9.0	6.6	5.0	14.0	14.0
Hungary	–6.9	–15.5	–3.7	–4.0	–6.4	–2.6	0.9	1.8	–6.9	0.4	0.5	–2.3	2.1	4.3
India	–1.2	–0.1	–0.1	–0.6	–7.8	2.8	5.0	7.2	10.3	7.0	5.0	–2.8	9.2	11.1
Indonesia	–0.3	–2.1	0.2	–5.1	–55.7	–13.3	–11.1	7.1	6.7	8.5	–5.2	–54.2	11.9	–39.0
Israel	–5.9	–3.1	–4.1	–3.3	–1.3	–1.2	4.6	–1.3	2.3	0.1	1.4	4.4	1.6	8.4
Korea, Rep. of	–1.4	0.5	–0.1	–0.9	–4.5	5.3	4.0	4.4	6.4	4.5	2.2	–0.5	10.8	8.0
Malaysia	4.7	5.5	5.3	4.4	–2.3	2.4	5.2	11.6	12.5	11.7	9.5	–0.2	7.1	8.9
Mexico	–5.7	–27.5	–21.3	–9.5	–7.6	–6.2	0.7	–8.0	–23.1	–11.3	1.3	–2.8	1.9	9.6
Pakistan	–1.0	–1.7	6.0	–3.2	–0.7	–1.1	5.1	17.9	8.4	20.7	6.1	12.5	25.0	14.3
Peru	–2.6	3.7	–7.5	–4.7	–5.2	–1.5	0.9	1.8	7.0	–6.9	–2.7	–4.6	–1.0	2.2
Philippines	–0.2	1.5	1.2	–0.9	–5.8	–3.1	2.5	1.1	11.1	3.6	1.3	–1.7	–2.9	5.9
Poland	–20.2	–17.0	–8.6	–6.6	–6.4	–2.4	–3.7	–18.5	–15.6	–7.7	–4.0	–3.6	0.3	–1.3
South Africa	–2.3	1.3	2.7	0.8	1.7	3.6	5.0	4.8	11.2	11.9	6.2	7.5	9.3	10.8
Taiwan	5.1	4.0	5.8	6.1	3.3	6.4	5.1	7.5	7.2	10.1	10.8	5.5	10.2	7.5
Thailand	3.3	2.3	1.5	–11.4	0.5	5.6	5.5	9.7	10.1	6.5	–19.2	15.9	10.4	12.9
Turkey	–87.8	–74.0	–69.9	–71.9	–81.5	65.5	–43.0	–75.8	–65.1	–58.0	–59.2	–78.3	408.3	–30.1
Venezuela	–58.3	–52.6	–87.1	–37.6	–33.4	–23.1	–12.0	–58.4	–49.4	–82.8	–33.9	–32.6	–23.9	–11.4
Group median	–0.6	0.6	0.4	–0.7	–3.9	3.7	3.5	6.2	6.3	5.7	3.1	–0.6	8.4	7.3
P value[a]	0.00	0.00	0.00	0.00	0.00	0.96	0.00	0.00	0.00	0.00	0.00	0.00	0.00	0.57
Global median	3.4	4.0	4.2	2.7	1.8	3.7	4.0	8.7	9.4	8.5	6.9	4.7	7.2	7.4

Source: Authors' calculations based on Osiris/BVD data.

n.a. Not available.

a. P value reports the results of test for equality of medians between the two country groups. P values less than 0.05 reject equality at the 5 percent level.

Figure 14-3. *Median Inflation-Adjusted Return on Assets in Emerging and Developed Markets, by Sector, 2000*

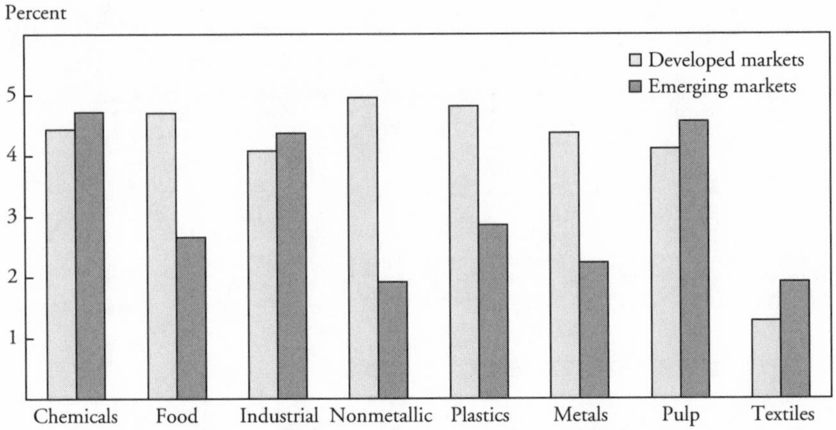

because of the lower number of firms in the individual sectors, the differences between the two country groups are statistically significant only for food, nonmetallic minerals, and metals, and in each of those cases the emerging-market median is below that of the developed-market group. Emerging-market group median returns exceed the corresponding developed-market group returns in four sectors, but those differences are not statistically significant.

The median returns on equity (inflation adjusted) reflect both changes in income over time as well as time variation in capital structure (table 14-10). Globally, returns peaked in 1995, dipped in 1998, and then recovered over 1999–2000. Differences between the two country groups are significant, both statistically (in all years) and economically. Returns in developed-market countries were high over 1994–97, approaching 10 percent in each year, compared to only about 6 percent in emerging-market countries for the first three years, falling to 3 percent in 1997. The Asian crisis hit returns hard in the emerging-market group in 1998, pushing them below zero, but recovery was both rapid and strong, with emerging-market returns well above their developed-market counterparts in 1999. A few countries have returns that exhibit low volatility over time—Australia and Singapore are examples—but many countries show considerable volatility in returns—the United States and Hong Kong are examples. Returns are quite high in a few countries, such as Ireland, the Netherlands, and

Argentina. Low returns correspond closely with high levels of inflation—Turkey and Venezuela are good examples.

Returns on both assets and equity have significant size, country, and sector effects, but there is no difference, on average, between the (inflation-adjusted) returns (in 2000) in the two country groups after controlling for these factors. In regressions not reported, a large number of countries have country fixed effects that are significantly greater than the returns on the base country (the United States). Several sectors have significant fixed effects, relative to the base sector (industrial and consumer products), but those effects are all negative. There is also a significant and positive size effect on returns. None of these factors accounts for much of the variation in returns across firms, however, as the R^2 of the regressions (for returns on assets) is a mere 1.1 percent, of which country factors account for the largest part by far.

Financing Growth

As companies expand their balance sheets through the acquisition of assets, they have choices to make in how that growth is financed. Previous-period earnings can be retained as a source of internal equity finance or be paid to shareholders in the form of dividends. External sources of finance include both the issuance of new shares—external equity—and the issuance of various debt instruments—liabilities. The final choice between these various financing options reflects the many factors discussed above. Using the growth in the balance sheet over the period 1995–2000 as the sample period, the financing of the growth in total assets is divided into these three components and expressed as a percentage of the change in total assets for the period. The means of these three ratios, which sum to 100 percent for each country, the two country groups, and the overall sample, are presented in table 14-11.[16]

Globally, liabilities account for 49 percent of total financing over the five-year period, which corresponds closely with the overall median value of total liabilities to total assets reported in table 14-5 for each of the individual years. Table 14-11 also tells us that, of the remaining 51 percent,

16. As mentioned, the sample used in this analysis is smaller than the sample used in most of the other tables. In particular, the sample has been reduced by eliminating all firms with financing ratios in excess of 200 percent (either positive or negative), which permits one to use mean values, rather than medians, making a comparison across ratios and countries easier.

Table 14-11. *Change in Total Assets, by Source of Financing, 1995–2000*[a]

Percent

Market	*Liabilities*	*External equity*	*Internal equity*
Developed markets			
Australia	58	32	11
Austria	52	3	45
Belgium	56	6	38
Bermuda	41	23	36
Canada	56	32	12
Cayman Islands	90	8	2
Denmark	72	6	23
Finland	53	26	22
France	61	7	31
Germany	62	5	33
Greece	52	34	14
Ireland	76	5	18
Italy	68	5	27
Japan	62	6	32
Netherlands	65	9	26
Norway	50	23	27
Singapore	66	15	19
Spain[b]	68	–9	40
Sweden	57	4	39
Switzerland	54	7	39
United Kingdom	52	21	27
United States	47	21	32
Group average	53	17	30
Emerging markets			
Argentina	46	16	38
Brazil	74	11	15
Chile	44	33	23
Colombia	73	16	11
Czech Republic	33	21	46
Hong Kong	44	20	35
Hungary	28	1	71
India	53	5	43
Indonesia	110	12	–23
Israel	54	6	40
Korea, Rep. of	27	48	25
Malaysia	40	18	42
Mexico	61	30	10
Pakistan	34	17	49
Peru	49	10	41
Philippines	59	40	1

Table 14-11. *(continued)*
Percent

Market	*Liabilities*	*External equity*	*Internal equity*
Poland	74	11	15
South Africa	61	18	21
Taiwan	27	54	19
Group average	35	39	27
Global average	49	22	29

Source: Authors' calculations based on Osiris/BVD data.

a. Companies are excluded if any of their ratios are outside [–200,+200]. The sample size is 3,360.

b. Spain has eighteen companies, one of which experienced a small decline in total assets over 1995–2000. That company also saw external equity increase, which resulted in a large negative value for the external equity ratio. Excluding that one company, the sample mean of the ratio is 3 percent; the internal equity ratio would decline accordingly.

internal equity represents 29 percent, with external equity equal to 22 percent of the total.

What is striking about table 14-11 is the substantial difference in the patterns across the two groups of countries and across individual countries. First, the use of liabilities to finance growth is much lower in the emerging-market group, with that lower level offset by higher levels of both internal and external equity. In particular, the use of external equity in emerging-market countries is well above the levels of the developed-market countries, which agrees with the findings of Domowitz, Glen, and Madhavan on the level of development of primary equity markets.[17] Second, in some of the emerging-market countries the use of liabilities is extremely low. In Korea, for example, few liabilities are used and growth is financed largely from external equity. Korea is also a country where the leverage ratios declined notably over the period 1994–2000. Third, in other countries the impact of the crisis makes the statistics more difficult to interpret. In Indonesia, there are only six companies in the sample, and the average growth in total assets is limited owing to the poor economic environment. In addition, neither internal nor external equity is a significant source of finance. Moreover, foreign currency–denominated liabilities increased significantly in value as the exchange rate depreciated. Hence liabilities are the dominant source of finance for Indonesian companies over the period.

Within the developed-market group, there is much less variation across countries in the use of external liabilities, with the United States having the

17. Domowitz, Glen, and Madhavan (2001).

lowest propensity (after Bermuda) for liabilities (47 percent), which corresponds with the low level of liabilities on its balance sheet. Other countries employ much higher levels of liability financing. Ireland has the highest level among the group (76 percent, ignoring the Cayman Islands), followed by Denmark (72 percent) and Italy and Spain (68 percent each).

There is also great variation across countries in both groups in the use of external equity. One country in the sample actually decreased the amount of external equity employed, but that country, Spain, has a small number of companies in the sample, and one of those is an outlier, with a small decrease in the value of total assets, which then translates a positive change in external equity into a negative ratio. Deleting that outlier produces an external finance ratio of 3 percent. The largest user of external equity is an emerging-market country—Korea—where nearly half of all growth was financed by external finance over the period. In contrast, external equity financed 21 percent of growth in the United States, the world's largest and most developed equity market, a level below that of the emerging-market average and below that of five emerging-market countries for this period.

One point to bear in mind when interpreting these financing ratios is the relative amount of capital being raised from the various sources. Over the sample period, the rate of growth, measured in dollars, was actually lower in the emerging-market group than the developed-market group. The average of the country growth rates was 18 percent in the emerging-market group compared to 28 percent in the developed-market group. Hence the emerging-market group had less growth to finance, which might account for its ability to finance more of that growth in the equity markets.

Conclusions

The main empirical results of the paper may be summarized as follows.

—First, regarding size as measured by total assets, (a) there is a significant difference in the distribution of emerging-market and developed-market firms in our sample; (b) emerging-market firms are smaller in most sectors; (c) country effects explain more of the variation among firms in the distribution of size than do sector effects; and (d) over the sample period the relationship between size and growth of the firm is broadly the same in the two groups of countries.

—Second, regarding firm leverage, (a) emerging-market firms currently have lower levels of leverage than do developed-market firms, and leverage has declined in emerging-market countries in recent years; (b) the use of current liabilities is much the same in the two groups of countries; (c) current liabilities finance a larger portion of total assets than do long-term liabilities in both groups of countries; and (d) neither country nor sector factors explain much of the variation in leverage among firms.

—Third, regarding asset structure, emerging-market firms employ a higher level of fixed assets than do their developed-market counterparts.

—Fourth, regarding returns on assets and equity, returns (adjusted for inflation) generally are lower in emerging-market countries, but they have increased in recent years.

—Fifth, regarding the financing of growth, (a) emerging-market firms use external equity finance more than developed-market firms, which use higher levels of liabilities, and (b) the use of internal finance is similar between the two groups of countries.

—Sixth, country effects account for more of the variation in all variables than do either sector or size effects, but individual firm effects account for most of the variation.

Although these results may be regarded as sample specific, they nevertheless raise broad issues that merit policy discussion. First, one finding that stands out above all others is the importance of the stock market in financing the growth of emerging-market firms. This suggests that stock market development in these countries has been important. However, whether further development of the stock market should take place and the form that it takes may depend on the particular circumstances of each country and should be the subject of serious policy discussion. Second, the finding that emerging-market firms use lower levels of liabilities to finance their balance sheet suggests that policymakers may need to spend more time on the development of credit markets. However, it could also mean that policies that reduce the riskiness of the environment within which emerging-market firms operate could accomplish the same goal. Third, contrary to a priori expectations, there are far fewer differences between the emerging-market and developed-market firms than one would expect. Consequently, the view that emerging-market firms are less subject to competition and market forces may not be valid. Indeed, our own research indicates that the intensity of competition in some emerging-market countries is at levels similar to those found in developed-market countries.[18] In order to maintain a competitive environment, policymakers will need to

18. Glen, Lee, and Singh (2001, 2002).

concentrate not only on capital structure and corporate finance issues but also on competition in product markets.

References

Aw, Bee Yan, Sukkyun Chung, and Mark J. Roberts. 2002. "Productivity, Output, and Failure: A Comparison of Taiwanese and Korean Manufacturers." NBER Working Paper 8766. Cambridge, Mass.: National Bureau of Economic Research, February.

Caves, Richard E. 1998. "Industrial Organization and New Findings on the Turnover and Mobility of Firms." *Journal of Economic Literature* 36 (4, December): 1947–82.

Claessens, Stijn, Simon Djankov, and Larry Lang. 2000. "The Separation of Ownership and Control in East Asian Corporations." *Journal of Financial Economics* 58 (1-2): 81–112.

Domowitz, Ian, Jack Glen, and Ananth Madhavan. 2001. "Liquidity, Volatility, and Equity Trading Costs across Countries and over Time." *International Finance* 4 (2, Summer): 221–25.

Glen, Jack, Kevin Lee, and Ajit Singh. 2001. "Persistence of Profitability and Competition in Emerging Markets." *Economics Letters* 72: 247–53.

———. 2002. "Corporate Profitability and the Dynamics of Competition in Emerging Markets: A Time-Series Analysis." Working Paper 248. ESRC Centre for Business Research, University of Cambridge.

Greenspan, Alan. 1998. "Testimony before the Committee on Banking and Financial Services." U.S. House of Representatives, January 30.

Khanna, Tarun. 2000. "Business Groups and Social Welfare in Emerging Markets: Existing Evidence and Unanswered Questions." *European Economic Review* 44: 748–61.

Laffont, Jean Jacques. 1999. "Competition, Information, and Development." *Annual World Bank Conference on Development Economics, 1998*, pp. 237–57. Washington: World Bank.

Leff, N. H. 1978. "Industrial Organization and Entrepreneurship in Developing Countries: The Economic Groups." *Economic Development and Cultural Change* 4 (26): 661–75.

Myers, Stewart C. 2001. "Capital Structure." *Journal of Economic Perspectives* 15 (2): 81–102.

Myers, Stewart C., and Nicholas S. Majluf. 1984. "Corporate Financing and Investment Decisions When Firms Have Information That Investors Do Not Have." *Journal of Financial Economics* 13 (2): 187–221.

Pomerleano, Michael, and Xin Zhang. 1999. "Corporate Fundamentals and the Behavior of Capital Markets in Asia." In Alison Harwood, Robert Litan, and Michael Pomerleano, eds., *Financial Markets and Development: The Crisis in Emerging Markets.* Brookings.

Roberts, Mark, and James Tybout. 1991. "Size Rationalization and Trade Exposure in Developing Countries." Working Paper 594. Washington: World Bank.

Shleifer, Andrei, and Daniel Wolfenzon. 2002. "Investor Protection and Equity Markets." *Journal of Financial Economics* 66 (2002): 3–27.

Singh, Ajit. 1995. *Corporate Financial Patterns in Industrializing Economies: A Comparative International Study.* IFC Technical Paper. Washington: International Finance Corporation.

———. 1997. "Financial Liberalisation, Stock Markets, and Economic Development." *Economic Journal* 107 (442, May): 771–82.

———. 1999. "'Asian Capitalism' and the Financial Crisis." In Jonathan Michie and John Grieve Smith, eds., *Global Instability: The Political Economy of World Economic Governance*, pp. 9–36. London: Routledge.

Singh, Ajit, Alaka Singh, and Bruce Weisse. 2002. "Corporate Governance, Competition, the New International Financial Architecture, and Large Corporations in Emerging Markets." Working Paper 50. University of Cambridge, ESRC Centre for Business Research.

Standard and Poor's. 2001. *Emerging Markets Fact Book, 2001.* New York.

Stiglitz, Joseph. 1999. "Reforming the Global Financial Architecture: Lessons from Recent Crises." *Journal of Finance* 54 (4): 1508–21.

Summers, Lawrence H. 1998. "Opportunities Out of Crises: Lessons from Asia." Remarks by the Undersecretary of the Treasury to the Overseas Development Council. Department of the Treasury, Office of Public Affairs, March 19.

Tybout, James. 2000. "Manufacturing Firms in Developing Countries: How Well Do They Do and Why?" *Journal of Economic Literature* 38 (1, March): 11–44.

Whittington, Geoffrey, Victoria Saporta, and Ajit Singh. 1997. *The Effects of Hyper-Inflation on Accounting Ratios: Financing Corporate Growth in Industrial Economies.* IFC Technical Paper 3. Washington: International Finance Corporation.

DILIP RATHA
PHILIP SUTTLE
SANKET MOHAPATRA

15

Corporate Financing Patterns and Performance in Emerging Markets

The sustainability of financial flows to developing countries depends heavily on the health of the corporate sector, which has been at the center of several recent crises. Corporate borrowers now account for more than a fifth of cross-border debt flows, compared with less than 5 percent in 1990, and flows of foreign direct investment (FDI), the dominant form of external financing for developing countries, are ultimately tied to corporate performance. This study examines corporate balance sheet data for major emerging markets to document trends in, and relationships between, corporate financial structure and corporate performance in the 1990s.

The chapter is organized as follows. The first section examines shifting patterns of corporate debt dependence in three major regions: East Asia and the Pacific, Europe and Central Asia, and Latin America and the Caribbean. The second section addresses vulnerability to short-term debt, while the third section examines trends in corporate profits. The final two sections are devoted to the benefits and risks associated with external borrowing.

The authors would like to thank Jack Glen and William Shaw for comments on an earlier draft.

Shifts in Corporate Sector Debt Dependence

It is widely accepted that excess corporate leverage was at the heart of the financial troubles of many East Asian developing countries in 1997–98.[1] Their total corporate debt grew at a compound annual rate of 16 percent between the end of 1990 and the end of 1997, swelling from $717 billion to $2.4 trillion (or from 80 to 105 percent of national income). Their debt-equity ratio, valued at the market price of equity, rose from 3.8 at the end of 1990 to 4.2 at the end of 1997. The foreign debt of the corporate sector (mainly debt owed to banks) grew at a compound annual rate of 27 percent during the same period, far more rapidly than overall debt. As a share of total corporate debt, foreign debt rose from 6 to 10 percent.

The corporate collapses in East Asia and the Pacific in 1997–98 produced sharp overall declines in gross domestic product (GDP) and forced severe and wrenching adjustments in corporate balance sheets; the severity of the adjustments reflected the need for a sharp and sustained shift in the private sector's financial balance. That shift has occurred. The aggregate current account balance of crisis countries in the region (the four crisis countries—Indonesia, Korea, Malaysia, and Thailand—plus the Philippines) shifted from a deficit of 4.8 percent of GDP in 1996 to a surplus of 2.6 percent in 1998. Over the same period, the budget balance of the region moved from a surplus of 0.2 percent of GDP to a deficit of 1.3 percent. The implied swing in the private sector's financial balance—equivalent to 8.9 percentage points of GDP—was carried out largely by a severe compression of spending.

One key result of this shift into financial surplus was that companies in East Asia were able, in the aggregate, to arrest and partly reverse the sustained rise in corporate debt relative to GDP that occurred through the first half of the 1990s.

The corporate "deleveraging" in East Asia had three other important dimensions. First, there was a sharp drop in foreign borrowing. The share of foreign debt in total corporate debt rose steadily between 1990 and 1997 for East Asian economies as a whole and through 1998 for the four crisis economies, but this ratio has fallen sharply since then. Asian companies paid dearly for their brief foray into international borrowing, and the experience has made them far more cautious about foreign currency borrowing, even as their economies have recovered. Also, the shift to a flexible exchange rate regime, by reducing implicit guarantees against

1. See Dadush, Dasgupta, and Ratha (2000); Dasgupta and others (2000); Radelet and Sachs (1998); World Bank (2000).

devaluation risks, has reinforced firms' reluctance to take on foreign debt. The result is that the foreign currency debt of Asian corporations is now in short supply relative to the demand and is trading at relatively tight spreads compared to similarly rated paper from borrowers in other regions.[2]

Second, some effort has been made to diversify sources of domestic funding. In East Asia, for example, important efforts have been made to strengthen bond markets, helping to reduce dependence on bank finance. However, the range of financing instruments available in emerging markets remains limited when compared with more developed markets such as the United States. One of the strengths of the U.S. financial system is its diversity of funding sources, ranging from commercial banks through a rich array of money and capital markets. Thus when bond market credit suddenly dried up in the United States in 1998, corporate borrowers were able to turn to banks. Likewise, when the market in short-term commercial paper slumped early in 2002, companies were able to issue longer-term bonds and swap into short-term liabilities.

Third, debt-equity ratios in the region have declined as the result of efforts to pare down debt (especially foreign debt) and raise equity participation in the economy. FDI in Asia has been relatively high since the crisis years, contributing to a shift in the pattern of foreign liabilities away from debt and toward equity. The shift has been far from uniform, however. China has been the key beneficiary of stepped-up FDI, while Indonesia has seen a steady exodus of foreign equity capital since 1998.[3]

These significant adjustments have helped Asian corporations to insulate themselves from global market pressures in recent quarters. In 2001–02, for example, Asian corporations were better insulated from the downturn in the global economy and the deterioration in high-risk debt markets than were their peers in the main industrial economies. In East Asia, with external financing (especially short-term financing) much reduced, there was no significant flight of foreign capital, and domestic lenders remained comfortable with their exposures.

One important difference between 1997–98 and 2001–02 was the trend in local interest rates. In 1997–98, these rose sharply, contributing to a serious deterioration in the quality of corporate credit and undermining the willingness of both domestic and external creditors to maintain exposures. By contrast, regional interest rates generally fell in 2001–02, giving companies a cushion that allowed them to ride out the downturn far more easily (figure 15-1).

2. See World Bank (2003, ch. 3).

3. See World Bank (2003, ch. 4).

Figure 15-1. *Benchmark Interest Rates and Consumer Price Index Inflation, East Asia, 1992–2002*

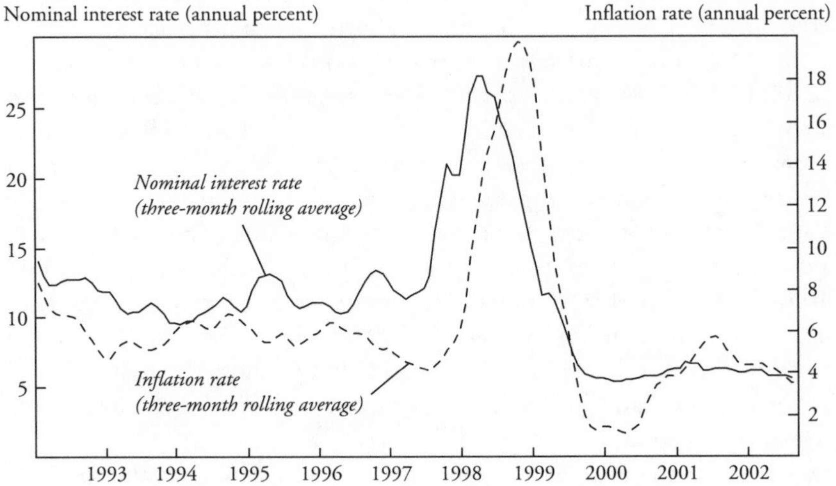

Indeed, the low level of regional interest rates is a key ingredient to the sustainability of what remains, after several years of painful adjustment, a very high ratio of corporate leverage. While corporate debt has been trimmed in some economies, it has risen sharply in others—notably China. As a result, debt levels (as a share of GDP) remain very high in East Asia compared to both Latin America and Eastern Europe (figure 15-2).

Similar regional trends (seen from top-down macro data) are also evident from firm-level data (see appendix A). The average debt-assets ratio for East Asian firms in the sample reached a peak of 68 percent in 1997; it has since fallen (see figure 15-3).[4] By contrast, the leverage ratio of Latin American firms dropped during the Mexican crisis in 1995 but has risen steadily ever since. By 2001 the leverage ratios of East Asia (54 percent) and Latin America (45 percent) had become similar.

While companies in East Asia have been reducing their dependence on foreign currency debt, however, companies in Latin America and Eastern Europe have been raising their dependence. The share of foreign lending to firms in East Asia has fallen steadily from its peak in 1996, whereas the share of Latin America and Eastern Europe has risen (figure 15-4). The

4. See also Mako (2001).

Figure 15-2. *Corporate Debt as a Percentage of GDP, by Region, 1995, 1997, and 2001*

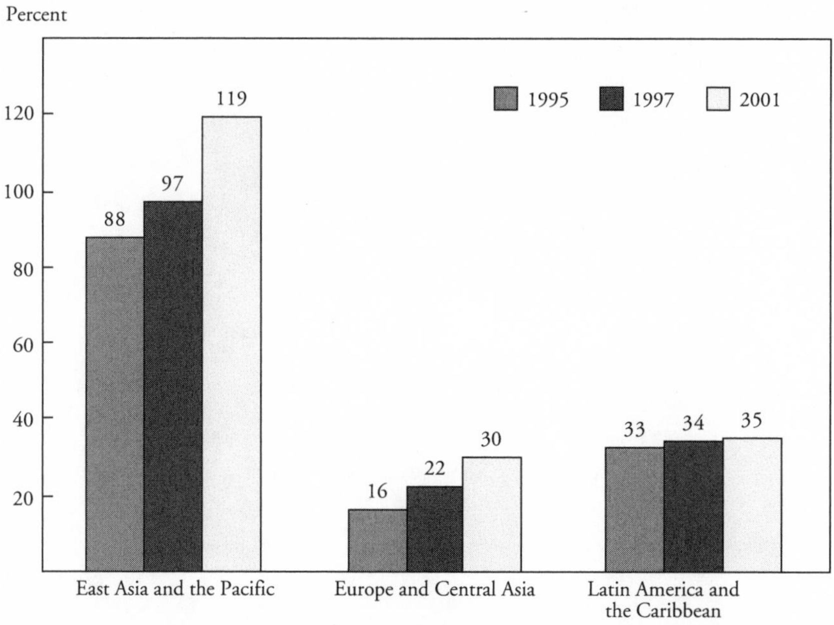

result? As of 2000, the share of total corporate debt accounted for by borrowing from abroad had risen to almost one-third in both Latin America and Eastern Europe (figure 15-5). Expressed as a share of GDP, the foreign debt of the corporate sectors in the two regions was at or above the peak seen in East Asia in 1997 (figure 15-6).

In conclusion, the overall level of corporate leverage remains the main risk facing East Asia; heavy dependence on external debt is the main risk for firms in Eastern Europe and Latin America.

Short-Term Corporate Debt Vulnerability

Companies in developing countries face the challenge of transforming, in a sustainable way, the typically short-term capital they raise from sources outside the firm into fixed, long-term capital suitable for financing the illiquid real assets that make up the physical capital of the firm. For com-

Figure 15-3. *Leverage Ratios, East Asia and Latin America, 1992–2001*[a]

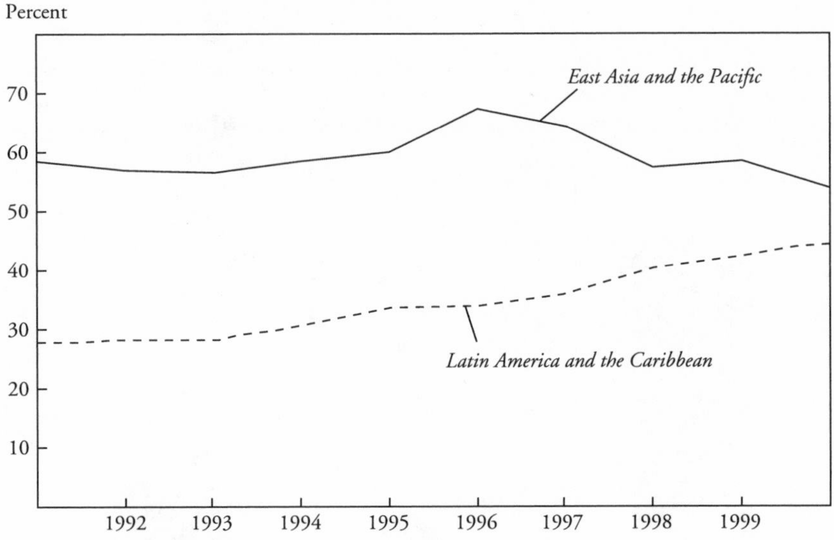

a. Ratio of debt to assets.

panies in mature economies with deep, well-developed equity markets, this transformation is usually not an insuperable challenge, although the evaporation of market access for several previously high-flying firms in the United States and Europe in 2001–02 illustrates that sudden corporate collapses can occur in even the most sophisticated capital markets.

Firms operating in developing countries, however, often have little choice but to finance fixed-asset accumulation with short-term liabilities. For companies operating in East Asia, such liabilities made up about 62 percent of total corporate debt in 2001. In Eastern Europe, the share was even higher—66 percent. Latin America had the lowest ratio of short-term debt to total debt: just 50 percent. The dependence on short-term finance in East Asia and Eastern Europe indicates that their primary source of funds remains banks: longer-term markets are either nonexistent or just beginning to reemerge after a period of dormancy.

The low dependence of Latin American firms on short-term finance does not reflect the availability of local long-term financing but rather the *overall* lack of local financing from outside the firm. That lack is a legacy of local instability. While more acute in some countries (Argentina) than

Figure 15-4. *Share in Foreign Lending to Emerging-Market Corporations, by Region, 1990–2001*

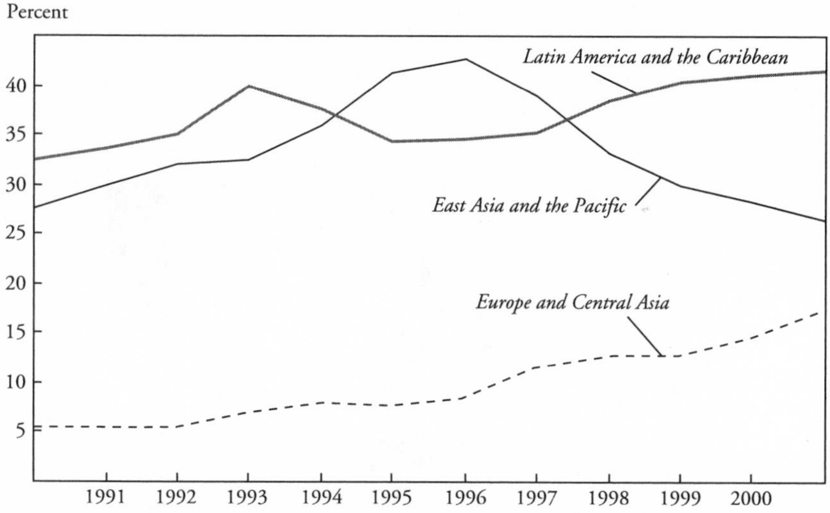

others (Chile), the low level for the region as a whole is a sign of poor financial intermediation. Firms in Latin America must depend on internal financing and, as previously noted, funds from abroad.

In Eastern Europe and Central Asia, persistent instability since the collapse of the Soviet Union, coupled with high and variable inflation, has kept corporate financial structures short. As convergence with the European Union proceeds, however, a lengthening of the maturities of corporate debt should be expected and encouraged.

The Downward Trend in Corporate Profits

Profitability is at the heart of corporate health. If the capital employed in an enterprise is not generating an adequate return, the flow of new capital to the firm will dry up. Eventually the holders of the existing stock of capital will seek to exit. The past five years have seen examples of such reversals in large parts of East Asia and in the telecom sectors of the G-7 economies.

To complicate the picture, recent accounting scandals in the United States have reminded us not only that the measurement of profits can be

Figure 15-5. *Share of External Financing in Corporate Sector Debt, by Region, 1995, 1997, 2001*

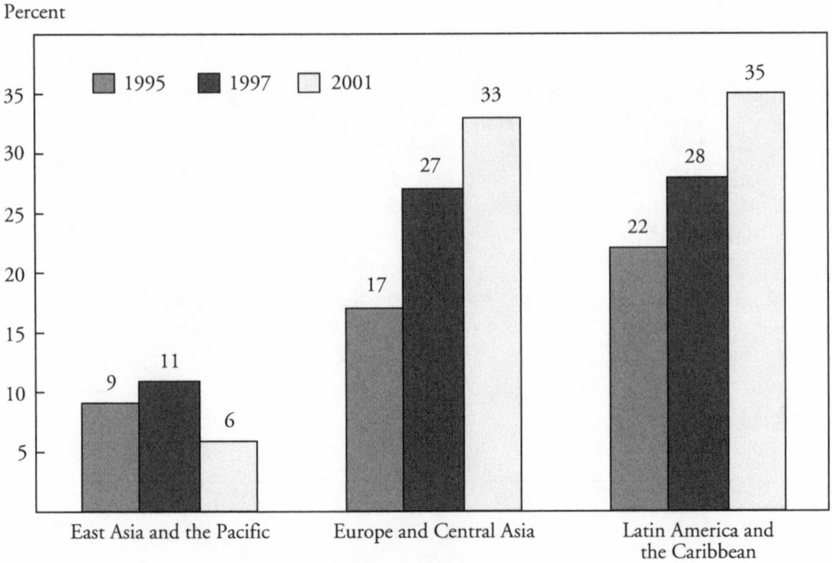

ambiguous but also that the quality of corporate accounting can leave much to be desired.

An examination of the trends in net earnings of the countries in our sample for the period 1992–2001 (table 15-1) yields several important conclusions.[5]

—Profits are low. In 1999–2001, profit margins were about 4.4 percent of sales and 3.0 percent of assets. By way of comparison, the return on assets achieved by the U.S. nonfinancial corporate sector in 1999–2001 was 4.9 percent.

5. The concept of earnings is total earnings, not the narrower and (more arbitrary) concept of operating earnings. In addition to uncertainty over how to measure earnings for a given company, the shifting sample size of our corporate database makes it difficult to compute measures of aggregate profitability that can be compared across time and countries. For example, it does not make sense to add profits, as the number of firms in our sample size varies each year. The alternative—to add together just the earnings of companies for which data are available for the full sample—involves a huge loss of information and a considerable risk of bias, as it would reflect (by definition) the selection of firms that existed throughout the period. As survivors, these firms might well be expected to have a higher-than-average rate of profitability. Given these constraints, the most meaningful measures of profitability that are available across regions and across time are net earnings of the sample companies as a percentage of sales (profit margins) and net earnings as a percentage of total assets.

Figure 15-6. *Corporate Foreign Debt as a Percentage of GDP, by Region, 1990–2001*

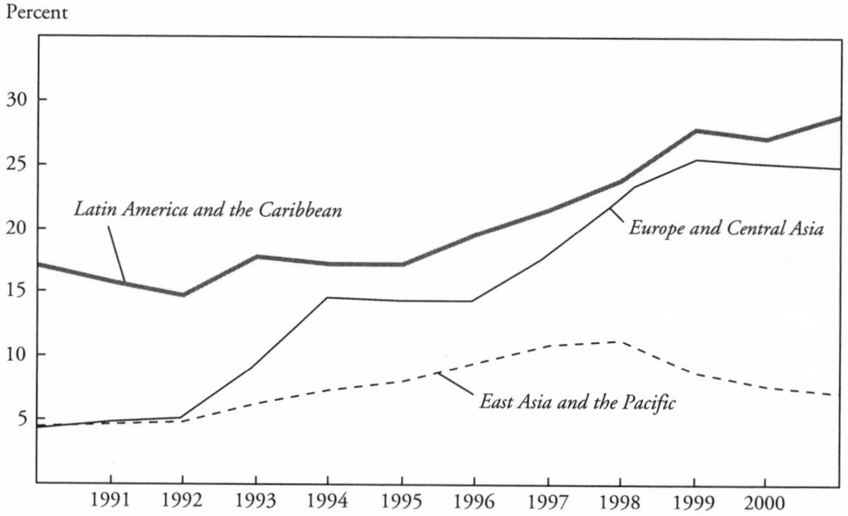

—Profits do not appear to be rising. The low point in 1998 is understandable in view of the recession that year in many developing countries, but average returns for 1999–2001, the last three years of data, were significantly worse than earlier in the decade. This evidence is consistent with the pattern of returns on FDI.[6]

—Profit margins and returns on assets are lowest in Asia. Both were negative in 1998; neither has recovered well. In part, the results reflect the higher leverage ratios of firms in the region; returns on equity are probably not as low as they appear.

—In the past two years, margins and returns have been higher in Europe and Central Asia than elsewhere in the developing world. Russia has bounced back strongly from collapse in 1998. Elsewhere in the region, profit rates have been relatively more stable than in Russia, consistent with the pattern of structural improvement in the region after the corporate collapses of the early 1990s.

To get a longer view of the evolution of profits, we combined the data from our sample with similar data available for the 1980s.[7] Although there

6. See World Bank (2003, p. 78).

7. For example, Glen, Singh, and Matthias (1999); Singh (1995).

Table 15-1. *Measures of Profitability for Nonfinancial Firms in Emerging Markets, 1992–2001*

Percent

	1992–2001											
Measure	*Average*	*Standard deviation*	*1992*	*1993*	*1994*	*1995*	*1996*	*1997*	*1998*	*1999*	*2000*	*2001*
Ratio of net income to assets												
All countries	3.1	0.9	3.9	4.0	3.4	3.7	3.2	2.4	1.1	2.5	3.2	3.2
Emerging Europe and Asia												
Total	5.9	2.3	6.1	7.1	7.1	7.7	5.8	4.5	–0.1	6.0	8.3	6.2
Excluding Russia	6.2	1.2	6.1	7.1	7.1	7.7	7.0	6.4	4.9	6.1	6.3	3.6
Asia												
Total	2.2	1.3	2.7	2.9	3.8	3.9	2.5	0.5	–0.3	1.9	1.5	2.2
Excluding China	1.9	1.4	2.7	2.8	3.8	3.8	2.5	0.4	–0.4	1.6	0.6	1.6
Latin America	3.5	1.0	4.9	4.8	2.6	2.6	3.3	4.3	3.1	2.0	3.8	3.4
Ratio of net income to sales												
All countries	4.6	1.2	5.2	5.5	5.8	5.6	5.1	4.2	1.8	4.0	4.6	4.6
Emerging Europe and Asia												
Total	6.7	2.8	5.5	6.3	6.6	6.9	7.5	7.5	–0.1	7.6	10.3	9.1
Excluding Russia	6.0	0.9	5.5	6.3	6.6	6.9	6.7	6.3	5.2	6.1	6.7	3.9
Asia												
Total	2.9	1.7	3.6	3.7	5.1	5.1	3.6	0.8	–0.4	2.8	1.9	2.8
Excluding China	2.6	1.9	3.5	3.6	5.0	4.9	3.5	0.5	–0.5	2.3	0.8	2.0
Latin America	7.5	2.1	10.3	10.2	6.7	6.3	7.8	10.0	6.4	4.2	7.0	6.0

is some discontinuity between the two data sets, their general patterns are similar, allowing a comparison of trends in profit margins since the mid-1980s (figure 15-7). Two trends stand out:

—Margins were generally lower in the 1990s than in the 1980s. India is the exception.

—Margins were more volatile in the 1990s. Again, there is one important exception (Brazil), where the relative stability offered by the successful currency program after 1994 stands in contrast with the earlier period of volatility and hyperinflation (1985–93).

Why were profits in many developing countries lower and more volatile in the 1990s, especially as the decade progressed? Because underlying nominal growth of GDP is the key driver of profits, the shocks to GDP brought on by the numerous crises of the 1990s are the main cause of the weakness in profits.

Other developments contributed as well. The trend toward lower inflation across the developing world added further downward pressure on nominal GDP growth and on profits. An otherwise welcome trend toward more open, integrated markets reduced the prices—and profits—of what had been local monopolies. In Brazil, for example, the liberalization of the trade regime in the early 1990s, which helped to bring greater competition to domestic goods industries, also restrained the margins of domestic producers.[8] Similarly, the emphasis on privatization of state-run monopolies, especially in utilities, helped to restrain both inflation and profits.

Finally, the rise in debt costs resulting from significant devaluations—and other events surrounding currency crises, such as sharp drops in real GDP—hit profit margins very hard in Mexico in 1994 and in Korea and Malaysia in 1998.[9]

Are profits in developing countries so low as to constitute a problem? Not necessarily. As nominal GDP grows in developing countries, so will profits. But policymakers and analysts would be well advised to pay attention to trends in these variables if, as expected, the primary flow of foreign capital (both debt and equity) to developing countries remains oriented largely to the private business sector. If profit performance continues to lag as the economy improves, the sustainability of the current pattern of financing flows dominated by FDI will be very much in question.

8. Glen, Lee, and Singh (2001).
9. Forbes (2002).

Figure 15-7. *Ratio of Net Income to Sales of Nonfinancial Firms, Select Countries, 1985–2001*

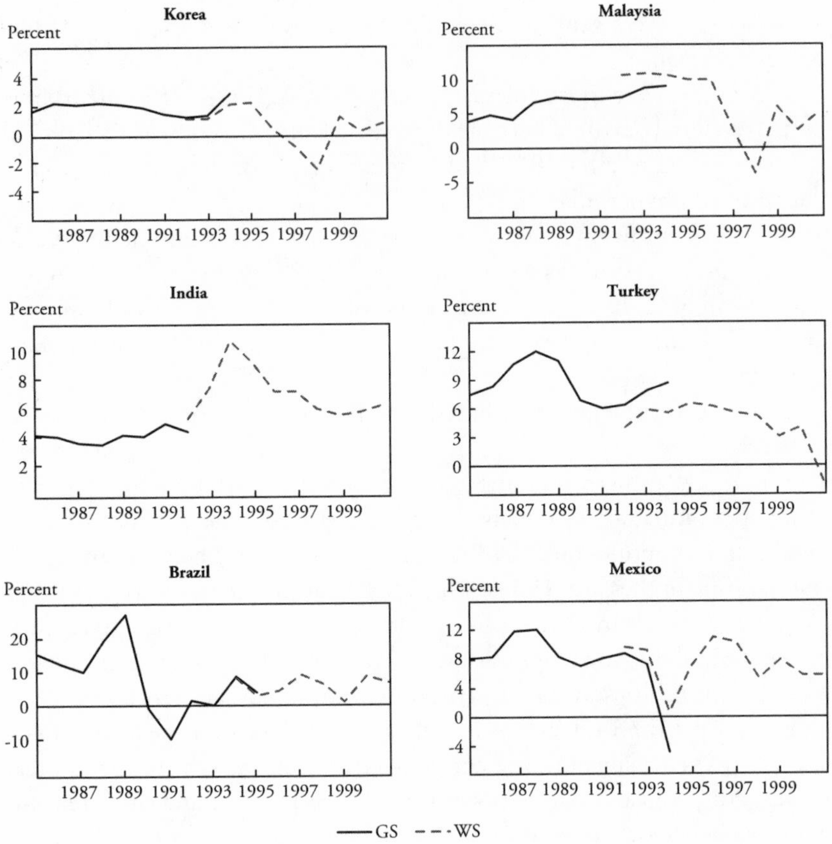

Source: Data for the 1980s are from Singh (1995); data for 1992–2001 are from Worldscope. Authors' estimates.

Borrowing from Abroad and Corporate Performance

Financing from abroad brings with it both risks and advantages. A firm can reduce its cost of capital by accessing international markets, which have a larger base of investors and are more liquid. And because international markets have better trading and clearance systems, more competition among traders and investment bankers, and better listing and monitoring standards, they are more efficient than local markets. International-market access, when successful, may also make a firm more attractive to domestic investors by signaling that the firm is willing to commit to higher standards of corporate governance and disclosure and to protection of minority rights.[10]

But international finance also entails risks. A currency devaluation may increase the debt burden of borrowing firms, especially those that have only local currency earnings.[11] Unanticipated changes in global interest rates can hurt profitability. And abrupt changes in investor sentiment may make it difficult to roll over debt. The various emerging-market crises of the last decade brought all these risks into sharp focus.

Indeed, an assessment of the relationship between external (international) financing and corporate performance reveals that among nonfinancial firms, market participants (that is, firms that had outstanding foreign debt) tended to show lower profitability than nonparticipants.[12] However, it would be wrong to conclude that borrowing abroad is excessively risky for all firms in developing countries. For example, firms that had foreign sales—and firms that were able to roll over debt—were, on average, more profitable than firms that did not.

Not surprising, market access over the period 1992–2001 was positively associated with firm size. The average assets of firms that participated in international markets were $2.4 billion during 1998–2001, more than five times the average size ($470 million) of firms that did not have outstanding foreign debt. Within the category of international-market participants, firms that were able to roll over debt (that is, continue market access) were even larger, having average assets of $4.9 billion. Firms that had outstanding debt but did not undertake new borrowing were much smaller, with assets averaging around $1.8 billion. The association between market access and size is to be expected, given that large firms are less vulnerable than small firms to adverse shocks and are more creditworthy in the eyes of investors.[13]

Firms that borrowed abroad were more highly leveraged than firms that did not. Foreign and domestic debt as a share of assets was 53 percent dur-

10. The growth of international market access in the 1990s was driven by improvements in macroeconomic environment in emerging-market economies, lifting of capital controls allowing firms to raise financing abroad, and establishment or improvement of legal systems that protect the rights of minority shareholders. See Levine (1997) for a review.

11. Forbes (2002).

12. International market participants among banks and other financial companies showed much higher profit rates than nonparticipants. When financial and nonfinancial companies are combined together, again market participants reported higher profit rates.

13. Besides, large firms tend to attract government support, especially during cyclical downturns ("too big to fail"), which further improves their ability to raise debt. Also, larger firms can negotiate better terms with creditors.

Figure 15-8. *Debt as a Percentage of Total Assets, by Market Participation and Region*

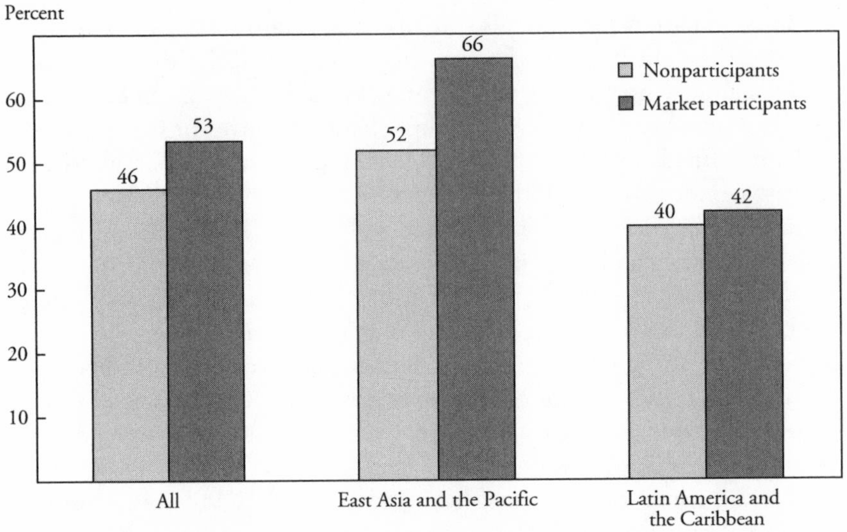

ing 1998–2001 for market participants—higher than the share of debt to assets (46 percent) for firms that did not borrow abroad (figure 15-8).

Even though market participants were more highly indebted, their average cost of credit—or average interest rate, defined as interest expenses as a percentage of debt—was lower than that of nonparticipants through much of the 1990s (figure 15-9).

Prior to the Asian crisis in 1997, average interest costs paid by firms declined as industrial countries cut interest rates during the mid-1990s and emerging-market spreads tightened. Following the Asian crisis, interest costs rose for all firms, but firms that had access to the wider international debt markets were able to obtain cheaper credit than those that did not, although they may also have suffered valuation losses as a result of denominating their debt in foreign currency prior to a sharp depreciation. Such mark-to-market debt losses are, however, reflected in the overall profit data analyzed below.[14]

14. For firms in developing countries, these valuation losses are one of the biggest components of the difference between operating earnings and overall earnings (we use the latter in this study).

Figure 15-9. *Corporate Profit Rates in Major Emerging Markets, by Market Participation, 1992–2001*

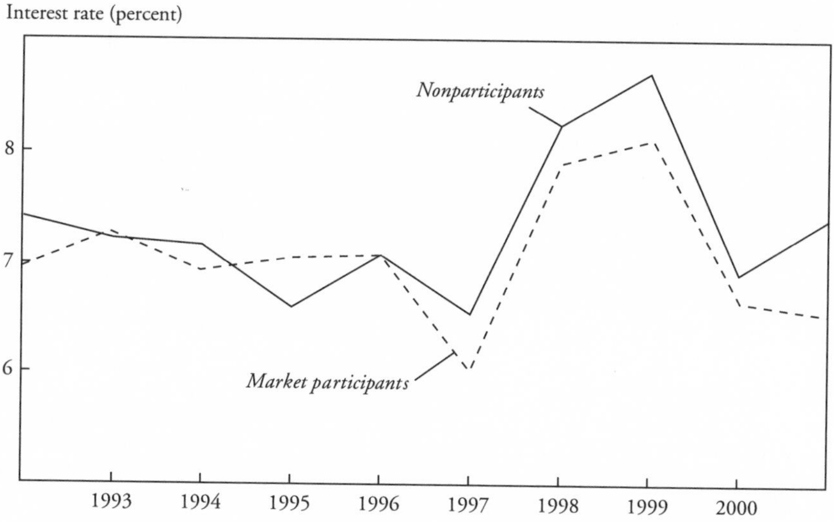

Except for the early 1990s (1992–94), firms that participated in international debt markets reported lower profits as a share of assets than did nonparticipating firms (figure 15-10). The average profit rate during 1998–2001 for market participants was 2 percent compared with 3 percent for nonparticipants (figure 15-11). Evidently, the lower interest costs available from market participation were not sufficient to generate a higher rate of profit for the participating firms, even though many of them had more assets than nonparticipating firms.[15] The profit rates between market participants and nonparticipants reached a low in 1998, the year interest rates spiked and currency-related losses were at their peak.

While this finding does highlight the risks associated with foreign borrowing, it does not necessarily imply that these risks outweigh the benefits (such as low interest rates) that market participation brings. In fact, this

15. This is similar to the view that smaller firms generate higher returns, a well-known result for small capitalized firms in the United States from Fama and French (1992). Some studies, however, have found evidence to the contrary: larger emerging-market firms tend to have larger returns on assets (see International Monetary Fund 2002a).

Figure 15-10. *Corporate Profits as a Percentage of Total Assets in Major Emerging Markets, by Market Participation, 1992–2001*

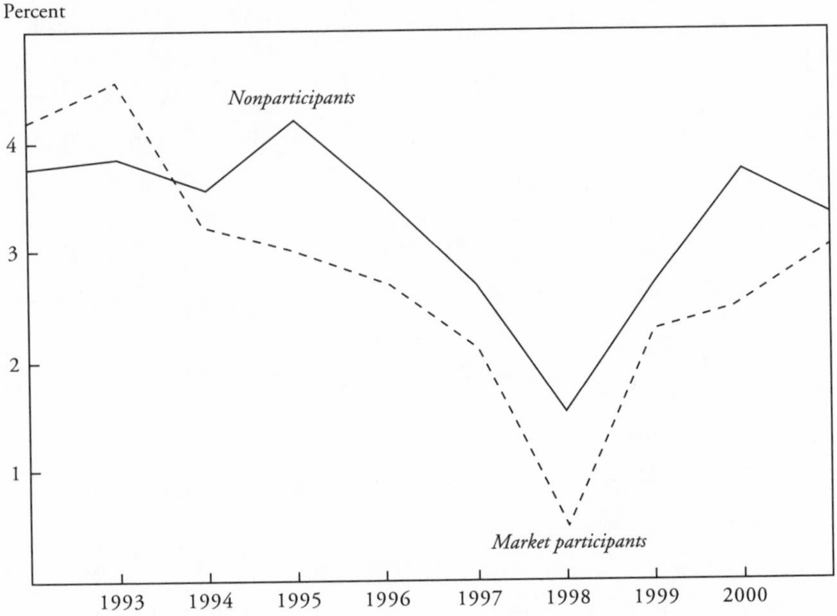

finding does not hold true in Latin America where, unlike in East Asia and in Europe and Central Asia, market-participating firms reported higher profit rates than nonparticipating firms (figure 15-11).[16] Even in East Asia, the lower profit rates reported by market-participating firms may be explained, in part, by the fact that only firms with low profitability (and high investment) may have needed external financing.[17] Also the profit performance of firms that were able to maintain access to external credit

16. The profit rates computed for nonparticipating firms may be underestimated due to sample selection bias, since firms that underperform may drop out of the sample and only relatively better-performing survivors are included in the calculation. Another factor that may affect the comparison of market participants and nonparticipants (especially in East Asia) is that commercial banks were borrowing internationally and on-lending the proceeds in local currency terms to domestic corporations (Dasgupta and others 2000, p. 332). As a result, foreign currency borrowing by nonbank financial corporations is underreported, reducing the number of market-participating firms. When both financial and nonfinancial firms are included, market participants reported higher profits than nonparticipants.

17. Claessens, Djankov, and Lang (1998).

Figure 15-11. *Profits as a Percentage of Total Assets, by Market Participation and Region, 1998–2001*

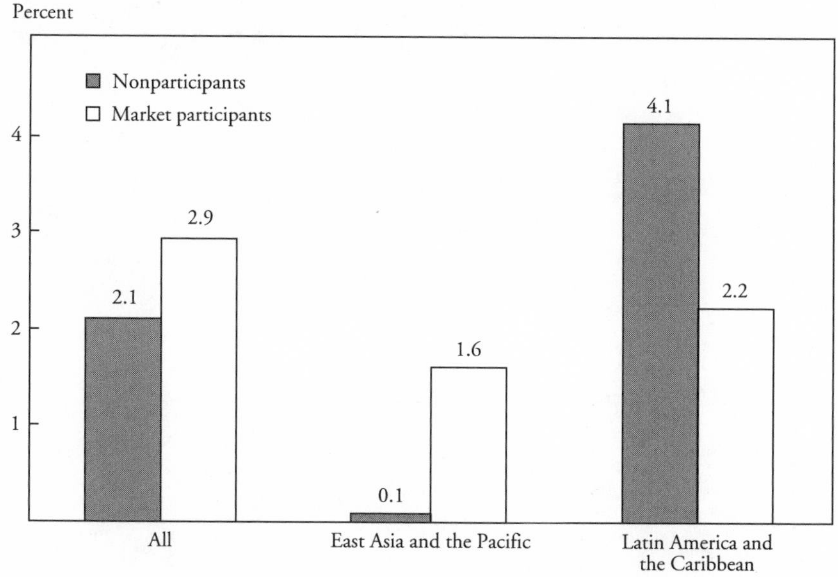

markets—and to roll over some of their foreign debt—was better and less affected by cycles than the profit rate of firms that had outstanding foreign debt but could not (or did not) roll it over (figure 15-12). Moreover, the most profitable firms in this sample were those that not only participated as borrowers in international markets but also had foreign sales (figure 15-13).[18] For this group, however, profit margins slipped significantly after 1997. This is somewhat surprising, as the more competitive real exchange rate enjoyed by many developing countries since then should have *raised* profit margins in the tradable sector. The exchange rate benefits must have been eroded by (a) deflationary pressures in global goods markets in recent years and (b) losses resulting from foreign currency debt, which the existence of foreign exchange earnings allowed some companies to take on.

Corporate finance is therefore a key influence, but it is not the only factor that affects corporate performance. Other factors, such as the domestic

18. Legal requirements for reporting foreign sales on firm balance sheets vary across countries. Thus the data used here can potentially underestimate the number of firms with foreign sales.

Figure 15-12. *Profits as a Percentage of Assets in Major Emerging Markets, by Type of Market Participant, 1992–2001*

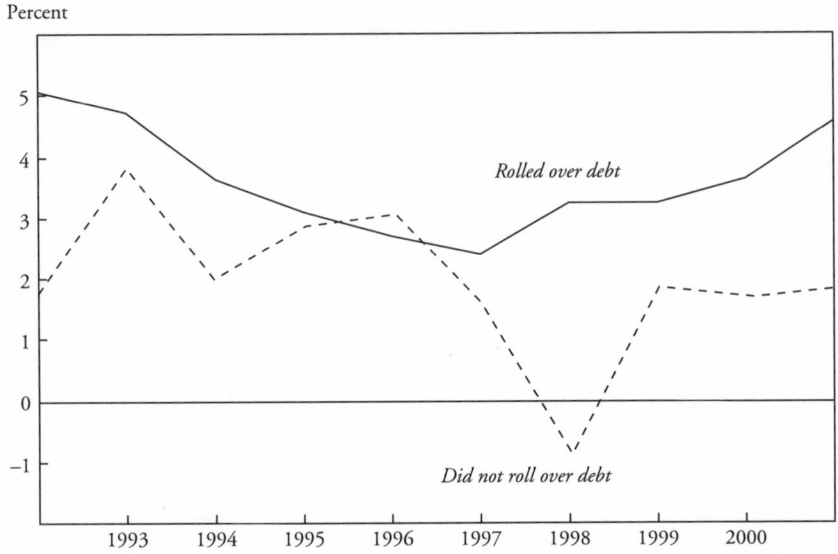

economic cycle, international economic cycles, and terms of trade changes, are also important. The most important determinant of corporate performance in the oil and gas sector seems to have been world crude oil prices (figure 15-14). Corporate profit rates for firms in the oil and gas sector declined sharply (from nearly 9 percent in 1996 to –1.3 percent in 1998 for market participants and from 6.5 percent to –2.2 percent for nonparticipants), when oil prices crashed from $18 a barrel to $12.5 a barrel. But during the upturn in oil prices in 1999 and 2000, the average profit rate of nonparticipants rose to 18 percent compared with only 11 percent for market participants. This divergence in profits seems to be related to the divergence in leverage (figure 15-15): while leverage for market participants rose from 38 to 43 percent from 1998 to 2000, the leverage for nonparticipants declined from 37 to 27 percent over the same period. Thus higher debt service associated with higher leverage could have cut into the profitability of market participants.

This example also sheds some light on the direction of causality between profitability and leverage: even if more profitable oil firms accessed international debt markets, an exogenous shock (in the form of changes in oil

Figure 15-13. *Profit as a Percentage of Assets in Major Emerging Markets, by Market Participation, 1993–2001*

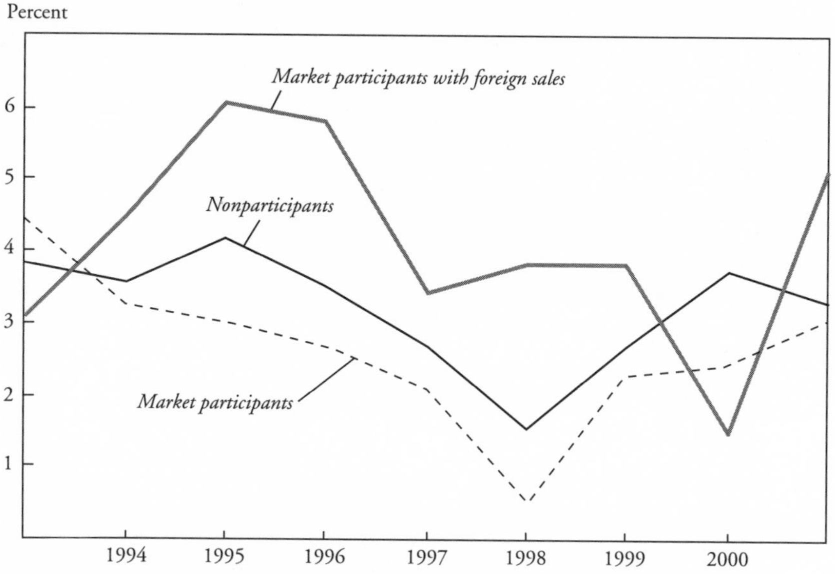

prices) produced a greater effect on firms that had higher leverage. In this case, an increase in leverage caused a reduction in profit rates.

Firm Leverage, Borrowing from Abroad, and Corporate Performance: Regression Analysis

In order to undertake a more formal analysis of the relationship between corporate performance (as measured by the profit rate or earnings before interest and taxes) and corporate finance (firm leverage), we performed regression analysis using variants of the following model:

$$(15\text{-}1) \quad Performance_{it} = c_0 + c_1{*}Leverage_{it-1} + c_2{*}Market\ participant + c_3{*}Leverage_{it-1}{*}Market\ participant_{it} + d{*}(Control\ Variables) + \varepsilon_{it},$$

where *Leverage* (debt as a percentage of assets) is lagged one period; the indicator for market participation takes the value of 1 for market partic-

Figure 15-14. *Profit Rates for Firms in Oil and Gas Sector in Major Emerging Markets and World Crude Oil Prices, by Market Participation, 1996–2000*

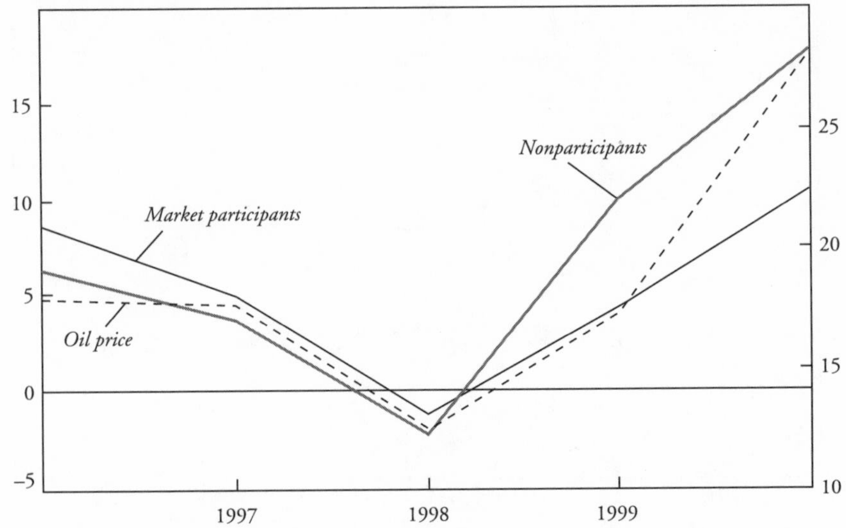

ipants and 0 for others.[19] The control variables are log(firm size), log(firm size) squared, capital intensity (proxied by capital stock as a ratio of assets), capital intensity squared, real GDP growth, lagged mean earnings, and lagged earnings volatility (the last two variables indicate expected returns and risks).[20] The indicator for market participation is also included in all the specifications in order to capture the difference in average performance of market participants and nonparticipants. Dummies to account for fixed effects relating to country and sector, and year effects to capture global shocks common to the sample of emerging markets, are added to the regressions. The specification does not explicitly include variables representing institutions that may affect profit rates and leverage; the time-

19. Market participants are firms that participated in international debt markets in the past and have foreign debt outstanding at the beginning of the current period (see appendix A).

20. Firm size is measured as the average of total assets in 1998–2001 in millions of U.S. dollars. Using the logarithm of firm size instead of actual firm size has the advantage that it gives a much smaller weight to large firms. Net profits and cash flows (as a percentage of assets) are used as measures of firm performance. Some analysts use earnings growth to measure firm performance (Forbes 2002).

Figure 15-15. *Leverage Ratios in the Oil and Gas Sector in Major Emerging Markets, by Market Participation, 1996–2000*

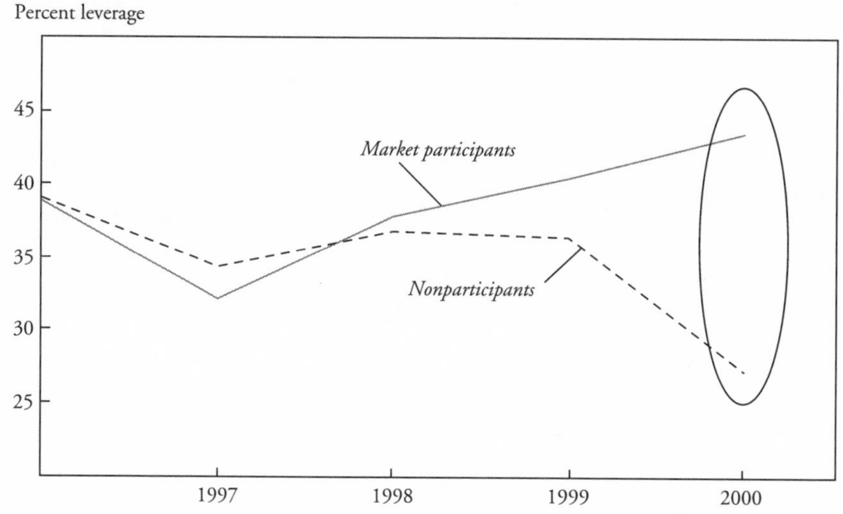

invariant component of these variables is captured indirectly through the inclusion of country fixed effects.[21] Similar regressions were run using earnings—earnings before interest, taxes, depreciation, and amortization as a percentage of assets—as the dependent variable. The results are summarized in table 15-2.

This regression analysis of the association between leverage and corporate profitability (controlling for other factors that also affect profitability) yields several interesting results. First, both profits and cash flows (earnings before interest, taxes) decline as a percentage of assets as firms take on more debt relative to their assets. This is similar to the finding of Harvey, Lins, and Roper that, although some debt may improve market discipline in

21. See IMF (2002a, p. 99); Klapper and Love (2002). Previous studies have identified historical origins of the contracting environment—creditor protection and laws favoring minority shareholders—as an important determinant of firm leverage, ownership structure, and firm performance (see Demirgüç-Kunt and Maksimovic 1999; Himmelberg, Hubbard, and Love 2002; La Porta and others 1997). Country fixed effects in our regressions control for such time-invariant differences in institutional variables across countries. But institutions also can change over time; for instance, financial liberalization can widen the investor base and make raising equity more attractive for firms. Similarly, deregulation of securities markets and easier access to foreign bank lending can encourage firms to increase their leverage. Severe financial crises can also produce a forced corporate "deleveraging."

Table 15-2. *Regression Results: The Relation between Leverage and Firm Profitability*[a]

	Net profit			*Cash flows*		
Variable	*(1)*	*(2)*	*(3)*	*(4)*	*(5)*	*(6)*
Leverage	–29.0	–27.7	–10.3	–15.4	–14.0	–0.3
Market participant	–0.677	1.029	1.339	–0.763	1.872	1.862
	–2.7	1.3	1.5	–2.8	2.1	1.9
Leverage*market participant		–0.031	–0.033		–0.047	–0.046
		–1.9	–1.8		–2.8	–2.6
log(size)	3.458	3.468	0.653	2.802	2.828	–0.114
	9.3	9.3	2.0	6.7	6.7	–0.3
log(size) squared	–0.219	–0.220	0.005	–0.185	–0.188	0.051
	–7.1	–7.1	0.2	–5.3	–5.3	1.7
Capital intensity	0.265	0.141	–1.798	19.095	18.947	15.487
	0.2	0.1	–0.9	9.2	9.2	6.4
Capital intensity squared	–7.644	–7.498	–3.270	–25.166	–24.980	–18.425
	–4.3	–4.2	–1.6	–11.5	–11.4	–7.2
Real GDP growth	0.182	0.180	0.165	0.071	0.067	0.034
	6.4	6.4	5.0	2.3	2.2	1.0
Mean earnings, five–year moving average (lagged)			0.653			0.722
			24.1			24.7
Earnings volatility, five–year rolling standard deviation (lagged)			0.019			0.085
			0.5			2.0
Number of observations	16,299	16,299	10,137	15,291	15,291	9,724
R^2	0.1872	0.1875	0.3099	0.1950	0.1955	0.3209

a. The dependent variable is net profit or firm cash flows as a percentage of assets. Leverage is lagged one period. The regressions include industry, country and regional fixed effects (not shown here). Year dummies were added to proxy for global business cycle effects. Five-year moving average of earnings and earnings volatility were calculated using at least three years of lagged earnings. t statistics were calculated using Huber-White heteroskedasticity-corrected robust standard errors and are reported below the coefficient estimates.

firms, the effect may be overcome by increasing financial risks at higher levels of leverage.[22] Second, the marginal (negative) effect of an increase in leverage on earnings is larger for firms that participate in international debt markets than for other firms.

Why do earnings decline as leverage increases? One reason may be diminishing returns. A firm may take on debt with a view to expanding its

22. Harvey, Lins, and Roper (2001).

operations, but revenue growth is likely to slow as it scales up. Moreover, revenue growth may slow faster in larger firms. This would explain the larger negative association between leverage and returns for market participants, which is usually significantly larger than for nonparticipants. Another reason is that at lower leverage ratios, the benefit of the lower cost of foreign borrowing may sufficiently offset losses due to currency depreciation and sudden collapses in investor confidence. As debt levels rise, however, these costs may become predominant.

The Effects of Financial Crisis

Some of the important emerging markets in our sample experienced devaluations and severe currency crises during the 1990s. How did crisis affect the performance of firms that were highly leveraged or had foreign currency debt? We estimated variants of the following regression for the two sets of firms in order to examine this question:

$$\text{(15-2)} \qquad Performance_{it} = c_0 + c_1{*}Leverage_{it-1} + c_2{*}EMCrisis_t + c_3{*}Leverage_{it-1}{*}EMCrisis_t + d{*}(Control\ Variables) + \varepsilon_{it},$$

where $EMCrisis_t$ is an indicator for emerging-markets currency crisis. The countries in our sample that experienced currency crises (or major episodes of devaluation) are Mexico (1994–95), Venezuela (1994, 1996), Indonesia, Korea, Malaysia, Philippines, and Thailand (1997–98), Russia (1998), Brazil (1999), and Turkey (2001). We allow for a lagged effect of currency crisis on firm performance by including the year subsequent to the initial devaluation as part of the crisis event. The set of control variables is similar to the earlier specification.[23] Since the timing, severity, and other aspects of currency crises differed across regions, we ran similar regressions separately for East Asia and for Latin America.[24] Table 15-3 summarizes the relation between leverage and firm performance for the major emerging regions during states of crisis and no crisis (the full set of regressions is

23. Lagged average earnings and lagged earnings volatility were excluded from the current and subsequent regressions in order to maximize the sample size, even though these variables improve the fit of the regression (including these variables causes the sample size to decrease more than a third). However, the sign and significance of the relevant coefficients and interaction terms are fairly robust to the exclusion of these and other control variables.

24. This allows the set of control variables to have different slope coefficients across the two emerging regions.

Table 15-3. Leverage and Firm Profitability during Emerging Markets Crisis: Marginal Effects of Leverage for Market Participants and Nonparticipants[a]

Dependent variable and region	*Nonparticipants*		*Market participants*	
	No crisis	*Crisis*	*No crisis*	*Crisis*
Net profit[b]				
All regions	−0.151	−0.225	−0.197	−0.280
East Asia and Pacific	−0.142	−0.192	−0.225	−0.268
Latin America and Caribbean	−0.148	−0.192	−0.045	−0.166
Cash flow[c]				
All regions	−0.085	−0.128	−0.142	−0.232
East Asia and Pacific	−0.087	−0.131	−0.161	−0.233
Latin America and Caribbean	−0.040	−0.120	−0.130	−0.223

a. The dependent variable is net profit or cash flows as a percentage of assets. Leverage is lagged one period. The regressions include the control variables, industry, country and regional fixed effects, and year dummies (not shown here). The sample period is 1992–2001. The full set of regressions is reported in appendix B.

b. The number of nonparticipants is 14,060, and the number of market participants is 2,239.

c. The number of nonparticipants is 13,147, and the number of market participants is 2,144.

reported in appendix B). The main messages from this set of regressions are as follows.

First, higher leverage is associated with lower firm profitability in all regions, during both no-crisis and crisis states. The magnitude of the coefficient of leverage is similar for nonparticipants in the full sample, in East Asia, and in Latin America during no-crisis states. This is noteworthy given the differences in institutional structure, level of economic and financial development, and macroeconomic policies and performance across the two emerging regions.

Second, market participants have a larger negative coefficient relative to nonparticipants for the full sample during both crisis and no-crisis states. Foreign borrowing is therefore associated with a larger decline in profitability per unit increase in leverage. However, there are important regional variations. A finding similar to that of the aggregate sample is observed for firms in East Asia.[25] For firms in Latin America, the effect of

25. The coefficient has the expected sign but is not statistically significant at the 5 percent level.

leverage on firm profitability is smaller for market participants during both crisis and no-crisis states. Latin American market participants therefore seem to benefit from foreign borrowing more than East Asian market participants during no-crisis states. There is also no significant difference in the effect of leverage on cash flows across crisis and no-crisis states for East Asian market participants.

Third, currency crises affect firm profitability and cash flows through leverage. In the event of a crisis, firms with higher leverage seem to be more adversely affected. This is true for both market participants as well as nonparticipants. There is also no independent effect of leverage for both market participants and nonparticipants (in the full sample and in East Asia) after including the interaction term for currency crisis and leverage. This indicates that leverage is particularly important during currency devaluations. However, the reason for higher sensitivity may be different for the two sets of firms. Nonparticipants with high leverage can be affected by a rise in domestic interest rates during a currency crisis, while market participants with high leverage and foreign exchange liabilities are likely to be adversely affected through the "balance sheet" effect of foreign exchange devaluation.

The next set of regressions explores this trade-off between devaluation risk and interest rate risk for market participants and nonparticipants. Market participants have access to a wider set of financing instruments and markets, which can allow them to fund their liabilities at a lower cost but subjects them to the risk of currency devaluation. Nonparticipants with high leverage do not face foreign exchange risk, but they do face the risk of an increase in interest rates, which often occur prior to or accompany currency devaluations (see figure 15-1 for benchmark short-term interest rates in East Asia during in 1997–98. Similar trends are observed for other emerging markets that faced large currency devaluations).[26] We test these two hypotheses formally below.

In order to measure the sensitivity of firm performance to currency risk, variants of the following regressions were estimated for both market participants and nonparticipants:

26. The purpose of a monetary contraction in such a situation is to stabilize the exchange rate and prevent capital outflows. Exchange rate stability can also be maintained through reserve losses (Eichengreen, Rose, and Wyplosz 1996). A large rise in domestic interest rates may also be part of an IMF stabilization program during a currency crisis (Stiglitz 2002).

$$\text{(15-3)} \quad Performance_{it} = c_0 + c_1{*}Leverage_{it-1} + c_2{*}Currency\ Depreciation_t + c_3{*}(Leverage_{it-1}){*}(Currency\ Depreciation_t) + d{*}(Control\ Variables) + \varepsilon_{it},$$

where *Currency Depreciation*$_t$ is the change in the logarithm of the nominal exchange rate over the previous period.[27] This specification follows the literature on measuring foreign exposure using firm- and industry-level returns.[28] The regressions control for differences in firm, industry, country, and regional characteristics, domestic fundamentals, global business cycle factors, and systematic differences in performance across market participants and nonparticipants. Since currency depreciations may be related with contemporaneous control variables (such a real GDP growth), we report separate regressions first with only firm size as a control variable and then with the full set of control variables in tables 15-4 and 15-5. The coefficient of the relevant interaction terms, and thus the main messages, are robust to the inclusion of control variables other than firm size. The results are presented in table 15-4. The messages that come from this set of regressions are as follows:

Currency devaluations are associated with an adverse effect on profitability of market participants. Nonparticipants, however, do not seem to be exposed to changes in the nominal exchange rate *on average.*[29] Domínguez and Tesar find that a fraction of firms in the developing countries in their sample were exposed to changes in the foreign exchange rate but are not able to identify specific channels for foreign exchange exposure.[30] Our results indicate that market participants in emerging markets are relatively more exposed to changes in the exchange rate than nonparticipants.[31] Second, higher leverage is associated with a larger sensitivity to changes in the nominal exchange rate for both market participants and

27. Using the logarithm of exchange rates instead of levels reduces the effect of extreme changes in the nominal exchange rate.

28. See Adler and Dumas (1984); Bartov and Bodnar (1994); Domínguez and Tesar (2001a, 2001b).

29. The performance of *market nonparticipant* firms can be adversely or beneficially affected by changes in the terms of trade following devaluation, but the average effect is expected to be independent of leverage. This is confirmed by our regression analysis.

30. Domínguez and Tesar (2001a, 2001b).

31. Domínguez and Tesar (2001b) do not find any evidence of a relationship between trade and foreign exchange exposure for the developing countries in their sample. Our subsequent regression shows that this finding could be due to the fact that they control only for trade effects rather than for *both* trade and foreign borrowing.

Table 15-4. *Nominal Exchange Rate Devaluation, Leverage, and Firm Profitability*[a]

Variable	*Nonparticipants* (1)	(2)	(3)	(4)	*Market participants* (5)	(6)	(7)	(8)
Leverage	−0.156	−0.142	−0.156	−0.142	−0.192	−0.168	−0.202	−0.177
	−27.0	−22.5	−27.3	−22.8	−9.9	−8.4	−9.9	−8.5
Currency depreciation$_{it}$	−3.87	3.42	−1.19	5.86	−7.37	7.05	−9.76	5.09
	−4.2	1.8	−1.1	3.1	−4.1	1.2	−4.4	0.9
Leverage*currency depreciation$_{it}$		−0.146		−0.144		−0.226		−0.236
		−3.8		−3.8		−2.4		−2.5
log(size)	1.05	1.05	4.08	4.08	1.22	1.20	4.38	4.45
	12.6	12.6	9.6	9.6	5.1	5.0	2.7	2.8
log(size) squared			−0.29	−0.29			−0.21	−0.22
			−7.9	−7.9			−2.0	−2.1
Capital intensity			1.1	0.8			−11.5	−11.2
			0.6	0.4			−2.4	−2.3
Capital intensity squared			−8.34	−8.07			4.41	4.03
			−4.4	−4.2			0.9	0.8
Real GDP growth			0.17	0.16			−0.17	−0.19
			4.8	4.6			−2.2	−2.3
Number of observations	14,089	14,089	14,060	14,060	2,246	2,246	2,239	2,239
R^2	0.1664	0.1683	0.1916	0.1935	0.2190	0.2270	0.2398	0.2485

a. The dependent variable is net profit as a percentage of assets. Leverage is lagged one period. Currency depreciation$_t$ is the change in logarithm of the nominal exchange rate (depreciation) over the previous period. The regressions include industry, country, and regional fixed effects (not shown here). Year dummies were added to proxy for global business cycle effects. t statistics were calculated using Huber-White heteroskedasticity-corrected robust standard errors and are reported below the coefficient estimates. The sample period is 1992–2001.

nonparticipants. However, highly leveraged market participants are 60 percent more sensitive to changes in the nominal exchange rate than nonparticipants with similar leverage. Highly leveraged market participants therefore face a direct adverse shock to profitability during devaluations. Nonparticipants are not exposed directly to changes in the exchange rate, but highly leveraged nonparticipants experience lower profitability during devaluations.

In order to measure the relative interest rate risk for market participants and nonparticipants during devaluations, we ran regressions similar to the one above, but with the interest expense as a percentage of assets as the dependent variable.[32] The results are presented in table 15-5. Nominal devaluations are associated with an increase in interest charges for both market participants and nonparticipant. Further, nominal devaluations are associated with a much larger effect of leverage on interest payments for nonparticipants relative to market participants (the size of this effect is almost three times larger than for market participants and is highly significant). Nonparticipants with higher leverage therefore face higher interest rate risk during devaluations than market participants with similar leverage.

At first glance, it may seem almost tautological that market participants with foreign debt would be adversely affected by currency devaluations relative to nonparticipants.[33] This is clearly not the case, since the effects on firm-level performance are net effects—net of optimizing decisions by firms regarding aggregate leverage, foreign debt, and possible hedging of foreign exchange risk, either through foreign trade or through the use of foreign exchange derivatives contracts. A strong and significant effect of devaluation on performance of market participants indicates an increased risk of foreign debt during devaluations *after* all possible measures that the firm may have taken to protect itself against such risk.[34] Moreover, the

32. Using interest charges relative to assets, instead of relative to total debt, makes the coefficients comparable to ones in the regressions reported in tables 15-2 through 15-4 and allows for interpretation of the interaction term. We control for the direct (positive) effect of leverage on interest expenses by including it as an explanatory variable.

33. The amount of foreign debt in local currency terms goes up by the percentage depreciation. Claessens, Djankov, and Ferri (1999) estimate the increase in firm-level foreign debt (in terms of local currency) for East Asian firms using foreign debt outstanding prior to the crisis and the percentage depreciation during the crisis.

34. Allayannis, Brown, and Klapper (2000) report that foreign exchange hedging by East Asian firms during 1996–98 was largely ineffective: firms that hedged foreign debt exposure actually did worse than firms that did not, after controlling for a variety of firm- and country-level factors. They

Table 15-5. *Interest Expenses of Firms during Nominal Devaluations*[a]

	Nonparticipants				*Market participants*			
Variable	*(1)*	*(2)*	*(3)*	*(4)*	*(5)*	*(6)*	*(7)*	*(8)*
Leverage	0.093 40.6	0.077 30.4	0.093 40.8	0.077 30.2	0.095 17.9	0.089 16.5	0.095 17.7	0.090 16.4
Currency depreciation$_{it}$	4.02 9.7	-4.32 -3.9	2.77 5.6	-5.44 -4.7	3.97 5.7	0.26 0.1	4.14 5.0	0.43 0.2
Leverage*currency depreciation$_{it}$		0.163 7.2		0.163 7.2		0.057 1.7		0.058 1.8
log(size)	-0.24 -8.6	-0.24 -8.6	-0.27 -2.6	-0.28 -2.7	-0.29 -3.8	-0.29 -3.7	0.00 0.0	-0.02 0.0
log(size) squared			0.003 0.3	0.004 0.4			-0.027 -0.9	-0.025 -0.9
Capital intensity			0.11 0.1	0.44 0.5			3.09 2.0	2.96 1.9
Capital intensity squared			0.90 1.0	0.59 0.6			-2.01 -1.3	-1.88 -1.2
Real GDP growth			-0.083 -5.1	-0.075 -4.8			0.010 0.3	0.012 0.4
Number of observations	13,476		13,476	13,453	13,453	2,206 2,206	2,200	2,200
R^2	0.3462	0.3593	0.3601	0.3735	0.4195	0.4227	0.4292	0.4324

a. The dependent variable is interest expenses as a percentage of assets. Leverage is lagged one period. Currency depreciation$_{t}$ is the change in the logarithm of the nominal exchange rate over the previous period. The regressions include industry, country, and regional fixed effects (not shown here). Year dummies were added to proxy for global business cycle effects. t statistics were calculated using Huber-White heteroskedasticity-corrected robust standard errors and are reported below the coefficient estimates. The sample period is 1992–2001.

larger increase in interest expense for nonparticipants during devaluations, relative to market participants with similar leverage, indicates that non-participants may face a higher cost of capital during a currency crisis due to a restricted set of financing options. Market participants, in contrast, are less vulnerable to domestic interest rate increases because they have access to external (international) finance. But the overall picture that emerges is that the lower cost of capital obtained by market participants is not sufficient to offset the direct adverse effect of currency depreciation on firm balance sheets.

This conclusion, however, should be taken with caution for purposes of policy formulation since the regression results are conditional on the sample period. The initial part of the sample period, or the "pre-crisis" period in emerging markets, was characterized by relatively stable or fixed exchange rates. The collective expectations of market participants may have been biased toward underestimating the risk of a future devaluation. The later part of the decade saw a broad shift (a forced and wrenching move in many cases) toward market-determined exchange rates. Since market-based exchange rates "price in" all available information, there is less chance of a systematic misalignment of expectations. Further, there has been significant growth in foreign exchange derivatives in recent years, indicating enhanced opportunities for risk-sharing.[35] These beneficial changes greatly reduce the currency risks that market participants may have faced during the last decade.

Our final specification considers the relation between foreign borrowing, foreign trade, and firm performance for market participants. Market participants in the tradable goods sector—for example, the oil and gas sector—might be able to raise foreign debt more easily because they have access to foreign currency earnings.[36] Further, access to foreign markets might make them less vulnerable to exchange rate devaluations even if they have a high ratio of foreign borrowing to assets. Market participants in nontradable sectors (such as utilities) that have primarily domestic earnings and high foreign debt thus are relatively more vulnerable.[37] In order to test

---

attribute this to illiquidity in foreign currency derivatives markets during the peak of the Asian crisis. The IMF provides some additional reasons: "While derivatives do play a positive role by reallocating risks and facilitating growth of capital flows to emerging markets, they can also allow market participants to take on excessive leverage, avoid prudential regulations, and manipulate accounting rules when financial supervision and internal risk management systems are weak or inadequate" (IMF 2002b, p. 67).

35. See IMF (2002b, ch. 3).

36. See Martínez and Werner (2002) for a case study of Mexico.

this hypothesis, variants of the following regression were estimated for the sample of market participants:

$$(15\text{-}4)\quad \mathit{Performance}_{it} = c_0 + c_1{*}\mathit{Leverage}_{it-1} + c_2{*}(\mathit{Foreign\ Debt/Total\ Debt})_{it} + c_3{*}\mathit{Tradable\ Dummy}_i + c_4{*}(\mathit{Foreign\ Debt/Total\ Debt})_{it}{*}\mathit{Tradable\ Dummy}_i + d{*}(\mathit{Control\ Variables}) + \varepsilon_{it},$$

where *(Foreign Debt/Total Debt)*$_{it}$ is the share of foreign debt in total debt and *Tradable Dummy*$_i$ is an indicator for whether the firm is in a tradable sector.[38] The set of control variables is similar to the earlier specifications. The results are summarized in table 15-6. The important messages that come from this analysis are as follows.

Among market participants, firms with higher foreign debt (as a share of total debt) do better on average in terms of both net profits and cash flows. This could be due to several reasons—market participants with higher foreign exposure are larger, are concentrated in tradable sectors, and may benefit from government-sponsored corporate "bailout" measures. When we include a differential effect of leverage for market participants in the tradable sectors, the relation between foreign debt and firm performance is positive and statistically significant for firms in tradable sectors. Further, there is no independent effect of foreign debt on the performance of market participants after controlling for trade effects (the effect of higher foreign debt is negative for market participants in nontradable sectors, but the coefficient is not statistically significant).[39] Market participants in the tradable sectors appear to benefit from foreign financing.

37. Foreign debt outstanding (or foreign debt as a share of total debt) was not used in the earlier specifications because firm debt issuance and debt maturity were used to estimate foreign debt outstanding. This measure of foreign debt outstanding is biased to some extent since (1) debt covenants can specify higher interest payments or early repayment following a rating downgrade or "rating trigger," (2) negotiated debt restructuring can reduce principal and interest payments and extend maturity of existing debt instruments, and (3) there may be significant cross-sectional variation in the amortization profile of international loan issues. The indicator for market participation is less affected by such measurement errors.

38. The classification of SIC (Standard Industrial Classification) two-digit sectors into "tradables" and "nontradables" is based on Forbes (2002). Using actual firm-level foreign sales is preferable, but the disadvantage with this approach is that firms in developing countries typically underreport foreign sales on their balance sheets. Domínguez and Tesar (2001a) report a similar issue for both developed and developing countries in their sample.

39. This result is conditional on the inclusion of control variables for firm productivity parameters and real GDP growth. The coefficient of the interaction term for trade sector and foreign debt is positive but not statistically significant in the absence of controls.

Table 15-6. *Foreign Debt Outstanding, Trade Exposure, and Firm Performance for Market Participants, 1992–2001*[a]

	Net profit		*Cash flows*	
Variable	*(1)*	*(2)*	*(3)*	*(4)*
Leverage	–0.175 –8.1	–0.172 –7.9	–0.125 –6.0	–0.122 –5.9
Ratio of foreign debt to total debt	0.049 4.5	–0.001 –0.1	0.038 3.3	–0.024 –1.4
Tradable sector dummy		–2.673 –0.3		4.109 1.5
Ratio of foreign debt to total debt* Tradable sector dummy		0.073 3.6		0.092 4.3
log(size)	6.03 3.0	5.89 2.9	2.34 1.3	2.21 1.2
log(size) squared	–0.312 –2.4	–0.297 –2.2	–0.090 –0.7	–0.075 –0.6
Capital intensity	–11.4 –2.2	–12.2 –2.3	0.0 0.0	–1.1 –0.2
Capital intensity squared	4.95 0.9	5.61 1.0	–4.43 –0.8	–3.53 –0.6
Real GDP growth	0.129 1.9	0.129 1.9	–0.001 0.0	0.001 0.0
Number of observations	2,083	2,083	1,997	1,997
R^2	0.2252	0.2295	0.2219	0.2288

a. The dependent variable is net profit or cash flows as a percentage of assets. Leverage is lagged one period. Tradable and nontradable sectors are based on the SIC two-digit classification of Forbes (2002). The regressions include industry, country, and regional fixed effects (not shown here). Year dummies were added to proxy for global business cycle effects. t statistics were calculated using Huber-White heteroskedasticity-corrected robust standard errors and are reported below the coefficient estimates. The sample period is 1992–2001.

Conclusions

Despite efforts to pay down debt since the 1997–98 crisis and the broad shift to flexible exchange rates, the corporate sector in developing countries remains subject to considerable risk. Corporate profitability in developing countries has shown a significant decline in recent years. Many Asian corporations remain highly leveraged, in part because they substituted domestic for external debt and also in part because the range of financing instruments available in emerging markets remains limited. Companies in Latin America and Eastern Europe, also highly leveraged, have increased their dependence on foreign finance. An excessive dependence on external finance hurt many Asian corporations in 1997–98. While firms (especially Latin American firms) active in international markets during the 1990s appear to have benefited from a lower cost of capital, high leverage remains a cause for concern in many emerging markets. These high levels of leverage appear sustainable in the low-interest environment prevailing currently, but they make firms vulnerable to interest rate risks.

The analysis presented in this chapter is as good as the quality of balance sheet data reported by companies in the major emerging markets. There may be inconsistencies in corporate reporting standards over the years and across emerging markets. Local accounting principles may allow for asset revaluations, which is an artificial way to mark up equity and "deleverage."[40] Foreign exchange losses and derivatives positions are frequently not marked-to-market and can be amortized over several years (for example, Indonesia). There is, therefore, a need to improve the quality and timeliness of corporate data in developing countries. Corporate scandals in industrial countries have brought to light the deficiencies of corporate information even in the major markets. There is considerable uncertainty over the true state of corporate balance sheets, especially over the nature and magnitude of off-balance-sheet risks. As the corporate sector is increasingly becoming the main conduit for development finance, and given the risks of rapid reversal of financial flows when corporate performance does not meet market expectations, it has become increasingly important for policymakers and market participants alike to be aware of the scope of corporate sector indebtedness (both domestic and foreign) and performance in emerging markets. That this is not easily achieved was underlined by recent corporate scandals in major industrial countries.

Appendix A. Methodology

Two types of data are especially useful in tracking trends in corporate finance in developing countries: (a) macroeconomic data, or "top-down" data, from surveys carried out by national and international data collectors and (b) microeconomic data, or "bottom-up" data, compiled from corporate reports. Each source has strengths and weaknesses.

40. This may partly explain why leverage ratios declined in Korea after the Asian crisis even while total debt was relatively stable.

The macro data are, in principle, the most comprehensive and generally quite timely. But they often provide little detail. If too highly aggregated, they make it impossible to distinguish the nonfinancial corporate sector from other parts of the private sector. The flow-of-funds data compiled for the United States by the Federal Reserve are a model of top-down data. Few developing countries, however, produce such complete accounts.

Firm-level data provide far more detail but suffer from the risk of sample bias. Often only the largest, most sophisticated enterprises are covered, because they are the ones that produce detailed reports. They may also have a time lag arising from the compilers' effort to gather comprehensive cross-country data.

The absence of comprehensive, timely data is more than a hindrance for researchers; it also is a concern for market participants and policymakers. With financial markets prone to sharp adjustments and given the easy availability of derivatives and other structuring products that allow corporates to both hedge and increase their risk exposures, it is increasingly important for market participants to be aware of the extent of exposure of the corporate sector as a whole. If the entire sector is over-exposed, individual companies are likely to have trouble rolling over their debt in times of market stress.

Four sources of macroeconomic data are used in this study to paint a picture of the liabilities on the aggregate balance sheet of the nonfinancial corporate sector:

—Data on domestic bank credit from the International Monetary Fund are used to estimate bank credit, the primary source of credit for most corporate entities in the developing world.[41] The IMF's *International Financial Statistics* (line 32d) includes all credit to the private sector (including households), but the publication does not disaggregate bank credit to consumers. Although this is small in most developing countries, it does bias the debt numbers up.

—The *BIS Quarterly Review* provides data on cross-border bank claims, foreign bond issuance, and local bond market issuance.[42]

—Domestic equity is estimated using the figures on market capitalization reported in Standard and Poor's Emerging Market Data Base. This source has two drawbacks. First, the use of market values rather than book values makes the equity component (and thus debt-equity ratios) more volatile. Second, the source does not include privately held equity.

41. IMF (various years).

42. Bank for International Settlements (various years).

—Foreign-held equity is estimated using the data on FDI stock from chapter 4 of *Global Development Finance, 2003.*[43]

The firm-level data used in this study are from the Worldscope database. We select only firms for which all the relevant balance sheet items are available. The regional breakdown of the sample is given in table A-1.

We built a database by matching firm-level balance sheets from Worldscope (December 2002 edition) with issuance data on bonds and syndicated loans from Dealogic Bondware and Loanware. On average, about half of annual bond issuance and about 35 percent of annual loan issuance are accounted for by firms matched with Worldscope balance sheet data.

The resulting database covers 4,682 firms in twenty-one emerging markets: Argentina, Brazil, Chile, China, Colombia, the Czech Republic, Hungary, India, Indonesia, Korea, Malaysia, Mexico, Pakistan, Peru, the Philippines, Poland, Russia, South Africa, Thailand, Turkey, and Venezuela. Because Worldscope data appear quite comprehensive for 1992–2001, the analysis in the main text focuses on this period. (Depending on the variable, the number of firms covered in the regression analysis ranges from 1,122 in 1992 to 3,629 in 2000 and 3,073 in 2001.)

The summary statistics presented in the analysis, unless otherwise mentioned, are weighted averages of the financial ratios (with firm assets used as weights). For example, the debt-asset ratio is computed as the ratio (expressed as a percentage) of the sum of debt for all firms to that of assets for all firms.

The findings related to foreign market access are derived as follows.

First, firms that had outstanding foreign debt in a given period (called "market participants") are compared with those that had no outstanding foreign debt ("nonparticipants" in the international debt markets, at least for that year). Outstanding foreign debt is calculated by summing all debt issues in international markets (syndicated loans and bonds) during 1990–2001 and subtracting debt that matured during the period. This method ignores outstanding debt issued before 1990, but because private debt flows to the corporate sector in emerging markets (and stocks in those markets) were small in the aftermath of the debt crisis of the 1980s, this omission is unlikely to affect the results presented here.

Second, considering all firms with outstanding foreign debt, firms that borrowed from international markets in the current period (that is, firms with "rollover") are compared with those that did not (firms without rollover).

43. World Bank (2003).

Table A-1. *Number of Firms in the Sample, 1992–2001*

Region	*1992*	*1993*	*1994*	*1995*	*1996*	*1997*	*1998*	*1999*	*2000*	*2001*
All	1,122	1,288	1,538	1,928	2,242	2,559	2,998	3,565	3,629	3,073
East Asia and Pacific	582	691	774	1,032	1,181	1,245	1,347	1,618	1,840	1,695
Latin America and the Caribbean	141	162	264	308	354	390	533	862	834	706
Europe and Central Asia	17	19	20	68	132	155	177	185	165	117
Others	382	416	480	520	575	769	941	900	790	555

Appendix B. Details of the Regressions Reported in Table 15-3

Table B-1. *Regressions for Net Profits of Nonparticipants and Market Participants, by Region, 1992–2001*[a]

	Nonparticipants			*Market participants*		
Variable	*All regions*	*East Asia and Pacific*	*Latin America and the Caribbean*	*All regions*	*East Asia and Pacific*	*Latin America and the Caribbean*
Leverage	–0.151	–0.142	–0.148	–0.197	–0.225	–0.045
	–26.3	–17.6	–10.1	–9.5	–7.6	–1.0
Crisis	0.723	–1.228	2.035	1.882	–0.889	3.644
	1.4	–1.2	2.5	1.6	–0.3	2.5
Crisis*leverage	–0.073	–0.051	–0.115	–0.083	–0.043	–0.122
	–5.8	–2.8	–3.9	–4.0	–1.0	–2.5
log(size)	4.07	2.59	4.90	4.30	5.45	4.51
	9.6	4.9	4.7	2.6	2.4	1.2
log(size) squared	–0.290	–0.156	–0.369	–0.206	–0.304	–0.133
	–7.9	–3.5	–4.4	–1.9	–2.0	–0.6
Capital intensity	0.959	7.303	–2.806	–12.389	–0.121	–25.953
	0.5	3.0	–0.6	–2.6	0.0	–2.8
Capital intensity squared	–8.27	–13.46	–1.10	5.38	–7.69	23.77
	–4.3	–5.1	–0.3	1.1	–1.0	2.6
Real GDP growth	0.203	0.038	0.302	0.184	–0.052	0.246
	5.7	0.6	3.9	2.0	–0.4	1.8
Number of observations	14,060	6,785	2,505	2,239	1,240	537
R^2	0.1952	0.1799	0.2365	0.2308	0.2371	0.2968

a. The dependent variable is net profit as a percentage of assets. Leverage is lagged one period. Crisis is an indicator for currency crisis (see text). Firm size is measured as average total assets in 1998–2001 in millions of U.S. dollars. The regressions include firm, industry, country, and regional fixed effects (not shown here). Year dummies are added to proxy for global business cycle effects. t statistics are calculated using Huber-White heteroskedasticity-corrected robust standard errors and are reported below the coefficient estimates.

Table B-2. *Regressions for Cash Flows of Nonparticipants and Market Participants, by Region, 1992–2001*[a]

	Nonparticipants			*Market participants*		
Variable	*All regions*	*East Asia and Pacific*	*Latin America and the Caribbean*	*All regions*	*East Asia and Pacific*	*Latin America and the Caribbean*
Leverage	–0.085	–0.087	–0.040	–0.142	–0.161	0.013
	–13.3	–9.8	–2.5	–7.1	–5.7	0.3
Crisis	0.851	–1.561	2.126	1.144	–1.090	3.721
	1.4	–1.4	2.2	1.0	–0.4	2.7
Crisis*leverage	–0.043	–0.044	–0.080	–0.090	–0.072	–0.093
	–3.1	–2.4	–2.1	–4.6	–1.5	–2.2
log(size)	3.54	1.52	5.97	1.57	1.85	–1.45
	7.3	2.3	4.5	1.0	0.9	–0.4
log(size) squared	–0.265	–0.075	–0.483	–0.042	–0.060	0.214
	–6.2	–1.3	–4.6	–0.4	–0.4	0.9
Capital intensity	20.8	24.4	20.0	–1.9	9.9	–7.7
	9.3	8.0	3.2	–0.4	1.5	–0.7
Capital intensity squared	–26.8	–29.1	–22.6	–3.6	–16.6	9.5
	–11.3	–8.5	–3.8	–0.7	–2.3	0.9
Real GDP growth	0.106	–0.076	0.403	0.016	–0.190	0.203
	2.5	–1.2	4.4	0.2	–1.2	1.6
Number of observations	13,147	6,453	2,213	2,144	1,206	482
R^2	0.2051	0.1514	0.1658	0.2306	0.2341	0.3489

a. The dependent variable is firm cash flows as a percentage of assets. Leverage is lagged one period. Crisis is an indicator for currency crisis (see text). Firm size is measured as average total assets in 1998–2001 in millions of U.S. dollars. The regressions include firm, industry, country, and regional fixed effects (not shown here). Year dummies are added to proxy for global business cycle effects. t statistics are calculated using Huber-White heteroskedasticity-corrected robust standard errors and are reported below the coefficient estimates.

References

Adler, Michael, and Barnard Dumas. 1984. "Exposure to Currency Risk: Definition and Management." *Financial Management* 13 (2): 41–50.

Allayannis, George, Gregory W. Brown, and Leora F. Klapper. 2000. *Exchange Rate Risk Management: Evidence from East Asia.* Policy Research Working Paper 2606. Washington: World Bank.

Bank for International Settlements. Various years. *BIS Quarterly Review.* Basel.

Bartov, Eli, and Gordon M. Bodnar. 1994. "Firm Valuation, Earnings Expectations, and the Exchange Rate Exposure Effect." *Journal of Finance* 5 (December): 1755–85.

Claessens, Stijn, Simon Djankov, and Giovanni Ferri. 1999. "Corporate Distress in East Asia: Assessing the Impact of Interest and Exchange Rate Shocks." *Emerging Markets Quarterly* 3 (2): 8–14.

Claessens, Stijn, Simeon Djankov, and Larry Lang. 1998. *Corporate Growth, Financing, and Risks in the Decade before East Asia's Financial Crisis.* Policy Research Working Paper 2017. Washington: World Bank, November.

Dadush, Uri, Dipak Dasgupta, and Dilip Ratha. 2000. "The Role of Short-Term Debt in Recent Crises." *Finance and Development* 37 (4, December): 54–57.

Dasgupta, Dipak, Dilip Ratha, Dennis Botman, and Ashish Narain. 2000. "Short-Term Debt and Financial Crises." In Charles Adams, Robert E. Litan, and Michael Pomerleano, eds., *Managing Financial and Corporate Distress: Lessons from Asia.* Brookings.

Demirgüç-Kunt, Aslı, and Vojislav Maksimovic. 1999. "Institutions, Financial Markets, and Firm Debt Maturity." *Journal of Financial Economics* 54 (3, December): 295–336.

Domínguez, Kathryn M., and Linda Tesar. 2001a. "A Re-Examination of Exchange Rate Exposure." *American Economic Review* 91 (2): 396–99.

———. 2001b. "Trade and Exposure." *American Economic Review* 91 (2): 367–70.

Eichengreen, Barry, Andrew Rose, and Charles Wyplosz. 1996. "Speculative Attacks on Pegged Exchange Rates: An Empirical Exploration with Special Reference to the European Monetary System." In Matthew Canzoneri, Wilfred Ethier, and Vittorio Grilli, eds., *New Trans-Atlantic Economy.* Cambridge University Press.

Fama, Eugene, and Kenneth French. 1992. "The Cross Section of Expected Stock Returns." *Journal of Finance* 47 (2): 427–65.

Forbes, Kristin J. 2002. "How Do Large Depreciations Affect Firm Performance?" NBER Working Paper 9095. Cambridge, Mass.: National Bureau of Economic Research. Available at www.nber.org./papers/w9095 [May 19, 2003].

Glen, Jack, Kevin Lee, and Ajit Singh. 2001. "Persistence of Profitability and Competition in Emerging Markets." *Economics Letters* 72 (2): 247–53.

Glen, Jack, Ajit Singh, and Rudolf Matthias. 1999. "How Intensive Is Competition in the Emerging Markets? An Analysis of Corporates Rates of Return in Nine Emerging Markets." IMF Working Paper 99/32. Washington: International Monetary Fund.

Harvey, Campbell R., Karl V. Lins, and Andrew H. Roper. 2001. "The Effect of Capital Structure When Expected Agency Costs Are Extreme." NBER Working Paper 8452. Cambridge, Mass.: National Bureau of Economic Research, September.

Himmelberg, Charles, Glenn Hubbard, and Inessa Love. 2002. *Investor Protection, Ownership and Investment.* Policy Research Working Paper 2834. Washington: World Bank, April.

International Monetary Fund. 2002a. "Essays on Trade and Finance." *World Economic Outlook,* ch. 2. Washington.

———. 2002b. "The Role of Financial Derivatives in Emerging Markets." Global Financial Stability Report. Washington, December.

———. Various years (1980–2002). *International Financial Statistics.* Washington.

Klapper, Leora, and Inessa Love. 2002. *Corporate Governance, Investor Protection, and Performance in Emerging Markets.* Policy Research Working Paper 2818. Washington: World Bank, March.

La Porta, Rafael, Florencio López-de-Silanes, Andrei Shleifer, and Robert Vishny. 1997. "Legal Determinants of External Finance." *Journal of Finance* 52 (3): 1131–50.

Levine, Ross. 1997. "Financial Development and Economic Growth: Views and Agenda." *Journal of Economic Literature* 35 (2): 688–726.

Mako, William P. 2001. "Corporate Restructuring in East Asia: Promoting Best Practices." *Finance and Development* 38 (1, March): 2–5.

Martínez, Lorenza, and Alejandro Werner. 2002. "The Exchange Rate Regime and the Currency Composition of Corporate Debt: The Mexican Experience." *Journal of Development Economics* 69 (2): 315–34.

Radelet, Steven, and Jeffrey Sachs. 1998. "The East Asian Financial Crisis: Diagnosis, Remedies, Prospects." *Brookings Papers on Economic Activity 1,* 1–74.

Ranciere, Romain. 2001. "Credit Derivatives in Emerging Markets." Unpublished manuscript. New York University, Stern School of Business.

Singh, Ajit. 1995. "Corporate Financial Patterns in Industrializing Economies: A Comparative International Study." IFC Technical Paper 14328. Washington: International Finance Corporation, April.

Stiglitz, Joseph E. 2002. *Globalization and Its Discontents.* New York: Norton.

World Bank. 2000. *Global Development Finance.* Washington.

———. 2003. *Global Development Finance.* Washington.

PANEL SUMMARY

The Role of Private Equity in the Development of Capital Markets

Michael Barth, chair of the panel and chief executive officer of the Netherlands Development Finance Company, initiated discussion by defining private equity as a medium- to long-term financial commitment in equity or quasi-equity in illiquid securities with the expectation that future performance of the company will generate both profits and an opportunity to divest with substantial returns. Private equity serves an important role in filling the financial gap between small companies, with sales generally of $15 million a year or less, and large, publicly tradable companies, with $250 million in annual revenue or more. Managers of private equity funds seek to expand a business by injecting not only finance but also business expertise and savvy. As a demonstration of how critical the second aspect is, Barth cited a study where 70 percent of private equity recipients in the United Kingdom stated that private equity managers had made substantial contributions through advice to their companies.

National macroeconomic impacts from private equity funding may include professionalization of the corporate sector and growth in employment and exports. Given its niche in transforming small domestic companies into internationally competitive businesses, this type of financing has the potential to build stronger, more balanced financial sectors.

While financial flows to the developing world have shrunk dramatically over the past few years, the fraction of those flows in foreign direct investment has continued to grow, reaching roughly 60 percent of the volume of flows in 1999, where it has remained since. However, private equity indexes in every developing region show a drop-off in both funds raised and investment over the past two years. Latin America and Russia suffered a massive decline in inflows over that time, while Asia and Central Europe fared better, with only modest decreases.

In contrast to public equity and fixed-income funds, the quality of private equity funds varies greatly. From 1980 to 1995, annual returns from the upper quartile of private equity funds exceeded returns from the bottom quartile of funds by 15 percent, while similar spreads were a modest 2.3 percent for equity funds and a scant 1 percent for fixed-income funds. A similar comparison of European private equity funds from 1993 to 1999 found a 25.2 percent differential between top and bottom quartiles.

What can be learned from these tremendous disparities in performance? Barth drew several conclusions. For one, management has a striking impact on the performance of private equity funds. Private equity operations must be adapted to local environments, as opposed to taking a one-model-fits-all approach. Such investment should be considered a craft requiring diligence and dedication in the pursuit of acceptable returns, not a commodity that requires no more work than cutting a deal and a check.

From a strategic side, firms must plan how they will divest in the future when making decisions to invest in the present, something that the past generation of equity investors may not have done. Managers must also incorporate into their investment planning and strategies the issues of the local environment—specifically poor investor protection and corporate governance laws—and not forget that they are operating in less sophisticated capital markets than the ones they are used to in the developed world.

Roger Leeds of Johns Hopkins School of Advanced International Studies offered an analysis of the numerous ways in which emerging-market private equity differs from venture capital investment in the United States and Europe, the role private equity can and should play in developing countries, why it fills an important hole in the financial infrastructure in these nations, and what adaptations can be made to bolster its success.

He began by sketching the recent history of private equity in emerging markets. In the mid-1990s, spurred by the booming success of venture capital funds in the developed world, investors began to apply the venture capital model, with few modifications, to previously untapped developing markets. They initiated private equity funds in these riskier markets, but the returns were abysmal, particularly compared with investment in Europe and the United States. As a result of this, private equity is now a relatively discredited asset class that must be revamped to restore its standing among investors. As a clear demonstration of this lack of confidence, institutional investors that participated in the initial round of financing are not returning with a second wave of liquidity.

Despite the underperformance of the first generation of private equity financing, private equity in developing nations continues to attract interest because it is the logical bridge between financing for small and very large firms. The current financial architecture fails to meet this critical need, as a vast portion of emerging-market capital flows are funneled to a handful of giant, very creditworthy firms, stunting the growth of smaller firms. The debt sector parallels its equity counterpart, as banks generally lend only to these conglomerates and governments. Domestic security markets either do not exist or are so shallow that they cannot fill the gap, and international financial markets are completely out of the question for mid-range companies in emerging markets.

Therefore, if a nation genuinely adheres to the prevailing belief in development through the private sector, it must welcome an intermediary form of finance to assist the maturation of juvenile mid-size firms to large, professional, competitive firms. Private equity is the obvious mechanism for incubating small and medium enterprises in private markets. Thus encouraging private equity would dramatically improve the business environment, expand the opportunities for private development, and stimulate economic growth in many countries. However, the venture capital model of the developed world has been applied to private equity in developing nations and failed in its first incarnation.

What can private equity practitioners learn from the initial fiascos and occasional successes? According to Leeds, a crucial lesson is that the environmental differences between the developed and developing world played a central role in rendering the venture capital structure highly ineffective when deployed ubiquitously around the globe. He detailed the laundry list of dissimilarities contributing to the difficulties facing private equity investors, including macroeconomic conditions, unfriendly national policies, substandard legal frameworks and enforcement, poor transparency and accountability, unprofessional managerial cultures, weak credit markets, and inferior exit conditions.

Healthy macroeconomic conditions, such as stability, growth, and steady exchange rates, are taken for granted in the United States and

European Union, yet they are far less certain in emerging markets, where macro fluctuations can have a tremendous and potentially devastating impact on the success of any private equity investment. Even high-yielding investments in local currency terms can quickly fall prey to currency devaluation triggered by economy-wide turmoil. For example, some companies in Brazil and Argentina fared extremely well in the mid- to late 1990s, with growth as high as 50 percent in local currency terms, but the tremendous erosion in currency value in both countries negated and even overwhelmed such extraordinary returns, leaving private equity funds with dollar losses.

As expected, the macroeconomic risk from investing in less-developed countries significantly affects private equity investment as well. Because investors may be unable to recall their funds in the short term, any suspicion that an economy may become dangerously volatile can lead to a long-term chilling effect, as seen in Asia since the 1998 crisis. Prior to making a decision to invest, macro instability poses challenges for the executives of a private equity fund or a recipient firm, as value projection—and therefore pricing negotiation—becomes far more uncertain in the face of strong macro fluctuations. According to Leeds, relative stability is a prerequisite to private equity investment, as its illiquid, long-term nature exacerbates the typical investment problems, and consequently the risk, posed by macroeconomic volatility.

In the past, fund managers erroneously assumed the presence of an environment receptive to private equity investment, and this environment was not always present. Many nations lack proper incentives to encourage investors to contribute to private equity funds or even a population willing to entertain the level of risk inherent in this sort of investing, much to the frustration of fund managers seeking domestic investors.

Drawing from the history of venture capital in developed countries, Leeds predicted that policy reform will have to come through industry groups similar to the National Venture Capital Association in the United States or its European counterpart, which have been quite successful in developing a positive environment for private equity investment. Groups such as these are important because the political stakeholders in developing nations, such as large firms, are not interested in this sort of investment and are unwilling to pressure governments to make the necessary changes. Although industrial groups have begun to form in some nations, the degree of mobilization necessary for real reform has yet to be attained.

Recent scandals have cast doubt on the quality of corporate governance—transparency and management accountability—even in the flagship economies of the developed world; in the developing world, weak corporate governance is a potent deterrent to private equity financing. Opacity and poor accountability greatly limit investors' ability to intervene on their own behalf, and private (as opposed to public) equity investments are particularly harmed because they are illiquid. The information asymmetries present in any financial transaction are especially severe in illiquid, nontransparent environments, giving management a tremendous advantage over investors.

In addition to compounding the problems of poor governance by limiting investor recourse and protection in the case of a crisis within a firm, the poor legal environment of many developing nations acts as a major and unintended deterrent to private equity investors. Particularly harmful flaws in the legal system include poor enforcement of bankruptcy laws, minority shareholder rights, disclosure requirements, and shareholder agreements. Without trust in the proper functioning of the system, the difficult business of equity investing becomes far riskier and more challenging. Leeds cautioned that investors should not discount the advantage that locals have in using the legal system to their full benefit.

The familial managerial culture in the developing-country companies that are typically targeted for private equity investment contrasts sharply with the professional culture of similar firms located in the United States and Europe, which can present a significant obstacle to investment success. The managers of these firms are frequently accustomed to tax evasion and secrecy and may view the independent audits and directors required by a private equity investor as hurdles to overcome or sidestep. Private equity managers must acknowledge and contend with this lack of professionalism, instead of assuming a transparent, accountable managerial approach.

Business plans that hinge on leveraging through credit markets may also fail, as weak credit markets and banking sectors can hinder a firm's ability to borrow. This may force the adoption of capital structures that are inefficient due to over-reliance on equity financing.

Leeds's final point regarding the differences between environments is that the tremendous difficulty in launching a successful initial public offering (IPO) in emerging markets dramatically alters the investment landscape relative to established markets. This wrinkle requires private equity investors to create a comprehensive exit strategy before taking a stake in a business. Of course, even when guided by a rigorous, analytically solid divestment plan, investors and management must devote significant energy to consummating viable alternatives to public sales, and these deals frequently offer a much lower return than an IPO would.

Leeds also examined the adaptations that can be made to improve the structure of private equity funds so as to increase the probability of success in a second generation of private equity financing. One hard lesson learned has been that the requisite set of skills for successful private equity investment in emerging markets is not limited to the traditional finance and deal-making skills demanded by venture capital and investment banking firms in the United States. Because private equity investing requires a blend of financial and managerial experience to enhance value in a firm, private equity managers must have operational experience. In this type of investment, the real work begins after funds are disbursed, distinctly unlike investment banking in the United States. Many first-generation private equity managers did not comprehend this, and the next wave of private equity managers has acquired greater operating experience in response to these initial strategic catastrophes. Many private equity investors now refuse to invest if they have no significant operating capacity.

Locating permanent, professional, locally knowledgeable staff in the country receiving funds is absolutely necessary and helps to build value in the portfolio companies through the provision of operational advice.

Leeds also wished to see greater industry collaboration, particularly to lobby governments to create a fertile, conducive environment for private equity investment but also to organize practitioner training and create mechanisms for sharing knowledge. The increased influence on governments would focus constructive legislative and regulatory attention on improving the framework for private equity investment and provide a viable avenue for financing the private sector growth that is the objective of almost every government. This pressure would not just guide policy at the macro level but also improve the framework at the micro level.

The development finance institutions should continue to be involved with private equity. In particular, withdrawal of the International Finance Corporation (IFC), given its status as a market leader, would be catastrophic for the industry. Leeds felt that the IFC should not only continue financing funds but also take the role of a hard-nosed promoter of government reform by collaborating more closely with the World Bank and other development finance institutions capable of giving policy advice. The IFC also could disseminate new ideas and best practices originating in developed countries.

Leeds concluded his presentation with a strong statement of support for the future of the private equity industry and his belief that private sector development is contingent on connection with proper financing, a condition that has not been achieved to date.

Alejandro Schwedhelm of Darby Oversees Investment agreed with several of the points made by both Barth and Leeds and added his own perspective as a private equity practitioner. Darby Oversees Investment, a financial services group, manages a fund of roughly $1 billion specializing in emerging markets.

Corroborating the perspective of Leeds, Schwedhelm stated that he has often seen entrepreneurs who become so attached to their firm that it becomes "their baby." They become major obstacles to selling the firm and obtaining a profitable exit following an investment. He offered two reactions to this, one positive and one negative. On the plus side, owner-managers who are deeply committed to the long-term success of a company enhance the firm's prospects for success. On the down side, consolidating too much power in one individual reduces transparency, which is important because a company becomes much more attractive to potential third-party investors if managers exercise leadership, but not absolute control.

Schwedhelm did not foresee private equity ever constituting the bulk of development finance, at least in terms of volume, due to the high returns demanded by investors for such risky ventures. He also observed that families and friends frequently act much like venture capital firms in the developing world, so the role of private equity is sometimes to bridge the gap between public listing and the venture capitalist stage.

He elaborated on the path by which private equity can stimulate and professionalize domestic investment. The high risk of such investments drives high expectations of earnings. This demand and the high administrative costs associated with any single investment encourage private equity managers to place their eggs in only a few baskets by making large, concentrated investments as opposed to smaller, dispersed investments. This concentration forces the private equity practitioner to participate in a firm and demand significant professional oversight. Schwedhelm agreed with Leeds that private equity investors not only professionalize a firm but also bring value by contributing the diverse viewpoints, practices, and experiences they have gained by working in multiple countries and sectors.

Schwedhelm shared a recent conversation he held with the head of the Central Bank of Costa Rica, in which both agreed that regulators and long-term, significant institutional investors have closely aligned interests in the financial sector. Both seek to achieve long-term stability and good management.

According to Schwedhelm, the success of any investment hinges on the rate of return, and return on an investment with limited (or sometimes nonexistent) opportunity for an IPO hinges on entry valuation and timing. Independent of these factors, firms can build rates of return in several ways. Organic and strategic growth is important; strategic growth might involve expanding into neighboring countries and horizontal or vertical integration. A strategic acquisition by the company, or the strategic sale of the company to another, can also enhance the profitability of an investment.

Schwedhelm also agreed with Leeds regarding the importance of quality management and cogent exit strategies prior to making an investment. Such exit plans could include a formulaic option agreement with other shareholders, a market sale, or gradual release of a significant position in the company. IPOs make for a very attractive option, although frequently these are impossible in emerging markets. Schwedhelm also stated that his fund patently refuses knowingly to invest in drug trafficking, money laundering, and other illicit activities.

On the future development of the private equity industry, Schwedhelm also remarked that governments and regulators should avoid over-regulating. As an example of what should not be done, he cited the case of Cincas, which are investment vehicles created in Mexico in the late 1980s. Cincas were widely anticipated to become a significant private equity mechanism, but a regulatory push to make them as "kosher" as possible led to their demise.

He concluded with two general comments. First, both the volume and quality of IPOs matter, not one or the other. However, private equity practitioners prefer markets that are conducive to IPOs, even at the expense of quality. Second, it is important to publicize and disseminate the true success stories—in which both private equity investors and shareholders of the company financed by them win—and the lessons learned from them. Sharing such information will facilitate development of the industry.

Alvaro Goncalves of Stratus Investimentos of Brazil provided both a policy and a domestic perspective on private equity. He manages a private equity fund in Brazil and serves on the board of the Brazilian Venture Capital Association, which has been active in recent policy initiatives to make the Brazilian environment more receptive to private equity.

Goncalves shared several insights about private equity that tend to be forgotten, even by practitioners, when trying to analyze the state and nature of the industry. First, the performance of private equity can be very difficult to assess in the short term, as private equity investments typically have long maturities. Goncalves has been working with several venture capital associations in Latin America on developing a consensus benchmark to compare funds' performance during the interim period before their investments reach full maturity, but no final standard has been adopted. Second, the best-performing private equity funds tend to start during the down cycle of their economies. Even in the United States, the top funds invested when the dollar was weak and interest rates were high, planning to divest later. Despite excellent final results, performance might look abysmal between the investment and the exit, so there must be some allowance for transient drop-offs in returns when evaluating fund performance.

Goncalves continued by recounting the brief history of private equity in Brazil. The nation first received a token wave of financing in 1993, but serious investment did not begin until the second half of the 1990s, when the Cardozo government's privatization plans drew attention from international investors. Since these funds have not yet had time to fully mature, assessing how conducive the Brazilian environment is to private equity remains quite difficult. This ambiguity has been exacerbated by the global downturn after 2000, which has restricted exit opportunities in Brazil, the United States, and elsewhere. Therefore, the first generation of financing did not mature until the second half of 2002 and first half of 2003, leaving an incomplete record for serious analysis. Complicating the assessment, many Brazilian companies have tracked the economic downtrend closely, making them appear to be terrible investments, although returns after controlling for the business cycle may not be nearly as bad as they appear.

Regardless, funds and international banks are panicking, desperately seeking to divest their interests at the trough of the business cycle. These institutional investors made the strategic mistake of buying at the peak valuation of Brazilian currency and further compounded their losses by entering the market during an influx of liquidity from numerous funds, forcing them into bidding wars. Goncalves noted that these funds should hold their investments and wait for the Brazilian economy to improve. As evidence of the wisdom of this strategy, he presented twenty-eight companies that, he believed, eventually will offer fivefold or even tenfold returns, in dollars, but whose gains have not yet been realized.

As a general comment on private equity in emerging markets, Goncalves agreed with the principle of diversifying through regionalization but concurred with others on the panel that the true key to the success of a private equity fund is careful monitoring of companies in the portfolio.

Many of the funds investing in Latin America badly exacerbated problems if and when they arose by positioning headquarters in one of the big financial hubs in the United States and leaving only junior staffers in the local market. If intervention in a firm's management or operations was needed, senior fund managers capable of adding value and resolving the issues typically were too far away to contribute. Spread among too many countries with too many differences, funds could not effectively cover any of them and failed. According to Goncalves, the two funds that organized with senior management on the ground—Darby and Advent—so far have avoided the poor performance prevalent in the industry.

Goncalves and others are working to develop a complete series of investment vehicles to finance a company from its incipient start-up phase to maturation as a public company. While private equity, designed to cover the later steps of that evolution, has taken root to some degree in Brazil, the early-stage venture capital financing needed for firms to reach the private equity stage has only just begun. Mezzanine finance holds great potential in emerging markets. Lastly, buyout-type private equity funds also could occupy a niche in emerging markets, resuscitating moribund public companies that have become illiquid.

Numerous measures have been implemented recently in Brazil to improve the investment environment. On the regulatory side, Brazil passed a new corporate law in 2001 that granted stronger rights to minority shareholders. Pension fund regulation also was revamped to increase transparency and require consistent asset allocation. The Brazilian Securities and Exchange Commission, known as the CVM, revised the regulation of funds to make different types of funds more compatible. The agency also held extensive public hearings on soon-to-be released regulations specifically for private equity. This step is quite important, as most funds were following mutual fund regulations, and this structure is poorly adapted to private equity usage. Regulations tailored specifically to private equity are very important for the transparency and professionalism of private equity in Brazil.

CVM has undergone significant modifications to complement changes in the regulations it enforces. Since 2000 the process for resolving shareholder conflicts has been shortened from two years to less than three months. The officers of the organization are now independent of the federal government, and the commission has disseminated a corporate governance guide.

In step with CVM's efforts to improve governance, the Brazilian stock exchange has embarked on a novel experiment by creating a new listing segment known as Novo Mercado for firms that voluntarily apply stringent corporate governance rules. Many corporations are moving to adopt the governance reforms necessary for listing under Novo Mercado, although the changes will take some time to implement.

The restructuring within Brazil's regulatory establishment has coincided with organization and maturation within the private equity industry. Brazil's Venture Capital Association was founded in 2000 and was followed in 2002 by creation of the Latin American Venture Capital Association. CVM's hearings dealing with the private equity law have involved more than forty private equity players, and the agency has received more than 200 suggestions for improving the process. To improve and disseminate best practices in the industry, a center for private equity and venture capital studies has been founded at a prestigious Brazilian business school.

Issues pending before the private equity community include the 20 percent tax on capital gains, the difficulties involved in disclosing pension fund performance when a portion of the portfolio includes investments that have failed to mature, and the difficulty of convincing asset managers and pension directors to invest a small fraction of their assets in private equity and venture capital. Long-term investing, in particular, can be quite difficult in Brazil's investment environment, which features interest rates of 25 percent.

In closing, Goncalves predicted that the value invested in Brazil in the 1990s will one day result in value created and that such investment is in line with investors' interests. However, creating a private equity track record takes a long time. To establish a successful track record, funds must maintain a physical presence close to the portfolio, a long-term commitment to the companies, portfolios, and investors, intense monitoring of portfolio firms, an experienced local team, and, obviously, an international capital connection.

Patricia Dinneen of Cambridge Associates ended the session by commenting on private equity from the investor's point of view. Investors see the high risk and low returns that characterize emerging-market private equity investment to date, and these clearly are not attractive qualities for any investment to have. For investors to sink funds into a given fund in a given country, they must feel confident that they will receive profits commensurate with the risk profile of the asset. Boding poorly for the asset class, investors have yet to receive such profits from private equity in the developing world.

Despite this discouraging trend, Dinneen foresaw hope for emerging-market private equity in the next five to ten years because institutional investors have accepted higher risk in exchange for higher returns over the past fifteen years. Funneling liquidity through the top quartile of managers could provide these sorts of investors with returns not attainable by lesser managers, justifying the risk undertaken.

To provide institutional investors with better information on what sort of risk-reward trade-off they are entering into, twelve international finance institutions, including the International Finance Corporation, are developing benchmarking capability. To enter the benchmarking database, the fund must be of institutional investor quality and disclose audited financial statements. Dinneen anticipated that, within a year, performance for 200–300 funds will have been quantified and that the improved quantification from this and other efforts will professionalize the asset class, enable institutional investors to allocate more of their portfolios to private equity, and result in an overall net increase in private equity investment.

PART V

Looking Forward

ALBERTO R. MUSALEM
THIERRY TRESSEL

16

Institutional Savings and Financial Markets: The Role of Contractual Savings Institutions

Contractual savings (the assets of pension funds and life insurance companies) have been growing at much faster rates than gross domestic product (GDP) in many developed countries (for example, the Netherlands, the United Kingdom, the United States, and Switzerland) and developing countries (for example, Chile, Malaysia, Singapore, and South Africa) over the past twenty to thirty years (see table 16-1). The institutionalization of savings by pension funds and life insurance companies is bound to develop further in the future, as demographic trends push countries to reform their pension systems in order to increase the funding ratio of mandatory pension systems and to encourage voluntary long-term savings plans through private pension funds and life insurance instruments.[1]

Although the primary function of these institutions is to provide sufficient, sustainable, and affordable retirement income and survivor benefits, recent work by Impávido, Musalem, and Tressel suggests that the spillovers on the financial system are significant by changing the composition of

We are grateful to Gaston Gelos, Robert Litan, Jorge Roldos, and participants at the Future of Domestic Capital Markets in Developing Countries conference for their comments. All remaining errors are ours.

1. Poterba and Samwick (1995) provide empirical evidence of institutionalization of savings in the United States. They notice how the principal postwar trend in ownership has been a decline in stock owned by households directly and an increase in stock owned through various financial intermediaries.

Table 16-1. *Assets of Contractual Savings Institutions as a Percentage of GDP in Select Countries, 1970–2000*

Country and type of asset	*1970*[a]	*1980*[a]	*1990*	*2000*
Chile	n.a.	1.10	29. 94	67.49
Life	n.a.	n.a.	5.59	16.58
Pension	n.a.	1.10	24.35	50.91
Malaysia	18.00	20.12	44.29	64.18
Life	n.a.	3.07	5.97	11.14
Pension	n.a.	17.05	38.32	53.04
Singapore	17.00	41.15	117.86	78.11
Life	2.81	6.16	11.17	21.64
Pension	14.19	34.99	106.69	56.47
South Africa	40.00	39.27	78.13	134.92
Life	n.a.	17.20	43.94	79.63
Pension	n.a.	22.07	34.19	55.29
Netherlands	45.00	66.90	108.11	182.82
Life	n.a.	21.13	36.06	67.62
Pension	n.a.	45.77	72.05	115.20
United Kingdom	43.00	38.81	86.91	176.57
Life	n.a.	17.77	36.87	91.57
Pension	n.a.	21.04	50.04	85.00
United States	40.00	43.31	69.20	99.79
Life	n.a.	17.72	25.85	29.89
Pension	n.a.	25.59	43.35	69.90
Switzerland	51.00	70.00	88.51	162.74
Life	n.a.	n.a.	32.29	60.74
Pension	n.a.	n.a.	56.22	102.00

Source: For Chile, data from the Superintendencia de Administradoras de Fondos de Pensiones and Superintendencia de Valores y Seguros 2002. For Malaysia, data from Employees Provident Fund and Life and General Insurance Funds 2002. For Singapore, data from Employees Provident Fund and Monetary Authority of Singapore 2002. For South Africa, data from South Africa Reserve Bank 2002; OECD (2001, 2002). For 1970, data are from Davis (1995).

n.a. Not available.

a. Prior to 1990, the data do not include the funds invested directly by individual workers in housing and other approved assets.

financial flows in favor of securities markets, thus modifying firms' financing patterns and banks' balance sheets.[2] Recent evidence shows that domestic securities markets are increasingly important sources of funding for the corporate sector as well as for the public sector.[3] This suggests that the

2. Impávido, Musalem, and Tressel (2002a, 2002b, 2003).

3. The Global Financial Stability Report of the International Monetary Fund (2003) shows that there has been a surge of local corporate bond issuance in Asia and Latin America, particularly in

development of contractual savings institutions can be a "pull" as well as a "push" factor of financial globalization.

These works also show that the impact of contractual savings institutions depends on the characteristics of the financial system as well as on the transparency and regulations of securities markets. This implies that governments aiming to encourage contractual savings plans should take into account these factors when providing incentives to invest in equities or bonds. Specifically, contractual savings should be encouraged to invest in equities when disclosure rules and corporate governance are adequate. In the context of a financially integrated world economy, domestic governance, transparency, and the degree of domestic financial development are indeed crucial for emerging economies to benefit from financial globalization.[4]

This chapter integrates the results of previous research in order to understand the channels through which the institutionalization of savings in the form of contractual savings contributes to financial market development, builds an economy more resilient to interest rates and demand shocks, and potentially stimulates economic growth.

This chapter has five sections. The first section analyzes the impact of contractual savings on the national saving rate. The second discusses how the development of contractual savings stimulates the development of securities markets. The third discusses how contractual savings improve the risk management of firms, while the fourth deals with the impact on banks. The discussion is based on the results obtained in papers written by Impávido, Musalem, and Tressel on a sample of developed and emerging economies.[5] These papers generate robust empirical evidence, and the results are consistent across the sectors covered in the papers, providing further support for our conclusions. The fifth section is devoted to policy recommendations and concludes.

Contractual Savings and National Saving

A key channel through which the development of contractual savings might contribute to improved economic performance and higher eco-

2000–01. Moreover, local bond markets have been the dominant source of funding for the public sector in all regions.

4. Prasad and others (2003) provide evidence that the quality of domestic institutions plays a role in the ability of a country to increase the benefits and control the risks of financial globalization.

5. Impávido, Musalem, and Tressel (2002a, 2002b, 2003).

nomic growth is the encouragement of a higher rate of national saving. Higher aggregate saving leads to higher growth by establishing a greater pool of resources available for productive investment.[6] What is less clear is whether changes in contractual savings translate into changes in aggregate savings.

The theoretical literature on the question is ambiguous. On the one hand, pension reforms that simply replace one form of voluntary saving with another are unlikely to affect household saving, since households will simply substitute one form of saving for another one. Moreover, even if pension funds offer greater (long-term) returns than other saving instruments, the effect of a higher real return on saving is ambiguous, as the income effect might offset the substitution effect. But there are other reasons for supposing that the development of pension funds might stimulate household saving. To the extent that participation in retirement plans is mandatory, individuals will save more than they would otherwise.[7] This is particularly true of individuals with low incomes, who may face binding borrowing constraints and therefore be unable to offset the impact of additional forced saving on consumption. Furthermore, even if participation is voluntary, the development of funded pension schemes may well raise awareness among the general population of the need to save for retirement, leading to a "recognition effect" that could stimulate household saving.

The short-run impact of pension fund development on aggregate saving depends primarily on government policy and, in particular, on how the government decides to finance the transition from a pay-as-you-go pension system to a partially or fully funded system.[8] If current unfunded liabilities are financed through debt, the short-run impact will be neutral, as the implicit debt of the pay-as-you-go system is transformed into an explicit liability. If, on the other hand, this transitional cost is financed via adjustments in the nonpension budget—through either increases in taxation or reductions in other expenditures—there may be an increase in national saving. In particular, in the presence of credit constraints, or if prior saving

6. Another channel is the allocative efficiency of a given pool of savings that is fostered by more efficient financial systems. See Levine (1997) for a survey of the role of the financial system in stimulating growth. See also Schmidt-Hebbel and Serven (1999).

7. Bailliu and Reisen (2000).

8. See, for instance, Holzmann (1997).

was motivated by precautionary rather than life-cycle reasons, agents will be unwilling to reduce their saving in response to a transition tax.[9]

Furthermore, if the government decides to encourage voluntary contractual savings plans through income tax incentives, the effect on national saving would depend primarily on the government's fiscal stance. A positive effect on aggregate saving would require that the reduction in income tax revenue be compensated either through increases in other tax revenues or through reductions in expenditures.

Several empirical studies attempt to assess more directly the impact of different types of pension systems on private saving. For example, Dayal-Gulati and Thimann conclude from a study of a sample of Southeast Asian and Latin American countries over the period 1975–95 that fully funded systems can be expected to increase saving provided that early withdrawals are prohibited.[10] Similarly, Samwick finds that developing countries that shift from a pay-as-you-go to a funded system tend, over time, to experience an increase in saving even though the initial impact of such reforms may be negative.[11] He also finds that countries that operate unfunded, pay-as-you-go systems tend to have lower saving rates, with the magnitude of the effect increasing with the degree of coverage of the system.[12]

Bailliu and Reisen use panel data, covering ten countries over the period 1982–93, to measure the effect of pension fund assets on saving.[13] They find a statistically significant effect among developing countries but none among developed countries. However, the positive relationship between pension funds and the national saving rate is weakly robust.

Finally, the development of contractual savings institutions is not likely to affect national saving via financial deepening. Indeed, as Loayza, Schmidt-Hebbel, and Serven show, private saving rates are highly autocorrelated and are not significantly associated with financial deepening.[14]

9. On credit constraints, see, for instance, Cifuentes and Valdes-Prieto (1996). On life-cycle reasons, see Samwick (1998a).

10. Dayal-Gulati and Thimann (1997).

11. Samwick (1998b).

12. With a larger sample that includes developed countries as well, Samwick (2000) finds little evidence that countries implementing defined-contribution reforms have higher trends in saving rates after the reform. However, cross-sectionally, countries with pay-as-you-go systems tend to have lower saving rates, and this effect increases with the coverage rate of the system. Recent additional single-case studies include those of Coronado (2002) on Chile, Loayza and Shankar (1998) on India, and Burnside (1998) on Mexico.

13. Bailliu and Reisen (2000).

14. Loayza, Schmidt-Hebbel, and Serven (2000).

Contractual Savings and Securities Markets

There is also a rapidly expanding literature on the role of contractual savings in promoting financial market development.[15] As seen in figure 16-1, the financial assets of contractual savings institutions are larger than money plus quasi-money (M2) in about half of the sample, including Chile and South Africa.

Contractual savings institutions affect securities markets through different channels. First, their development provides an institutional framework favoring the accumulation of long-term capital. For instance, the existence of transaction costs in capital markets, the ability to diversify risk, and the long-term commitments of contractual savings institutions explain why they may be more willing to hold long-term securities than individual investors and require lower risk and liquidity premiums.[16] By increasing the demand for long-term financial assets, contractual savings could thus promote the development of securities markets.[17]

Next, whether the development of contractual savings stimulates further the demand for securities—and in turn stimulates supply by lowering issuance costs—will depend on the supervisory and regulatory mechanisms, fostered by transparent accounting practices, among other factors. Moreover, contractual savings institutions, because of their size, have the potential to enhance market discipline and promote the interests of minority shareholders of the firms in which they invest.

Finally, the development of contractual savings institutions may have an indirect impact on domestic financial markets. For instance, it may signal a sound and stable domestic financial system to foreign investors, hence leading to significant cross-border transactions of securities.[18] On the con-

15. This suggests that the development of contractual savings institutions may have an indirect positive effect on growth. Indeed, there is a substantial literature on the relationship between financial market development and economic growth. It is now accepted that capital market development exerts a strong and independent influence on growth by raising capital accumulation and productivity (Demirgüç-Kunt and Levine 1996; Levine and Zervos 1996; Neusser and Kugler 1998). A more detailed discussion of this topic can be found in Catalán, Impávido, and Musalem (2000); Blommestein (2001); Blommestein and Funke (1998); Davis and Steil (2001); Impávido, Musalem, and Tressel (2002a, 2002b, 2003); Reisen (2000); Vittas (1999).

16. Contrary to contractual savings institutions, mutual funds and other investment funds prefer liquid financial assets.

17. Allen and Santomero (1997) argue that the institutionalization of saving is strongly associated with the development of capital markets over the past twenty years.

18. For instance, pension funds hardly invest in stocks in Malaysia, Singapore, and Switzerland, all countries with large contractual savings and stock markets.

Figure 16-1. *Share of Financial Assets of Contractual Savings Institutions and M2 in Total Assets of Contractual Savings Institutions plus M2, by Country, 2000*[a]

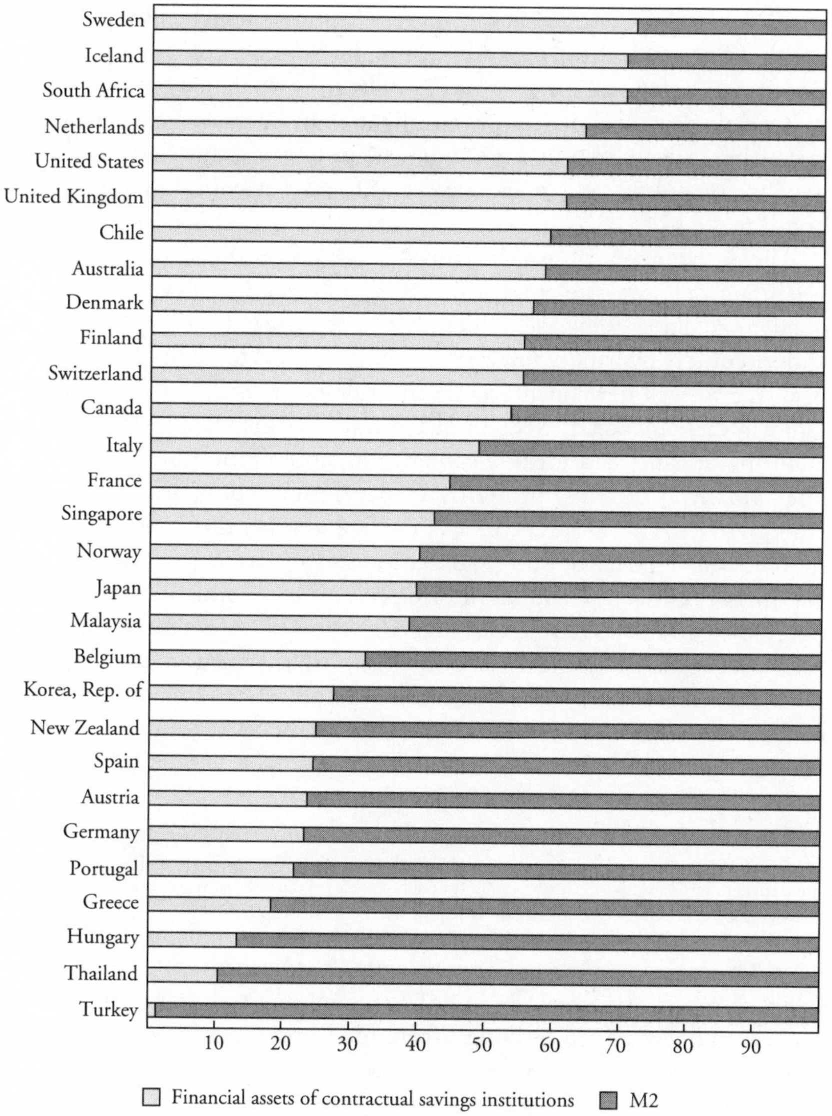

a. Since the financial assets of contractual savings institutions include deposits, one should, in principle, subtract these deposits from M2 (money plus quasi-money). This correction would increase the relative share of the financial assets of contractual savings and decrease the other component.

trary, the development of domestic financial markets is less stimulated when contractual savings institutions invest a larger proportion of their funds abroad.[19]

The development of securities markets also is stimulated if the additional demand of contractual savings institutions is matched by additional supply of government debt. Indeed, the development of contractual savings creates a demand for long-term public debt (matched by the issuance of bonds instead of short-term instruments), which provides a benchmark for setting interest rates and eventually helps to build the yield curve. The issuance of public debt may, however, crowd out equity and corporate bond markets.

The development of securities markets may, in turn, affect the access of small and medium-size enterprises (SME) to financial services. In developed financial systems, debt finance is a specialized activity performed almost entirely by banks, and SMEs have full access to bank credit in great part due to well-developed accounting rules and legal and judiciary systems. In these markets, SMEs also have access to financial services through factoring, leasing, and venture capital companies. However, in less developed financial systems, primarily in developing countries, SMEs have either restricted or no access to bank credit and other financial services due to lower legal and accounting standards, less supportive judiciary systems, and higher transaction and monitoring costs.[20] As a consequence, SMEs in developing countries have access to credit from the corporate sector, either exclusively or as a complement to institutionalized financial services. This is particularly the case of industrial structures where large corporations operate in collaboration with a large number of SMEs and the linkages between them are quite strong, involving supply of inputs, purchase of output, quality control, technology transfer, and financing.

Overall, there are many reasons why one would expect to observe substantial heterogeneity across countries' experiences, as indeed is observed. This may have implications for the macroeconomic impact of contractual savings development, specifically its impact on economic growth. As the development of contractual savings shifts financial intermediation from banks to capital markets, one could argue that it also shifts resources from higher- to lower-return activities (from SME to corporate sector projects,

19. However, restricting the foreign investments of contractual savings for the sole purpose of stimulating the domestic financial system is likely to be counterproductive; see Impávido, Musalem, and Vittas (2002) for a discussion.

20 See Beck, Demirgüç-Kunt, and Maksimovic (2002); Berger, Klapper, and Udell (2001).

if SMEs indeed have greater returns); hence the impact on growth would be negative. However, in developing countries there are strong financial linkages between SMEs and the corporate sector. Furthermore, in competitive financial systems, banks and factoring, leasing, and venture capital companies are able to capture funds in the capital market by issuing bonds or by offering attractive deposit rates to contractual savings institutions. This would enable them to maintain the flow of finance to SMEs. Furthermore, to the extent that contractual savings development would increase the availability of long-term funds to financial intermediaries, they, in turn, would be able to allocate a higher proportion of their loan portfolio in long-term credit to the enterprise sector without themselves undertaking excessive term transformation risks. In fact, the analysis conducted by Impávido, Musalem, and Tressel shows that the share of short-term loans in banks' loan portfolios decreases when contractual savings institutions develop.[21] Furthermore, in bank-based systems, the share of long-term debt to total debt in the corporate sector increases when contractual savings institutions develop.[22] Finally, the lengthening maturity of debt is likely to imply a shift of resources from low-return, short-term projects to higher-return, long-term projects, thus fostering growth.[23]

The most recent and robust analysis of the impact of contractual savings on securities markets is derived from the latest work of Impávido, Musalem, and Tressel.[24] It is based on panel data and focuses on the short-term dynamics of stock market depth, liquidity, and bond market depth.[25] The main results are as follows.

When we control for several sources of bias that may affect the correlation between financial market variables and the development of contractual savings,[26] the institutionalization of savings is associated with the deepening of stock and bond markets.

There is evidence of substantial heterogeneity across countries. First, the development of contractual savings is associated with an increase in stock market depth in countries that structurally rely more on stock market

21. Impávido, Musalem, and Tressel (2002b).

22. Impávido, Musalem, and Tressel (2002a).

23. If more productive projects are less liquid, an increase in the availability of long-term capital should, on average, increase the returns of projects.

24. Impávido, Musalem, and Tressel (2003).

25. Market depth and liquidity are defined as market capitalization and value traded relative to gross domestic product, respectively. Bond market capitalization is the value of bonds outstanding (the aggregate of public and private bonds).

26. In particular, we control for the level of development, measured with income per capita.

finance,[27] and it is associated with an increase in bond market depth in countries that structurally rely more on bank finance. Second, contractual savings development leads to an increase in stock market depth and stock market liquidity in countries in which pension contributions are mandatory, while these two effects are less clear in countries in which pension contributions are voluntary. Third, the impact on stock market depth is significant when cross-border transactions in securities are not too large. Finally, structural features of the securities market, such as transparency, also matter: the impact of contractual savings is greater in countries with better accounting standards.

The impact of contractual savings on the short-term dynamics of securities markets is not explained by other structural characteristics of the economies, such as the overall level of development, openness to trade, legal environment, and demographic structure. This result can be interpreted as evidence that policy decisions that shape the evolution of contractual savings institutions do matter and that the impact of contractual savings on securities markets is not due solely to slow-moving country characteristics.

Accordingly, we conclude that contractual savings institutions have an independent and positive impact on securities market development,[28] which may have indirect positive effects on economic growth. However, even in bank-based financial systems, contractual savings institutions may have a positive impact on growth by (a) lengthening debt maturities and flattening the yield curve, which enable the undertaking of higher-return, long-term projects, and by (b) developing the bond market and the yield curve, which are keys to financial sector innovation and development.

Contractual Savings Institutions and the Mitigation of Firms' Financial Risks

This section focuses on the channels through which contractual savings institutions mitigate firms' financial risks. Assessing whether the development of institutional investors reduces the vulnerability of firms to various

27. Using macroeconomic indicators of financial development, Demirgüç-Kunt and Levine (1999) classify countries in two subgroups: (a) economies with bank-based financial structures and (b) economies with market-based financial structures. Our results are based on their classification.

28. Davis and Steil (2001) also find that the institutionalization of saving is associated with larger stock markets and larger financial systems.

shocks has important implications because the resulting reduction in the cost of capital is likely to foster investment and growth.

In the recent context of currency and financial crisis associated with asset-liability mismatch in the balance sheets of banks and firms and excessive reliance on (foreign currency–denominated) short-term debt,[29] there is a growing consensus about the need to evaluate whether the presence of domestic institutional investors tends to reduce the vulnerability of banks, firms, and other economic agents to interest rate variations and other shocks. In a more general context, Caprio and Demirgüç-Kunt show that the lack of long-term finance in emerging economies is not totally explained by the characteristics of banks and firms.[30] The institutional environment and macroeconomic factors affect significantly the supply of long-term finance.

Determinants of Firms' Financing Patterns

In a world of asymmetric information, the financial institutions and legal environment shape the capital structures of firms, leading to systematic differences across countries.[31] To the extent that contractual savings institutions may modify the set of information available to all investors, push for compliance with transparency rules and legal rights, or simply modify the relative supply of different securities, one should indeed expect to observe significant cross-country differences associated with contractual savings' characteristics. In particular, the effects would be minimal if contractual savings institutions invest primarily in government debt.

Impávido, Musalem, and Tressel emphasize informational issues and refinancing risks.[32] Their work provides a simple framework in which firms choose the debt maturity and can also issue equity. It discusses the potential benefits associated with the development of stock markets and the nature of investors in a framework in which banks may be subject to term transformation risks. In particular, the model suggests that the develop-

29. See, for instance, Aghion, Banerjee, and Piketty (1999); Aghion, Bacchetta, and Banerjee (2000); Rodrik and Velasco (1999) for theoretical models of monetary policies in such a context.

30. Caprio and Demirgüç-Kunt (1997).

31. Demirgüç-Kunt and Levine (1999); Demirgüç-Kunt and Maksimovic (1996a, 1996b, 1999); La Porta and others (1998). See Shleifer and Vishny (1997) for a survey on corporate governance; see La Porta and others (1998) for the impact of the legal environment on external finance.

32. More specifically, Impávido, Musalem, and Tressel (2002a) develop a model focusing on adverse selection issues and the role of private information in the credit relationship.

ment of contractual savings institutions may affect firms' financing choices if it (a) leads to an increase in the supply of long-term debt, (b) reduces equity rationing, and (c) fosters information disclosure and better corporate governance mechanisms on the stock market. More generally, the framework predicts that the equilibrium capital structures of firms will be a function of (a) their characteristics (for example, maturity of assets, profitability, risks, asymmetry of information), (b) the efficiency of the financial system (for instance, in generating—ex ante and interim—private and public information), and (c) the supply of funds to capital markets that depend on the nature of investors.

The empirical analysis assesses the impact of the development of contractual savings institutions on firms' capital structures. It focuses on (a) the choice between debt and equity and (b) the maturity structure of debt. Three sets of explanatory variables explain firms' financing patterns: firms' characteristics, macroeconomic factors, and financial system characteristics. Hence we have:

Capital structure = *F* (firms' characteristics; macroeconomic factors; financial system characteristics).

FIRMS' CHARACTERISTICS. The following firms' characteristics are controlled for: (1) the market-to-book ratio, as a proxy for Tobin's Q, (2) the ratio of net fixed assets to total assets, (3) the ratio of net sales to total assets, (4) size, (5) profitability, and (6) firm-level risk.[33]

33. First, regarding the market-to-book ratio and in accord with Myers's theory of underinvestment (Myers 1977), Barclay and Smith (1995) show that firms with more growth options in their set of investment opportunities have less long-term debt in their capital structure because stockholders have incentives to reject profitable investments when they have to share their benefits with debt holders. Myers argues that, for a given indebtedness, this incentive problem can be mitigated by shortening the maturity of debt. Second, regarding the ratio of net fixed to total assets, theories of lending under asymmetric information show that the debt capacity of a firm depends on the availability of collateral. Moreover, Stohs and Mauer (1996) show that firms in the United States match the maturity of assets and liabilities, as suggested by Hart and Moore (1994), but this is also the case if firms try to limit the risks of illiquidity. Third, regarding the ratio of net sales to total assets, as argued by Demirgüç-Kunt and Maksimovic (1999), a high ratio of net sales to total assets may signal a need for short-term financing. Fourth, regarding size, the size of the firm may be an important determinant of firms' indebtedness. A positive correlation between leverage and size is expected if the size is a proxy for the public information and the reputation of the firm. A similar correlation is expected with the debt maturity. Fifth, regarding profitability, several studies—Rajan and Zingales (1995) for developed economies and Demirgüç-Kunt and Maksimovic (1996b) for emerging countries—have found a negative correlation between profitability and leverage. Finally, regarding firm-level risk, risk considerations seem to be important determinants of corporate financing decisions (Graham and Harvey 2001). The risk control variable *at the firm level* is defined as the ratio of the standard deviation of earnings and the average of earnings over the period (in absolute value).

MACROECONOMIC FACTORS. Various macroeconomic factors may affect firms' financing patterns. More developed economies have, in general, more efficient institutions and better compliance with the legal system in general and with investor rights, accounting standards, and transparency rules (on the stock market) in particular. The inflation rate is an indicator of the government's management of the economy and whether long-term contracting is likely to be widespread.[34] Two other control variables for asset market conditions are the real interest rate and the cost of equity. Finally, the volatility of inflation is a proxy for macroeconomic instability.

FINANCIAL SYSTEM CHARACTERISTICS. The financing patterns of firms, especially their access to external finance, depend on the characteristics of the financial system.[35] This, in turn, affects the ability of firms to reach a higher rate of growth than the one permitted by their internal resources.[36] The stock market and banking sector variables provide a control group guaranteeing that the contractual savings variables are not simply a proxy for the level of development of the financial system.[37]

34. It also characterizes the opportunity cost of holding money. Debt contracts may be specified in nominal terms. So the authors expect a negative correlation between the rate of inflation and firms' indebtedness, if this supply effect dominates.

35. Carlin and Mayer (1999); Demirgüç-Kunt and Maksimovic (1996b, 1999); Rajan and Zingales (1998).

36. See Beck and others (2000) for a synthetic approach.

37. First, the size of the stock market is measured by the stock market capitalization (in percentage of gross domestic product). The ability of the stock market to provide risk diversification opportunities and information also depends on its level of activity and liquidity (Levine and Zervos 1998). Greater liquidity will indeed encourage investors to acquire stakes in risky firms (and make efficient restructuring decisions)—see Maug (1998) for a theoretical argument—and will enhance information acquisition by large investors (Holmstrom and Tirole 1993). Greater informational content of prices will improve the efficiency of capital allocation. Moreover, better public information may have a spillover effect on the long-term debt market by reducing initial informational asymmetries. Activity on the stock market is measured by the total value traded in proportion to stock market capitalization. Second, banks have a comparative advantage in acquiring private information on borrowers and in monitoring their actions. A sound and efficient banking sector is obviously essential for firms, especially those that do not have access to capital markets. The use of short-term debt reduces the scope for opportunistic behavior, thus reducing the cost of monitoring. But the implication for the debt maturity of firms is not clear. A developed banking system implies lower monitoring costs in general. This will lead to an increase in the supply of short-term debt, but also in the supply of long-term debt in the sense that long-term debt will be able to finance more projects. The overall impact may be negative or positive. Moreover, monitoring per se is not the only issue. The market structure of the banking sector (that is, the degree of competition among banks and the indirect competition from other financial institutions) will have an impact on the lending behavior of banks. For instance, greater information disclosure on the stock market and in general easier outside options for firms will affect the lending behavior of banks: their ex post informational rent may be reduced, which may reduce their ex ante incentive to invest in information (see Stulz 2000). On the contrary, greater information disclosure and

CONTRACTUAL SAVINGS INSTITUTIONS. The study measures the development and investment behavior of contractual savings institutions by their size relative to capital markets. It is defined as the ratio of the financial assets of contractual savings institutions to market capitalization plus total bonds outstanding. There are two motivations for this variable: (a) it grasps, although imperfectly, the relative importance of contractual savings as a provider of finance relative to total supply of long-term finance, and (b) it partially corrects for movements in the price of shares that may introduce a spurious correlation between the firm-level variable and this explanatory variable.[38]

The Empirical Analysis

Impávido, Musalem, and Tressel agree that endogeneity may be an issue in their analysis. However, they argue that the simultaneity bias may be small given the variables considered.[39]

---

better accounting standards associated with capital market development are likely to increase the supply of bank credit by limiting managerial slack. Activity of the banking sector is measured by total credit to the private sector as a percentage of gross domestic product.

38. Consider, for instance, an exogenous rise in stock prices. Then the value of contractual savings assets and stock market capitalization will increase, implying a correlation that has no economic meaning. Similarly, this may also introduce a negative correlation with firms' debt-equity ratio. This effect is likely to be stronger when measuring firm equity by the market value of the firm. Still, in principle, a negative (but presumably weaker) correlation may remain because firms are sensitive to their market value when they decide to issue new shares. Pagano, Panetta, and Zingales (1998) show, for instance, that initial public offerings are partly motivated by stock overvaluation in the industry in which the firm operates. Finally, the behavior of contractual savings institutions may significantly depend on their investments. For instance, they will have greater incentive to invest actively in the stock market when they hold a large share of their assets in stocks; conversely, explanations favoring corporate governance issues are less likely to be relevant in countries in which contractual savings hardly invest in the stock market. It is likely that the incentive for contractual savings institutions to be active minority shareholders is positively correlated with the proportion of shares in the portfolio of contractual savings institutions. Therefore, this variable aims at capturing cross-country and time-series differences in the behavior of these institutions.

39. See Impávido, Musalem, and Tressel (2002a). The size and characteristics of the financial system may indeed evolve to respond to the aggregate demand of capital by the corporate sector and the public sector. Moreover, shocks affect the financial sector and the corporate sector simultaneously. For instance, unexpected good news on profit opportunities will increase the demand for external finance by firms, and banks also will tend to offer more loans. Hence, it will increase simultaneously the size of the banking sector and firms' indebtedness. In the case of contractual savings, however, it is less clear why their size is significantly affected by firms' demand for capital, unless one is willing to argue that pension contributions and insurance premiums are significantly affected by the current business environment. Endogeneity may arise because the value of contractual savings assets will move with stock

CONTRACTUAL SAVINGS AND FIRMS' FINANCING PATTERNS. Impávido, Musalem, and Tressel obtain the following results.[40] First, after controlling for firms' characteristics, for macroeconomic factors, and for financial system characteristics, the level of development of contractual savings institutions is positively correlated with leverage and with the maturity of debt. The mechanism seems to work through an increase in long-term debt relative to equity and long-term debt relative to short-term debt. These results tend to support the hypothesis of an independent impact of contractual savings development on leverage. Moreover, the development of contractual savings institutions seems to foster the use of long-term debt.

Furthermore, an increase in the proportion of financial assets invested in shares is associated with a decrease in corporate leverage. It also leads to a decrease in short-term debt relative to equity. This set of results is consistent with the claim that the investment behavior of contractual savings institutions matters for corporate financing patterns. The investment decisions of contractual savings institutions have a significant impact on firms' capital structure: for instance, if contractual savings institutions had had the same investment behavior in Korea as in South Africa (where institutions invested 44 percent of their financial assets in shares on average over the period, compared to 12 percent in Korea), the debt-equity ratio of Korean firms would have decreased from 4.9 to a range of between 3.9 and 4.6.

Overall these results strongly suggest that (a) any attempt to understand cross- and within-country variations in corporate financing patterns needs to assess the role of nonbank financial intermediaries such as institutional

market capitalization of the firm. The authors provide three controls for this source of simultaneity bias. First, firms' net worth is measured at their book value; second, the ratio of contractual savings financial assets to market capitalization variable should, in principle, partially correct for price movements; finally, the stock market capitalization variable should capture these effects. Portfolio decisions will, of course, depend on the relative returns of the different assets; for this reason, the asset allocation of pension funds may be endogenous. However, the authors expect this endogeneity problem to be limited because (a) price movements affecting the corporate financing patterns should be captured in the stock market capitalization variable; (b) investment regulations may be binding, especially in developing countries (see, for instance, Srinivas and Yermo 1999); and (c) in many developed economies, implicit limits or strong (conservative) asset management traditions may be as important as relative returns in determining the allocation of assets when return differentials are not too large. (For instance, in the case of Germany, it seems difficult to attribute the 2.77 percent of equity in total financial assets to low stock returns relative to other assets.)

40. Impávido, Musalem, and Tressel (2002a).

investors and that (b) policy interventions that remove binding constraints on portfolios may have sizable effects on the pattern of corporate sector financing.

The results displayed in the next section shed light on the channels through which contractual savings institutions affect corporate financing choices. They provide a basis for better-targeted policy interventions.

MACROECONOMIC FINANCIAL CHANNELS. Impávido, Musalem, and Tressel use the classification of macroeconomic financial structures developed by Demirgüç-Kunt and Levine.[41] Countries are divided in two subgroups: (a) economies with bank-based financial structures and (b) economies with market-based financial structures. This classification is constructed using a large set of indicators for size, activity, and efficiency of the banking sector and the stock market. It provides a rough evaluation of whether savings are channeled to productive activities mainly through the banking system or through the stock market.[42] Therefore, this is a relevant classification for our purposes: in market-based economies, for instance, the contractual savings industry accounts for 46 percent of the size of long-term capital markets, and equity investments are 31 percent of total financial assets and 29 percent of stock market capitalization; in bank-based economies, the same figures are, respectively, 22, 12, and 12 percent. Therefore, the contractual savings industry is less developed in bank-based countries than in market-based countries. Moreover, pension funds and life insurance companies invest significantly less on the stock market in bank-based economies than in market-based economies.

This classification is used in order to disentangle different channels through which contractual savings institutions affect firms' capital structure by identifying different impacts on firms' leverage and debt maturity. Despite the lack of information on the maturity of debt instruments held by contractual savings institutions, the authors break their assets into two categories—(a) bills and bonds and (b) loans—for a significant number of countries. In market-based economies, bills and bonds represent 43 percent of total financial assets, and loans represent only 14 percent. In bank-based economies, the same figures are, respectively, 45 and 32 percent. On

41. Demirgüç-Kunt and Levine (1999); Impávido, Musalem, and Tressel (2002a).

42. Beck and others (2000) show that the financial structure does not explain economic growth and reliance on external financing after controlling for the level of financial development. Our point is not inconsistent with their claim: our result is not normative in the sense that we do not claim that one financial structure dominates from a welfare point of view: we simply show that financial channels differ across countries and that this classification is useful for this purpose.

average, the lower equity investments in bank-based economies are explained mainly by the higher proportion of loans in their portfolio.

The relative importance of pension funds and life insurance companies differs in the two groups of countries. Pension funds account, on average, for 30 and 20 percent of the total financial assets of contractual savings institutions, respectively, in market-based and bank-based economies. In particular, Anglo-Saxon and continental Europe exhibit strongly different contractual savings industries. Pension funds hold 70, 54, and 50 percent of the financial assets of contractual savings institutions, respectively, in the United States, the United Kingdom, and Australia. In Germany, Italy, and France, the figures are 12, 37, and less than 1 percent.

The results are the following. First, in market-based economies, the choice of contractual savings portfolio has a strongly significant impact on the financing patterns of firms: an increase in equity investments by contractual savings leads to a decline in leverage, and its effect is economically large. The impact of contractual savings development is somewhat weaker, although it affects leverage in a similar way. Debt maturity is also negatively correlated either with the level of development of contractual savings or with the proportion of equity investments in the portfolio of contractual savings. These results are consistent with intuition. As contractual savings are large in these countries on average, it is likely that their marginal effect on firms' financing patterns goes through their investment choices rather than through an increase in their size.[43] As they increase their equity holdings, firms tend to substitute equity finance for debt finance. These results suggest that banks and institutional investors are indirect competitors. The fall in the maturity of debt may be attributed partly to the fact that banks concentrate on their core activity, which is short-term lending.

Second, in the case of bank-based economies, firms' capital structures are affected through noticeably different channels. The dominant effect is the level of development of the contractual savings industry, while asset allocation hardly affects firms' capital structure. The no-correlation result with the portfolio variable makes sense: because the investment of contractual savings institutions in equity is no more than 12 percent of stock market capitalization, a change in their behavior is very unlikely to affect significantly the aggregate corporate financing choices. Hence, the level of

43. More precisely, it seems that the characteristics of contractual savings portfolios are more important than the size of share holdings relative to stock market capitalization. This result favors a corporate governance explanation.

development of the contractual savings industry has a positive effect on leverage and a positive effect on the maturity of debt. These results suggest that the channel through which contractual savings affect the patterns of corporate financing does not go through the stock market. Indeed, contractual savings development is associated with an increase in debt finance—and an increase in debt maturity. As explained above, it is very unlikely that this can be explained by higher investments in bonds in bank-based economies than in market-based economies. Rather the explanation is likely to be related to loans: either (a) contractual savings institutions lend directly to the productive sector or (b) they complement the banking sector. More specifically, by reducing the risk of liquidity in the banking system, they may increase the incentive of banks to issue more long-term loans in proportion to total loans.

SUMMARY. The development of contractual savings institutions, as well as their portfolio decisions, is significantly associated with firms' financing patterns across and within countries and after controlling for firms' characteristics and macroeconomic determinants. The empirical results are consistent with the comparative advantage of contractual savings institutions in the supply of long-term finance to the corporate sector.

Moreover, contractual savings affect the financing decisions of firms through various channels. In bank-based economies, the development of contractual savings is associated with an increase in firms' leverage and maturity of debt. In market-based economies, instead, the asset allocation affects firms' leverage: an increase in the proportion of shares in the portfolio of contractual savings is associated with a decrease in firms' leverage. These results suggest that there might be an efficiency gain at the firm level: an increase in the array of external financing possibilities is associated with increased maturity of firms' liabilities.

Increased maturity of the corporate sector's liabilities should strengthen its resilience to various shocks (such as refinancing risks and bankruptcy risks). The impact goes through several possible channels; in market-based economies, the main effect seems to be through the stock market and equity finance. In bank-based economies, it seems to be through the supply of long-term bank loans or through the bond market.

The results of this section and the analysis describing the impact of contractual savings on securities markets have important policy implications. They show that public intervention encouraging the development of contractual savings will benefit the corporate sector. However, both sets of results clearly imply that the decision to encourage investments in equities (or bonds) depends on the financial structure of the economy and the adequacy of information disclosure, accounting rules, and general regulation of securities markets. Equity investment should be encouraged, relative to bonds, when security markets are more transparent; conversely, investment in bonds may be more appropriate when regulation of securities markets is still underdeveloped.

Contractual Savings Institutions and Banks' Stability and Efficiency

The broad movement of financial liberalization that started in the early 1980s has deeply modified the functioning of banking systems in many countries. Increased competitive pressures may improve the efficiency of the banking system but also may increase instability when proper regulation and supervision are not set. Surprisingly few studies have analyzed the efficiency, profitability, and balance sheets of banks on a cross-country basis.[44] In particular, whereas financial liberalization often has been associated with competitive pressures from nonbank financial institutions, there has been, to date, no attempt to analyze both empirically and theoretically the interaction between the banking system and other financial institutions (except the stock market) in cross-country regressions.[45]

First, Impávido, Musalem, and Tressel assess the association between the development of contractual savings institutions and the banking system across countries and over time.[46] They evaluate the impact of contractual savings institutions on the pricing and asset structure of banks, after controlling for banks' characteristics, financial sector development, and the macroeconomic environment.

Contractual savings institutions act as competing suppliers of funds; hence competitive pressure on the banking systems may increase, either indirectly or directly, when contractual savings institutions develop. The development of contractual savings institutions will indirectly exert competitive pressures on the banking system because it is associated with the development and liquidity of the capital markets. The cost of issuing secu-

44. See, however, Claessens, Demirgüç-Kunt, and Huizinga (2001); Davis and Tuori (2001); Demirgüç-Kunt and Huizinga (1999a, 1999b).

45. Allen and Santomero (1997) claim that the broad movement toward more market finance that was initiated in the 1980s has led to a greater importance of nonbank financial intermediation.

46. Impávido, Musalem, and Tressel (2002b).

rities will decrease, hence reducing the market power of banks.[47] Moreover, contractual savings institutions may increase the supply of public information on capital markets and have positive spillover effects on banks' monitoring of borrowers. In addition, the development of contractual savings institutions directly increases competitive pressures on the banking system. First, these institutions compete on the saving side.[48] Second, they compete on the lending side, either directly or indirectly, by increasing the demand for securities on the primary markets. Hence, one would expect to observe an impact on banks' behavior. Competition, however, is likely to be two-dimensional. First, competition will be in *price*; thus we would expect a decrease in bank net interest margins as contractual savings institutions develop. Second, banks may modify the *maturity* of their loans. As contractual savings institutions have a comparative advantage in supplying long-term finance,[49] banks may shorten the maturity of their loans. Therefore, one might expect to observe a decrease in the maturity of bank loans.

However, contractual savings institutions may also complement banks. First, as Demirgüç-Kunt and Maksimovic note, banks and stock markets may be complementary.[50] Information disclosure requirements and generally the improved transparency associated with capital market development may stimulate the monitoring activity of banks, lowering the credit risk borne by the banking sector.[51] Bank lending and total profitability may increase as capital markets develop. Second, contractual savings institutions may provide long-term resources to banks, thus reducing the interest rate and liquidity risk in the banking system by limiting the term transformation activity of banks.[52] Therefore, the maturity of bank loans may lengthen if such complementarity effects dominate.

47. Underwriting costs may decrease, as argued by Vittas (1999), and the supply of funds will increase on capital markets. See Rajan (1992), which analyzes the welfare gains of increasing firms' outside financial opportunities. See also Petersen and Rajan (1995).

48. In France, the development of life insurance over the past ten years has implied a significant reallocation of savings from more "classic" banking savings instruments.

49. Contractual savings institutions have long-term liabilities.

50. Demirgüç-Kunt and Maksimovic (1996b). Bank and market finance are complementary also because they finance different segments of the population of firms; see Diamond (1991); Bolton and Freixas (2000), among others.

51. However, the theoretical relation between stock market transparency, liquidity, and monitoring of firms by claimants (banks or investors) is not clear-cut. See Holmstrom and Tirole (1993). Davis (2001) stresses the "multiple avenues" of financial systems by comparing aggregate net flows of bank loans and market debt finance.

52. Following Diamond and Dybvig (1983), systemic risk in the banking system has been identified as a consequence of maturity transformation and the "sequential service" constraint on bank liabil-

The development of contractual savings institutions may increase the stability of the banking system, thus reducing systemic risks that may potentially lead to banking crisis.[53] This is the case if the development of contractual savings institutions reduces the risks borne by the banking sector. First, credit risk may be reduced if the development of contractual savings institutions leads directly or indirectly to an increase in bank monitoring. Second, the development of contractual savings institutions may reduce interest rate risks and liquidity risks associated with the term transformation of assets realized in the banking system. On the one hand, if contractual savings institutions compete with banks, banks may indeed respond to competitive pressures by concentrating on their core comparative advantage (associated with narrow banking, which is their superior ability to monitor firms) and by issuing more short-term loans. Banks will therefore be able to avoid losses caused either by unexpected increases in short-term interest rates or by sudden withdrawals. On the other hand, if contractual savings institutions provide resources to the banking system (either in the form of loans or deposits or in the purchase of securities issued by banks), banks will be less subject to liquidity risks for a given level of long-term assets. They may therefore increase the supply of long-term loans.[54] Finally, the recent crises in emerging economies have stressed the risks associated with short-term capital flows. Excessively volatile capital movements have exacerbated the structural weaknesses of these economies, which were magnified by fragile banking systems.[55] This financial risk is associated with the difficulty (or impossibility) for these economies to borrow abroad in their own currencies and long term. One solution is to deepen the domestic financial system in order to develop domestic sources of long-term finance, which is the comparative advantage of contractual savings.[56]

---

ities; in addition, imperfect information and moral hazard increase this fragility of the banking system (Chen 1999). Freixas and Rochet (1997) provide a guidebook to microeconomic theories of banking.

53. Increased competitive pressures and financial stability are not incompatible. For a recent theoretical analysis, see for instance Koskela and Stenbacka (2000), who show that loan market competition leads to a reduction in lending rates and higher investments without increasing the equilibrium bankruptcy risk of firms. In addition, whether a reduction in term transformation risk in the banking system leads to more- or less-efficient lending decisions is an empirical question.

54. The results of Impávido, Musalem, and Tressel (2002b) are consistent with this assertion.

55. See the recent literature, such as Aghion, Bacchetta, and Banerjee (2000); Caballero and Krishnamurthy (2000); Chang and Velasco (1999); Deckle and Kletzer (2001); Rodrik and Velasco (1999). For empirical analysis, see Demirgüç-Kunt and Detriagache (1997, 1998, 2000); Harwood, Litan, and Pomerleano (1999).

56. See, for instance, Caballero (2001).

Empirical Strategy

Limited evidence is available on the impact of contractual savings institutions on the stability and efficiency of the banking system, given adequate regulation and supervision.[57] Impávido, Musalem, and Tressel make a first step in assessing this impact.[58] More specifically, they analyze (a) profitability, (b) the maturity structure of loans, (c) credit risk, and (d) the structure of liabilities. They assess the association between contractual savings institutions and the following variables: (a) net interest margin, defined as the accounting value of a bank's net interest income over total assets; (b) profitability, defined as profit before taxes over total assets;[59] (c) loan maturity, defined as short-term loans (with maturity less than one year) over total loans; (d) credit risk, proxied by loan loss provisions (over total assets or over total loans); and (e) short-term liabilities, proxied by customer plus short-term funding (over total assets).

The first two variables describe the profitability of banks, hence proxy for their efficiency. The net interest margin variable accounts for banking spreads; the objective is to assess whether the pricing behavior of banks may be affected by the development of contractual savings institutions. The net interest margin is also affected by the credit risk borne by the banks: it is an ex post measure taking into account the *realized* default rate. For these reasons, in subsequent work Impávido, Musalem, and Tressel also use the profit variable that accounts for all sources of bank profits.[60]

The third variable captures the maturity transformation activity realized in the banking system; more specifically, the authors test whether the development of contractual savings institutions has an impact on the maturity of bank loans. In other words, do banks increase or decrease long-term lending when contractual savings institutions develop?

The fourth set of variables aims at describing the credit risk borne by the banks. The authors use two measures: (a) loan loss provisioning over total assets is the relevant variable for understanding the indirect impact of contractual savings on profitability via the reduction in credit risk, and (b) loan loss provisions over total loans roughly describe the risk of the loan portfolio.

57. See Barth, Caprio, and Levine (2001) for an analysis of the prudential regulation of banks; see also Dewatripont and Tirole (1994). Generally, La Porta and others (1997, 1998) claim that laws are important determinants of cross-country differences in firms' choice of external finance.

58. Impávido, Musalem, and Tressel (2002a).

59. See, for instance, Demirgüç-Kunt and Huizinga (1999a, 1999b).

60. Impávido, Musalem, and Tressel (2002a).

The authors use three sets of explanatory variables: (a) banks' characteristics, (b) macroeconomic factors, and (c) financial system characteristics.[61] The second and third sets of characteristics are the same as those in the study discussed earlier in the paper.

Bank-Specific Characteristics

The first bank characteristic is the book value of equity divided by total assets. Recent studies show a positive relationship between bank profitability and capitalization.[62] High capitalization and profitability may indeed reflect a high franchise value.[63] Moreover, well-capitalized banks may face lower bankruptcy risks, thereby reducing their costs of funding. In addition, this variable ensures that loan maturity is not explained by the structure of bank liabilities.

The second variable controlling for the structure of bank liabilities is customer and short-term funding over total assets. It includes all short-term and long-term deposits plus other nondeposit short-term funding. Again, this variable ensures that loan maturity is not driven by the structure of liabilities. This is important insofar as we want to test whether the development of contractual savings institutions has an independent impact on bank loan maturity that is not driven by other bank-specific characteristics.

The study includes two variables describing the structure of bank activities. The first is total loans over total assets. The second is noninterest earnings assets over total assets. Noninterest earnings assets are mainly cash and noninterest earnings deposits at other banks.

Finally, the study controls for overhead expenses, expressed as a percentage of total assets. This implies that differences between net interest margin and profits before taxes are explained by variations in noninterest income (or taxes and provisions for loan losses).

Empirical Results

The data show some interesting dispersion. For example, credit risk seems to be negatively correlated with the development of contractual savings

61. In order to provide comparable results, Impávido, Musalem, and Tressel (2002b) use explanatory variables similar to those used by Demirgüç-Kunt and Huizinga (1999a, 1999b).

62. See, for instance, Demirgüç-Kunt and Huizinga (1999a, 1999b) for cross-country comparisons.

63. Caprio and Summers (1993).

institutions. There are large cross-country differences: the top four countries in terms of credit risk are Hungary (2.36 percent), Argentina (1.56 percent), Thailand (1.18 percent), and Brazil (1.16 percent), while banks face the lowest credit risk in Germany (0.06 percent), Austria (0.10 percent), Belgium (0.21 percent), and Ireland (0.24 percent). The financial assets of contractual savings institutions constitute 4.3 percent of GDP on average in the first group and 29.6 percent on average in the second group. This suggests that the development of contractual savings institutions is likely to explain part of the variation in credit risks across countries.

The econometric analysis confirms that the correlation between the activity of institutional investors and banks' profitability and loan policy is not merely a function of banks' characteristics and other macroeconomic factors. The main results are the following.

There is a logarithmic relation between contractual savings development and net interest margin; this suggests that *the magnitude of the impact depends on the initial development of contractual savings institutions.* The impact is large at low initial levels of development, and it decreases as contractual savings institutions develop. Therefore, the results are consistent with the initial hypothesis that the development of contractual savings institutions is associated with increased competitive pressures in the banking system, leading banks to reduce the spreads between loan and deposit rates.

While banks tend to choose lower spreads when contractual savings institutions are more developed, the total impact on profit is surprisingly positive, and the impact is likely to go through a reduction in credit risk.

The level of development of contractual savings institutions has a positive and significant effect on loan maturity. This suggests that, even if banks seem to face higher competitive pressures when contractual savings institutions develop (thus reducing interest spreads), they do not reduce the maturity of loans (in other words, they do not seem to concentrate on their core activity). On the contrary, there seems to be complementarity between the two institutions when concentrating on the loan maturity dimension.[64]

There is a negative correlation between credit risk borne by the banking system and the level of development of contractual savings institutions. It is worthwhile underlining that this strong result does not reflect cross-

64. For various aspects of the role of long-term finance, see the discussion in Impávido, Musalem, and Tressel (2002b).

country differences, for instance, the level of economic development. This result complements the conclusions of the analysis of firms showing that the corporate sector is more resilient to various shocks when contractual savings institutions are more developed or invest more on the stock exchange.

The development of contractual savings implies a reduction in the short-term liabilities of the banking sector. This result is also consistent with complementarity between banks and contractual savings institutions.

The paper by Impávido, Musalem, and Tressel constitutes a first attempt to assess the interaction between the banking system and contractual savings institutions.[65] The results are consistent with the view that the development of contractual saving is associated with a more efficient banking system. Moreover, these results support the argument that the banking system is more resilient to liquidity and credit risks when contractual savings institutions are more developed. Furthermore, they are consistent with conclusions concerning the financing patterns of firms.[66]

Conclusions and Policy Recommendations

Our analysis is based on recent research on a topic that is not well explored. More analysis is needed to identify the precise channels through which contractual savings institutions interact with the financial system. In particular, country case studies may provide useful insights.

In spite of these restrictions, there is scope for policy recommendations. If demographic, institutional, and political preconditions for pension reforms (or reform of the life insurance industry) are met, policymakers should bear in mind that development of contractual savings instruments is a complex undertaking requiring the synchronization of macroeconomic and financial sector policies. The commitment of the government must be strong in these areas to minimize uncertainties.

First, only countries with sustainable macroeconomic policy frameworks, including low expected inflation rates, will generate the enabling environment for the successful development of long-term saving instruments. This includes budget surpluses, which could be used to absorb the budgetary impact of policies promoting these instruments.

65. Impávido, Musalem, and Tressel (2002b).
66. Impávido, Musalem, and Tressel (2002a).

Second, particular attention should be paid to financial sector development policies that enhance the efficiency of the contractual savings industry as a major provider of noncaptive funds. The regulation, in particular of equity investments, may have a large impact when portfolio limits affect actual investments. Investment regulations should seek to maximize the benefits to plan members. This is achieved by basing regulation on the prudent person rule (maximizing investment returns with due consideration to risks) rather than on picking winners (regulating quantitative portfolio allocations). In addition, policy intervention should be based on a precise evaluation of the interaction between institutional investors and other components of the financial system. For instance, one may want to assess the importance of liberalizing the domestic banking system before undertaking pension reform.

Moreover, adoption of internationally accepted standards on governance, accounting, disclosure, and accountability through effective enforcement mechanisms would enhance financial sector development, including contractual savings. Furthermore, sound contractual savings plans require that funds be segregated as sole property of plan members, be independent from fund managers, and be kept with reputable custodians.

Next, regulations (on foreign investment) should assess the potential effects on the external balance. On the one hand, if the return on foreign financial assets is imperfectly correlated with the return on domestic financial assets, then plan members would benefit from international diversification of the portfolio. However, this should be traded off against potential macroeconomic risks for financing the current account, so that a gradual approach to liberalizing investment could also be considered. Hence a careful assessment of the impact of substantial capital outflows, in the context of an open capital account, caused by the investment of pension funds may be important.

Finally, contractual savings plans deal with future claims on output. To the extent that they promote growth, they facilitate the distribution of future output between active workers and beneficiaries. However, this does not mean that mandatory funded plans should be supported without limit. Excessive mandatory contributions to funded plans may be welfare reducing. The level of mandatory contributions to pension plans should be such as to generate retirement income sufficient to keep people from falling into poverty after retirement and not to pursue other objectives.

References

Aghion, Philippe, Philippe Bacchetta, and Abhijit Banerjee. 2000. "Currency Crisis and Monetary Policy in an Economy with Credit Constraints." CEPR Discussion Paper 2529. London: Centre for Economic Policy Research.

Aghion, Philippe, Abhijit Banerjee, and Thomas Piketty. 1999. "Dualism and Macroeconomic Volatility." *Quarterly Journal of Economics* 114 (4, November): 1359–97.

Allen, Franklin, and Anthony M. Santomero. 1997. "The Theory of Financial Intermediation." *Journal of Banking and Finance* 21 (11-12, December): 1461–85.

Bailliu, Jeannine, and Helmut Reisen. 2000. "Do Funded Pensions Contribute to Higher Aggregate Savings? A Cross-Country Analysis." In Helmut Reisen, ed., *Pensions, Savings, and Capital Flows—From Ageing to Emerging Markets*, pp. 113–31. Paris: Organization for Economic Cooperation and Development.

Barclay, Michael J., and Clifford W. Smith. 1995. "The Maturity Structure of Corporate Debt." *Journal of Finance* 50 (2, June): 609–31.

Barth, James, Gerard Caprio, and Ross Levine. 2001. "Bank Regulation and Supervision: What Works and What Doesn't." Unpublished manuscript. Washington: World Bank.

Beck, Thorsten, Aslı Demirgüç-Kunt, Ross Levine, and Vojislav Maksimovic. 2000. "Financial Structure and Economic Development: Firm, Industry, and Country Evidence." Working Paper 2423. Washington: World Bank.

Beck, Thorsten, Aslı Demirgüç-Kunt, and Vojislav Maksimovic. 2002. *Financial and Legal Constraints to Firm Growth: Does Size Matter?* Policy Research Paper 2784. Washington: World Bank.

Berger, Allen N., Leora F. Klapper, and Gregory F. Udell. 2001. "The Ability of Banks to Lend to Informally Opaque Small Business." *Journal of Banking and Finance* 25 (May): 2127–67.

Blommestein, Hans. 2001. "Ageing, Pension Reform, and Financial Market Implications in the OECD Area." CeRP Working Paper 9/01. Moncalieri, Italy: Centre for Research on Pensions and Welfare Policies.

Blommestein, Hans, and Norbert Funke, eds. 1998. *Institutional Investors in the New Financial Landscape*. Paris: Organization for Economic Cooperation and Development.

Bolton, Patrick, and Xavier Freixas. 2000. "Equity, Bonds, and Bank Debt: Capital Structure and Financial Market Equilibrium under Asymmetric Information." *Journal of Political Economy* 108 (2): 324–51.

Burnside, Craig. 1998. "Private Saving in Mexico, 1980–95." Washington: World Bank. Available at www.worldbank.org/research/projects/savings/mexico.htm [July 2, 2003].

Caballero, Ricardo J. 2001. "Macroeconomic Volatility in Latin America: A View and Three Case Studies." Unpublished manuscript. Massachusetts Institute of Technology.

Caballero Ricardo J., and Arvind Krishnamurthy. 2000. "Dollarization of Liabilities: Underinsurance and Domestic Financial Development." Unpublished manuscript. Massachusetts Institute of Technology.

Caprio, Gerard Jr., and Aslı Demirgüç-Kunt. 1997. "The Role of Long-Term Finance: Theory and Evidence." Washington: World Bank, Policy Research Department.

Caprio, Gerard Jr., and Lawrence Summers. 1993. *Finance and Its Reform, Beyond Laissez-Faire.* Policy Research Paper 1171. Washington: World Bank.

Carlin, Wendy, and Colin Mayer. 1999. "Finance, Investment, and Growth." CEPR Discussion Paper 2233. London: Centre for Economic Policy Research.

Catalán, Mario, Gregorio Impávido, and Alberto R. Musalem. 2000. "Contractual Savings or Stock Market Development: Which Leads?" *Journal of Applied Social Science Studies* 120 (3): 445–87. Also available at wbln0018.worldbank.org/html/FinancialSectorWeb.nsf/(attachmentweb)/wp002421/$FILE/wp002421.pdf [June 18, 2003].

Chang, Roberto, and Andres Velasco. 1999."Liquidity Crisis in Emerging Markets: Theory and Evidence." NBER Working Paper 7272. Cambridge, Mass.: National Bureau of Economic Research.

Chen, Yehning. 1999. "Banking Panics: The Role of the First-Come, First-Served Rule and Information Externalities." *Journal of Political Economy* 107 (5): 946–68.

Cifuentes, Rodrigo, and Salvador Valdes-Prieto. 1996. "Transitions in the Presence of Credit Constraints." In Salvador Valdes-Prieto, ed., *The Economics of Pensions.* Cambridge University Press.

Claessens, Stijn, Aslı Demirgüç-Kunt, and Harry Huizinga. 2001. "How Does Foreign Entry Affect Domestic Bank Markets?" *Journal of Banking and Finance* 25 (5, April): 891–911.

Coronado, Julia Lynn. 2002. "The Effects of Social Security Privatization on Household Saving: Evidence from the Chilean Experience." *Contributions to Economic Analysis and Policy* 1 (1): art. 7.

Davis, E. Philip. 1995. *Pension Funds, Retirement Income Security, and Capital Markets: An International Perspective.* Oxford University Press.

———. 2001. "Multiple Avenues of Intermediation, Corporate Finance, and Financial Stability." IMF Working Paper. Washington: International Monetary Fund.

Davis, E. Philip, and Benn Steil. 2001. *Institutional Investors.* MIT Press.

Davis, E. Philip, and Klaus Tuori. 2001. "The Changing Structure of Banks' Income: An Empirical Investigation." Working Paper 00-11. London: Brunel University.

Dayal-Gulati, Anuradha, and Christian Thimann. 1997. "Saving in South East Asia and Latin America Compared: Searching for Policy Lessons." IMF Working Paper 97/11. Washington: International Monetary Fund.

Deckle, Robert, and Ken Kletzer. 2001. "Domestic Bank Regulation and Financial Crisis: Theory and Empirical Evidence from East Asia." NBER Working Paper 8322. Cambridge, Mass.: National Bureau of Economic Research.

Demirgüç-Kunt, Aslı, and Enrica Detragiache. 1997. "The Determinants of Banking Crisis: Evidence from Developed and Developing Countries." Unpublished manuscript. Washington: World Bank.

———. 1998. "Financial Liberalization and Financial Fragility." Unpublished manuscript. Washington: World Bank.

———. 2000. "Does Deposit Insurance Increase Banking System Stability? An Empirical Investigation." Unpublished manuscript. Washington: World Bank.

Demirgüç-Kunt, Aslı, and Harry Huizinga. 1999a. "Determinants of Commercial Bank Interest Margins and Profitability: Some International Evidence." *World Bank Economic Review* 13 (2): 379–408.

———. 1999b. "Financial Structure and Bank Profitability." Unpublished manuscript. Washington: World Bank.

Demirgüç-Kunt, Aslı, and Ross Levine. 1996. "Stock Markets, Corporate Finance, and Economic Growth: An Overview." *World Bank Economic Review* 10 (2, May): 223–39.

———. 1999. "Bank-Based and Market-Based Financial Systems: Cross-Country Comparisons." Unpublished manuscript. Washington: World Bank.

Demirgüç-Kunt, Aslı, and Vojislav Maksimovic. 1996a. *Institutions, Financial Markets, and Firms' Choice of Debt Maturity.* Policy Research Paper 1686. Washington: World Bank.

———. 1996b. "Stock Market Development and Financing Choices of Firms." *World Bank Economic Review* 10 (2, May): 341–69.

———. 1999. "Institutions, Financial Markets, and Firm Debt Maturity." *Journal of Financial Economics* 54 (3, December): 295–336.

Dewatripont, Mathias, and Jean Tirole. 1994. *The Prudential Regulation of Banks.* MIT Press.

Diamond, Douglas W. 1991. "Monitoring and Reputation: The Choice between Bank Loans and Directly Placed Debt." *Journal of Political Economy* 99 (4): 689–721.

Diamond, Douglas, and Philip Dybvig. 1983. "Bank Runs, Deposit Insurance, and Liquidity." *Journal of Political Economy* 91 (3): 401–19.

Freixas, Xavier, and Jean-Charles Rochet. 1997. *Microeconomics of Banking.* MIT Press.

Graham, John R., and Campbell R. Harvey. 2001. "The Theory and Practice of Corporate Finance: Evidence from the Field." *Journal of Financial Economics* 60 (1): 187–243.

Hart, Oliver, and John A. Moore. 1994. "Theory of Debt Based on the Inalienability of Human Capital." *Quarterly Journal of Economics* 109 (4): 841–79.

Harwood, Alison, Robert Litan, and Michael Pomerleano, eds. 1999. *Financial Markets and Development: The Crisis in Emerging Markets.* Brookings.

Holmstrom, Bengt, and Jean Tirole. 1993. "Market Liquidity and Performance Monitoring." *Journal of Political Economy* 101 (4): 678–709.

Holzmann, Robert. 1997. "Fiscal Alternatives of Moving from Unfunded to Funded Pensions." Technical Paper 126. Paris: OECD Development Center.

Impávido, Gregorio, Alberto R. Musalem, and Thierry Tressel. 2002a. "Contractual Savings and Firms' Financing Choices." In Shantayana Devarajan and F. Halsey Rogers, eds., *World Bank Economists' Forum,* vol. 2, pp. 179–222. Washington: World Bank.

———. 2002b. *Contractual Savings Institutions and Banks' Stability and Efficiency.* Policy Research Paper 2752. Washington: World Bank.

———. 2003. *The Impact of Contractual Savings Institutions on Securities Markets.* Policy Research Paper. Washington: World Bank. Forthcoming.

Impávido, Gregorio, Alberto R. Musalem, and Dmitri Vittas. 2002. "Contractual Savings in Countries with a Small Financial System." In James Hanson, Patrick Honohan, and Giovanni Majnoni, eds., *Globalization and Financial Systems in Small Developing Countries.* Washington: World Bank.

International Monetary Fund. 2003. *Global Financial Stability Report.* World Economic and Financial Surveys. Washington.

Koskela, Erkki, and Rune Stenbacka. 2000. "Is There a Trade-off between Bank Competition and Financial Fragility?" *Journal of Banking and Finance* 24 (12): 1853–73.

La Porta, Rafael, Florencio López-de-Silanes, Andrei Shleifer, and Robert W. Vishny. 1997. "Legal Determinants of External Finance." *Journal of Finance* 52 (3): 1131–50.

———. 1998. "Law and Finance." *Journal of Political Economy* 106 (6, December): 1113–55.

Levine, Ross. 1997. "Financial Development and Economic Growth: Views and Agenda." *Journal of Economic Literature* 5 (2): 688–726.
Levine, Ross, and Sara Zervos. 1996. "Stock Market Development and Long-Run Growth." *World Bank Economic Review* 10 (2): 323–39.
———. 1998. "Stock Markets and Economic Growth." *American Economic Review* 88 (3, June): 537–58.
Loayza, Norman, Klaus Schmidt-Hebbel, and Luis Serven. 2000. "What Drives Private Saving across the World?" *Review of Economics and Statistics* 82 (2): 165–81.
Loayza, Norman, and Rashmi Shankar. 1998. "Private Saving in India." *World Bank Economic Review* 14 (3): 571–94.
Maug, Ernst. 1998. "Large Shareholders as Monitors: Is There a Trade-Off between Liquidity and Control?" *Journal of Finance* 62 (February): 65–99.
Myers, Stewart C. 1977. "Determinants of Corporate Borrowing." *Journal of Financial Economics* 5 (November): 147–75.
Neusser, Klaus, and Maurice Kugler. 1998. "Manufacturing Growth and Financial Development: Evidence from OECD Countries." *Review of Economics and Statistics* 80 (4): 638–46.
OECD (Organization for Economic Cooperation and Development). 2001. *Institutional Investors Statistical Year Book 2001*. Paris.
———. 2002. *Insurance Statistics Year Book 2002.* Paris.
Pagano, Marco, Fabio Panetta, and Luigi Zingales. 1988. "Why Do Companies Go Public? An Empirical Analysis." *Journal of Finance* 53 (1, February): 27–63.
Petersen, Mitchell A., and Raghuram Rajan. 1995. "The Effect of Credit Market Competition on Lending Relationships." *Quarterly Journal of Economics* 110 (2, May): 407–43.
Poterba, James M., and Andrew A. Samwick. 1995. "Stock Ownership Patterns, Stock Market Fluctuations, and Consumptions." *Brookings Papers on Economic Activity 2*.
Prasad, Eswar, Kenneth Rogoff, Shang-Jin Wei, and M. Ayhan Kose. 2003. "Effects of Financial Globalization on Developing Countries: Some Empirical Evidence." Board paper. Washington: International Monetary Fund.
Rajan, Raghuram. 1992. "Insiders and Outsiders: The Choice between Informed and Arm's-Length Debt." *Journal of Finance* 47 (September): 1367–400.
Rajan, Raghuram, and Luigi Zingales. 1995. "What Do We Know about Capital Structure? Some Evidence from International Data." *Journal of Finance* 50 (5): 1421–60.
———. 1998. "Financial Dependence and Growth." *American Economic Review* 88 (3): 559–86.
Reisen, Helmut. 2000. *Pensions, Savings, and Capital Flow.* Northampton, Mass.: Edward Elgar Publishing.
Rodrik, Dani, and Andres Velasco. 1999. "Short-Term Capital Flows." Paper presented at the Annual Conference on Development Economics, World Bank, Washington.
Samwick, Andrew A. 1998a. "Discount Rate Heterogeneity and Social Security Reform." *Journal of Development Economics* 57 (October): 117–46.
———. 1998b. "Is Pension Reform Conducive to Higher Saving?" Paper presented at the Saving Workshop, World Bank, Washington, September.
———. 2000. "'Is Pension Reform Conductive to Higher Saving?" *Review of Economic Statistics* 82 (2, May): 264–72.

Schmidt-Hebbel, Klaus, and Luis Serven. 1999. *The Economics of Saving and Growth.* Cambridge University Press.

Shleifer, Andre, and Robert W. Vishny. 1997. "A Survey of Corporate Governance." *Journal of Finance* 52 (2, June): 737–83.

Srinivas, Pulle S., and Juan Yermo. 1999. "Do Investment Regulations Compromise Pension Fund Performance?" Washington: World Bank, Latin American and Caribbean Studies.

Stohs, Mark Hoven, and David C. Mauer. 1996. "The Determinants of Corporate Debt Maturity Structure." *Journal of Business* 69 (3): 279–312.

Stulz, René. 2000. "Does Financial Structure Matter for Economic Growth? A Corporate Finance Perspective." Unpublished manuscript. Washington: World Bank.

Vittas, Dimitri. 1999. *Pension Reform and Financial Markets.* Development Discussion Paper 697. Harvard Institute for International Development.

PANEL SUMMARY

The Future of Domestic Capital Markets in Developing Countries

Cesare Calari, chair of the panel and vice president of the World Bank's Financial Sector Division, stated that the panel was going to revisit the model of capital market development followed by the World Bank Group and the International Finance Corporation (IFC) in the 1970s and 1980s. This model was based on relatively large middle-income countries such as Brazil, Korea, and Thailand, where the IFC worked to develop financial, regulatory, and legal infrastructure. After they attained a certain level of development, the IFC helped open these countries to foreign investment so that they could be linked with global markets. However, the landscape has changed in the past decade, and many of the countries seeking to benefit from capital markets today are very small relative to the global marketplace. Given the importance of economies of scale in the financial industry, should the World Bank alter the advice it provides? Are domestic capital markets still relevant, given that many larger companies are now listing in New York and London to take advantage of assured liquidity and lower trading costs? Are there advantages to outsourcing trading, market, and regulatory infrastructure to regional or foreign markets? What role does financial reform have in promoting the development of domestic capital markets, and how do the benefits from domestic development measure against the benefits of cost efficiencies and diversification gained from investing in foreign funds? What role should international financial institutions play in promoting international "soft law," the best practices embodied in standards and codes in developing countries? Does one basic set of practices and codes indeed fit all nations?

Calari recognized the difficulty of these questions and called on the two panelists, both of whom were trailblazers in the development of equity markets, particularly in emerging markets. According to Calari, Antoine van Agtmael was the first to coin the term "emerging market," and Frank Veneroso predicted and prescribed remedies for the developing-world debt crisis in the mid-1970s, among their many other notable achievements.

Antoine van Agtmael, president and chief investment officer of Emerging Markets Management, set the tone of the discussion by stating that he was quite upbeat about the future of domestic capital markets in developing countries.

Addressing the question of whether there is a need for small capital markets, he stated that first we must recognize that the world is very, very different from what it was twenty years ago, when he and others began their careers in developing capital markets. At that time, economies and markets were quite closed. Today, they are inextricably linked, and interest rates and trading are global. Yet, while globalization has created fierce competition for domestic capital markets over the past two decades, the cost of running a market has declined precipitously as inexpensive computers have replaced the costly physical infrastructure previously necessary to run a capital market. These titanic shifts have altered the calculus of whether to run a market or not.

Obviously, the costs of operating a capital market stem not only from the expenses of running an exchange but also from the additional investment in the infrastructure of governance, regulation, and transparency. However, van Agtmael felt that these costs could be quite low if countries simply would adopt the international standards that, he believed, most eventually will accept—reinventing the wheel in every country being wasted effort. Of course, a nation with a domestic capital market will need a regulatory commission, but such a commission need not be a burdensome expense, given the savings that can be realized by mimicking the regulatory structures of other nations.

Van Agtmael offered the following rule of thumb for countries contemplating whether to support or not support a domestic capital market: countries with their own central bank could consider equity and bond markets, while countries without a central bank should not. Under this rule,

Europe—now that it has one central bank and one currency—should have only one market.

To balance his appraisal of the costs, van Agtmael cited one of the main benefits of domestic capital markets. People, up to a limit, are sympathetic to local companies and want to invest in companies they know. If there was only one global market, many companies would never have a chance to develop, because local investors would be deprived of the opportunity to invest in domestic firms. Thus local markets serve as an incubator in which to cultivate and develop local companies.

Van Agtmael strongly supported local capital markets and suggested that others should not be too quick to discount them. He considered attempts to discourage domestic markets as resulting from superpower megalomania. He also pointed to the emergence of markets like Korea or Taiwan, which, to everyone's surprise, became huge, active domestic securities markets despite their small populations: in the 1950s these countries had per capita income equal to that of Peru. Most people thought that Argentina had a much better chance of developing than Singapore, for example. Perhaps even more unlikely was the development of markets in China, Russia, and India, which twenty years ago would have been unthinkable.

In response to Calari's question about the role of pension funds in the development of local capital markets, he agreed that they were extremely important but disagreed that they should be restricted to socially useful investing. If the only task of pension funds is to make money for investors, they should be free to do so wherever and however they see fit. However, the rapid departure of pension funds in markets in which such funds are major players could be quite disruptive, so such a transition should not be rushed. However, in the long run, pension funds unquestionably should be unrestricted. Even in an economy free of capital restrictions, pension funds probably will continue to invest a reasonable amount of money in the local market.

Frank Veneroso, president of Veneroso Associates, began by discussing why capital and equity markets exist. When he first entered this arena, he believed their raison d'être was to mobilize savings. However, as time passed, he became convinced that the real benefit stemmed from improving the allocation of real resources by funneling savings through discriminating capital (particularly equity) markets and that this was the correct reason to develop these markets.

Yet when this was attempted in emerging economies, the markets rapidly became highly unstable, which severely hampered their efficient allocation of resources. If market behavior is speculative and disregards long-term real returns to capital, then the allocation of resources is inefficient. So instability counteracted the real reason to have markets in the first place.

As a response to the instability produced in developing-world capital markets, in the 1970s Veneroso sought to replicate the equity markets of the developed world, because he was confident that the first-world markets were reasonably efficient. Valuations and accounting were reasonable, corporate governance was solid, and markets fluctuated in a normal, cyclical fashion. Such markets were net issuers of capital and functioned essentially as intended. Given their fairly utopian performance, the bulk of Veneroso's attention was focused on containing financial instability, which he viewed as necessary to provide the smoothly functioning, rational investment environment that would yield efficient allocations.

Since that time, he has watched the developed world's stock markets transform from rational allocative mechanisms to casinos producing speculative bubbles of an unprecedented degree. This phenomenon has sent signals to consumers and firms to spend in excess of their incomes, which in turn has resulted in excessive leveraging and credit bubbles. Accounting rules have been dismissed, corporate governance has been thrown out the window, and equity markets have failed to raise capital. Many net issuers have been fraudulent firms luring unsuspecting investors, as companies with genuine cash flows have been buying back equity to leverage themselves and inflate executive stock options. Veneroso said he never would have pushed such an economy on developing nations in the 1970s. Markets only increase welfare when they are efficient, oscillating around an even keel. If they fail in that, then a country is better off without them.

Given the speculative nature of many markets today, it is essential for countries to have sovereignty over their markets. Blindly designing their own market or putting themselves at the whim of markets in developed nations bodes ominously for them. In work co-authored with Robert Wade, Veneroso weighed the idea of using capital controls to maintain sovereignty, despite the great difficulty in implementing them, but was unable to arrive at a satisfactory way to do so. To predict the future of capital markets, it is necessary to remember that sovereignty may be a prerequisite for achieving allocational efficiency. Given that most countries with a central bank believe they will, are likely to, or will want to have the wisdom to conduct their own affairs in a rational way, respect for national sovereignty in the area of financial markets is essential.

Calari interjected that the panelists seem to agree that there is still room for domestic markets, at least in countries that feel competent to manage their monetary affairs through a central bank. However, given Veneroso's assessment of the present state of the world's financial markets, he wondered whether it is time to reconsider the market development model that has been promoted for developing countries.

Van Agtmael responded that the model needs to be not reconsidered but reshaped and concurred with Veneroso on the importance of national sovereignty. One factor influencing the new shape should be the tight linkage of nations through financial flows, and van Agtmael felt that organizing markets without recognizing that linkage would be foolish. A solution could be for companies large enough to be noticed in international markets to trade in other markets, but at the same time the next generation of companies should not be blocked from investors in the local markets of these firms, as this is the group of investors most likely to be sympathetic to them and to provide them with capital.

Calari countered Veneroso's criticism of forcing developed-country markets on developing nations by saying that, despite the inefficiencies of the Western capitalist system, the systems it replaced were no better at allocating or mobilizing real resources. Such structures frequently were dominated by fraudulent elites who took advantage of asset bubbles.

He then questioned van Agtmael about the regulatory cost of running a market today, particularly in nations with scarce human capital. Calari doubted that the savings due to advances in computer technology are readily applicable to human capital–intensive activities such as regulation and wondered how the migration of large, liquid companies to major markets will affect the financial viability of smaller domestic markets. Van Agtmael responded that markets are very dynamic, due to an intense battle for survival of the fittest, and that one should keep that aspect in mind when analyzing them. A firm with a high cost of capital due to illiquidity will either move to another market or pressure the market it is listed in to become more efficient. He felt that such a process is desirable and that regulators, policymakers, and exchanges should focus on holding the door open for the next generation of companies of interest to investors.

Calari then opened the floor to questions. Mallam Suleiman Ndanusa of Nigeria's SEC asked how a developing market could retain investors and funds when confronted with the speciously attractive returns of casino markets in developed nations. Veneroso replied that sovereignty is essential for nations to insulate themselves from the vagaries of casino markets in other nations. If even highly knowledgeable entrepreneurs are unable to predict long-run returns to capital accurately, how do unsophisticated investors attempt such valuation? Keynes would have answered that people simplify the problem and assume that the historical paper returns to equities will continue indefinitely. This is clearly contrary to the rational expectations approach in which an investor considers the anticipated future real returns of the underlying assets and makes investment decisions based on that prediction.

The herd mentality will drive the market and create self-fulfilling prophecies in markets where the former approach dominates. Free markets from time to time may develop this behavior, which creates serious problems of misinvestment, credit and asset bubbles, and volatility severe enough to frighten away some investors permanently. To prevent this behavior, policymakers should attempt to curb market fundamentalism. However, Alan Greenspan and others in the United States adopted the exact opposite approach, as the laissez-faire attitudes of the nation's top economic policymakers stoked the herd and casino behavior that contributed prominently to the asset bubbles of the late 1990s. This decision to neglect regulation directly contradicted what Veneroso, Joseph Stiglitz, the Bank for International Settlements, and others believed was the wise and proper path to take, namely curbing asset bubbles.

According to Veneroso, a small nation seeking to protect its interests by ensuring a rational capital market must have sovereignty to do so in the face of massive economic mood swings in the world's economic powers. Were a nation to hand over its economic decisions to other countries, it would lose the ability to curb asset bubbles or embark on any other policy it wished to pursue. These swings create inefficiencies in the allocation of real resources that could have very significant impacts on a small nation.

Robert Kapler of the World Bank's Financial Sector Operations and Policy Department followed and asked whether the panelists agreed or not with three assertions of a recent World Bank report on capital markets. First, access to high-quality financial services is a key variable for growth, but whether those services are provided by domestic or foreign companies is irrelevant. Second, the type of financial structure—bank based or capital market based—makes no difference; if anything, the two tend to complement one another. Thus governments should focus on developing infrastructure to support a healthy financial sector but not worry about what the financial sector looks like in terms of nationality and so forth. Third, governments should worry about the incentives governing the financial sector, not simply scratch off items from a checklist for liberalization and consider the job done. The financial sector is very complex, so nations should reject simple solutions and instead realize that one must continually work to understand and regulate the sector.

Veneroso agreed with all of the points and reiterated his thesis that policies should be in place to keep markets on an even keel, but he was unsure that handing over the reins on financial activity to foreign markets and models would accomplish that. Van Agtmael agreed that access to financial services should be made available wherever possible, but without limiting access to local sources of capital. He also expanded on one of Kapler's points, in that he felt a mix of capital markets and banks is essential to stability, because financial sectors weighted heavily to one extreme or another have experienced serious problems in the past. Although the point should be obvious, the general macroeconomic environment stands as a fundamental component of financial sector policy.

Japheth Katto of Uganda's Capital Market Authority offered several comments and posed a question. He felt that in many developing economies even the biggest firms will never list on the New York or London stock exchange, and therefore domestic capital markets are essential for financing the growth of firms in these locations. He also agreed with presenters throughout the conference that public firms must be encouraged to provide and receive the benefits from good governance and agreed with van Agtmael that technology can enable exchanges to be smaller and more efficient. He cited the examples of Uganda and Tanzania, which are developing a single shared depository system.

Katto asked the panel whether regulation can be cost-effective if it is not financially self-sufficient. Van Agtmael responded that the cost of regulation is quite small as a percentage of gross national product (GNP) or as a share of the benefits of better resource allocation, which supports his view that healthy markets can exist only in the presence of good regulation. He reiterated that the adoption of another nation's standards of transparency, governance, and so forth will bring down the cost of regulation and consequently improve its cost-effectiveness. He qualified the importance of good financial sector regulations, however, by adding that a nation's legal and enforcement systems have a dramatic impact on the effectiveness of regulation. Unfortunately, these are typically outside the province of even the most influential financial sector policymakers. As an example of the importance of the interaction of legal, enforcement, and regulatory systems, he cited a lesson from the United States, where lax enforcement of white-collar crime encouraged tremendous excesses in the financial sector, causing impacts outside the influence of any financial regulator. In his opinion, enforcement should have been, and should now be, brutal to curb such problems and avoid their damaging consequences.

Concurring fully with van Agtmael about the low cost of regulation, Veneroso added that the reason people focus on regulatory and transaction costs is their firm belief that laissez-faire markets function more efficiently than regulated ones. Predicated on the belief that market participants are rational, this view remains a common bias of academic economists in the United States. Market participants in the United States also dislike interference, because many of them feel that, since unregulated markets work so well, small costs incurred by regulation have a significant impact on their bottom line. He felt that such an attitude may change when the bubble in the United States fully pops, which he felt has not occurred to date, and the population sees what damage has been wrought by such great instability. When that time comes, he predicted that citizens will understand the rationale for regulation and be willing to incur the costs associated with it in exchange for transparency. Veneroso's final point was that the costs of regulation are not large and that, over time, people will come to see their value.

Richard Simons of the World Bank's Legal Department asked how the securities authorities, even in the United States, could gain prominence and influence in financial markets, especially in the face of the prevailing free-market philosophy. He commented that some nations have given their central bank the authority it needs to function appropriately, but that independence generally has not been extended to securities commissions. Even in the United States, the SEC's power to regulate was weakened in the late 1990s by Congress, which forced Chairman Arthur Levitt to stop calling attention to conflicted auditors and the unrealistic profit statements produced by American corporations.

Veneroso agreed strongly with this, saying that the immense importance of regulation must be both recognized and prioritized. Unless citizens recognize that the market must be contained by political bodies, there will be minimal support for those institutions. As an example, the Federal Reserve has the support and power it does now because the price deflations of the first forty years of the twentieth century were so devastating that people were willing to grant it that power. He felt that the free market must produce devastating outcomes, such as the Great Depression, before adequate authority and resources are given to regulatory bodies. Securities regulators have by and large not been given such autonomy and support. As confirmation of this, and in accord with Simons, he pointed out that the Financial Accounting Standards Board acted quite similarly to the SEC in the late 1990s and that Congress threatened to eviscerate its authority if it continued with market reforms.

A participant reinforced the point that the cost of regulation pales in comparison to its benefits. He mentioned that the SEC budget is roughly 0.005 percent of the total U.S. gross domestic product (GDP), while the wealth recently erased in markets equals $4 trillion, or 40 percent of GDP. In light of the damage done to investment portfolios and pension plans, devoting such a miniscule amount to regulation makes little sense. He also participated in a World Bank program that examined what worked and what did not work to preempt bubbles or mitigate the damage from their collapse. The consensus of that conference was that monetary policy is too blunt an instrument, as well as politically untenable, and that the only effective measures are enhanced transparency and effective regulation.

Veneroso reflected on those comments, assessing the evolutionary process of market behavior, regulation, and moral hazard of participants in the United States. He believed that the recent asset and credit bubble is rooted in this evolution. In response to the price deflation of 1929–33, national policy shifted dramatically to combat deflation. The central bank was unleashed to become an aggressive lender of last resort, deposit insurance was introduced, and other mechanisms were instituted to prevent certain debt deflation dynamics. The net effect of these policies was to make the economy less cyclical, and these successfully eliminated the price deflations that had crushed debtors in the past. As people adjusted to this fact, they also shifted their risk appetite to incur more debt and adopt riskier financial structures, enabling smaller shocks to precipitate financial crises. In response to this, policy had to become ever more proactive, and this ethos led to bailouts in the 1970s and 1980s.

In order to maintain macroeconomic stability as financial structures become more fragile, policy must become more aggressive, and this attitude eventually is incorporated into behavior, leading to a continual increase in moral hazard. Veneroso commented that one should take this historical perspective into account when looking at capital market trends.

Continuing with the theme of economic theory, van Agtmael speculated on the research that would win three of the next ten Nobel Prizes in economics. The first paper would contradict the "free market is wonderful" ideology by stating that a free market without regulation works poorly. The second would show that diversification, an important ingredient, is based on the faulty premise of short-term correlations. The third would demonstrate that markets are inefficient, as they are driven by herd instinct, psychology, and nothing else. He felt a complete overhaul of modern finance is called for, because three of the field's basic tenets are simply erroneous.

In opposition to the third point, Calari noted that long-term returns on categories of investment closely match economic predictions and that this demonstrates the long-term efficiency of markets. While Agtmael acknowledged the long-term accuracy of predictions, he noted that a century is longer than the lives of most people, so such a guide is useful only to those wealthy enough to create estates. Calari felt that the data are fairly consistent over a much shorter period of twenty years, while Agtmael doubted whether the trend would even hold up over fifty years. Effectively, he felt such rules of thumb are only useful for lifetime investment and are useless for any shorter time frame. Veneroso agreed that, although Calari is correct in the long run, the long-run efficiency of markets has been made moot at times, as some nearer-term fluctuations in asset values have been too large for societies to tolerate.

Daochi Tong of the Department of Listed Companies Supervision in China's Securities Regulatory Commission felt that it is useless to debate whether developing countries should have domestic capital markets, given that most already have them. Instead, he suggested that the debate should hinge on whether developing countries should create secondary markets, such as a Nasdaq-like entity. He felt that this may make sense, given that more and more small firms are demanding equity financing in the face of the limited availability of bank financing and that many of those firms are unable to access the major global markets due to quality concerns and other reasons.

Calari disagreed that debate on capital markets is unnecessary. Should impoverished countries from Africa with less than 2 million people establish an SEC, demanding the attention of its twenty or thirty best lawyers and economists? Does it have the critical mass to make a market work efficiently without crowding out other productive uses of its limited human capital? The capital markets model is applicable to large middle-income countries, not necessarily the smallest and poorest nations. As a potential alternative, a regional market or cooperation over an even larger zone may make more sense. The market in West Africa exemplifies this approach. However, Calari did not disagree with the assertion that a second layer of capital market would satiate demand unmet as of now. Van Agtmael agreed completely and concurred that a critical mass is needed to support a market, but he felt that the necessary mass is fairly small.

Van Agtmael then began his closing comments. In contrast with much of the downbeat nature of the conference, he was quite positive about the future of capital markets in emerging economies. As an example, he stated that his investment clients earned 10 percent a year over the past fifteen years, which is not an extraordinary return but greatly exceeds that of treasury bills, and submitted this as proof that one can make money in emerging markets over extended periods.

Volatility decreased in emerging markets while it increased in developed markets, so that volatilities in the two regions are now roughly equal. Therefore, this particular argument for not maintaining a domestic capital market or for investing in one no longer holds water. In fact, over the past few of years, while emerging markets have done poorly in absolute terms, they have fared well relative to the major markets, which have performed terribly.

One major change van Agtmael has witnessed in his two decades in the industry has been the broad improvement in macroeconomic policies in many countries, and this change has provided a stable base for financial market development. Similarly important has been the transformation of companies in his firm's portfolio into professionally run, focused organizations gaining market share. Many companies in his firm's portfolio have realized returns to equity of 15 percent or greater, among other solid financial statistics. He was quite confident that it is difficult to lose money on such investments.

Finally, the best-performing markets, at least for equities in his firm's portfolio over the past ten years, have been the African markets. Not only have they had better returns, but they have also been half as volatile as other markets. In agreement, Veneroso said that his global policy committee, at one of the largest institutions in the world, is pessimistic about the long-run prospects of the U.S. market but extremely positive about the prospects in emerging markets over the same time frame.

Contributors

Reena Aggarwal
Georgetown University

Alan Cameron
Sydney Futures Exchange Corporation

Mierta Capaul
World Bank

Patrick K. Conroy
World Bank

Clemente del Valle
Superintendencia de Valores, Colombia

Jennifer Elliott
International Monetary Fund

Olivier Frémond
World Bank

Amar Gill
Credit Lyonnais Securities Asia, Hong Kong

Jack D. Glen
International Finance Corporation

Peter Blair Henry
Stanford University

Glenn Hoggarth
Bank of England

Gerd Häusler
International Monetary Fund

Patricia Jackson
Bank of England

Cem Karacadag
International Monetary Fund

Ruben Lee
Oxford Finance Group, London

Robert Litan
Brookings Institution

Peter Lombard Lorentzen
Stanford University

Donald J. Mathieson
International Monetary Fund

Sanket Mohapatra
Columbia University

Alberto R. Musalem
World Bank

Erlend Nier
Bank of England

Arne B. Petersen
International Monetary Fund

Michael Pomerleano
World Bank

Dilip Ratha
World Bank

Jorge Roldos
International Monetary Fund

Ajit Singh
University of Cambridge

V. Sundararajan
International Monetary Fund

Philip Suttle
World Bank

Thierry Tressel
International Monetary Fund

Philip Turner
Bank for International Settlements

Piero Ugolini
International Monetary Fund

Index